Lecture Notes in Computer Science 15890

Founding Editors

Gerhard Goos
Juris Hartmanis

The series Lecture Notes in Computer Science (LNCS), including its subseries Lecture Notes in Artificial Intelligence (LNAI) and Lecture Notes in Bioinformatics (LNBI), has established itself as a medium for the publication of new developments in computer science and information technology research, teaching, and education.

LNCS enjoys close cooperation with the computer science R & D community, the series counts many renowned academics among its volume editors and paper authors, and collaborates with prestigious societies. Its mission is to serve this international community by providing an invaluable service, mainly focused on the publication of conference and workshop proceedings and postproceedings. LNCS commenced publication in 1973.

Osvaldo Gervasi · Beniamino Murgante ·
Chiara Garau · Yeliz Karaca ·
Maria Noelia Faginas Lago · Francesco Scorza ·
Ana Cristina Braga
Editors

Computational Science and Its Applications – ICCSA 2025 Workshops

Istanbul, Turkey, June 30 – July 3, 2025
Proceedings, Part V

Springer

Editors
Osvaldo Gervasi ⓘ
University of Perugia
Perugia, Italy

Beniamino Murgante ⓘ
University of Basilicata
Potenza, Italy

Chiara Garau ⓘ
University of Cagliari
Cagliari, Italy

Yeliz Karaca ⓘ
University of Massachusetts
Worcester, MA, USA

Maria Noelia Faginas Lago ⓘ
University of Perugia
Perugia, Italy

Francesco Scorza ⓘ
University of Basilicata
Potenza, Italy

Ana Cristina Braga ⓘ
University of Minho
Braga, Portugal

ISSN 0302-9743   ISSN 1611-3349 (electronic)
Lecture Notes in Computer Science
ISBN 978-3-031-97605-6   ISBN 978-3-031-97606-3 (eBook)
https://doi.org/10.1007/978-3-031-97606-3

Preface

The compiled 14 volumes (LNCS volumes 15886–15899) consist of the peer-reviewed papers from the 68 Workshops of the 2025 International Conference on Computational Science and Its Applications (ICCSA 2025), which was held between June 30 – July 3, 2025 in Istanbul (Türkiye). The peer-reviewed papers of the main conference tracks are published in a separate set made up of three volumes (LNCS 15648–15650).

The conference was held in a hybrid form, with the large majority of participants in presence, hosted by Galatasaray University, Istanbul, Türkiye. We enabled virtual participation for those who did not attend the event in person due to logistical, political and economic problems, by adopting a technological infrastructure via open-source software (jitsi + riot) and a commercial Cloud infrastructure.

With the 2025 edition, ICCSA celebrated its 25th anniversary, a quarter of a century as a memorable moment that is harmoniously aligned with Istanbul, an extraordinary city located at the crossroads and acting as a bridge connecting Asia and Europe, representing different cultures, beliefs as well as lifestyles, which highlights its intercultural fabric.

ICCSA 2025 marked another fruitful and thought-provoking academic event in the International Conferences on Computational Science and Its Applications (ICCSA) conference series, previously held in Hanoi, Vietnam (2024), Athens, Greece (2023), Málaga, Spain (2022), Cagliari, Italy (hybrid with a few participants in presence in 2021 and completely online in 2020), whilst earlier editions took place in Saint Petersburg, Russia (2019), Melbourne, Australia (2018), Trieste, Italy (2017), Beijing, China (2016), Banff, Canada (2015), Guimaraes, Portugal (2014), Ho Chi Minh City, Vietnam (2013), Salvador, Brazil (2012), Santander, Spain (2011), Fukuoka, Japan (2010), Suwon, South Korea (2009), Perugia, Italy (2008), Kuala Lumpur, Malaysia (2007), Glasgow, UK (2006), Singapore (2005), Assisi, Italy (2004), Montreal, Canada (2003), and (as ICCS) Amsterdam, the Netherlands (2002) and San Francisco, USA (2001).

Computational Science constitutes the main pillar of most present research, industrial and commercial applications, and plays a unique role in exploiting ICT innovative technologies, and the ICCSA conference series has, accordingly, provided ample opportunities to researchers and industry practitioners to discuss new ideas, to share complex problems and their solutions, and to shape new trends in Computational Science. As the conference mirrors society from a scientific point of view, this year's undoubtedly dominant theme was large language models, machine learning and Artificial Intelligence (AI) and their applications in the most diverse technological, economic and industrial fields, amongst the others.

The ICCSA 2025 conference was structured in six general tracks covering the fields of computational science and its applications: Computational Methods, Algorithms and Scientific Applications – High Performance Computing and Networks – Geometric Modeling, Graphics and Visualization – Advanced and Emerging Applications – Information Systems and Technologies – Urban and Regional Planning. In addition, the conference consisted of 68 workshops, focusing on topical issues of utmost importance to science, technology and society: from new computational approaches for earth science, to mathematical methods for image processing, new statistical and optimization methods, several Artificial Intelligence approaches, sustainability issues, smart cities and related technologies, to name some.

In the Workshops' proceedings, we accepted 362 full papers, 37 short papers and 2 Ph.D. Showcase papers from total of 1043 submissions (Acceptance rate 38.4%). In the Main Conference Proceedings, we accepted 71 full papers, 6 short papers and 1 Ph.D. Showcase paper from 269 submissions to the General Tracks of the Conference (with an acceptance rate of 29.9%). We would like to convey our sincere appreciation to the workshops' chairs and co-chairs and program committee members for their diligent work, commitment and dedication.

The success and consistent maintenance of the ICCSA conference series in general, and of ICCSA 2025 in particular, rely upon the support of many people: authors, presenters, participants, keynote speakers, workshop chairs, session chairs, organizing committee members, student volunteers, Program Committee members, Advisory Committee members, International Liaison chairs, reviewers and other individuals in various roles. Thus, we take this opportunity to wholehartedly thank each and everyone.

We additionally wish to thank publisher Springer for their agreement to publish the proceedings, besides sponsoring part of the best papers awards and for their kind assistance and cooperation during the editing process.

We would cordially like to invite you to refer to the ICCSA website https://iccsa.org, where you can find the relevant details regarding this academic endeavor and event of ours.

June 2025

Osvaldo Gervasi
Yeliz Karaca
Beniamino Murgante
Chiara Garau

A Welcome Message from the Organizers

The International Conference on Computational Science and Its Applications (ICCSA) reflects a culmination of meticulous and dedicated efforts and academic endeavors toward the progress of science and technology.

One of the most noteworthy aspects of ICCSA is its fostering of a collective spirit, bringing together a plethora of participants from all over the world. Correspondingly, this merging power manifests itself in the 25th anniversary of ICCSA, which is a quarter of a century, in Istanbul, Türkiye, which connects and acts as a bridge between two continents, namely Asia and Europe. This unique location in the world hosts the 25th year of ICCSA at Galatasaray University, located on Çırağan Avenue by Istanbul's Bosphorus, which is an established international university bestowed with a distinctive past of teaching tradition, research and education exceeding five centuries.

Istanbul, having served as the capital city of four empires, namely the Roman Empire (330–395), the Byzantine Empire (395–1204 and 1261–1453), the Latin Empire (1204–1261) and the Ottoman Empire (1453–1922), is an exceptional city of the Republic of Türkiye founded by Mustafa Kemal Atatürk.

Situated at a strategic location along the historic Silk Road, Istanbul is at the core of extending rail networks which span across Europe and West Asia along with the only sea route between the Black Sea and the Mediterranean.

The cultural, historical and economic pulses of the country are evident in Istanbul whose rooted origins have embraced varying beliefs, lifestyles and populace, which highlights the city's mosaic quality with blended fabric in a constant harmonious flow. This has enabled cultures to grow and be nurtured, which is profoundly rooted in its urban culture.

Computational Science constitutes the main pillar of most present research, industrial and commercial activities besides manifesting a unique role in exploiting and addressing innovative Information and Communication Technologies. Thus, the 25-year-old ICCSA conference series provides remarkable opportunities to get acquainted with leading researchers, scientists, scholars, practitioners and many more while exchanging innovative ideas and initiating new partnerships, associations and bonds.

With the hosting of Galatasaray University, I would personally and on behalf of the Local Organizing Committee, with the members Emre Alptekin, Gülfem Işıklar Alptekin, Cengiz Kahraman, Abdullah Çağrı Tolga and Ayberk Zeytin, like to convey our sincere gratitude and thanks to everyone who exerted their efforts in and contributed to the realization of ICCSA 2025. With these notes and remarks, welcome to Istanbul!

Cordially yours,

On behalf of the Local Organizing Committee.

June 2025   Yeliz Karaca

A Welcome Message from the Organizers

Organization

Honorary General Chairs

Bernady O. Apduhan	Kyushu Sangyo University, Japan
Kenneth C. J. Tan	Sardina Systems, UK

General Chairs

Yeliz Karaca	University of Massachusetts, USA
Osvaldo Gervasi	University of Perugia, Italy
David Taniar	Monash University, Australia

Program Committee Chairs

Beniamino Murgante	University of Basilicata, Italy
Chiara Garau	University of Cagliari, Italy
Ana Maria A. C. Rocha	University of Minho, Portugal
A. Çağrı Tolga	Galatasaray University, Turkey

International Advisory Committee

Jemal Abawajy	Deakin University, Australia
Dharma P. Agarwal	University of Cincinnati, USA
Rajkumar Buyya	Melbourne University, Australia
Claudia Bauzer Medeiros	University of Campinas, Brazil
Manfred M. Fisher	Vienna University of Economics and Business, Austria
Pierre Frankhauser	University of Franche-Comté/CNRS, France
Marina L. Gavrilova	University of Calgary, Canada
Sumi Helal	University of Florida, USA & Lancaster University, UK
Bin Jiang	University of Gävle, Sweden
Yee Leung	Chinese University of Hong Kong, China

International Liaison Chairs

Ivan Blečić	University of Cagliari, Italy
Giuseppe Borruso	University of Trieste, Italy
Elise De Donker	Western Michigan University, USA
Maria Noelia Faginas Lago	University of Perugia, Italy
Maria Irene Falcão	University of Minho, Portugal
Robert C. H. Hsu	Chung Hua University, Taiwan
Yeliz Karaca	University of Massachusetts Chan Medical School, USA
Tae-Hoon Kim	Zhejiang University of Science and Technology, China
Vladimir Korkhov	Saint Petersburg University, Russia
Takashi Naka	Kyushu Sangyo University, Japan
Rafael D. C. Santos	National Institute for Space Research, Brazil
Maribel Yasmina Santos	University of Minho, Portugal
Anastasia Stratigea	National Technical University of Athens, Greece

Workshop and Session Organizing Chairs

Beniamino Murgante	University of Basilicata, Italy
Chiara Garau	University of Cagliari, Italy

Award Chair

Wenny Rahayu	La Trobe University, Australia

Publicity Committee Chairs

Elmer Dadios	De La Salle University, Philippines
Nataliia Kulabukhova	Saint Petersburg University, Russia
Daisuke Takahashi	Tsukuba University, Japan
Shangwang Wang	Beijing University of Posts and Telecommunications, China

Local Organizing Committee Chairs

Emre Alptekin	Galatasaray University, Turkey
Gülfem Işıklar Alptekin	Galatasaray University, Turkey
Cengiz Kahraman	İstanbul Technical University, Turkey
A. Çağrı Tolga	Galatasaray University, Turkey
Ayberk Zeytin	Galatasaray University, Turkey

Technology Chair

Damiano Perri	University of Perugia, Italy

Program Committee

Vera Afreixo	University of Aveiro, Portugal
Vladimir Alarcon	Northern Gulf Institute, USA
Filipe Alvelos	University of Minho, Portugal
Debora Anelli	Polytechnic University of Bari, Italy
Hartmut Asche	Hasso-Plattner-Institut für Digital Engineering Ggmbh, Germany
Nizamettin Aydın	İstanbul Technical University, Turkey
Ginevra Balletto	University of Cagliari, Italy
Nadia Balucani	University of Perugia, Italy
Socrates Basbas	Aristotle University of Thessaloniki, Greece
David Berti	ART SpA, Italy
Michela Bertolotto	University College Dublin, Ireland
Sandro Bimonte	CEMAGREF, TSCF, France
Ana Cristina Braga	University of Minho, Portugal
Tiziana Campisi	Kore University of Enna, Italy
Yves Caniou	Université Claude Bernard Lyon 1, France
Alessandra Capolupo	Polytechnic University of Bari, Italy
José A. Cardoso e Cunha	Universidade Nova de Lisboa, Portugal
Rui Cardoso	University of Beira Interior, Portugal
Leocadio G. Casado	University of Almería, Spain
Mete Celik	Erciyes University, Turkey
Maria Cerreta	University of Naples Federico II, Italy
Ta Quang Chieu	Thuyloi University, Vietnam
Rachel Chien-Sing Lee	Sunway University, Malaysia
Birol Ciloglugil	Ege University, Turkey
Mauro Coni	University of Cagliari, Italy

Workshops

Workshop on Advancements in Applied Machine-Learning and Data Analytics (AAMDA 2025)

Workshop Organizers

Alessandro Costantini	INFN, Italy
Daniele Cesini	INFN, Italy
Elisabetta Ronchieri	INFN, Italy
Barbara Martelli	INFN, Italy

Workshop Program Committee Members

Alessandro Costantini	Istituto Nazionale di Fisica Nucleare (INFN), Italy
Daniele Cesini	Istituto Nazionale di Fisica Nucleare (INFN), Italy
Elisabetta Ronchieri	Istituto Nazionale di Fisica Nucleare (INFN), Italy
Barbara Martelli	Istituto Nazionale di Fisica Nucleare (INFN), Italy
Luca Dell'Agnello	Istituto Nazionale di Fisica Nucleare (INFN), Italy

Advanced and Innovative Web Apps 2025 (AIWA 2025)

Workshop Organizers

Damiano Perri	University of Perugia, Italy
Osvaldo Gervasi	University of Perugia, Italy
Stelios Kouzeleas	International Hellenic University, Greece
Sergio Tasso	University of Perugia, Italy

Workshop Program Committee Members

David Berti	ART SpA, Italy
JungYoon Kim	Gachon University, South Korea
TaiHoon Kim	Zhejiang University of Science and Technology, China

Advanced Processes of Mathematics and Computing Models in Complex Data-Intensive Computational Systems (AMCM 2025)

Workshop Organizers

Yeliz Karaca	University of Massachusetts Chan Medical School and Massachusetts Institute of Technology, USA
Dumitru Baleanu	Lebanese American University, Lebanon
Osvaldo Gervasi	University of Perugia, Italy
Yudong Zhang	University of Leicester, UK
Majaz Moonis	University of Massachusetts Chan Medical School and Massachusetts Institute of Technology, USA

Workshop Program Committee Members

TaeHoon Kim	Zhejiang University of Science and Technology, China
Martin Bohner	Missouri University of Science and Technology, USA
Shuihua Wang	University of Leicester, UK
Khan Muhammad	Sungkyunkwan University, South Korea
Mahmoud Abdel-Aty	Sohag University, Egypt
Aziz Dursun	Virginia Polytechnic Institute and State University, USA
Kemal Güven Gülen	Namık Kemal University, Turkey
Akif Akgül	Hitit Üniversitesi, Turkey

Advanced Numerical Approaches for Assessment and Design of No-Tension Masonry Structures (ANAMS 2025)

Workshop Organizers

Antonino Iannuzzo	Universitá degli studi del Sannio, Italy
Carlo Olivieri	Universitá Telematica Pegaso, Italy
Andrea Montanino	CIMNE, Spain
Elham Mousavian	University of Edinburgh, UK

Workshop Program Committee Members

Pietro Meriggi	Roma Tre University, Italy
Francesca Perelli	University of Naples Federico II, Italy
Marialuigia Sangirardi	University of Oxford, UK
Sam Cocking	University of Cambridge, UK

Matteo Salvalaggio	University of Minho, Portugal
Vittorio Paris	University of Bergamo, Italy
Luigi Sibille	Norwegian University of Science and Technology, Norway
Natalia Pingaro	Politecnico di Milano, Italy
Martina Buzzetti	Politecnico di Milano, Italy
Generoso Vaiano	Pegaso Telematic University, Italy
Alessandra Capolupo	Politecnico di Bari, Italy
Amal Gerges	Università degli Studi di Cagliari, Italy
Fabian Orozco	National Autonomous University of Mexico, Mexico
Nathanael Savalle	Polytech Clermont and Université Clermont Auvergne, France
Luca Umberto Argiento	University of Naples Federico II, Italy
Bartolomeo Pantó	Durham University, UK

Unveiling the Synergies Between Air Quality and Climate PlAnning (AQCliPA 2025)

Workshop Organizers

Angela Pilogallo	University of L'Aquila, Italy
Luigi Santopietro	University of Basilicata, Italy
Filomena Pietrapertosa	IMAA CNR, Italy
Monica Salvia	IMAA CNR, Italy
Carlo Trozzi	IMAA CNR, Italy
Valeria Scapini	Central University of Chile, Chile

Workshop Program Committee Members

Lucia Saganeiti	IMAA-CNR, Italy
Lorena Fiorini	University of L'Aquila, Italy
Antonio Mazza	IMAA-CNR, Italy
Gabriele Nolè	IMAA-CNR, Italy
Carmen Guida	University of Naples "Federico II", Italy
Floriana Zucaro	University of Naples "Federico II", Italy
Sabrina Lai	University of Cagliari, Italy
Chiara Garau	University of Cagliari, Italy

Advancements in Spatial assessment of Socio-Ecological SystemS (ASSESS 2025)

Workshop Organizers

Daniele Cannatella	TU Delft, The Netherlands
Giuliano Poli	University of Naples Federico II, Italy
Eugenio Muccio	TU Delft, The Netherlands
Claudiu Forgaci	TU Delft, The Netherlands

Workshop Program Committee Members

Daniele Cannatella	TU Delft, The Netherlands
Giuliano Poli	University of Naples Federico II, Italy
Eugenio Muccio	University of Naples Federico II, Italy
Claudiu Forgaci	TU Delft, The Netherlands
Maria Cerreta	University of Naples Federico II, Italy
Maria Somma	University of Naples Federico II, Italy
Laura Di Tommaso	University of Naples Federico II, Italy
Sabrina Sacco	Politecnico di Milano, Italy
Piero Zizzania	University of Naples Federico II, Italy
Gaia Daldanise	CNR IRISS, Italy
Benedetta Grieco	University of Naples Federico II, Italy
Giuseppe Ciciriello	University of Naples Federico II, Italy
Marta Dell'Ovo	Politecnico di Milano, Italy
Francesco Piras	University of Cagliari, Italy
Diana Rolando	Politecnico di Torino, Italy
Stefano Cuntò	University of Naples Federico II, Italy
Ludovica La Rocca	University of Naples Federico II, Italy

Blockchain and Distributed Ledgers: Technologies and Applications (BDLTA 2025)

Workshop Organizers

Vladimir Korkhov	Saint Petersburg State University, Russia
Elena Stankova	Saint Petersburg State University, Russia
Nataliia Kulabukhova	Saint Petersburg State University, Russia

Workshop Program Committee Members

Adam Belloum	University of Amsterdam, the Netherlands
Dmitrii Vasiunin	Deutsche Telekom Cloud Services E.P.E., Greece
Serob Balyan	Osensus Arm LLC, Armenia
Suren Abrahamyan	Osensus Arm LLC, Armenia
Ashot Sergey Gevorkyan	NAS of Armenia, Armenia

Michal Hnatic	Univerzita Pavla Jozefa Šafárika v Košiciach, Slovakia
Michail Panteleyev	Saint Petersburg Electrotecnical University, Russia
Martin Vala	Univerzita Pavla Jozefa Šafárika v Košiciach, Slovakia
Nodir Zaynalov	Tashkent University of Information Technologies named after Muhammad al Khwarizmi, Uzbekistan
Michail Panteleyev	Saint Petersburg Electrotecnical University, Russia
Alexander Degtyarev	Saint Petersburg University, Russia
Alexander Bogdanov	St. Petersburg State University, Russia

Bio and Neuro Inspired Computing and Applications (BIONCA 2025)

Workshop Organizers

Nadia Nedjah	State University of Rio de Janeiro, Brazil
Luiza de Macedo Mourelle	State University of Rio de Janeiro, Brazil

Workshop Program Committee Members

Nadia Nedjha	State University of Rio de Janeiro, Brazil
Luiza de Macedo Mourelle	State University of Rio de Janeiro, Brazil
Luigi Maciel Ribeiro	State University of Rio de Janeiro, Brazil
Joelmir Ramos	Federal University of Rio de Janeiro, Brazil
Rogério Moraes	Brazilian Navy, Brazil
Marcos Santana Farias	Institute of Nuclear Energy, Brazil
Luneque Silva Jr.	Federal University of ABC, Brazil
Alan Oliveira	University of Lisboa, Portugal
Brij Bhooshan Gupta	Asia University, Taiwan

Computational and Applied Mathematics (CAM 2025)

Workshop Organizers

Maria Irene Falcão	University of Minho, Portugal
Fernando Miranda	University of Minho, Portugal

Workshop Program Committee Members

Fernando Miranda	University of Minho, Portugal
Graça Tomaz	Polytechnic of Guarda, Portugal
Helmuth Malonek	University of Aveiro, Portugal

Isabel Cacao	University of Aveiro, Portugal
João Morais	Autonomous Technological Institute of Mexico, Mexico
Lidia Aceto	University of Eastern Piedmont, Italy
Luís Ferrás	University of Porto, Portugal
M. Irene Falcão	University of Minho, Portugal
Patrícia Beites	University of Beira Interior, Portugal
Paulo Amorim	FGV EMAp, Brazil
Regina de Almeida	University of Trás-os-Montes e Alto Douro, Portugal
Ricardo Severino	University of Minho, Portugal

Computational and Applied Statistics (CAS 2025)

Workshop Organizer

Ana Cristina Braga	ALGORITMI Research Centre, LASI, University of Minho, Portugal

Workshop Program Committee Members

Adelaide Freitas	University of Aveiro, Portugal
Andreas Futschik	Johannes Kepler University Linz, Austria
Ana Cristina Braga	University of Minho, Portugal
Ângela Silva	University of Minho, Portugal
Arminda Manuela Gonçalves	University of Minho, Portugal
Carina Silva	Polytechnic Intitute of Lisbon, Portugal
Elisete Correia	University of Trás-os-Montes e Alto Douro, Portugal
Frank Westad	Norwegian University of Science and Technology, Norway
Isabel Natario	New University of Lisbon, Portugal
Irene Oliveira	University of Trás-os-Montes e Alto Douro, Portugal
Ivan Rodriguez Conde	University of Vigo, Spain
Joaquim Gonçalves	Instituto Politécnico do Cávado e do Ave, Portugal
Lino Costa	University of Minho, Portugal
Marco Reis	University of Coimbra, Portugal
Maria Filipa Mourão	Polytechnic Institute of Viana do Castelo, Portugal
Maria João Polidoro	Polytechnic Institute of Porto, Portugal
Martin Perez Perez	University of Vigo, Spain
Michal Abrahamowicz	McGill University, Canada
Vera Afreixo	University of Aveiro, Portugal

Werner G. Müller	Johannes Kepler University Linz, Austria
Bruna Silva Ramos	University Lusiada de Famalicão, Portugal
Inês Sousa	University of Minho, Portugal
Luís Miguel Rocha Matos	University of Minho, Portugal
Manuel Carlos Figueiredo	University of Minho, Portugal

Cyber Intelligence and Applications (CIA 2025)

Workshop Organizer

Gianni D'Angelo	University of Salerno, Italy

Workshop Program Committee Members

Gianni D'Angelo	University of Salerno, Italy
Francesco Palmieri	University of Salerno, Italy
Massimo Ficco	University of Salerno, Italy
Arcangelo Castiglione	University of Salerno, Italy

Computational Methods for Business Analytics (CMBA 2025)

Workshop Organizers

Cláudio Alves	Universidade do Minho, Portugal
Telmo Pinto	Universidade do Minho, Portugal

Workshop Program Committee Members

Abdulrahim Shamayleh	American University of Sharjah, United Arab Emirates
Ana Rocha	University of Minho, Portugal
Angelo Sifaleras	University of Macedonia, Greece
Cristóvão Silva	University of Coimbra, Portugal
José Valério de Carvalho	University of Minho, Portugal
Miguel Vieira	Universidade Lusófona, Portugal
Rita Macedo	Université de Lille, France
Ana Moura	Universidade de Aveiro, Portugal
Cristina Lopes	ISCAP, Portugal
Eliana Costa e Silva	Instituto Politécnico do Porto, Portugal

Computational Methods, Statistics and Industrial Mathematics (CMSIM 2025)

Workshop Organizers

Maria Filomena Teodoro	IST ID, Instituto Superior Técnico, Portugal
Marina Alexandra Pedro Andrade	ISCTE – Lisbon University Institute, Portugal
Paula Simões	University of Lisbon, Portugal
Teresa A. Oliveira	IST ID, Instituto Superior Técnico, Portugal

Workshop Program Committee Members

Amilcar Oliveira	Universidade Aberta and Universidade de Lisboa, Portugal
Victor Lobo	Escola Naval and NOVA IMS Almada, Portugal
António Pacheco	IST Universidade de Lisboa, Portugal
Eliana Costa	Escola Superior de Tecnologia e Gestão IPPorto, Portugal
Aldina Correia	Escola Superior de Tecnologia e Gestão IPPorto, Portugal
Fernando Carapau	University of Évora, Portugal
Ricardo Moura	Portuguese Naval Academy, Portugal
Ana Borges	Escola Superior de Tecnologia e Gestão IPPorto, Portugal
Cristina Lopes	ISCAP IPPorto, Portugal
Fernanda Costa	University of Minho, Portugal
Cabrita Carlos	IPBeja, Portugal
Maria Luísa Morgado	University of Trás os Montes e Alto Douro and University of Lisbon, Portugal
Rosário Ramos	Universidade Aberta, Portugal
Sofia Rézio	Iscal, Instituto Politécnico de Lisboa, Portugal
Matteo Sacchet	University of Turin, Italy
Marina Marchisio Conte	University of Turin, Italy
António Seijas-Macias	University of Coruña, Spain
Luís F. A. Teodoro	University of Glasgow, UK and University of Oslo, Norway
Christos Kitsos	University of West Attica, Greece
M. Filomena Teodoro	Universidade de Lisboa, Portugal
Marina A. P. Andrade	Instituto Universitário de Lisboa, Portugal
Paula Simões	Military Academy and Universidade Nova de Lisboa, Portugal
Teresa Oliveira	Universidade Aberta and Universidade de Lisboa, Portugal

Computational Optimization and Applications (COA 2025)

Workshop Organizers

Ana Rocha   ALGORITMI Research Centre, LASI, University
                         of Minho, Portugal, Portugal
Humberto Rocha   ALGORITMI Research Centre, LASI, University
                         of Minho, Portugal, Portugal

Workshop Program Committee Members

Florbela Fernandes   Polytechnic Institute of Bragança, Portugal
Clara Vaz   Polytechnic Institute of Bragança, Portugal
Ana Pereira   Polytechnic Institute of Bragança, Portugal
Filipe Alvelos   University of Minho, Portugal
Joana Dias   University of Coimbra, Portugal
Eligius M. T. Hendrix   University of Málaga, Spain
Emerson José de Paiva   Federal University of Itajubá, Brazil
Ana Paula Teixeira   University of Trás-os-Montes and Alto Douro,
                         Portugal
Lino Costa   Universidade do Minho, Portugal

Coastal Cities Versus Inland Areas. Hypotheses for Sustainable Regeneration Through Ecosystem Services of 'Hooking' and Rehabilitation of Brownfield Sites (CoastalCities_VS_InlandAreas 2025)

Workshop Organizers

Celestina Fazia   Università di Enna Kore, Italy
Angrilli Massimo   University of Chieti-Pescara, Italy
Valentina Ciuffreda   University of Chieti-Pescara, Italy
Maurizio Oddo   Università di Enna Kore, Italy
Marcello Sestito   Università di Enna Kore, Italy
Clara Stella Vicari Aversa   University of Reggio Calabria, Italy

Workshop Program Committee Members

Alessandro Camiz   Università d'Annunzio, Italy
Thowayeb Hassan   King Faisal University, Saudi Arabia
Alessandro Barracco   Università Kore di Enna, Italy
Mario Morrica   University of Urbino, Italy
Mariana Ratiu   University of Oradea, Romania
Alanda Akamana   Mohammed VI Polytechnic University, Morocco
Kaoutare Amini Alaoui   Mohammed VI Polytechnic University, Morocco

Computational Astrochemistry 2025 (CompAstro 2025)

Workshop Organizers

Marzio Rosi	University of Perugia, Italy
Daniela Ascenzi	University of Trento, Italy
Nadia Balucani	University of Perugia, Italy
Stefano Falcinelli	University of Perugia, Italy

Workshop Program Committee Members

Dario Campisi	Università degli Studi di Perugia, Italy
Giacomo Giorgi	Università degli Studi di Perugia, Italy
Andrea Giustini	Università degli Studi di Perugia, Italy
Luca Mancini	Università degli Studi di Perugia, Italy
Albert Rimola	Universitat Autònoma de Barcelona, Spain
Gianmarco Vanuzzo	Università degli Studi di Perugia, Italy
Dimitrios Skouteris	Master-Tec, Italy
Piero Ugliengo	Università degli Studi di Torino, Italy
Franco Vecchiocattivi	Università degli Sudi di Perugia, Italy
Giacomo Pannacci	Università degli Studi di Perugia, Italy
Costanza Borghesi	Università degli Studi di Perugia, Italy
Marco Parriani	Università degli Studi di Perugia, Italy
Marta Loletti	Università degli Studi di Perugia, Italy
Fernando Pirani	Università degli Studi di Perugia, Italy
Andrea Lombardi	Università degli Studi di Perugia, Italy
Noelia Faginas Lago	Università degli Studi di Perugia, Italy
Paolo Tosi	Università di Trento, Italy
Cecilia Coletti	Università degli Studi Chieti-Pescara, Italy
Nazzareno Re	Università degli Studi Chieti-Pescara, Italy
Linda Podio	Osservatorio Astrofisico di Arcetri INAF, Italy
Claudio Codella	Osservatorio Astrofisico di Arcetri INAF, Italy
Gabriella Di Genova	Università degli Studi di Perugia, Italy

Computational Methods for Porous Geomaterials (CompPor 2025)

Workshop Organizers

Vadim Lisitsa	IPGG SB RAS, Russia
Evgeniy Romenski	IPGG SB RAS, Russia

Workshop Program Committee Members

Vadim Lisitsa	Institute of Petroleum Geology and Geophysics SB RAS, Russia
Evgeniy Romenski	Sobolev Institute of Mathematics SB RAS, Russia
Vladimir Cheverda	Sobolev Institute of Mathematics SB RAS, Russia
Tatyana Khachkova	IPGG SB RAS, Russia
Dmitry Prokhorov	IPGG SB RAS, Russia
Mikhail Novikov	Sobolev Institute of Mathematics SB RAS, Russia
Sergey Solovyev	Sobolev Institute of Mathematics SB RAS, Russia
Kirill Gadylshin	LLC RNBashNIPIneft, Russia
Olga Stoyanovskaya	Lavrentev Institute of Hydrodynamics SB RAS, Russia
Yerlan Amanbek	Nazarbaev University, Kazakstan

Workshop on Computational Science and HPC (CSHPC 2025)

Workshop Organizers

Elise de Doncker	Western Michigan University, USA
Hideo Matsufuru	High Energy Accelerator Research Organization, Japan

Workshop Program Committee Members

Elise de Doncker	Western Michigan University, USA
Hideo Matsufuru	High Energy Accelerator Research Organization (KEK), Japan
Fukuko Yuasa	KEK, Japan
Issaku Kanamori	RIKEN, Japan
Hiroshi Daisaka	Hitotsubashi University, Japan
Norikazu Yamada	KEK, Japan
Naohito Nakasato	University of Aizu, Japan
Robert Makin	Western Michigan University, USA

Cities, Technologies and Planning 2025 (CTP 2025)

Workshop Organizers

Giuseppe Borruso	University of Trieste, Italy
Beniamino Murgante	University of Basilicata, Italy
Malgorzata Hanzl	Lodz University of Technology, Poland
Anastasia Stratigea	National Technical University of Athens, Greece
Ljiljana Zivkovic	Republic Geodetic Authority, Serbia
Ginevra Balletto	University of Trieste, Italy

Workshop Program Committee Members

Giuseppe Borruso	University of Trieste, Italy
Beniamino Murgante	University of Basilicata, Italy
Malgorzata Hanzl	Lodz University of Technology, Poland
Anastasia Stratigea	National Technical University of Athens, Greece
Ljiljiana Zivkovic	Republic Geodetic Authority of Serbia, Serbia
Ginevra Balletto	University of Cagliari, Italy
Silvia Battino	University of Sassari, Italy
Mara Ladu	University of Cagliari, Italy
Maria del Mar Munoz Leonisio	University of Cádiz, Spain
Ahinoa Amaro Garcia	University of Las Palmas of Gran Canaria, Spain
Maria Attard	University of Malta, Malta
Enrico D'agostini	World Maritime University, Sweden
Francesca Krasna	University of Trieste, Italy
Brisol Garcia Garcia	Polytechnic University of Quintana Roo, Mexico
Tu Anh Trinh	UEH University, Vietnam
Giovanni Mauro	Università degli Studi della Campania, Italy
Maria Ronza	University of Naples Federico II, Italy
Massimiliano Bencardino	University of Salerno, Italy
Tomasz Bradecki	Silesian University of Technology, Poland
Dorota Kamrowska-Załuska	Gdańsk University of Technology, Poland
Iwona Jażdżewska	University of Lodz, Poland
Yiota Theodora	National Technical University of Athens, Greece
Apostolos Lagarias	University of Thessaly, Greece
George Tsilimigkas	University of the Aegean, Greece
Akrivi Leka	National Technical University of Athens, Greece
Maria Panagiotopoulou	National Technical University of Athens, Greece
Andrea Gallo	Ca' Foscari University of Venice, Italy
Francesca Sinatra	University of Trieste, Italy

Digital Transition: Effects on Housing Mobility, Market, Land Governance (DIGITRANS 2025)

Workshop Organizers

Fabrizio Battisti	University of Florence, Italy
Fabiana Forte	University of Campania, Italy
Orazio Campo	Sapienza University of Rome, Italy
Alessio Pino	Kore University of Enna, Italy
Carlo Pisano	University of Florence, Italy
Mariolina Grasso	Kore University of Enna, Italy

Workshop Program Committee Members

Fabrizio Battisti	University of Florence, Italy
Fabiana Forte	Università della Campania Luigi Vanvitelli, Italy
Orazio Campo	University of Rome "La Sapienza", Italy
Alessio Pino	Kore University of Enna, Italy
Carlo Pisano	University of Florence, Italy
Mariolina Grasso	Università Kore di Enna, Italy

Evaluating Inner Areas Potentials (EIAP 2025)

Workshop Organizers

Diana Rolando	Politecnico di Torino, Italy
Alice Barreca	Politecnico di Torino, Italy
Manuela Rebaudengo	Politecnico di Torino, Italy
Giorgia Malavasi	Politecnico di Torino, Italy

Workshop Program Committee Members

John Accordino	Virginia Commonwealth University, USA
Francesco Bruzzone	Università Iuav di Venezia, Italy
Maria Cerreta	Università degli Studi di Napoli Federico II, Italy
Maddalena Chimisso	Università degli Studi del Molise, Italy
Chiara Chioni	Università degli Studi di Trento, Italy
Annalisa Contato	Università degli Studi di Palermo, Italy
Cristina Coscia	Politecnico di Torino, Italy
Marta Dell'Ovo	Politecnico di Milano, Italy
Benedetta Di Leo	Università Politecnica delle Marche, Italy
Sara Favargiotti	Università degli Studi di Trento, Italy
Maddalena Ferretti	Università Politecnica delle Marche, Italy
Salvo Giuffrida	Università degli Studi di Palermo, Italy
Barbara Lino	Università degli Studi di Palermo, Italy
Umberto Mecca	Politecnico di Torino, Italy
Beatrice Mecca	Politecnico di Torino, Italy
Giuliano Poli	Università degli Studi di Napoli Federico II, Italy
Marco Rossitti	Politecnico di Milano, Italy
Alexandra Stankulova	Politecnico di Torino, Italy
Elena Todella	Politecnico di Torino, Italy
Asja Aulisio	Politecnico di Torino, Italy
Giulia Datola	Politecnico di Milano, Italy

Francesco Calabrò	Università degli Studi Mediterranea di Reggio Calabria, Italy
Valeria Saiu	Università degli Studi di Cagliari, Italy
Maria Rosa Trovato	Università di Catania, Italy

Econometric and Multidimensional Evaluation in Urban Environment (EMEUE 2025)

Workshop Organizers

Maria Cerreta	University of Naples Federico II, Italy
Carmelo Maria Torre	Polytechnic University of Bari, Italy
Pierluigi Morano	Polytechnic University of Bari, Italy
Simona Panaro	University of Naples Federico II, Italy
Felicia Di Liddo	University of Naples Federico II, Italy
Debora Anelli	University of Naples Federico II, Italy

Workshop Program Committee Members

Carmelo Maria Torre	Polytechnic University of Bari, Italy
Maria Cerreta	University of Naples Federico II, Italy
Pierluigi Morano	Polytechnic University of Bari, Italy
Francesco Tajani	Sapienza University of Rome, Italy
Simona Panaro	University of Naples Federico II, Italy
Felicia di Liddo	Polytechnic University of Bari, Italy
Debora Anelli	Sapienza University of Rome, Italy
Giuliano Poli	University of Naples Federico II, Italy
Maria Somma	University of Naples Federico II, Italy
Simona Panaro	University of Campania Luigi Vanvitelli, Italy
Laura Di Tommaso	University of Naples Federico II, Italy
Caterina Loffredo	University of Naples Federico II, Italy
Ludovica La Rocca	University of Naples Federico II, Italy
Sabrina Sacco	Politecnico di Milano, Italy
Piero Zizzania	University of Naples Federico II, Italy
Gaia Daldanise	CNR IRISS, Italy
Benedetta Grieco	University of Naples Federico II, Italy
Giuseppe Ciciriello	University of Naples Federico II, Italy
Marta Dell'Ovo	Politecnico di Milano, Italy
Daniele Cannatella	TU Delft University, The Netherlands
Eugenio Muccio	University of Naples Federico II, Italy
Sveva Ventre	University of Naples Federico II, Italy

Governance of Energy Transition: Environmental, Landscape, Social and Spatial Planning (ENERGY_PLANNING 2025)

Workshop Organizers

Mara Ladu	University of Cagliari, Italy
Ginevra Balletto	University of Cagliari, Italy
Emilio Ghiani	University of Cagliari, Italy
Alessandra Marra	University of Salerno, Italy
Roberto De Lotto	University of Pavia, Italy
Balázs Kulcsár	Chalmers University of Technology, Sweden

Workshop Program Committee Members

Riccardo Trevisan	University of Cagliari, Italy
Marco Naseddu	University of Cagliari, Italy
Giuseppe Borruso	University of Trieste, Italy
Andrea Gallo	University of Trieste, Italy
Francesca Sinatra	University of Trieste, Italy
Maria Attard	University of Malta, Malta
Tu Anh Trinh	UEH University Ho Chi Minh City, Vietnam
Marcello Tadini	University of Eastern Piedmont, Italy
Luigi Mundula	University for Foreigners of Perugia, Italy
Silvia Battino	University of Sassari, Italy
Maria del Mar Munoz Leonisio	University of Cádiz, Spain
Anna Richiedei	University of Brescia, Italy
Michele Pezzagno	University of Brescia, Italy
Federico Mertellozzo	University of Firenze, Italy
Marco Mazzarino	IUAV University Venice, Italy

Ecosystem Services in Spatial Planning for Climate Neutral Urban and Rural Areas (ESSP 2025)

Workshop Organizers

Sabrina Lai	University of Cagliari, Italy
Francesco Scorza	University of Basilicata, Italy
Corrado Zoppi	University of Cagliari, Italy
Beniamino Murgante	University of Basilicata, Italy
Carmela Gargiulo	University of Naples Federico II, Italy
Floriana Zucaro	University of Naples Federico II, Italy

Workshop Program Committee Members

Alfonso Annunziata	University of Basilicata, Italy
Ginevra Balletto	University of Cagliari, Italy
Ivan Blečić	University of Cagliari, Italy
Giuseppe Borruso	University of Trieste, Italy
Barbara Caselli	University of Parma, Italy
Maria Cerreta	University of Naples Federico II, Italy
Chiara Garau	University of Cagliari, Italy
Carmen Guida	University of Naples Federico II, Italy
Federica Isola	University of Cagliari, Italy
Francesca Leccis	University of Cagliari, Italy
Federica Leone	University of Cagliari, Italy
Silvia Rossetti	University of Parma, Italy
Luigi Santopietro	University of Basilicata, Italy
Carmelo Torre	Polytechnic of Bari, Italy

The 15th International Workshop on Future Information System Technologies and Applications (FiSTA 2025)

Workshop Organizers

Bernady O. Apduhan	Kyushu Sangyo University, Japan
Rafael Santos	Brazilian National Institute for Space Research, Brazil

Workshop Program Committee Members

Agustinus Borgy Waluyo	Monash University, Australia
Andre Ricardo Abed Grégio	Federal University of Paraná, Brazil
Eric Pardede	La Trobe University, Australia
Kai Cheng	Kyushu Sangyo University, Japan
Ching-Hsien Hsu	Asia University, Taiwan
Fenghui Yao	Tennessee State University, USA
Yusuke Gotoh	Okayama University, Japan
Alvaro Fazenda	Federal University of São Paulo, Brazil
Kazuaki Tanaka	Kyushu Institute of Technology, Japan
Tengku Adil	MARA Technological University, Malaysia
Toshihiro Yamauchi	Okayama University, Japan
Yasuaki Sumida	Kyushu Sangyo University, Japan
Earl Ryan Aleluya	MSU-Iligan Institute of Technology, Philippines
Cherry Mae G. Villame	MSU-Iligan Institute of Technology, Philippines
Anton Louise De Ocampo	Batangas State University, Philippines
Krishnamoorthy Ranganthan	Chennai Institute of Technology, India

Flow Management in Urban Contexts (FMUC 2025)

Workshop Organizers

Alessio Pino	Kore University of Enna, Italy
Giovanna Acampa	Kore University of Enna, Italy

Workshop Program Committee Members

Giovanna Acampa	University of Florence, Italy
Alessio Pino	Kore University of Enna, Italy
Mariolina Grasso	Università Kore di Enna, Italy
Fabrizio Battisti	University of Florence, Italy
Fabrizio Finucci	Roma Tre University, Italy
Antonella G. Masanotti	Roma Tre University, Italy
Daniele Mazzoni	Roma Tre University, Italy

Geographical Analysis, Urban Modeling, Spatial Statistics 2025 (Geog-And-Mod 2025)

Workshop Organizers

Beniamino Murgante	University of Basilicata, Italy
Giuseppe Borruso	University of Trieste, Italy
Hartmut Asche	University of Potsdam, Germany
Rodrigo Tapia McClung	CentroGeo, Mexico
Andreas Fricke	University of Potsdam, Germany

Workshop Program Committee Members

Giuseppe Borruso	University of Trieste, Italy
Beniamino Murgante	University of Basilicata, Italy
Hartmut Asche	University of Potsdam, Germany
Rodrigo Tapia-McClung	Centro de Investigación en Ciencias de Información Geoespacial (CentroGeo), Mexico
Andreas Fricke	University of Potsdam, Germany
Malgorzata Hanzl	Lodz University of Technology, Poland
Anastasia Stratigea	National Technical University of Athens, Greece
Ljiljiana Zivkovic	Republic Geodetic Authority of Serbia, Serbia
Ginevra Balletto	University of Cagliari, Italy
Silvia Battino	University of Sassari, Italy
Mara Ladu	University of Cagliari, Italy
Maria del Mar Munoz Leonisio	University of Cádiz, Spain
Ahinoa Amaro Garcia	University of Las Palmas of Gran Canaria, Spain
Maria Attard	University of Malta, Malta

Enrico D'agostini	World Maritime University, Sweden
Francesca Krasna	University of Trieste, Italy
Brisol García García	Polytechnic University of Quintana Roo, Mexico
Tu Anh Trinh	UEH University, Vietnam
Giovanni Mauro	Università degli Studi della Campania, Italy
Maria Ronza	University of Naples Federico II, Italy
Massimiliano Bencardino	University of Salerno, Italy
Andrea Gallo	Ca' Foscari University of Venice, Italy
Francesca Sinatra	University of Trieste, Italy
Salvatore Dore	University of Trieste, Italy

Geogames for Sustainable Development (Geogames 2025)

Workshop Organizer

| Alenka Poplin | Iowa State University, USA |

Workshop Program Committee Members

Alenka Poplin	Iowa State University, USA
Bruno Amaral de Andrade	Portucalense University, Portugal
Brian Tomaszewski	Rochester Institute of Technology, USA
Deepak Marhatta	Tribhuvan University, Nepal
Alessandro Plaisant	University of Sassari, Italy
David Schwartz	Rochester Institute of Technology, USA
Silvia Rossetti	University of Parma, Italy
Floriana Zucaro	University of Naples Federico II, Italy
Alfonso Annunziata	University of Basilicata, Italy
Reza Askarizad	University of Cagliari, Italy
Chiara Garau	University of Cagliari, Italy
Tanja Congiu	University of Sassari, Italy

Geomatics for Resource Monitoring and Management (GRMM 2025)

Workshop Organizers

Alberico Sonnessa	Politecnico di Bari, Italy
Eufemia Tarantino	Politecnico di Bari, Italy
Alessandra Capolupo	Politecnico di Bari, Italy

Workshop Program Committee Members

| Umberto Fratino | Politecnico di Bari, Italy |
| Valeria Monno | Politecnico di Bari, Italy |

Antonino Maltese	Università degli studi di Palermo, Italy
Athos Agapiou	Cyprus University of Technology, Cyprus
Michele Mangiameli	Università di Catania, Italy
Angela Gorgoglione	Universidad de la República de Uruguay, Uruguay
Roberta Ravanelli	University of Liège, Belgium
Ester Scotto di Perta	Università degli studi di Napoli Federico II, Italy
Giacomo Caporusso	CNR, Italy
Andrea Montanino	International Centre for Numerical Methods in Engineering of Barcelona, Spain
Antonino Iannuzzo	Università degli studi del Sannio, Italy
Alessandro Pagano	Politecnico di Bari, Italy
Francesco Di Capua	Università degli Studi della Basilicata, Italy
Albertini Cinzia	CNR-IREA, Italy
Alessandra Saponieri	Università degli studi del Salento, Italy
PierFrancesco Recchi	Università degli studi di Napoli Federico II, Italy
Vincenzo Totaro	Politecnico di Bari, Italy
Stefania Santoro	CNR Water Research Institute, Italy
Francesco Bimbo	University of Foggia, Italy
Cristina Proietti	Istituto Nazionale di Geofisica e Vulcanologia, Italy
Carla Cavallo	University of Salerno, Italy
Gaetano Falcone	Università degli Studi di Napoli Federico II, Italy
Valeria Belloni	Sapienza University of Rome, Italy
Alessandra Mascitelli	University of Chieti-Pescara, Italy

HERitage and CLIMAte neutrality. Resilient approach for nature centered/based sustainable cities (HERCLIMA 2025)

Workshop Organizers

Celestina Fazia	Università di Enna Kore, Italy
Angrilli Massimo	University of Chieti-Pescara, Italy
Clara Stella Vicari Aversa	University of Reggio Calabria, Italy
Dorina Camelia Ilies	University of Oradea, Romania
Mariana Ratiu	University of Oradea, Romania

Workshop Program Committee Members

Alessandro Camiz	Università d'Annunzio, Italy
Mario Morrica	University of Urbino, Italy
Thowayeb Hassan	King Faisal University, Saudi Arabia
Alessandro Barracco	Università Kore di Enna, Italy
Kaoutare Amini Alaoui	Mohammed VI Polytechnic University (UM6P), Morocco

Mariana Ratiu   University of Oradea, Romania
Valentina Ciuffreda   Università Chieti-Pescara, Italy

International Workshop on Information and Knowledge in the Internet of Things (IKIT 2025)

Workshop Organizers
Teresa Guarda   Universidad Estatal Península de Santa Elena, Ecuador
Luis Enrique Chuquimarca Jimenez   Universidad Estatal Península de Santa Elena, Ecuador
Gustavo Gatica   Universidad Andrés Bello, Chile
Filipe Mota Pinto   Polytechnic Institute of Leiria, Portugal
Arnulfo Alanis   Instituto Tecnológico de Tijuana, Mexico
Luis Mazon   Universidad Estatal Península de Santa Elena, Spain

Workshop Program Committee Members
Arnulfo Alanis   Instituto Tecnológico de Tijuana, Mexico
Bruno Sousa   University of Coimbra, Portugal
Carlos Balsa   Instituto Politécnico de Bragança, Portugal
Filipe Mota Pinto   Instituto Politécnico de Leiria, Portugal
Gustavo Gatica   Universidad Andrés Bello, Chile
Isabel Lopes   Instituto Politécnico de Bragança, Portugal
José-María Díaz-Nafría   Universidad a Distancia, Spain
Maria Fernanda Augusto   BiTrum Research Group, Spain
Maria Isabel Ribeiro   Instituto Politécnico Bragança, Portugal
Modestos Stavrakis   University of the Aegean, Greece
Simone Belli   Universidad Complutense de Madrid, Spain
Walter Lopes Neto   Instituto Federal de Educação, Brazil

International Workshop on territorial Planning to integrate Risk prevention and urban Ontologies (IWPRO 2025)

Workshop Organizers
Beniamino Murgante   University of Basilicata, Italy
Roberto De Lotto   University of Pavia, Italy
Elisabetta Maria Venco   University of Pavia, Italy
Caterina Pietra   University of Pavia, Italy

Workshop Program Committee Members

Stefano Borgo	Consiglio Nazionale delle Ricerche ISTC, Italy
Valentina Costa	Università di Genova, Italy
Hamid Danesh Pajouh	Middle East Technical University, Turkey
Ilaria Delponte	Università di Genova, Italy
Lorena Fiorini	Università de L'Aquila, Italy
Veronica Gazzola	Politecnico di Milano, Italy
Ghazaleh Goodarzi	Islamic Azad University, Iran
Michele Grimaldi	Università degli Studi di Salerno, Italy
Alessandra Marra	Università degli Studi di Salerno, Italy
Naghmeh Mohammadpourlima	Åbo Akademi University, Finland
Francesca Pirlone	Università di Genova, Italy
Silvia Rossetti	Università di Parma, Italy
Bahareh Shahsavari	University of Minnesota, USA
Ilenia Spadaro	Università di Genova, Italy
Maria Rosaria Stufano Melone	Politecnico di Bari, Italy

Regional Connectivity, Spatial Accessibility and MaaS for Social Inclusion (MaaS 2025)

Workshop Organizers

Mara Ladu	University of Cagliari, Italy
Ginevra Balletto	University of Cagliari, Italy
Gianfranco Fancello	University of Cagliari, Italy
Tanja Congiu	University of Sassari, Italy
Patrizia Serra	University of Cagliari, Italy
Francesco Piras	University of Cagliari, Italy

Workshop Program Committee Members

Marco Naseddu	University of Cagliari, Italy
Italo Meloni	University of Cagliari, Italy
Giuseppe Borruso	University of Trieste, Italy
Andrea Gallo	University of Trieste, Italy
Francesca Sinatra	University of Trieste, Italy
Maria Attard	University of Malta, Malta
Tu Anh Trinh	UEH University, Vietnam
Marcello Tadini	University of Eastern Piedmont, Italy
Luigi Mundula	University for Foreigners of Perugia, Italy
Silvia Battino	University of Sassari, Italy
Brunella Brundu	University of Sassari, Italy
Veronica Camerada	University of Sassari, Italy

Maria del Mar Munoz Leonisio	University of Cádiz, Spain
Anna Richiedei	University of Brescia, Italy
Michele Pezzagno	University of Brescia, Italy
Marco Mazzarino	IUAV University Venice, Italy

The Development of Urban Mobility Management, Road Safety and Risk Assessment (MANTAIN 2025)

Workshop Organizers

Antonio Russo	Università degli Studi di Enna, Italy
Corrado Rindone	University of Reggio Calabria, Italy
Antonio Polimeni	University of Messina, Italy
Florin Rusca	Politehnica University of Bucharest, Romania
Grigorios Fountas	Aristotle University of Thessaloniki, Greece
Antonio Comi	University of Rome Tor Vergata, Italy

Workshop Program Committee Members

Massimo Di Gangi	University of Messina, Italy
Orlando Marco Belcore	University of Messina, Italy
Antonio Polimeni	University of Messina, Italy
Socrates Basbas	Aristotle University of Thessaloniki, Greece
Claudia Caballini	Polytechnic of Torino, Italy
Efstathios Bouhouras	Aristotle University of Thessaloniki, Greece
Stefano Ricci	Sapienza University of Rome, Italy
Marina Zanne	University of Lubljana, Slovenia
Kh Md Nahiduzzaman	Mohammed VI Polytechnic University, Morocco
Alexsandra Deluka Tibljaš	University of Rijeka, Croatia
Guilhermina Torrao	Aston University, UK

Multidimensional Evolutionary Evaluations for Transformative Approaches (MEETA 2025)

Workshop Organizers

Maria Cerreta	University of Naples Federico II, Italy
Giuliano Poli	University of Naples Federico II, Italy
Maria Somma	University of Naples Federico II, Italy
Gaia Daldanise	CNR IRISS, Italy
Ludovica La Rocca	University of Naples Federico II, Italy

Workshop Program Committee Members

Maria Cerreta	University of Naples Federico II, Italy
Giuliano Poli	University of Naples Federico II, Italy
Maria Somma	University of Naples Federico II, Italy
Laura Di Tommaso	University of Naples Federico II, Italy
Sabrina Sacco	Politecnico di Milano, Italy
Piero Zizzania	University of Naples Federico II, Italy
Gaia Daldanise	CNR IRISS, Italy
Benedetta Grieco	University of Naples Federico II, Italy
Giuseppe Ciciriello	University of Naples Federico II, Italy
Marta Dell'Ovo	Politecnico di Milano, Italy
Daniele Cannatella	TU Delft, The Netherlands
Eugenio Muccio	University of Naples Federico II, Italy
Francesco Piras	University of Cagliari, Italy
Diana Rolando	Politecnico di Torino, Italy
Sveva Ventre	University of Naples Federico II, Italy
Caterina Loffredo	University of Naples Federico II, Italy
Ludovica La Rocca	University of Naples Federico II, Italy
Simona Panaro	University of Campania Luigi Vanvitelli, Italy

Building Multi-dimensional Models for Assessing Complex Environmental Systems (MES 2025)

Workshop Organizers

Vanessa Assumma	University of Bologna, Italy
Caterina Caprioli	Politecnico di Torino, Italy
Giulia Datola	Politecnico di Milano, Italy
Federico Dell'Anna	University of Bologna, Italy
Marta Dell'Ovo	Politecnico di Milano, Italy
Marco Rossitti	Politecnico di Milano, Italy

Workshop Program Committee Members

Vanessa Assumma	Università di Bologna, Bologna
Caterina Caprioli	Politecnico di Torino, Italy
Giulia Datola	DAStU Politecnico di Milano, Italy
Federico Dell'Anna	Politecnico di Torino, Italy
Marta Dell'Ovo	Politecnico di Milano, Italy
Marco Rossitti	Politecnico di Milano, Italy
Francesca Torrieri	Politecnico di Milano, Italy
Mariarosaria Angrisano	Università Telematica Pegaso, Italy
Maksims Feofilovs	Riga Technical University, Latvia

Danny Caprini	Politecnico di Milano, Italy
Giulio Cavana	Politecnico di Torino, Italy
Sebastiano Barbieri	Politecnico di Torino, Italy
Marta Bottero	Politecnico di Torino, Italy
Francesco Cosentino	Politecnico di Milano, Italy
Silvia Ronchi	Politecnico di Milano, Italy
Chiara Mazzarella	TU Delft, Netherlands
Marco Volpatti	Politecnico di Torino, Italy
Chiara D'Alpaos	Università degli Studi di Padova, Italy
Alessandra Oppio	Politecnico di Milano, Italy
Alessia Crisopulli	Politecnico di Milano, Italy
Domenico D'Uva	Politecnico di Milano, Italy
Giorgia Malavasi	Politecnico di Torino, Italy
Rubina Canesi	Università degli Studi di Padova, Italy
Elena Todella	Politecnico di Torino, Italy
Beatrice Mecca	Politecnico di Torino, Italy
Giulia Marzani	University of Bologna, Italy
Isabella Giovanetti	University of Bologna, Italy
Lucia Petronio	University of Bologna, Italy
Franco Corti	University of Padova, Italy
Salvatore De Pascalis	Politecnico di Milano, Italy
Valeria Vitulano	Politecnico di Torino, Italy
Lorenzo Diana	Università degli studi di Napoli Federico II, Italy
Maksims Feofilovs	Riga Technical University, Latvia
Marco De Luca	Politecnico di Torino, Italy
Ilaria Cazzola	Politecnico di Torino, Italy
Andrea De Toni	Politecnico di Milano, Italy
Eugenio Muccio	University of Naples Federico II, Italy
Giuliano Poli	University of Naples Federico II, Italy
Francesco Sica	University "La Sapienza" of Rome, Italy
Elena Di Pirro	Università degli Studi del Molise, Italy
Riccardo Alba	Università di Torino, Italy
Irene Regaiolo	Università di Torino, Italy
Francesca Cochis	Università di Torino, Italy

Modelling Liveable Cities: Techniques, Methods, Challenges, and Perspectives Behind the 'X-Minute' City (MLC 2025)

Workshop Organizers

Federico Mara	University of Pisa, Italy
Valerio Cutini	University of Pisa, Italy
Alessandro Araldi	Université Côte d'Azur, France

Flávia Lopes   Chalmers University of Technology, Sweden
Giovanni Fusco   Université Côte d'Azur, France

Workshop Program Committee Members
Simone Rusci   University of Pisa, Italy
Lorena Fiorini   University of L'Aquila, Italy
Chiara Di Dato   University of L'Aquila, Italy
Francesco Zullo   University of L'Aquila, Italy
Alfonso Annunziata   University of Basilicata, Italy
Beniamino Murgante   University of Basilicata, Italy
Alessandro Araldi   Universitè Côte d'Azur, France
Chiara Garau   University of Cagliari, Italy
Giampiero Lombardini   Università di Genova, Italy
Flavia Lopes   Chalmers University of Technology, Sweden
Giovanni Fusco   Universitè Côte d'Azur, France

Mathematical Methods for Image Processing and Understanding 2025 (MMIPU 2025)

Workshop Organizers
Ivan Gerace   Università degli Studi di Perugia, Italy
Gianluca Vinti   Università degli Studi di Perugia, Italy
Arianna Travaglini   Università degli Studi della Basilicata, Italy

Workshop Program Committee Members
Ivan Gerace   University of Perugia, Italy
Gianluca Vinti   University of Perugia, Italy
Arianna Travaglini   University of Basilicata, Italy
Marco Baioletti   University of Perugia, Italy
Marco Donatelli   University of Insubria, Italy
Anna Tonazzini   C.N.R. Pisa, Italy
Muhammad Hanif   Ghulam Ishaq Khan Institute of Engineering
                                Sciences and Technology, Pakistan
Francesco Marchetti   University of Padua, Italy
Wolfgang Erb   University of Padua, Italy
Danilo Costarelli   University of Perugia, Italy
Francesco Santini   University of Perugia, Italy
Valentina Giorgetti   University of Perugia, Italy

Mobility Opportunities Bridging Inequalities: Social Inclusion and Gender Equity Initiatives Strategies Against Fragmentation and Complexity of Mobility (MOBIL-EGI 2025)

Workshop Organizers

Tiziana Campisi	University of Enna Kore, Italy
Guilhermina Torrao	Aston University, UK
Socrates Basbas	Aristotle University of Thessaloniki, Greece
Tanja Congiu	University of Sassari, Italy
Stefanos Tsigdinos	National Technical University of Athens, Greece
Florin Nemtanu	Politehnica University of Bucharest, Romania

Workshop Program Committee Members

Massimo Di Gangi	University of Messina, Italy
Orlando Marco Belcore	University of Messina, Italy
Francesco Russo	Mediterranean University of Reggio Calabria, Italy
Alexandros Nikitas	University of Huddersfield, UK
Marilisa Nigro	Rome Tre University, Italy
Kh Md Nahiduzzaman	Mohammed VI Polytechnic University, Morocco
Efstathios Bouhouras	Aristotle University of Thessaloniki, Greece
Antonio Comi	University of Rome Tor Vergata, Italy
Edouard Ivanjko	University of Zagreb, Slovenia
Osvaldo Gervasi	University of Perugia, Italy
Beniamino Murgante	University of Basilicata, Italy
Chiara Garau	University of Cagliari, Italy

MOdels and indicators for assessing and measuring the urban settlement deVElopment in the view of NET ZERO by 2050 (MOVEto0 2025)

Workshop Organizers

Lorena Fiorini	University of L'Aquila, Italy
Lucia Saganeiti	CNR-IMAA, Italy
Angela Pilogallo	CNR-IMAA, Italy
Alessandro Marucci	University of L'Aquila, Italy
Francesco Zullo	University of L'Aquila, Italy

Workshop Program Committee Members

Ginevra Balletto	University of Cagliari, Italy
Giuseppe Borruso	University of Trieste, Italy
Chiara Garau	University of Cagliari, Italy

Beniamino Murgante	University of Basilicata, Italy
Giulia Desogus	University of Cagliari, Italy
Ljiljana Zivkovic	Republic Geodetic Authority, Serbia
Luigi Santopietro	University of Basilicata, Italy
Ilaria Delponte	University of Genoa, Italy
Carmen Guida	University of Naples Federico II, Italy
Chiara Di Dato	University of L'Aquila, Italy

5th Workshop on Privacy in the Cloud/Edge/IoT World (PCEIoT 2025)

Workshop Organizers

Lelio Campanile	Università degli Studi della Campania Luigi Vanvitelli, Italy
Mauro Iacono	Università degli Studi della Campania Luigi Vanvitelli, Italy
Michele Mastroianni	Università degli Studi di Foggia, Italy

Workshop Program Committee Members

Arcangelo Castiglione	Università degli Studi di Salerno, Italy
Maria Ganzha	Warsaw University of Technology, Poland
Daniel Grzonka	Cracow University of Technology, Poland
Antonio Iannuzzi	Università degli Studi Roma Tre, Italy
Armando Tacchella	Università degli Studi di Genova, Italy
Biagio Boi	University of Salerno, Italy
Marco De Santis	University of Salerno, Italy
Fiammetta Marulli	Università degli Studi della Campania "L. Vanvitelli", Italy
Christian Riccio	Università degli Studi della Campania "L. Vanvitelli", Italy
Luigi Piero Di Bonito	Università degli Studi di Napoli Federico II, Italy

Preserving Our Past: Spatial and Remote Sensing Technologies for Cultural Heritage in a Changing Climate (POP 2025)

Workshop Organizers

Maria Danese	CNR-ISPC, Italy
Nicola Masini	CNR-ISPC, Italy
Rosa Lasaponara	CNR-IMAA, Italy

Workshop Program Committee Members

Maria Danese	CNR-ISPC, Italy
Nicola Masini	CNR-ISPC, Italy
Rosa Lasaponara	CNR-IMAA, Italy
Dario Gioia	CNR-ISPC, Italy
Giuseppe Corrado	Università degli Studi della Basilicata, Italy
Canio Sabia	CNR-ISPC, Italy

Processes, methods and tools towards RESilient cities and cultural and historic sites prone to SOD and ROD disasters (RES 2025)

Workshop Organizers

Elena Cantatore	Polytechnic University of Bari, Italy
Dario Esposito	Polytechnic University of Bari, Italy
Alberico Sonnessa	Polytechnic University of Bari, Italy

Workshop Program Committee Members

Elena Cantatore	Politecnico di Bari, Italy
Dario Esposito	Politecnico di Bari, Italy
Alberico Sonnessa	Politecnico di Bari, Italy
Valeria Belloni	Sapienza University of Rome, Italy
Michela Ravanelli	Sapienza University of Rome, Italy
Silvano Dal Sasso	University of Basilicata, Italy
Francesco Chiaravalloti	CNR - IRPI, Italy
Roberta Ravanelli	University of Liège, Belgium
Alessandra Mascitelli	University of Chieti-Pescara, Italy
Francesco Di Capua	University of Basilicata, Italy
Gabriele Bernardini	Università Politecnica delle Marche, Italy
Vito Domenico Porcari	University of Basilicata, Italy
Carmen Rosa Fattore	University of Basilicata, Italy
Stefania Santoro	Water Research Institute, Italy

Scientific Computing Infrastructure (SCI 2025)

Workshop Organizers

Vladimir Korkhov	Saint Petersburg State University, Russia
Elena Stankova	Saint Petersburg State University, Russia
Nataliia Kulabukhova	Saint Petersburg State University, Russia

Workshop Program Committee Members

Adam Belloum	University of Amsterdam, the Netherlands
Dmitrii Vasiunin	Deutsche Telekom Cloud Services E.P.E., Greece
Serob Balyan	Osensus Arm LLC, Armenia
Suren Abrahamyan	Osensus Arm LLC, Armenia
Ashot Sergey Gevorkyan	NAS of Armenia, Armenia
Michal Hnatic	Univerzita Pavla Jozefa Šafárika v Košiciach, Slovakia
Michail Panteleyev	Saint Petersburg Electrotecnical University, Russia
Martin Vala	Univerzita Pavla Jozefa Šafárika v Košiciach, Slovakia
Nodir Zaynalov	Tashkent University of Information Technologies named after Muhammad al Khwarizmi, Uzbekistan
Michail Panteleyev	Saint Petersburg Electrotecnical University, Russia
Alexander Degtyarev	Saint Petersburg University, Russia
Alexander Bogdanov	St. Petersburg State University, Russia

Ports and Logistics of the Future - Smartness and Sustainability (SmartPorts 2025)

Workshop Organizers

Andrea Gallo	Università degli Studi di Trieste, Italy
Gianfranco Fancello	University of Cagliari, Italy
Giuseppe Borruso	Università degli Studi di Trieste, Italy
Enrico D'agostini	World Maritime University, Sweden
Silvia Battino	Università degli Studi di Sassari, Italy
Veronica Camerada	Università degli Studi di Sassari, Italy

Workshop Program Committee Members

Giuseppe Borruso	University of Trieste, Italy
Beniamino Murgante	University of Basilicata, Italy
Ginevra Balletto	University of Cagliari, Italy
Silvia Battino	University of Sassari, Italy
Mara Ladu	University of Cagliari, Italy
Maria del Mar Munoz Leonisio	University of Cádiz, Spain
Ahinoa Amaro Garcia	University of Las Palmas of Gran Canaria, Spain
Maria Attard	University of Malta, Malta
Enrico D'agostini	World Maritime University, Sweden
Francesca Krasna	University of Trieste, Italy

Tu Anh Trinh	UEH University - Ho Chi Minh City, Vietnam
Giovanni Mauro	Università degli Studi della Campania, Italy
Maria Ronza	University of Naples Federico II, Italy
Massimiliano Bencardino	University of Salerno, Italy
Andrea Gallo	Ca' Foscari University of Venice, Italy
Francesca Sinatra	University of Trieste, Italy
Salvatore Dore	University of Trieste, Italy
Veronica Camerada	University of Sassari, Italy
Brunella Brundu	University of Sassari, Italy
Gianfranco Fancello	University of Cagliari, Italy
Marcello Tadini	University of Eastern Piedmont, Italy
Marco Mazzarino	IUAV University Venice
José Ángel Hernández Luis	University of Las Palmas de Gran Canaria, Spain
Marco Naseddu	University of Cagliari, Italy
Maurizio Cociancich	Adriafer, Italy
Giovanni Longo	University of Trieste, Italy
Luca Toneatti	University of Trieste, Italy
Martina Sinatra	University of Cagliari, Italy
Enrico Vanino	University of Sheffield, UK
Patrizia Serra	University of Cagliari, Italy
Agostino Bruzzone	University of Genoa, Italy
Marco Petrelli	University of Roma 3, Italy

Smart Transport and Logistics - Smart Supply Chains (SmarTransLog 2025)

Workshop Organizers

Francesca Sinatra	University of Trieste, Italy
Maria del Mar Munoz	Universidad de Cádiz, Spain
Brunella Brundu	University of Sassari, Italy
Patrizia Serra	University of Cagliari, Italy
Salvatore Dore	University of Trieste, Italy
Marco Naseddu	University of Cagliari, Italy

Workshop Program Committee Members

Giuseppe Borruso	University of Trieste, Italy
Beniamino Murgante	University of Basilicata, Italy
Ginevra Balletto	University of Cagliari, Italy
Silvia Battino	University of Sassari, Italy
Mara Ladu	University of Cagliari, Italy
Maria del Mar Munoz Leonisio	University of Cádiz, Spain
Ahinoa Amaro Garcia	University of Las Palmas of Gran Canaria, Spain

Maria Attard	University of Malta, Malta
Enrico D'agostini	World Maritime University, Sweden
Francesca Krasna	University of Trieste, Italy
Tu Anh Trinh	UEH University, Vietnam
Giovanni Mauro	Università degli Studi della Campania, Italy
Maria Ronza	University of Naples Federico II, Italy
Massimiliano Bencardino	University of Salerno, Italy
Andrea Gallo	Ca' Foscari University of Venice, Italy
Francesca Sinatra	University of Trieste, Italy
Salvatore Dore	University of Trieste, Italy
Veronica Camerada	University of Sassari, Italy
Brunella Brundu	University of Sassari, Italy
Gianfranco Fancello	University of Cagliari, Italy
Marcello Tadini	University of Eastern Piedmont, Italy
Marco Mazzarino	IUAV University Venice
José Ángel Hernández Luis	University of Las Palmas de Gran Canaria, Spain
Marco Naseddu	University of Cagliari, Italy
Maurizio Cociancich	Adriafer, Italy
Giovanni Longo	University of Trieste, Italy
Luca Toneatti	University of Trieste, Italy
Martina Sinatra	University of Cagliari, Italy
Enrico Vanino	University of Sheffield, UK
Patrizia Serra	University of Cagliari, Italy
Agostino Bruzzone	University of Genoa, Italy
Marco Petrelli	University of Roma 3, Italy

Smart Tourism (SmartTourism 2025)

Workshop Organizers

Silvia Battino	University of Sassari, Italy
Francesca Krasna	University of Trieste, Italy
Ainhoa Amaro	University of Las Palmas de Gran Canaria, Spain
Maria del Mar Munoz	University of Cádiz, Spain
Brisol García García	Polytechnic University of Quintana Roo, Mexico
Marta Meleddu	University of Sassari, Italy

Workshop Program Committee Members

Giuseppe Borruso	University of Trieste, Italy
Beniamino Murgante	University of Basilicata, Italy
Gianfranco Fancello	University of Cagliari, Italy
Mara Ladu	University of Cagliari, Italy

Martina Sinatra	University of Cagliari, Italy
Salvatore Dore	University of Trieste, Italy
Marco Mazzarino	IUAV University Venice, Italy
Veronica Camerada	University of Sassari, Italy
Brunella Brundu	University of Sassari, Italy
Maria Attard	University of Malta, Malta
Ginevra Balletto	University of Cagliari, Italy
Giovanni Mauro	University degli Studi della Campania, Italy
Salvatore Lampreu	University of Sassari, Italy
Maria Ronza	University of Naples, Italy
Massimiliano Bencardino	University of Salerno, Italy

Sustainable evolution of long-Distance frEight and paSsenger Transport (SOLIDEST 2025)

Workshop Organizers

Francesco Russo	University of Reggio Calabria, Italy
Andreas Nikiforiadis	Democritus University of Thrace, Greece
Orlando Marco Belcore	University of Messina, Italy
Antonio Comi	University of Rome Tor Vergata, Italy
Tiziana Campisi	Kore University of Enna, Italy
Aura Rusca	Politehnica University of Bucharest, Romania

Workshop Program Committee Members

Massimo Di Gangi	University of Messina, Italy
Orlando Marco Belcore	University of Messina, Italy
Antonio Polimeni	University of Messina, Italy
Socrates Basbas	Aristotle University of Thessaloniki, Greece
Efstathios Bouhouras	Aristotle University of Thessaloniki, Greece
Marina Zanne	University of Lubljana, Slovenia
Marilisa Nigro	Rome Tre University, Italy
Edoardo Marcucci	Molde University College, Norway
Eugen Rosca	Polytechnic University of Bucharest, Romania
Kh Md Nahiduzzaman	Mohammed VI Polytechnic University, Morocco
Beniamino Murgante	University of Basilicata, Italy
Chiara Garau	University of Cagliari, Italy

Sustainability Performance Assessment: Models, Approaches, and Applications Toward Interdisciplinary and Integrated Solutions (SPA 2025)

Workshop Organizers

Francesco Scorza	University of Basilicata, Italy
Sabrina Lai	University of Cagliari, Italy
Francesco Rotondo	Università Politecnica delle Marche, Italy
Jolanta Dvarioniene	Kaunas University of Technology, Lithuania
Michele Campagna	University of Cagliari, Italy
Corrado Zoppi	University of Cagliari, Italy

Workshop Program Committee Members

Federico Amato	University of Lausanne, Switzerland
Ferdinando Di Carlo	University of Basilicata, Italy
Maddalena Floris	University of Cagliari, Italy
Federica Isola	University of Cagliari, Italy
Giuseppe Las Casas	University of Basilicata, Italy
Federica Leone	University of Cagliari, Italy
Giampiero Lombardini	University of Genoa, Italy
Federico Martellozzo	University of Florence, Italy
Alessandro Marucci	University of L'Aquila, Italy
Ana Clara Moura	Universidade Federal de Minas Gerais, Brazil
Beniamino Murgante	University of Basilicata, Italy
Silviu Nate	Lucian Blaga University of Sibiu, Romania
Anastasia Stratigea	National Technical University of Athens, Greece
Francesco Zullo	University of L'Aquila, Italy
Luigi Santopietro	University of Basilicata, Italy
Benedetto Manganelli	University of Basilicata, Italy

Specifics of Smart Cities Development in Europe (SPEED 2025)

Workshop Organizers

Chiara Garau	University of Cagliari, Italy
Katarína Vitálišová	Matej Bel University, Slovak Republic
Marco Fanfani	University of Florence, Italy
Anna Vaňová	Matej Bel University, Slovak Republic
Kamila Borsekova	Matej Bel University, Slovak Republic
Paola Zamperlin	University of Florence, Italy

Workshop Program Committee Members

Claudia Loggia	University of KwaZulu-Natal, South Africa
Francesca Maltinti	University of Cagliari, Italy
Alessandro Plaisant	University of Sassari, Italy
Alenka Poplin	Iowa State University, USA
Silvia Rossetti	University of Parma, Italy
Gerardo Carpentieri	University of Naples Federico II, Italy
Carmen Guida	University of Naples Federico II, Italy
Floriana Zucaro	University of Naples Federico II, Italy
Anastasia Stratigea	National Technical University of Athens, Greece
Yiota Theodora	National Technical University of Athens, Greece
Giovanna Concu	University of Cagliari, Italy
Paolo Nesi	University of Florence, Italy
Emanuele Bellini	University of Roma Tre, Italy
Mana Dastoum	Polytechnic University of Madrid, Spain
Barbara Caselli	University of Parma, Italy
Martina Carra	University of Brescia, Italy
Alfonso Annunziata	University of Basilicata, Italy
Elisabetta Venco	University of Pavia, Italy
Caterina Pietra	University of Pavia, Italy
Enrico Collini	University of Florence, Italy
Luciano Alessandro Ipsaro Palesi	University of Florence, Italy

Smart, Safe, and Healthy Cities (SSHC 2025)

Workshop Organizers

Chiara Garau	University of Cagliari, Italy
Gerardo Carpentieri	University of Naples Federico II, Italy
Carmen Guida	University of Naples Federico II, Italy
Tanja Congiu	University of Sassari, Italy
Martina Carra	University of Brescia, Italy
Alenka Poplin	Iowa State University, USA

Workshop Program Committee Members

Rosaria Battarra	Istituto di Studi sul Mediterraneo, Italy
Barbara Caselli	University of Parma, Italy
Francesca Maltinti	University of Cagliari, Italy
Romano Fistola	Università degli Studi di Napoli Federico II, Italy
Alessandro Plaisant	University of Sassari, Italy
Silvia Rossetti	University of Parma, Italy
Marco Fanfani	University of Florence, Italy
Reza Askarizad	University of Cagliari, Italy

Floriana Zucaro	University of Naples Federico II, Italy
Anastasia Stratigea	National Technical University of Athens, Greece
Yiota Theodora	National Technical University of Athens, Greece
Giovanna Concu	University of Cagliari, Italy
Francesco Zullo	University of L'Aquila, Italy
Paola Zamperlin	University of Florence, Italy
Vincenza Torrisi	University of Catania, Italy
Tiziana Campisi	University of Enna Kore, Italy
Katarína Vitálišová	Matej Bel University, Slovakia
Tazyeen Alam	University of Cagliari, Italy
Mana Dastoum	Polytechnic University of Madrid, Spain
Martina Carra	University of Brescia, Italy
Alfonso Annunziata	University of Basilicata, Italy
Elisabetta Venco	University of Pavia, Italy
Caterina Pietra	University of Pavia, Italy

Smart and Sustainable Island Communities (SSIC 2025)

Workshop Organizers

Chiara Garau	University of Cagliari, Italy
Anastasia Stratigea	National Technical University of Athens, Greece
Yiota Theodora	National Technical University of Athens, Greece
Giovanna Concu	University of Cagliari, Italy

Workshop Program Committee Members

Milena Metalkova-Markova	University of Portsmouth, UK
Tarek Teba	University of Portsmouth, UK
Alenka Poplin	Iowa State University, USA
Gerardo Carpentieri	University of Naples Federico II, Italy
Carmen Guida	University of Naples Federico II, Italy
Floriana Zucaro	University of Naples Federico II, Italy
Silvia Rossetti	University of Parma, Italy
Barbara Caselli	University of Parma, Italy
Martina Carra	University of Brescia, Italy
Alfonso Annunziata	University of Basilicata, Italy
Maria Panagiotopoulou	National Technical University of Athens, Greece
Apostolos Lagarias	University of Thessaly, Greece
Paola Zamperlin	University of Florence, Italy
Vincenza Torrisi	University of Catania, Italy
Giuseppina Vacca	University of Cagliari, Italy
Roberto Minunno	Curtin University, Australia
Marco Zucca	University of Cagliari, Italy

Elisabetta Venco   University of Pavia, Italy
Caterina Pietra   University of Pavia, Italy
Pietro Crespi   Politecnico di Milano, Italy

From STreet Experiments to Planned Solutions (STEPS 2025)

Workshop Organizers
Silvia Rossetti   Università degli Studi di Parma, Italy
Angela Ricciardello   Kore University of Enna, Italy
Francesco Pinna   Università degli Studi di Cagliari, Italy
Chiara Garau   Università degli Studi di Cagliari, Italy
Tiziana Campisi   Kore University of Enna, Italy
Vincenza Torrisi   University of Catania, Italy

Workshop Program Committee Members
Martina Carra   University of Brescia, Italy
Barbara Caselli   University of Parma, Italy
Tanja Congiu   University of Sassari, Italy
Gabriele D'Orso   University of Palermo, Italy
Matteo Ignaccolo   University of Catania, Italy
Md Kh Nahiduzzaman   Mohammed VI Polytechnic University, Morocco
Muhammad Ahmad Al-Rashid   University of Malaya, Malaysia
Alessandro Plaisant   University of Sassari, Italy
Marianna Ruggieri   University of Enna Kore, Italy
Michele Zazzi   University of Parma, Italy

Sustainable Tourism Evaluations: approaches, methods and indicators (STEva 2025)

Workshop Organizers
Mariolina Grasso   Università Kore di Enna, Italy
Fabrizio Finucci   Roma Tre University, Italy
Daniele Mazzoni   Roma Tre University, Italy
Antonella G. Masanotti   Roma Tre University, Italy
Giovanna Acampa   University of Florence, Italy

Workshop Program Committee Members
Giovanna Acampa   University of Florence, Italy
Fabrizio Finucci   Roma Tre University, Italy
Mariolina Grasso   "Kore" University of Enna, Italy

Alberto Marzo	Ministero della Cultura, Italy
Antonella G. Masanotti	Roma Tre University, Italy
Daniele Mazzoni	Roma Tre University, Italy
Rocco Murro	Sapienza University of Rome, Italy
Claudio Piferi	University of Florence, Italy
Alessio Pino	"Kore" University of Enna, Italy
Nicoletta Setola	University of Florence, Italy
Laura Calcagnini	Roma Tre University, Italy
Antonio Magarò	Roma Tre University, Italy
Janos Ghyerghyak	University of Pécs, Hungary
Ágnes Borsos	University of Pécs, Hungary
Fabrizio Battisti	University of Florence, Italy

Sustainable Development of Ports (SUSTAINABLEPORTS 2025)

Workshop Organizers

Tiziana Campisi	University of Enna KORE, Italy
Giuseppe Musolino	University of Reggio Calabria, Italy
Efstathios Bouhouras	Aristotle University of Thessaloniki, Greece
Elen Twrdy	University of Ljubljana, Slovenia
Elena Cocuzza	University of Catania, Italy
Aura Rusca	Politehnica University of Bucharest, Romania

Workshop Program Committee Members

Massimo Di Gangi	University of Messina, Italy
Orlando Marco Belcore	University of Messina, Italy
Antonio Polimeni	University of Messina, Italy
Claudia Caballini	Polytechnic of Torino, Italy
Gianfranco Fancello	University of Cagliari, Italy
Marina Zanne	University of Lubljana, Slovenia
Stefano Ricci	Sapienza University of Rome, Italy
Beniamino Murgante	University of Basilicata, Italy
Chiara Garau	University of Cagliari, Italy

Theoretical and Computational Chemistry and Its Applications (TCCMA 2025)

Workshop Organizers

Noelia Faginas Lago	Università di Perugia, Italy
Andrea Lombardi	Università di Perugia, Italy
Marcos Mandado Alonso	University of Vigo, Spain

Workshop Program Committee Members

Noelia Faginas-Lago	University of Perugia, Italy
Andrea Lombardi	University of Perugia, Italy
Marcos Mandado	University of Vigo, Spain
Angeles Peña	University of Vigo, Spain
Luca Mancini	Universiy of Perugia, Italy
Massimiliano Bartolomei	CSIC, Spain
Cecilia Coletti	University of Chieti-Pescara, Italy
Iñaki Tuñón	Universidad de Valencia, Spain
Albert Rimola Gilbert	Universitat Autònoma de Barcelona, Spain
Stefano Falcinelli	University of Perugia, Italy
Dario Campisi	University of Perugia, Italy
Ernesto García Para	University of the Basque Country, Spain
Giacomo Giorgi	University of Perugia, Italy
Tomás González Lezana	IFF CSIC, Spain
Enrique M. Cabaleiro Lago	Universidade de Santiago de Compostela, Spain
Aurora Costales	Universidad de Oviedo, Spain
Angel Martin	Universidad de Oviedo, Spain
Jose Manuel	University of Vigo, Spain
Annarita Laricchiuta	CNR ISTP Bari, Italy
Fernando Pirani	University of Perugia, Italy

Transport Infrastructures for Smart Cities (TISC 2025)

Workshop Organizers

Francesca Maltinti	University of Cagliari, Italy
Mauro Coni	University of Cagliari, Italy
Benedetto Barabino	University of Brescia, Italy
Nicoletta Rassu	University of Cagliari, Italy
James Rombi	University of Cagliari, Italy

Workshop Program Committee Members

Francesco Pinna	University of Cagliari, Italy
Chiara Garau	University of Cagliari, Italy
Mauro D'Apuzzo	University of Cassino, Italy
Roberto Minunno	Curtin University, Australia
Tiziana Campisi	University of Enna Kore, Italy
Roberto Ventura	University of Brescia, Italy
Alessandro Plaisant	University of Sassari, Italy
Massimo Di Francesco	University of Cagliari, Italy

| Vincenza Torrisi | University of Catania, Italy |
| Paola Zamperlin | University of Florence, Italy |

Transforming Urban Analytics: The Impact of Crowdsourced Mapping and Advanced AI Techniques on Future Cities (Tr-UrbAna 2025)

Workshop Organizers

Ayse Giz Gulnerman Gengec	Ankara Hacı Bayram Veli University, Turkey
Müslüm Hacar	Tildiz Technical University, Turkey
Himmet Karaman	Istanbul Technical University, Turkey

Workshop Program Committee Members

Beniamino Murgante	University of Basilicata, Italy
Abdulkadir Memduhoğlu	Harran University, Turkey
Zeynel Abidin Polat	İzmir Katip Çelebi University, Turkey
Güzide Miray Perihanoğlu	Van Yüzüncü Yıl University, Turkey
Tugba Memisoglu Baykal	Ankara Hacı Bayram Veli University, Turkey

From structural to TRAnsformative-change of City Environment: challenges and solutions and perspectives (TRACE 2025)

Workshop Organizers

Pierluigi Morano	Polytechnic University of Bari, Italy
Maria Rosaria Guarini	Sapienza University of Rome, Italy
Francesco Sica	Sapienza University of Rome, Italy
Francesco Tajani	Sapienza University of Rome, Italy
Marco Locurcio	Polytechnic University of Bari, Italy
Debora Anelli	Polytechnic University of Bari, Italy

Workshop Program Committee Members

Felicia di Liddo	Politecnico di Bari, Italia
Valeria Saiu	Università di Cagliari, Italia
Emma Sabatelli	Sapienza Università di Roma, Italia
Antonella Roma	Sapienza Università di Roma, Italia
Giuseppe Cerullo	Sapienza Università di Roma, Italia
Lucia della Spina	Università di Reggio Calabria, Italia
Alejandro Segura de la Cal	Politecnico di Madrid, Spain
Yilsy Nuñez	Politecnico di Madrid, Spain
Gabriella Maselli	Università di Salerno, Italy
Maria Rosa Trovato	Università di Catania, Italy

Manuela Rebaudengo	Politecnico di Torino, Italy
Pierfrancesco De Paola	Università di Napoli Federico II, Italy
Daniela Tavano	Università della Calabria, Italy
Maria Saez	University of Granada, Spain
Paola Amoruso	LUM "Giuseppe Degennaro" University, Italy

Temporary Real Estate management: Approaches and methods for Time-integrated impact assessments and evaluations (TREAT 2025)

Workshop Organizers

Chiara Mazzarella	TUDelft, The Netherlands
Hilde Remoy	TUDelft, The Netherlands
Maria Cerreta	University of Naples Federico II, Italy

Workshop Program Committee Members

Chiara Mazzarella	TU Delft, The Netherlands
Hilde Remoy	TU Delft, The Netherlands
Maria Cerreta	University of Naples Federico II, Italy
Maria Somma	University of Naples Federico II, Italy
Simona Panaro	University of Campania Luigi Vanvitelli, Italy
Laura Di Tommaso	University of Naples Federico II, Italy
Caterina Loffredo	University of Naples Federico II, Italy
Ludovica La Rocca	University of Naples Federico II, Italy
Sabrina Sacco	Politecnico di Milano, Italy
Piero Zizzania	University of Naples Federico II, Italy
Gaia Daldanise	CNR IRISS, Italy
Benedetta Grieco	University of Naples Federico II, Italy
Giuseppe Ciciriello	University of Naples Federico II, Italy
Marta Dell'Ovo	Politecnico di Milano, Italy
Daniele Cannatella	TU Delft, The Netherlands
Eugenio Muccio	University of Naples Federico II, Italy
Sveva Ventre	University of Naples Federico II, Italy

Supporting the Transition to Ecological Economy in Cities Regeneration: Circular Model Tools for Reusing Architecture and Infrastructures (TReE 2025)

Workshop Organizers

Mariarosaria Angrisano	Pegaso University, Italy
Giulio Cavana	Politecnico di Torino, Italy
Francesca Buglione	CNR-ISPC, Italy

| Antonia Gravagnuolo | CNR-ISPC, Italy |
| Piera Della Morte | Pegaso University, Italy |

Workshop Program Committee Members

Giulia Datola	Politecnico di Milano, Italy
Vanessa Assumma	University of Bologna, Italy
Marco Volpatti	Politecnico di Torino, Italy
Sebastiano Barbieri	Politecnico di Torino, Italy
Caterina Caprioli	Politecnico di Torino, Italy
Marta Dell'Ovo	Politecnico di Milano, Italy
Federico Dell'Anna	Politecnico di Torino, Italy
Elena Todella	Politecnico di Torino, Italy
Danny Casprini	Politecnico di Milano, Italy
Grazia Neglia	Università Telematica Pegaso, Italy
Francesca Nocca	Università degli Studi di Napoli Federico II, Italy
Giulio Cavana	Politecnico di Torino, Italy
Francesca Buglione	CNR-IPSC, Italy
Marco Rossitti	Politecnico di Milano, Italy
Jhon Escorcia	Politecnico di Torino, Italy
Beatrice Mecca	Politecnico di Torino, Italy
Sara Biancifiori	Politecnico di Torino, Italy

Urban Digital Twins and Data Spaces: Shaping the Future of Sustainable Cities (TwinAbleCities 2025)

Workshop Organizers

Dessislava Petrova Antonova	Sofia University, GATE Institute, Bulgaria
Beniamino Murgante	University of Basilicata, Italy
Senthil Rajendran	RMSI, Bahrain
Tiziana Campisi	Kore University of Enna, Italy
Mila Koeva	University of Twente, The Netherlands

Workshop Program Committee Members

Dessislava Petrova-Antonova	Sofia University, Bulgaria
Mila Koeva	The University of Twente, The Netherlands
Beniamino Murgante	University of Basilicata, Italy
Senthil Rajendran	RMSI, Bahrain
Tiziana Campisi	Kore University of Enna, Italy

Urban Regeneration: Innovative Tools and Evaluation Model (URITEM 2025)

Workshop Organizers

Fabrizio Battisti	University of Florence, Italy
Giovanna Acampa	University of Florence, Italy
Orazio Campo	Sapienza University of Rome, Italy
Melania Perdonò	University of Florence, Italy

Workshop Program Committee Members

Fabrizio Battisti	University of Florence, Italy
Giovanna Acampa	University of Florence, Italy
Orazio Campo	University of Rome "La Sapienza", Italy
Melania Perdonò	Università degli Studi di Firenze, Italy

Urban Space Accessibility and Mobilities (USAM 2025)

Workshop Organizers

Chiara Garau	DICAAR, University of Cagliari, Italy
Alessandro Plaisant	University of Sassari, Italy
Barbara Caselli	University of Parma, Italy
Mauro D'Apuzzo	University of Cassino and Southern Lazio, Italy
Gabriele D'Orso	University of Palermo, Italy
Matteo Ignaccolo	University of Catania, Italy

Workshop Program Committee Members

Mauro Coni	University of Cagliari, Italy
Martina Carra	University of Brescia, Italy
Tiziana Campisi	University of Enna Kore, Italy
Tanja Congiu	University of Sassari, Italy
Francesca Maltinti	University of Cagliari, Italy
Silvia Rossetti	University of Parma, Italy
Barbara Caselli	University of Parma, Italy
Angela Pilogallo	University of L'Aquila, Italy
Lorena Fiorini	University of L'Aquila, Italy
Reza Askarizad	University of Cagliari, Italy
Francesco Pinna	University of Cagliari, Italy
Aime Tsinda	University of Rwanda, Rwanda
Youssef El Ganadi	International University of Rabat, Morocco
Marco Migliore	University of Palermo, Italy
Alessio Salvatore	Italian National Research Council, Italy
Giuseppe Stecca	Italian National Research Council, Italy

Paola Zamperlin	University of Florence, Italy
Vincenza Torrisi	University of Catania, Italy
Gerardo Carpentieri	University of Naples Federico II, Italy
Carmen Guida	University of Naples Federico II, Italy
Floriana Zucaro	University of Naples Federico II, Italy
Alfonso Annunziata	University of Basilicata, Italy
Elisabetta Venco	University of Pavia, Italy
Caterina Pietra	University of Pavia, Italy
Tazyeen Alam	University of Cagliari, Italy
Valerio Cutini	University of Pisa, Italy

UX Mobility 2025: Placing User Experience at the Center of Urban Mobility: Methods and Frameworks (UXM 2025)

Workshop Organizers

Carmen Guida	Università degli Studi di Napoli Federico II, Italy
Gerardo Carpentieri	Università degli Studi di Napoli Federico II, Italy
Federico Messa	Systematica srl, Italy
Lamia Abdelfattah	Systematica srl, Italy

Workshop Program Committee Members

Rosaria Battarra	Istituto di Studi sul Mediterraneo CNR, Italy
Romano Fistola	Università degli Studi di Napoli Federico II, Italy
Lucia Saganeiti	IMAA-CNR, Italy

Virtual Reality and Augmented reality and applications (VRA 2025)

Workshop Organizers

Damiano Perri	University of Perugia, Italy
Osvaldo Gervasi	University of Perugia, Italy
Chau Ma Thi	University of Engineering and Technology, Vietnam National University, Hanoi, Vietnam
Paolo Nesi	University of Florence, Italy
Pierfrancesco Bellini	University of Florence, Italy

Workshop Program Committee Members

| David Berti | ART SpA, Italy |
| JungYoon Kim | Gachon University, South Korea |

TaiHoon Kim	Zhejiang University of Science and Technology, China
Marcelo de Paiva Guimares	Federal University of São Paulo, Brazil
Sergio Tasso	University of Perugia, Italy

Workshop on Advanced and Computational Methods for Earth Science Applications (WACM4ES 2025)

Workshop Organizers

Luca Piroddi	University of Cagliari, Italy
Patrizia Capizzi	University of Palermo, Italy
Marilena Cozzolino	University of Molise, Italy
Sebastiano D'Amico	University of Malta, Malta
Chiara Garau	University of Cagliari, Italy
Giuseppina Vacca	University of Cagliari, Italy

Workshop Program Committee Members

Andrea Angelini	CNR ISPC, Italy
Ilaria Barone	Università degli Studi di Padova, Italy
Patrizia Capizzi	University of Palermo, Italy
Luigi Capozzoli	CNR, Italy
Alberto Carletti	University of Cagliari, Italy
Emanuele Colica	University of Malta, Malta
Marilena Cozzolino	Università del Molise, Italy
Sebastiano D'Amico	University of Malta, Malta
Chiara Garau	University of Cagliari, Italy
Luciano Galone	University of Malta, Malta
Peter Iregbeyen	University of Malta, Malta
Mariano Lisi	Basilicata Aerospace Cluster CLAS, Italy
Raffaele Martorana	Università di Palermo, Italy
Paolo Mauriello	Università del Molise, Italy
Veronica Pazzi	University of Florence, Italy
Raffaele Persico	Università della Calabria, Italy
Luca Piroddi	University of Cagliari, Italy
Sina Saneiyan	Binghamton University, USA
Mercedes Solla	Universidade de Vigo, Spain
Deodato Tapete	ASI, Italy
Giuseppina Vacca	University of Cagliari, Italy
Enrica Vecchi	University of Cagliari, Italy

Sponsoring Organizations

ICCSA 2025 would not have been possible without the tremendous support of many organizations and institutions, for which all organizers and participants of ICCSA 2025 express their sincere gratitude:

Galatasaray University, Istanbul, Türkiye
(https://gsu.edu.tr/en)

African Mathematical Union
(https://www.africanmathunion.org/)

Springer Nature Switzerland AG, Switzerland
(https://www.springer.com)

The University of Massachusetts, USA
(https://www.umass.edu/)

University of Perugia, Italy
(https://www.unipg.it)

University of Basilicata, Italy
(http://www.unibas.it)

Monash University, Australia
(https://www.monash.edu/)

Kyushu Sangyo University, Japan
(https://www.kyusan-u.ac.jp/)

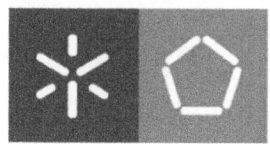

Universidade do Minho
Escola de Engenharia

University of Minho, Portugal
(https://www.uminho.pt/)
Venue
ICCSA 2025 took place in: **Galatasaray University, Istanbul, Türkiye**

Additional Reviewers

Reviewers
The review tasks for each workshop have been carried out by the workshop Organizers
and the members of the workshop Program Committee.

Plenary Lectures

Sky Safe with GAI and Post-quantum Computing

Elizabeth Chang

Professor of Cyber Security and Head of Discipline, University of the Sunshine Coast, Australia

Abstract. Professor Chang's talk in this presentation has two distinct parts. To start, she will introduce the landscape of cybersecurity development, attacks, threats, and vulnerabilities, as well as state-of-the-art cyber protection, cyber defence, and cyber incident prevention. This is followed by a discussion of the impact of Generative AI (GAI) and quantum-safe cryptographic computing, highlighting the major issues and challenges in research, education, and training. In conclusion, she will present a vision for Sky Safe solutions, aiming to achieve cyber resilience that supports business and economic stability, enhances human capabilities, and promotes environmental sustainability.

Disaster Preparedness and Risk Profiling in the Digital Era from Earth Observation Lens

Jagannath Aryal

Department of Infrastructure Engineering, University of Melbourne, Australia

Abstract. Natural hazards which turn into disasters result in severe losses of lives, infrastructure, and property. Disasters such as earthquakes and landslides and their impacts on transportation safety, infrastructure resilience, and displacement of people to new places are challenges. To address such challenges, earth observation data and intelligent methods can provide potential solutions in developing decision support systems. This talk will present the state of the art in Earth observation for disaster resilience using intelligent methods. In the Earth observation space, digitalisation has revolutionised the way we map, monitor, and develop decision support systems. Global case study examples covering earthquake-induced landslides from the Himalayan region will cover the digital capabilities. The digital capabilities will embrace object recognition, interpretation, and their accurate and precise capture to integrate into digital models. The developed digital models from representative case studies can be leveraged in other jurisdictions in profiling risks to protect lives and infrastructure and creating disaster preparedness in the era of digital age and digital economy.

Intelligent Image Enhancement for Real-World Applications in Adverse Atmospheric Conditions

Khan Muhammad

Department of Global Convergence, Sungkyunkwan University, South Korea

Abstract. The adverse impacts of atmospheric conditions such as haze, fog, and low-light environments pose significant challenges for real-world applications reliant on computer vision, including autonomous driving, surveillance, and remote sensing. This keynote explores cutting-edge advancements in intelligent image enhancement, drawing insights from two pivotal studies. The first introduces HazeSpace2M, a comprehensive dataset and novel classification-guided dehazing framework that improves image clarity across diverse atmospheric conditions, addressing the gap between synthetic and real-world dehazing performance. The second focuses on LoLI-Street, a benchmark for low-light image enhancement tailored to urban environments, extending beyond enhancement to enable robust object detection and scene understanding. Taken together, these contributions demonstrate how integrating domain-specific datasets, advanced algorithms, and performance benchmarks can significantly elevate the reliability of computer vision systems under challenging weather and lighting conditions. Attendees will gain valuable insights into the methodologies, datasets, and practical applications driving innovation in this field, with implications for research and industry alike.

In Memory of Carmelo Torre

Unfortunately, Professor Carmelo Torre, one of the cornerstones of the ICCSA Conference, passed away last December, leaving everyone stunned and deeply saddened. His loss has created a profound void within our academic community. Carmelo was not only a respected scholar and dedicated contributor to the success and growth of ICCSA, but also a generous colleague, mentor, and friend to many. His intellectual rigor, warm personality, and unwavering commitment to advancing research will be remembered with great admiration. As we continue the work he helped shape, we honor his legacy and the indelible mark he left on all of us. Carmelo Torre graduated in engineering at the Polytechnic of Bari with a thesis on urban planning under Dino Borri's guidance. He began his research career by collaborating with Franco Selicato. During his PhD at the University of Naples Federico II under Luigi Fusco Girard, he specialized in real estate market analysis and multi-criteria evaluation methods. He explored the social impacts of urban transformations with his lifelong friend Maria Cerreta. His first ICCSA participation was in Perugia in 2008, in the session Geographical Analysis, Urban Modeling, Spatial Statistics. Instantly captivated by the conference, his charisma enabled him to involve various Italian scientific communities, including those in real estate and statistics. ICCSA became a yearly commitment for him, where he valued the high editorial quality of the proceedings and the dynamic post-presentation discussions and debates he passionately and expertly enriched. In 2012, alongside Maria Cerreta and Paola Perchinunno, he organized the workshop Econometrics and Multidimensional Evaluation in the Urban Environment (EMEUE), fostering dialogue on critical topics. His influence steadily grew, drawing numerous research groups to ICCSA and establishing real estate and assessment as one of the conference's leading fields. A pillar of ICCSA, he was involved across all facets of the event. Torre's contributions to academic discourse were marked by intellectual rigor and innovative thinking. His conference interventions consistently challenged conventional wisdom, offering insights transcending disciplinary boundaries. Beyond the conference, he passionately advocated for equity and social justice. His left-leaning ideology, though firm, earned respect from those with differing views, thanks to his sincerity and loyalty. He was creative, generous, and always willing to help, even at a personal cost. Despite battling illness, he maintained his characteristic optimism, warmth, cheerfulness, and commitment, supported by his partner, Caterina Rinaldo. His legacy lives on in his ideas, dedication, and unmatched generosity.

Contents – Part V

**The 15th International Workshop on Future Information System
Technologies and Applications (FiSTA 2025)**

Geogames for Sustainable Development (GeoGames 2025)

Geographical Analysis, Urban Modeling, Spatial Statistics 2025 (Geog- And-Mod 2025)

HERitage and CLIMAte Neutrality. Resilient Approach for Nature Centered/Based Sustainable Cities. (HERCLIMA 2025)

Workshop on Computational Science and HPC (CSHPC 2025)

Development of AFCAL: An Asteroid Flux Density Calculator for ALMA Observations

Shigeru Takahashi[1]([✉])[iD], Hikaru Kubota[2][iD], Hideo Sagawa[1,3][iD],
Takashi Tsukagoshi[1,4][iD], Fumi Yoshida[5,6][iD], Junya Kawase[1],
and Takahiro Iino[1][iD]

[1] Information Technology Center, The University of Tokyo, 2-11-16 Yayoi,
Bunkyo-ku, Tokyo 113-8658, Japan
{shigeru.takahashi,iino.takahiro}@mail.u-tokyo.ac.jp,
j.kawase@ds.itc.u-tokyo.ac.jp
[2] Division of Science, Graduate School, Kyoto Sangyo University, Kamigamo
Motoyama, Kita, Kyoto 603-8555, Japan
i2485049@cc.kyoto-su.ac.jp
[3] Faculty of Science, Kyoto Sangyo University, Kamigamo Motoyama, Kita, Kyoto
603-8555, Japan
sagawa@cc.kyoto-su.ac.jp
[4] Department of Innovative Engineering, Faculty of Engineering, Ashikaga
University, 268-1 Omae-cho, Ashikaga 326-8558, Tochigi, Japan
takashi.tsukagoshi.astro@gmail.com
[5] University of Occupational and Environmental Health, Japan, 1-1 Iseigaoka,
Yahata, Kitakyusyu 807-8555, Fukuoka, Japan
fumi-yoshida@med.uoeh-u.ac.jp
[6] Planetary Exploration Research Center, Chiba Institute of Technology, 2-17-1
Tsudanuma, Narashino, Chiba 275-0016, Japan

Abstract. We developed AFCAL (An Asteroid Flux Density Calculator
for ALMA Observations), Python-based software designed to simulate
the brightness temperature and radio flux of asteroids using thermophysical modeling (TPM) calculations. AFCAL numerically solves the
heat conduction equation while accounting for thermal radiation from
subsurface layers, enabling accurate simulations. By utilizing multiprocessing, AFCAL efficiently performs TPM calculations for each facet of
a polygonal-shaped model, fully leveraging all CPU cores for faster computation.

We validate AFCAL using ALMA observations of the dwarf planet (1)
Ceres. Additionally, we present simulation results for the asteroid (3200)
Phaethon, the target of Japan's upcoming asteroid exploration mission.
AFCAL enhances the interpretation of ALMA observations, contributing
to a deeper understanding of asteroid thermal properties and supporting
future research in planetary science.

Keywords: Asteroid · ALMA · Thermal Radiation · Numerical
Simulation

O. Gervasi et al. (Eds.): ICCSA 2025 Workshops, LNCS 15890, pp. 3–19, 2026.
https://doi.org/10.1007/978-3-031-97606-3_1

1   Introduction

Asteroids are considered primordial bodies that have undergone minimal thermal evolution compared to the major planets and retain relatively more information about the formation of the solar system. Therefore, the study of asteroids is indispensable for understanding the history of the solar system. Research on asteroids has been conducted from various perspectives, theoretical, observational studies, laboratory experiments and in-situ observations by spacecraft (e.g., [12]). In observational studies, research has mainly focused on the visible to mid-infrared wavelength ranges using ground-based telescopes and obtained numerous significant results.

On the other hand, observations of asteroids in the radio wavelength range, such as submillimeter and millimeter waves, have been relatively scarce. Two primary reasons for this are: (1) since asteroids' thermal emission in the radio wavelength ranges is lower compared to the mid-infrared, observations have been done for relatively large asteroids; (2) Models for describing thermal emission in the radio wavelength range were not sufficiently developed.

However, the advent of large aperture telescopes such as ALMA (Atacama Large Millimeter/submillimeter Array) has become possible to observe smaller bodies in the solar system (e.g., [2,8]). ALMA has solved the problems of the past, especially the observation sensitivity problem caused by (1) above, and made it possible to observe even smaller asteroids.

In order to promote more effective observational studies of asteroids using ALMA, the above mentioned problem (2), i.e., the lack of a thermal emission model of asteroids in the radio wavelength, has become a recent issue.

This study aims to develop software to calculate the radio intensity of asteroids for ALMA. The software will be based on an asteroid thermal emission model that integrates physical parameters required for the radio wavelength range.

2   Thermophysical Model (TPM)

Asteroidal thermal radiation arises from the process in which absorbed solar radiation is re-emitted as thermal energy. The intensity of this radiation is an essential tool for investigating the physical properties of asteroids and can be inferred from their surface temperatures. The temperature of an asteroid is determined by three primary physical processes: (1) absorption of solar radiation (mainly in the visible spectrum), (2) thermal re-emission in the infrared and radio wavelengths, and (3) heat conduction into the subsurface. Most asteroids are not composed of bare rock surfaces but are instead covered by regolith, a fine-grained rocky material that influences all of the above described three thermal processes. Therefore, studying an asteroid's thermal radiation allows us to estimate the physical parameters of its regolith, such as thermal conductivity, specific heat, and density.

A fundamental thermal model used to describe asteroid thermal radiation is the Standard Thermal Model (STM). This model assumes: (1) the asteroid is either non-rotating or rotating very rapidly, (2) the nighttime temperature is zero, (3) there is no subsurface heat conduction, and (4) an empirical beaming factor η is used to correct for surface roughness effects. STM was successfully employed in creating a catalog of asteroid diameters and albedos based on infrared data from the IRAS satellite [1].

However, since actual asteroids rotate, the temperature of a given surface point varies throughout the day, decreasing at night as it radiates away stored heat. To accurately determine asteroid diameters from thermal radiation, it is essential to consider rotational effects. Thus, the Thermophysical Model (TPM) was developed, incorporating both rotation and subsurface heat conduction (e.g., see Delbo et al. in [12].

2.1   1D Conductive Heat Flow Equation

The TPM framework follows the approach outlined by Spencer et al. (1989) [18]. Considering a sufficiently small region of an asteroid's surface relative to its diameter, heat conduction can be treated as a one-dimensional process. This requires that the polygonal surface elements in TPM are small compared to the asteroid's diameter. The heat conduction equation is expressed as:

$$\frac{\partial T(z,t)}{\partial t} = \frac{k}{\rho c} \frac{\partial^2 T(z,t)}{\partial z^2}, \tag{1}$$

where $T(z,t)$ is the temperature at depth z and time t, ρ is the material density, c is the specific heat capacity, k is the thermal conductivity.

Although in reality, ρ may vary with depth and both c and k may depend on temperature, the TPM in this study assumes them to be constant values.

The thermal inertia Γ is defined as:

$$\Gamma = \sqrt{k\rho c}, \tag{2}$$

and has a unit $[\mathrm{Jm^{-2}s^{-0.5}K^{-1}}] \equiv \mathrm{tiu}$. This parameter represents the resistance of a material to temperature changes. A low thermal inertia asteroid exhibits large day-night temperature variations, whereas a high thermal inertia asteroid stores and releases heat more gradually, reducing diurnal temperature fluctuations. Generally speaking, regolith has low thermal inertia, while solid rock has high thermal inertia.

Defining the thermal skin depth l_s as:

$$l_s = \sqrt{\frac{k}{\rho c \omega}}, \tag{3}$$

where ω is the rotational angular velocity [rad/s], l_s represents the depth at which temperature variations decay to $1/e$ of their surface values.

2.2   Surface Boundary Condition

In the basic TPM, the energy balance at the asteroid surface is given by:

$$k\left(\frac{\partial T(z,t)}{\partial z}\right)_{z=0} = \epsilon\sigma T^4(0,t) - (1-A)F_s(t), \tag{4}$$

where the left-hand term represents subsurface heat conduction, and the right-hand terms include $\epsilon\sigma T^4(0,t)$: thermal radiation following Stefan-Boltzmann's law, $(1-A)F_s(t)$: absorbed solar energy, ϵ: emissivity, σ: the Stefan-Boltzmann constant and A: the Bond albedo. The solar flux received by a surface element is given by:

$$F_s(t) = S_0 \cdot \frac{1}{r(t)^2} \cdot \cos\theta(t), \tag{5}$$

where S_0 is the solar constant at 1 AU (1361 W/m^2), $r(t)$ is the asteroid's distance from the Sun (AU) and $\theta(t)$ is the solar incidence angle.

A rough surface creates shadowing and thermal re-radiation effects. To account for these, a surface roughness correction factor X is introduced as follows:

$$S_0(1-A)\cos\theta/r^2 = X\sigma T^4 + k\frac{\partial T}{\partial z}, \tag{6}$$

where $X = (1 - \epsilon\xi)\epsilon$, with ξ being the roughness parameter [3]. It is noted that the NASA Dawn mission applied this model to determine thermal inertia values for the mean surface and some specific craters of Ceres (e.g., Haulani and Occator craters) [16]).

2.3   Internal Boundary Condition

For the asteroid interior, the deep subsurface is assumed to maintain a constant temperature beyond a depth d. Since we confirmed no temperature variation was observed for $d > 10 \cdot l_s$, we set $d = 20 \cdot l_s$ in this study:

$$\left(\frac{\partial T(z,t)}{\partial z}\right)_{z=d} = 0. \tag{7}$$

No internal heat flux is assumed.

2.4   Subsurface Thermal Radiation (STR)

The above model effectively calculates thermal radiation intensity in the mid-infrared to far-infrared wavelength range. However, observations at millimeter and submillimeter wavelengths have revealed lower observed temperatures than those predicted by this model [15]. This discrepancy is attributed to the exclusion of subsurface thermal radiation (STR) in the millimeter and submillimeter regimes [9]. Since electromagnetic waves in these wavelength ranges partially penetrate asteroid material, STR must also be considered. Consequently, several studies have incorporated this approach into their models (e.g., [4,5,10]).

Total Transmissivity. Thermal radiation from the subsurface is described using the complex dielectric permittivity $\tilde{\varepsilon}$ (or the complex refractive index $\tilde{n}$). If the constituent material is non-magnetic and non-conductive, the relationship between complex dielectric permittivity $\tilde{\varepsilon} = \varepsilon_1 + i\varepsilon_2$ and complex refractive index $\tilde{n} = n + i\kappa$ is given by:

$$\tilde{\varepsilon} = \tilde{n}^2, \quad \varepsilon_1 = n^2 - \kappa^2, \quad \varepsilon_2 = 2n\kappa, \tag{8}$$

$$n = \sqrt{\frac{|\tilde{\varepsilon}| + \varepsilon_1}{2}}, \quad \kappa = \sqrt{\frac{|\tilde{\varepsilon}| - \varepsilon_1}{2}}. \tag{9}$$

In addition, the loss tangent ($\tan\delta$) is often used in simulations to quantify energy dissipation in dielectric materials. It is defined as the ratio of the imaginary part to the real part of the permittivity:

$$\tan\delta = \frac{\varepsilon_2}{\varepsilon_1}. \tag{10}$$

Thermal radiation from the subsurface refracts and reflects at the asteroid surface. Given an incident angle θ_i within the asteroid and an exit angle θ_t into space, Snell's law applies:

$$n \sin\theta_i = \sin\theta_t. \tag{11}$$

Using Fresnel's equations, the reflection and transmission coefficients are derived. The reflection coefficients for s-polarized (r_s) and p-polarized (r_p) waves are:

$$r_s = \frac{n\cos\theta_i - \cos\theta_t}{n\cos\theta_i + \cos\theta_t}, \quad r_p = \frac{\cos\theta_i - n\cos\theta_t}{\cos\theta_i + n\cos\theta_t}. \tag{12}$$

The reflectance R_s and R_p are given by:

$$R_s = |r_s|^2, \quad R_p = |r_p|^2. \tag{13}$$

The total reflectance R is the mean of R_s and R_p:

$$R = \frac{R_s + R_p}{2}. \tag{14}$$

Similarly, the transmission coefficients for s-polarized (T_s) and p-polarized (T_p) waves are:

$$T_s = \left(\frac{2n\cos\theta_i}{n\cos\theta_i + \cos\theta_t}\right)^2, \quad T_p = \left(\frac{2\cos\theta_i}{\cos\theta_i + n\cos\theta_t}\right)^2. \tag{15}$$

The total transmissivity T_{tr} is given by:

$$T_{tr} = \frac{T_s + T_p}{2}. \tag{16}$$

By the principle of energy conservation, the relationship between total transmissivity and reflectance is:

$$T_{tr} + R = 1. \tag{17}$$

Electrical Skin Depth. Thermal radiation generated in the subsurface is attenuated as it propagates to the surface due to absorption by the internal material. The characteristic distance over which this attenuation occurs is called the electrical skin depth δ_{elec}, given by:

$$\delta_{elec} = \frac{\lambda}{4\pi\kappa}. \tag{18}$$

Flux Density (Intensity). With the above model, the surface and subsurface temperature distribution of the asteroid can be determined. The brightness temperature T_B observed from a given facet is computed using the Rayleigh-Jeans approximation by integrating the subsurface temperature profile $T(z)$ along the propagation direction;

$$T_B = (1 - R) \int T(z) \exp\left(-\frac{z}{\delta_{elec}\cos\theta_i}\right) \frac{dz}{\delta_{elec}\cos\theta_i}. \tag{19}$$

For an asteroid subtending a solid angle Ω as seen by the observer, the total observed flux density (intensity per unit frequency) I is:

$$I = \int_\Omega I_\nu \, d\Omega = \int_\Omega B_\nu(T) \, d\Omega. \tag{20}$$

In radio astronomy, the unit Jansky (Jy) is commonly used to measure radio flux density:

$$1 \text{ Jy} = 10^{-26} \text{ W m}^{-2} \text{ Hz}^{-1}. \tag{21}$$

Since asteroid thermal emission is a continuum spectrum, assuming that the spectral intensity remains approximately constant within the instrumental bandwidth BW, the observed intensity I_{obs} is expressed as:

$$I_{obs} = I \cdot BW. \tag{22}$$

3   Simulation

3.1   Overview

The AFCAL is developed using Python 3.11.5. To achieve efficient and high-precision calculations, it utilizes the numerical computation libraries *NumPy* and *SciPy*. For visualization of results, the graphing library *Matplotlib* is employed. AFCAL performs calculations on the high-performance computing system **mdx (a platform for building data-empowered society)** provided by the Information Technology Center at the University of Tokyo. The mdx is equipped with Intel Xeon Platinum 8368 CPUs and NVIDIA A100 Tensor Core GPUs. In this study, we used the Xeon CPUs for all computations. However, AFCAL is not restricted to the mdx and can be executed on any platform where Python 3.11.5 and the aforementioned modules are available, including Windows, macOS, Linux and Unix.

The calculation flow of AFCAL consists of six steps (Fig. 1). Here, we explain each step in detail.

3.2   Data Set Input

This step involves loading and pre-processing the input data set required for calculations.

Polygon Model. In AFCAL, asteroid shapes are modeled using polygon meshes. The model shapes are based on data provided by DAMIT (Database of Asteroid Models from Inversion Techniques) [6]. DAMIT is a database of asteroid shape models operated and managed by the Faculty of Mathematics and Physics at Charles University in the Czech Republic[1]. The shape models in DAMIT are derived by inverting asteroid lightcurve data. The database includes hundreds of asteroid models, each containing detailed information about their shape, rotational axis, and spin period. The format of DAMIT's shape models is a custom format but is similar to the Wavefront OBJ format. Additionally, the orientation of asteroid rotational axes is also provided by the same database. In this study, we use the models of (1) Ceres and (3200) Phaethon for the calculations.

Ephemeris. The ephemeris for asteroids is obtained from the Horizons System provided by NASA's Jet Propulsion Laboratory (JPL)[2]. The Horizons System is a tool that provides information on orbital elements, positions and velocities, apparent brightness, distances, and more for celestial bodies such as major planets, asteroids and comets within the solar system. It is widely used in scientific research, astronomical observations, and educational activities.

Data can be obtained via a web interface, email, telnet, and an API interface using HTTP GET and POST methods. In this study, the position information of asteroids at calculation times was obtained by interpolating values from prepared ephemeris.

3.3   Initial Preparation

We perform the rotation calculations to align the polygon with the spin axis. Additionally, we calculate the normal vectors of the facets for each rotational phase.

Rotation of Asteroids. Since asteroids rotate, it is necessary to perform polygon rotation calculations. Methods for rotation calculations include using matrices or Euler angles, but in this study, quaternions were used.

Quaternions are an extension of complex numbers and are expressed as follows:

$$q = w + xi + yj + zk, \tag{23}$$

---

[1] https://astro.troja.mff.cuni.cz/projects/damit/.
[2] https://ssd.jpl.nasa.gov/horizons/.

where w, x, y, z are real components, and i, j, k are imaginary units with the following properties:

$$i^2 = j^2 = k^2 = ijk = -1, \tag{24}$$

$$ij = k, \quad jk = i, \quad ki = j, \tag{25}$$

$$ji = -k, \quad kj = -i, \quad ik = -j. \tag{26}$$

Quaternions are widely used in computer graphics because they can represent rotations in three-dimensional space concisely and efficiently.

To rotate a three-dimensional vector $\mathbf{v}$ around an axis $\mathbf{u} = (u_x, u_y, u_z)$ by an angle θ, a unit quaternion q is defined as follows:

$$q = \cos\frac{\theta}{2} + \sin\frac{\theta}{2}(u_x i + u_y j + u_z k). \tag{27}$$

To rotate the vector $\mathbf{v}$ using the quaternion q, represent $\mathbf{v}$ as a pure imaginary quaternion and compute as follows:

$$\mathbf{v}' = q\mathbf{v}q^{-1}, \tag{28}$$

where q^{-1} is the inverse of quaternion q, and $\mathbf{v}'$ is the quaternion representing the rotated vector.

3.4   Initial TPM Calculation

Initial Condition. We obtain the initial temperature distribution of the asteroid as follows. First, the asteroid was fixed at the position of the initial calculation time (t_0), and the surface and internal temperatures were uniformly set to $T = 0$ K. Starting from this initial state, TPM calculation was done. The TPM calculation method will be described in the next section.

As the number of rotations increased, the temperature distribution stabilized and converged over time. In this simulation, the asteroid was rotated typically 100–1000 times to confirm that the temperature distribution had sufficiently converged. The resulting stable temperature distribution was adopted as the initial condition at the start of the calculation.

In AFCAL, numerical calculations of heat conduction are performed for multiple surface elements (polygons). For models with a large number of polygons, single-threaded calculations are computationally expensive and time-consuming. To address this, AFCAL employs Python's robust parallel processing module, *multiprocessing*.

By utilizing *multiprocessing*, AFCAL generates multiple processes, each of which independently handling the calculations for specific surface elements. This approach fully utilizes all available CPU cores, achieving significant acceleration through parallel computing.

3.5   TPM Calculation

TPM simulations are conducted, refining thermal models based on the results from the initial calculations as changing geometric parameters of the asteroid.

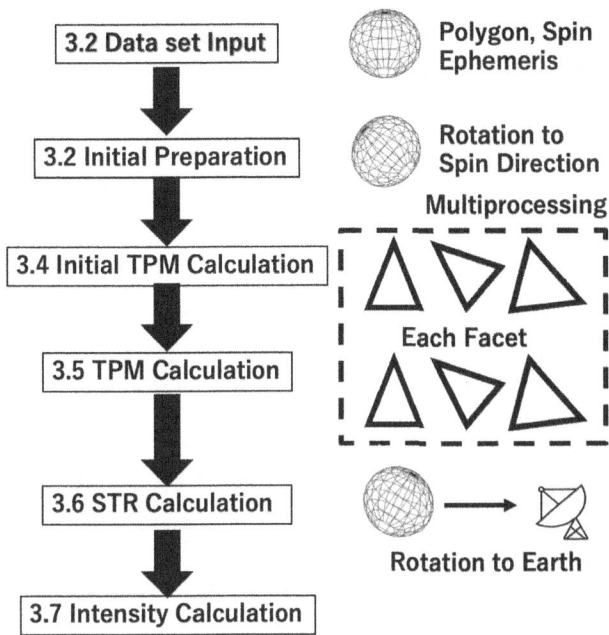

Fig. 1. Calculation Sequence of AFCAL.

1D Conductive Heat Flow Equation. An explicit finite difference method was used to solve the one-dimensional heat conduction equation. The finite difference equation is as follows:

$$T_i^{j+1} = T_i^j + \frac{\alpha \Delta t}{\Delta z^2} \left(T_{i+1}^j - 2T_i^j + T_{i-1}^j \right), \tag{29}$$

where:

- T_i^j: Temperature at spatial position $z = i\Delta z$ and time $t = j\Delta t$
- Δz: Spatial step size
- Δt: Time step size
- α: Thermal diffusivity
- $i = 0, 1, 2, \ldots, N$: Spatial index
- $j = 0, 1, 2, \ldots$: Time index

Introducing the parameter:

$$r = \frac{\alpha \Delta t}{\Delta z^2}. \tag{30}$$

The partial differential equation can be rewritten as:

$$T_i^{j+1} = T_i^j + r \left(T_{i+1}^j - 2T_i^j + T_{i-1}^j \right). \tag{31}$$

For stability in the explicit method, the following condition must be satisfied:

$$r = \frac{\alpha \Delta t}{\Delta z^2} \leq \frac{1}{2}. \tag{32}$$

Since the above equation cannot determine T_0^{j+1} and T_N^{j+1}, the following boundary conditions are used:

For the asteroid's interior:

$$T_{N-1}^{j+1} = T_N^{j+1}. \tag{33}$$

For the asteroid's surface, the boundary condition in finite difference form is:

$$\left(\frac{\partial T}{\partial z}\right)_{z=0} = \frac{1}{\Delta z}\left(T_1^{j+1} - T_0^{j+1}\right). \tag{34}$$

Thus:

$$T_0^j = T_1^j - \frac{1}{k}\left[X\sigma\left(T_0^j\right)^4 - (1-A)F(t)\right]\Delta z. \tag{35}$$

To solve this equation and obtain T_0^{j+1}, several methods such as self-consistent method can be used. In this study, Newton-Raphson method was adopted.

3.6 STR Calculation

To calculate STR as observed from Earth, the polygonal shape model was rotated toward Earth. Then, the STR for each facet was calculated using Eq. (19). Numerical integration was required for Eq. (19). Since the function decreases exponentially, Gauss-Laguerre Quadrature was used for the calculation.

3.7 Flux Density (Intensity) Calculation

In this step, the final flux density (intensity) values are calculated based on the previous calculations. Using Eq. (20), the STR (Spectral Thermal Radiation) from each facet is summed to determine the observed intensity. Additionally, visualize the asteroid's shape and temperature distribution at the time of observation and create an animation.

4 Results

4.1 (1) Ceres

(1) Ceres is the largest dwarf planet located in the main asteroid belt of the solar system. It orbits the Sun at an average distance of approximately 2.8 AU (4.2×10^8 km) and completes one revolution around the Sun in about 4.6 years (see Fig. 2). Additionally, Ceres rotates on its axis approximately every

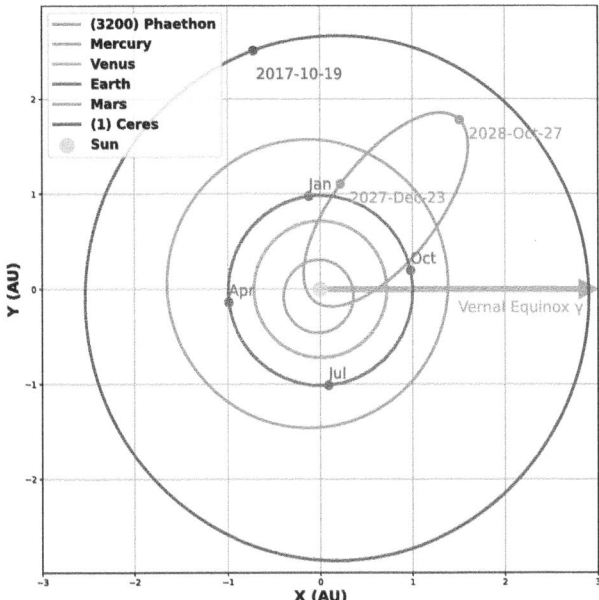

Fig. 2. Orbital Diagram of Planets, (1) Ceres and (3200) Phaethon.

9 h (Russell et al., 2016). Its shape closely resembles a triaxial ellipsoid, with principal radii of $a = 483.1$ km, $b = 481$ km, and $c = 445.9$ km, giving it an almost spherical structure [17].

Detailed observations by NASA's Dawn spacecraft revealed that the surface of Ceres contains partially bright regions. Around the Occator Crater, transient hazes have been reported [13], suggesting that Ceres is a relatively active celestial body. Moreover, (1) Ceres is sometimes used as a calibrator (reference source) in ALMA observations.

In this software, validation was performed by comparing the results with ALMA observations conducted on October 19, 2017. (1) Ceres was observed using ALMA Band 6 (1.1 mm, 265 GHz), and physical parameters such as thermal inertia and dielectric permittivity were estimated [10]. The used parameters are summarized in Table 1 and the results are shown in Fig. 3. Figure 3a shows the distribution of brightness temperature when observed in the mid-infrared and Fig. 3b the calculated distribution of brightness temperature when observed with ALMA Band 6.

The brightness temperature observed by ALMA on October 19, 2017, was 179 ± 5 K, and the radio intensity was 1.60 ± 0.05 Jy. In comparison, the calculated results were 173 K and 1.62 Jy, which is approximately 1 K lower than the observational value. However, in the simulation the brightness temperature varies between 172 K and 174 K due to rotational effects during the observation period. Therefore, the calculation results are considered to be in good agreement with the observational data. In the mid-infrared calculations, the average

Table 1. Physical Parameters Used for the Calculation of (1) Ceres

Parameter	Value	Reference/Comment
Facet number	800	DAMIT
Shape (a,b,c)	$(482.64 \times 480.64 \times 445.57)$ km	Russell et al. (2016) [17]
Rotation Period	9.074170 hr	Chamberlain et al. (2007)
Pole direction (λ,β)	$(11°, 81°)$	Park et al. (2016) [14]
Emissivity ϵ	0.95	Keihm et al. (2013) [9]
Bond albedo A	0.037	Li et al. (2019) [11]
Roughness parameter ξ	0.0	Lambertian scattering
Thermal inertia Γ	80 tiu	Li et al. (2020) [10]
Dielectric constant ϵ_r	2.25	Li et al. (2020) [10]
Loss tangent $\tan\delta$	0.03	Li et al. (2020) [10]
Frequency f_{rq}	264.985 GHz	ALMA Observation [10]

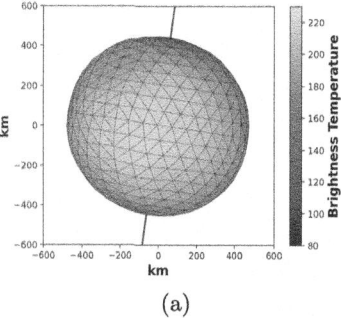 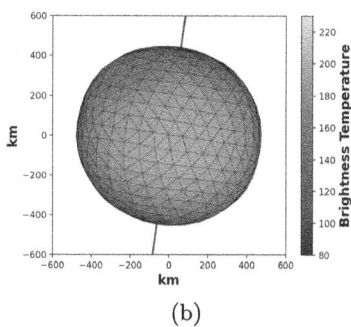

(a)   (b)

Fig. 3. (a) Calculated Surface Temperature of (1) Ceres, (b) Calculated Brightness Temperature Considering STR for (1) Ceres.

brightness temperature was 200 K, and the intensity was 1.88 Jy. In contrast, the brightness temperature observed in ALMA Band 6 was approximately 27 K lower and the intensity was 0.26 Jy lower, representing a difference of about 15%.

This decrease in observed temperature can be influenced by various factors such as thermal inertia, and complex dielectric permittivity etc. Although the same 15% decrease may not be observed for other asteroids, this value would serve as a useful reference.

4.2   (3200) Phaethon

(3200) Phaethon is an asteroid with an approximate diameter of 5 km and a rotation period of about 3.6 h. It has a highly eccentric elliptical orbit, with a perihelion distance of 0.14 AU ($\sim$21 million km) and an aphelion distance of 2.4

AU ($\sim$360 million km). This distinctive orbit brings (3200) Phaethon closer to the Sun than Mercury's orbit and farther than Mars' orbit.

Moreover, (3200) Phaethon is classified as a Near-Earth Object (NEO) and is known as the parent body of the Geminid meteor shower. To investigate this peculiar asteroid in more detail, JAXA is planning an exploration mission to (3200) Phaethon with the Deep Space Exploration Technology Demonstrator (DESTINY$^+$) spacecraft[3]. Research on the thermophysical parameters of (3200) Phaethon is limited, but its thermal inertia is estimated to be $\Gamma = 600 \pm 200$ tiu [7]. In this study, we used this value, while other physical parameters were assumed to be the same as those for (1) Ceres (Table 2).

For the Roughness parameter (ξ), the value $\xi = 0.55$ observed at the Occator Crater on (1) Ceres was used [16]. This choice was made because the Occator Crater has a higher thermal inertia ($\Gamma = 115$ - 136 tiu) compared to other regions on Ceres. However, it should be noted that this choice is not based on theoretical or observational reason for (3200) Phaethon possesses this same roughness value.

Table 2. Physical Parameters Used for the Calculation of (3200) Phaethon

Parameter	Value	Reference/Comment
Facet number	2040	DAMIT
Diameter	5.1 km	Hanuš et al. 2016 [7]
Rotation Period	3.603957 hr	DAMIT
Pole direction (λ,β)	(318°, −47°)	DAMIT
Emissivity ϵ	0.95	Substituting the value used for (1) Ceres
Bond Albedo A	0.048	Hanuš et al. 2016 [7]
Roughness parameter ξ	0.55	Substituting the value used for Occator Crater
Thermal inertia Γ	600 tiu	Hanuš et al. 2016 [7]
Dielectric constant ϵ_r	2.25	Substituting the value used for (1) Ceres
Loss tangent $\tan\delta$	0.03	Substituting the value used for (1) Ceres
Frequency f_{rq}	264.985 GHz	ALMA Observation

We investigated the brightness temperature and radio intensity of (3200) Phaethon at two distinct orbital positions; closest approach to Earth on December 23 and near aphelion on October 27, 2028 (Fig. 4). The brightness temperature on December 23, 2027 was calculated to be 280 K, and the radio intensity was 7.4 mJy (Fig. 4a). Conversely, near aphelion on October 27, 2028, the brightness temperature was estimated to be 199 K, with the radio intensity of 169 μJy (Fig. 4b). We also confirmed that the uncertainty of ± 200 in the thermal inertia of (3200) Phaethon leads to only about a $1-2\%$ variation in the brightness temperature. These calculations reveal a significant intensity difference by a factor of approximately 44 between the two orbital positions.

---

[3] https://www.perc.it-chiba.ac.jp/en/projects/destiny-plus/.

This variation in brightness temperature and intensity is attributed to the substantial change in the heliocentric distance of (3200) Phaethon along its highly elliptical orbit. When Phaethon approaches the Sun, the surface temperature increases, resulting in higher brightness temperature and radio intensity. Conversely, as it moves away from the Sun towards aphelion, the surface temperature decreases, leading to lower observed values.

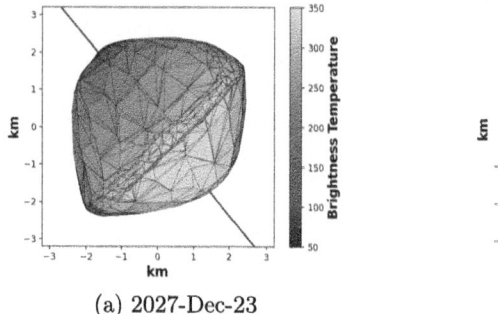 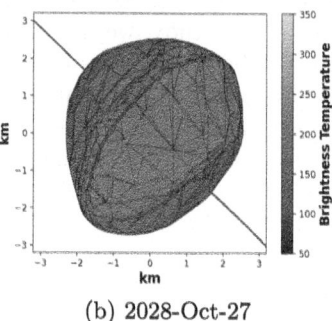

(a) 2027-Dec-23   (b) 2028-Oct-27

Fig. 4. Brightness Temperature and Apparent Shape Variations of (3200) Phaethon at Different Positions: (a) during closest approach to Earth, (b) at aphelion.

This information is particularly valuable for planning future observations, including those by the DESTINY$^+$ mission.

5   Evaluation of Parallelization in AFCAL

We evaluated the performance of parallelization in AFCAL (Asteroid Flux Calculator for ALMA), using Python's `multiprocessing` module to run radiative transfer calculations.

To assess scalability, we defined the parallel speedup as:

$$s(p) = \frac{t(1)}{t(p)}.$$

The test case was based on the dwarf planet (1) Ceres, and the execution time using a single processor was measured as $t(1) = 4.98$ h. The results are shown in Fig. 5. The ideal linear speedup is also plotted for comparison.

Assuming software-related factors dominate the overhead, we applied Amdahl's law. From the maximum speedup $s_{\max} \approx 55$, the parallelizable fraction was estimated as:

$$f = 1 - \frac{1}{s_{\max}} \approx 0.982.$$

This indicates that about 98.2% of AFCAL's computation can be parallelized. Further improvements will depend on reducing the remaining serial components such as I/O and initialization.

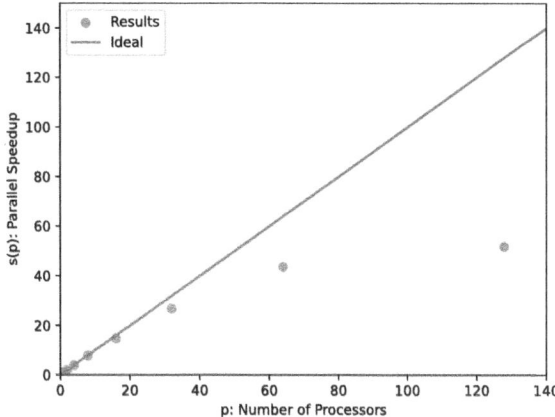

Fig. 5. Measured speedup $s(p)$ as a function of processor count p, compared with ideal scaling, for the case of (1) Ceres.

6   Future Prospects

The current implementation of AFCAL has demonstrated high parallel efficiency. However, further improvements in total computation time remain desirable, particularly when applying TPM to a large number of small bodies or high-resolution datasets.

A promising direction for future development lies in the adoption of novel algorithms. Zhao et al. (2024) [20] recently proposed an approach that applies a deep operator neural network to the computation of asteroid surface temperature. Their method achieved a reduction in computational cost by five orders of magnitude compared to traditional TPM techniques. Incorporating such algorithmic advances into AFCAL could offer substantial speedup and extend its applicability to real-time or large-scale modeling scenarios.

7   Summary

This study presents a thermophysical modeling software, AFCAL, developed using Python to simulate the brightness temperature and flux density of asteroids for millimeter and submillimeter wavelength observations, with a particular focus on ALMA. It simulates thermal radiation not only from the asteroid's surface but also from the subsurface layers. Additionally, the software utilizes Python's multiprocessing module to achieve high-speed and efficient parallel computing.

To validate the results of our developed software, we used ALMA Band 6 observational data of (1) Ceres from October 19, 2017. A comparison between the observational data and simulation results confirmed high accuracy and reliability in brightness temperature and flux density calculations. Furthermore, as a demonstration of the software's capability, brightness temperatures and flux

densities of (3200) Phaethon were calculated for two orbital positions: the closest approach to Earth and near aphelion. These simulations demonstrated the
software's applicability to other asteroid observations.

Acknowledgments. The author would like to thank the three anonymous referees
for their constructive and insightful comments. This research was supported by MEXT
as "Developing a Research Data Ecosystem for the Promotion of Data-Driven Science"
and as the JSPS Kakenhi (21H01142, 21H05420, 23K20872 and 24K07097). We used
the "mdx: a platform for building data-empowered society" for the data analysis [19].

References

1. Asteroids. 2. Univ. of Arizona Pr, Tucson, Ariz (1989)
2. ALMA Partnership, Hunter, T.R., et al.: THE 2014 ALMA LONG BASELINE
   CAMPAIGN: OBSERVATIONS OF ASTEROID 3 JUNO AT 60 KILOMETER
   RESOLUTION. Astrophys. J. **808**(1), L2 (2015). https://doi.org/10.1088/2041-
   8205/808/1/L2
3. Davidsson, B.J., Gutiérrez, P.J., Rickman, H.: Physical properties of morphological
   units on Comet 9P/Tempel 1 derived from near-IR Deep Impact spectra. Icarus
   201(1), 335–357 (2009). https://doi.org/10.1016/j.icarus.2008.12.039
4. De Kleer, K., et al.: Ganymede's surface properties from millimeter and infrared
   thermal emission. Planet. Sci. J. **2**(1), 5 (2021). https://doi.org/10.3847/PSJ/
   abcbf4
5. De Kleer, K., Cambioni, S., Shepard, M.: The surface of (16) psyche from thermal
   emission and polarization mapping. Planet. Sci. J. **2**(4), 149 (2021). https://doi.
   org/10.3847/PSJ/ac01ec
6. Ďurech, J., Sidorin, V., Kaasalainen, M.: DAMIT: a database of asteroid models. Astron. Astrophys. **513**, A46 (2010). https://doi.org/10.1051/0004-6361/
   200912693
7. Hanuš, J., et al.: Near-Earth asteroid (3200) phaethon: characterization of its orbit,
   spin state, and thermophysical parameters. Astron. Astrophys. **592**, A34 (2016).
   https://doi.org/10.1051/0004-6361/201628666
8. Iino, T., Sagawa, H., Tsukagoshi, T., Nozawa, S.: A belt-like distribution of gaseous
   hydrogen cyanide on Neptune's equatorial stratosphere detected by ALMA. Astrophys. J. Lett. **903**(1), L1 (2020). https://doi.org/10.3847/2041-8213/abbb9a
9. Keihm, S., et al.: Reconciling main belt asteroid spectral flux density measurements
   with a self-consistent thermophysical model. Icarus **226**(1), 1086–1102 (2013).
   https://doi.org/10.1016/j.icarus.2013.07.005
10. Li, J.Y., Moullet, A., Titus, T.N., Hsieh, H.H., Sykes, M.V.: Disk-integrated ther-
    mal properties of ceres measured at millimeter wavelengths. Astron. J. **159**(5), 215
    (2020). https://doi.org/10.3847/1538-3881/ab8305
11. Li, J.Y., et al.: Spectrophotometric modeling and mapping of Ceres. Icarus **322**,
    144–167 (2019). https://doi.org/10.1016/j.icarus.2018.12.038
12. Michel, P., DeMeo, F.E., Bottke, W.F.: Asteroids IV. The University of Arizona
    Space Science Series, The University of Arizona press in collaboration with Lunar
    and planetary institute, Tucson (2015)
13. Nathues, A., et al.: Sublimation in bright spots on (1) Ceres. Nature **528**(7581),
    237–240 (2015). https://doi.org/10.1038/nature15754

14. Park, R.S., et al.: A partially differentiated interior for (1) Ceres deduced from its gravity field and shape. Nature **537**(7621), 515–517 (2016). https://doi.org/10.1038/nature18955

15. Redman, R.O., Feldman, P.A., Matthews, H.E.: High-Quality photometry of asteroids at millimeter and submillimeter wavelengths. Astron. J. **116**(3), 1478–1490 (1998). https://doi.org/10.1086/300495

16. Rognini, E., et al.: High thermal inertia zones on ceres from dawn data. J. Geophys. Res. Planets **125**(3), e2018JE005733 (2020). https://doi.org/10.1029/2018JE005733

17. Russell, C.T., et al.: Dawn arrives at ceres: exploration of a small, volatile-rich world. Science **353**(6303), 1008–1010 (2016). https://doi.org/10.1126/science.aaf4219

18. Spencer, J.R., Lebofsky, L.A., Sykes, M.V.: Systematic biases in radiometric diameter determinations. Icarus **78**(2), 337–354 (1989). https://doi.org/10.1016/0019-1035(89)90182-6

19. Suzumura, T., eta l.: mdx: A cloud platform for supporting data science and cross-disciplinary research collaborations. In: 2022 IEEE International Conference on Dependable, Autonomic and Secure Computing, International Conference on Pervasive Intelligence and Computing, International Conference on Cloud and Big Data Computing, International Conference on Cyber Science and Technology Congress (DASC/PiCom/CBDCom/CyberSciTech), pp. 1–7 (2022). https://doi.org/10.1109/DASC/PiCom/CBDCom/Cy55231.2022.9927975

20. Zhao, S., Lei, H., Shi, X.: Deep operator neural network applied to efficient computation of asteroid surface temperature and the Yarkovsky effect. Astron. Astrophys. **691**, A224 (2024). https://doi.org/10.1051/0004-6361/202451789

Methods for Expansion of 3-Loop 2-Point Feynman Integrals

E. de Doncker[1]([✉]), F. Yuasa[2], T. Ishikawa[2], and K. Kato[3]

[1] Western Michigan University, Kalamazoo, MI 49008, U.S.A.
elise.dedoncker@wmich.edu
[2] High Energy Accelerator Research Organization (KEK), Ibaraki 1-1 OHO Tsukuba,
305-0801, Japan
{fukuko.yuasa,tadashi.ishikawa}@kek.jp
[3] Department of Physics, Kogakuin University, Shinjuku, Tokyo 163-8677, Japan
katok@kute.tokyo

Abstract. We explore various approaches to expand 3-loop 2-point Feynman integrals with respect to the dimensional regularization parameter. These methods are tailored to the range of the squared momentum. Below a threshold in the squared momentum, we can use lattice integration rules and a linear extrapolation for the integral expansion. An expansion of the integrand and adaptive integration of the individual terms can also be employed. We further rely on the latter techniques for the computations above the threshold.

Keywords: Feynman loop diagrams · dimensional regularization · adaptive/non-adaptive integration · lattice rules · GPUs

1 Introduction

Marked improvements in the technology of high energy physics experiments impose the need for accurate theoretical predictions, which can be contributed by higher-order corrections in the perturbation method.

The Feynman diagrammatic approach introduces Feynman loop integrals in the calculation of higher-order corrections to the cross section of particle interactions. The one-loop level has been completely established in an analytic manner [13] and implemented in packages such as LoopTools [12]. A general and analytic treatment is not possible for multi-loop integrals with general mass and momentum values.

Although challenging Feynman integral computations can presently be performed using existing symbolic or symbolic/numerical software packages such as pySecDec [2], we target the development of fully numerical methods using "automatic" integration strategies that require little or no knowledge of the problem or the underlying numerical analysis.

The scalar loop integral is defined as

$$\mathbf{I} = \prod_{k=1}^{L} \int \frac{d^{\nu}\ell_k}{(2\pi)^{\nu}} \frac{1}{D_1 \cdots D_N} \tag{1}$$

O. Gervasi et al. (Eds.): ICCSA 2025 Workshops, LNCS 15890, pp. 20–30, 2026.
https://doi.org/10.1007/978-3-031-97606-3_2

where $D_r = p_r^2 - m_r^2$ is the inverse propagator of the r-th internal line with mass m_r, N is the number of lines, and L is the number of loops. When we deal with the UV singularity by dimensional regularization, the space-time dimension, ν, is set to $4 - 2\varepsilon$.

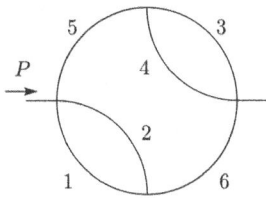

Subsequently we explore 3-loop 2-point integrals associated with the "baseball" diagram of Fig. 1 with $N = 6$ internal lines and the external momentum P. According to the Nakanishi formalism [3,16], for $L = 3$ and $N = 6$ and without the prefactor, we denote

$$\mathcal{I} = \int_{\mathcal{C}_6} \prod_{r=1}^{6} dx_r\, \delta(1 - \sum x_r)\, U^{\varepsilon-2}(V - i\varrho)^{-3\varepsilon} \tag{2}$$

Fig. 1. 3-loop *baseball* diagram with $N = 6$ lines. The numbers denote the index r in Eq. (2).

where x_r is the Feynman parameter of the r-th internal line, $V = M^2 - sW/U$ with squared momentum $s = P^2$, $M^2 = \sum_r m_r^2 x_r$; U is an L-th order polynomial of x_r and W is of order $(L+1)$; ε is an infinitesimal parameter, and (with the goal to obtain an approximation), it is the objective to expand $\mathcal{I}$ as a series in powers of ε. We include ϱ also as an infinitesimal parameter, which is set to 0 unless V vanishes in the domain; in the latter case, an extrapolation with respect to ϱ can help alleviate the effect of some singularities within the domain. $\mathcal{C}_d$ is the d-dimensional unit hypercube. In the dimensional regularization method the integral is given by the Laurent series in ε of the form

$$\mathcal{I} = \frac{C_{-2}}{\varepsilon^2} + \frac{C_{-1}}{\varepsilon} + C_0 + C_1\varepsilon + \cdots. \tag{3}$$

Here, C_{-2}, C_{-1}, C_0 and C_1 are leading expansion coefficients. In this paper we focus on the numerical expansion with respect to ε and the behavior of the coefficients as a function of s and we compute the equal mass case as $m_r = m, 1 \leq r \leq 6$.

In integral computations, transformations are basic tools to simplify the integrand and/or smoothen its behavior (see also Sect. 3.4). We perform the variable transformation $x_r = y_r$, $1 \leq r \leq 4$ and $x_5 = y_5 z$, $x_6 = y_5 \bar{z}$ where $\bar{z} = 1 - z$. The U and W can be written as follows:

$$U = y_1 y_2 y_3 + y_1 y_2 y_4 + y_1 y_3 y_4 + y_2 y_3 y_4 + (y_1 + y_2)(y_3 + y_4) y_5 \tag{4}$$

$$W = y_1 y_2 y_3 y_4 + y_1 y_2 (y_3 + y_4) y_5 z + (y_1 + y_2) y_3 y_4 y_5 \bar{z} + (y_1 + y_2)(y_3 + y_4) y_5^2 z \bar{z}. \tag{5}$$

In our previous work [6,7], several 3-loop diagrams and their associated integrals were treated analytically and numerically after separating the ultra-violet divergence by use of the sector decomposition(SD) method.

For the diagram in Fig. 1, we divide the integration region R

$$R = \{(y_1, y_2, y_3, y_4, y_5) \mid \sum_{j=1}^{5} y_j = 1\} \tag{6}$$

into regions $R(k, l, m, n, p)$.

In this decomposition, the integrals are labeled by the $120 = 5!$ permutations of the quintuple $(1, 2, 3, 4, 5)$, but only fifteen distinct cases (regions) remain after taking symmetries into account. We studied the $\mathcal{I}_{51234}$ integral in [7]. In this paper, we will demonstrate our numerical techniques for $\mathcal{I}_{12345}$ and $\mathcal{I}_{12534}$. We have already touched on a preliminary study for the full calculation of the 15 regions and it shall be presented in a future publication.

In the region $R(k, l, m, n, p)$, the variables are transformed as

$$y_k = s_k, \quad y_l = s_k t_l, \quad y_m = s_k t_l u_m, \quad y_m = s_k t_l u_m v_n, \quad y_p = s_k t_l u_m v_n w_p \quad (7)$$

where $0 \leq t_l, u_m, v_n, w_p \leq 1$ and $s_k^{-1} = 1 + t_l(1 + u_m(1 + v_n(1 + w_p)))$. Hereafter, we omit the index for t, u, v, w when it is redundant.

The U function is a sum of monomials and each monomial is a product of three different y's with coefficient 1. We call a region $R(k, l, m, n, p)$ and the corresponding integral in the region as Type-I(II) when the term $y_k y_l y_m$ is (not) in U^1

The U and W functions are

$$
\begin{array}{ll}
U = s_k^3 t^2 u f, & W = s_k^4 t^2 u q, \quad (\text{Type} - \text{I}) \\
U = s_k^3 t^2 u v f, & W = s_k^4 t^2 u v q, \quad (\text{Type} - \text{II}) ,
\end{array}
\tag{8}
$$

$$V s_k^{-1} = G = m^2 g - s \frac{q}{f}, \qquad h = y_5 s_k^{-1}, \qquad g = (1 + t(1 + u(1 + v(1 + w)))) \quad (9)$$

where functions f, q, G, h are defined.

Section 2 will specify the integrals in detail. Section 3 will develop the methods used, based on lattice-rule non-adaptive integration, and an iterated adaptive method. Results will be presented in Sect. 4 and Conclusions in Sect. 5.

2 Integrals

Summed over the regions, the integral of Eq. (2) becomes $\mathcal{I} = \sum_\alpha \mathcal{I}_\alpha$, with $\alpha = (k, l, m, n, p)$; here we focus on $\mathcal{I}_{12345}$ of Type-I and $\mathcal{I}_{12534}$ of Type-II. The variable transformation in SD works to specify the ultra-violet divergence clearly. As shown in the following equations, in Type-I, the t-integral is of order $1/\varepsilon$, while in Type-II both the t- and v- integrals are in $1/\varepsilon$. The singularity can be softened by a factor h. Then for $\mathcal{I}_{12345}$ of Type-I the Laurent series in Eq.(3) starts from the C_0 term and for $\mathcal{I}_{12534}$ of Type-II the series starts from C_{-1}. With $H = G^{-3\varepsilon}/f^{2-\varepsilon}$, these are given by

$$\mathcal{I}_{12345} = \int_{C_5} dz\, dt\, du\, dv\, dw\; h\, v\, t^{2\varepsilon-1} u^\varepsilon H, \quad \text{with} \tag{10}$$

$h = tuvw,$

$f = 1 + v + uv(1 + w + vw + t + tw + tvw),$

$q = tuv(1 + wz + vwz + uvw\bar{z} + uvw^2\bar{z}z + uv^2 w^2 \bar{z}z +$

$tuvw\bar{z} + tuvw^2\bar{z}z + tuv^2 w^2 \bar{z}z),$

---

[1] In Ref [6], we studied the case of a 'complete' U function, which is the sum of all possible monomials. In this case, all regions are Type-I and the f in Eq. (8) is identical for all regions.

and

$$\mathcal{I}_{12534} = \int_{\mathcal{C}_5} dz\, dt\, du\, dv\, dw\; h\, v^{\varepsilon-1}\, t^{2\varepsilon-1}\, u^{\varepsilon}\, H, \quad \text{with} \tag{11}$$

$h = tu,$

$f = 1 + w + u + uw + uvw + tu + tuw + tuvw,$

$q = tu(z + wz + vw + u\bar{z}z + uw\bar{z}z + uvw\bar{z} + tu\bar{z}z + tuw\bar{z}z + tuvw\bar{z}).$

$\mathcal{I}_{12534}$ can further be expressed as

$$I = I_0 + I_1 \quad \text{with} \tag{12}$$

$$I_0 = \int_0^1 dz \int_0^1 dt \int_0^1 du \int_0^1 dw \frac{1}{\varepsilon} \frac{(h/t)}{t^{-2\varepsilon} u^{-\varepsilon}} \frac{G_b^{-3\varepsilon}}{f_b^{2-\varepsilon}}, \tag{13}$$

$$I_1 = \int_0^1 dz \int_0^1 dt \int_0^1 du \int_0^1 dv \int_0^1 dw \frac{(h/t)}{t^{-2\varepsilon} u^{-\varepsilon} v^{1-\varepsilon}} \left(\frac{G^{-3\varepsilon}}{f^{2-\varepsilon}} - \frac{G_b^{-3\varepsilon}}{f_b^{2-\varepsilon}} \right), \tag{14}$$

where the h, f, f_b ($f_b = f|_{v=0}$), G and G_b ($G_b = G|_{v=0}$) functions are different for each case.

Note that, for $\mathcal{I}_{12345}$, we will expand the integral with respect to ε using a linear extrapolation (see Sect. 3.3), whereas for $\mathcal{I}_{12534}$ we expand the integrands of I_0 and I_1. The integrands F_0 of I_0 and F_1 of I_1 can be expanded with respect to ε as

$$F_0 \sim \frac{h}{f_b^2 t} \frac{1}{\varepsilon} + \frac{h}{f_b^2 t} \left(\log f_b - 3 \log G_b + 2 \log t + \log u \right)$$

$$+ \frac{h}{2 f_b^2 t} \left[\log^2 f_b - 6 \log f_b \log G_b + 9 \log^2 G_b + 4 \log f_b \log t \right.$$

$$- 12 \log G_b \log t + 4 \log^2 t + 2 \log f_b \log u - 6 \log G_b \log u$$

$$+ 4 \log t \log u + \log^2 u \left. \right] \varepsilon$$

$$+ \mathcal{O}(\varepsilon^2) \tag{15}$$

and

$$F_1 \sim \frac{h}{tv} \left(\frac{1}{f^2} - \frac{1}{f_b^2} \right) - \frac{h}{f^2 f_b^2 tv} [-f_b^2 \log f + f^2 \log f_b + 3 f_b^2 \log G - 3 f^2 \log G_b$$

$$+ 2 f^2 \log t - 2 f_b^2 \log t + f^2 \log u - f_b^2 \log u + f^2 \log v - f_b^2 \log v] \varepsilon$$

$$+ O(\varepsilon^2). \tag{16}$$

With these expansions, we can integrate each term analytically and/or numerically. The first term of (15) corresponding to C_{-1} of I_0 is s-independent and it can be integrated numerically by Mathematica or other numerical integration methods. The second and the third term of (15) corresponding to C_0 and C_1 of I_0 include s-independent and s-dependent parts and as a whole they are s-dependent. Similarly, C_0 of I_1 in (16) is s-independent and C_1 of I_1 is s-dependent. Table 1 indicates the s-dependency of each coefficient.

Table 1. s-dependency of expansion coefficients

	C_{-1} real	C_0 real	C_1 real	C_{-1} imag.	C_0 imag.	C_1 imag.
I_0	s-independent (constant value)	s-dependent	s-dependent	-	s-dependent	s-dependent
I_1	-	s-independent (constant value)	s-dependent	-	-	s-dependent

3   Numerical Methods

3.1   Rank-1 Lattice Rules

Eliminating the δ-function in (2) yields an integral over an $(N-1)$-dimensional simplex, which can then be transformed to the $(N-1)$-dimensional unit cube. Lattice rules are applied with a periodizing transformation that flattens the integrand at the boundaries of the cube. A rank-1 lattice rule is given by $Qf = \frac{1}{n}\sum_{j=0}^{n-1} f(\{\frac{j}{n}\mathbf{z}\})$ where n is the number of integrand evaluations (see, e.g., [22]). Here $\mathbf{z}$ is an integer *generator* vector of length d with components $z \in \mathcal{Z}_n = \{1 \leq z < n \mid gcd(z,n) = 1\}$, where $\{\mathbf{x}\}$ denotes the vector obtained by taking the fractional part of each component of $\mathbf{x}$. Classically n is prime [14,15] and $\mathcal{Z}_n = \{1, 2, \ldots, n-1\}$. We precomputed the generators $\mathbf{z}$ for various numbers of points n using the component by component (CBC) algorithm [17,18]. The CBC algorithm runs in $\mathcal{O}(d\,n\,\log(n))$ time and $\mathcal{O}(n)$ space.

3.2   Composite/embedded Lattice Rules

An embedded sequence is given in [22], based on m copies of a rank-1 rule in r coordinate directions; m and n are assumed relatively prime.

Q_r is the m^r-copy rule of the original rule; has $m^r n$ points and is of rank r for $1 \leq r \leq d$. The points of Q_r are embedded in those of Q_{r+1}. An error estimate is also calculated.

Because of their regular structure, lattice rules are very well-suited for parallelization on GPUs (see, e.g., [1,4] implemented on Kepler-20 GPU. For the GPU computations we used CUDA, where the rule evalutions are laid out over the GPU cores. Later work included [8,11]. For this paper we made use of a GV100 Quadro GPU, which is specified with 5120 CUDA cores, 80 SMs, 32 GB of memory, and bandwidth of 868.4 GB/s. The theoretical performance is fast at 8.33 TFLOPS for FP64 (double). It is 33.32 TFLOPS for FP16 (half), and 16.66 TFLOPS for FP32 (float).

Note that an adaptive procedure is much harder to implement on a many-core system (see, e.g., [9]).

3.3   Linear Extrapolation

Linear extrapolation for an integral $\mathcal{I}$ is based on an asymptotic expansion of the form

$$\mathcal{I}(\varepsilon) \sim \sum_{k \geq \kappa} C_k\,\varphi_k(\varepsilon), \qquad \text{as } \varepsilon \to 0$$

where the sequence of $\varphi_k(\varepsilon)$ is known. The expansion is truncated after $2, 3, \ldots$ terms to form linear systems of increasing size in the C_k variables.

3.4 Transformations

For an integral $\mathcal{I}f = \int_0^1 f(x)\,dx$, we use a periodizing transformation $x = \Psi_p(t)$ of rather high order, $p = 6$ [20,21], so that the function can be extended periodically and which will help alleviate boundary singularities. We have

$$\Psi_p(t) = \frac{\theta_p(t)}{\theta_p(1)}, \qquad \text{where}$$

$$\theta_p(t) = \int_0^t \sin^p(\pi u)\,du, \qquad p = 1, 2, \ldots,$$

in particular,

$$\Psi_6(t) = t - (45\sin(2\pi t) - 9\sin(4\pi t) + \sin(6\pi t))/(60\pi)$$

$$\text{with } \Psi_6'(t) = \frac{16}{5}\sin^6(\pi t). \tag{17}$$

3.5 Iterated Automatic Adaptive Integration

The goal of automatic integration is to employ a blackbox approach to approximate integrals. For a user-specified function, required accuracy and a limit on the number of integrand evaluations, the procedure seeks to return an approximation $\mathcal{Q}f$ to an integral $\mathcal{I}f$, and estimated error $\mathcal{E}f$, such that the actual error Ef satisfies

$$Ef = |\mathcal{Q}f - \mathcal{I}f| \le \mathcal{E}f \le \mathcal{A}f,$$

where $\mathcal{A}f$ is the requested (absolute) accuracy.

An adaptive integration procedure relies on partitioning the domain to gain accuracy, especially in the vicinity of singularities. An adaptive strategy is generally based on a meta-algorithm of the type shown in Fig. 2. The subdivisions are performed in a loop that runs while the termination conditions are not yet achieved.

```
Evaluate initial region and update results
Initialize priority queue with initial region
while (evaluation limit not reached and
         estimated error too large)
    Retrieve region from priority queue
    Split region into subregions
    Evaluate new subregions and update results
    Insert new subregions into priority queue
```

Fig. 2. Adaptive Integration Meta-Algorithm

Iterated integration allows multivariate integration routines to apply one- or low-dimensional strategies in consecutive coordinate directions. For the computations in this paper, we made ample use of the QUADPACK routine DQAGSE [19], which adds an extrapolation cycle around the adaptive partitioning strategy [5, 10, 19].

4   Results

In the numerical computation, we take the value of $m = 1$, so that the value of s hereafter is in the unit of m^2.

4.1   Results for s-Independent Part

Table 2. s-independent part (constant value) obtained by Mathematica INTEGRATE function

Integral	C_{-1} real of I_0	C_0 real of I_1
$\mathcal{I}_{12534}$	$\frac{1}{4}\log\left(\frac{4}{3}\right) = 0.07192051811294521$	Eq. (18) = -0.013612949401830665

We give results of the s-independent part obtained by the Mathematica INTEGRATE function and of the s-dependent part by DQAGSE. For example, results of the s-independent part for $\mathcal{I}_{12534}$ are presented in Table 2. The s value corresponding to the threshold can be derived for each region. It was also obtained as $s = 4$ for $\mathcal{I}_{51234}$ in [7]. An imaginary part emerges for s above the threshold.

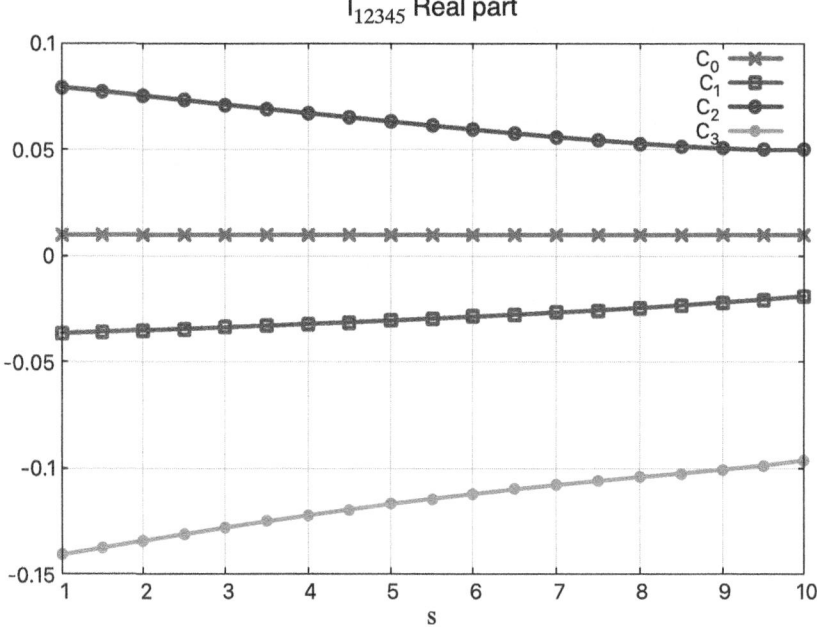

Fig. 3. Expansion coefficients for (real part) integral $\mathcal{I}_{12345}$ for $1 \leq s \leq 10$.

Table 3. C_1 values real part for $\mathcal{I}_{12345}$

s	C_1 real	C_1 err. est.	avg. time per extrapolation [sec]
1.0	-0.366254912683067133E-01	0.694E-17	0.435671
2.0	-0.352734663409193724E-01	0.694E-17	0.339906
3.0	-0.338343803945274912E-01	0.338E-19	0.349586
4.0	-0.322942491257907777E-01	0.694E-17	0.358567
5.0	-0.306349922082456046E-01	0.104E-16	0.367252
6.0	-0.288324846083721949E-01	0.694E-17	0.381545
7.0	-0.268531677116918728E-01	0.269E-19	0.433463
8.0	-0.246475664169333170E-01	0.243E-16	0.428521
9.0	-0.221359473140998880E-01	0.347E-17	0.435893
10.0	-0.191666104338030566E-01	0.153E-15	1.9738
11.0	-0.153079145751799286E-01	0.306E-09	2339.34
12.0	-0.101543652050236598E-01	0.328E-08	21444.5

Table 4. C_1 values imaginary part for $\mathcal{I}_{12345}$.

s	C_1 imag.	C_1 err. est.	avg. time per extrapolation [sec]
1.0	-0.539335522750480990E-18	0.166E-18	0.351519
2.0	-0.195362252749212056E-18	0.132E-18	0.423981
3.0	-0.246070315045975660E-18	0.424E-18	0.34778
4.0	0.104498913122451924E-17	0.633E-18	0.315143
5.0	0.192999922779541645E-17	0.694E-17	0.316811
6.0	0.348030100973042225E-18	0.351E-19	0.306804
7.0	0.114283270307553195E-17	0.830E-18	0.292358
8.0	-0.173579618677075613E-17	0.125E-18	0.293527
9.0	-0.941990468210273017E-18	0.145E-18	0.367719
10.0	0.931979443642864929E-17	0.665E-17	3.25767
11.0	0.102394384403092849E-03	0.710E-10	9435.61
12.0	0.142349044122052379E-02	0.134E-10	58581.9

A general expression (valid for C_0 real of I_1) is

$$\frac{1}{4}[-36 \log 2 - 2 \log^2 2 + 8 \log 3 + \log 2 \log 3 + 10 \log 5 \tag{18}$$

$$-2\mathrm{Li}_2\left(\frac{1}{6}\right) - 2\mathrm{Li}_2\left(\frac{1}{4}\right) + 3\mathrm{Li}_2\left(\frac{1}{3}\right)]$$

where $\mathrm{Li}_2(z)$ is the Spence function defined as $\mathrm{Li}_2(z) = -\int_0^z \frac{\ln(1-x)}{x}\,dx$.

4.2   Results for s-Dependent Part

For $\mathcal{I}_{12345}$, Fig. 3 shows results for the expansion coefficients C_0, C_1, C_2, C_3 of the error expansion using a composite lattice rule $Q_m = Q_2$ where two scaled copies of the rule are applied in each coordinate direction. The integral is real in the range $1 \leq s \leq 10$ up to the threshold of the squared momentum, and the coefficients show a smooth behavior.

Tables 3 and 4 give numerical values for the C_1 coefficient of $\mathcal{I}_{12345}$ for $s = 1.0, \ldots, 12.0$. The threshold can be seen at $s = 10$, where the imaginary part emerges. These are computed by the DQAGSE. The computation of Feynman integrals generally becomes more time-consuming for s above the threshold. Even after performing SD of a Feynman integral, this property remains valid in each resulting regional integral. Our results, as shown in the tables, agree with this observation. Note, however, that the thresholds of the integrals obtained after sector decomposition may differ from those of the original Feynman integral. In case of $\mathcal{I}_{12345}$ the threshold is 10 and the computation time above the threshold is significantly long.

Figure 4 and Fig. 5 plot the real and imaginary parts, respectively, for the coefficients C_0 and C_1 of $\mathcal{I}_{12534}$. A threshold can clearly be seen at $s = 8$, where the imaginary part emerges. The integrations were performed adaptively with DQAGSE from QUAD-PACK [19], iterated for the integration over the 5D unit cube in Eqs. (6-7).

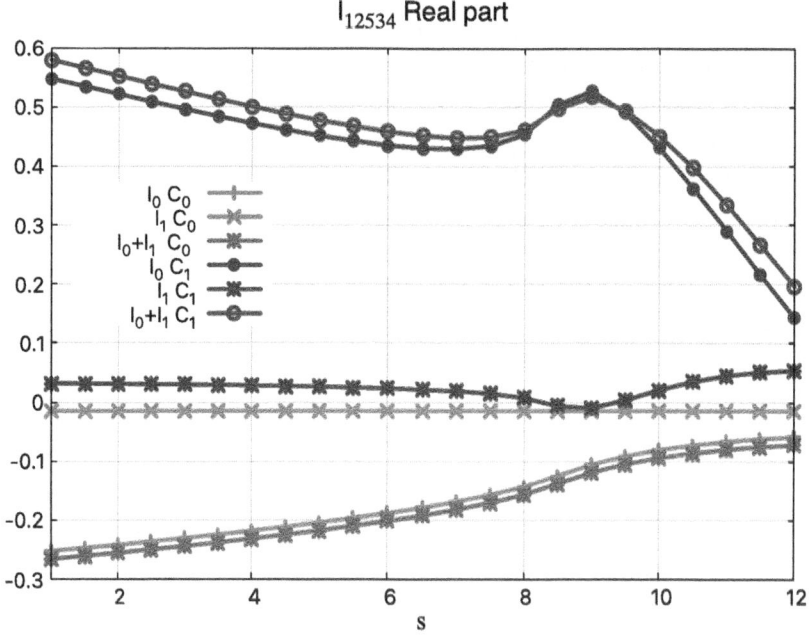

Fig. 4. Real part of expansion coefficients for integral $\mathcal{I}_{12534}$ as a function of s

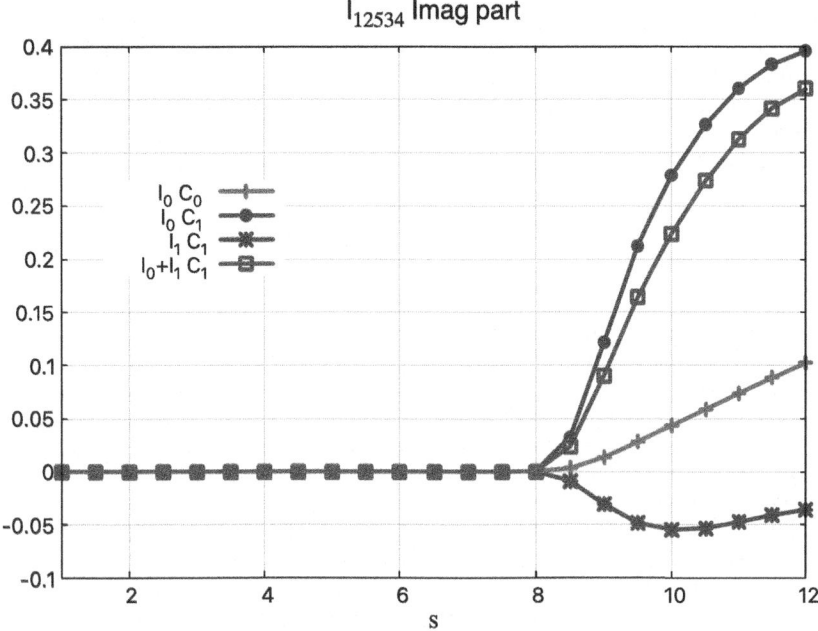

Fig. 5. Imaginary part of expansion coefficients for integral $\mathcal{I}_{12534}$ as a function of s

5   Conclusions

Higher-order corrections can contribute to accurate theoretical predictions of the cross section of particle interactions, which are fundamental to match increased accuracy in high energy physics experiments. The dimensionality and degree of difficulty increases with the number of loops and lines in the diagram. Since it is generally not possible to treat multi-loop instances with arbitrary masses and momenta, numerical approaches – in particular for higher-dimensional numerical integration in the presence of singularities, are needed to offer solutions. Lattice rules with suitable transformations provide an important tool for boundary singularities. In future work, we plan on further parallelizations of adaptive integration. We are also planning on the full computation of the 15 contributing integrals and the overall Feynman integral associated with the baseball diagram.

Acknowledgments. We acknowledge the support by JSPS KAKENHI Grant Number JP20K11858, JP20K03941 and JP21K03541. We also thank the referees for their valuable comments and suggestions.

References

1. Almulihi, A., de Doncker, E.: Accelerating high-dimensional integration using lattice rules on GPUs. In: Proc. 2017 Int. Conf. on Computational Science and Computational Intelligence (CSCI'17). CPS IEEE (2017)

2. Borowka, S., Heinrich, G., Jahn, S., Jones, S. P., Kerner, M., Schlenk, J.: A GPU compatible quasi-monte carlo integrator interfaced to pySecDec. Comput. Phys. Commun. **240**, 120–137 (2019). arXiv:1811.11720

3. Cvitanović, P., Kinoshita, T.: Feynman-Dyson rules in parametric space. Phys. Rev. D **10**, 3978 (1974)

4. de Doncker, E., Almulihi, A., Yuasa, F.: High speed evaluation of loop integrals using lattice rules. J. Phy. Conf. Ser. (JPCS) IOP Series **1085**(052005) (2018). http://iopscience.iop.org/article/10.1088/1742-6596/1085/5/052005

5. de Doncker, E., et al.: Quadpack computation of Feynman loop integrals. J. Comput. Sci. (JoCS) **3**(3), 102–112 (2011). https://doi.org/10.1016/j.jocs.2011.06.003

6. de Doncker, E., Ishikawa, T., Kato, K., Yuasa, F.: Analytic and numerical approaches for depictive 3-loop integrals using sector decomposition. Prog. Theor. Exp. Phys. **083B08** (2024). https://doi.org/10.1093/ptep/ptae122

7. de Doncker, E., Yuasa, F., , Ishikawa, T., Kato, K.: 3-loop Feynman integral extrapolations for the baseball diagram. In: (2024) the 22nd International Workshop on Advanced Computing and Analysis Techniques in Physics Research (ACAT 2024). Accepted. arXiv:2408.6551 [hep-ph]

8. de Doncker, E., Yuasa, F.: Self-energy Feynman diagrams with four loops and 11 internal lines. Springer Lecture Notes Comput. Sci. (LNCS) **12953**, 160–175 (2021)

9. de Doncker, E., Yuasa, F., Kapenga, J., Olagbemi, O.: Scalable software for multivariate integration on hybrid platforms. In: Conference on Computational Physics (CCP 2014), vol. 640. The Journal of Physics: Conf. Series (JPCS) (2015). https://doi.org/10.1088/1742-6596/640/1/012062

10. de Doncker, E., Yuasa, F., Kato, K., Ishikawa, T., Kapenga, J., Olagbemi, O.: Regularization with numerical extrapolation for finite and UV-divergent multi-loop integrals. Comput. Phys. Commun. **224**, 164–185 (2018). arXiv:1702.04904

11. de Doncker, E., Yuasa, F., Olagbemi, O., Ishikawa, T.: Large scale automatic computations for Feynman diagrams with up to five loops. Springer Lecture Notes Comput. Sci. (LNCS) **12253**, 145–162 (2020)

12. Hahn, T., Pérez-Victoria, M.: Automated one-loop calculations in four and D dimensions. Comput. Phys. Commun. **118**(2–3), 153–165 (1999). hep-ph/9807565

13. 't Hooft, G., Veltman, M.: Scalar one-loop integrals. Nucl. Phys. B **153**, 365–401 (1979)

14. Korobov, N.M.: The approximate computation of multiple integrals. Dokl. Akad. Nauk SSSR **124**, 1207–1210 (1959). (Russian)

15. Korobov, N.M.: Properties and calculation of optimal coefficients. Doklady Akademii Nauk SSSR 132, 1009–1012,: Russ. Eng. trans. Soviet Math. Doklady **1**, 696–700 (1960)

16. Nakanishi, N.: General integral formula of perturbation term in the quantized field theory. Prog. Theor. Phys. **17**, 401–418 (1957)

17. Nuyens, D., Cools, R.: Fast algorithms for component-by-component construction of rank-1 lattice rules in shift-invariant reproducing kernel Hilbert spaces. Math. Comp. **75**, 903–920 (2006)

18. Nuyens, D., Cools, R.: Fast component-by-component construction of rank-1 lattice rules with a non-prime number of points. J. Complex. **22**, 4–28 (2006)

19. Piessens, R., de Doncker, E., Überhuber, C.W., Kahaner, D.K.: QUADPACK, A Subroutine Package for Automatic Integration, Springer Series in Computational Mathematics, vol. 1. Springer-Verlag (1983)

20. Sidi, A.: A new variable transformation for numerical integration. Int. Ser. Numer. Math. **112**, 359–373 (1993)

21. Sidi, A.: Extension of a class of periodizing transformations for numerical integration. Math. Comp. **75**(253), 327–343 (2005)

22. Sloan, I., Joe, S.: Lattice Methods for Multiple Integration. Oxford University Press (1994)

Assessing the Performance of Mixed-Precision ILU(0)-Preconditioned Multiple-Precision Real and Complex Krylov Subspace Methods

Tomonori Kouya$^{(\boxtimes)}$ (iD)

Otemon Gakuin University, 2-1-15 Nishiai, Ibaraki, Osaka 567-8502, Japan
t-koya@haruka.otemon.ac.jp
https://www.otemon.ac.jp

Abstract. Krylov subspace methods are linear solvers based on matrix-vector multiplications and vector operations. While easily parallelizable, they are sensitive to rounding errors and may experience convergence issues. ILU(0), an incomplete LU factorization with zero fill-in, is a well-known preconditioning technique that enhances convergence for sparse matrices. In this paper, we implement a double-precision and multiple-precision ILU(0) preconditioner, compatible with product-type Krylov subspace methods, and evaluate its performance.

Keywords: preconditioning · Krylov subspace method · multiple-precision floating-point arithmetic

1 Introduction

With the continuous progress of digital transformation (DX), computing infrastructures capable of efficiently processing large-scale data are increasingly essential. The operation and training of AI systems, primarily based on machine learning and deep learning, are expected to drive DX forward. Consequently, faster and more efficient computers are needed, and the demand for computational power continues to grow. However, further increases in CPU and GPU clock speeds are limited, making adopting architectures optimized for parallel processing, such as those supporting single instruction, multiple data (SIMD) instructions and multi-core configurations essential. Software should likewise be optimized to run effectively on these modern architectures.

While AI applications frequently use floating-point formats with short mantissas (e.g., IEEE754 binary32 or binary16), scientific computing requires higher precision formats such as binary64 or above. Hardware advancements are driven by market demand, which often favors the former. For ill-conditioned problems requiring high precision or mixed-precision computing that combines short and long mantissa floating-point formats is a promising approach to achieve both accuracy and performance.

© The Author(s), under exclusive license to Springer Nature Switzerland AG 2026
O. Gervasi et al. (Eds.): ICCSA 2025 Workshops, LNCS 15890, pp. 31–41, 2026.
https://doi.org/10.1007/978-3-031-97606-3_3

To address such ill-conditioned problems, we developed an optimized basic linear algebra library, BNCmatmul, supporting multiple-precision formats beyond binary64. Libraries such as QD [1], MPFR [11], and MPC [3] offer reliable multi-component and arbitrary-precision arithmetic. MPLAPACK/MPBLAS [9] extends LAPACK/BLAS functionality to support these formats. However, current parallel architecture optimizations are limited to what is provided by C++ compilers. Similar to machine-optimized libraries like Intel MKL [8] and Open-BLAS [10], optimized multiple-precision BLAS libraries are required.

Our BNCmatmul library is optimized primarily for x86 environments. As of March 2025, we have completed the implementation of real and complex various multiple-precision floating-point operations, along with random sparse matrix-vector multiplication (SpMV). Details on SpMV are reported in [7], and although further tuning is possible, the current implementation is usable functionally.

This paper reports on applying ILU(0), factorization-free of fill-ins-as a pre-conditioner to product-type Krylov subspace methods: BiCG, CGS, BiCGSTAB, and GPBiCG. Unlike our AVX2-optimized SpMV, the current ILU(0) implementation is not optimized or parallelized and is, therefore, slow. Nevertheless, the implementation supports mixed-precision ILU(0) using binary64, enabling performance evaluation with test matrices from the SuiteSparse matrix collection [2]. This evaluation offers insight into the utility of the method and provides a foundation for future optimization.

The remainder of this paper is structured as follows. Section 2 describes the features of BNCmatmul. Section 3 explains the ILU(0) algorithm. Section 4 presents benchmark test results on an EPYC machine and discussions. Section 5 concludes with future work.

2   Multiple-Precision Optimized Basic Linear Algebra Library: BNCmatmul

An overview of the features of BNCmatmul [5] is shown in Fig. 1. As of March 2025, Version 0.21 has been released as open-source software, primarily supporting real-valued linear algebra routines and their optimized/parallelized versions. Version 0.22, currently under development, extends functionality to complex linear algebra based on real implementations.

The library supports the following five floating-point types:

Double (D). IEEE754 binary64 format with a 53-bit mantissa (52-bit + 1 hidden bit).

Multi-component-type. Formats based on binary64 that extend mantissa length using multiple components:
  Double-double (DD). 106-bit mantissa using two binary64 values.
  Triple-double (TD). 159-bit mantissa using three binary64 values.
  Quadruple-double (QD). 212-bit mantissa using four binary64 values.

Multi-digit-type. Arbitrary precision types provided by MPFR (real) and MPC (complex), built on GMP's multiple-precision natural number (MPN) kernel.

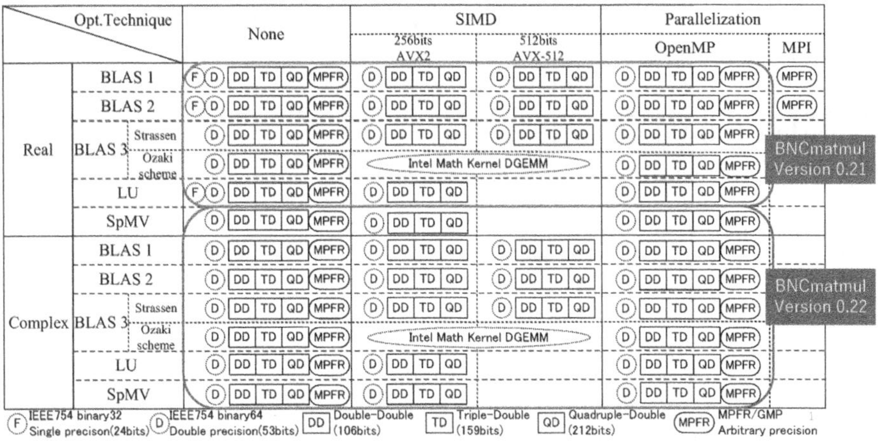

		None	SIMD 256bits AVX2	SIMD 512bits AVX-512	Parallelization OpenMP	MPI
	Opt.Technique					
Real	BLAS 1	(F)(D)[DD][TD][QD](MPFR)	(D)[DD][TD][QD]	(D)[DD][TD][QD]	(D)[DD][TD][QD](MPFR)	(MPFR)
	BLAS 2	(F)(D)[DD][TD][QD](MPFR)	(D)[DD][TD][QD]	(D)[DD][TD][QD]	(D)[DD][TD][QD](MPFR)	(MPFR)
	BLAS 3 Strassen	(D)[DD][TD][QD](MPFR)	(D)[DD][TD][QD]	(D)[DD][TD][QD]	(D)[DD][TD][QD](MPFR)	BNCmatmul Version 0.21
	BLAS 3 Ozaki scheme	(D)[DD][TD][QD](MPFR)	Intel Math Kernel DGEMM		(D)[DD][TD][QD](MPFR)	
	LU	(F)(D)[DD][TD][QD](MPFR)	(D)[DD][TD][QD]		(D)[DD][TD][QD](MPFR)	
	SpMV	(D)[DD][TD][QD](MPFR)	(D)[DD][TD][QD]		(D)[DD][TD][QD](MPFR)	
Complex	BLAS 1	(D)[DD][TD][QD](MPFR)	(D)[DD][TD][QD]	(D)[DD][TD][QD]	(D)[DD][TD][QD](MPFR)	
	BLAS 2	(D)[DD][TD][QD](MPFR)	(D)[DD][TD][QD]	(D)[DD][TD][QD]	(D)[DD][TD][QD](MPFR)	BNCmatmul Version 0.22
	BLAS 3 Strassen	(D)[DD][TD][QD](MPFR)	(D)[DD][TD][QD]	(D)[DD][TD][QD]	(D)[DD][TD][QD](MPFR)	
	BLAS 3 Ozaki scheme	(D)[DD][TD][QD](MPFR)	Intel Math Kernel DGEMM		(D)[DD][TD][QD](MPFR)	
	LU	(D)[DD][TD][QD](MPFR)	(D)[DD][TD][QD]		(D)[DD][TD][QD](MPFR)	
	SpMV	(D)[DD][TD][QD](MPFR)	(D)[DD][TD][QD]		(D)[DD][TD][QD](MPFR)	

Legend: (F) IEEE754 binary32 Single precison(24bits); (D) IEEE754 binary64 Double precision(53bits); [DD] Double-Double (106bits); [TD] Triple-Double (159bits); [QD] Quadruple-Double (212bits); (MPFR) MPFR/GMP Arbitrary precision

Fig. 1. Current development status of BNCmatmul

The SpMV implemented in this work builds on our prior implementation of MPFR-based arbitrary-precision compressed row storage (CRS) multiplication [6], extended to support all five floating-point types. This feature is included in Version 0.22, and detailed performance evaluation results can be found in [7].

Version 0.22 is scheduled for release soon. Looking ahead, Version 0.23 will expand the capabilities of the library for nonlinear computations based on the current linear algebra core. It will also introduce SIMD-optimized "pair arithmetic" for multi-component types. Additionally, we plan to adapt the library for consumer-grade computing platforms, including environments with 128-bit SIMD support such as Arm NEON, WebAssembly (WASM), and x86 SSE.

3 Product-Type Krylov Subspace Methods and Mixed-Precision ILU(0) Preconditioner

We consider solving the linear system:

$$Ax = b \tag{1}$$

where $A \in \mathbb{C}^{n \times n}$ is a complex-valued square coefficient matrix, $\mathbf{b} \in \mathbb{C}^n$ is a known n-dimensional vector, and $\mathbf{x} \in \mathbb{C}^n$ is the unknown n-dimensional vector to be solved. In this study, we assume A is non-singular. For comparison purposes, we also consider real-valued cases where $A \in \mathbb{R}^{n \times n}$, $\mathbf{b} \in \mathbb{R}^n$, and $\mathbf{x} \in \mathbb{R}^n$.

When A is sparse, iterative methods such as Krylov subspace methods and GMRES are effective due to their reliance on matrix-vector multiplication, which is easy to parallelize. However, these algorithms are highly sensitive to rounding errors and may fail to converge within the theoretical limit of n iterations. To improve convergence, preconditioning is commonly applied. One such technique is the incomplete LU factorization (ILU) that approximates $A \approx LU$ while controlling fill-ins. We use ILU(0), which introduces no fill-in, as defined in the Algorithm 1.

Algorithm 1. ILU(0) Factorization

Require: Sparse matrix $A \in \mathbb{C}^{n \times n}$ (non-singular)
Ensure: Matrices $\tilde{L}, \tilde{U} \in \mathbb{C}^{n \times n}$ such that $A \approx \tilde{L}\tilde{U}$
 1: Initialize $\tilde{L} := I$, $\tilde{U} := 0$
 2: **for** $k = 1$ to n **do**
 3:   **if** $U_{kk} := A_{kk} \neq 0$ **then**
 4:     **for** each $i > k$ such that $A_{ik} \neq 0$ **do**
 5:       $\tilde{L}_{ik} := A_{ik}/\tilde{U}_{kk}$
 6:       **for** each $j > k$ such that $A_{kj} \neq 0$ **do**
 7:         **if** $A_{ij} \neq 0$ **then**
 8:           $A_{ij} := A_{ij} - \tilde{L}_{ik} \cdot \tilde{U}_{kj}$
 9:         **end if**
10:       **end for**
11:     **end for**
12:     **for** each $j > k$ such that $A_{kj} \neq 0$ **do**
13:       $\tilde{U}_{kj} := A_{kj}$
14:     **end for**
15:   **end if**
16: **end for**

Once the ILU(0) factorization is complete, we apply the preconditioner $M = \tilde{L}\tilde{U}$ before starting the iterations. During each iteration, we solve $M\mathbf{z} = \mathbf{r}$ using forward and backward substitutions, as described in Algorithm 2.

Among the product-type Krylov methods, applying ILU(0) preconditioning to the BiCG method results in Algorithm 3:

In BiCG, both $M\mathbf{z} = \mathbf{r}$ and $M^H\mathbf{z} = \mathbf{r}$ must be solved at each iteration. In contrast, other product-type methods such as CGS, BiCGSTAB, and GPBiCG require only one preconditioning solve per iteration.

Our ILU(0) implementation supports both real and complex CRS sparse matrices and handles Hermitian systems. In line with previous research by Hishinuma et al. [4], the SuiteSparse Matrix Collection [2] provides only binary64 matrices, therefore, we implemented mixed-precision SpMV and forward/backward substitutions with binary64 and higher precisions to assess the impact of mixed-precision ILU(0) on convergence and performance. In the BiCG method described in Algorithm 3, all computations are performed entirely in high-precision arithmetic. Only when binary64 ILU(0) is used, Lines 5, 6, 19, and 20 in Algorithm 3 are executed using binary64 $\tilde{L}_{ij}$ and $\tilde{U}_{ij}$, along with high-precision y_i and z_i in Algorithm 2.

4   Benchmark Test

This section presents and discusses the results of benchmark tests conducted on the following 32-core EPYC computing environment:

Algorithm 2. Preconditioning via ILU(0): Solving $M^{-1}\mathbf{r} = \mathbf{z}$

Require: Residual vector $\mathbf{r} \in \mathbb{C}^n$, ILU(0) factors $\tilde{L}$, $\tilde{U}$
Ensure: Preconditioned vector $\mathbf{z} \in \mathbb{C}^n$
 1: Forward substitution to solve $\tilde{L}\mathbf{y} = \mathbf{r}$
 2: **for** $i = 1$ to n **do**
 3:     $y_i := r_i$
 4:     **for** $j = 1$ to $i - 1$ **do**
 5:         **if** $\tilde{L}_{ij} \neq 0$ **then**
 6:             $y_i := y_i - \tilde{L}_{ij} \cdot y_j$
 7:         **end if**
 8:     **end for**
 9: **end for**
10: Backward substitution to solve $\tilde{U}\mathbf{z} = \mathbf{y}$
11: **for** $i = n$ downto 1 **do**
12:     $z_i := y_i$
13:     **for** $j = i + 1$ to n **do**
14:         **if** $\tilde{U}_{ij} \neq 0$ **then**
15:             $z_i := z_i - \tilde{U}_{ij} \cdot z_j$
16:         **end if**
17:     **end for**
18:     $z_i := z_i / \tilde{U}_{ii}$
19: **end for**

Hardware: AMD EPYC 9354P, 3.7 GHz, 32 cores, Ubuntu 20.04.6 LTS
Software: Intel Compiler version 2021.10.0, GNU MP 6.2.1, MPFR 4.1.0, MPC
1.2.1

For the linear system defined in Eq. 1, the exact solution vector $\mathbf{x}$ is set as
follows:

- For real matrices: $\mathbf{x} := \sqrt{2} \begin{bmatrix} 1 & 2 & \dots & n \end{bmatrix}^T$
- For complex matrices: $\mathbf{x} := \sqrt{2 + 3\mathrm{i}} \begin{bmatrix} 1 & 2 & \dots & n \end{bmatrix}^T$

The right-hand side vector is computed as $\mathbf{b} := A\mathbf{x}$.

The performance of sparse matrix preconditioning strongly depends on the
structure of the matrix and the target computing environment. In this test,
we selected the following two example matrices from the SuiteSparse Matrix
Collection, shown in Fig. 2:

- Real sparse matrix: mcfe ($n = 765$)
- Complex sparse matrix: dwg961b ($n = 961$)

As demonstrated subsequently, neither matrix converges without ILU(0) preconditioning under floating-point precision below 256 bits. Since both are originally stored in binary64 precision, we evaluated the performance using:

- Mixed-precision SpMV implementations using binary64 and DD/TD/QD
  (BiCG_d, etc.)

Algorithm 3. Preconditioned BiCG Method for Complex Systems

Require: Complex matrix $A \in \mathbb{C}^{n \times n}$, RHS vector $\mathbf{b} \in \mathbb{C}^n$, initial guess $\mathbf{x}_0 := 0$
Require: Preconditioner $M \approx A$, tolerance ϵ
Ensure: Approximate solution $\mathbf{x}$

1: $\mathbf{x} := \mathbf{x}_0$
2: $\mathbf{r}_0 := \mathbf{b} - A\mathbf{x}$
3: $\mathbf{r} := \mathbf{r}_0$
4: $\tilde{\mathbf{r}} := \mathbf{r}$
5: Solve $M\mathbf{z} := \mathbf{r}$
6: Solve $M^H\tilde{\mathbf{z}} := \tilde{\mathbf{r}}$
7: $\mathbf{p} := \mathbf{z}, \tilde{\mathbf{p}} := \tilde{\mathbf{z}}$
8: $\rho := \langle \tilde{\mathbf{z}}, \mathbf{r} \rangle$
9: **for** $k = 1$ to max_iter **do**
10:    $\mathbf{q} := A\mathbf{p}$
11:    $\tilde{\mathbf{q}} := A^H\tilde{\mathbf{p}}$
12:    $\alpha := \rho / \langle \tilde{\mathbf{p}}, \mathbf{q} \rangle$
13:    $\mathbf{x} := \mathbf{x} + \alpha\mathbf{p}$
14:    $\mathbf{r} := \mathbf{r} - \alpha\mathbf{q}$
15:    $\tilde{\mathbf{r}} := \tilde{\mathbf{r}} - \overline{\alpha}\tilde{\mathbf{q}}$
16:    **if** $\|\mathbf{r}\| < \varepsilon_r\|\mathbf{r}_0\| + \varepsilon_a$ **then**
17:       **break**
18:    **end if**
19:    Solve $M\mathbf{z} := \mathbf{r}$
20:    Solve $M^H\tilde{\mathbf{z}} := \tilde{\mathbf{r}}$
21:    $\rho_{\text{new}} := \langle \tilde{\mathbf{z}}, \mathbf{r} \rangle$
22:    $\beta := \rho_{\text{new}} / \rho$
23:    $\mathbf{p} := \mathbf{z} + \beta\mathbf{p}$
24:    $\tilde{\mathbf{p}} := \tilde{\mathbf{z}} + \overline{\beta}\tilde{\mathbf{p}}$
25:    $\rho := \rho_{\text{new}}$
26: **end for**

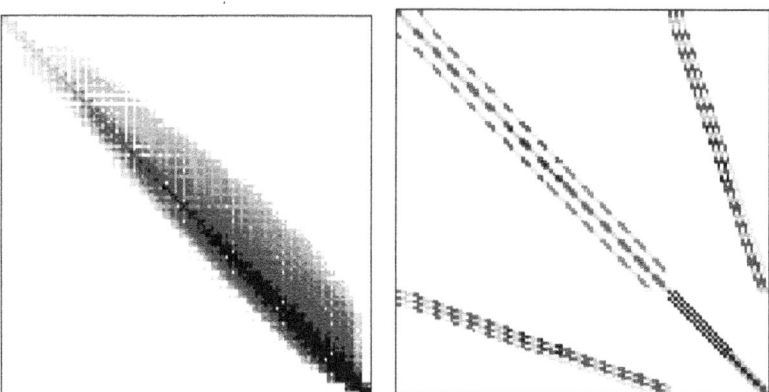

Fig. 2. Structures of non-zero elements in the example matrices: mcfe (left) and dwg961b (right) adapted from [2].

Table 1. Real linear equation: mcfe

mcfe, $n = 765$	DD			TD			QD		
Algorithm	[1]	[2]	[3]	[1]	[2]	[3]	[1]	[2]	[3]
BiCG	2295	0.26	0.11	2295	3.00	1.31	2295	3.64	1.58
BiCG_p	2295	0.23	0.10	2295	1.14	0.50	2295	1.70	0.74
BiCG_ILU(0)	13	0.67	51.31	13	0.74	56.85	13	0.78	59.77
BiCG_d	2295	0.25	0.11	2295	2.88	1.25	2295	3.47	1.51
BiCG_dp	2295	0.27	0.12	2295	1.13	0.49	2295	1.61	0.70
BiCG_d_ILU(0)	13	0.67	51.31	13	0.69	53.23	13	0.73	56.23
CGS	2295	0.25	0.11	2295	3.10	1.35	2295	4.01	1.75
CGS_p	2295	0.09	0.04	2295	0.70	0.30	2295	0.93	0.41
CGS_ILU(0)	9	0.52	57.67	9	0.55	60.67	9	0.59	66.00
CGS_d	2295	0.23	0.10	2295	2.98	1.30	2295	3.84	1.67
CGS_dp	2295	0.22	0.10	2295	0.69	0.30	2295	0.91	0.40
CGS_d_ILU(0)	9	0.47	52.56	9	0.51	56.56	9	0.54	59.78
BiCGSTAB	2295	0.25	0.11	2295	3.19	1.39	2295	4.23	1.84
BiCGSTAB_p	2295	0.08	0.04	2295	0.81	0.35	2295	1.12	0.49
BiCGSTAB_ILU(0)	9	0.51	56.89	9	0.52	58.11	9	0.56	62.56
BiCGSTAB_d	2295	0.24	0.10	2295	3.08	1.34	2295	4.06	1.77
BiCGSTAB_dp	2295	0.24	0.10	2295	0.83	0.36	2295	1.11	0.48
BiCGSTAB_d_ILU(0)	9	0.47	52.44	9	0.49	54.11	9	0.51	57.00
GPBiCG	2295	0.26	0.12	2295	3.53	1.54	2295	4.57	1.99
GPBiCG_p	2295	0.12	0.05	2295	1.20	0.52	2295	1.49	0.65
GPBiCG_ILU(0)	8	0.46	57.63	8	0.50	62.38	8	0.54	67.38
GPBiCG_d	2295	0.26	0.11	2295	3.42	1.49	2295	4.40	1.92
GPBiCG_dp	2295	0.23	0.10	2295	1.13	0.49	2295	1.47	0.64
GPBiCG_d_ILU(0)	8	0.43	53.50	9	0.51	56.56	8	0.49	61.13

- Mixed-precision ILU(0) forward/backward substitution using binary64 (BiCG_d_ILU(0), etc.)
- Parallel implementations using 32-thread OpenMP without preconditioning (BiCG_p, etc.)

Although our 32-threaded parallelized SpMVs are not optimized for any particular type of sparse matrix, they were used for this benchmarking.

We first present results using DD, TD, and QD multi-component precision formats. Table 1 lists the results for the real matrix mcfe ($n = 765$) under a maximum iteration count of $3n = 2295$, with convergence thresholds $\varepsilon_r = 10^{-13}$ and $\varepsilon_a = 10^{-100}$. The metrics in each column are as follows:

[1] Number of iterations
[2] Total computation time (in seconds)
[3] Average time per iteration (in milliseconds), calculated as [2] divided by [1]

As shown, without ILU(0) preconditioning, all methods hit the iteration limit without converging, regardless of the precision format. Mixed-precision SpMV does not negatively impact convergence, nor does it reduce the effectiveness of ILU(0). Mixed-precision forward/backward substitution maintains the same number of iterations.

Next, Table 2 lists the results for the complex sparse matrix dwg961b ($n = 961$), again with DD, TD, and QD precision formats. As in the previous case, none of the Krylov subspace methods converge without ILU(0) preconditioning.

Table 2. Complex linear equation: dwg961b

dwg961b, $n = 961$	DD			TD			QD		
Algorithm	[1]	[2]	[3]	[1]	[2]	[3]	[1]	[2]	[3]
BiCG	2883	0.79	0.27	2883	8.96	3.11	2883	13.10	4.55
BiCG_p	2883	1.61	0.56	2883	6.73	2.33	2883	10.77	3.73
BiCG_ILU(0)	758	199.67	263.41	516	170.33	330.09	442	206.52	467.24
BiCG_d	2883	0.76	0.26	2883	8.64	3.00	2883	12.66	4.39
BiCG_dp	2883	1.83	0.63	2883	6.71	2.33	2883	10.36	3.59
BiCG_d_ILU(0)	758	62.74	82.77	512	45.34	88.55	438	82.33	187.96
CGS	2883	0.85	0.29	2883	9.89	3.43	2883	15.49	5.37
CGS_p	2883	0.70	0.24	2883	3.67	1.27	2883	6.04	2.10
CGS_ILU(0)	1057	268.15	253.69	666	215.51	323.59	529	244.34	461.88
CGS_d	2883	0.81	0.28	2883	9.60	3.33	2883	14.99	5.20
CGS_dp	2883	1.67	0.58	2883	3.72	1.29	2883	6.07	2.10
CGS_d_ILU(0)	1064	84.79	79.69	664	57.05	85.92	526	48.36	91.93
BiCGSTAB	2883	0.93	0.32	2883	10.51	3.65	2883	17.56	6.09
BiCGSTAB_p	2883	0.69	0.24	2883	4.27	1.48	2883	8.19	2.84
BiCGSTAB_ILU(0)	2209	551.94	249.86	1242	401.85	323.55	778	354.55	455.72
BiCGSTAB_d	2883	0.89	0.31	2883	10.21	3.54	2883	17.10	5.93
BiCGSTAB_dp	2883	1.50	0.52	2883	4.23	1.47	2883	8.17	2.83
BiCGSTAB_d_ILU(0)	1998	159.13	79.65	1117	96.01	85.96	831	76.92	92.56
GPBiCG	2883	1.12	0.39	2883	12.53	4.35	2883	21.92	7.60
GPBiCG_p	2883	0.92	0.32	2883	6.30	2.18	2883	12.64	4.38
GPBiCG_ILU(0)	1954	489.50	250.51	1143	370.68	324.31	869	396.26	456.00
GPBiCG_d	2883	1.08	0.37	2883	12.23	4.24	2883	21.42	7.43
GPBiCG_dp	2883	2.09	0.72	2883	6.33	2.20	2883	12.67	4.39
GPBiCG_d_ILU(0)	1871	149.19	79.74	1162	100.73	86.68	896	84.30	94.09

Compared to the real-valued case, solving complex linear systems takes more time, consistent with our previous benchmark study [7]. Furthermore, the cost per iteration when using ILU(0) preconditioning is significantly higher.

We also benchmarked arbitrary-precision arithmetic using MPFR and MPC with a 256-bit mantissa to observe the impact on convergence. Results indicate that like the multi-component case, no convergence is achieved without ILU(0). The effect of mixed-precision in these settings is summarized in Table 3.

Table 3. MPFR and MPC 256-bit benchmark results

MPFR and MPC 256bits	mcfe			dwg961b		
Algorithm	[1]	[2]	[3]	[1]	[2]	[3]
BiCG	2295	11.93	5.20	2883	7.60	2.64
BiCG_p	2295	7.31	3.19	2883	1.43	0.50
BiCG_ILU(0)	13	1.10	84.46	401	0.90	2.25
BiCG_d	2295	17.70	7.71	2883	13.37	4.64
BiCG_dp	2295	7.33	3.20	2883	1.68	0.58
BiCG_d_ILU(0)	13	0.86	66.31	2883	72.52	25.15
CGS	2295	11.84	5.16	2883	9.78	3.39
CGS_p	2295	5.47	2.38	2883	1.34	0.46
CGS_ILU(0)	9	0.82	91.44	468	0.59	1.26
CGS_d	2295	17.60	7.67	2883	17.80	6.17
CGS_dp	2295	5.33	2.32	2883	1.68	0.58
CGS_d_ILU(0)	9	0.63	70.00	2087	0.47	0.22
BiCGSTAB	2295	12.12	5.28	2883	13.40	4.65
BiCGSTAB_p	2295	5.74	2.50	2883	2.00	0.69
BiCGSTAB_ILU(0)	9	0.79	87.22	716	0.59	0.83
BiCGSTAB_d	2295	17.88	7.79	2883	24.65	8.55
BiCGSTAB_dp	2295	5.53	2.41	2883	2.49	0.86
BiCGSTAB_d_ILU(0)	9	0.60	66.89	2883	0.47	0.16
GPBiCG	2295	13.82	6.02	2883	17.60	6.10
GPBiCG_p	2295	7.30	3.18	2883	3.40	1.18
GPBiCG_ILU(0)	8	0.76	95.00	674	0.76	1.13
GPBiCG_d	2295	19.97	8.70	2883	31.06	10.77
GPBiCG_dp	2295	7.50	3.27	2883	3.96	1.37
GPBiCG_d_ILU(0)	8	0.58	72.50	2883	0.49	0.17

Finally, Table 4 summarizes the reduction ratios in computation time when using ILU(0) and mixed-precision ILU(0) substitutions.

The results indicate the following for real-valued systems:

Table 4. Computation time ratio: real vs. complex systems

Ratio	mcfe				dwg961b			
Algorithm	DD	TD	QD	MPFR	DD	TD	QD	MPC
ILU(0)/BiCG	456.4	43.5	37.7	16.2	960.1	106.2	102.8	15.1
ILU(0)_d/BiCG_d	476.7	42.4	37.2	8.6	313.6	29.5	42.8	8.2
ILU(0)/ILU(0)_d	1.0	1.1	1.1	1.3	3.2	3.7	2.5	1.2
ILU(0)/CGS	538.0	45.0	37.8	17.7	863.5	94.3	86.0	14.5
ILU(0)_d/CGS_d	515.4	43.5	35.7	9.1	284.3	25.8	17.7	7.8
ILU(0)/ILU(0)_d	1.1	1.1	1.1	1.3	3.2	3.8	5.0	1.2
ILU(0)/BiCGSTAB	526.5	41.8	34.0	16.5	773.7	88.8	74.8	13.5
ILU(0)_d/BiCGSTAB_d	505.7	40.4	32.2	8.6	258.0	24.3	15.6	7.5
ILU(0)/ILU(0)_d	1.1	1.1	1.0	1.3	3.1	3.8	4.9	1.2
ILU(0)/GPBiCG	500.9	40.6	33.8	15.8	644.8	74.6	74.8	10.5
ILU(0)_d/GPBiCG_d	481.5	40.4	32.2	8.3	212.9	20.4	12.7	6.4
ILU(0)/ILU(0)_d	1.1	1.1	1.1	1.3	3.1	3.7	4.8	1.2

- ILU(0) preconditioning increases total time by factors of 456.4 – 538.0 (DD), 40.6 – 45.0 (TD), and 33.8 – 37.8 (QD).
- Mixed-precision substitutions reduce time by -4.5 – 5.3% compared to standard ILU(0).
- For MPFR 256-bit, mixed-precision yields up to 47.1 – 48.5% reduction in ILU(0) cost.

In complex systems, mixed-precision preconditioning significantly improves performance, especially for multi-component formats. However, in MPC-based arbitrary precision, the effect is less pronounced.

- ILU(0) preconditioning increases total time by factors of 644.8 – 960.1 (DD), 74.6 – 106.2 (TD), and 74.8 – 102.8 (QD).
- Mixed-precision substitutions reduce time by 58.4 – 83.1% compared to standard ILU(0).
- For MPFR 256-bit, mixed-precision yields up to 39.2 – 46.0% reduction in ILU(0) cost.

5 Conclusion and Future Work

The benchmark results presented above indicate that, for cases where preconditioning is essential, the computational cost of ILU(0) increases with higher arithmetic precision. Specifically, DD precision incurs a 456x to 960x overhead, TD incurs 41x to 106x, and QD incurs 34x to 103x compared to un-preconditioned runs. In such cases, the use of mixed-precision SpMV and mixed-precision forward/backward substitution provides a modest reduction in computational cost, typically around 58.4 – 83.1% for multi-component types in complex Krylov subspace methods.

In the MPFR 256-bit precision tests, the benefit of using mixed-precision substitution was even more evident, reducing ILU(0) computation time by approximately 39.2 – 48.5%. This shows that even a naive mixed-precision implementation can yield significant performance improvements, especially in high-precision environments.

Furthermore, for complex-valued systems, the benefit of mixed-precision is more pronounced when using multi-component types (DD, TD, QD). In contrast, the MPC-based arbitrary-precision results demonstrated minimal variation, likely due to the already high cost of complex arithmetic in those settings.

Currently, our ILU(0) implementation is not optimized or parallelized. The ILU factorization itself and the forward/backward substitutions are implemented sequentially, leading to significant computational overhead. To further improve performance, especially for practical use in high-precision environments, future work should include:

- SIMD optimization and OpenMP parallelization of ILU(0) routines
- Improved memory access patterns and cache-aware implementations
- Enhanced support for mixed precision preconditioning techniques
- Benchmarking on wider hardware platforms including Arm NEON, WASM, and SSE

Acknowledgment. This research was supported by JSPS KAKENHI Grant Number 23K11127. We thank all anonymous referees for their helpful comments, which greatly contributed to the revision of this paper.

References

1. D.H. Bailey. QD. https://www.davidhbailey.com/dhbsoftware/
2. The SuiteSparse Matrix Collection. https://sparse.tamu.edu/
3. Andreas Enge, Philippe Théveny, and Paul Zimmermann. MPC. http://www.multiprecision.org/mpc/
4. Hishinuma, T., Fujii, A., Tanaka, T., Hasegawa, H.: AVX acceleration of DD arithmetic between a sparse matrix and vector. In: Wyrzykowski, R., Dongarra, J., Karczewski, K., Waśniewski, J., (eds.) Parallel Processing and Applied Mathematics, pp. 622–631, Berlin, Heidelberg. Springer (2014)
5. Tomonori Kouya. BNCmatmul. https://github.com/tkouya/bncmatmul
6. Kouya, T.: A highly efficient implementation of multiple precision sparse matrix-vector multiplication and its application to product-type krylov subspace methods. Int. J. Num. Meth. Appl. **7**(2), 107–119 (2012)
7. Kouya, T.: Performance evaluation of accelerated real and complex multiple-precision sparse matrix-vector multiplication. In: 2024 International Conference on Engineering and Emerging Technologies (ICEET), pp. 1–6 (2024)
8. Intel Math Kernel Library. http://www.intel.com/software/products/mkl/
9. MPLAPACK/MPBLAS. Multiple precision arithmetic LAPACK and BLAS. https://github.com/nakatamaho/mplapack
10. OpenBLAS. http://www.openblas.net/
11. MPFR Project. The MPFR library. https://www.mpfr.org/

Stochastic Variational Method as a Machine Learning Approach to Large-Scale Few-Body System Calculations

Shigeyoshi Aoyama[1,2]($\boxtimes$)(iD), Takayuki Myo[3,4](iD), and Daisuke Yoshida[5](iD)

[1] Computing Research Center, High Energy Accelerator Research Organization
(KEK), Tsukuba, Ibaraki 305-0801, Japan
shigeyoshi.aoyama@kek.jp
[2] RIKEN Nishina Center, Wako 351-0198, Japan
[3] General Education, Faculty of Engineering, Osaka Institute of Technology,
Osaka 535-8585, Japan
takayuki.myo@oit.ac.jp
[4] Research Center for Nuclear Physics (RCNP), Osaka University,
Ibaraki 567-0047, Japan
[5] Department of Physics, Tohoku University, Sendai 980-8578, Japan
daisuke.yoshida.b1@touhoku.ac.jp

Abstract. Stochastic variational method as a machine learning approach to large-scale few-body system calculations is performed with
Gaussian expansion method. As a basic research to far beyond the three-
body systems, the methodology is confirmed in three-body system called
^{4}He trimer. When the number of particles is large, it becomes impossible
to perform the calculations at around seven-body system even with a
massively parallel computer such as Fugaku supercomputer, mainly due
to memory capacity limitations, but this limitation can be significantly
alleviated by reducing the number of necessary basis functions. Therefore, a machine learning approach that searches for basis functions with
as few basis functions as possible is expected. In the present calculation
with a machine learning approach based on SVM, the calculated minimum energ with 625 basis functions, which is a standard number in
GEM, is reproduced with learned significantly less 54 basis functions.

Keywords: few-body system · machine learning · massive parallel
computing

1 Introduction

In the research field of quantum few-body systems, several method are proposed
and applied to solve few-body problems. One of standard and powerful methods
has been known as Gaussian Expansion Method (GEM) [1–8]. Currently, the
cutting edge of many methods for few-body system calculations is around five-
body systems although there have been successful cases of more than six-body

© The Author(s), under exclusive license to Springer Nature Switzerland AG 2026
O. Gervasi et al. (Eds.): ICCSA 2025 Workshops, LNCS 15890, pp. 42–53, 2026.
https://doi.org/10.1007/978-3-031-97606-3_4

systems through simplification and ingenuity of the problems. On the other hand, in the region with a large number of particles, other methods such as density functional theory are used, but there are not practical methods for the region of about 10-body systems, and there is no direct relationship between few-body calculations and model calculations for many bodies. When large-scale few-body system calculations more than 10-body is possible, there is possibility to gives a strong foundation for model calculations.

In GEM, the relative wave function is expanded in Gaussians basis functions with the order of 10. When the number of particles is increased by one, the number of basis functions in GEM describing that degree of freedom takes effect as a product of those for the previous degrees of freedom. That is 10 times larger at least when the number of particles increases by one. Therefore, the computing time for matrix elements and computer memories are required 100 times the amount compared to the case where there is one less particle. Furthermore, since it is known that the computational time of the diagonalization is $\mathcal{O}(N^3)$, reducing the number of basis functions N is important. Actually, the limitation of GEM using cutting-edge massively parallel computers like Fugaku is 7-body or 8-body systems even with optimistic estimates.

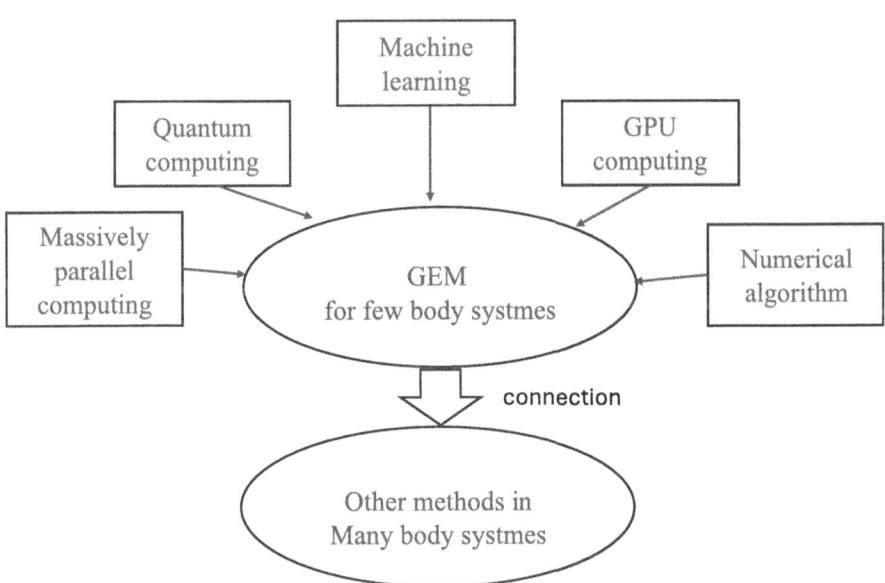

Fig. 1. Schematic diagram of GEM's development and expansion.

We have a plan revising and expanding the GEM calculation code with the aim of applying it to up to 10-body systems and connecting to many-body system calculations (Fig. 1). However, if we want to expand it to beyond 10-body systems, the calculation code needs to be revised as two points:

i) accelerating calculation of individual matrix elements,
ii) reducing the number of basis functions for the diagonalization.

First one (i) would be achieved by the so called hybrid computing with parallel computer+GPU and/or parallel computer+quantum computer, and revisions of numerical algorithms. The calculation of GEM matrix elements involves extensive use of algebraic and matrix operations, so it is also expected that GPU programming will speed up the process. Energy variation problems are expected to be a representative application of quantum computers, and GEM is a method for solving typical energy variation problems. Second one (ii) would be achieved by the machine learning. In GEM, as the number of basis functions increases, non-important basis functions are searched for to reduce the computation time with like craftsmanship approach. Or the stochastic variational method (SVM) [9–13] has been used to find automatically unimportant basis functions. The purpose of this research is investigate the availability of of SVM as a first example of a machine learning approach. The machine learning approach is expected to be powerful in other point of views. Since N-body system is a sub-system of more than $N+1$-body systems, the learned important basis functions would be also important in more than $N+1$-body systems.

In Sect. 2, GEM and SVM as a machine learning approach are explained. In Sect. 3, the calculation results and discussions for them are given. Finally, summary and conclusions are given.

2   Method

2.1   Gaussian Expansion Method

Here, we briefly explain GEM for three body bosonic system with Jacobi coordinate. The detail is given in review papers [3,14]. In GEM, the wave function Ψ_{JM} (J is the total angular momentum and M is its z-component) of the Schrödinger equation,

$$(H - E)\Psi_{JM} = 0, \tag{1}$$

is obtained by diagonalizing the Hamiltonian in a space spanned by basis functions which are constructed on Jacobi coordinates. ^{4}He-^{4}He potential in the Hamiltonian used in this research is B2+B2, which is two range (attractive and repulsive) Gaussian potential [15]. In Fig. 2, the Jacobi coordinate for three body system is displayed. R_i is i-th Jacobi coordinate, L_i is angler momentum, b_i is a range parameter of Gaussian type basis functions.

The total wave function Ψ_{JM} is written as

$$\Psi_{JM} = \sum_{i=1}^{i_{max}} c_i \mathcal{S}\Phi_i \left(R_1, R_2 \right). \tag{2}$$

where $\mathcal{S}$ is symmetrization operator to the bosonic systems and Φ_i is three-body basis functions. In a three-body bosonic system with the same mass, the

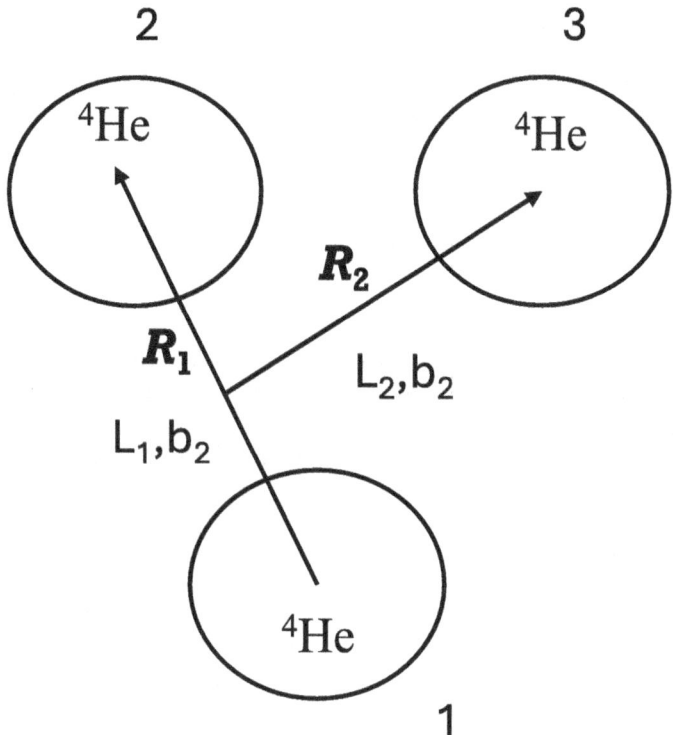

Fig. 2. Jacobi coordinate for three body system.

symmetrization for the wave function is equivalent to rearranging the Jacobi coordinates [3,14].

The three body basis functions are taken as

$$\Phi_i\left(\boldsymbol{R_1}, \boldsymbol{R_2}\right) = \phi_{n_1 L_1}\left(R_1\right)\phi_{n_2 L_2}\left(R_2\right)\left[Y_{L_1}\left(\widehat{R}_1\right)Y_{L_2}\left(\widehat{R}_2\right)\right]_{JM}, \tag{3}$$

$$i \equiv \{n_1 L_1, n_2, L_2\}. \tag{4}$$

R_i is i-th Jacobi coordinate, L_i is angler momentum of the spherical harmonic function Y_L, n_i is the basis number. Radial dependence of the basis functions $\phi_{nl}(r)$ is taken as Gaussians multiplied by r^L with ranges in geometric progression [3,14],

$$\phi_{nL}(r) = N_{nL}r^L e^{-a_n r^2}, \tag{5}$$

$$a_n = 1/b_n^2, \tag{6}$$

$$b_n = b_{min}\gamma^{n-1} \quad (n = 1, \ldots, n_{\max}), \tag{7}$$

b_i is a range parameter and N_{nL} is a normalization constant.

2.2   Stochastic Variational Method

Here, SVM is explained in brief. In the next subsection, its extension are explained from the perspective of machine learning approach to solving few-body problems.

As a prerequisite, suppose that we have i-1 basis functions $\{\Phi_1, \ldots, \Phi_{i-1}\}$ and know the lowest energy $\mathcal{E}^{i-1}$ with them by diagonalizing the Hamiltonian matrix. This can be achieved by following the steps below from the single basis function. The basis function would be selected as follows:

(i) the i-th basis function Φ_i is generated randomly,
(ii) determine the corresponding lowest energy $\mathcal{E}^i$ with $\{\Phi_1, \ldots, \Phi_i\}$,
(iii) when the calculated energy difference $\mathcal{E}^{i-1} - \mathcal{E}^i$ is larger than a standard energy (for example, we employ $0.0001K$ for the ^{4}He trimer calculation in this paper), we employ the basis function as the i-th basis function and increase the dimension to i, return to i) until the calculated energy converges. The larger calculated energy difference, $\mathcal{E}^{i-1} - \mathcal{E}^i$, means that the calculated energy is closer to the true energy. In other words, the h in the regression equation of Eq.(8) in the next subsection is better.

Thus, the SVM automatically selects the important basis function through steps (i)→(iii). The advantage of this algorithm is that relatively small number of matrix elements (i-th row or column) need to be calculated for each step and the unimportant basis functions because of non-orthogonal basis function is automatically removed.

2.3   SVM as a Machine Learning Approach

Regression is known as a typical machine learning technique. Concept of SVM is very related to a regression using function expansions. As one of regression expressions, we can describe,

$$\Delta E = |E_{min} - h(N, b_1, b_2, \ldots, b_N)|, \qquad (8)$$
$$\rightarrow 0. \qquad (9)$$

E_{min} is the minimum energy for the given Hamiltonian, h is a lowest energy function, b's correspond to the range parameters in the Gaussian expansion,

$$\phi(r) = \sum_{j=1}^{N} c_j \exp(-\frac{r^2}{b_j^2}), \qquad (10)$$

the angler momentum part is dropped for simplicity. The problem to be solved in regression is to find $N, b_1, b_2, \ldots, b_N$ so that ΔE is as close to 0 as possible. The algorithm of (i)-(iii) in subsection 2.2 is a practical method to determine $N, b_1, b_2, \ldots, b_N$. The energy variation principle dictates that the energy will always go down when good basis functions are adopted, so we can choose the variation parameter $b's$ to get closer and closer to E_{min}. However, it is easy to imagine that the energy minimum state is not realized by stochastically selecting bad basis functions only. Also, there is no guarantee that the number of basis functions will be extremely smaller than the standards calculations using ranges in geometric progression. In that sense, there is some room for improvement in SVM that are currently used.

In this paper, we propose and investigate an additional procedure called SVM+:

iv)many SVM calculations of (i)-(iii) is performed at the same time,

v)by using the basis functions used for the wave functions that give the lower energies, the SVM calculation of the procedure of (i)-(iii) is performed again. Adding iv) and v) is easy and the computational time is also not so much different at present thanks to the development of the parallel computer unlike when it was first proposed a quarter century ago. In other words, the calcurational time for 1000 times SVM calculation (as performed in the present paper) is essentially takes the same for just one time SVM calculation if we use 1000 cores. When SVM was first proposed (1977) and the methodology subsequently developed in late 90's, supercomputers were not equipped with the capabilities to anticipate an algorithm that could run 1,000 or 10,000 times SVM calculations simultaneously. The practical application of iv) and v) is shown later in the next section.

3   Results

Figure 3 shows the convergence of the ground state energy for ^{4}He trimer when SVM is performed. The solid line represents the calculated energy with SVM and the dashed line represents the calculated energy with GEM. ^{4}He-^{4}He potential is 2B+2B (Gaussian type) [15], which reproduce the scattering length, and the ground and excited state energies. The horizontal axis represents the number of trials and the vertical axis represents the calculated energy. Note that the horizontal axis is the number of diagonalization attempts, not the dimension of the matrix that is being diagonalized. For example, the dimension of a matrix diagonalized at 100 on the horizontal axis is 69.

In this calculation, the trial basis functions are selected from the same ones as those for GEM. In Table 1 to compare the energy calculated by GEM. L_1, L_2, L are orbital angular momentum. b^i_{min} and b^i_{max} are minimum and maximum range parameters for Gaussian basis functions. i represents the Jacobi coordinate. N^i is a number of basis function superpositions for the i-th Jacobian coordinate. So the total number of basis functions is 625 (400=20×20 for channel1 and 225 = 15×15 for channel2. Since typical number of basis function in GEM for three body system is around 1,000–2,000 which is depend on systems of course, 625 basis functions would be reasonable to the present purpose. In GEM, the energy is calculated with all (625) basis functions considered. The calculated energy for the 625 basis functions is E= −0.125 K. Hereafter, the main question is whether this energy can be reproduced with fewer than 625 basis functions.

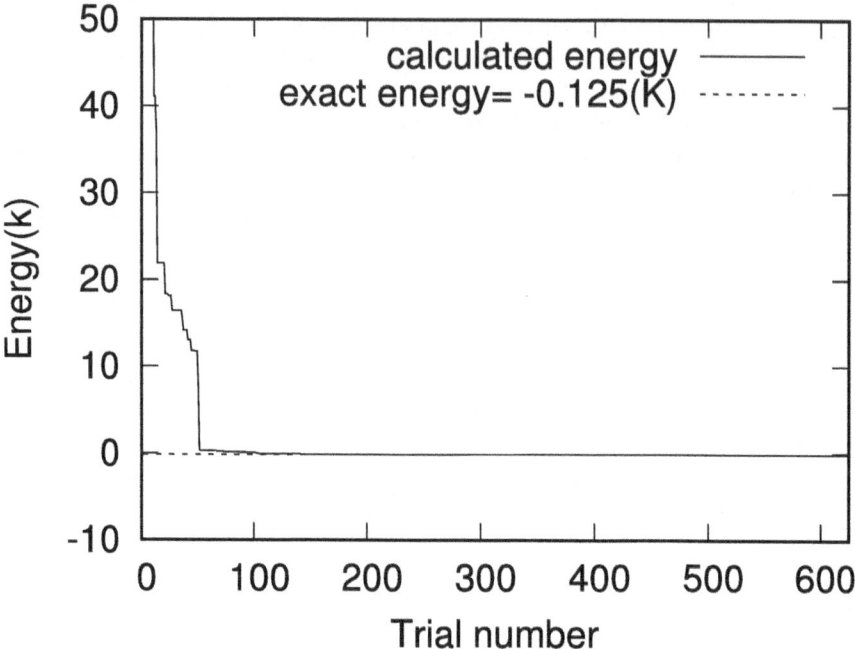

Fig. 3. Convergence of energy for ^{4}He trimer with increasing trial basis function. The horizontal axis represents the number of trials. The solid line represents the calculated energy with SVM. The dashed line represents the exact energy.

Table 1. Basis functions of GEM for ^{4}He trimer

Channel	L_1	L_2	J	$b^1_{min.}(\text{Å})$	$b^1_{max.}(\text{Å})$	N_1	$b^2_{min.}(\text{Å})$	$b^2_{max.}(\text{Å})$	N_2
1	0	0	0	0.2	30	20	0.2	30	20
2	2	2	0	0.2	15	20	0.2	30	15

In Fig. 3, the calculated energy with (solid line) approaches to that of GEM with three-digit accuracy with at 460 trial. The number of basis function is 129 smaller than 625. In other words, of the 625 basis functions employed in conventional GEM, approximately 500 are redundant to make the wave function with three-degit accurate energy. The main reason why the number of basis functions can be small is that the basis functions are overcomplete in two respects. One respect is that Gaussian basis functions are not orthogonal. Another is that the channel with rearranged Jacobi coordinates represents overcomplete basis functions before the original Jacobichannel.

In Fig. 4, the convergences of energy for ^{4}He trimer are displayed when SVM is performed. The difference in the line colors represents five trials (try1, try2, try3, try4, try5). In these trials, the 625 basis functions are same but the order in which the basis functions are selected from 625 ones is different. As seen from

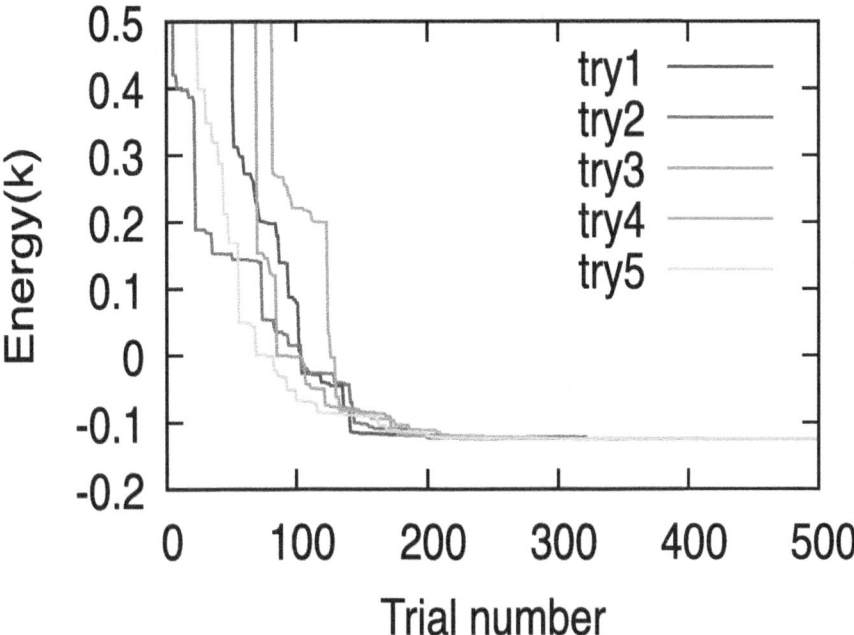

Fig. 4. Convergence of energy for ^{4}He trimer with increasing trial basis function. The horizontal axis represents the number of trials. The difference in the line colors represents five trials.

Fig. 4, the calculated energies converge the same energy ($E = -0.125$K) even if the order of the selection is different. We can not distinguish the difference from the figure at around 200–300 trials where about 100 basis functions are employed.

In Table 2, number of try and number of basis function employed to obtain convergent energy for ^{4}He trimer. The second column represents number of trial to reproduce the exact energy $E=-0.125$ K. The third column represents number of basis functions to reproduce the exact energy. About 100 basis functions (instead of 625) are enough to reproduce the exact energy. The least number of basis functions is 90 for try 2(green line).

Furthermore, we search the smallest number of basis functions among 1000 trial (step (iv)). The motivation for this research is how to reduce the number of basis functions. Thanks to the progress of parallel computing such as MPI over the last quarter century, it is now possible to use SVM algorithms that were not possible when originally proposed. Since each SVM try is completely independent, the calculation time can essentially be the same for 1,000 trials as for one trial when we have enough cores and memory. In Fig. 5, we show the tendency of number of the employed basis functions. The horizontal axis represents trials and the vertical represents the number of the employed basis functions. The all calculated energies are $E = -0.125$K (or -0.124K as a rare case) for

Table 2. Number of trial and number of basis function employed to obtain convergent energy for ^{4}He trimer. Different combinations of trial basis functions are used in Tyr1-Try5.

Basis function set	Number of try	Number of basis functions employed	Energy(k)
try1	460	129	−0.125
try2	410	90	−0.125
try3	337	126	−0.125
try4	443	138	−0.125
try5	485	110	−0.125

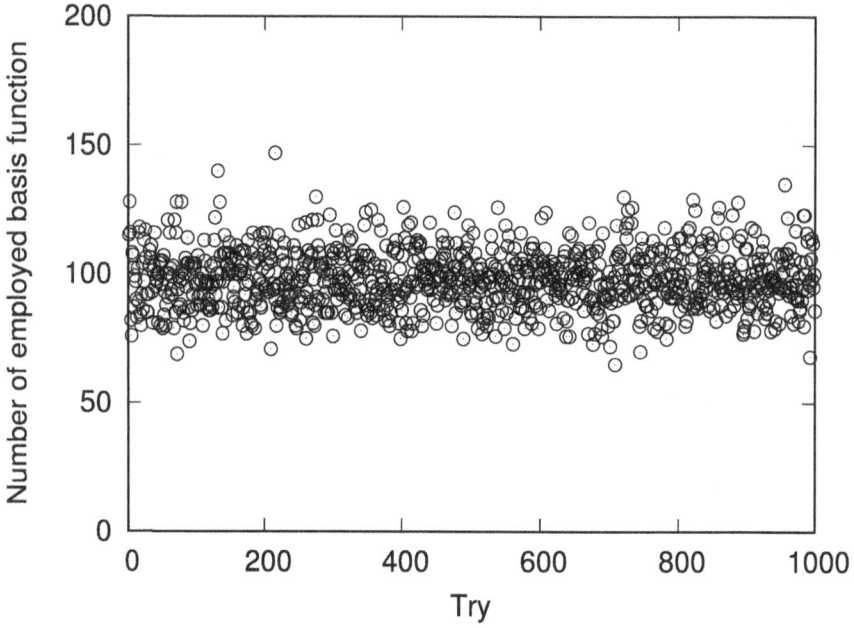

Fig. 5. The tendency of number of the employed basis functions.

the standard energy $\delta E = 0.0001$K and there were no failed trials. The smallest number of the employed basis function is 68 and the largest number is 146. It is found that about 90% of the basis functions are redundant to describe the wave function with the energy minimum.

We compare the employed basis functions between the smallest number of basis functions and the second smallest number of basis functions to check whether the selected basis function is almost the same. Although 18 basis function are consistent, the selected basis functions are not essencially the same. This is expected to be originating from non-orthogonal property for the Gaussian type basis function, a basis function is almost replaced by the superposition of other

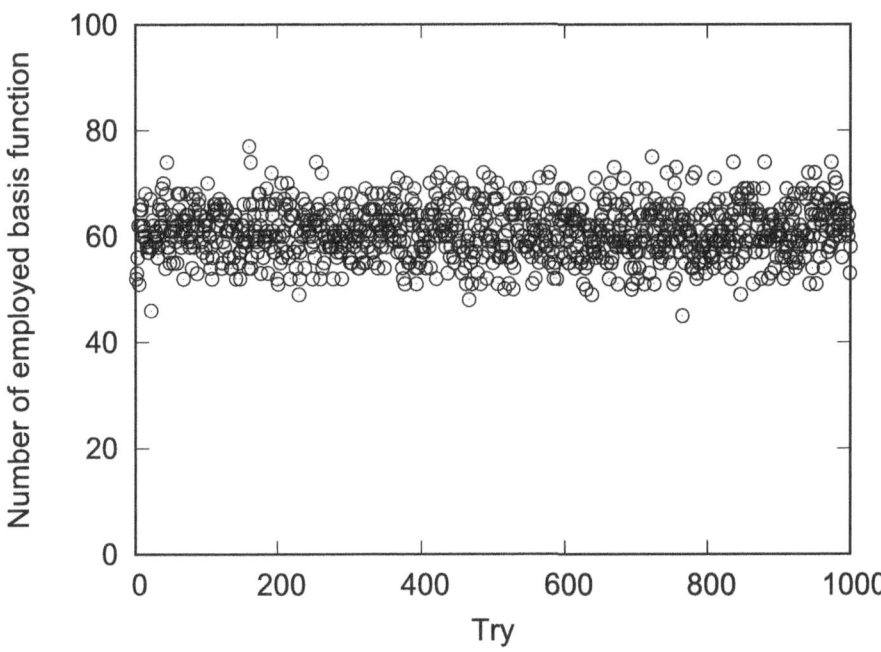

Fig. 6. The tendency of number of the employed basis functions from 119 basis functions. The 119 basis functions are the smallest number of basis functions and the second smallest number of basis functions employed from the first 625 basis functions.

basis functions. This is a good property because the energy minimum state is obtained independently of the basis functions initially chosen.

To verify the above procedure, the important 119 basis functions, which are used in the energy minimum state with the smallest number of 68 basis functions and the second smallest number of 69 basis function. Since 18 basis functions are same, the total number is 119 = 68+69-18.

In Fig. 6, the tendency of number of the employed basis functions from 119 basis functions is displayed. The lowest number of basis functions are 46, but the calculated energy is $E = -0.123(K)$. This is considered to be some important basis functions are not employed for diagonalization steps, although it may be recovered adding other remained (625–119) basis functions. However, many energy minimum states of $E = -0.125(K)$ are also obtained. The lowest number of basis functions are 54 for the energy minimum state. Thus, by adding the procedure (iv) and (v), the lowest number of basis functions becomes 54 from 68. Thus, the important 54 basis functions are learned from 625 basis functions. As mentioned before, three body system is a sub system of more than four body system, the corresponding part of basis functions is replaced with the learned basis functions in three body system, we can expect to be reduced the number of basis function for more than 7-body systems.

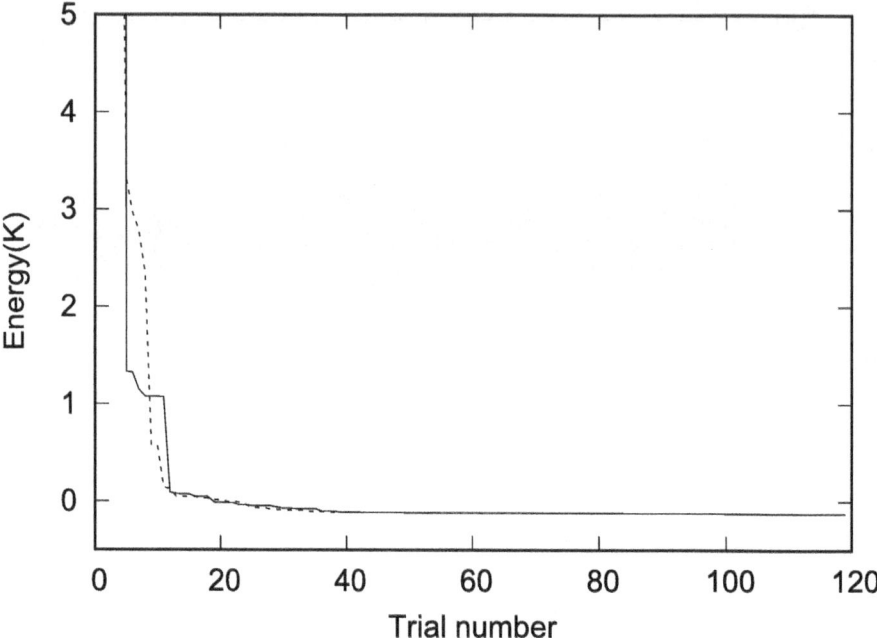

Fig. 7. Convergence of energy for ^{4}He trimer with increasing trial basis functions for the smallest 54 basis number employed.

In Fig. 7, we display convergence of energy for ^{4}He trimer with increasing trial basis functions for the smallest 54 basis number employed. There are two cases for the smallest 54 basis number employed. We can easily see quick convergence for both cases.

4   Summary and Conclusion

In this paper, we calculate ^{4}He trimer using SVM as a machine learning approach with GEM. When we proceed to more few-body systems, the reduction of the number of the basis functions becomes important. By using the present procedure which is employed in this paper, the number of basis functions for the energy minimum states of ^{4}He trimer reduced significantly. That is 54 instead of a standard number 625.

We conclude the present added procedures iv) and v) are very reasonable to learn the energy minimum wave function with a smaller basis numbers. Therefore, starting from three-body system to larger body systems, the limits are being pushed even further large body systems.

In the near future, we apply this method to the larger body systems and investigate its applicability.

Acknowledgements. This work was supported by Japan Society for the Promotion of Science (JSPS) KAKENHI with Grant Number 25H01270, 20K03967 and JP22K03643 and by the ERATO TOMOE project with Grant Number JPMJER 2304.

This research used computational resources of Wisteria/BDEC-01 Odyssey (the University of Tokyo) and Fugaku (the RIKEN Center for Computational Science, Project ID: hp240299). And we also use Miyabi (the University of Tokyo), provided by the Multidisciplinary Cooperative Research Program in the Center for Computational Sciences, University of Tsukuba.

References

1. Kamimura, M.: Phys. Rev. A **38**, 621 (1988)
2. Kameyama, H., Kamimura, M., Fukushima, Y.: Phys. Rev. C **40**, 974 (1989)
3. Hiyama, E., Kino, Y., Kamimura, M.: Prog. Part. Nucl. Phys. **51**, 223 (2003)
4. Hiyama, E.: Few-Body Syst. **53**, 189 (2012)
5. E. Hiyama, Prog. Theor. Exp. Phys. 01A204 (2012)
6. Varga, K., Suzuki, Y., Lovas, R.G.: Nucl. Phys. A **571**, 447 (1994)
7. Mitroy, J., et al.: Rev. Mod. Phys. **85**, 693 (2013)
8. Aoyama, S., K., Arai, Y., Suzuki, P., Descouvemont, D., Baye, Few-Body Syst. **52**, 97 (2012)
9. Suzuki, Y., Varga, K., Usukura, J.: Nucl. Phys. A **631**, 91 (1998)
10. Suzuki,Y., Varga, K.: Stochastic variational approach to quantum-mechanical few-body problems. Lecture notes in physics, Vol. 54 Springer, Berlin (1998)
11. Kukulin, V.I., Krasnopol'sky, V.M.: J. Phys. G: Nucl. Phys. **3**, 79 (1977)
12. Arai, K., Aoyama, S., Suzuki, Y., Descouvemont, P., Baye, D.: Phys. Rev. Lett. **107**, 132502 (2011)
13. Aoyama, S., Arai, K., Suzuki, Y., Descouvemont, P., Baye, D.: Few-Body Syst. **52**, 97 (2012)
14. Hiyama, E., Kamimura, M.: Front. Phys. **13**(6), 132106 (2018)
15. Naidon,P.: (RIKEN Nishina Centre), private communication

Accelerating Iterative Linear Equation Solver Using Modified Domain-Wall Fermion Matrix in Lattice QCD Simulations

Wei-Lun Chen[1]([✉])[iD], Issaku Kanamori[2][iD], Hideo Matsufuru[3][iD], and Hartmut Neff[4]

[1] Particle and Nuclear Physics, Graduate Institute for Advanced Studies, Graduate University for Advanced Studies (SOKENDAI), Oho 1-1, Tsukuba 305-0801, Japan
wlchen@post.kek.jp
[2] RIKEN Center for Computational Science, 7-1-26 Minatojima-minami-machi, Chuo-ku, Kobe, Hyogo 650-0047, Japan
kanamori-i@riken.jp
[3] Computing Research Center, High Energy Accelerator Research Organization (KEK), Accelerator Science Program, Graduate University for Advanced Studies (SOKENDAI), Oho 1-1, Tsukuba 305-0801, Japan
hideo.matsufuru@kek.jp
[4] Luzernerstrasse 43, 6330 Cham, Switzerland
hartmutneff@aol.com

Abstract. Lattice simulations of Quantum Chromodynamics (QCD) enable one to calculate low-energy properties of the strong interaction among quarks and gluons based on the first principle. The most time-consuming part of the numerical simulations of lattice QCD is typically solving a linear equation for the quark matrix. In particular, a discretized quark formulation called the domain-wall fermion operator requires a large numerical cost while retaining the lattice version of the chiral symmetry to good precision. The domain-wall operator is defined on a five-dimensional (5D) space extending the four-dimensional (4D) spacetime with an extra fifth coordinate. After solving the linear equation in 5D space, the result vector is projected onto the original 4D space. There is a variant of the domain-wall operator that improves the convergence of the 5D linear equation while unchanging the 4D solution vector. In this paper, we examine how this variant of the domain-wall operator accelerates the iterative linear equation solver in practical setups. We also measure the eigenvalues of the operator and compare the condition number with the convergence of the solver. We use a generic lattice QCD code set Bridge++ that is planned to be released including the improved form of the domain-wall operator examined in this work with code for GPU.

Keywords: lattice QCD · iterative linear equation solver · high performance computing

© The Author(s), under exclusive license to Springer Nature Switzerland AG 2026
O. Gervasi et al. (Eds.): ICCSA 2025 Workshops, LNCS 15890, pp. 54–69, 2026.
https://doi.org/10.1007/978-3-031-97606-3_5

1 Introduction

Large-scale simulations of lattice Quantum Chromodynamics (QCD) have been a challenge of the high performance computing for long time. The QCD is the fundamental theory of the strong interaction among quarks and gluons, which is formulated based on the invariance under the local SU(3) gauge transformation on the color degree of freedom of the quark and gluon fields. While the fundamental theory is known, it is quite difficult to solve it analytically because of the strong coupling of this theory. The lattice QCD is a field theory formulated on the Euclidean discretized spacetime. Employing the path integral quantization, this theory enables numerical evaluation of the physical quantities using the Monte Carlo algorithms. Thus the lattice QCD simulations provide a general procedure to investigate the QCD based on the first principle. Such calculation is particularly important in the search for phenomena beyond the Standard Model of particle physics through precision evaluation of the hadronic scattering processes. Lattice QCD is also important in the quantitative understanding of the nuclear force among hadrons, the phase structure of QCD at finite temperature and density, and so on.

The most time-consuming part of lattice QCD simulation is solving a linear equation for the quark (fermion) matrix, which is typically large and sparse, and thus solved by iterative Krylov subspace methods. There is a variety in the form of a fermion matrix since the only required condition is that it approaches QCD in the continuum limit. In this paper, we focus on the type of matrix called the domain-wall fermion operator. This fermion matrix has an important feature that preserves the chiral symmetry, an important symmetry of QCD, on the lattice with good precision. The domain-wall operator is defined in the five-dimensional (5D) space, which extends the four-dimensional (4D) spacetime by adding the fifth-coordinate. The physical modes in the original four-dimensional space are picked up from the two edges in the fifth direction. Since the domain-wall fermion matrix is defined in the 5D space, the numerical cost is higher than other formulations. Thus improving the convergence of the fermion matrix solver is a quite important subject in numerical simulations.

One of the authors (H. Neff) proposed a form of the domain-wall operator that improves the convergence of the solver while unchanging the physical modes in the 4D space [16]. This paper aims to conduct a systematic and practical investigation of Neff's form and how it improves the convergence of solvers. While Ref. [16] already examined the effect of the improved form on several parameter sets, we add several new setups including the operator with the link smearing. We determine the condition number of the matrix by measuring the lowest and highest eigenvalues of the Hermitian domain-wall matrix and compare with the convergence of the Conjugate Gradient (CG) solver. In numerical study, we employ the Bridge++ code set [1] with an extension to incorporate Neff's improved form of the domain-wall matrix. We use the code for GPU implemented with OpenACC [7].

This paper is organized as follows. The next section introduces the lattice QCD and our target fermion matrix in a certain depth. While the equations necessary to implement the fermion matrix used in this work are displayed to make the description self-contained, the essential ingredient is the introduction of a tunable parameter α in the 5D matrix that does not change the 4D solution vector. Section 3 shows our numerical results. We examine the effect of α in the modified matrix on the convergence of the CG solver. The last section is devoted to the conclusion and outlook.

2   Lattice QCD

2.1   Lattice QCD and Chiral Symmetry

The lattice QCD action in four-dimensional Euclidean space is written as follows:

$$S_{\text{QCD}} = \sum_x \left\{ (S_G[U_\mu(x)] + \bar{\psi}(x) D_F[U]\psi(x) \right\}, \tag{1}$$

where S_G is a gauge action, $\psi(x)$ and $\bar{\psi}(x)$ anti-commuting Grassmann fields representing quark and anti-quark, $D_F[U]$ a fermion operator depending on the link variable $U_\mu(x)$, $x = (x_1, x_2, x_3, x_4)$ a lattice site, where the lattice spacing a is set to unity for simplicity. $U_\mu(x)$ is a 3×3 complex matrix field representing the gauge field. ψ has the color and spinor degrees of freedom in addition to the lattice site x. The spinor has four components that represent the up and down spin for quark and anti-quark. Thus the quark field has $3 \times 4 = 12$ complex components on each site x.

Employing the path integral quantization, the QCD partition function reads

$$\int \mathcal{D}U \mathcal{D}\psi \mathcal{D}\bar{\psi} \exp\left[-S_G - \bar{\psi}(x) D_F[U]\psi(x) \right] = \int \mathcal{D}U \det(D_F) e^{-S_G}$$

$$= \int \mathcal{D}U \mathcal{D}\phi \mathcal{D}\phi^\dagger \exp\left[-S_G - \frac{1}{2}\phi^\dagger(x) D_F[U]^{-1}\phi(x) \right], \tag{2}$$

where complex (ordinary number) field $\phi(x)$ is introduced as Gaussian integration variables. Applying a Monte Carlo method, an expectation value of physical observable $\mathcal{O}$ is represented as

$$\langle \mathcal{O}[U, \psi, \bar{\psi}] \rangle = \frac{1}{N} \sum_i^N O[U^{(i)}, S_q^{(i)}]. \tag{3}$$

Here, the gauge field configurations $\{U^{(i)}\}$ are assumed to be generated with the Boltzmann weight $\exp[-S_G] \det(D_F)$, and $S_q^{(i)}$ is a quark propagator obtained by solving a linear equation for the fermion matrix D_F,

$$D_F[U^{(i)}]_{y,x} S_q^{(i)}(x) = b_y, \tag{4}$$

where the color and spinor indices are omitted for simplicity. To obtain the physical quantities with high precision, one needs to solve this linear equation many times to calculate $O[U^{(i)}, S_q^{(i)}]$. Furthermore, the linear equation solver is called many times during the Monte Carlo generation of the gauge configurations. Thus solving this linear equation is a typical bottleneck of lattice QCD simulations.

In discretizing the continuum QCD action, there is a variation of the action on the lattice, since the only required condition is that the lattice action approaches to the QCD action in the continuum limit, $a \to 0$, where a is the lattice spacing. Thus there has been proposed a number of lattice actions intending rapid approach to the continuum limit. Each lattice fermion action has its pros and cons. One of the most popular fermion operators is the Wilson fermion,

$$
D_W(x, y; M) = (4 + M)\delta_{x,y} - \frac{1}{2} \sum_{\mu=1}^{4} \big\{ (1 - \gamma_\mu)U_\mu(x)\delta_{x+\hat{\mu},y}
$$

$$
+ (1 + \gamma_\mu)U_\mu^\dagger(x - \hat{\mu})\delta_{x-\hat{\mu},y} \big\}, \qquad (5)
$$

where M is quark mass, $\hat{\mu}$ is a unit vector in μ-th direction ($\mu = 1, 2, 3, 4$), γ_μ is a 4×4 complex matrix acting on the spinor components. The improved form of the Wilson fermion action called clover fermion is extensively used in large-scale simulations of lattice QCD. It has a disadvantage, however, that a symmetry called chiral symmetry, which is satisfied by the QCD action for vanishing quark mass, is explicitly violated even with setting $M = 0$.

In the continuum QCD, the chiral symmetry is represented as

$$
\gamma_5 D_F + D_F \gamma_5 = 0, \qquad (6)
$$

where $\gamma_5 = \gamma_1 \gamma_2 \gamma_3 \gamma_4$. This symmetry concerns the left- and right-handed components of the quark field. The spontaneous break-down of this symmetry at low-energy ensures the smallness of the pion masses and is attributed to the most of the masses of proton and neutron. The chiral symmetry is also the basis of the phenomenological properties of the hadrons, as typically represented by the soft pion theorem that declares that the coupling between a hadron and a pion vanishes as the transferred energy becomes small. Thus the quark action that respects the chiral symmetry is particularly important in understanding the chiral dynamics of QCD. For the Wilson fermion action, the chiral symmetry is restored only in the continuum limit.

On the lattice, the chiral symmetry had been a difficulty for a long time. Understanding of the chiral symmetry on the lattice was proceeded by the discovery that the exact chiral symmetry on the lattice is represented by the Ginsparg-Wilson relation [11],

$$
\gamma_5 D_F + D_F \gamma_5 = a D_F R \gamma_5 D_F, \qquad (7)
$$

where R is a certain constant [12, 14]. Thereafter several fermion actions that satisfies the Ginsparg-Wilson relation exactly or approximately have been proposed. The Domain-wall fermion is the latter kind of formulation and in the limit of the infinite extent of the fifth direction, $L_s \to \infty$, it satisfies the Ginsparg-Wilson relation exactly.

2.2   Domain-Wall Fermion Matrix

The domain-wall fermion was proposed by Kaplan [13] intending to formulate the chiral gauge theory. The domain-wall fermion is defined on the five-dimensional space by adding the fifth coordinate, $s = 1, \ldots, L_s$, to the four-dimensional spacetime and by introducing a large negative mass to the Wilson operator kernel (5). The light modes appear in the two edges of the fifth direction. After the realization of the domain-wall fermion as a light fermion formulation [10, 17], several improved forms have been proposed [3, 6, 8]. These variants are described by the following form [6]:

$$
D_{DW} = \begin{pmatrix}
D_+^{(1)} & D_-^{(1)}P_- & 0 & \cdots & 0 & -mD_-^{(1)}P_+ \\
D_-^{(2)}P_+ & D_+^{(2)} & D_-^{(2)}P_- & & & 0 \\
0 & D_-^{(3)}P_+ & D_+^{(3)} & D_-^{(3)}P_- & & 0 \\
\vdots & & \ddots & \ddots & \ddots & \vdots \\
0 & & & D_-^{(L_s-1)}P_+ & D_+^{(L_s-1)} & D_-^{(L_s-1)}P_- \\
-mD_-^{(L_s)}P_- & 0 & \cdots & 0 & D_-^{(L_s)}P_+ & D_+^{(L_s)}
\end{pmatrix}, \qquad (8)
$$

where m is the quark mass, $P_- = (1 - \gamma_5)/2$, $P_+ = (1 + \gamma_5)/2$,

$$
D_+^{(s)} = b_s D_W + 1, \qquad D_-^{(s)} = c_s D_W - 1, \qquad (9)
$$

$D_W = D_W(-M_0)$ is the Wilson operator (5) with large negative mass $-M_0$, where $M_0 = O(1)$ is called the domain-wall height. There are several choices for the parameters b_s and c_s: $(b_s, c_s) = (1, 0)$ [10, 17], $(b_s, c_s) = (1, 1)$ [3], $b_s - c_s =$ const. (independent of s) called the Möbius fermion [6], and $b_s = c_s$ chosen depending on s so as to optimize the Ginsparg-Wilson relation [8]. In this paper we only examine the cases $(b_s, c_s) = (b, c)$ independent of s.

In the fifth direction, the following boundary condition is imposed at $s = 1$ and L_s:

$$
P_+ \psi(s = 0) = P_- \psi(s = L_s + 1) = 0. \qquad (10)
$$

The fermion field in four-dimensional space is given as[1]

$$
q(x) = P_- \, \psi(x, s=1) + P_+ \, \psi(x, s=L_s),
$$
$$
\bar{q}(x) = \bar{\psi}(x, s=1)(-D_-^{(1)})P_+ + \bar{\psi}(x, s=L_s)(-D_-^{(L_s)})P_-. \qquad (11)
$$

In the limit of $L_s \to \infty$, the lattice chiral symmetry is satisfied exactly. This limit corresponds to the overlap fermion operator, $D_{ov} = \mathrm{sign}(\gamma_5 D_W)$, which practically requires large numerical resources.

Link Smearing. Recently link smearing is frequently adopted as an improvement procedure for fermion actions. The link smearing is essentially the integration of the surrounding gauge field into the link variable, $U_\mu(x)$. We consider the stout projection combined with the APE smearing [15]:

$$
C_\mu(x) = \sum_{\nu \neq \mu} \rho \left[U_\nu(x) U_\mu(x+\hat{\nu}) U_\nu^\dagger(x+\hat{\mu}) + U_\nu^\dagger(x-\hat{\nu}) U_\mu(x-\hat{\nu}) U_\nu(x-\hat{\nu}+\hat{\mu}) \right],
$$

---

[1] This definition of $\bar{q}(x)$ corresponds to $\tilde{q}_x$ called "traditional choice" in Ref. [5].

$$U_\mu(x)' = \exp\left([C_\mu(x)U_\mu^\dagger(x)]_{\rm AT}\right)U_\mu(x),\tag{12}$$

where $[\cdots]_{\rm AT}$ represents anti-Hermitian and traceless operation, and ρ is a tunable parameter. This smearing step (12) can be repeatedly applied. The fermion operator can be improved by adopting the smeared link variable instead of the original one.

2.3 Better Conditioned Form of Domain-Wall Operator

An improved form of the domain-wall fermion operator which unchanges the four-dimensional fermion field was proposed by H. Neff [16]. This form is represented as follows.

$$D_{DW}^{(\alpha)} = \begin{pmatrix} D_+^{(1)}(P_- + \alpha P_+) & \alpha D_-^{(1)}P_- & 0 & \cdots & -mD_-^{(1)}P_+ \\ \alpha D_-^{(2)}P_+ & \alpha D_+^{(2)} & \alpha D_-^{(2)}P_- & & 0 \\ \vdots & \ddots & \ddots & \ddots & \vdots \\ -mD_-^{(N)}P_- & 0 & \cdots & \alpha D_-^{(N)}P_+ & D_+^{(N)}(P_+ + \alpha P_-) \end{pmatrix}\tag{13}$$

Note that except for the four corners of the fifth coordinate matrix, each four-dimensional block is multiplied by α. The top-left and bottom-right blocks are modified by multiplied by $(P_\mp + \alpha P_\pm)$, respectively, and top-right and bottom-left blocks are unchanged. This modification does not change the four-dimensional quark field, while affecting the convergence of the linear equation in five-dimensional space.

There is a relation between $D_{DW}^{(\alpha)}$ and $D_{DW} = D_{DW}^{(\alpha=1)}$ that

$$D_{DW}^{(\alpha)}\,\mathcal{P} = D_{DW}^{(\alpha=1)}\,\mathcal{P}\mathcal{A},\tag{14}$$

where

$$\mathcal{P} = \begin{pmatrix} P_- & P_+ & 0 & \cdots & 0 \\ 0 & P_- & P_+ & \ddots & \vdots \\ \vdots & \ddots & \ddots & \ddots & 0 \\ 0 & & \ddots & P_- & P_+ \\ P_+ & 0 & \cdots & 0 & P_- \end{pmatrix}, \qquad \mathcal{A} = \begin{pmatrix} 1 & 0 & & \cdots & 0 \\ 0 & \alpha & 0 & & \vdots \\ \vdots & \ddots & \ddots & \ddots & \vdots \\ \vdots & & \ddots & \alpha & 0 \\ 0 & \cdots & \cdots & 0 & \alpha \end{pmatrix}.\tag{15}$$

We need to solve a 5D equation

$$D_{DW}^{(\alpha=1)}x_5 = b_5,\tag{16}$$

where according to Eq. (11), $b_5 = (-D_-)\mathcal{P}^\dagger(0,\cdots,0,b_4)^T$ for a 4D source vector b_4 with $D_- = \mathrm{diag}(D_-^{(1)},\cdots,D_-^{(L_s)})$. Once a 5D solution vector x_5 is determined, the 4D solution vector x_4 is provided as $x_4 = [\mathcal{P}^\dagger x_5]_{s=1}$. Due to the relation (14), the solution of $D_{DW}^{(\alpha)}x_5^{(\alpha)} = b_5$ gives the same 4D solution x_4, since

$$\mathcal{P}^\dagger x_5 = (D_{DW}\mathcal{P})^{-1}b_5 = (D_{DW}^{(\alpha)}\mathcal{P}\mathcal{A}^{-1})^{-1}b_5 = \mathcal{A}\mathcal{P}^\dagger(D_{DW}^{(\alpha)})^{-1}b_5 = \mathcal{A}\mathcal{P}^\dagger x_5^{(\alpha)},\tag{17}$$

where $\mathcal{P}^\dagger = \mathcal{P}^{-1}$, and $[\mathcal{A}\mathcal{P}^\dagger x_5^{(\alpha)}]_{s=1} = [\mathcal{P}^\dagger x_5^{(\alpha)}]_{s=1}$. Thus if the linear equation with $\alpha \neq 1$ can be solved faster than the original equation (16), the numerical cost would be reduced.

Even-Odd Preconditioning. Noting that the D_W and D_{DW} contain nearest neighbor coupling, by dividing sites into even and odd sites, $D_{DW}x = b$ is represented as

$$D_{DW}\, x = \begin{pmatrix} D_{ee} & D_{eo} \\ D_{oe} & D_{oo} \end{pmatrix} \begin{pmatrix} x_e \\ x_o \end{pmatrix} = \begin{pmatrix} b_e \\ b_o \end{pmatrix} = b. \tag{18}$$

One arrives at the even-odd preconditioned linear equation,

$$D\, x_e \equiv (1 - D_{ee}^{-1} D_{eo} D_{oo}^{-1} D_{oe})\, x_e = \tilde{b}_e, \tag{19}$$

$$\tilde{b}_e = D_{ee}^{-1}(b_e - D_{eo} D_{oo}^{-1} b_o), \tag{20}$$

$$x_o = D_{oo}^{-1}(b_o - D_{oe} x_e). \tag{21}$$

One needs to solve Eq. (19) whose matrix D usually has a smaller condition number than D_{DW}. There are two ways to divide the sites into even and odd: In the five-dimension space, or four-dimensional space. We adopt the latter for simplicity and similarity with other fermion formulations. Since this paper focuses on the effect of α on the convergence of iterative solver, we do not concern the details of implementation and its performance, which is described in [7].

Note that there is another version of even-odd preconditioned equation,

$$(1 - D_{eo} D_{oo}^{-1} D_{oe} D_{ee}^{-1})\, y_e = b_e', \tag{22}$$

where $b_e' = b_e - D_{eo} D_{oo}^{-1} b_o$ and $x_e = D_{ee}^{-1} y_e$. However, the relation (14) means $D_{DW}^{(\alpha)} = D_{DW}(\mathcal{P}\mathcal{A}^{-1}\mathcal{P}^\dagger)$, and thus $D_{ee}^{(\alpha)} = D_{ee}^{(\alpha=1)}(\mathcal{P}\mathcal{A}^{-1}\mathcal{P}^\dagger)$ and so on. In Eq. (22), $(\mathcal{P}\mathcal{A}^{-1}\mathcal{P}^\dagger)$ and $(\mathcal{P}\mathcal{A}^{-1}\mathcal{P}^\dagger)^{-1} = \mathcal{P}\mathcal{A}\mathcal{P}^\dagger$ cancel each other, which results in no effect on the convergence of solver.

In lattice QCD simulations, the BiCGStab algorithm works in many cases as a good choice. However, for the domain-wall fermion matrix, the BiCGStab does not converge in general. This is because the eigenvalues of D_{DW} distribute in the region of negative real part. Thus the CG algorithm for $D^\dagger D$ is applied, where "$\dagger$" denotes Hermitian conjugate, $i.e.$, taking complex conjugate and transpose of the matrix D in Eq. (19).

It is well-known that a single precision solver can work as a preconditioner in the solver in the double precision which is the precision practically required in numerical simulations. In such a multi-precision solver, most of the time is consumed in the single precision solver and hence the performance of matrix multiplication to a vector in single precision determines the efficiency of solver algorithms. It is also expected that the convergence property of the iterative solver is not much different for double and single precision. Thus in the following we show the solver convergence for the single precision solver only.

3   Results

3.1   Numerical Setup

We perform a numerical experiment to investigate how the introduction of the parameter α improves the convergence of five-dimensional solver. For practical investigation, we generate three ensembles of gauge configuration generated with quenched approximation, namely without the quark vacuum polarization effect. They are generated with the plaquette gauge action at the gauge coupling $\beta = 6.0$ and 5.7, which roughly correspond to the values of lattice spacing $a \simeq 0.1$ and 0.2 fm, respectively. For $\beta = 6.0$, two lattice volumes 16^4 and 32^4 are adopted. For the $\beta = 5.7$, we generate a 16^4 lattice that roughly corresponds to the same physical volume as the 32^4 lattice with $\beta = 6.0$. On these configurations, the parameter of the domain-wall operator $M_0 = 1.8$ is used as a typical value in practical simulations, as adopted by the RBC/UKQCD Collaboration [2].

To examine the effect of the link smearing, we apply three steps of the stout projection [15] with the APE smearing with $\rho = 0.1$. This setup corresponds to that adopted by the JLQCD collaboration [9]. In this case $M_0 = 1.0$ is adopted since the lattice artifact to shift the best value of M_0 from 1 due to the interaction is largely suppressed.

On these ensembles, the parameters $(b, c) = (1.5, 0.5)$ and $(1.0, 1.0)$ are adopted with two values of $L_s = 8$ and 16. The values of parameters $(b, c) = (1.5, 0.5)$ are adopted by JLQCD Collaboration [9] and RBC/UKQCD Collaboration [2], and $(b, c) = (1.0, 1.0)$ corresponds to the Borici's form [3]. We observe the convergence of the CG solver for several values of quark mass in the range of $m = 0.001$–0.01, with varying the value of α.

As the simulation code, we employ the Bridge++ code set [1,4] with an extension to offloading code for GPU implemented using OpenACC [7]. The numerical computation is performed on the Pegasus system at University of Tsukuba, whose each node is composed of one Intel Xeon processor and one NVIDIA H100 GPU. All the computation is performed on a single process with a single GPU device. Since this work concerns the algorithmic convergence of an iterative solver, we do not discuss the performance of the code which is described in [7].

3.2   Result for $\beta = 6.0$ on the 16^4 Lattice

Let us start with examining the effect of α on the convergence of CG solver on the 16^4 lattice generated with the gauge coupling $\beta = 6.0$. In the unsmeared cases, we set $M_0 = 1.8$ as aforementioned. The CGNR solver is applied in the single precision with the convergence criterion $|r|^2 < 10^{-14}$.

Figure 1 shows the converged iteration number against α on a single configuration without the link smearing. Fluctuation against the gauge configuration will be discussed later. The top panels of Fig. 1 display the result for $(b, c) = (1.5, 0.5)$ with $L_s = 8$ and 16. For $L_s = 8$, setting $\alpha \simeq 0.6$ gives the best-improved result and reduces the interation counts by 25% compared to the $\alpha = 1$ case independently of the quark mass. While $L_s = 16$ requires slightly more iterations until convergence, the result shows the same tendency that $\alpha \simeq 0.6$ is the best, while the amount of improvement decreases as the quark mass becomes larger, from 25% for $m = 0.001$ to 20% for $m = 0.01$.

The bottom panels of Fig. 1 display the result for $(b, c) = (1.0, 1.0)$ (Borici's setting). For the both of $L_s = 8$ and 16 cases, $\alpha \simeq 0.5$ improves the conver-

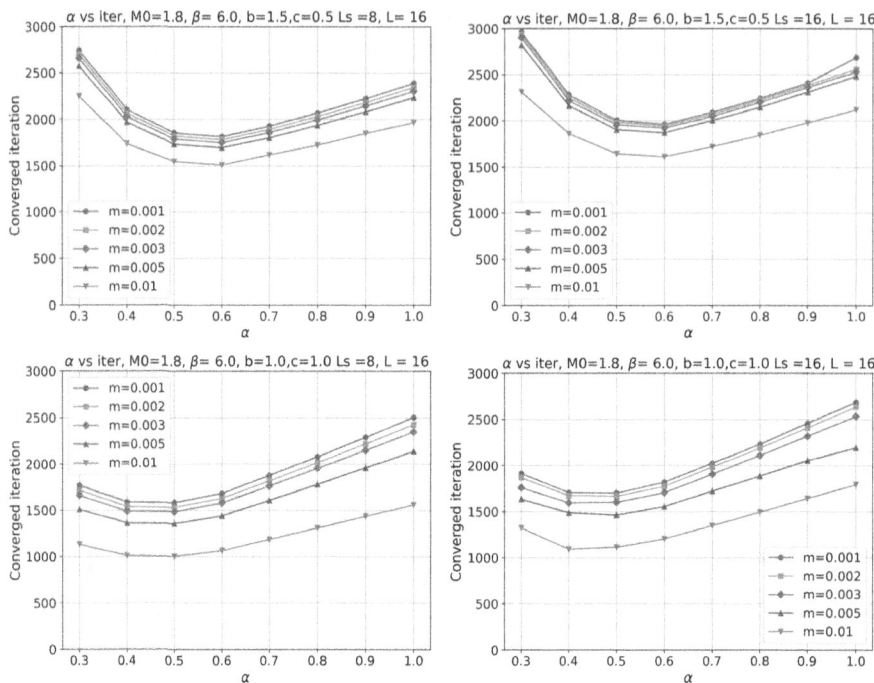

Fig. 1. Converged number of CG iteration for $\beta = 6.0$ on $(L = 16)^4$ lattice, $M_0 = 1.8$ (without smearing), $(b, c) = (1.5, 0.5)$ (top panels) $L_s = 8$ (left) and 16 (right) and $(b, c) = (1.0, 1.0)$ (bottom panels).

gence most, for which about 36% acceleration is achieved independently of the quark mass and L_s. As an observation, the quark mass dependence of converged iteration is larger than the case of $(b, c) = (1.5, 0.5)$.

Next we observe the effect of the link smearing. For the domain-wall operator with the smeared link, we set $M_0 = 1.0$. The top panels of Fig. 2 show the result for $(b, c) = (1.5, 0.5)$. Together with the link smearing, this choice of the parameters corresponds to the setup adopted by JLQCD Collaboration, except for the configuration in this work is in the quenched approximation. Around $\alpha \simeq 0.5$, the converged number of CG iteration becomes minimum where 37% acceleration is achieved for $m = 0.001$. We find that changing L_s does not affect the optimal value of α, and has only little effect on the iteration number for the convergence.

The bottom panels of Fig. 2 shows the result for $(b, c) = (1.0, 1.0)$. A similar tendency to the $(b, c) = (1.5, 0.5)$ case is found while the best value of α becomes around 0.4. The achieved speed-up is about 40 % for $m = 0.001$. Also a small effect of L_s on the convergence is observed.

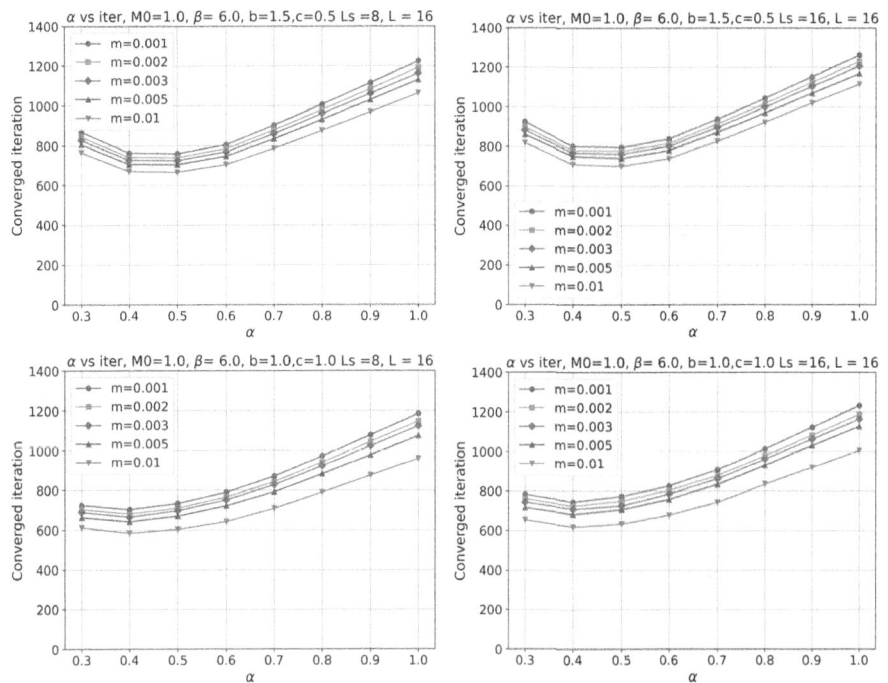

Fig. 2. Converged number of CG iteration for $\beta = 6.0$ on $(L = 16)^4$ lattice, $M_0 = 1.0$ (with smearing), $(b, c) = (1.5, 0.5)$ (top panels) $L_s = 8$ (left) and 16 (right) and $(b, c) = (1.0, 1.0)$ (bottom panels).

Condition Number. The convergence of the CG algorithm is represented by the condition number which is defined as the ratio of the maximum and minimum eigenvalues of the matrix. We measure the minimum and maximum eigenvalues of $D^\dagger D$ by applying the implicitly restarted Lanczos algorithm in the double precision, which is implemented in the Bridge++ code.

In Fig. 3, the measured condition number against the value of α is displayed for the domain-wall operators $D^\dagger D$ without the link smearing. We display the result for $(b, c) = (1.5, 0.5)$ (top panels) and $(b, c) = (1.0, 1.0)$ (bottom) for $m = 0.001$. The left panels show the values of the computed condition number on three configurations. While the fluctuation of the condition number against configuration is substantial, as displayed in the right panels of Fig. 3, normalizing by the values at $\alpha = 1$, the effect of α itself is stable. The α dependence of the condition number exhibits similar behavior as the converged number of iteration shown in Fig. 1, which is consistent with the theoretical expectation.

Figure 4 shows the condition numbers and those normalized by the values at $\alpha = 1.0$ for $D^\dagger D$ with the link smearing. Similarly to the case without smearing, the behavior of the condition numbers is consistent with the converged num-

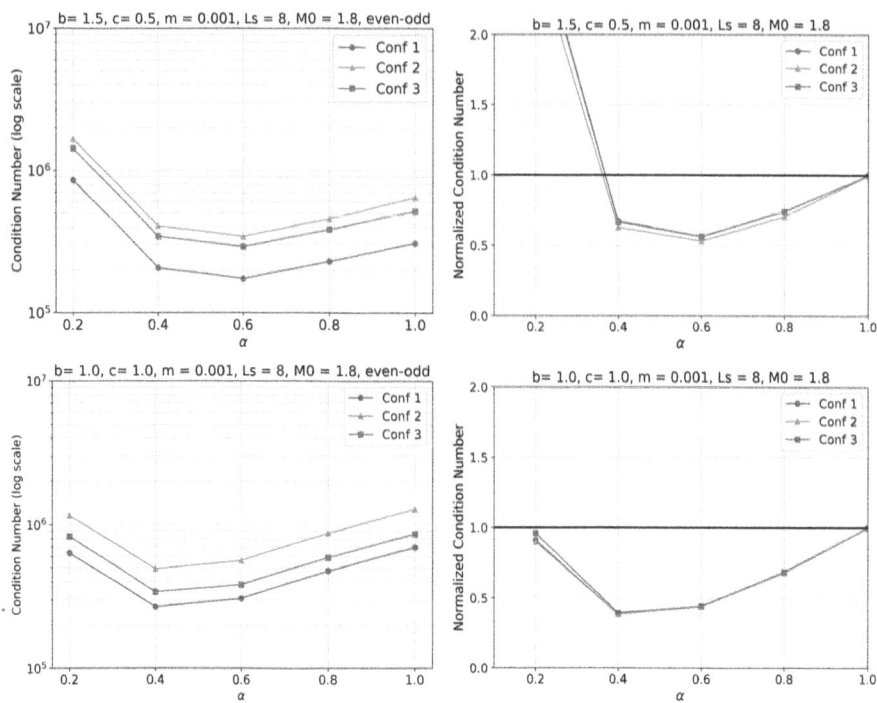

Fig. 3. The result of the condition number on the 16^4 lattice at $\beta = 6.0$ for the domain-wall operator without link smearing with parameters $M_0 = 1.8$, $(b, c) = (1.5, 0.5)$ (top panels) and $(1.0, 1.0)$ (bottom), $m = 0.001$. The left panels show the observed condition number on three configurations. The right panels show the condition numbers normalized by the values for $\alpha = 1$.

ber of CG iterations in Fig. 4. It is also observed that the fluctuation against configuration is absorbed by normalizing with the values at $\alpha = 1$.

3.3 Result for $\beta = 6.0$ on the 32^4 Lattice

To examine the effect of lattice volume on the convergence of the CG algorithm, we measure the converged iteration number against α on a 32^4 lattice with configurations generated at the gauge coupling $\beta = 6.0$. This means that the lattice volume is doubled in each direction compared to the lattice examined in the previous subsection. On this lattice size, we only show the results for $L_s = 8$.

Figure 5 shows the results of the converged number of CG iteration for unsmeared and smeared cases with $(b, c) = (1.5, 0.5)$ and $(1.0, 1.0)$. The acceleration of CG convergence for $m = 0.001$, the severest one of the measured quark masses, is in the range of 22% (top-left panel)–39% (bottom panels).

As a different feature from the results on 16^4 lattice in Figs 1 and 2, large dependence on the quark mass is observed. This is considered that the 16^4 lattice

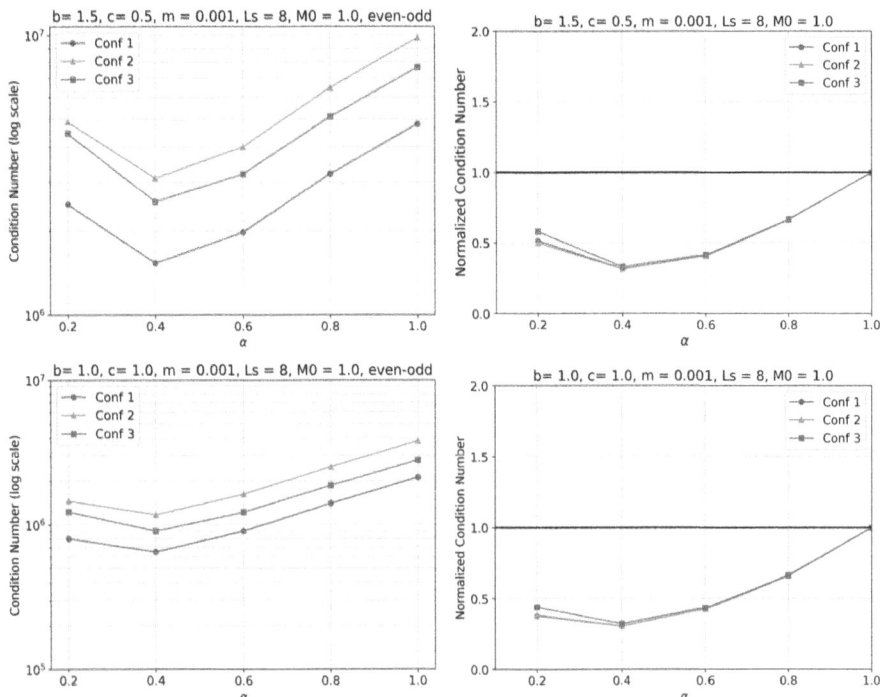

Fig. 4. The result of the condition number on the 16^4 lattice at $\beta = 6.0$ for the domain-wall operator with link smearing with parameters $M_0 = 1.0$, $(b, c) = (1.5, 0.5)$ (top panels) and $(1.0, 1.0)$ (bottom), $m = 0.001$. The left panels show the observed condition number on three configurations. The right panels show the condition numbers normalized by the values for $\alpha = 1$.

may be affected by finite volume effect, since for the present small values of quark mass, the lattice size of about 1.6 fm is not sufficiently larger than the pion Compton wavelength. This should be examined by observing the pion spectrum by varying the lattice volume.

In the context of this paper, we focus on the effect of α on the convergence number of iterations. As Fig. 5 shows, the optimal values of α are almost unchanged from those on the 16^4 lattice at the same β with similar improving rates. This result implies that incorporating α in the domain-wall operator results in improved convergence of the even-odd preconditioned CG solver almost independently of lattice volume.

3.4 Result for $\beta = 5.7$ on the 16^4 Lattice

We also examine a 16^4 lattice with configurations generated at $\beta = 5.7$, which roughly corresponds to the lattice spacing $a \simeq 0.2$ fm. This implies that the physical volume is almost the same as that of 32^4 lattice at $\beta = 6.0$. We adopt

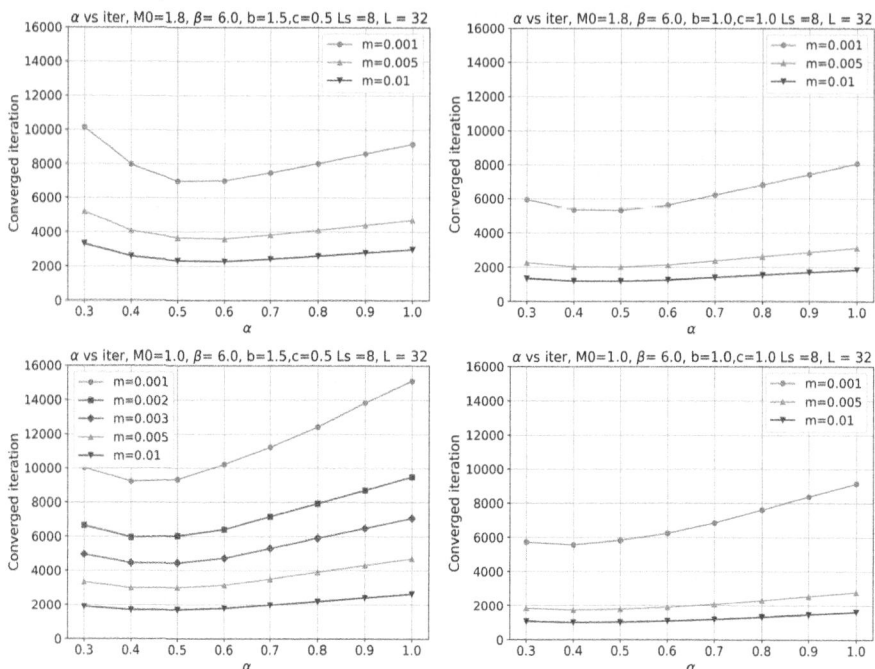

Fig. 5. Converged numbers of CG iteration on 32^4 lattice at $\beta = 6.0$. Top panels show $M_0 = 1.8$ (without smearing), $(b, c) = (1.5, 0.5)$ (left) and $(b, c) = (1.0, 1.0)$ (right). The bottom panels show $M_0 = 1.0$ (with smearing), $(b, c) = (1.5, 0.5)$ (left) and $(b, c) = (1.0, 1.0)$ (right). In both cases, $L_s = 8$ is used.

the same values of the quark mass m in lattice units as those for $\beta = 6.0$, which means that the mass in physical units is halved correspondingly.

Figure 6 shows that the α improvement effect diminishes as the quark mass increases. Similar to the case of $\beta = 6.0$, the optimal improvement is observed when α is in the range of 0.4 to 0.6. The acceleration of CG convergence for $m = 0.001$ is in the range of 24% (bottom-left panel)–39% (top-right).

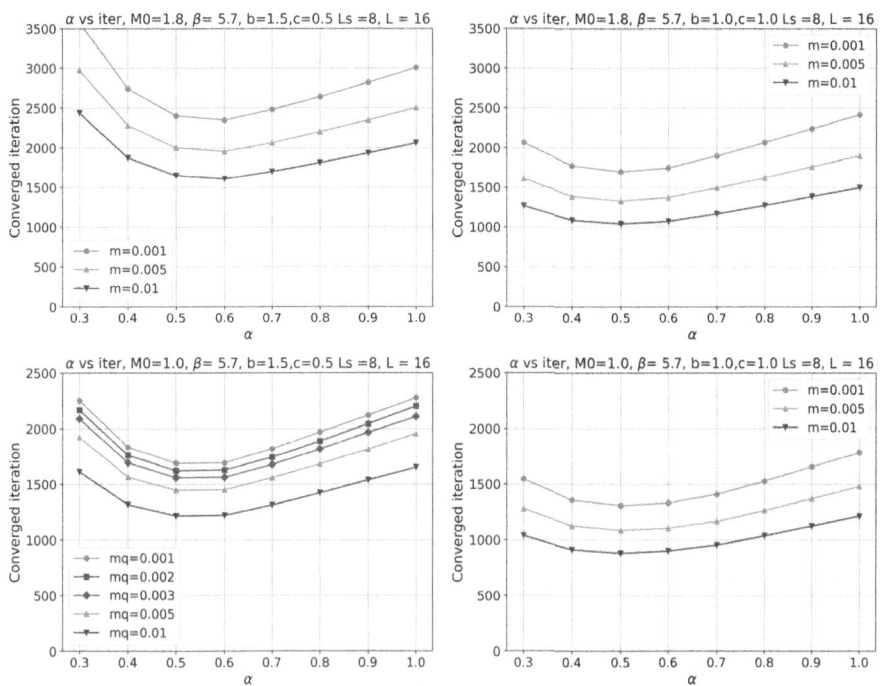

Fig. 6. Converged numbers of CG iteration on 16^4 lattice at $\beta = 5.7$. Top panels show $M_0 = 1.8$ (without smearing), $(b, c) = (1.5, 0.5)$ (left) and $(b, c) = (1.0, 1.0)$ (right). The bottom panels show $M_0 = 1.0$ (with smearing), $(b, c) = (1.5, 0.5)$ (left) and $(b, c) = (1.0, 1.0)$ (right). In both cases, $L_s = 8$ is used.

Table 1. Summary of the results. The values of α most accelerating the convergence is chosen for $m = 0.001$ and $L_s = 8$.

lattice	β	a [fm]	Smearing	M_0	(b, c)	Best α	Acceleration
16^4	6.0	~ 0.1	no	1.8	$(1.5, 0.5)$	0.6	25%
					$(1.0, 1.0)$	0.5	36%
			yes	1.0	$(1.5, 0.5)$	0.5	37%
					$(1.0, 1.0)$	0.4	40%
32^4	6.0	~ 0.1	no	1.8	$(1.5, 0.5)$	0.6	22%
					$(1.0, 1.0)$	0.5	30%
			yes	1.0	$(1.5, 0.5)$	0.4	39%
					$(1.0, 1.0)$	0.4	39%
16^4	5.7	~ 0.2	no	1.8	$(1.5, 0.5)$	0.6	38%
					$(1.0, 1.0)$	0.5	39%
			yes	1.0	$(1.5, 0.5)$	0.5	24%
					$(1.0, 1.0)$	0.5	34%

4   Conclusion and Outlook

In this paper, we examined the effect of the improved form of the domain-wall fermion operator on the convergence of the linear equation solver. The results are summarized in Table 1 for $m = 0.001$ and $L_s = 8$. In a wide range of parameters, the modified form indeed improves the convergence of the even-odd preconditioned CG solver about several tens percent, in the range of 20–40% for our smallest value of the quark mass that requires iterations until convergence most. The required modification of the simulation code is small and the increase in the arithmetic operations is negligible compared to the observed gain. Indeed, in a modern simulation environment where the memory bandwidth or communication overhead is more relevant to the performance than the arithmetic operations, this modification has little effect on the simulation time. Thus the practical use of the improved form of domain-wall fermion matrix is highly attractive.

In a future release, the Bridge++ code set will incorporate the improved form as the standard implementation of the domain-wall fermion matrix.

Acknowledgment. We thank the members of the Bridge++ project, Tatsumi Aoyama, Kazuyuki Kanaya, Yusuke Namekawa, Hidekatsu Nemura, and Keigo Nitadori, for useful discussions. The code development and measurement were performed on the Cygnus and Pegasus systems at University of Tsukuba and Wisteria/BDEC-01 at University of Tokyo through the Multidisciplinary Cooperative Research Program in Center for Computational Sciences, University of Tsukuba. The code development was also done on the Supercomputer Fugaku (through Usability Research ra000001) at RIKEN Center for Computational Science. This work is supported by JSPS KAKENHI (JP20K03961, JP22H00138, JP23K22495), MEXT as "Program for Promoting Researches on the Supercomputer Fugaku" (Simulation for basic science: approaching the new quantum era, PMXP1020230411) and Joint Institute for Computational Fundamental Science (JICFuS).

References

1. Akahoshi, Y., et al.: General purpose lattice QCD code set Bridge++ 2.0 for high performance computing. J. Phys. Conf. Ser. **2207**(1), 012053 (2022). https://doi.org/10.1088/1742-6596/2207/1/012053
2. Arthur, R., et al.: Domain Wall QCD with Near-Physical Pions. Phys. Rev. D **87**, 094514 (2013). https://doi.org/10.1103/PhysRevD.87.094514
3. Borici, A.: Truncated overlap fermions: the link between overlap and domain wall fermions. NATO Sci. Ser. C **553**, 41–52 (2000)
4. Bridge++ project: Lattice QCD code Bridge++. https://bridge.kek.jp/Latticecode/ (2012)
5. Brower, R.C., Neff, H., Orginos, K.: The Möbius domain wall fermion algorithm. Comput. Phys. Commun. **220**, 1–19 (2017). https://doi.org/10.1016/j.cpc.2017.01.024
6. Brower, R.C., Neff, H., Orginos, K.: Mobius fermions: improved domain wall chiral fermions. Nucl. Phys. B, Proc. Suppl. **140**, 686–688 (2005). https://doi.org/10.1016/j.nuclphysbps.2004.11.180

7. Chen, W.L., Kanamori, I., Matsufuru, H.: Lattice QCD code on GPUs: implementation and performancecomparison with OpenACC and CUDA. In: Proceedings of the International Conference on High Performance Computing in Asia-Pacific Region, pp. 80–89. HPCASIA '25, Association for Computing Machinery, New York, NY, USA (2025). https://doi.org/10.1145/3712031.3712327

8. Chiu, T.W.: Optimal domain wall fermions. Phys. Rev. Lett. **90**, 071601 (2003). https://doi.org/10.1103/PhysRevLett.90.071601

9. Colquhoun, B., Hashimoto, S., Kaneko, T., Koponen, J.: Form factors of $B \to \pi \ell \nu$ and a determination of —VUB— with Möbius domain-wall fermions. Phys. Rev. D **106**(5), 054502 (2022). https://doi.org/10.1103/PhysRevD.106.054502

10. Furman, V., Shamir, Y.: Axial symmetries in lattice QCD with Kaplan Fermions. Nucl. Phys. B **439**, 54–78 (1995). https://doi.org/10.1016/0550-3213(95)00031-M

11. Ginsparg, P.H., Wilson, K.G.: A Remnant of chiral symmetry on the lattice. Phys. Rev. D **25**, 2649 (1982). https://doi.org/10.1103/PhysRevD.25.2649

12. Hasenfratz, P., Laliena, V., Niedermayer, F.: The Index theorem in QCD with a finite cutoff. Phys. Lett. B **427**, 125–131 (1998). https://doi.org/10.1016/S0370-2693(98)00315-3

13. Kaplan, D.B.: A Method for simulating chiral fermions on the lattice. Phys. Lett. B **288**, 342–347 (1992). https://doi.org/10.1016/0370-2693(92)91112-M

14. Luscher, M.: Exact chiral symmetry on the lattice and the Ginsparg-Wilson relation. Phys. Lett. B **428**, 342–345 (1998). https://doi.org/10.1016/S0370-2693(98)00423-7

15. Morningstar, C., Peardon, M.J.: Analytic smearing of SU(3) link variables in lattice QCD. Phys. Rev. D **69**, 054501 (2004). https://doi.org/10.1103/PhysRevD.69.054501

16. Neff, H.: A better conditioned Domain Wall Operator (2015). 1501.04950 [hep-lat]

17. Shamir, Y.: Chiral fermions from lattice boundaries. Nucl. Phys. B **406**, 90–106 (1993). https://doi.org/10.1016/0550-3213(93)90162-I

Governance of Energy Transition: Environmental, Landscape, Social and Spatial Planning (ENERGY_PLANNING 2025)

A Comparative Analysis of Energy Transition and Carbon Footprint in the Mediterranean Islands

Ginevra Balletto[1]([✉]) [iD], Mara Ladu[1] [iD], Antonio Puddu[1] [iD], Marco Naseddu[1] [iD], Emilio Ghiani[2] [iD], and Balázs Kulcsár[3] [iD]

[1] DICAAR - Department of Civil, Environmental Engineering and Architecture, University of Cagliari, Cagliari, Italy
{balletto,mara.ladu,antonio.puddu3,marco.naseddu}@unica.it

[2] DIEE - Department of Electrical and Electronic Engineering, University of Cagliari, Cagliari, Italy
emilio.ghiani@unica.it

[3] Institute of Industrial Process Management - Department of Basic Technical Studies, University of Debrecen, Debrecen, Hungary
kulcsarb@eng.unideb.hu

Abstract. Energy transition is a global objective. Moving towards cleaner and more sustainable energy sources requires the progressive abandonment of fossil fuels such as coal, oil and gas. The transition also arises from concerns about climate change and national security that require a more secure and resilient energy system.

The European Union aims to be climate neutral by 2050. Key strategies include the European Green Deal, which promotes renewable energy, energy efficiency and sustainable mobility. Significant investments are supporting the transition, including the Just Transition Fund and the InvestEU programme. Italy is actively participating in the energy transition with the National Recovery and Resilience Plan (NRRP) prioritising green initiatives. However, challenges remain, especially for island regions.

The study proposes a method to compare the monthly trend of the carbon footprint in the islands of Sardinia (Italy), Sicily (Italy) and Cyprus, analyzing data for the period 2021–2024, in respect to the following indicators: direct carbon intensity, percentage of low-carbon energy and energy from renewable sources. The results reveal an overall improvement in renewable energy production across the three islands from 2021 to 2024, with a positive trend towards greater adoption of low-carbon and renewable energy sources. The comparison proved to be valuable for informing policy decisions to support energy transitions in the Mediterranean islands.

Keywords: Energy Transition · Carbon Footprint · Mediterranean Islands

O. Gervasi et al. (Eds.): ICCSA 2025 Workshops, LNCS 15890, pp. 73–90, 2026.
https://doi.org/10.1007/978-3-031-97606-3_6

1 Introduction

The energy transition represents a pivotal ongoing transformation posing specific challenges for land governance at the international level. It is a global process with the aim of reshaping the modalities of energy production and consumption. Promoting a shift from a system based on fossil fuels to one centred on renewable and sustainable energy sources [1]. The European Union (EU) is characterized by a significant reliance on energy imports, a factor that impinges upon its global competitiveness, particularly in comparison to China and the self-sufficiency of the United States [2]. In order to address the exigencies of climate change and ensure security of supply, the EU launched the "European Green Deal" in 2019 (European Commission, 2019) [3], an ambitious strategy designed to achieve climate neutrality by 2050, with an interim target of a 55% reduction in greenhouse gas emissions by 2030 (UN, 2015) [4]. This transition is supported by three key principles: security of energy supply, the advancement of a renewable energy sector in order to improve energy efficiency, and the formation of an integrated energy market [5]. The Green Deal is part of an international commitment to sustainability, in line with the United Nations Sustainable Development Goals and the Paris Agreement. The urgency of this transition is underlined by the IPCC reports, which call for the need to limit the increase in global temperature [6]. In addition, a 'just transition' that supports workers and communities affected by change is crucial to ensuring inclusivity [7]. Currently, the EU's energy mix is characterised by an increasing share of renewables, but there is still a significant reliance on fossil fuels to meet overall energy demand and electricity generation. There are also different views among member states on the role of nuclear energy in the transition. Germany, with its 'Energiewende', is a case study illustrating the complexity of this transition [8]. Furthermore, the heterogeneity of EU countries in terms of economic conditions and energy infrastructure has led to the emergence of an "energy gap", which makes the implementation of a coherent energy policy very complex [9]. The energy crisis, exacerbated by the war in Ukraine, has prompted the EU to step up its efforts through the REPowerEU plan [7]. This plan aims to reduce dependence on Russian fossil fuels and accelerate the transition to renewable energy through measures such as demand reduction, diversification of import sources and increased use of clean energy technologies [10]. These plans stipulate that a minimum of 37% of the allocated resources must be directed towards climate objectives, with Italy allocating approximately 40% of its NRRP funds for this purpose [11]. A comparative analysis with the Italian situation reveals both similarities and distinct differences relative to the previously described European context. In Italy, a notable decline in fossil fuel consumption has been observed since 2008, a reduction closely correlated with the decrease in primary energy demand, which is, in turn, linked to GDP per capita [12]. Coal constitutes a limited share (only 3.5% of primary energy demand), but a potential resurgence in its consumption could occur due to the reduction in gas supplies. The demand for oil, following a period of stability between the early 1990s and the early 2000s, has commenced a downward trend. Conversely, the demand for natural gas experienced consistent growth from the 1980s until 2005, subsequently declining from 2008 onwards, a reduction that can be attributed, at least partially, to the decrease in GDP per capita triggered by the economic crisis of 2007–2008. This decline persisted until 2014, whereupon a phase of recovery began. Italy holds the leading position within the EU for electricity generation via natural gas. The Italian decision to diversify its supply through the construction of the TAP (Trans Adriatic Pipeline), which transports gas from Azerbaijan and initially faced opposition, is now considered a crucial solution in response to the reduction in gas supplies from Russia. Regarding renewable energies, they represent a substantial portion of Italian energy demand (11.5% in 2020), but after a growth phase until 2013, they have experienced a deceleration and even a decline. This shift in trend is attributable to several factors, including the reduction of subsidies for renewables under the "conto energia" scheme, the sluggish post-crisis economic recovery, and protracted administrative procedures for project approval [13]. In this context, the development of the National Recovery and Resilience Plan (NRRP) assumes a role of considerable importance in establishing concrete pathways towards a just ecological transition. The NRRP represents a fundamental instrument for overcoming the economic and social crisis precipitated by the pandemic and offers a significant opportunity to expedite the transition towards an economic development model based on circularity and energy-environmental sustainability. The National Recovery and Resilience Plan (NRRP) defines the allocation criteria for the European funds from Next Generation EU (NGEU) for the post-Covid recovery. Italy submitted its proposal, which was approved by the EU in July 2021. Mission 2 of the NRRP, with a budget of 59.33 billion euros, is dedicated to the "green revolution and ecological transition" and is structured into four components: Circular economy and sustainable agriculture (M2C1), Renewable energy, hydrogen, network and sustainable mobility (M2C2), Energy efficiency and building renovation (M2C3), and Protection of the territory and water resources (M2C4) [14]. Mission M2C2, with a planned investment of 23.78 billion euros, focuses on five key areas: increasing the share of renewable energy, enhancing and digitizing networks, promoting hydrogen, developing sustainable local transport, and fostering industrial and research leadership in the transition. A total of 5.9 billion euros are allocated to augmenting production from RES, with anticipated investments in utility-scale plants (unlocking potential through regulatory and market reforms and valorizing agrivoltaics), energy communities and small-scale distributed systems (particularly pertinent in Italy due to the limited availability of large land areas), innovative solutions (including integrated and offshore technologies), and the strengthening of biomethane [15]. The government intends to operate at two levels: incentivizing large-scale RES plants and promoting energy communities, with a focus on municipalities with populations under 5,000 inhabitants. Despite the substantial allocation for energy communities (2.2 billion euros), a contrast remains with large-scale plants in terms of localization strategies and resource utilization. The plan allocates significant funding to "*agrivoltaics*", aiming to integrate sustainable agricultural and energy production, although its actual innovative scope requires careful evaluation regarding its impact on the territory and biodiversity. Substantial investments are directed towards long-term energy vectors such as green hydrogen, while some argue for greater investment in energy efficiency and RES. Furthermore, reference is made to PITESAI for hydrocarbon exploration, indicating a continued anticipated role for fossil fuel sources. The government's rationale is to facilitate private investments in renewables by streamlining procedures, but this could potentially lead to a relaxation of territorial protections [16]. The diffusion of renewable energy sources in Italy, supported by various national regulations and strategies (including the Bersani Decree, Burden Sharing, SEN 2017, PNIEC 2018, the "Mille Proroghe" Decree, and Legislative Decree 199/2021), exhibits substantial stagnation, with slow and insufficient growth to meet the 2030 targets. This growth has been primarily driven by photovoltaics and wind power. At the international level, Italy ranks behind China and other European countries in terms of new RES installations, despite a total installed capacity that places it in a more favorable position [13, 14]. However, it is essential that the National Recovery and Resilience Plan (NRRP) supports the crucial role of just transition policies to ensure an inclusive ecological transformation [15]. Following the pandemic emergency, trade unions presented a unified document on energy policy, anticipating their positions on the Recovery Fund and the priorities for the utilization of European funds at the national level. Key concerns include the historical institutional and administrative inability to spend, the slowness of bureaucratic procedures, the limited valorization of synergies between projects, an insufficient assessment of the socio-economic impact (particularly on employment), and the necessity for a more defined governance system and greater involvement of social partners and territorial institutions, all of which are crucial elements for the implementation of just transition policies [16].

1.1 The Mediterranean Scenario

The Mediterranean area presents a notable potential for the development of renewable energies, owing to the abundance of solar irradiance and wind resources, as well as the declining costs of relevant technologies, within a context of robust growth in energy demand, particularly for electricity. The International Energy Agency projects that renewable capacity in the Middle East and North Africa region will double within the next five years, propelled by solar photovoltaics and incentivized by private investments [17]. This potential is geographically dispersed throughout the area, spanning from Morocco to Turkey and the Balkans. Southeastern Europe alone boasts an estimated technical capacity of 740 GW [18], with recent studies by IRENA indicating that 127 GW could already be cost-competitive. North Africa follows this trend, exhibiting solar irradiation three times greater than that of Europe and significant wind potential [19].

Regarding natural gas, in addition to the established reserves of North Africa, the Eastern Mediterranean is reassessing its own resources, estimated at 3,500 billion cubic meters [20], as corroborated by recent offshore explorations, including the discovery of the Zohr field by Eni in Egypt. Despite the substantial potential, the Mediterranean region has exhibited a slow rate of renewable energy adoption, with coal and oil dominating (especially in Turkey and the Western Balkans), leading to elevated CO_2 emissions. It is crucial to harness the potential of both renewable energy and gas for a rapid energy transition. The political, economic, and social transformations in the Southeastern Mediterranean are intrinsically linked to regional energy dynamics, influenced by crises and instability that impede the sustainable development of the sector. Political uncertainty and reduced investments, coupled with geopolitical tensions and territorial disputes, constrain the exploitation of resources, despite demographic and economic growth that augment energy demand. A significant increase in energy consumption is anticipated, accompanied by macroeconomic risks and environmental impacts associated with the extensive utilization of fossil fuels. The transition towards cleaner sources, energy efficiency, the integration of energy markets, and infrastructural development are paramount, also considering the potential of biogas and green hydrogen. The Mediterranean region necessitates substantial investments, particularly within the renewable energy sector. In this regard, private investment is crucial for bridging the financial gap, enhancing technologies, and generating commercial opportunities within the energy sector, as such synergies foster political dialogue and sustainable economic development. In this context, Italy, alongside Germany and France, is a prominent actor, with major companies such as Eni, Enel, Snam, Terna, and Edison, and international players like TAP AG, constituting key drivers of the energy transition in the Mediterranean, encompassing both the gas and renewable energy sectors. The paucity of infrastructure represents a constraint on the development of gas and renewable energy sources in the Mediterranean. The Italian private sector is actively involved in various energy infrastructure projects in the Mediterranean: Snam participates in the TAP gas pipeline to diversify European supply and support the decarbonization of the Balkans, and explores collaborations in Egypt (Snam, 2018); Edison contributes to the EastMed gas pipeline to bolster the EU's energy security; Terna plays a fundamental role in electricity interconnections, such as Sicily-Tunisia and Pescara-Kotor; Enel invests in wind power projects in Morocco, Spain, the Balkans, and Greece. Islands represent ideal sites for the study of the socio-spatial dimensions of the energy transition, owing to their isolation and the necessity to ensure energy security, in addition to their aspirations for political autonomy [21, 22]. The central objective of this paper is to examine the evolution of the carbon footprint within the context of the energy transition, with a specific focus on the Mediterranean islands, particularly those large and geographically isolated from the mainland: Sardinia, Sicily, and Cyprus. Through a comparative analysis of data pertaining to carbon intensity, the percentage of low-emission energy, and the proportion derived from renewable sources, for the period 2021–2024, the intention is to evaluate the monthly trend of this footprint. Concurrently, the study aims to elucidate the specificities of island contexts in their energy transition pathway, considering both the vulnerabilities and the opportunities arising from local renewable resources. Consequently, the investigation intends to provide a detailed and comparative analysis of the impact of the energy transition on the carbon footprint in the Mediterranean islands, with the aim of identifying sustainable strategies and models for the future.

2   Method

This study proposes a method to compare the monthly trend of carbon footprint in Mediterranean islands. The employment of a comparative method offers numerous substantial advantages [23], enabling the examination of multiple cases to identify both similarities and differences in the trends of the indicators analysed. This methodological approach facilitates the identification of both commonalities and distinctions between the indicators, thereby enabling the discernment of specificities and shared characteristics. A crucial strength of this approach is its enhanced ability to understand the causes of these trends. By comparing islands with different characteristics and energy policies, it is possible to identify the factors that most influence carbon intensity, the share of low-carbon energy and the use of renewables. Furthermore, the comparison of different islands enables the identification of best practices and areas for improvement. The analysis of multiple case studies, especially over a temporal comparison between years, constitutes an ongoing assessment, allowing to distinguish significant trends from temporary fluctuations. Finally, the findings from comparative studies are invaluable in guiding policy decisions, thereby providing a foundation for the development of more effective strategies for the energy transition. The comparison method proposed by the present study analyzes the following indicators over the year 2021–2024: Carbon Intensity (direct) [gCO_2eq/kWh], Percentage of Low-Carbon Energy, and Percentage of Energy from Renewable Sources. Specifically, the first indicator, termed "Carbon Intensity (direct)", measures the quantity of greenhouse gases directly emitted for each unit of electricity produced and consumed. It is expressed in grams of CO_2 equivalent per kilowatt-hour (gCO_2eq/kWh) and illustrates the direct contribution of electricity generation to emissions. The second indicator, labeled "Percentage of Low-Carbon Energy", indicates the percentage share of electricity generated from sources that produce low carbon emissions. This category includes renewable energies (biomass, geothermal, hydroelectric, solar, and wind) and nuclear energy, excluding fossil fuels. Lastly, the final indicator analyzed, namely the "Percentage of Energy from Renewable Sources", indicates the percentage share of electricity generated from renewable sources [24]. To better understand consumption patterns, the method stipulates that each indicator expressed in absolute value be related to the annual population within the reference territorial context, described according to the following socio-geographic and economic elements that exert a significant influence on energy consumption models: Area, Density, Population, Average Age, GDP, and Climate Zone according to the Köppen Climate Classification (KCC). The Köppen climate classification, a widely used system for defining climate classes [25], proves to be a relevant element in studies focused on analyzing the performance of the energy transition.

3   Case Studies

This study analyses the trend of the carbon footprint taking the Mediterranean islands as a case study, particularly those large and geographically isolated from the mainland: Sardinia and Sicily (Italy), and Cyprus. As a matter of fact, Islands represent ideal sites for the study of the socio-spatial dimensions of the energy transition, owing to their isolation and the necessity to ensure energy security, in addition to their aspirations for political autonomy.

Sardinia has been selected as a case study due to its complex energy situation. Its insularity, supply challenges, political relationships with the central State, and economic vulnerabilities render it a particularly interesting territory. Despite the notable potential of natural resources, such as wind and solar, the island's energy transition is progressing with difficulty. The island has made some progress, exceeding European targets in terms of renewable energy, reaching 24% of total consumption, and reducing CO2 emissions. Photovoltaics, particularly in greenhouses, have experienced significant expansion. However, important challenges persist. Dependence on fossil fuels, especially in transportation, remains high [26], and the development of RES (Renewable Energy Sources) in the electricity sector is limited (Fig. 1).

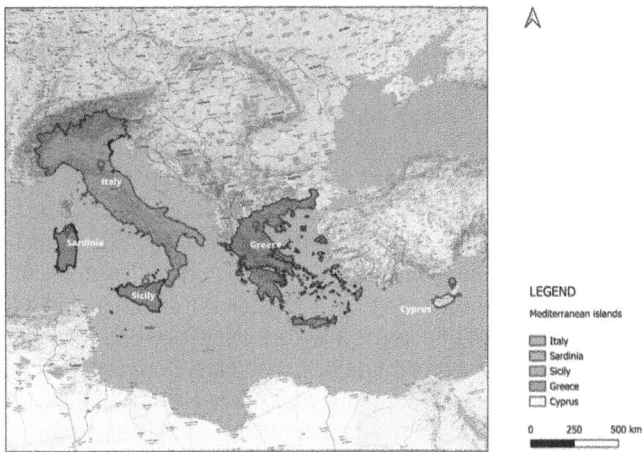

Fig. 1. Case studies: Sardinia, Sicily and Cyprus.

The region is at a crossroads, with a mix of progress and obstacles. On one hand, the expansion of photovoltaics in greenhouses is a positive development. On the other hand, resistance to large-scale renewable plants, such as CSP (Concentrated Solar Power), and the scarcity of storage systems hinder change. Regional policies, which promote smart grids and small local energy systems, clash with the strong lobbies of the fossil fuel industry, which impede a more rapid transition. The role of Terna, the operator of the national electricity grid, is crucial, with investments in power lines and storage. However, the lack of incentives and political uncertainty regarding storage make the island's energy future uncertain [27]. Sardinia, therefore, despite having significant renewable resource potential, finds itself in an intermediate position within the Italian energy landscape, with latent potential and the need to overcome resistance to fully embrace the transition towards a sustainable future.

Sicily, another Italian island taken as a case study, is establishing itself as a strategic hub in the European energy landscape, thanks to its privileged geographical position and rich potential for renewable resources. The Environmental Energy Plan of the Sicilian Region (PEARS) serves as a compass for this change, promoting the adoption of clean energy sources and cutting-edge technologies [28]. A pillar of this strategy is the incentivization of the installation of photovoltaic plants (which reached a capacity of 2637 MW in November 2024) and wind farms (2462 MW), with the aim of fostering energy self-production and self-consumption. Simultaneously, the installation of lithium battery storage systems (47,940 units) is supported, which are fundamental for stabilizing the electricity grid and strengthening the technological skills of local businesses [29]. For large-scale plants (over 1 MW), the PEARS has identified suitable areas through an inter-institutional mapping process involving various regional departments, in order to protect the island's environmental and cultural heritage. The plan also includes the development of wind power (with revamping, repowering, and offshore plants), concentrated solar power, and tidal energy in the Strait of Messina, aiming for a flexible and decentralized energy system, with particular attention to the smaller islands. The expected positive repercussions are both environmental and socio-economic: the PEARS estimates the creation of 14,000 new jobs and an impact of over 1 billion euros on the regional GDP by 2030. Sicilian ports, such as Augusta and Milazzo, are undergoing a transformation, becoming hubs of the energy transition, ready to host LNG (Liq-uefied Natural Gas) terminals and green hydrogen plants. Sicily's proximity to North Africa makes it a crucial point for energy interconnection between the two shores of the Mediterranean. The collaboration between the Sicilian Region and Terna translates into investments of 3.2 billion euros to strengthen electricity infrastructure, with key projects such as the Caracoli – Ciminna power line, the Fulgatore – Partinico connection, and the Priolo – Rossano submarine cable [30]. Sicily, therefore, through the PEARS 2030 and a series of infrastructural initiatives, proposes itself as a protagonist of the energy transition in the Mediterranean, promoting sustainable development, technological inno-vation, and the creation of new opportunities for the territory. Similar to the islands of Sardinia and Sicily, Cyprus is also making significant strides in the energy transition. The European program CITyFiED (2014–2019) promoted the transformation of cities into smart cities, creating a "Community of Interest" with 44 cities from 19 countries, including Cyprus. The primary objective was to reduce energy demand and emissions, increasing the use of renewable energies and developing replicable energy retrofitting models. Cyprus, as a member of the "Community of Interest", benefited from the sharing of retrofitting methodologies, with the aim of disseminating the project's solutions [31]. In the Mediterranean context, Cyprus, despite tensions with Turkey, is a potential energy player thanks to offshore natural gas reserves, such as the "Aphrodite" field. The EastMed project, which aims to connect the Eastern Mediterranean gas reserves to Europe, is hin-dered by territorial disputes with Turkey [32]. Despite the challenges, Cyprus explores options for exploiting its gas resources and invests in renewable energies. Geopolitical tensions, particularly with Turkey, influence energy cooperation projects, such as the EastMed pipeline [33].

4   Results

In accordance with the proposed methodology, the key geographic data have been col-lected for each case study (Fig. 2 and Fig. 3): Area, Density, Population, Average Age, GDP, and Climate Zone (according to the Köppen climate classification KCC). Specif-ically, for insular contexts, the Köppen climate classification served as a significant element in the analysis of energy transition, with regard to energy consumption and the associated carbon intensity.

Italy, including Sardinia and Sicily, is predominantly characterized by a Hot-summer Mediterranean climate (Csa), typical of latitudes between 30° and 45°, featuring mild, wet winters and hot, dry summers dominated by subtropical high pressure. Coastal areas may experience cooler summers and fog phenomena due to cold ocean currents. The majority of precipitation is concentrated in the winter and spring months, with generally arid summers. Local variations in rainfall may exist. The island of Cyprus also falls under the Csa climate classification. However, in specific areas such as the Alps and the Po Valley, a Monsoon-influenced humid subtropical climate (Cwa) is found, typical of lower latitudes (25°-40°). This climate features hot, humid summers and mild or

Region		Sardinia	Sicily	Italy
Area [km²]		24.090	25.711	302.073
Density [ab/km²]		64.8	185.12	195.4
Population [inhabitants]		1.578.146	4.814.016	58.997.201
Average age of population		48,4	45,2	46,6
GDP per capita [€]	2021	22.300	17.110	30.118
	2022	25.042	18.078	33.000
	2023	26.315,80	22.891	36.077
Climate Zone [Köppen climate classification (KCC)]		Csa	Csa	Csa, Cwa

Fig. 2. The key geographic data for each case study (Sardinia, Sicily and Italy).

Region		Cyprus	Greece
Area [km²]		9.251	131.957
Density [ab/km²]		132	84
Population [inhabitants]		1.260.138	10.413.982
Average age of population		38,4	46,5
GDP per capita [€]	2021	25.940	17.610
	2022	30.430	19.888
	2023	32.150	19.460
Climate Zone [Köppen climate classification (KCC)]		Csa	Csa

Fig. 3. The key geographic data for each case study (Cyprus and Greece).

cold winters, with abundant precipitation distributed throughout the year, peaking in the summer. Inland Cwa zones exhibit greater seasonal temperature variations, with potentially cold and foggy winters.

The comparative method has been applied to evolute the carbon footprint in each island and relative country, considering the following indicators: Direct Carbon Intensity, Low-Carbon Energy Percentage, and Renewable Energy Percentage, available on the Electricity Maps platform [34]. This study compares the three islands (Sardinia – Sicily – Cyprus) for the period 2021–2024, as this timeframe is representative of the post-COVID-19 phase and the subsequent acceleration towards the energy transition.

Carbon Intensity

The monthly trend of carbon intensity (gCO_2eq/kWh) for Sardinia, Sicily, and Cyprus over the period 2021 – 2024 is described both in absolute and normalized values (normalized by population: per capita values multiplied by 100000) in Fig. 4 and Fig. 5. Cyprus records the highest rank of emission intensity in both years. In 2021, absolute values consistently exceed 600.00 gCO_2eq/kWh, peaking in August (626.76 gCO_2eq/kWh) and remaining high until December (625.71 gCO_2eq/kWh). In 2024, an improvement is observed, ranging from a minimum in May (437.12 gCO_2eq/kWh) to a maximum in December (536.74 gCO_2eq/kWh). The normalized value as well, shows Cyprus leads with per capita values ranging from 41.14 to 50.35 gCO_2eq/kWh in 2021, and between 34.46 and 42.31 gCO_2eq/kWh in 2024, indicating a persistent strong reliance on fossil fuels in its energy system.

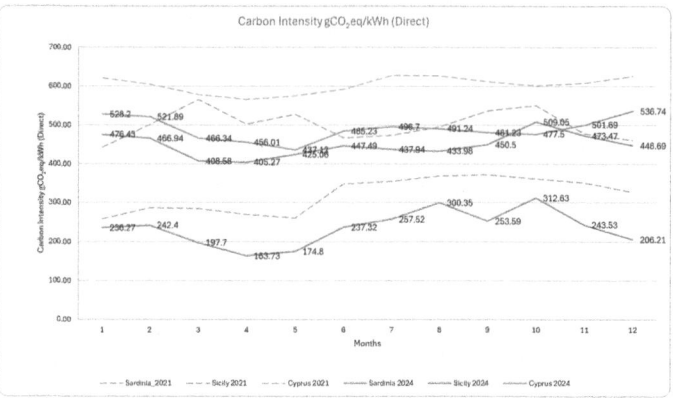

82   G. Balletto et al.

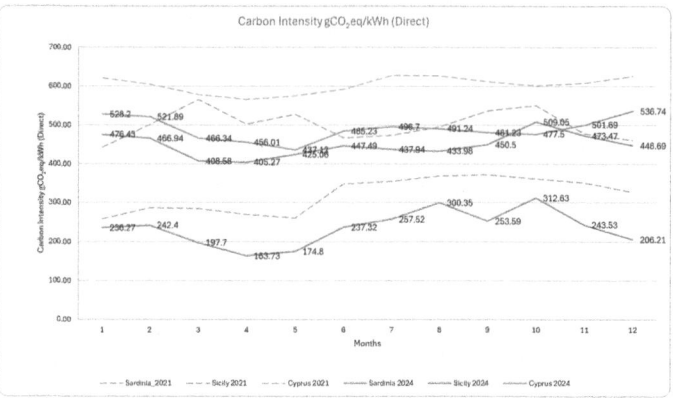

Fig. 4. Direct Carbon Intensity (gCO$_2$eq/kWh) for the three islands. Data source: [34].

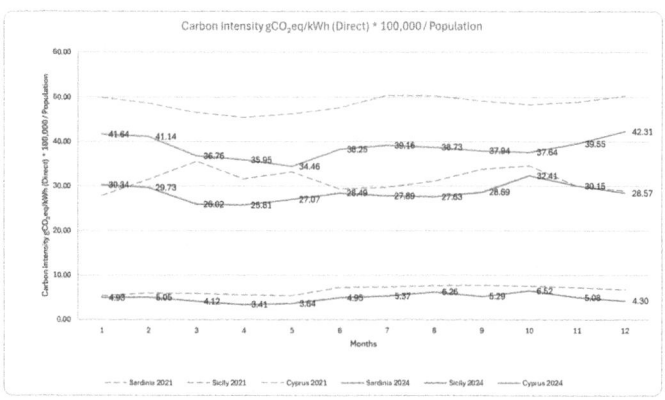

Fig. 5. Direct Carbon Intensity (gCO$_2$eq/kWh) *100000 / Population for the three islands. Data source: [34].

Sardinia records a high carbon intensity, albeit lower than Cyprus, with pronounced seasonal changes. In 2021, absolute values vary significantly between a peak in March (565.73 gCO$_2$eq/kWh) and a minimum in January (443.10 gCO$_2$eq/kWh). The phenomena appears more stable in 2024, fluctuating between a minimum in April (405.27 gCO$_2$eq/kWh) and an autumn peak in October (509.05 gCO$_2$eq/kWh). As regard the normalized value, Sardinia records a maximum of 35.58 gCO$_2$eq/kWh in March and a minimum around 27.87 gCO$_2$eq/kWh in January 2021, but a clear spring reduction in 2024 (minimum 25.81 gCO$_2$eq/kWh in April), with a slight autumn increase culminating in October (32.41 gCO$_2$eq/kWh). This evolution reflects a slight but significant rationalization in the use of energy sources.

Sicily ranks as the region with the lowest and most stable emission intensity in both years. In 2021, absolute values fluctuate between a minimum in January (258.73 gCO$_2$eq/kWh) and a maximum in October (373.39 gCO$_2$eq/kWh). A clear improvement is observed in 2024, particularly in the spring months, with values dropping to 163.73

gCO_2eq/kWh in April, before rising to 312.63 gCO_2eq/kWh in October. The normalized value highlights that Sicily records values between 5.35 and 7.72 gCO_2eq/kWh in 2021, while further improving in 2024, with a minimum of 3.41 gCO_2eq/kWh in April and a maximum of 6.52 gCO_2eq/kWh in October. This trend indicates increasing energy efficiency and a reduced reliance on fossil fuels.

The described comparison highlights Cyprus as the island with the highest carbon intensity, despite an improvement in 2024. Sardinia shows significant progress in terms of stability and emission reduction, although remaining at average levels higher than Sicily. The latter stands out positively, confirming itself as the most virtuous region in terms of carbon intensity, with a consolidated trend towards a more sustainable and less emissive energy system.

Low-Carbon Energy

The comparison of the monthly trends in the share of electricity generated from low-carbon sources (%) in Sardinia, Sicily, and Cyprus during the period 2021–2024, including both absolute and normalized values (normalized by population: multiplied by 100000) is represented in Fig. 6 and 7.

Regarding absolute values, Sicily dominated in terms of the quantity of energy produced from low-carbon sources in 2021, with an initial peak in January (49.01%), a second in May (48.13%), and a subsequent progressive decline in the following months. Sardinia recorded lower but stable levels, with values ranging from 24.25% (October) to 38.38% (January), showing continuity with a slight recovery at the end of the year. Cyprus registered more modest levels at the beginning of the year (12.47% in January), followed by a significant increase until April (20.31%), and then a progressive decrease in the second half of the year.

The analysis of population-normalized values reveals that Sardinia emerged as the leader in per capita terms, with values exceeding 1.50% for most of the year and a maximum of 2.53% in February. Cyprus ranked second, with an increase up to 1.63% in April, maintaining values around 1.00% in the following months, while Sicily fell to third place, showing more moderate values (between 0.58% and 1.00%) and less seasonal variability.

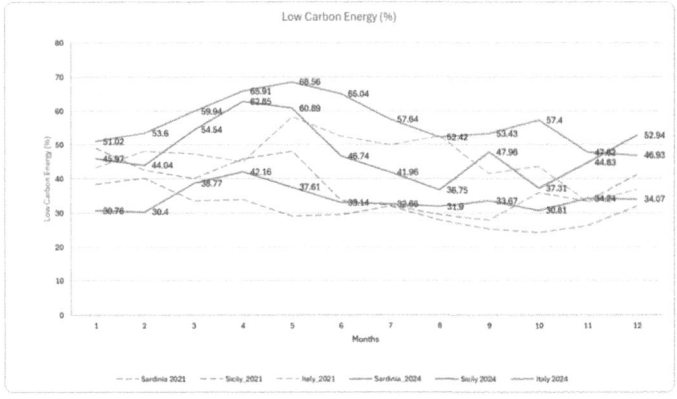

Fig. 6. Low-Carbon Energy Percentage for the three islands. Data source: [34].

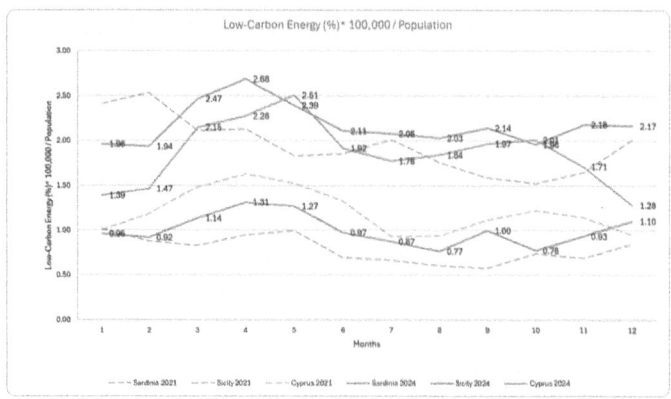

Fig. 7. Low-Carbon Energy Percentage *100000 / Population for the three islands. Data source: [34].

A general strengthening of low-carbon energy production was recorded in the three islands in 2024. Regarding absolute values, Sicily confirmed and reinforced its leading position, maintaining levels above 40.00% for most of the year, with the maximum reached in April (62.85%). Sardinia showed a more moderate but stable performance, ranging from a minimum in January (30.78%) to a maximum in April (42.16%). Cyprus remained the region with the lowest absolute share, reaching its maximum in May (31.82%) and its minimum in December (16.28%), indicating a slower decarbonization process compared to the other regions.

The normalized value confirms Sardinia as the most effective region in per capita terms also in 2024, with values close to or above 2.00% and a peak of 2.68% in April. Significant was the improvement in Cyprus during the first part of the year, which exceeded Sardinia between March and May (maximum of 2.51% in May), followed, however, by a decrease in the second half of the year (closing at 1.28% in December). Sicily also showed a positive trend compared to 2021, consistently exceeding 1.00% in the first months of the year with a maximum of 1.31% in April, then decreasing in the summer and recovering slightly at the end of the year (December: 1.10%).

The comparison highlights a general increase in low-carbon energy production from 2021 to 2024. Sicily leads in absolute terms, Sardinia leads in the energy-to-population ratio, while Cyprus shows initial improvements, particularly in the first part of 2024.

Renewable Energy

The comparison of the monthly trend of electricity produced from renewable sources (%) in Sardinia, Sicily, and Cyprus during the period 2021–2024, including both absolute and normalized values (normalized by population: multiplied by 100,000) is shown in Fig. 8 and 9.

Regarding the absolute values, Sicily emerges as the region with the highest renewable energy production in 2021, recording a peak in May (48.03%) and a marked decrease during the summer months, reaching a minimum in August (27.86%). Sardinia shows a lower but more stable production compared to Sicily, fluctuating between 38.77% and 40.26% with peaks in the winter months (February) and a slight decrease in summer. Cyprus presents lower absolute values compared to the other two islands, starting from low levels in January (12.47%), progressively increasing until April with a peak of 20.31%, but experiencing a significant drop during the summer months down to July (11.59%).

The scenario changes significantly when considering the population-normalized data in 2021. Sardinia leads in terms of per capita production, with values generally above 2.0%, reaching a maximum of 2.53% in February, followed by a minimum in October (1.52%), with a final recovery in December (2.01%). Cyprus, despite its low absolute values, ranks second in per capita share, growing to a maximum of 1.63% in April before decreasing in the second half of the year. Sicily ranks third in per capita terms, with lower and more stable values between 0.58% and 1.00%, while dominating in absolute values. Moreover, Sicily confirms and strengthens its leading position in absolute values in 2024, showing a significant increase compared to 2021, with values above 40.00% for most of the year and reaching a peak in April (62.75%), maintaining high levels also in May (60.80%), followed by a summer decrease and a new increase in December (52.87%). However, it remains the region with the lowest values in per capita terms, although improved compared to the past, ranging between 0.76% and a maximum of 1.31% recorded in April, showing greater continuity throughout the year.

Sardinia remains the leading region for per capita renewable energy also in 2024, with a share close to or above 2.0%, and a maximum of 2.68% in April, while maintaining lower absolute values than Sicily (annual maximum of 42.10% in April). The monthly trend is more stable compared to 2021, indicating greater regularity and robustness of renewable energy production throughout the year, with a slight summer decrease and a final recovery (2.16% in December).

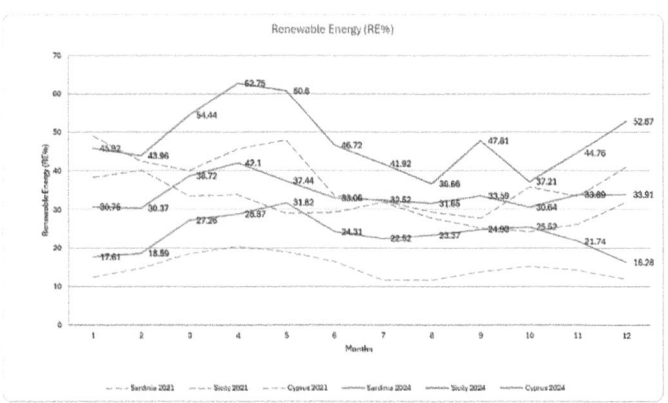

Fig. 8. Renewable Energy Percentage for the three islands. Data source: [34].

Cyprus shows an interesting evolution in 2024: in absolute terms, it reaches a maximum in May (31.82%), followed by a gradual decrease to the annual minimum in December (16.28%). Regarding the population-normalized values, it records a significant increase in the first months of 2024, surpassing Sardinia in April and May, reaching a peak of 2.51% in May. However, this positive dynamic is not maintained throughout the year, and the share progressively decreases in the second half, ending the year in December at 1.28%.

The comparison shows an overall improvement from 2021 to 2024 in renewable energy production: Sicily consolidates its absolute leadership; Sardinia confirms a position of per capita excellence; Cyprus shows significant signs of progress in the first half of the year, although remaining at lower values.

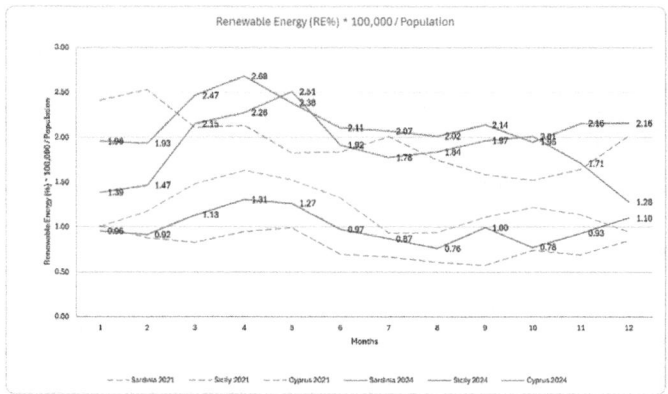

Fig. 9. Renewable Energy Percentage *100,000 / Population for the three islands. Data source: [34].

5 Discussions

The present study provides a comparative analysis of carbon intensity, low-carbon energy production, and renewable energy trends across Cyprus, Sardinia, and Sicily between 2021 and 2024. The findings reveal distinct energy profiles for each island, highlighting their progress and challenges in transitioning towards more sustainable energy systems.

As regards the carbon intensity, Cyprus consistently registered the highest levels in both absolute and per capita terms throughout the study period. While there was an improvement observed in 2024, this still indicates a significant and persistent reliance on fossil fuels within its energy mix. Sardinia exhibited a high carbon intensity as well, albeit lower than Cyprus, with noticeable seasonal fluctuations in 2021 that became more stable with a slight reduction by 2024. This suggests a gradual optimization in the utilization of energy sources. In contrast, Sicily demonstrated the lowest and most stable carbon intensity in both absolute and per capita values. It showed further improvement in 2024, particularly during the spring months, signifying increasing energy efficiency and a decreasing dependence on fossil fuels. This positions Sicily as the most environmentally sustainable of the three islands in terms of carbon intensity, demonstrating a clear trajectory towards a less emissive energy system.

In 2021, Sicily led in absolute low-carbon energy production with peaks early in the year, while Sardinia maintained lower but stable levels, and Cyprus recorded the lowest initial production with mid-year growth. Regarding population-normalized values in 2021, Sardinia was the per capita leader, followed by Cyprus, and then Sicily. By 2024, all three islands showed increased low-carbon energy production. Sicily strengthened its absolute lead, Sardinia maintained a stable performance, but Cyprus still had the lowest absolute share, indicating a slower decarbonization. In normalized terms for 2024, Sardinia remained the per capita leader. Cyprus showed significant improvement in the first half of the year, temporarily surpassing Sardinia, before a subsequent decrease. Sicily also demonstrated a positive trend compared to 2021. Overall, low-carbon energy production increased across the islands from 2021 to 2024. Sicily led in absolute terms, Sardinia in per capita ratio, and Cyprus showed initial progress, particularly in early 2024.

The trends in renewable energy production from 2021 to 2024 indicate that Sicily had the highest absolute production in 2021, peaking in May. Sardinia presented lower but more stable production, and Cyprus recorded the lowest absolute values with a peak in April. Considering population-normalized data in 2021, Sardinia led in per capita renewable energy, followed by Cyprus, with Sicily ranking third despite its absolute dominance. In 2024, Sicily solidified its absolute leadership with a significant increase in renewable energy production. Sardinia remained the per capita leader with a stable monthly trend, and Cyprus showed an interesting evolution with an absolute peak in May followed by a decrease. Focusing on per capita renewable energy in 2024, Sardinia continued to lead, while Cyprus demonstrated a notable increase in the first half of the year, temporarily surpassing Sardinia, before a decline in the latter half. Sicily, despite its absolute leadership in production volume, remained the region with the lowest per capita renewable energy, although showing improvement compared to 2021.

6 Conclusions

The study proposed a comparative analysis of the trend of the energy transition in the Mediterranean islands considering significant factors such as Carbon Intensity [gCO$_2$eq/kWh], Low-Carbon Energy [%] and Energy from Renewable Sources [%]. Three large islands have been selected as a case study - Sardinia and Sicily (Italy), and Cyprus - understood as ideal sites for the analysis of the socio-spatial dimensions of the energy transition, owing to their isolation and the necessity to ensure energy security, in addition to their aspirations for political autonomy.

The analysis of multiple case studies, particularly over an extended period (temporal comparison across years 2021–2024), highlighted different trends and temporary fluctuations. Moreover, each indicator has been expressed in absolute value and normalized value (related to the annual population), within a specific context well described by socio-geographic and economic characteristics to better understand consumption patterns.

Sicily, Sardinia, and Cyprus show distinct characteristics and varying paces of transition towards sustainability between 2021 and 2024. Sicily emerges as a leader in mitigating climate impact, consistently demonstrating the lowest carbon intensity and a strong absolute production of both low-carbon and renewable energy, showcasing a clear trajectory towards a less emissive energy system. Sardinia excels in per capita renewable and low-carbon energy production, indicating a strong commitment to cleaner energy sources relative to its population, despite having a moderate carbon intensity. Cyprus, while showing improvements in reducing carbon intensity and increasing low-carbon and renewable energy production, particularly in the first half of 2024, still lags behind the other two islands, showing the highest carbon intensity and the lowest absolute share of low-carbon energy, suggesting a slower decarbonization process and a persistent reliance on fossil fuels.

In conclusion, the study reveals an overall improvement in renewable energy production across the three islands from 2021 to 2024, with a positive trend towards greater adoption of low-carbon and renewable energy sources, demonstrating unique strengths for further development in energy transitions. In this sense, the results are valuable for informing policy decisions, providing a basis for developing more effective strategies for the energy transition in the Mediterranean islands.

More precisely, Sardinia faces a crucial stage regarding the energy transition. The increase in the utilization of renewable sources is essential to guarantee a sustainable energy future, but it requires necessary interventions to adapt the existing electricity grid. This is fundamental also to integrate renewable energy communities (RECs) as a tool to overcome geographical barriers and bring clean energy to the most remote areas. Therefore, the challenge for Sardinia and for other countries with low population density is to strengthen and implement new infrastructure to ensure that renewable resources are effectively used to meet local energy demands, thus contributing to face climate change in the Mediterranean region.

Acknowledgments. This study was partially carried out within the Ecosystem of Innovation for Next Generation Sardinia (e.INS) and received funding from the European Union Next-GenerationEU (PIANO NAZIONALE DI RIPRESA E RESILIENZA (PNRR) –MISSIONE 4 COMPONENTE 2, INVESTIMENTO 1.5 – ECS00000038). In particular, Sects. 1-5 were funded by eINS; Sect. 6 was funded by the research grant CUP__F73C23001680007 for the project "Geodesign for climate change mitigation and adaptation in the Mediterranean region" funded in 2022 by Fondazione di Sardegna.

Author Contributions. G.B. and M.L. wrote Sect. 1, Sect. 1.1, Sect. 2, and Sect. 6; G.B. and A.P. wrote Sect. 3, G.B., M.L., and A.P. wrote Sect. 4; G.B., M.L, M.N., E.G. and B.K. wrote Sect. 5. All authors have read and agreed to the published version of the manuscript.

Disclosure of Interests. The authors have no competing interests to declare that are relevant to the content of this article.

References

1. Balletto, G., Ladu, M., Camerin, F., Ghiani, E., Torriti, J.: More circular city in the energy and ecological transition: a methodological approach to sustainable urban regeneration. Sustainability **14**(22), 14995 (2022)
2. de Vincenzo, D.: La transizione energetica nell'attuale contesto globale. Rivista Geografica Italiana **1** (2022)

3. Szpilko, D., Ejdys, J.: European Green Deal–research directions. A systematic literature review. Ekonomia i Środowisko **2**, 8–38 (2022)
4. Trevisan, R., Ladu, M., Ghiani, E., Balletto, G.: Achieving net zero condominiums through energy community sharing. Sustainability **16**(5), 2076 (2024)
5. Balletto, G., Ladu, M.: Indicatori per la Città Circolare nella transizione ecologica ed energetica. BDC Bollettino Del Centro Calza Bini **22**(2), 255–270 (2022)
6. Kikstra, J.S., et al.: The IPCC Sixth Assessment Report WGIII climate assessment of mitigation pathways: from emissions to global temperatures. Geoscientific Model Development **15**(24), 9075–9109 (2022)
7. Siddi, M., Zuddas, A.: Il Piano REPowerEU dell'Unione Europea tra Transizione Energetica e Geopolitica. In: Ucraina, 2022: un'analisi storica, giuridica e politica, pp. 95–115. Jovene (2023)
8. Tutak, M., Brodny, J., Bindzár, P.: Assessing the level of energy and climate sustainability in the european union countries in the context of the european green deal strategy and agenda 2030. Energies **14**, 1767 (2021)
9. Ladu, M., Milesi, A., Balletto, G.: Transizione energetica, tra tutela e valorizzazione per una strategia circolare dei centri storici. In: I processi di pianificazione urbanistica e territoriale nella gestione delle crisi energetica e alimentare, vol. 10., pp. 108–115. Planum Publisher e Società Italiana degli Urbanisti (2024)
10. European Commission. Italy's Recovery and Resilience Plan (2021). https://ec.europa.eu/info/business-economy-euro/recovery-coronavirus/recovery-and-resilience-facility/italys-recovery-and-resilience-plan_en. Accessed 04 Nov 2025
11. de Vincenzo, D.: NextGenerationEU tra pandemia, guerra e transizione energetica. Documenti geografici **1**, 23–36 (2022)
12. de Vincenzo, D.: Transizione ambientale e transizione Energetica. Il caso dell'Unione Europea. Documenti geografici **2**, 343–358 (2021)
13. Legambiente: Comunità Rinnovabili. GF Pubblicità - Grafiche Faioli (2021)
14. Global Energy Monitor. https://globalenergymonitor.org/projects/global-integrated-power-tracker/tracker-map/. Accessed 04 Nov 2025
15. Balletto, G., Borruso, G., Murgante, B., Milesi, A., Ladu, M.: Resistance and resilience. A methodological approach for cities and territories in Italy. In: Computational Science and Its Applications–ICCSA 2021: 21st International Conference, Proceedings, Part IV 21, pp. 218–229. Springer (2021)
16. Balletto, G., Mundula, L., Milesi, A., Ladu, M.: Cohesion policies in Italian metropolitan cities. Evaluation and challenges. In: Computational Science and Its Applications–ICCSA 2020: 20th International Conference, Cagliari, Italy, July 1–4, 2020, Proceedings, Part VII 20, pp. 441–455. Springer (2020)
17. International Energy Agency (IEA): Renewables 2019. IEA, Paris (2019)
18. Ścigan, M., et al.: Cost-Competitive Renewable Power Generation: Potential across South East Europe. IRENA (2017)
19. Sartori, N., Bianchi, M.: Energia nel Mediterraneo e il ruolo del settore privato. Istituto Affari Internazionali (IAI) (2019)
20. Schenk, C.J., et al.: Assessment of undiscovered oil and gas resources of the Levant Basin Province, Eastern Mediterranean: U.S. Geological Survey Fact Sheet 2010-3014 (2010)
21. Williams, R.H.: Toward zero emissions for transportation using fossil fuels. In: Transportation, Energy, and Environmental Policy, pp: 63–104, Washington (2001)
22. Berlinguer, A.: La 'questione' insulare. In: La transizione ecologica nelle isole minori, pp. 17–19. CNR-IIA e Legambiente (2024)
23. Hopkin, J.: The comparative method. Theory and methods in political science **3**, 285–307 (2010)

24. Electricity Maps. https://portal.electricitymaps.com/datasets. Accessed 31 Mar 2025
25. Fratianni, S., Acquaotta, F.: The climate of Italy. Landscapes and landforms of Italy, 29–38 (2017)
26. Pellizzoni, L.: Energia di comunità: Una ricognizione critica della letteratura. Biblioteca della società aperta. Studi e ricerche **5**, 17–41 (2018)
27. Terna. https://www.terna.it/it. Accessed 28 Mar 2025
28. Regione Siciliana: Aggiornamento Piano Energetico Ambientale della Regione Siciliana PEARS 2030. Regione Siciliana (2021)
29. Innovation Island. https://innovationisland.it/sicilia-cuore-della-transizione-energetica-del-med/. Accessed 29 Mar 2025
30. Regione Siciliana e Terna. https://www.terna.it/it/media/comunicati-stampa/dettaglio/terna-regione-siciliana-protocollo-intesa-richieste-connessione-impianti-rinnovabili. Accessed 22 Mar 2025
31. Barbaro, S.: Net Zero Energy District: norme, strumenti finanziari e modelli decisionali per la transizione energetica urbana (2023)
32. Sartori, N., Bianchi, M.: Energia nel Mediterraneo e il ruolo del settore privato. Istituto Affari Internazionali (IAI) IAI PAPERS **19**(21), 1–15 (2019)
33. Hafner, M., Tagliapietra, S.: Ripartire dall'energia per rilanciare la cooperazione euro-mediterranea. Equilibri, Rivista per lo sviluppo sostenibile **2**, 207–210 (2016)
34. Electricity Maps. https://portal.electricitymaps.com/datasets. Accessed 04 Nov 2025

Ecosystem Services in Spatial Planning for Climate Neutral Urban and Rural Areas (ESSP 2025)

The Update of the Provincial Structural Plan of Potenza to Strengthen Climate Change Adaptation Policies in the Governance of Basilicata

Alessandro Attolico[1], Rosalia Smaldone[1,2], Antonio Santandrea[1], Michele Sanseviero[1], and Francesco Scorza[2(✉)] [iD]

[1] Province of Potenza, MCR2030 Resilience HUB, P.Zza M.Pagano 1, 85100 Potenza, Italy
alessandro.attolico@provinciapotenza.it,
rosalia.smaldone@unibas.it
[2] Department of Engineering, University of Basilicata, Viale dell'Ateneo Lucano, Potenza, Italy
francesco.scorza@unibas.it

Abstract. The UN's 2050 biodiversity vision aims to achieve thriving ecosystems, reduced species extinction risks, and long-term benefits for humanity. Climate change and biodiversity loss are interlinked global challenges that demand urgent and comprehensive action. Local ecological networks support both climate change adaptation and biodiversity protection by fostering interconnected green spaces that enhance ecosystem resilience. Through targeted policies and nature-based solutions, such as native reforestation and wildlife corridors, these networks mitigate extreme climate events and support species survival. This contribution illustrates the activities of the Province of Potenza in the planning of ecological networks, updating the Provincial Structural Plan as a government tool, seeking strategies for multi-functional development of the territory. With the increase in catastrophic weather events, the identification of new strategies and new tools assumes an important role in adapting to climate change and the challenges that changes in society reflect on the territory. The Province of Potenza is actively involved in European projects promoting participatory governance, territorial resilience, and sustainable ecosystem management, contributing to integrated and lasting environmental transformation.

Keywords: ecological network · governance · climate change adaptation · biodiversity

1 Introduction

Biodiversity is the variety of life on Earth, from genes and bacteria to entire ecosystems like forests and coral reefs. It has evolved over 4.5 billion years, with increasing influence from human activity. Up to one million species are threatened with extinction, many within decades. Important ecosystems such as the Amazon rainforest, are shifting from carbon sinks to carbon sources due to deforestation, while 85% of carbon-absorbing wetlands have vanished [1].

O. Gervasi et al. (Eds.): ICCSA 2025 Workshops, LNCS 15890, pp. 93–105, 2026.
https://doi.org/10.1007/978-3-031-97606-3_7

The Convention on Biological Diversity (CBD), ratified by 196 nations in 1993, aims to conserve biodiversity, promote sustainable use, and ensure fair sharing of genetic resources. It covers ecosystems, species, and genetic resources, extending to areas like biotechnology, education, and agriculture. The Conference of the Parties (COP) meets biennially to review progress and set priorities [2]. While human land use remains the main driver of biodiversity loss, climate change is increasingly contributing by disrupting ecosystems, causing species loss, increasing diseases, and leading to the first climate-driven extinctions [1]. In 2023, many temperature and ice extent records were shattered, with global and North Atlantic sea surface temperatures significantly exceeding their 1991–2024 averages, a trend continuing into 2024. While Antarctic and global sea ice extent has returned to levels seen in previous years, it remains well below the 1993–2024 average. Global daily mean temperatures reached record highs for much of 2023 and 2024 [3] (Fig. 1).

Climate change is a major driver of biodiversity loss, causing species extinctions through habitat disruption, stress, and threats to keystone species. Efforts to address this include climate action, mass reforestation, habitat restoration, and targeted conservation. While progress has been made with increased protected areas, challenges remain in integrating climate policies with biodiversity goals. Nature-based solutions, such as enhancing genetic diversity and leveraging ecosystems for carbon sequestration (e.g., whales' role in marine ecosystems), are vital for resilience. Collaboration, funding, and effective management are essential. The UN's 2050 biodiversity vision aims to reduce extinction risks and ensure long-term benefits for humanity by aligning biodiversity conservation with climate strategies.

2   The European and National Strategies and Plans to Address Climate Change and Biodiversity Loss

Climate change and biodiversity loss are interlinked global challenges that demand urgent and comprehensive action. Europe has taken a leading role in developing and implementing strategies to address these issues, aiming to promote environmental sustainability while ensuring economic and social resilience.

The key initiatives to tackle Climate Change are the European Green Deal, introduced in 2019, is the cornerstone of Europe's climate action plan. This ambitious framework sets forth the goal of achieving carbon neutrality by 2050. To reach this target, the European Union (EU) has prioritized:

– Decarbonization: Transitioning to renewable energy sources, promoting energy efficiency, and phasing out fossil fuels.
– Circular Economy: Reducing waste and encouraging sustainable production and consumption patterns.
– Climate Adaptation: Implementing measures to mitigate the impacts of extreme weather events, rising sea levels, and other climate-related challenges.

Moreover, the Fit for 55 package underscores the EU's commitment to reducing greenhouse gas emissions by at least 55% by 2030 compared to 1990 levels. These initiatives are complemented by international cooperation under the Paris Agreement.

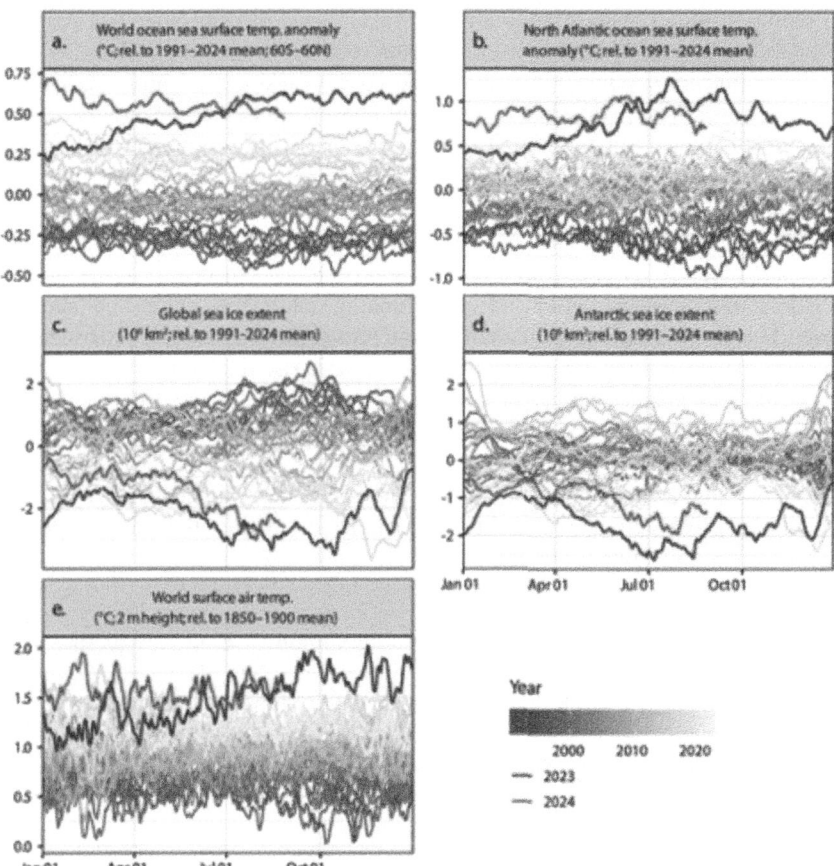

Fig. 1. Unusual climate anomalies in 2023 and 2024. Ocean temperatures (a, b) are presently far outside their historical ranges. These anomalies reflect the combined effect of long-term climate change and short-term variability. Sources and additional details about each variable are provided in supplemental file S1. Each line corresponds to a different year, with darker gray representing later years. All of the variables shown are daily estimates [3].

Biodiversity is essential for ecological balance and climate resilience. The EU Biodiversity Strategy for 2030 outlines critical steps to halt and reverse biodiversity loss, including:

– Habitat Restoration: Restoring degraded ecosystems, such as forests, wetlands, and marine areas, to improve carbon sequestration and protect species.
– Protected Areas: Expanding the coverage of protected land and marine zones to conserve key biodiversity hotspots.
– Sustainable Land Use: Promoting sustainable agricultural and forestry practices to minimize habitat destruction and support ecosystem health.

In addition, the EU Nature Restoration Law sets legally binding targets for ecosystem restoration, aiming for long-term environmental recovery and sustainability.

Integration Strategy integration plays a key role: Europe recognizes the interconnectedness of climate action and biodiversity conservation. The integration of these strategies is evident in nature-based solutions, such as afforestation, which simultaneously reduce carbon emissions and enhance biodiversity. Collaboration with local communities, industries, and global partners is vital for achieving sustainable outcomes.

Through innovative policies and ambitious targets, Europe is addressing climate change and biodiversity loss with a holistic approach. The success of these strategies relies on robust implementation, adequate funding, and cross-sectoral collaboration. As the EU continues to lead global efforts, the preservation of natural ecosystems and climate resilience will remain central to its vision for a sustainable future.

Italy has implemented a range of strategies to tackle the interconnected challenges of climate change and biodiversity loss, aligning its efforts with European and international frameworks.

Regarding the Italian framework on these topics, Italian Climate Change Strategies Italy aims to achieve climate neutrality by 2050, as outlined in its National Integrated Plan for Energy and Climate (PNIEC).

Key measures include:

- Greenhouse Gas Reduction: A target of reducing emissions by 55% by 2030 compared to 1990 levels.
- Renewable Energy Transition: Expanding the use of renewable energy sources and improving energy efficiency.
- Adaptation Measures: The National Adaptation Plan to Climate Change (PNACC) incorporates over 361 actions to enhance climate resilience, including ecosystem-based solutions and infrastructure improvements2.

Regarding the biodiversity conservation issue, the National Biodiversity Strategy for 2030 focuses on preserving and restoring ecosystems.

Key objectives include:

- Protected Areas: Expanding legally protected land and marine areas to cover at least 30% of the national territory.
- Ecosystem Restoration: Restoring degraded ecosystems, such as forests and wetlands, to enhance carbon sequestration and biodiversity.
- Sustainable Practices: Promoting sustainable agriculture and forestry to minimize habitat destruction.

Italy's ecological transition strategy emphasizes the integration of climate and biodiversity goals. Collaborative governance frameworks, involving local communities and private stakeholders, are essential for effective implementation. Funding can be sourced from national budgets, EU programs, and private investments.

Italy's comprehensive approach to addressing climate change and biodiversity loss reflects its commitment to sustainability. By aligning national strategies with European and global goals, Italy is working towards a resilient and biodiverse future.

3   Programmatic Framework: Policies and Strategies of the Province of Potenza

The Province of Potenza (PPZ), through the adoption of its Provincial Structural Plan in 2013, has outlined, developed, and strengthened territorial development policies under the #weResilient strategy. This initiative focuses on disaster risk reduction and integrates environmental sustainability, territorial safety, and climate change mitigation, leveraging extensive local experience in civil protection and territorial safety.

Since 2014, Potenza has actively contributed to the UNDRR "Making Cities Resilient" (2010–2020) initiative, fostering a network among 100 municipalities to implement a shared territorial development strategy at both urban and local scales. A multi-stakeholder platform has been established to engage public and private institutions, citizens, and interest groups in institutional activities.

In 2015, PPZ adopted the Strategic Framework to Combat Climate Change, followed by joining the Covenant of Mayors as regional coordinator in 2016 to support and coordinate territorial initiatives.

Additionally, PPZ turned its enrolment as a supporting authority to the UNDRR MCR2030 (2020–2030), advocating for local resilience enhancement through knowledge-sharing, technical expertise, and collaborative governance.

PPZ's commitment aligns with global strategies such as the Sendai Framework, and its efforts have led to recognition as a UNDRR Resilience HUB in 2022 and as a key partner in European initiatives supporting the Green Deal and Climate Adaptation Strategy.

Potenza Province has introduced tools like the "House of the 100 Municipalities" for real-time information sharing and the Resilience HUB, a coordination structure for education, collaboration, and stakeholder and communities' engagement.

A key element of the strategy is the active engagement of communities in local decision-making for territorial policies, including sustainable development, disaster risk reduction, and climate change adaptation/mitigation. This involves coordinating actions with municipalities and establishing permanent platforms to promote community resilience, ensuring inclusivity across social groups. The goal is to strengthen the capacity of individuals and communities to pursue sustainable development by raising awareness of biodiversity conservation and involving them in relevant policy decisions. The participation of institutional stakeholders further enhances this process [16, 17].

4   The Provincial Structural Plan from Approval to Date

After many years of elaborations and analyses, the PPZ adopted its territorial policy instrument in 2013. Providing, for the first time, knowledge frameworks on environmental, demographic and urban issues to support the definition of a territorial project within the four strategic territorial areas, directing the local territorial government through the action of municipalities and their own governance instruments.

The plan in recent years has worked as collector of organized data and information from different territorial authorities, in support of the only instrument of territorial governance approved in Basilicata, that is the PSP - Provincial Structural Plan.

Over the years, the provincial government has introduced new themes into the local urban planning landscape, such as addressing actions to adapt to climate change or adopting good practices aimed at territorial resilience.

The measures and strategies for adaptation to climate change and land protection, implemented in the Provincial Structural Master Plan (PSP) have been an experience that in recent years allowed to safeguard the qualities trying to intervene on environmental criticalities through the protection of the ecological network in competition with the Italian landscape and environmental legislation.

In the spatial planning of Basilicata, the Ecological Network project of the PPZ's (REP) represented an element that made it possible to recognize an environmental system consisting of protected areas and ecosystems characterized by an intrinsic quality not protected but equally important to guarantee the diffuse environmental quality (core areas), the residual elements and habitats of passage of living species (stepping stones), the corridors of river and land interconnection and areas of poor environmental quality where to direct improvement actions (restoration areas).

The identification of a network of interconnections between habitats of territorial importance represented the first step in an environmental restoration project that was carried out with the contribution of actors and stakeholders who actually act on the territory. The REP has set itself the objective of guaranteeing the high degree of naturalness that has historically characterized the territory, ensuring the preservation and improvement of the most valuable areas and improving the connections between the different habitats with actions that guarantee the efficiency of ecological corridors and territorial security climate change.

The guidelines provided by the project represent a fundamental step to be implemented with specific interventions by local actors in order to improve quality and to intervene on criticalities increasing the detail of the information and the possibility of interventions punctual.

The contribution of PPZ through this instrument has mainly aimed to ensure the interconnection between habitats through the improvement of ecological corridors identified by ensuring territorial security with actions improving officiousness hydraulic.

The regional territory of Potenza, described through the ecological network, is characterized by large areas predominantly forested distributed from north to south along the mountains of the Southern Apennines. These areas, through less extensive and more fragmented woodlands, find a greater spatial continuity of the terrestrial ecological corridors, mainly along mountain ridges and hills, also thanks to the abandoned pastures that slowly evolve towards the forest (Fig. 2).

The blueways have been identified within rivers protected by national landscape legislation (D. lgs. 42/2004 art. 142 lett. c), as considered the most correct criterion by virtue of the scale of representation and the characteristic of representing watercourses with a permanent and non-episodic water regime.

The most critical areas identified relate to the most populated areas, with reference to the rural context, where urban, agricultural and industrial development has been concentrated, due to the northern territory with widespread urbanization and intensive agriculture that has depleted the naturalistic components of the agricultural landscape.

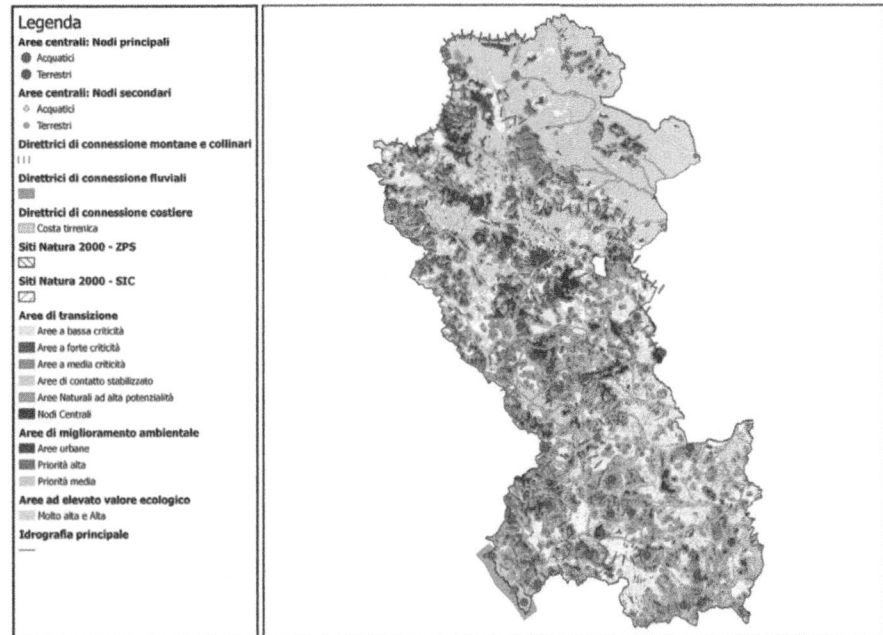

Fig. 2. Provincial Ecological Network. Source: Provincial Structural Plan of the Province of Potenza (PSP)

The PSP in these areas provides, through special provisions for the common guidelines for the implementation of green ways along the paths, in order to enhance the historical landscapes and introducing elements for soil protection such as hedgerows rows and trees able to increase connectivity but also to protect soils from the risk of erosion by carrying out a windbreak action and providing organic material for the land. This type of strategy seeks to repair the environmental connections put to the test by the excessive functionalization of intensive agriculture. In this respect it should be noted that the contribution of the office has been to identify priorities for intervention aimed at environmental improvement based on the degree of anthropogenic pressure suffered. Through the identification of transition bands (buffer areas) have been highlighted the dynamics of pressure on the areas of greater environmental value, preparing different actions according to the pressure in place, For example, by protecting and managing the spontaneous re-naturalisation of pastures and fallow crops, or where high-level criticalities have been identified, medium or low, mitigation or containment measures have been suggested to which the municipal administrations will have to respond at the planning stage (Fig. 3).

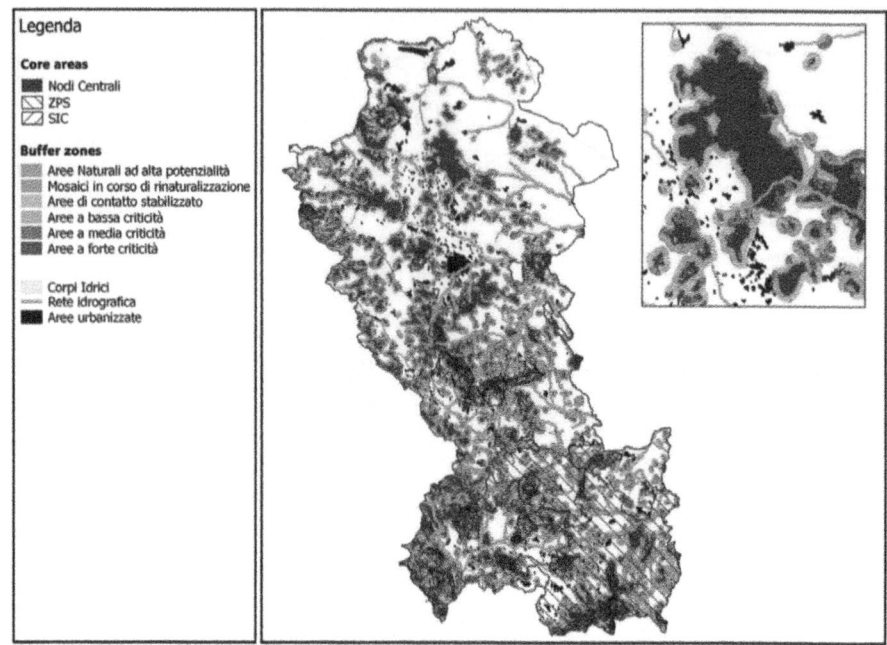

Fig. 3. Core and Buffer Areas of the Ecological Network of the Province of Potenza. Source: Provincial Structural Plan of the Province of Potenza

5 New Approaches and Challenges for the Provincial Ecological Network (REP)

After more than fifteen years since the publication of the Regional Functional Ecological Scheme, which was the methodological structure from which the Provincial Ecological Network was developed, the Basilicata Region through the Regional Landscape Plan (PPR) has redefined a methodology and an approach, adopting that of the National Strategy for Biodiversity and that is to get out of the rigid distinction between territory with high natural value and territory with low or no value.

Also in the National Strategy for Biodiversity (MATTM 2010) and in particular of the work area "Species, habitat and landscape" are highlighted the strong criticalities for biodiversity identified in the abandonment of the countryside, the progressive closure of open areas in favour of shrub and tree formations, the general simplification of agro-ecosystems (mostly in hilly and lowland areas) with the elimination of traditional elements of the agricultural landscape (hedges, rows, pools, fountains), the spread of invasive alien species, and it is recognized the urgency to develop and implement conservation and restoration policies in which the design, construction and maintenance of "ecological networks" Large-area can be the operational tools for this desired synergy between landscape policies and biodiversity conservation.

This new approach in the regional vision finds its implementation in the introduction already in the Landscape Plan with the publication of the guidelines for the design by the municipalities of the Local Ecological Network.

The identification of elements of the ecological network at municipal level, the improvement of the ecological relations between nature and the built environment aims to strengthen contact with ecological elements on a larger scale, in particular ditches, trees, corridors connecting with the Ecological Network at regional scale.

The ultimate goal is to preserve the residual nature in the urban centres, but also to reconstruct a new ecosystem scenario oriented to the model of contemporary sustainable city, in which greater emphasis is placed on human-environment with the idea of the designers that this choice can prove to be an added value for a traditionally agricultural territory rich in excellent agri-food products. The experimental, didactic and educational value of this vademecum will make it possible to see small local actions of great ecological-landscape significance in the search for the possible balance between man and nature.

The ecological network has a strategic importance both from the technical point of view, and from the planning decisions point of view, because it allows to "design" in an integrated way the territory starting from the contact areas between nature and man's work.

In this way, ecological networks represent the moment of redevelopment of natural space in built and artificial contexts of local urban planning, and regulate issues such as land use, territorial fragmentation, the sustainability of settlement development, territorial reputation, quality of life.

This new approach, while breaking with previous ecological network models, represents a more ecosystem-based vision of the territory, beyond conservation measures for protected sites, and also recognizes a value to natural elements of the territory that in a scientific approach might not be considered recognizable in a network as an interconnected system of core areas.

As can be seen from the methodology published with the PPR, the natural elements of the territory assume a connective or centrality function according to the scale in which they are observed, from the regional to the corporate scale.

The regional project provides that starting from a regional project, through methodological guidelines, each municipality can represent its own ecological network, through a look at the current, the implementation/improvement policy of the network is identified with ecological improvement guidelines. For example:

- Re-naturalization of native species reforestation
- Restoration of streams and ditches
- By pass for wildlife on transport infrastructure
- Establishment of plant mitigation bands
- Urban green with native plants peculiar to the area
- Creating green walls to mitigate within the urban perimeter
- Remediation and restoration
- Crop wastage for wildlife
- Grass bands in the presence of extensive monocultures.

What can be the support of the Provincial ecological network in this new methodological vision?

The Provincial Ecological Network, as in general the contribution of the PSP, being at an intermediate level between regional and municipal planning, can assume a coordinating role towards a shared vision of the territory, for its administrative functions.

PPZ can certainly give a vision of the projects to be carried out to realize a network of connection through green infrastructures, multifunctional green ways and blue ways that enhance a new use of the naturalistic landscape. The role that the new REP will have to undertake is therefore to repair natural areas by intervening also with Nature Based Solutions in fragile contexts characterized by hydrogeological hazards or going to intervene in urban and peri-urban area for the reduction of flooding and a more careful management of rainwater.

6   Actions to Improve Blue Infrastructure

The rivers of Basilicata Region constitute a special and important ecosystem to be protected, preserved and enhanced not only for natural and landscape aspects, but also for tourism and sustainable development of the territory. This heritage, as already mentioned above, can become a critical because of the continuous emergency situations, given by increasingly violent weather events able to create huge damage to the populations.

From these considerations arise the actions implemented by the PPZ consisting, essentially, in the implementation of maintenance activities of the hydrographic grid, with the consequent reduction of the hydrogeological risk and redevelopment of the territorial system (both environmental and landscape).

The maintenance activity stems from a regional programming initiative and has, in fact, as its general objective that of revaluing the water courses, returning to the Lucanian rivers the historical and multipurpose role of sources of life, wellness, wealth and security; of energy and productive sources in agriculture and industry; generators of quality urban, agricultural and natural landscapes, cultures, lifestyles with a crucial qualitative function for the territory.

In more detail, on a technical level, the strategic objectives, in line with those set by the PPZ, within the framework of the government policies of its territory are:

• the mitigation of hydraulic risk,
• the structural and functional upgrading of the ecological network and environmental systems,
• the qualitative and quantitative protection of water,
• sharing of information.

The poor and sometimes total absence of maintenance of watercourses has as its effect an intense proliferation of uncontrolled infesting vegetation, briers and dense bushes in riverbed that, in some cases, generates both widespread and localized obstructions, Causing rise of the water shackles and, consequently, the risk of disastrous floods.

The interventions affect many sections of the provincial river network, which coincides with the ecological river corridors of the REP, and they also bring considerable benefits from the point of view of the redevelopment of sites.

In the context of the works, a key role is occupied by the functional recovery of existing hydraulic works and the restoration of the hydraulic officiality of the lights of crossings, bridges and manholes, in many cases dangerously obstructed by vegetation, from debris and other material trapped in it.

Obviously, the interventions guarantee the maintenance of the ecological functionality of the river ecosystem and safeguard, where possible, the conservation of plant species that permanently colonize the sheltered habitats.

The knowledge of detail that is being acquired can allow the development of programmes and action systems, for the full sharing of information and for the dissemination of information, Encouraging and enabling, soon, the full participation of citizens in initiatives aimed at the development, protection and rational use of water resources. In this way, the foundations are laid for hypotheses of connection of open spaces of river environments, through the realization of historical-ecological routes (green infrastructures) that allow to travel rivers from their sources to the sea, in a green network that includes river-relevant areas, protected areas and existing parks with the aim of creating an ecological network that is multifunctional, able to ensure the connectivity of all living species, including humans.

7   Conclusions

The approach based on local/provincial ecological networks can harmonize climate change adaptation and biodiversity protection by fostering interconnected green spaces that support both ecological resilience and species survival. The provincial policies for preserving and restoring habitats, such as wetlands, and forests, are based on these networks that can act as natural buffers against climate impacts like floods, heatwaves, and soil erosion, while simultaneously providing safe havens for diverse species. Integrating climate-smart conservation strategies, such as planting native and climate-resilient vegetation, enhances ecosystem stability and carbon sequestration. Connecting fragmented habitats through wildlife corridors ensures species mobility, enabling adaptation to shifting environmental conditions. The ecological networks create a synergistic approach, where biodiversity thrives and ecosystems better withstand the effects of climate change [18–22].

In the pursuit of these important objectives and using direct European funds, PPZ is currently engaged in several project and actions and, amongst the most relevant:

- it is leading the CIBIOGO Project "Citizen Participation in Biodiversity Governance", within the "INTERREG EUROPE" 2021–2027 Program. The general objective of the project consists in improving policy-making tools to increase biodiversity governance and sustainable management of ecosystem services and will have to be implemented within the initiatives conducted by the Resilience HUB of the PPZ capitalized in the broader MCR2030 initiative on territorial resilience;

- it is a partner in the Project "DesirMED", "Demonstration and mainstrEaming of nature-based Solutions for clImate Resilient transformation in the MEDiterranean", within the Operational Programme "HORIZON EUROPE" 2021–2027. The Project is based on the idea that climate change (CC) represents a growing threat on a European and global scale, affecting social stability, public health and well-being. Adapting to the demands of CC requires a radical shift from fragmented strategies and approaches to transformative approaches, supporting the development of policies at all levels and promoting transversal and multi-level governance solutions. Nature-based solutions (NBS) to preserve and restore ecosystems, increase climate resilience, sustainably manage the environment, while providing broader long-term socio-economic benefits, are at the core of the goal of the Adaptation Plan of the European CC Adaptation (CCA) mission to be supported globally and of which PPZ is part;

- it is partner in the NBS4RESILIENCE Project within the Interreg IPA ADRION Programme. The Project addresses the complex issue of various negative climate events and presents several NBS suitable for the problem to increase climate resilience, territorial security and to improve the overall state of the environment in the IPA ADRION Programme region. The main objective of NBS4RESILIENCE is to co-create and transfer into policy choices and planning actions the conditions for the widespread use of NBS for climate resilient territories.

References

1. https://www.un.org/en/climatechange/science/climate-issues/biodiversity
2. https://www.un.org/en/observances/biological-diversity-day/convention
3. Ripple, W.J, Wolf, C.: The 2024 state of the climate report: Perilous times on planet Earth: BioScience. Oxford University Press (2024)
4. Badr, A, El-Shazly, H..: Climate Change and Biodiversity Loss: Interconnected Challenges and Priority Measures. Catrina: The International Journal of Environmental Sciences (Serial Number 29), pp. 69–78 (2024)
5. https://commission.europa.eu/strategy-and-policy/priorities-2019-2024/european-green-deal_it
6. https://www.consilium.europa.eu/en/policies/fit-for-55/
7. https://environment.ec.europa.eu/strategy/biodiversity-strategy-2030_en
8. Regulation (EU) 2024/1991 of the European Parliament and of the Council of 24 June 2024 on nature restoration and amending Regulation (EU) 2022/869
9. Piano Nazionale di adattamento ai cambiamenti climatici – PNACC
10. Piano Nazionale Integrato per l'Energia e il Clima (PNIEC)
11. Santandrea, A., Moretti V., Attolico, A.: L'importanza della Carta della Natura nella definizione della rete ecologica all'interno del Piano Strutturale provinciale della Provincia di Potenza. RETICULA 16/2017, pp. 73–81 (2017)
12. Santandrea, A., Smaldone, R., D'onofrio, D., Moretti, V., Attolico, A.: Coniugare la sicurezza territoriale e la riqualificazione funzionale della rete ecologica a fronte dei cambiamenti climatici. RETICULA 4/2013, pp. 20–23 (2013)
13. Regione Basilicata: Piano Paesaggistico Regionale – Relazione Metodologica della Rete Ecologica (2023)
14. Provincia di Potenza: Piano Strutturale Provinciale della Provincia di Potenza (2013)
15. Regione Basilicata: Sistema Ecologico Funzionale Territoriale (2009)
16. Attolico, A., Smaldone, R., The Province of Potenza #weResilient multiscale and multilevel holistic approach in downscaling local Resilience and Sustainable Development: the case of the Province of Potenza and its Municipalities of Potenza and Pignola. Contributing Paper. The "State of DRR at the Local Level" A 2019 Report on the Patterns of Disaster Risk Reduction Actions at Local Level, Unisdr, Geneva (2019)
17. Attolico, A.: "Implementation of the 'resilience of communities' policy in land use planning on the provincial territory of Potenza", Contributing Paper, Global Assessment Report on Disaster Risk Reduction 2015. United Nations International Strategy for Disaster Reduction, Geneva (2014)

18. Attolico, A., Smaldone, R.: The #weResilient strategy for downscaling local resilience and sustainable development: the Potenza province and municipalities of Potenza and Pignola case. Disaster Prevention Manage. Int. J. **29**, 793–810 (2020). https://doi.org/10.1108/DPM-04-2020-0130/FULL/XML

19. Scorza, F., Attolico, A.: Innovations in promoting sustainable development: the local implementation plan designed by the Province of Potenza. In: Computational Science and Its Applications–ICCSA 2015, pp. 756–766. Springer (2015). https://doi.org/10.1007/978-3-319-21407-8_54

20. Attolico, A., Scorza, F.: A transnational cooperation perspective for "low carbon economy." In: Gervasi, O., et al. (eds.) Computational Science and Its Applications – ICCSA 2016: 16th International Conference, Beijing, China, July 4–7, 2016, Proceedings, Part I, pp. 636–641. Springer, Cham (2016). https://doi.org/10.1007/978-3-319-42085-1_54

21. Attolico, A., Smaldone, R., Scorza, F., De Marco, E., Pilogallo, A.: Investigating good practices for low carbon development perspectives in basilicata. In: Lecture Notes in Computer Science (including subseries Lecture Notes in Artificial Intelligence and Lecture Notes in Bioinformatics), pp. 763–775. Springer (2018). https://doi.org/10.1007/978-3-319-95174-4_58

22. Scorza, F., Attolico, A., Moretti, V., Smaldone, R., Donofrio, D., Laguardia, G.: Growing sustainable behaviors in local communities through smart monitoring systems for energy efficiency: RENERGY outcomes. Lecture Notes in Computer Science (including subseries Lecture Notes in Artificial Intelligence and Lecture Notes in Bioinformatics), vol. 8580. LNCS, pp. 787–793 (2014). https://doi.org/10.1007/978-3-319-09129-7_57

A Systematic Review of Climate Action Plans: A Focus on Urban Green Spaces for Adaptation and Energy Saving

Laura Ascione ⓘ, Carmela Gargiulo ⓘ, and Carmen Guida^(✉) ⓘ

Department of Civil, Building and Environmental Engineering, University of Naples Federico II, Naples, Italy
carmen.guida@unina.it

Abstract. Given the rising temperatures and more frequent and intense events typical of the climate crisis, urban areas are increasingly subject to severe effects. In the search for effective adaptation, Climate Action Plans (CAPs) are seen as one of the main strategic approaches, and within these, greening interventions emerge as cross-cutting solutions, achieving goals in both mitigation and adaptation and generating multiple benefits for urban systems.

The research reported in the current contribution is part of a broader project aimed at developing a tool in support of decision-making by policy makers for the development of more resilient cities. The present study systematically analyzes the CAPs of a sample of twenty cities recognized globally for their commitment to climate action. The objective is to identify significant relationships between the adaptation strategies put in place by the different cities and their urban, climatic, physical, social, and environmental characteristics, searching in particular to understand the role of green spaces in mitigating the effects of global warming.

To achieve this objective, a three-step methodology is proposed. In the first step, multivariate statistical analysis is used to identify clusters of cities based on their climatic, physical, social, and environmental characteristics. In the second step, topic modeling techniques are used in the systematic analysis of the classes of adaptation actions contained in the CAPs. Finally, the results of the first two steps are used to conduct a comparative analysis of cities versus classes of actions, revealing the strengths and weaknesses of the measures in the individual CAPs. This knowledge forms the basis for construction the final tool, aimed at supporting decision-makers in selecting effectively contextualized measures for application in urban scenarios.

Keywords: green space · climate action plans · urban characteristics

1 Introduction

More than half of the global population resides in urban areas and cities account for over 80% of global GDP. They serve as strategic nodes for economic activity, governance, and innovation and are central to global systems. With rising temperatures and more frequent

O. Gervasi et al. (Eds.): ICCSA 2025 Workshops, LNCS 15890, pp. 106–121, 2026.
https://doi.org/10.1007/978-3-031-97606-3_8

and intense climatic events, the impacts on cities are thus highly complex and extensive. The risks to urban citizens, infrastructure, and ecosystems are devastatingly profound, however given their role as engines of development and innovation, cities can also lead in implementing actions for climate resilience [1, 2]. Recognizing the climate risks, decision-makers have adopted strategies aiming to mitigate the most dramatic effects, however it is becoming clear that planning must also include actions for adaptation [3–7]. Actions for climate adaptation generate positive effects on other aspects of the urban system, such as in public health, enhancement of biodiversity, reduction of inequalities and promotion of economic development.

Cities are in themselves dynamic engines of change. Worldwide, numerous city administrations have joined networks to fight, adapt to and prepare for climate change [8]. Furthermore, a growing number of cities have developed a Climate Action Plan (CAP), outlining a roadmap addressing the multiple impacts of climate change and contributing to sustainable development. Such plans typically place strong emphasis on emissions reduction, but given the realities of climate change, also on adaptation [9]. In this scenario, urban greening interventions have gained ground on urban agendas as measures that contribute to both adaptation and mitigation, thereby strengthening urban resilience while simultaneously reducing greenhouse gas emissions [10, 11].

Researchers have attempted to define the range of factors, among which climatic conditions, physical morphology and socio-economic variables, which influence the exposure of a city to climate risks, its vulnerability to climate-related impacts, and its capacity to effectively implement context-specific strategies of response and adaptation. Urban climate vulnerability describes the degree to which a system is susceptible to, or unable to cope with, adverse effects of climate change. It is typically a function of exposure, sensitivity, and adaptive capacity. Urban areas with high population densities, aging infrastructure, or socio-economic inequalities tend to be more vulnerable [12]. Yılmaz and Işınkaralar [13] emphasize the crucial role of the morphological characteristics of cities in defining climate resilience policies, suggesting that CAPs should directly address such characteristics. Less concerned with actions in regard to physical context, Aboagye and Sharifi [8] instead propose a holistic approach to the socio-economic and political dimensions of urban areas. Reinwald et al. [14] share this approach, recommending climate analyses and planning maps of local characteristics to identify both risks and opportunities for adaptation and mitigation. Wamsler et al. [4] explore how urban form shapes climate resilience, offering insights into the transition from theoretical planning to practical implementation. In general these studies stress the need for CAPs tailored to the specific vulnerabilities and capacities of individual cities. It is noteworthy, however, that few studies focus on understanding the inter-relations of the climatic, physical and environmental characteristics of different cities with their specific adaptation-mitigation plans.

This contribution is part of a broader research project aimed at developing a tool that will assist policymakers and urban planners in considering the characteristics of their specific cities in making decisions on the design of climate resilience. In particular, through a systematic analysis of the CAPs of a global sample of cities that are among the most active in climate action, it investigates the relationships between urban characteristics and implemented adaptation actions, with a specific focus on the role of green spaces in mitigating the effects of global warming. To achieve this objective, a three-part methodology is developed. The first step defines clusters of cities based on their climatic, physical, social, and environmental characterization, through a series of multivariate statistical analyses. Using topic modeling techniques, the second step identifies and systematically analyzes the classes of adaptation actions proposed in the CAPs. The results from these first two steps then allow the final comparative analyses of the groups of cities versus classes of actions, thereby highlighting the strengths and weaknesses of the measures included in the CAPs.

Following this introduction, the next section of the paper provides a detailed description of the methodology developed. The third presents the results derived from the application of the method to twenty selected cities. Finally, the last section summarizes the main results and proposes directions of future research.

2   Materials and Method

The core hypothesis of the current research is that the decision-makers responsible for the development and implementation of CAPs require instruments for comprehensive understanding and analysis of urban systems, enabling them to identify climate risks and tailor approaches to address the unique vulnerabilities and capacities of each city. The methodology developed here allows systematic analysis of the interventions defined in CAPs relative to the physical, socio-economic and environmental characteristics of the cities adopting them. The specific objective of the current paper is to assess the alignment of greening actions with city profiles. The general benefits of greening approaches in urban contexts are well recognized, however for optimal effectiveness, the specific actions must be meticulously customized to suit the distinct characteristics of each city, including in terms of integration with other sectors of potential intervention, among which energy efficiency, mobility, water management and social equity, so as to foster synergies of climate resilience. Supported by tools for examination of the inter-connections, decision-makers can gain valuable insights into the way nature-based solutions contribute to broader climate adaptation and mitigation goals. Subsequently, the implementation of greening actions as part of a cohesive strategy sensitive to the specific urban characteristics, rather than in isolation, can achieve the desired synergies for the specific urban environment.

The methodology workflow (Fig. 1) is structured in three steps, as described in Fig. 1 below.

The methodology is applied to a sample of global cities selected according multiple criteria, ensuring a diverse and representative dataset. Geographic diversity is prioritized, with at least two cities from each continent, and the sample is also heterogeneous in terms of the population size, density, morphology and socio-economic conditions of the cities, all of which influence the planning and implementation of climate strategies. The cities are also selected based on their exposure to different climate hazards, among which excessive heat, rising sea levels rise and precipitation events. Finally, the cities were selected from those belonging to the C40 Climate Leadership network, formally committed to mitigation and adaptation for climate change through adoption of policies and allocation of resources, and in general for their strategic importance at the national and international levels.

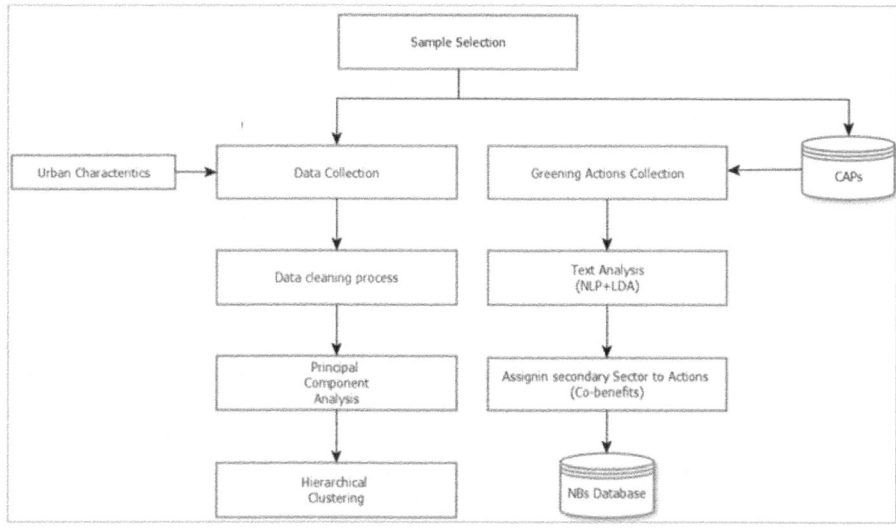

Fig. 1. Methodology workflow

Once the sample of cities is defined, two parallel analyses are conducted. The first focuses on classifying cities into groups based on urban features that influence their climate response. The second identifies the climate actions promoted in CAPs and categorizes them according to their primary and secondary sectors of focus.

The step of classifying the cities consists of four main tasks. The first two consist of collecting and cleaning data so as to accurately represent the urban characteristics that influence climate response. Based on a significant body of scientific literature, these factors can be categorized into four main domains: climate, physical environment, social dynamics, and environmental systems. For example, variables associated with the climatic domain include the maximum annual temperature recorded in each city, the Cooling Degree Days (CDD) which represents the amount of energy required to maintain indoor thermal comfort as outdoor temperatures increase. Rising cooling demand is often associated with higher electricity consumption and increased greenhouse gas emissions in cities [15]. For what concerns the physical domain, examples of relevant variables are the extension of green areas within the city and the range of elevation, defined as the difference between the highest and lowest points in the urban area. The socio-anthropic domain includes variables such as the percentage of the elderly population, considered among the most vulnerable groups, and the average monthly salary. Finally, the environmental domain encompasses variables such as the reduction in CO_2 emissions that refers to the release of carbon dioxide into the atmosphere, primarily due to the combustion of fossil fuels for electricity, transportation, heating, and industrial activities. CO_2 is the most prevalent anthropogenic greenhouse gas and a major driver of global warming [16]. All the characteristics within these domains are summarized in the table below (Table 1).

Once data collection is completed, a cleaning process is performed, followed by calculation of a correlation matrix. To ensure the stability of the dataset, variables exhibiting strong correlations are removed [17]. Then the Bartlett test of sphericity is performed to confirm whether PCA (Principal Component Analysis) would be justified on the database. Using PCA to reduce its dimensionality, hierarchical clustering is then performed to cluster cities according to their similarities in urban characteristics. This clustering helps identify patterns in the characteristics of cities that may influence the selection and implementation of greening actions.

Alongside the PCA (Principal Component Analysis) and hierarchical clustering analysis, the second step is to analyze the actions proposed in the CAPs of the selected cities, using information collected in a detailed database.

The Climate Action Plans (CAPs) of the sample cities are systematically assessed to identify the full range of promoted climate actions, and on this basis construct a structured database of actions. Once identified, the actions are classified into primary sectors using topic modeling and Natural Language Processing (NLP) [18]. Each action is assigned to a thematic category, with an additional sector representing any possible generation of co-benefits. A specialized dictionary, developed by integrating climate plan descriptions and academic literature, refines the classification process [19]. NLP techniques, such as tokenization, stop-word removal and lemmatization, ensure accurate and consistent classification of actions.

The final step of the methodology is a comparative analysis of the trends in how cities with different characteristics implement greening actions, by comparing the characteristics of the city clusters derived in the first step with the climate actions outlined in their CAPs. The development of diagrams and charts serves to accentuate patterns, similarities, and differences among cities and to identify congruencies between greening initiatives and urban characteristics. This analysis assists in understanding which urban profiles are more prone to implement specific greening actions and how these interventions contribute to the cities' climate adaptation strategies. Finally, the methodology aims to uncover insights into how urban characteristics influence the selection and effectiveness of greening actions as nature-based solutions for climate adaptation.

Based on the criteria describe above, a sample of twenty cities is selected for application of the three-step methodology, with at least two from each inhabited continent: from North America, New York, New Orleans, Los Angeles, and San Francisco; from South America, Buenos Aires and Rio de Janeiro; from Africa, Accra and Cape Town; from Europe, Milan, Paris, Barcelona, Copenhagen, Rotterdam, Istanbul; from Asia, Mumbai, Ahmedabad, Wuhan, Seoul; from Australia, Sydney and Auckland.

The selected cities are heterogeneous in population density, ranging from the very high densities of cities such as Istanbul, Mumbai and Rio de Janeiro to the lesser densities of Auckland and San Francisco. These differences can be crucial in terms of the policies and strategies needed for climate adaptation.

Moreover, the sample represents exposure to a range of climate hazards. Cities such as Rotterdam, Cape Town and New Orleans face rising sea levels, while Milan, Ahmedabad and Paris are increasingly subject to longer periods of very high temperatures. Accra and Los Angeles face problems of drought and desertification, while Mumbai, New York and Rio de Janeiro experience periodic storms of heavy rain.

Although not all of the selected cities are national capitals, all serve as important economic, social and cultural hubs at regional or global levels.

Table 1. Urban system characteristics affecting cities response to extreme events, according to literature review

System	Variable	Description	References
Climatic	Average annual temperature	Annual average of temperatures recorded in a year	[12, 20]
	Maximum annual temperature	Maximum temperature recorded from October 2023 to September 2024	
	Cooling degrees days	Summation over a year of the days with average temperature in excess of thermal comfort temperature (25 °C)	[12]
	Difference between the average temperature of urban and rural area	Annual average of the difference in average temperature between urban and surrounding rural areas	[12, 21]
	Maximum wind speed	Annual maximum wind speed	
	Average wind speed	Annual average wind speed	
	Maximum monthly average of mm of precipitation	Maximum value of average monthly rainfall over one year	[22]
	Average number of days per month when a rain event occurred	Annual average of number of days per month with a rainfall event	
	Standard deviation of the number of days per month in which a rainfall event occurred	Annual standard deviation of the number of days per month with a rainfall event	
Physical	Range of elevation	Difference between maximum and minimum elevation	[23]
	Linear extension of coast	Linear measure of any coastal frontage	[24]
	Altitude	Weighted average altitude with respect to the territorial extension of the city, compared to the average sea level	[23]
	Green space extension	Percentage of extension of total green spaces relative to extension of the entire city	[20, 25]
	Percentage of water coverage	Percentage of extension of water bodies relative to extension of the entire city	[25]

(*continued*)

Table 1. (*continued*)

System	Variable	Description	References
	Extension of urban area	Extension of the surface of the urbanized area	
	Building Coverage Ratio	Percentage of land occupied by buildings relative to extension of the entire city	
Socio-anthropic	Population	Total number of residents	[22, 25]
	Population density	Ratio between population and urban area extension	[25]
	Percentage of elderly population	Percentage of elderly inhabitants (over age 65) out of total population	[22]
	Percentage of population below the poverty line	Percentage of population living below the poverty threshold, defined at national or local level	[22, 26]
	Unemployment rate	Percentage of the population that is unemployed	[25, 26]
	Average monthly salary	Average monthly salary (net after tax) in euros	
Environmental	Percentage of renewable energy used	Percentage of energy consumed from renewable sources relative to total energy consumed per year	[12, 27]
	Percentage of energy consumed in the transport sector	Percentage of total energy consumed for transport relative to total energy consumed per year	[28]
	Percentage reduction in CO2 emissions over the past ten years	Percentage reduction in CO_2 emissions over the past 10 years	[12, 29]
	Percentage of use of sustainable modes of transport	Percentage of journeys made using sustainable modes of transport, i.e. walking, cycling, public transport	[12, 30]

The collection of data on the variables outlined in Table 1 relied on open sources. Some data, in particular on reductions in CO_2 emissions, were not always available from open sources. In these cases, the existing data on current emissions were used as a substitute.

3 Results

This section presents the findings from the application of the three methodological steps, as outlined above.

The first step was the set of statistical multivariate analyses to assess the robustness of the sample and then cluster the selected cities based on features affecting their response to climate hazards, as identified through review of the scientific literature.

First, to address multi-collinearity, two highly correlated variables identified in the analysis, Max TY (annual maximum temperature) and MaxPrecipIntensity (annual maximum precipitation intensity) for selected locations, were removed from the dataset. The Bartlett test was then conducted, yielding a p-value lower than 0.0005, confirming the statistical significance necessary to proceed with Principal Component Analysis (PCA).

The PCA results show that the first five principal components explain over 70% of the total variance, indicating a strong explanatory power of the selected variables. PC1 combines both climatic factors (patterns of temperature and precipitation) and socio-economic factors (e.g. CO_2 emissions), revealing relationships between cooling demand, climate vulnerability, and emissions.

The higher emissions of this component are linked with increased climate vulnerability, suggesting that areas with greater emissions are more susceptible to climate-related risks. PC2 primarily captures socio-economic dynamics, involving factors such as income distribution and urban infrastructure with physical variables such as range of elevation. The inclusion of this latter factor would reflect its role in shaping local climate impacts. PC3 integrates physical characteristics, such as land use and density, with sustainable mobility patterns. PC4 is influenced by both physical features and socio-economic elements (such as population density), capturing the complexity of urbanization and its effects on environmental sustainability. PC5 is primarily shaped by CO_2 emissions and urban sprawl, with lower-density cities showing greater reliance on private transport and less sustainable mobility, which reflects the challenges posed by urban expansion. The contribution of all urban, climatic, and socio-economic variables in these principal components reveals their relevance for further analysis and provides a solid foundation for understanding the multifaceted nature of urban climate adaptation.

The combination of correlated variables into composite components was used to provide a clearer understanding of the key factors driving urban resilience and, consequently, how cities have been clustered. The hierarchical clustering (Fig. 2) categorizes cities based on the selected variables, with these groupings further clarified through PCA.

Cities in Cluster 1 (Cape Town, Auckland, Istanbul, Seoul, Rio de Janeiro, and Los Angeles) are characterized by their coastal positioning, variable elevations, extensive green space, and moderate cooling demand. However, these cities exhibit a lower level of reliance on sustainable mobility measures.

The second cluster is comprised exclusively of Wuhan, a city that merits particular attention due to its minimal seasonal climate variability, its substantial reliance on sustainable transportation, and its low population density dispersed across an extensive urban area.

Cluster 3, which includes Accra, Ahmedabad, and Mumbai, is characterized by high cooling demand, significant climate variability, low CO_2 emissions, extreme population

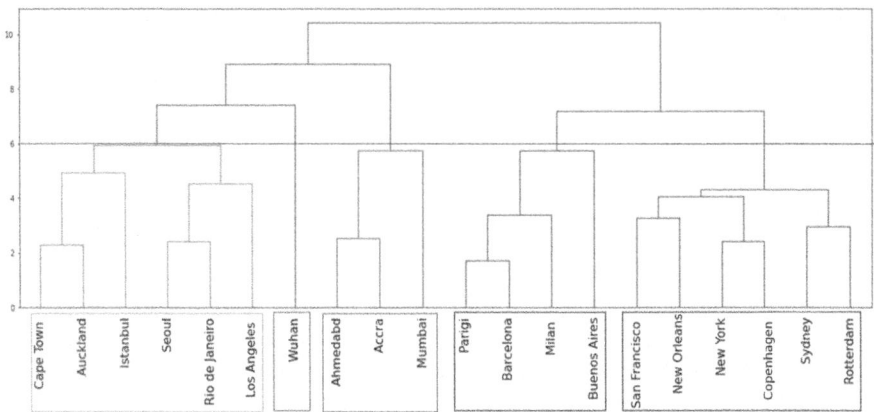

Fig. 2. Hierarchical cluster analysis dendrogram

density in small urban areas, and predominantly young populations. Cluster 4, which includes the cities of Barcelona, Buenos Aires, Milan, and Paris, is characterized by stable annual precipitation patterns, moderate population density, and a high proportion of sustainable mobility. These factors suggest that cities may have prioritized climate action through mitigation policies, such as more sustainable mobility.

Cluster 5, which includes the cities of San Francisco, New Orleans, New York, Copenhagen, Sydney, and Rotterdam, is characterized by a low demand for cooling, temperate climates with high carbon dioxide emissions, and high average incomes. However, some of these cities are low-lying and therefore particularly vulnerable to climate risks such as rising sea levels.

This clustering approach offers a structured understanding of how different urban characteristics and climate risks shape city-level adaptation strategies, providing a foundation for further analysis of climate action plans.

The second methodological step involved a systematic review of CAPs and the actions they promote. To categorise climate interventions by sector, a refined dictionary was developed. This dictionary serves to augment the NLP and Topic Modeling process by referencing two sources: the actions delineated in Climate Action Plans (CAPs) and the findings of Jin et al. [19]. The latter applied a similar topic modeling approach to climate action documents.

The dictionary classifies actions into ten sectors. The Urban Planning and Policies sector encompasses measures pertaining to territorial planning. The Energy and Buildings sector focuses on the adoption of renewable energy sources and enhancement of building energy efficiency. Mobility and Transport encompasses strategies for sustainable mobility. The Waste Management and Resource Management sector focuses on optimization of resources and waste recycling. The Climate Emergency sector encompasses emergency response actions, particularly related to extreme weather events, public health and urban safety. Community Engagement and Communications encompasses initiatives to raise public awareness and engage residents in climate planning. The Sustainable Economy and Finance sector encompasses initiatives promoting a circular economy, while actions under Responsible Consumption and Sustainable Lifestyles promote more sustainable everyday behaviors. The Monitoring and Evaluation sector encompasses actions for assessing the effectiveness of adaptation and mitigation strategies.

Finally, the sector of Green Space and Biodiversity, of particular interest to the current study, encompasses urban greening initiatives and actions for conservation of biodiversity. This sector includes interventions for enhancing, preserving, and managing urban natural assets, at both neighborhood and city-wide levels. Examples seen among the twenty selected cities would include tree planting campaigns in Milan and Los Angeles, creation and connection of blue-green corridors in Rotterdam and San Francisco, and promotion of green roofs in Barcelona and Mumbai. In the Ahmedabad CAP we see the critical role of green spaces in the action of opening parks and gardens for extended hours during heat alerts. Among many of the twenty cities there are programs of assistance, advice and training to build the capacities and capabilities of local communities in developing and protecting green areas. Given the multifaceted nature of these actions and interventions, which often extend across multiple sectors, a secondary sector classification was assigned to each action. However, for the purpose of this contribution, only actions classified under Green Space and Biodiversity as either their primary or secondary sector were considered.

The final methodological step was the comparative analysis integrating the results from cluster analysis with the database of actions for green spaces. The initial result of this analysis is a pie chart, seen in Fig. 3, displaying the ten sectors of all of actions planned under the CAPs, in which Green Space and Biodiversity is seen to account for 9% of aggregate actions. A second pie chart relating to the first one focuses on Green Space and Biodiversity, assigning the actions to the five clusters of cities identified in the first methodological step. This approach facilitates the identification of the clusters that implement the most actions.

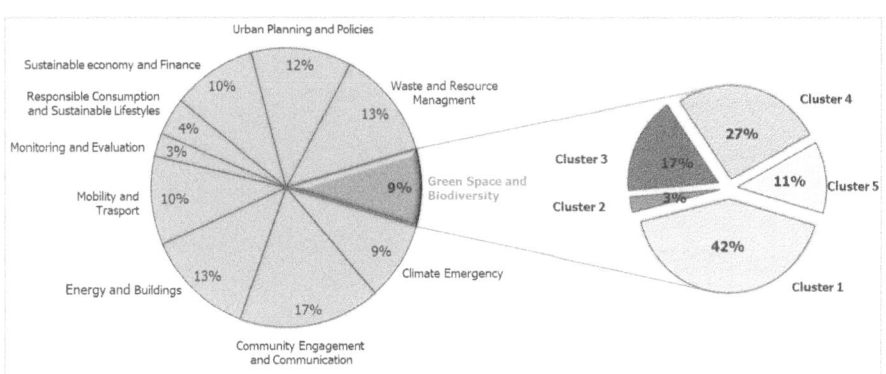

Fig. 3. The first pie illustrates the distribution of actions across ten sectors. The second pie provides a detailed analysis of Green Space and Biodiversity actions, by cluster.

Within these percentages, it is notable that clusters 1 and 4 have the highest number of planned green space actions, while cluster 2 shows the lowest absolute number. However, relating the total number of actions within each cluster to the numerosity of cities, it can be observed that green space actions never exceed 20% of total actions in a cluster, while in clusters 3, 4 and 5, green space actions are always less than 10% of the total actions.

Figure 4b instead illustrates planned actions in other sectors that have the potential to positively impact green space and biodiversity. The analysis indicates that the Waste and Resource Management sector is the most significant contributor, with a percentage of 31%. This finding suggests a robust correlation between circular economy initiatives and the enhancement of urban ecological systems. Community Engagement and Communication also plays a role, with 21% of association. This finding underscores the

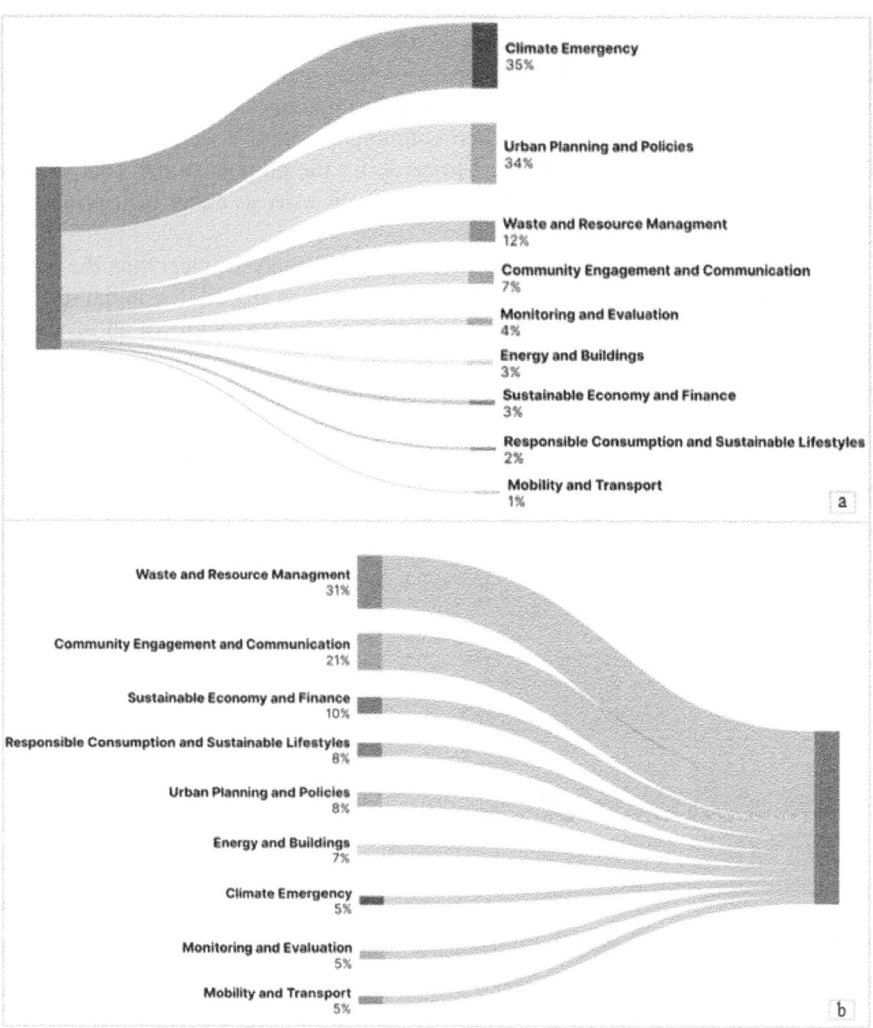

Fig. 4. (a) Sectors benefiting from greening and biodiversity actions. (b) Sectors generating benefits for greening and biodiversity

significance of participatory and awareness-raising initiatives in fostering stewardship of greenspace and enhancing biodiversity protection.

Other sectors, among which Climate Emergency, Monitoring and Evaluation, and Mobility and Transport, exhibit a mere 5% of actions yielding co-benefits in the green space sector. These percentages suggest that greater attention could be directed toward identifying and enhancing green co-benefits in the relative sectors, and may reflect underexplored potentials. The diagrams also demonstrate that green space actions are multifunctional and can provide co-benefits in a broad spectrum of urban governance domains.

4 Conclusions

This contribution represents the first result in research aimed at building a tool to support the decisions of policymakers and urban planners in designing more resilient cities in relation to their specific characteristics.

In particular, the current study provides an updated framework for the analysis and understanding of how very large cities equip themselves to respond to the challenges posed by climate change, through the identification of strategies and actions for mitigation and adaptation within their Climate Action Plans (CAPs). The particular interest of the current study is to understand the results achieved through actions of greening and promotion of biodiversity. The proposed methodology proceeds in three steps, aimed at identifying the relationships between the characteristics of cities and the adaptive actions and interventions for minimization of effects from climate change [31]. The first research step applies multivariate statistical analysis to classify the sample of cities based on their urban characteristics (climatic, physical, socio-economic, environmental, etc.). The second step applies topic modeling to classify the actions of the CAPs into different categories, following a preliminary review of scientific literature aimed at identifying all the possible actions and interventions considered effective in respect of the various urban characteristics (physical, functional, environmental, climatic, etc.). The last methodological step consists of a comparative analysis between city clusters to identify specific actions adopted in the plans relative to the actual urban characteristics.

While it presents the overall results of sectors of CAP actions relative to urban characteristics for the twenty cities under study, this contribution focuses on the actions taken for green spaces. The study identified how the different clusters of cities implement greening interventions in respect of their specificities and strategies for climate-related management. As shown in Fig. 3, Clusters 1 and 4 have the highest absolute number of actions for green spaces. Cluster 1 includes cities such as Cape Town and Rio de Janeiro, known for their coastal location and important range of altitude. Cluster 4, includes cities such as Barcelona and Paris, characterized by stable precipitation patterns and high levels of sustainable mobility. In contrast, Cluster 3, which includes cities like Ahmedabad and Mumbai, characterized by a high cooling demand and high population density, and Cluster 5, which includes cities like New York and Rotterdam, known for their temperate climates and high CO_2 emissions, show relatively low percentages of actions for green spaces. It is noteworthy that actions for green spaces never exceed 20% in any cluster and are less than 10% in clusters 3, 4, and 5, indicating that while greening is considered, it is often not the primary objective of the CAP. As illustrated in Fig. 4(a), which outlines the sectors in which greening initiatives also generate benefits in other sectors, such positive impacts are predominantly concentrated in the sectors of climate emergency (35%) and urban planning and policies (34%). This underscores that green spaces are not only beneficiaries of other urban strategies but are deemed essential for mitigating climate-related emergencies and defining strategic urban development. The significant role of green spaces in urban planning and policies indicates that cities recognize the need for holistic approaches, integrating green space planning into broader urban development frameworks. In contrast, Fig. 4(b), which illustrates the sectors that generate benefits for green spaces, highlights Waste and Resource Management (31%) and Community Engagement and Communication (21%). This suggests that cities recognize the multiple impacts of greening beyond environmental benefits, acknowledging its potential to promote broader sustainability goals, such as waste reduction and increased community engagement.

These results, taken together, emphasize the recognition of green spaces as strategic elements for implementing urban resilience and sustainability, highlighting their dual role as contributors and beneficiaries of various urban sectors [32–35]. The research and methodology proposed in the current work represent a fundamental step towards the broader research aim of defining a comprehensive decision-support tool for climate adaptation actions tailored in respect of the main characteristics of urban areas, thereby avoiding maladaptation. By analyzing the relationships between CAPs and the specific characteristics of the cities that adopted them, this study has developed a valuable collection of actions and insights. This collection can serve as a basis for future research and development activities, with the goal of providing urban planners and policymakers with concrete and specific recommendations integrate green space initiatives into their climate adaptation strategies in manners suitable for their specific context.

Despite the fact that the study yielded significant results, it is important to note that it is not without certain limitations. It is acknowledged that reliance on open data sources, while promoting replicability of the methodology, can result in inconsistencies and missing values due to variations in update frequency, spatial and temporal resolutions, and data collection protocols. In order to limit such inconsistencies, when specific selected indicators were unavailable, proxy variables were employed to approximate the intended dimensions of analysis. Although proxies can be useful, they may also introduce additional uncertainty, particularly when their relevance or correlation with the variables is context dependent. In the context of ongoing research, the analysis of cities from the same region is proposed as a solution to mitigate potential biases arising from collecting data exclusively from open sources.

The topic modeling approach, while effective, may overly simplify the complex language of the CAP, overlooking important details. Furthermore, the categorization of complex climate actions into primary and secondary sectors may overly abstract the interconnected nature of these interventions, reducing the understanding of other benefits and synergies. Given these limitations, and considering that the current study has been limited to twenty cities, future research will expand the sample of cities to include a broader range of urban contexts, refine data collection methodologies to minimize inconsistencies and gaps and also incorporate qualitative data, such as interviews with stakeholders and case studies, to provide a more articulated understanding of the decision-making processes underlying the development of the CAP.

References

1. Batty, M.: Complexity in city systems: understanding, evolution, and design. In: Healey, P. (ed.) A Planner's Encounter with Complexity, pp. 99–122. Routledge, London (2016)
2. Portugali, J.: Handbook on Cities and Complexity. Edward Elgar Publishing, Cheltenham (2021) https://doi.org/10.4337/9781789900125
3. Laukkonen, J., Blanco, P.K., Lenhart, J., Keiner, M., Cavric, B., Kinuthia-Njenga, C.: Combining climate change adaptation and mitigation measures at the local level. Habitat Int. **33**(3), 287–292 (2009). https://doi.org/10.1016/j.habitatint.2008.10.003
4. Wamsler, C., Brink, E., Rivera, C.: Planning for climate change in urban areas: from theory to practice. J. Clean. Prod. **50**(2), 68–81 (2013). https://doi.org/10.1016/j.jclepro.2012.12.008
5. Papa, R., Galderisi, A., Vigo Majello, M.C., Saretta, E.: European cities dealing with climate issues: ideas and tools for a better framing of current practices. TeMA – J. Land Use Mobility Environ. 63–80 (2015). https://doi.org/10.6092/1970-9870/3658
6. Zucaro, F., Morosini, R.: Sustainable land use and climate adaptation: a review of European local plans. TeMA – J. Land Use Mobility Environ. **11**(1), 7–26 (2018). https://doi.org/10.6092/1970-9870/5343
7. Scorza, F., Santopietro, L.: A systemic perspective for the sustainable energy and climate action plan (SECAP). Eur. Plan. Stud. **32**(2), 281–301 (2024). https://doi.org/10.1080/09654313.2021.1954603
8. Aboagye, P.D., Sharifi, A.: Urban climate adaptation and mitigation action plans: a critical review. Renew. Sustain. Energy Rev. **189**, 113886 (2024). https://doi.org/10.1016/j.rser.2023.113886
9. Stone, B., Vargo, J., Habeeb, D.: Managing climate change in cities: will climate action plans work? Landsc. Urban Plan. **107**(3), 263–271 (2012). https://doi.org/10.1016/j.landurbplan.2012.05.014
10. Kabisch, N., et al.: Nature-based solutions to climate change mitigation and adaptation in urban areas: perspectives on indicators, knowledge gaps, barriers, and opportunities for action. Ecol. Soc. **21**(2) (2016). http://www.jstor.org/stable/26270403
11. Mazzeo, G., Polverino, S.: Nature-based solution for climate change adaptation and mitigation in urban areas with high natural risk. TeMA – J. Land Use Mobility Environ. **16**(1), 47–65 (2023). https://doi.org/10.6093/1970-9870/9736
12. Intergovernmental Panel on Climate Change (IPCC): Climate Change 2022: Impacts, Adaptation, and Vulnerability. Contribution of Working Group II to the Sixth Assessment Report of the Intergovernmental Panel on Climate Change. In: Pörtner, H.-O., et al. (eds.) Cambridge University Press, Cambridge (2022). https://doi.org/10.1017/9781009325844
13. Yılmaz, D., Işınkaralar, Ö.: Climate action plans under climate-resilient urban policies. Kastamonu Univ. J. Eng. Sci. **7**(2), 140–147 (2021)
14. Reinwald, F., Thiel, S., Kainz, A., Hahn, C.: Components of urban climate analyses for the development of planning recommendation maps. Urban Clim. **57** (2024). https://doi.org/10.1016/j.uclim.2024.102090
15. Santamouris, M., et al.: On the impact of urban heat island and global warming on the power demand and electricity consumption of buildings—a review. Energy Build. **98**, 119–124 (2015)
16. Environmental Protection Agency (EPA): Carbon Dioxide Emissions. https://www.epa.gov/ghgemissions/carbon-dioxide-emissions (2023)

17. Asuero, A.G., Sayago, A., González, A.G.: The correlation coefficient: an overview. Crit. Rev. Anal. Chem. **36**(1), 41–59 (2006). https://doi.org/10.1080/10408340500526766

18. Jelodar, H., et al.: Latent dirichlet allocation (LDA) and topic modeling: models, applications, a survey. Multimedia Tools Appl. **78**, 15169–15211 (2019). https://doi.org/10.1007/s11042-018-6894-4

19. Jin, S., Stokes, G., Hamilton, C.: Empirical evidence of urban climate adaptation alignment with sustainable development: Application of LDA. Cities **136**, 104254 (2023). https://doi.org/10.1016/j.cities.2023.104254

20. Ferranti, E., Cook, S., Greenham, S., Grayson, N., Futcher, J., Salter, K.: Incorporating heat vulnerability into local authority decision making: an open access approach. Sustainability **15**(18), 13501 (2023). https://doi.org/10.3390/su151813501

21. Isinkaralar, O., Sharifi, A., Isinkaralar, K.: Assessing spatial thermal comfort and adaptation measures for the antalya basin under climate change scenarios. Clim. Change **177**, 118 (2024). https://doi.org/10.1007/s10584-024-03781-8

22. Ramli, M.W.A., et al: Spatial multidimensional vulnerability assessment index in urban area – a case study Selangor, Malaysia. Prog. Disaster Sci. **20**, 100296 (2023). https://doi.org/10.1016/j.pdisas.2023.100296

23. Ahmadi, S., Amjadi, H., Chapi, K., Soodmand Afshar, R., Ebrahimi, B.: Fuzzy flash flood risk and vulnerability assessment for the city of Sanandaj, Kurdistan Province. Iran. Nat. Hazards **115**, 237–259 (2023). https://doi.org/10.1007/s11069-022-05552-z

24. Wu, T.: Quantifying coastal flood vulnerability for climate adaptation policy using principal component analysis. Ecol. Ind. **129**, 108006 (2021). https://doi.org/10.1016/j.ecolind.2021.108006

25. Sun, Y., Li, Y., Ma, R., Gao, C., Wu, Y.: Mapping urban socio-economic vulnerability related to heat risk: a grid-based assessment framework by combining the geospatial big data. Urban Climate **43**, 101169 (2022). https://doi.org/10.1016/j.uclim.2022.101169

26. Leichenko, R., Silva, J.A.: Climate change and poverty: vulnerability, impacts, and alleviation strategies. Wiley Interdisc. Rev. Clim. Change **5**(4), 539–556 (2014). https://doi.org/10.1002/wcc.287

27. Olabi, A.G., Abdelkareem, M.A.: Renewable energy and climate change. Renew. Sustain. Energy Rev. **158**, 112111 (2022). https://doi.org/10.1016/j.rser.2022.112111

28. Chapman, L.: Transport and climate change: review. J. Transp. Geogr. **15**(5), 354–367 (2007). https://doi.org/10.1016/j.jtrangeo.2006.11.008

29. Hansen, J., et al.: Assessing "dangerous climate change": Required reduction of carbon emissions to protect young people, future generations and nature. PLOS ONE **8**(12), e81648 (2013). https://doi.org/10.1371/journal.pone.0081648

30. Mashayekh, Y., et al.: Potentials for sustainable transportation in cities to alleviate climate change impacts. Environ. Sci. Technol. **46**(5), 2529–2537 (2012). https://doi.org/10.1021/es203353q

31. Codemo, A., Favargiotti, S., Albatici, R.: Fostering the climate-energy transition with an integrated approach. TeMA – J. Land Use Mobility Environ. **14**(1), 5–20 (2021). https://doi.org/10.6092/1970-9870/7157

32. Gargiulo, C., Tulisi, A., Zucaro, F.: Climate change-oriented urban green network design: a decision support tool. In: Network Design and Optimization for Smart Cities, pp. 255–278 (2017). https://doi.org/10.1142/9789813200012_0011

33. Gargiulo, C., Lombardi, C.: Urban retrofit and resilience: the challenge of energy efficiency and vulnerability. TeMA – J. Land Use Mobility Environ. **9**(2), 137–162 (2016). https://doi.org/10.6092/1970-9870/3922

34. Gargiulo, C., Zucaro, F.: A method proposal to adapt urban open-built and green spaces to climate change. Sustainability **15**, 8111 (2023). https://doi.org/10.3390/su15108111

35. Zucaro, F., Gargiulo, C.: Greening networks for smart and resilient cities: from methodology to application in densely built urban contexts. Archivio di studi urbani e regionali 127(Suppl. 1), Franco Angeli, Milano (2020)

Carbon Sequestration and Provision of Ecosystem Services: Evidence from Campania Region, Italy

Federica Isola⬤, Francesca Leccis⬤, Federica Leone$^{(\boxtimes)}$⬤, and Corrado Zoppi⬤

Department of Civil and Environmental Engineering and Architecture, University of Cagliari, Cagliari, Italy
{federica.isola,francescaleccis,federicaleone,zoppi}@unica.it

Abstract. A methodological approach is implemented here that aims to study the relationships between climate neutrality and the supply of ecosystem services (ESs), with reference to regional spatial contexts. The measure of carbon sequestration (CS) is taken as a reference to estimate the status and evolutionary dynamics of this phenomenon, which is analyzed and evaluated as associated with the supply of certain types of ESs, in relation to the reference spatial context. The study is developed as follows.

First, the spatial framework of the CS is characterized through density maps, using the "Carbon Storage and Sequestration" model of the InVEST suite. Second, a methodology for characterizing the supply of ESs is identified. Based on in-depth analyses of environmental, landscape and cultural contexts, the supply of ESs in relation to the Campania regional territory is characterized in this study by the following types: preservation of habitat quality; regulation of the local climate through mitigation of land surface temperature; production of agricultural and wood crops; protection and enhancement of the attractiveness of spatial contexts in relation to recreational and cultural activities; and preservation and enhancement of landscape values that ground regional identity.

Finally, the correlations between the spatial taxonomies of CS and ESs supply with regard to the regional context of Campania are analyzed to assess how the characteristics and specificities of ESs supply can be used to foster climate neutrality. These correlations allow, also, to identify specific recommendations related to plan policies, finalized to improve the quality of life of local communities.

Keywords: Carbon Sequestration · Climate Neutrality · Ecosystem Services

1 Introduction

In this study, a methodological approach that aims to implement climate neutrality through spatial planning policies is defined and applied. The measure of carbon sequestration (CS) is taken as a reference to estimate the status and evolutionary dynamics of this phenomenon, analyzed and evaluated as associated with the supply of certain types of ecosystem services (ESs), in relation to the reference spatial context.

O. Gervasi et al. (Eds.): ICCSA 2025 Workshops, LNCS 15890, pp. 122–139, 2026.
https://doi.org/10.1007/978-3-031-97606-3_9

Climate change is affecting both rural and urban areas with increasing intensity, compromising well-being and quality of life. Its consequences, which are now evident, call for urgent action, especially to meet the Paris Agreement target of limiting global warming to 1.5 °C by 2030. The European Union (EU) has initiated several mitigation and adaptation strategies, including the Green Deal and the "Ready for 55" package, aimed at climate neutrality by 2050 and a 55% reduction in emissions by 2030 compared to 1990 levels. These actions are based on the European Climate Act, which obliges Member States to fulfil their commitments. The strategies are implemented at the national, regional and local scales.

In order to effectively integrate CS issues into policies and strategies at different planning levels, a thorough understanding of this process and the aspects that most contribute to achieving climate neutrality, including in terms of multiple provision of ESs, is required. Natural ecosystems provide multiple services that mutually influence each other, positively or negatively. In order to define effective planning choices, it is necessary to fully exploit the potential of nature by considering the existing relationships between different ESs in terms of synergies and trade-offs, since, if not properly studied and implemented, measures aimed at increasing CS in habitats could have negative effects on biodiversity and other services produced by the same ecosystem.

The study is developed as follows.

First, the spatial framework of the CS is characterized through density maps, using the "Carbon Storage and Sequestration" model of the InVEST (Integrated Valuation of Ecosystem Services and Tradeoffs) suite, which estimates the amount of carbon stored in spatial units of reference using raster maps of land cover. The model estimates the state of CS, also allowing for appreciation of its variation over time. The spatial context targeted by the implementation of the methodology is Campania, an administrative region in southern Italy.

Second, a methodology to characterize the supply of ESs is identified. Based on previous studies and in-depth analyses of environmental, landscape, and socio-cultural contexts, the supply of ESs in relation to the regional territory of Campania is characterized, in this study, by the following types: preservation of habitat quality levels suitable for sustaining the life cycles of wild plants and animals that can be useful to humans; climate regulation through mitigation of land surface temperature; production of agricultural and wood crops; protection and enhancement of the attractiveness of spatial contexts in relation to nature- and natural resource-based recreational and cultural activities; preservation and enhancement of landscape values that ground the regional identity.

Finally, the correlations between the spatial taxonomies of CS capacity and ESs supply with regard to the regional Campanian context are detected and analyzed, in order to assess how the characteristics and specificities of the multifunctional supply of ESs can be effectively used in order to maximize CS capacity, and, thus, the contribution of the Campania Region to the improvement of global climate neutrality. The identification of these correlations makes it possible, also, to identify specific recommendations in terms of plan policies in order to improve the quality of life of local societies in Campania.

2 Materials and Methods

This section is organized as follows. First, the regional context of Campania is presented, as regards its features as for supply of CS and the other ESs which are involved in this study. Secondly, the methodology used to detect the spatial taxonomy of the provision of CS and of the other ESs is described, which is implemented through the identification of the spatial taxonomies of CS capacity, levels of habitat quality, land surface temperature (LST) mitigation, agricultural and forestry production, landscape value and outdoor recreation features. Finally, a multiple regression is estimated, in order to detect spatial correlations between CS and the ESs supply.

2.1 Campania Region

Campania, located in Southern Italy, covers about 13,700 square kilometers and borders Latium, Molise, Apulia, Basilicata, and the Tyrrhenian Sea. The Region's geography is predominantly hilly and mountainous, with 51% of its surface being hills and 35% mountains. The plains, mostly alluvial, cover only 14% of the area. Campania features coastal plains like the Campana and Sele Plains, as well as ancient lake basins between mountainous regions such as the Matese, Sannio, Irpinia, and Alburni Mountains. The Region also has volcanic areas, such as Vesuvius and Phlegraean Plain.

2.2 Provision of Ecosystem Services

This subsection reports synthetic descriptions of the six ecosystem services whose influence on CS is assessed and, therefore, whose impact on climate neutrality is analyzed. The description includes the measurement methods and spatial taxonomy of ES provision.

Land Surface Temperature

LST is an important climate variable to identify phenomena related to thermal emissions that are produced between the Earth's surface and the overlying atmosphere. This temperature directly affects air temperature and is one of the main parameters in physics of processes occurring between land and surface, both on regional and global scales. The methodological approach to LST mapping and assessment implemented here provides the identification of temperature anomalies and peaks in the study area, and it is applied as follows.

LST is obtained from the satellite images through the United States Geological Survey (USGS)'s Earth Explorer interface, specifically utilizing the Landsat 2 - Level 2 collection (Landsat 8–9 OLI/TIRS C2 L2)[1], which provides 30-m LST raster maps[2]. The LST variable was detected during Summer 2023, the date range was set from the last week of June (June 25, 2023) to the first week of September (September 2, 2023), with a maximum cloud cover threshold of 6%. Specifically, the information utilized is

---

[1] The Landsat collection 8-9 incorporates the Operational Land Imager (OLI) and Thermal Infra-Red Sensor (TIRS) sensors.

[2] Earth Explorer by U.S. Geological Survey. Available from https://earthexplorer.usgs.gov/. [Accessed: 2025.03.26].

derived from the Landsat B10 thermal band, which provides data on the Earth's surface temperature. To obtain the mean values in Celsius degrees (°C), the scale factor provided by the USGS Guide is utilized using the digital number (DN) values in raster images:

$$0.00341802 * DN + 149.0 - 273.15 \; (°C) \tag{1}$$

Satellite scenes do not cover the whole Campania Region; to create a complete map, therefore, several raster images are required. Different scenes' merged raster images are needed. Merged images with high mean values are selected to compose the LST map.

Habitat Quality

Habitat quality denotes the ability of a habitat to sustain species survival and population persistence [1], nevertheless, it is increasingly imperiled by anthropogenic land-use transformations. These alterations fragment the landscape and reduce its connectivity, thereby undermining ecosystem health and their capacity to deliver crucial services [2].

The InVEST Habitat Quality model is acknowledged as a reliable and efficient tool for assessing habitat quality. This GIS-based software maps the distribution of habitats while accounting for their degree of degradation, using habitat quality and rarity as proxies for biodiversity.

The model computes the Habitat Quality Index (HQI) by incorporating five essential factors: (i) Land Use Land Cover (LULC), (ii) threats and their corresponding impacts, (iii) habitat proximity to threats, (iv) habitat suitability, and (v) habitat sensitivity [3]. Mandatory inputs encompass the land cover data; threat raster layers, the threat table detailing the maximum impact distance, impact intensity, spatial decay function, and storage path for each threat raster; the sensitivity table indicating habitat suitability and relative sensitivity to each threat, and the half-saturation constant.

Habitat quality is mapped and measured using a dimensionless index ranging from 0 to 1. Although not a direct biodiversity metric, this score enables comparative evaluations. Higher values indicate superior habitat quality in relation to surrounding areas, whereas lower scores highlight areas with poor habitat quality. Results are visualized in a habitat quality gradient map, which illustrates the spatial distribution of habitat quality and the extent of habitat degradation across the Region.

Value of Agricultural and Forestry Production

Agricultural and forestry production qualifies as a provisioning ES. Provisioning ESs are material goods such as food, fresh water, timber, fiber, and energy resources. There are multiple methodological approaches that can be implemented to assess this ES.

The method used in this study assesses agricultural and forestry production (VAFP) based on location, altitude, morphology, and orography, by means of two datasets: the National Dataset for agricultural areas, which shows the land monetary value per unit area, provided by the National Research Council of Agriculture and Agricultural Economics (CREA); and, the National Dataset for forestry areas, which shows the mean values (MVs) per unit area, provided by the National Revenue Agency (NRA). The data on agrarian regions are reported in the "List of agrarian regions associated to municipalities, subdivided by region, province and elevation zone", related to the CREA's Land values Database[3].

Subsequently, correspondences between the 2018 CORINE Land Cover classes and the types of agricultural crops defined by CREA for the agricultural value, and the taxonomy of the NRA for the forestry value were established. Finally, to analyze spatial distribution of mean agricultural and forestry land values, a land cover vector map to be overlaid on the agroforestry value vector map. This allows the value of agricultural and forestry production to be identified for each spatial unit of land cover.

Landscape Value

Landscape value is strictly associated to individual perception and personal experience, yet various methodologies have been developed, and different indicators have been defined to objectively assess landscape quality, on the assumption that consensus on landscape quality perception is shared among individuals [4]. Scenic beauty assumes a crucial aesthetic role as it serves as a measurable indicator of landscape beauty, determining whether its visual qualities inspire human admiration [5]. Scenic beauty, a fundamental aesthetic measure, is positively influenced by natural elements such as vegetation and water features, which elevate perceived value [6]. In contrast, anthropogenic infrastructure such as wind turbines and solar farms, commonly diminishes its perceived quality. These principles are operationalized by the InVEST Scenic Quality model, which measures visual disamenities to determine landscape quality. It creates viewshed maps from observer perspectives and calculates the visibility of landscape detractors while taking topography and terrestrial curvature into consideration. These viewsheds are defined using the region's Digital Elevation Model (DEM) and geospatial markers of visually impactful features. They reflect the unobstructed 360-degree area visible from an observation site.

Landscape quality is mapped and quantified with integer Impact Values (IV) ranging from 0 to 4. This score is unitless and does not correspond to any specific measurement of landscape quality; instead, it serves as a relative index of visual quality within the landscape studied. Higher values indicate higher visual impact, and, consequently, diminished visual quality in relation to surrounding areas, whereas lower scores indicate a reduced visual impact, and, consequently, superior visual quality. Locations completely unaffected by visual disamenities are assigned a score of 0.

Recreational Service Supply

Recreational services are a sub-category of cultural ESs [7], including activities like walking and cycling, and provide non-material benefits that enhance mental, physical, and social well-being. Accessibility, landscape features, and proximity to nature are key factors in making these services attractive and beneficial.

The assessment of recreational service value (RECVA) relies on ESTIMAP (Ecosystem Service Mapping Tool), a GIS-based model developed in 2013 by a group of the

---

[3] Documentation on agricultural regions is available online at: https:// www.crea.gov.it/docume nts/68457/0/Regioni+agrarie+indagine+MF+INEA.xlsx/8019a0cb-f3d4-dcd9-6639-d178e9 f2e89e?t=1561366035978 (Accessed: 2025.03.26).

Joint Research Centre (JRC) of the European Commission. The ESTIMAP recreation model helps assess how ecosystems support outdoor activities and contact with nature. In this study, only the first part of the original ESTIMAP model, developed by Vallecillo et al. [8] and Barton et al. [9] is applied to evaluate the recreational potential of Campania Region, based on Isola et al. [10].

The methodological approach follows three key phases. The first phase examines the availability of natural areas for recreation, considering their degree of naturalness, measured using the hemeroby index (HI) [11]. HI determines how much human activity has altered an ecosystem. HI ranges from 0 (completely natural) to 9 (highly artificial) [10]. The second phase studies the presence of protected areas and landscape assets, assigning scores based on conservation objectives [12]. Areas are classified according to IUCN categories, and their importance is reflected in a raster map, where higher values indicate greater recreational potential. The third phase focuses on coastal elements, considering three factors: proximity to the coastline [12], which influences attractiveness; coastal geomorphology, based on geological classifications; and bathing water quality. Once all these elements are analyzed, the final step is to combine the results from the three phases. The outcome is a detailed raster map that highlights the potential for nature-based recreational activities in Campania (Table 1).

Table 1. Selected ecosystem services: list, definition, and data sources.

Variable	Definition and unit of measurement	Input data	Data sources
LST_Cmax	Maximum land surface temperature in a census tract [°C]	Landsat, Collection 2-Level 2 imagery (Landsat 8–9 OLI/TIRS C2 L2)	USGS Earth Explorer
HAQUA	Habitat quality index [0–1]	2018 CORINE Land cover	Copernicus land monitoring service
		Threat rasters	Open Street Map
		Threat table	Sallustio et al. [13]
		Sensitivity table	Sallustio et al. [13]
		Half saturation constant	Model's default value
VAFPR		2018 CORINE Land cover	Copernicus land monitoring service
	Land monetary value per unit area [€/ha]	National Dataset for agricultural areas on the land monetary value	"National Research Council of Agriculture and Agricultural Economics" (CREA)

(*continued*)

Table 1. (*continued*)

Variable	Definition and unit of measurement	Input data	Data sources
	Mean agricultural value (MAV) per unit area [€/ha]	National Dataset for forestry areas concerning MAV	National Revenue Agency (NRA)
LANVA	Classes of landscape value [0–4]	Area of Interest	ISTAT
		Aesthetic detractors	Global Energy Monitor [14]
		Digital Elevation Model	Copernicus GLO-30
		Refractivity coefficient	Model's default value
RECVA	Values of recreational service provision [0–1]	Hemeroby index	ISTAT National Livestock Database[a]
			Map of potential natural vegetation[b]
		CORINE land cover map	Copernicus Land Monitoring Service
		Protected areas and landscape assets	Italian national geoportal[c]
			Campania - Regional geoportal[d]
			European Environment Agency[e]
		Coastal geomorphology	European Environment Agency – Eurosion. Coastal erosion and defense[f]
		Bathing water quality	European Environment Agency – Bathing Water Directive. Status of bathing water[g]

[a]Data are available online at: https://www.vetinfo.it/j6_statistiche/#/, last accessed 2025/03/30.
[b]Data are available online at: https://land.copernicus.eu/en/products/corine-land-cover/clc2018, last accessed 2025/03/30.
[c]Data are available online at: https://gn.mase.gov.it/portale/wfs, last accessed 2025/03/30.
[d]Data are available online at: https://sit2.regione.campania.it/content/decreti-ministeriali-art-136, last accessed 2025/03/30.
[e]Data are available online at: https://www.eea.europa.eu/en/datahub/datahubitem-view/6fc8ad2d-195d-40f4-bdec-576e7d1268e4, last accessed 2025/03/30.
[f]Data are available online at: https://www.eea.europa.eu/en/datahub/datahubitem-view/ba6d7fe6-c79f-48c7-b738-f78260730538?activeAccordion=1090218, last accessed 2025/03/30.
[g]Data are available online at: https://www.eea.europa.eu/en/datahub/datahubitem-view/c3858959-90da-4c1b-b9ca-492db0e514df, last accessed 2025/03/30

2.3 Multiple Regression Model

The multiple linear regression model implemented here allows the spatial distribution of CS to be associated with the taxonomies of the five identified ESs. The model operationalizes as follows.

$$CASQT = \beta_0 + \beta_1 LSURT + \beta_2 HAQUA + \beta_3 VAFPR \\ + \beta_4 LANVA + \beta_5 RECVA + \beta_6 CSLAG \tag{2}$$

Measurements of the CS variable and related covariates are related to a four-hectare square cell:

- CASQT is the carbon sequestration per unit area (Mg/m^2);
- LSURT is the LST, which is a reference for urban heat variation and, therefore, for the measure of its variation, which, if it were decreasing, would put in evidence an improvement in the quality of life of local communities ($°C$);
- HAQUA is the measure of the level of habitat quality, and takes decimal values between 0 and 1, as described in Subsect. 2.2;
- VAFPR measures the value of agricultural and forestry production (€/ha);
- LANVA measures the value of landscape, and takes decimal values between 0 and 1, as described in Subsect. 2.2;
- RECVA is the measure of recreational value, and takes decimal values between 0 and 1, as described in Subsect. 2.2;
- CSLAG is a spatially-lagged control variable for the spatial autocorrelation of CASQT (Mg/m^2).

The coefficient estimates of the covariates and the spatially-lagged variable express the marginal effect of these variables on CASQT. Multiple linear regression is generally used when there is evidence of the impossibility of priors regarding correlations between dependent and explanatory variables.

The multiple linear regression model represents the equation of a plane, tangent to a surface of unknown shape, in an n-dimensional spatial domain consisting of the variable associated with the CS, the five explanatory variables and the control variable. Around the tangency point, the linear relationship linking the seven variables, expressed by the estimate of model (2), effectively approximates the unknown surface equation above.

The control variable, CSLAG, is the spatially-lagged variable whose distribution is related to the spatial distribution of CS, and allows control of the phenomenon of spatial autocorrelation. This distribution is identified through the methodology proposed by Anselin [15].

The significance of the coefficient estimates of the explanatory and control variables is assessed by the p-value test.

3 Results

This section is organized as follows.

First, the spatial taxonomies related to the regional spatial context of Campania are presented as for the variables associated with CS and to the covariates of model (2). Secondly, the correlations implied by the estimates of the coefficients of the covariates of regression (2) are shown, so as to detect evidence concerning the association of CS to the explanatory variables.

3.1 Spatial Taxonomies of Ecosystem Services

Carbon Sequestration

Figure 1, panel A, displays the carbon storage values in the Campania Region, which range from 0 to 21.55 megagrams per 900 square meters. The highest values are distributed in distinct clusters, with two large ones located in the central and southern parts of the Region, while smaller clusters are found in the northern areas. The southern part of the Region, particularly the National Park of Cilento and Vallo di Diano, also holds substantial carbon storage values. The areas with medium-low values concern: in the north-west, the Metropolitan City of Naples, characterized by an almost totally urbanized land and the Volturno-Litorale Domizio Plain, characterized by a rural landscape that includes both specialized arboreta and arable land.

Land Surface Temperature

A total of 21 satellite images from Summer 2023 were analyzed, with only those from the same date merged into three sets. The merged images' mean values were compared, and those with the highest means were selected. The LST map is created using four Landsat images, two related to July 17, 2023 (scene 189), and two related to August 25, 2023 (scene 190).

In the Campania Region, the LST values are within the range of 27.5–64.5 °C (see Fig. 1, panel B). The highest LST values are observed in urban and artificial areas in the north-western part of the Region, with reference to the Metropolitan City of Naples. These areas include the Campana Plain, the Phlegraean Plain and the coastal hills of Naples, as well as the areas in the crown of the Vesuvius Volcano. A concentration of elevated LST values is observed in the north-eastern portion of the provinces of Avellino and Benevento as well, specifically within the agrarian regions of Alto Tammaro and Alto Fortore. The lowest LSTs are observed in the green belt extending along the Dorsale Appenninica from the north-eastern border of the Region, in areas characterized by widespread mountains and hills.

Habitat Quality

Figure 1, panel C displays the habitat quality values in the Campania Region, where the average value is 0.49. Specifically, 40.61 percent of the Region comprises low-quality habitats ($0 < HQ \leq 0.33$), 27.96 percent consists of medium-quality habitats ($0.33 < HQ \leq 0.66$), while the remaining 31.43 percent exhibits high-quality habitats ($0.66 < HQ \leq 1$). The highest values are concentrated in green areas, particularly in forested regions, frequently safeguarded by parks and reserves. In contrast, the lowest values occur in large urban zones and areas characterized by intensive agriculture. The second-lowest values are observed in "open urban areas" (aggregated from CLC 141, 142) and "intensive agricultural lands" (aggregated from CLC 211, 212, 213, 221, 222, 223), with mean values of 0.22 and 0.24, respectively. Higher mean values are found in "inland unvegetated or sparsely vegetated areas" (aggregated from CLC 332, 333, 334, 335) with a mean of 0.53.

Value of Agricultural and Forestry Production

Four types of elevation zones can be identified: hills, mountains, coastal hills, and plains. The spatial layout of agrarian regions and elevation zones through the spatial layout of municipalities in Campania are detected, based on agrarian regions identified with groups of contiguous municipalities. Regarding forestry areas, a preliminary correspondence is established between the taxonomy of the NRA and that of the subclasses of the second level of 2018 CORINE Land cover forestry classes (3.1 - Forests and 3.2 - Areas characterized by shrub and/or herbaceous vegetation). The final step is to aggregate the data referring to VAFPR. Figure 1, panel D shows the spatial distribution of the VAFPR for the Region related to 2023 in thousands €/ha. The value ranges from zero, in case the areas were not classified as agricultural or forestry, to a maximum value of 82,316 €/ha. VAFPR is zero as for 22.08% of the Region; the average land value is 12,552 €/ha. 52.11% of land values are less than 10,000 €/ha and are concentrated in the eastern mountainous areas of the Campanian Apennines and in the Cilento area. The peaks are observed in the agrarian regions of the coastal hills of Naples and in the coastal regions of the Sorrento Peninsula, characterized by the crops "Arable and horticultural crops."

Landscape Value

Figure 1, panel E illustrates the landscape quality values in the Campania Region, indicating a regional average value of 1.33. Specifically, over half of the Region (54 percent) maintains areas with unaffected landscape quality (VI = 0), 17 percent consists of landscapes with moderate quality (VI = 2), 18 percent includes areas of low landscape quality (VI = 3), while the remaining 11 percent exhibits poor landscape quality (VI = 4). The highest values of VI are predominantly concentrated in agricultural areas. However, agricultural areas in the Province of Salerno are an exception, where landscape values commonly range from low to unaffected, with only small portions of the territory displaying poor visual quality. Protected areas are not immune from visual degradation. While landscape quality remains largely unaffected in the Cilento National Park, the Guardaregia-Campochiaro Natural Oasis, and the Roccamonfina – Foce Garigliano Regional Park, this pattern deviates in the Taburno-Camposauro Regional Park, the Monti Picentini Regional Park, and the Partenio Regional Park, where extensive areas exhibit poor visual quality. Preserved landscapes persist in the southern part of the Region, in the Province of Salerno.

Recreational Service Supply

Figure 1, panel F displays the distribution of recreational service provision across Campania, with values ranging from 0.1 to 3, indicating that no area has the lowest potential value of 0. The highest values are concentrated along the coastline, with the exception of the area within the administrative boundaries of the Metropolitan City of Naples.

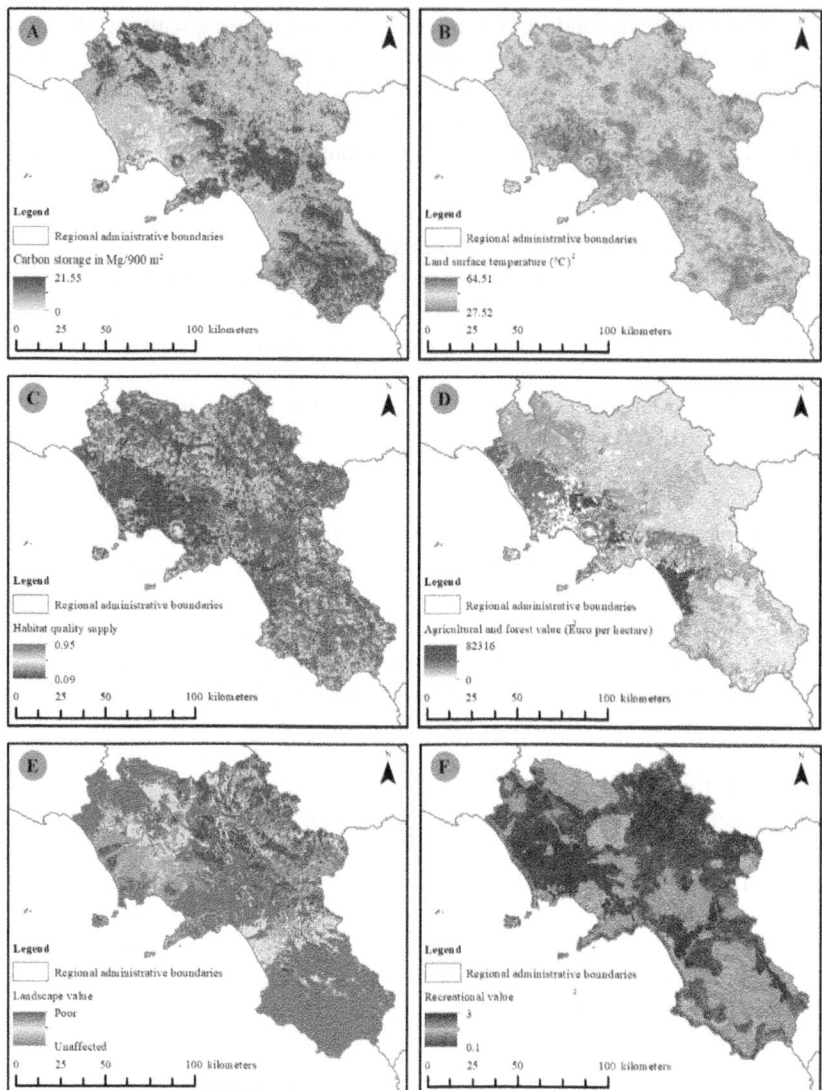

Fig. 1. Spatial distribution related to Carbon storage (panel A), Land surface temperature (panel B), Habitat quality supply (panel C), Agricultural and forest values (panel D), Landscape value (panel E), and Recreational value (panel F) in the Campania Region (Regional boundaries retrieved from: https://www.istat.it/statistiche-per-temi/ambiente-e-territorio/territorio-e-cartografia/).

Medium to high values are found in several key parts of the Region. In contrast, areas with the lowest recreational service values are located in the northeastern and northwestern parts of the Region. These areas show a lower potential for providing recreational services due to their agricultural use and less natural landscape features. These data are confirmed by the mean values that each land cover class assumes. Natural cover classes, such as salt marshes, beaches, water bodies, bare rock, water courses and coastal lagoons have the highest mean values, from 2.79 to 1.80. Conversely, the lowest mean values, between 0.23 and 0.96, are associated with agricultural and artificial land cover types.

3.2 Multiple Regression Model

The results of the estimates of model (2) are described, in the following, as shown in Table 2, which reports the marginal effects related to CS as for a unitary increase in the variables associated to the five ESs and spatially-lagged variables, and the p-value significance tests, that account for the reliability of these estimates.

Table 2. Regression outcomes.

Variable	Coefficient	t-Statistic	p-Value	Mean of the explanatory variable	Elasticity at the mean values of CASQT and expl. Var's $[(\Delta y/y)/(\Delta x/x)]$
Dependent variable: Carbon sequestration (CASQT)					
LSURT	−0.39144	−44.47850	0.00000	42.47074	−0.18892
HAQUA	75.20223	308.71536	0.00000	0.49840	0.42593
VAFPR	0.00023	114.84450	0.00000	16484.56641	0.04279
LANVA	0.84426	10.948531	0.00000	0.33133	0.00318
RECVA	−10.18535	−50.90622	0.00000	0.31506	−0.03647
CSLAG	35.24651	508.05586	0.00000	0.08111	0.03249

Mean and Standard deviation of dependent variable: 87.9987, 56.2533 - Adjusted R-squared: 0.92109

The outcomes of model (2) should be read taking account that the positive sign of an estimated coefficient implies that a growth in the availability of the associated ES corresponds to a growth in the CS and vice versa. An exception is the case of LANVA, the variable expressing landscape value, in which the availability of the corresponding ES increases as the value of the covariate decreases. All estimated coefficients, as shown in Table 2, have highly significant p-values. The estimated values of the coefficients are, therefore, reliable in identifying the relationships between CS and the supply of the ESs corresponding to the covariates. The absolute values of the elasticities are always less than unity and, therefore, configure an inelastic behavior of the CS availability with respect to the covariates, although significant differences between them are evident.

The results posit that a 1% increase in the LSURT covariate, i.e., an average gradient of just over 0.4 °C, corresponds to an average decrease in CS of about 0.17 Mg/ha, or just under 0.2%. It should be emphasized, in this regard, how the temporal trend, on an annual basis, of thermal gradients is generally smaller than this value and, therefore, how the association of CASQT and LSURT, consistent with the results of several scientific articles available in the literature, indicates a reduced and, in any case, significant impact of LST on CS.

Of particular note is habitat quality, whose associated variable, HAQUA, shows the highest value among elasticities, at about 43%. This implies that a 1% increase in this covariate is associated with a 0.43% increase in CS, or about 0.38 Mg/ha. Since habitat quality can be significantly improved in relation to land policies geared toward direct or indirect protection of areas, especially in relation to mitigation of threats, it is evident that the HAQUA variable emerges as the most important one with regard to what concerns the establishment of land policies geared toward contributing to overall climate quality.

As for the variable representing agricultural and forestry production, the elasticity value associated with it is positive and rather low, at about 4%, thus about one-tenth of the elasticity related to habitat quality. This implies that only changes in VAFPR of the order of 10%, or about 1.650 €/ha, or more, are associated with changes of some significance in CS, amounting to about 0.35 Mg/ha, thus of the order of magnitude of those associated with habitat quality or with decreasing LST.

With regard to landscape value, which is related to the significance of scenic views in relation to aesthetic detractors such as, for example, wind turbines and photovoltaic installations, the positive and significant value of the coefficient estimated through model (2) indicates how an increase in CS is associated with a decrease in landscape value, i.e., scenic significance. The value of the elasticity is, however, very low at about 3‰. This outcome highlights a substantial indifference of CS with respect to landscape value, although it implies, as well, a strong indication in the direction of avoiding, as much as possible, the location of energy production plants in areas of particular scenic importance.

The value of the ES representing the supply of nature-based services behaves similarly to the landscape value, but with a significantly larger elasticity of about 3.6%. In this case, a 10% decrease in RECVA supply is associated with an increase in CS of about 0.30 Mg/ha. The negative correlation can be attributed to the fact that recreational potential is closely linked to the accessibility of areas available for outdoor activities, thus to the presence, albeit with limited extent, of mobility infrastructure.

4   Discussion

The discussion developed in the following subsections is based on the implications of model (2), with reference to the relationships between the supply of CS and the availability of the other ESs.

4.1   Carbon Sequestration and Land Surface Temperature

The link between CS and LST, evidenced by the use of the methodology presented here in the regional spatial context of Campania, is supported by multiple research in the literature. Momo and Devi [16] examine the trends in LST and CS over ten years (2011–2021), focusing on the western district of Imphal, which is the capital of the Indian State of Manipur. They compare the results achieved through different methodologies based on satellite data, showing how they converge, both qualitatively and quantitatively, and demonstrate that the steady decrease in CS is associated with an equally steady increase in LST. Similar results, albeit with different methodological approaches, are presented and discussed by Wang et al. [17], with reference to the metropolitan context of Shenzen, located in a subtropical area of China, by Dibaba [18], regarding the urban contexts of Nekemte and Jimma, in western Ethiopia.

4.2   Carbon Sequestration and Habitat Quality

There are many studies showing a positive relationship between CS and habitat quality, covering a wide range of spatial scales including continental, regional, and local contexts, as well as different definitions of the spatial distribution of ESs associated with habitat quality. Based on Bayley [19], in the context of the Falkland Islands, a link emerges between improved habitat quality and increased CS capacity. The research by Hua et al. [20] focuses on the Xiamen metropolitan area, located in the Min Delta Region of China. In addition, two articles are significant, that of Del Vecchio et al. [21] on the progress of dune vegetation along the Veneto coast of northeastern Italy, and that of Zullo et al. [22] on the coastal area of Abruzzo, in eastern Italy.

4.3   Carbon Sequestration and Value of Agricultural and Forestry Production

Many studies highlight the connection between CS and VAFPR. Al Kafy et al. [23] examined the influence of changes in land use and land cover on CS capacity in forest ecosystems in the Chittagong Hill Tracts Region (Bangladesh) using remote sensing techniques. This study, conducted for the years 1996 to 2021, revealed a loss of 21.65 $\times 10^6$ Mg of CS due to a 21% reduction in vegetation cover.

Regarding agricultural areas, Paris et al. [24] and Frank et al. [25] have evidence that agricultural and forestry techniques contribute to ecological intensification of productivity. This is demonstrated in a recent research on olive groves in the Umbria Region of Italy [26] which indicates how significant portion of soil carbon is concentrated in the top 30 to 60 cm of agricultural land. Maintaining olive grove cultivation is a key strategy for protecting soil organic carbon and minimizing atmospheric carbon release due to land use change or intensive soil management.

4.4   Carbon Sequestration and Landscape Value

CS and landscape value are very strongly intertwined such that scholars identified Agroforestry systems of High Nature and Cultural Value (HNCV) [27], where CS and landscape aesthetics are mutually enhanced. Specifically, agroforestry systems of high nature value are defined as areas characterized by the prevalence of semi-natural habitats and trees that typically support rich biodiversity [28] and provide numerous services, including CS [29], while simultaneously offering pleasant landscapes [30]. However, Renewable Energy Source (RES) infrastructures, such as the here examined wind turbines and solar farms, often disrupt the scenic views that characterize these landscapes, sacrificing their aesthetic value in the name of green energy supply.

4.5 Carbon Sequestration and Recreational Service Supply

The results point to a negative correlation between RECVA supply and CS, potentially associated with issues related to the accessibility of such areas for recreational activities. Costanza [31] describes recreational services as "user movement related," highlighting accessibility as one of the three core elements of recreational services, alongside ecosystem functions and the spatial distribution of potential demand. Moreover, according to Paracchini et al. [32], one key factor influencing a place's attractiveness is its proximity. When it comes to everyday recreational activities, people tend to favor locations within approximately 8 km of their residence. High CS values are associated with wooded areas, which are very often located in natural and semi-natural areas far from built-up areas.

5 Conclusions

This study proposes a methodological itinerary aimed at identifying the association between climate neutrality conditions, represented by CS capacity, and ESs supply, structured through a spatial system consisting of two regulating ESs, namely LST control and habitat quality, one provisioning ES, such as agricultural and forestry production, and two cultural ESs, namely landscape value and outdoor recreation. The methodology was experimentally implemented with reference to the regional context of Campania.

There are two significant profiles that characterize the study. First, the definition and application, in a single interpretative model, of different methodological approaches, based on current scientific and technical literature, concerning the identification of the spatial supply of some ESs, typical of spatial, urban, peri-urban and rural contexts, and their integration in a single model that configures their association with the global climate situation, represented by CS capacity. In this way, the spatial configuration of this situation is read and interpreted with reference to an integrated supply of ESs and not only in relation to the impacts of the individual ES. The results, with reference to Campania, indicate how habitat quality is the most relevant ES in relation to the impact on climate neutrality, how, likewise, effects of medium importance are found with regard to LST control, agricultural and forestry production, and nature-based recreation, and how, finally, the influence of landscape value is significantly less significant, although, in the latter case, the model estimate identifies a relationship between the provision of this ES and climate neutrality that signals the need for special attention of the location of renewable energy production facilities as environmental detractors of landscape scenic value.

Secondly, the model's easily readable and interpretable outcomes allow, with regard to the results just mentioned, to recognize implications for regional and local planning policies based on the integration of enhancing the supply of different services provided by natural ecosystems. The ecosystem approach represents, certainly, a highly innovative conceptual horizon, probably still revolutionary today, for the practice of spatial planning.

Authors' Contributions. Federica Isola (F.I.), Francesca Leccis (F.L.), Federica Leone (F.Le.) and Corrado Zoppi (C.Z.) collaboratively designed this study. Individual contributions are as follows: F.Le. And C.Z. collaboratively wrote Sects. 1; F.Le. Wrote Sect. 2.1, Subsections "Recreational service supply" in Sects. 2.2 and 3.1, and Sect. 4.5; F.I. wrote Subsections "Land surface temperature" and "Value of agricultural and forestry production" in Sects. 2.2 and 3.1, and Sect. 4.3; F.L. wrote Subsections "Habitat quality" and "Landscape value" in Sects. 2.2 and 3.1, and Sect. 4.4; C.Z. wrote Sects. 2.3, 3.2, 4.1, 4.2 and 5.

Acknowledgments. This study was carried out: i. within the RETURN Extended Partnership funded by the European Union – NextGenerationEU (National Recovery and Resilience Plan – NRRP, M4, C2, In-VESTment 1.3 – D.D. 1243 2/8/2022, PE0000005); ii. Within the NRRP, M4, C2, In-VESTment 1.1, Call for tender no. 1409 published on 14.9.2022 by the Italian Ministry of University and Research (MUR), funded by the European Union – NextGenerationEU – Project Title "Definition of a guidelines handbook to implement climate neutrality by improving ecosystem service effectiveness in rural and urban areas" – CUP F53D23010760001 – Grant Assignment Decree no. 1378 adopted on September 1, 2023, by MUR; iii. Within the research grant CUP F73C23001680007 for the project "Geodesign for climate change mitigation and adaptation in the Mediterranean region," funded in 2022 by Fondazione di Sardegna.

Disclosure of Interests. The authors declare no competing interests.

References

1. Hall, L.S., Krausman, P.R., Morrison, M.L.: The habitat concept and a plea for standard terminology. Wildlife Soc. Bull. (1973–2006), **25**, 173–182 (1997). https://www.jstor.org/stable/3783301
2. Lorilla, R.S., Poirazidis, K., Kalogirou, S., Detsis, V., Martinis, A.: Assessment of the spatial dynamics and interactions among multiple ecosystem services to promote effective policy making across Mediterranean island landscapes. Sustainability **10**, 3285 (2018). https://doi.org/10.3390/su10093285
3. Yang, S., et al.: Nature-based solution for climate change adaptation: coastal habitats restoration in Xiamen Bay, China. Forests**15**(11), 1844 (2024). https://doi.org/10.3390/f15111844
4. Bader, P.: Understanding landscape change. The. Environment **3**, 16–18 (2020)
5. Mundher, R., et al.: Aesthetic quality assessment of landscapes as a model for urban forest areas: a systematic literature review. Forests **13**, 991 (2022). https://doi.org/10.3390/f13070991
6. Zhang, N., Zheng, X., Wang, X.: Assessment of aesthetic quality of urban landscapes by integrating objective and subjective factors: a case study for riparian landscapes. Front. Ecol. Evol. **9** (2021). https://doi.org/10.3389/fevo.2021.735905
7. MA (Millennium Ecosystem Assessment): ecosystems and human well-being: a framework for assessment. Island Press: Washington, DC, USA (2003). https://wedocs.unep.org/bitstream/handle/20.500.11822/8768/Ecosystem_and_human_well_being_a_framework_for_assessment.pdf?sequence=3&amp%3BisAllowed=, Accessed 30 Mar 2025

8. Vallecillo, S., La Notte, A., Zulian, G., Ferrini, S., Maes, J.: Ecosystem services accounts: valuing the actual flow of nature-based recreation from ecosystems to people. Ecol. Model. **392**, 196–211 (2019). https://doi.org/10.1016/j.ecolmodel.2018.09.023

9. Barton, D.N., et al.: Discussion paper 10: recreation services from ecosystems (2019). https://www.researchgate.net/publication/333263149_Recreation_services_from_ecosystems, Accessed 30 Mar 2025

10. Isola, F., Lai, S., Leone, F., Zoppi, C.: Green infrastructure and regional planning. An operational framework. FrancoAngeli, Milan, Italy (2022)

11. Paracchini, M.L., Capitani, C.: Implementation of a EU Wide Indicator for the Rural-Agrarian Landscape. Publications Office of the European Union, Luxembourg (2011)

12. Zulian, G., Paracchini, M.L., Maes, J., Liquete, C.: ESTIMAP: ecosystem services mapping at European scale. JRC (European Commission – Joint Research Centre – Institute for Environment and Sustainability) Technical Report EUR 26474 ENG. Publications Office of the European Union: Luxembourg (2013). https://doi.org/10.2788/6436

13. Sallustio, L., et al.: Assessing habitat quality in relation to the spatial distribution of protected areas in Italy. J. Environ. Manage. **201**, 129–137 (2017). https://doi.org/10.1016/j.jenvman.2017.06.031

14. GEM (Global Energy Monitor): global solar power tracker, global energy monitor and TransitionZero, June 2024 release. https://globalenergymonitor.org/projects/global-solar-power-tracker/, Accessed 30 Mar 2025

15. Anselin, L., Syabri, I., Kho, Y.: GeoDa: an introduction to spatial data analysis. Geogr. Anal. **38**(1), 5–22 (2006). https://doi.org/10.1111/j.0016-7363.2005.00671.x

16. Momo, M., Devi, T.T.: Assessment of land surface temperature and carbon sequestration using remotely sensed satellite data in the Imphal-West district, Manipur, India. J. Earth Syst. Sci. **131**, 229 (2022). https://doi.org/10.1007/s12040-022-01944-8

17. Wang, J., Xiang, Z., Wang, W., Chang, W., Wang, Y.: Impacts of strengthened warming by urban heat island on carbon sequestration of urban ecosystems in a subtropical city of China. Urban Ecosyst. **24**, 1165–1177 (2021). https://doi.org/10.1007/s11252-021-01104-8

18. Dibaba, W.T.: Urbanization-induced land use/land cover change and its impact on surface temperature and heat fluxes over two major cities in Western Ethiopia. Environ. Monit. Assess. **195**, 1083 (2023). https://doi.org/10.1007/s10661-023-11698-5

19. Bayley, D.T.I., Brickle, P., Brewin, P.E., Golding, N., Pelembe, T.: Valuation of kelp forest ecosystem services in the Falkland Islands: a case study integrating blue carbon sequestration potential. One Ecosyst. **6**, e62811 (2021). https://doi.org/10.3897/oneeco.6.e62811

20. Hua, Y., Yan, D., Liu, X.: Assessing synergies and trade-offs between ecosystem services in highly urbanized area under different scenarios of future land use change. Environ. Sustain. Indicat. **22**, 100350 (2024). https://doi.org/10.1016/j.indic.2024.100350

21. Del Vecchio, S., Rova, S., Fantinato, E., Pranovi, F., Buffa, G.: Disturbance affects the contribution of coastal dune vegetation to carbon storage and carbon sequestration rate. Plant Sociol. **59**(1), 37–48 (2022). https://doi.org/10.3897/pls2022591/04

22. Zullo, F., Montaldi, C., Di Pietro, G., Cattani, C.: Land use changes and ecosystem services: the case study of the Abruzzo Region coastal strip. ISPRS Int. J. Geo Inf. **11**, 588 (2022). https://doi.org/10.3390/ijgi11120588

23. Al Kafy, A., et al.: Integrating Forest cover change and carbon storage dynamics: leveraging google earth engine and In-VEST model to inform conservation in hilly regions. Ecol. Indicat. **152**, 110374 (2023). https://doi.org/10.1016/j.ecolind.2023.110374

24. Paris P., et al.: Agroselvicoltura ed intensificazione ecologica. Forest@ **16**, 10–15 (2019). https://doi.org/10.3832/efor3053-016

25. Frank, S., Lessa Derci Augustynczik, A., Havlík, P., et al.: Enhanced agricultural carbon sinks provide benefits for farmers and the climate. Nat. Food **5**, 742–753 (2024). https://doi.org/10.1038/s43016-024-01039-1

26. Bateni, C., Ventura, M., Tonon, G., Pisanelli, A.: Soil carbon stock in olive groves agroforestry systems under different management and soil characteristics. Agrofor. Syst. **95**, 951–961 (2021). https://doi.org/10.1007/s10457-019-00367-7
27. Beaufoy, G., BaldocK, D. E ClarK, J.: The nature of farming. Low intensity farming systems in nine European countries Report IEEP/WWF/JNCC, London, Gland, Peterborough (1994). https://ieep.eu/wp-content/uploads/2023/01/TheNatureOfFarming_1994_.pdf, Accessed 25 Mar 2025
28. Andersen E., et al.: Developing a high nature value indicator. Report for the European Environment Agency, Copenhagen (2003)
29. Rolo, V., et al.: Challenges and innovations for improving the sustainability of European agroforestry systems of high nature and cultural value: stakeholder perspectives. Sustain. Sci. **15**, 1301–1315 (2020). https://doi.org/10.1007/s11625-020-00826-6
30. Moreno, G., et al.: Agroforestry systems of high nature and cultural value in Europe: provision of commercial goods and other ecosystem services. Agroforest Syst. **92**, 877–891 (2018). https://doi.org/10.1007/s10457-017-0126-1
31. Costanza, R.: Ecosystem services: multiple classification systems are needed. Biol. Cons. **141**(2), 350–352 (2008). https://doi.org/10.1016/j.biocon.2007.12.020
32. Paracchini, M.L., et al.: Mapping cultural ecosystem services: a framework to assess the potential for outdoor recreation across the EU. Ecol. Ind. **45**, 371–385 (2014). https://doi.org/10.1016/j.ecolind.2014.04.018

Mapping Recreational Services and Beneficiaries in the Sardinia Region Using ESTIMAP with Tourism Insights

Bilge Kobak$^{(\boxtimes)}$ (ID)

IUSS Pavia & DICAAR Università degli Studi di Cagliari,
Via Marengo 2, Cagliari 09123, CA, Italy
`bilge.kobak@iusspavia.it`

Abstract. Ecosystem services (ESs) knowledge is key for urban planning as they provide essential resources to society. Mapping the beneficiaries of these services helps identify the levels of access to certain ESs, such as nature-based recreation, while also assessing residents' and tourists' dynamics and patterns across the region. This information aids in decision-making for planning green infrastructure that meets the needs of both residents and visitors. In this study, the ESTIMAP model is applied at a regional scale and subsequently a methodology for mapping the distribution of beneficiaries of recreational ES is introduced. The study further outlines the calculation of beneficiaries within varying buffer zones, considering both population and tourist numbers as well as different modes of transportation, including walking, cycling, public transportation, and private cars. The findings reveal that areas that potentially supply high levels of recreational ES (ROS9) in Sardinia are spread out across the region, ensuring accessibility by car for everyone within a 30-min drive. When walking is considered, the percentage of the population within 1 km of ROS9 areas is almost half that of tourists, as accommodation facilities tend to be situated nearer to ROS9 areas compared to population settlements. This highlights a disparity in walking access, which decreases when considering public transportation. The adaptable method highlights the effectiveness of the ES approach in guiding urban planning while supporting nature-based tourism.

Keywords: Ecosystem Services · Nature-based recreation · GIS

1 Introduction

The relationship between nature and society is at the core of urban planning studies. To understand and improve this relationship, Ecosystem Services (ESs) have become a prominent research domain in related fields. While many studies focus on the provision of ESs, the distribution and accessibility of these service is equally important [1]. Urban planning is a key tool for authorities to shape the distribution of ecosystems and ESs in cities, determining the number, location, and types of beneficiaries [1, 2]. Failing to disaggregate the distribution of environmental resources limits a full understanding of the various dimensions of equitable well-being, ultimately leading to the unequal provisioning of ESs among potential beneficiaries [1].

O. Gervasi et al. (Eds.): ICCSA 2025 Workshops, LNCS 15890, pp. 140–155, 2026.
https://doi.org/10.1007/978-3-031-97606-3_10

Identifying the relationship between the supply and demand of nature-based recreation is key for integrating the ES approach into policy and decision-making processes that support sustainable tourism [3], since rapid urban sprawl is increasing the mismatch between supply and demand [4]. Addressing these imbalances can help identify areas in need of improvement and inform spatial and regional planning, enhancing sustainable tourism management and safeguarding natural ecosystems [3].

Research on methods to calculate the demand for ESs and map their flows remains ongoing. Models such as ESTIMAP provide frameworks for mapping both the provision and the demand of ESs; however, studies predominantly emphasize their economic valuation [5, 6]. At the European level, Vallecillo et al. compare the "actual flow of nature-based recreation in relative terms at the country level" [7, Fig. 7] with Italy ranking among the bottom three countries, indicating one of the lowest percentages of potential visits per inhabitant. Baró et al. [8] identify the unsatisfied demand for ESs in the metropolitan region of Barcelona, while Isola et al. [9] map the spatial distribution of both met and unmet demand for daily nature-based recreation in Sardinia, measured by the number of trips per year to areas that provide high levels of recreational services. Within this framework, this study aims to explore the provision of recreational ESs and offers a novel approach that integrates within the traditional ESTIMAP model both tourists' demand for outdoor recreation, and accessibility by different means of transportation. Since the demand for nature-based recreation varies, with some people seeking local ecosystems like urban parks and forests for activities such as walking or cycling, while others travel longer distances to visit national parks or hike in the mountains [7], mapping both the provision of ESs and different beneficiary groups enables practical strategies to enhance accessibility and ensure the equitable distribution of ES.

2   Case Study: Sardinia Region, Italy

2.1   Location

Sardinia, one of the 20 regions of Italy (Fig. 1), is located in the southern part of the country. The region is the Mediterranean's second-largest island after Sicily, covering an area of 24,100.02 km^2. With a coastline stretching 1,897 km, when considered together with its surrounding smaller islands, it has the most extensive coastal development of any Italian region, accounting for more than a quarter of Italy's total coastline [10].

Fig. 1. Sardinia and regional borders in Italy.

3 Materials and Methodology

3.1 Methodology

The ESTIMAP recreation model, developed by the European Commission's Joint Research Centre, is a GIS-based tool designed to assess ESs across Europe [11, 12]. The model comprises two modules: the Human Input (Proximity) map and the Recreation Potential (RP) map. As seen in Fig. 2, these two modules are cross-tabulated to produce the Recreation Opportunity Spectrum (ROS) map, which shows recreational opportunities according to their distance from the road network and populated areas.

The first module, RP, is an ecosystem-based potential map. The original model uses three parameters to map RP: i) the degree of naturalness in land cover, ii) the presence of protected areas, and iii) the presence of water-related features. However, these parameters are often adapted to fit the context of specific studies [9, 13, 14]. In this study, the parameters for the first module follow those established in Kobak [14], where the input parameters for the RP map were chosen as follows: i) the degree of naturalness in land cover, ii) the presence of protected areas, and iii) the presence of areas of interest.

The second module, HI, measures the distance from human settlements and road networks. The traditional ESTIMAP model focuses on non-motorized recreational activities, accounting for ESs that are supplied by high-quality ecosystems near urban centers, which shows only a portion of the total potential [9]. The proximity to population and the proximity to transportation infrastructure; road network and slow-mobility routes such as biking routes are the two parameters that create the HI. The data layers used to create these intermediate maps are presented in Table 1. After obtaining the final rasters for the RP map and HI modules, cross-tabulation is performed in QGIS to generate the final ROS map. This process results in nine distinct values representing the intersections between RP and HI classes, as shown in Fig. 3.

The ROS map can be considered as the final output of the adapted ESTIMAP model that aids in understanding which areas have high recreation potential while also showing

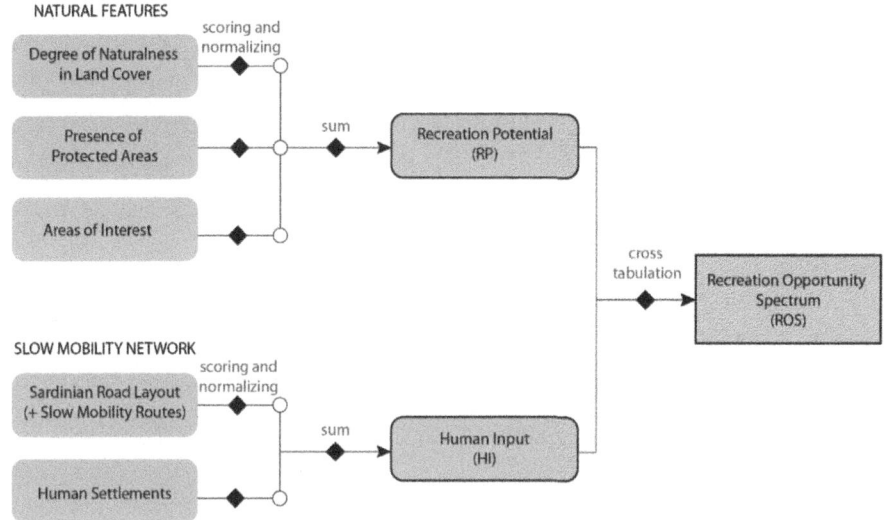

Fig. 2. Adaptation of ESTIMAP-Recreation Model for Sardinia. Modified after Zulian et al. (2013).

high accessibility levels. In order to further investigate the met and unmet demand of beneficiaries, an additional step is applied to the Sardinia Region.

To assess the demand for ES, the methodology presented in Vallecillo et al. [6] is used. In their study, also applied by Isola et al. [9], the met and unmet demand for daily nature-based recreation is calculated in terms of the number of trips per year to areas offering high levels of recreational services with the focus on trips within an 8 km round-trip distance, considering only resident populations, and excluding tourists and motorized transportation. Therefore, to provide a more inclusive analysis, this study considers additional parameters, including tourists and access by bus, train, and car within the proposed framework and it calculates the number of people that live or lodge within these vicinity buffers.

As shown in Fig. 4, the proposed methodology to calculate the beneficiaries of recreational services uses mainly two groups of data. The first group consists of raster files representing the number of people per pixel, including both residents and tourists residing in the region. These pixels are considered as starting points for potential visits to high-score recreational areas, defined as areas with a maximum score of nine on the ROS map (ROS9 areas). The second group of data consists of areas of interest, meaning specifically ROS9 areas, areas in their vicinity, and areas with transportation options that enable people to access them. These transportation options include walking, biking, taking the bus, train or car.

The first group of data, i.e., the number of people per pixel, is obtained for two groups: residents and tourists. While for the information regarding the distribution of population per pixel, the global data layer "GHS-POP R2023A - GHS population grid multitemporal (1975–2030)" [15] is used; the information on tourists is obtained by using a combination of different sources listed in Table 2.

Table 1. Input data for the intermediate maps of the ESTIMAP Model.

Data layer name	Data source	Parameter	Module
Corine Land Cover 2018	Copernicus Land Monitoring Service[a]	degree of naturalness in land cover	RP
N2000 sites, Sites of Community Importance (SCI), Special Conservation Zones (SCZ), Special Protection Areas (SPA)	Ministero dell'Ambiente e della Sicurezza Energetica (MASE)[b]	presence of protected areas	
Art. 142 - Parchi e riserve nazionali o regionali (dati indicativi)	Aree tutelate Sardegna Geoportale[c]		
cultural sites, caves, BP (Landscape assets), BI (Identity assets), ARCHEO (Archaeological assets), monumental trees, monuments	Aree tutelate Sardegna Geoportale[c]	presence of areas of interest	
Località italiane	2021 National Census[d]	Human settlements	HI
layer 01 "roads, mobility, and transport"	DBGT[e] Sardegna Geoportale	Road layout	
Biking Routes	Courtesy of Sardegna Ciclabile[f]	Slow mobility routes	

[a]Copernicus Land Monitoring Service. (2018). Corine Land Cover 2018. European Environment Agency. https://land.copernicus.eu/en/products/corine-land-cover/clc2018.
[b]Ministero dell'Ambiente e della Sicurezza Energetica (MASE) [Ministry of the Environment and Energy Security]. https://www.mase.gov.it [last accessed 5 March 2024].
[c]Aree tutelate Sardegna Geoportale [Official Website for geospatial data of the Sardinia Region]. https://www.sardegnageoportale.it/webgis2/sardegnamappe/?map=aree_tutelate [last accessed 5 December 2024].
[d]Istituto Nazionale di Statistica (ISTAT). [National Institute of Statistics] https://www.istat.it/notizia/basi-territoriali-e-variabili-censuarie/ [Last accessed 5 December 2024].
[e]Datatabase Geotopografico [Geotopographic Database]. https://www.sardegnageoportale.it/index.php?xsl=2420&s=40&v=9&c=95645&es=6603&na=1&n=100&esp=1&tb=14401 [Last accessed 9 October 2024].
[f]Sardegna Ciclabile [Official website showing all cycling routes in Sardinia] http://www.sardegnaciclabile.it/site/itinerari/ [last accessed 23 February 2024].

The second group of data, i.e., areas of interest, defined as the ROS9 areas, includes zones that facilitate transportation methods such as walking, biking, bus, train, or car. These areas are identified through buffer zones, whose size is determined based on studies specific to each transportation mode. Implementing more types of transportation methods as well as introducing the number of tourists was a strategical choice to overcome some of the limitations mentioned in earlier studies [7, 9].

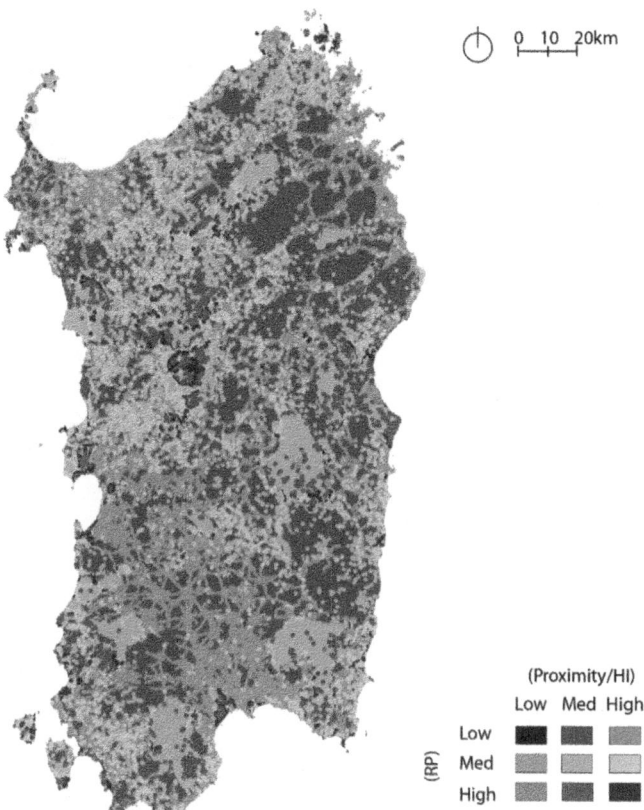

Fig. 3. Recreation Opportunity Spectrum (ROS) map.

Considering the access by walking, a 4-km buffer distance is considered as "met demand", representing the maximum distance people are typically willing to walk to a recreational area [7]. To account for variations in walking willingness, buffer distances of 1 km, 2 km, and 4 km were analysed, and the population within each distance was calculated to identify the number of beneficiaries.

For biking, an 8-km buffer distance is considered, reflecting the fact that most cycling trips are typically under 15 km, which aligns with the distance that greenway users travel to access the trail [16–18]. Regarding the number of people who might benefit from this service, physical ability is considered since not all people are able to bike. Even though most kids learn how to ride a bike at the age of 4–7 according to the American Academy of Pediatrics' bicycle guidance [19], for traveling by bike, adolescence is considered a suitable minimum age. For the maximum age, 64 is here considered as 65 is regarded as senior citizenship in most countries. According to the World Health Organization, adolescence[1], begins at the age of 10, while adulthood is defined as the age range of

---

[1] WHO. (2019). Adolescent health. https://www.who.int/health-topics/adolescent-health#tab= tab_1.

CALCULATION OF BENEFICIARIES

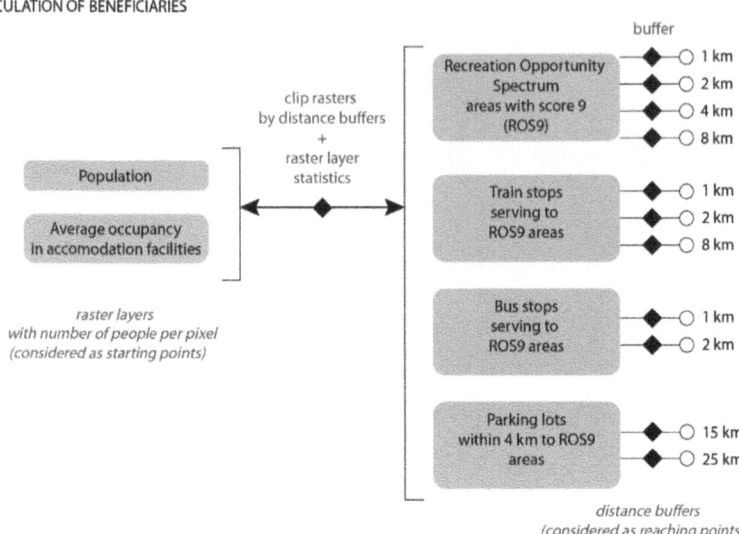

Fig. 4. Calculation of beneficiaries.

Table 2. Input data used to create raster layers for the calculation of beneficiaries.

Data layer name	Data source	Final Output
GHS-POP R2023A - GHS population grid (1975–2030) [raster layer]	European Commission, Joint Research Centre (JRC)	Raster layer depicting population per pixel for residents
«Strutture_Ricettive_RAS_20240833» [vector layer]	Courtesy of Directorate General of Tourism, Crafts, and Trade of Sardinia	Raster layer depicting population per pixel for tourists
Private accommodation capacity (Airbnb listings) [csv table]	BNB Toolbox Scraper for Airbnb	
OSM Tag: "amenity = parking" [vector layer]	Overpass Turbo Tool - Open Street Map (OSM)[a]	Parking lots
Dati fermate trasporti [Transport stops]	Sardegna Mobilità[b]	Bus stops / Train stops
Percorsi di linea TPL [Public Transport Line Routes]		

[a]Data mining by Overpass Turbo. OSM. https://overpass-turbo.eu/?template=key-value&key=amenity&value=parking [Last accessed November 10, 2024].
[b]Sardegna Mobilità. Open data – Percorsi [Routes]. https://www.sardegnamobilita.it/open-data/percorsi [Last accessed November 10, 2024].

18 to 64 [20]. Therefore, individuals aged 10 to 64 are considered capable of biking. Considering this age range, a rate of 68% was applied to population in Sardinia calculated according to the age distribution data of ISTAT [21] and a rate of 78% is applied to tourist numbers calculated according to the "Tourist Movement Data" available from Sardegna Turismo [22]. The data here is limited to individuals aged 15 to 64, as information for the 10 to 14 age group is unavailable.

For travelling by car, distances under 100 km are considered accessible, as traveling 100 km or more is generally regarded as a long-distance trip [23]. Parking lots within

4 km from ROS9 areas are considered as destination and buffer layers were created around those parking lots.

For travelling by bus, bus stops located within a 4-km radius of ROS9 areas were identified. Subsequently, the bus lines serving these stops were mapped, and all stops along these lines were regarded as stops that people can use to reach a ROS9 location. Individuals residing within 1 km and 2 km from these bus stops were identified as having the opportunity to access a ROS9 area via bus. For travelling by train, the same method used for calculating bus accessibility was applied, with one additional consideration: an 8 km buffer was included alongside the 1-km and 2-km buffers, accounting for the possibility that people might use bicycles to reach train stations, as bikes are permitted on trains and can also be utilized within recreational areas.

For the calculation of the number of people who benefit from at least one ROS9 area, the average occupancy rates (O.R.) are applied to both tourist numbers. This rate is 22% in for the AIRBNB listings in Sardinia in 2019, calculated by the percentage of days with a reservation out of the total number of days either reserved or available in a year, excluding blocked days [24]. For the other types of accommodation such as hotels, no information is available specific to Sardinia, but it is available for Italy. According to the statistics provided by Eurostat [25, 26], the average rate of occupancy in hostels and similar establishments in Italy is 51.6% in 2019, calculated by dividing the total sum of bedrooms in use by the total bedrooms available, adjusted for seasonal and temporary closures.

4 Results

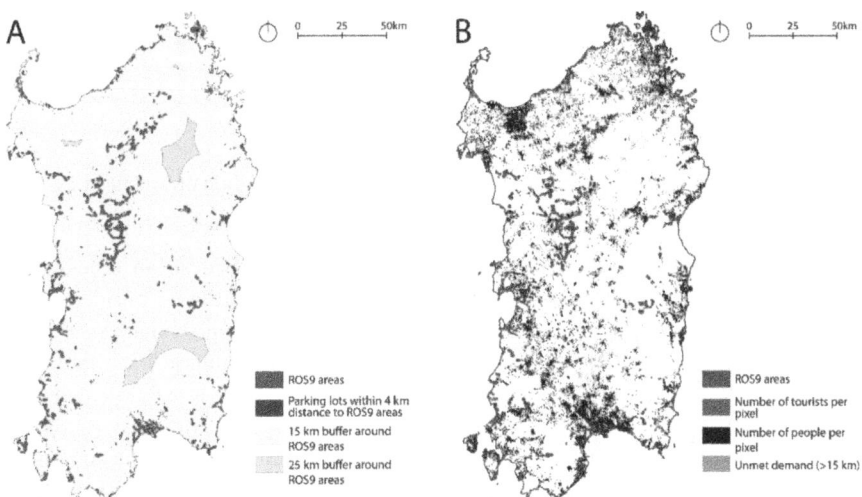

Fig. 5. Access by car; distances to ROS9 areas (A), distribution of beneficiaries (B).

Figure 5(A) shows the buffer layers around parking lots within a 4-km distance of ROS9 areas. Given the scattered distribution of ROS9 areas, a 25-km threshold was deemed sufficient to cover the entire island. This indicates that everyone in Sardinia lives within a 30-min (at 50 km/h) driving distance of at least one ROS9 area. If we consider a 15-km trip to a parking lot near a ROS9 area, approximately 97.97% of the population residing on the island can access a recreational area (ROS9) by car within around 15 min (at 60 km/h). This percentage is 98.43% for tourists, indicating that accommodation facilities are situated closer to recreational areas. The spatial distribution of residents and tourists staying in accommodation facilities is shown in Fig. 5(B). Since different sources are combined to calculate the tourist numbers, in Table 3, more detail is provided on the number of tourists, showing the difference in capacity between private accommodation facilities such as Airbnb, and other types of facilities. Table 3 also provides a summary of all distance buffers considered per transportation type and the numbers corresponding to those buffers.

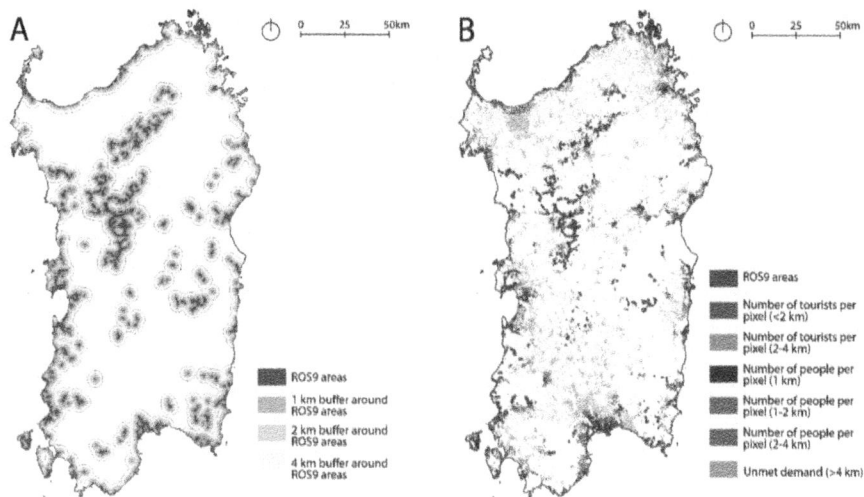

Fig. 6. Access by walking; distances to ROS9 areas (A), distribution of beneficiaries (B).

Figure 6(A) shows the buffer distances considered for pedestrian access, while Fig. 6(B) shows the distribution of beneficiaries within those buffers. Considering 4 km as the maximum distance people might be willing to walk (approximately 80 min of walking), 60.49% of the population (937,482 people) live within a 4 km radius of a ROS9 area, leaving around 40% of the population without access to a ROS9 area within walking distance. However, a 4 km distance may not be equally attractive to everyone. Therefore, distances of 2 km and 1 km should be considered more realistic and relevant for access to ROS9 areas. When considering a 2 km distance (around 30–40 min of walking), about 60% of the population does not have access to a ROS9 area. In contrast, 86.22% of tourists lodge within 4 km of a ROS9 area, and 71.49% within 2 km. Moreover, while 22.56% of the population lives within 1 km of ROS9 areas, this percentage rises to 54.09% for tourists, which indicates that accommodation facilities are more likely to be located closer to ROS9 areas, as reflected in the higher accessibility percentages for tourists compared to the general population.

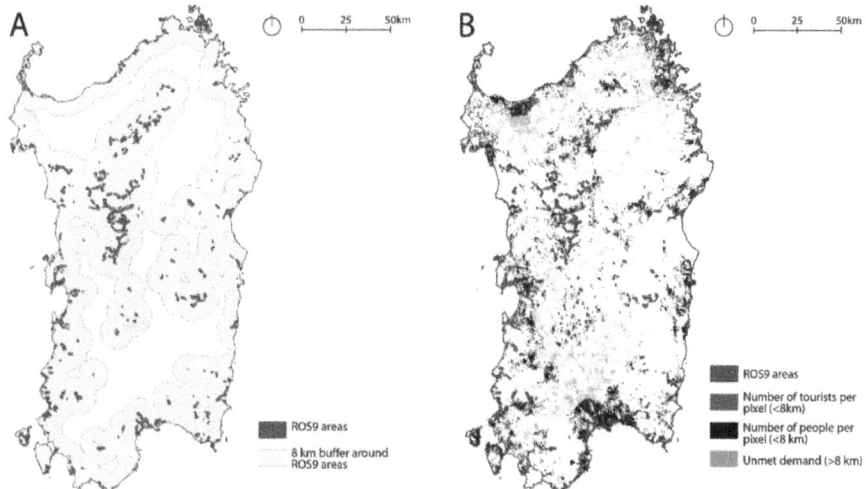

Fig. 7. Access by biking; distances to ROS9 areas (A), distribution of beneficiaries (B).

Regarding accessibility by biking, an 8 km buffer distance is considered, as shown in Fig. 7(A). For Fig. 7(B), after determining the number of people within the 8 km buffer, a rate of 67% is applied to the population of Sardinia, and a rate of 78% is applied to the tourist population, based on the age range identified, which reflects the physical ability to bike. For the tourist numbers, the occupancy rates are applied first, then the biker rate when biking is involved, as shown in Table 3. The results show that 94.81% of tourists capable of biking have at least one ROS9 area within 8 km of their accommodation, while 78.75% of the population in Sardinia capable of biking have at least one ROS9 area within 8 km of their residence. However, it should be noted that some places in Sardinia, such as the main city Cagliari, may not be suitable for biking due to high levels of slope and challenging topographical conditions. Therefore, while these percentages are promising, a more detailed analysis considering the topographical conditions is needed.

To calculate the number of people who can reach a ROS9 area by train, the train stops within a 4-km distance of ROS9 areas are first identified, and the train lines serving these stops are mapped, shown in Fig. 8(A). Buffers are then created around the stops along these lines. Distances of 1 and 2 km are considered as walking distances to a train station, while an 8 km distance is also taken into account to accommodate the fact that bikes are allowed on trains, and some individuals may prefer this option. The total distribution of beneficiaries is seen in Fig. 8(B). At a 1 km distance from train stations serving ROS9 areas, 145,968 residents (9.42%) and 1,006 tourists (1.62%) are within reach. At 2 km, the resident number increases to 302,642 (19.53%), and the tourist number rises to 1,733 (2.79%). Within an 8 km distance, 491,689 residents (47.35% of the population within the identified age range for biking) and 5,261 tourists (10.86%) can

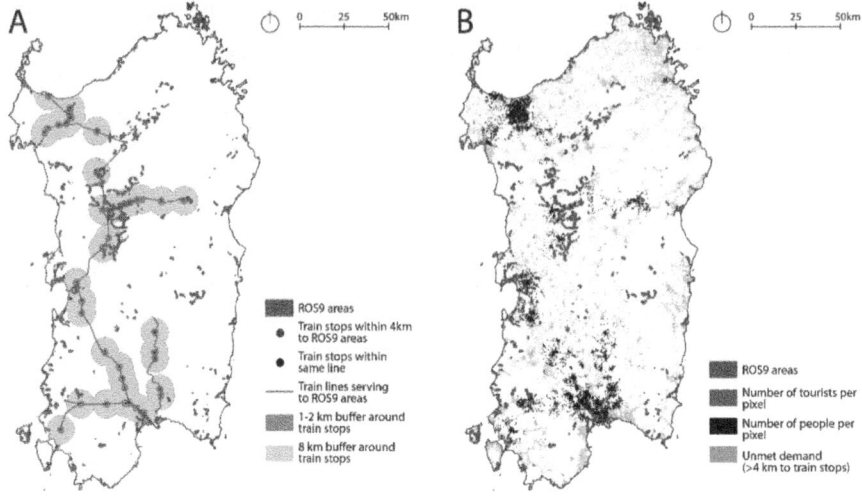

Fig. 8. Access by train; distances to train stops (A), distribution of beneficiaries (B).

access a ROS9 area by bike. Here, only people who live in close vicinity to a train station are considered, which explains the lower percentages compared to earlier calculations. For a more comprehensive analysis, if walking or biking directly to a ROS9 area is also preferred, Table 4, which shows all buffers cumulatively, should be considered for the calculation.

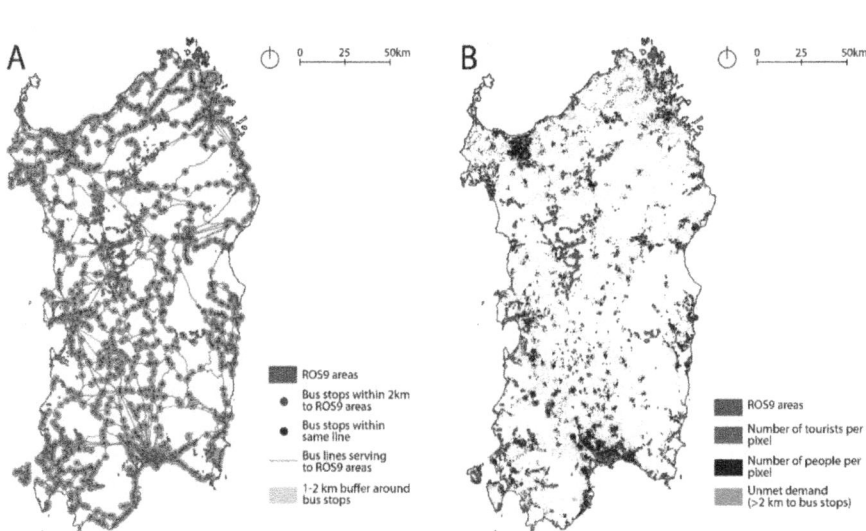

Fig. 9. Access by bus; distances to bus stops (A), distribution of beneficiaries (B).

To calculate the beneficiaries who can reach a ROS9 area by bus, the same method used for train stops is applied, considering only 1 km and 2 km distances as bikes are not allowed on buses. The results show that 1,467,368 people (94.68% of the population) live within 1 km of a bus stop that serves a ROS9 area, while for tourists this number is 46,855 corresponding to 75.46% of the total tourist numbers. Within 2 km, the population increases to 1,509,164 (97.38%), while tourists to 54,638 (87.99%). This indicates that the majority of people live in close proximity to a bus stop from which they can access a bus line to reach a ROS9 area. Here, the length of the bus trip is not considered. However, as shown in Fig. 9, ROS9 areas are not clustered in a few locations but are rather scattered across the region with numerous bus lines available to provide access. Therefore, it is assumed that the bus trip to reach a ROS9 area will not take too long. In the case of other regions, the trip duration could be considered.

Table 3. Distribution of population in terms of access to ROS9 areas, divided by type of transport.

	Population	Tourists in private accommodation (O.R. 22%)	Tourists in hotels and other facilities (O.R. 51.6%)	Tourists total O.R. applied
All Sardinia	**1549772**	Max capacity: 67150 O.R. applied: **14773**	Max capacity: 91701 O.R. applied: **47318**	**62091**
WALKING (distances around ROS9 areas)				
Distances	Population	% relative to the total in Sardinia	Tourists in private accommodation (O.R. 22%)	Tourists in hotels and other facilities (O.R. 51.6 %)	Tourist total O.R. applied	% relative to the total in Sardinia
1 km	**349624**	22.56%	Max capacity: 29867 O.R. applied: **6571**	Max Capacity: 52358 O.R. applied: **27016**	**33587**	54.09%
2 km	**633313**	40.86%	Max capacity: 45445 O.R. applied: **9998**	Max capacity: 66648 O.R. applied: **34391**	**44389**	71.49%
4 km	**937482**	60.49%	Max Capacity: 55863 O.R. applied: **12290**	Max capacity: 79927 O.R. applied: **41243**	**53533**	86.22%
BIKING (distances around ROS9 areas)				
8 km	Total: 1204902 Biker: **807284**	77.75%	Max capacity: 63142 O.R. applied: **13892**	Max capacity: 87168 O.R. applied: **44979**	Total: 58871 Biker: **45919**	94.81%
BY TRAIN (distances around train stops that serve to ROS9 areas)				
1 km	**145968**	9.42 %	Max capacity: 993 O.R. applied: **219**	Max capacity: 1527 O.R. applied: **787**	**1006**	1.62%
2 km	**302642**	19.53%	Max capacity: 2090 O.R. applied: **460**	Max capacity: 2467 O.R. applied: **1273**	**1733**	2.79%
8 km (biking)	Total: 733864 Biker: **491689**	47.35%	Max capacity: 7953 O.R. applied: **1750**	Max capacity: 9681 O.R. applied: **4995**	Total: 6745 Biker: **5261**	10.86%
BY BUS (distances around bus stops that serve ROS9 areas)				
1 km	**1467368**	94.68%	Max capacity: 52977 O.R. applied: **11654**	Max capacity: 68219 O.R. applied: **35201**	**46855**	75.46%
2 km	**1509164**	97.38%	Max capacity: 60418 O.R. applied: **13292**	Max capacity: 80128 O.R. applied: **41346**	**54638**	88%
BY CAR (distances around parking lots within 4km to ROS9 areas)				
15 km	**1518354**	97.97%	Max capacity: 65553 O.R. applied: **14422**	Max capacity: 90492 O.R. applied: **46694**	**61116**	98.43%

Figure 10 illustrates the aggregation of all buffers and transportation types considered, with scores assigned on a scale from 1 to 8, where 1 represents the highest preference. To prevent double-counting of beneficiaries, overlapping areas have been avoided. In cases of overlap, the area is assigned the higher score. The number of beneficiaries corresponding to these scores are presented in Table 4. This table provides the opportunity to calculate the sum of different transportation types while also providing

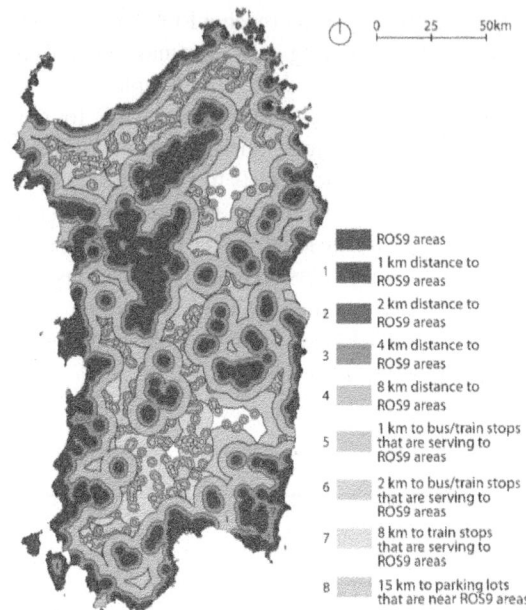

Fig. 10. Access to ROS9 areas by different types of transportation, distances with scores.

the option to include scores 1, 2, and 3 in the calculation to account for individuals who may walk directly to a ROS9 area. To calculate the sum, a cumulative addition from 1 to 8 is necessary.

5   Conclusion and Future Work

Results show that the ratio of tourists in vicinity to ROS9 areas is always higher considering access by walking and biking (see Table 3). Considering the vicinity to transportation options such as train or buses, the ratio of beneficiaries is higher in residents than tourists. This is logical since the active users of these stops are residents. However, when considering walking distance, while more than half of tourists can access ROS9 areas within 1 km and 2 km, less than a quarter of residents can reach a ROS9 area within 1 km, and this ratio is still under half within 2 km. This highlights the necessity for regional policies that focus on improving access for residents, ensuring equitable distribution of recreational services, and improving the overall quality of life for local communities; as uneven accessibility and availability of these services can limit marginalized communities' opportunities for nature-based recreation and the associated health and well-being benefits [27]. On the other hand, improving public transportation access in areas with accommodation facilities could be improved to promote sustainable tourism.

Acknowledging the importance of equitable distributions of ES across different target groups is key for environmental justice [27]. Research that aims to understand more deeply the relationship between supply and demand of ESs, as well as how policies can address inequalities in access, will enhance our understanding and help shape more

Table 4. Distribution of population in terms of access to ROS9 areas, all options scored.

	ALL TYPES OF TRANSPORT (distances around ROS9 areas and bus/train stops)					
SCORES	Population	% relative to the total in Sardinia	Tourists in private accommodation (O.R. 22%)	Tourists in hotels and other facilities (O.R. 51.6%)	Tourists total O.R. applied	% relative to the total in Sardinia
1	349624	22.56%	Max capacity: 29867 O.R. applied: **6571**	Max capacity: 52358 O.R. applied: **27017**	33588	54.09%
2	283688	18.31%	Max capacity: 15578 O.R. applied: **3427**	Max capacity: 14290 O.R. applied: **7374**	10801	17.40%
3	304169	19.63%	Max capacity: 10418 O.R. applied: **2292**	Max capacity: 13279 O.R. applied: **6852**	9144	14.73%
4	Total: 267420 Biker: **179171**	17.26%	Max capacity: 7279 O.R. applied: 1601 Biker: **1249**	Max capacity: 7241 O.R. applied: 3736 Biker: **2915**	Total: 5337 Biker: **4164**	8.60%
5	328383	21.19%	Max capacity: 2986 O.R. applied: **657**	Max capacity: 3658 O.R. applied: **1888**	2545	4.10%
6	8347	0.54%	Max capacity: 547 O.R. applied: **120**	Max capacity: 273 O.R. applied: **141**	261	0.42%
7	Total: 2337 Biker: **1566**	0.15%	Max capacity: 19 O.R. applied: 4 Biker: **3**	Max capacity: 13 O.R. applied: 7 Biker: **5**	Total: 11 Biker: **8**	0.02%
8	5610	0.36%	Max capacity: 261 O.R. applied: **57**	Max capacity: 221 O.R. applied: **114**	171	0.28%
TOTAL [exc. (8)]	1454948	99.63%	14376	46306	60682	99.35%

This table corresponds to Fig. 10. Overlapping areas are counted only under the highest score (1 being the highest, 8 being the lowest).

inclusive strategies for sustainable ES management. Green Infrastructure planning is a valuable approach to respond to the challenge of ensuring equitable access to ESs, aiming to provide equal opportunities for all citizens while promoting both social well-being and sustainable urban development.

This method, applied in Sardinia, provides a framework that can be easily adapted to other regions, demonstrating its versatility and potential for broader and cross-scale application. It allows to introduce different types of transportation possibilities to access recreational services. To avoid creating a complex framework, demographic information is only included for biking distances, considering the age range capable of biking to ensure more realistic figures. Introducing a survey to assess people's willingness to use these transportation options, combined with more comprehensive data such as including topographical variations in terrain, would be beneficial for future studies.

Acknowledgments. This article was produced while attending the PhD program in Sustainable Development and Climate Change at the University School for Advanced Studies IUSS Pavia & University of Cagliari, Cycle XXXIX, with the supervision of Prof. Sabrina Lai and the support of a scholarship financed by the Ministerial Decree no. 118 of March 2nd 2023, based on the NRRP - funded by the European Union - NextGenerationEU - Mission 4 "Education and Research", Component 1 "Enhancement of the offer of educational services: from nurseries to universities"

- Investment 4.1 "Extension of the number of research doctorates and innovative doctorates for public administration and cultural heritage".

Disclosure of Interests. The authors have no competing interests to declare that are relevant to the content of this article.

References

1. Ernstson, H.: The social production of ecosystem services: a framework for studying environmental justice and ecological complexity in urbanized landscapes. Landsc. Urban Plan. **109**, 7–17 (2013). https://doi.org/10.1016/j.landurbplan.2012.10.005
2. Zardo, L.: Analyzing ecosystem services and green urban infrastructures to support urban planning. http://eprints-phd.biblio.unitn.it/2086/ (2017)
3. Ghasemi, M., González-García, A., Charrahy, Z., Serrao-Neumann, S.: Utilizing supply-demand bundles in Nature-based Recreation offers insights into specific strategies for sustainable tourism management. Sci. Total. Environ. **922**, 171185 (2024). https://doi.org/10.1016/j.scitotenv.2024.171185
4. González-García, A., Palomo, I., González, J.A., López, C.A., Montes, C.: Quantifying spatial supply-demand mismatches in ecosystem services provides insights for land-use planning. Land Use Policy **94**, 104493 (2020). https://doi.org/10.1016/j.landusepol.2020.104493
5. Barton, D.N.: Monetary valuation of urban ecosystem services - operationalization or tragedy of well-intentioned valuation? An illustrated example. In: Ecosystem Services: concepts, methodologies and instruments for research and applied use. Documenta Universitaria, Girona (2016)
6. Vallecillo, S., et al.: Ecosystem services accounting. Part I, Outdoor recreation and crop pollination. EUR 29024 EN. Publications Office of the European Union, Luxembourg (2018)
7. Vallecillo, S., La Notte, A., Zulian, G., Ferrini, S., Maes, J.: Ecosystem services accounts: valuing the actual flow of nature-based recreation from ecosystems to people. Ecol. Model. **392**, 196–211 (2019). https://doi.org/10.1016/j.ecolmodel.2018.09.023
8. Baró, F., Palomo, I., Zulian, G., Vizcaino, P., Haase, D., Gómez-Baggethun, E.: Mapping ecosystem service capacity, flow and demand for landscape and urban planning: a case study in the Barcelona metropolitan region. Land Use Policy **57**, 405–417 (2016). https://doi.org/10.1016/j.landusepol.2016.06.006
9. Isola, F., Lai, S., Leone, F., Zoppi, C.: Green Infrastructure and Regional Planning: An Operational Framework: An Operational Framework. FrancoAngeli (2022)
10. Rossetti, I.: La Sardegna. (2012). Sardegna Natura. https://www.sardegnanatura.com/sardegna.html. Accessed 2025/02/05
11. Paracchini, M.L., et al.: Mapping cultural ecosystem services: a framework to assess the potential for outdoor recreation across the EU. Ecol. Indic. **45**, 371–385 (2014). https://doi.org/10.1016/j.ecolind.2014.04.018
12. Zulian, G., Paracchini, M.L., Liquete, C., Joachim, M.: ESTIMAP: Ecosystem services mapping at European scale. EUR 26474. Joint Research Centre: Institute for Environment and Sustainability. Publication Office., Luxembourg (2013)
13. Cortinovis, C., Geneletti, D.: Ecosystem services in urban plans: what is there, and what is still needed for better decisions. Land Use Policy **70**, 298–312 (2018). https://doi.org/10.1016/j.landusepol.2017.10.017
14. Kobak, B.: Transformation of disused railways based on ES assessment: sassari case. In: Gervasi, O., Murgante, B., Garau, C., Taniar, D., C. Rocha, A.M.A., Faginas Lago, M.N. (eds.) Computational Science and Its Applications – ICCSA 2024 Workshops. pp. 370–386. Springer, Cham (2024). https://doi.org/10.1007/978-3-031-65273-8_24

15. Schiavina, M., Freire, S., MacManus, K.: GHS-POP R2023A - GHS population grid multitemporal (1975–2030). http://data.europa.eu/89h/2ff68a52-5b5b-4a22-8f40-c41da8332cfe (2023). https://doi.org/10.2905/2FF68A52-5B5B-4A22-8F40-C41DA8332CFE

16. Heinen, E., Maat, K., Wee, B.V.: The role of attitudes toward characteristics of bicycle commuting on the choice to cycle to work over various distances. Transp. Res. Part Transp. Environ. **16**, 102–109 (2011). https://doi.org/10.1016/j.trd.2010.08.010

17. Price, A.E., Reed, J.A., Muthukrishnan, S.: Trail user demographics, physical activity behaviors, and perceptions of a newly constructed greenway trail. J. Community Health **37**, 949–956 (2012). https://doi.org/10.1007/s10900-011-9530-z

18. Senes, G., Rovelli, R., Bertoni, D., Arata, L., Fumagalli, N., Toccolini, A.: Factors influencing greenways use: definition of a method for estimation in the Italian context. J. Transp. Geogr. **65**, 175–187 (2017). https://doi.org/10.1016/j.jtrangeo.2017.10.014

19. Biking (Care of the Young Athlete). Pediatr. Patient Educ. (2021). https://doi.org/10.1542/peo_document278

20. WHO Guidelines on Physical Activity and Sedentary Behaviour. World Health Organization, Geneva (2020)

21. Istituto Nazionale di Statistica (ISTAT): Popolazione residente al 1° gennaio: Per fascia di età [Resident population on 1 January: By age group] (2024). http://dati.istat.it/Index.aspx?QueryId=42869

22. Sardegna Turismo: Dati 2022 [Data 2022] - Movimenti Turistici [Tourist Movements] (2022). http://osservatorio.sardegnaturismo.it/it/dashboard/dati-2022

23. Malichová, E., Cornet, Y., Hudák, M.: Travellers' use and perception of travel time in long-distance trips in Europe. Travel Behav. Soc. **27**, 95–106 (2022). https://doi.org/10.1016/j.tbs.2021.12.003

24. Contu, G., Conversano, C., Frigau, L., Mola, F.: Identifying factors affecting the status of superhost: evidence from Sardinia and Sicily. Qual. Quant. **54**, 1633–1653 (2020). https://doi.org/10.1007/s11135-019-00925-2

25. Eurostat: Tourism statistics - occupancy rates in hotels and similar establishments. https://ec.europa.eu/eurostat/statistics-explained/index.php?title=Tourism_statistics_-_occupancy_rates_in_hotels_and_similar_establishments (2019)

26. Eurostat: Net occupancy rates of bed places in hotels and similar establishments, December 2019, 4th quarter 2019, and January to December 2019 compared with the same periods of 2018 (%) (2019). https://ec.europa.eu/eurostat/statistics-explained/images/e/e2/Net_occupancy_rates_of_bed-places_in_hotels_and_similar_establishments%2C_December_2019%2C_4th_quarter_2019_and_January_to_December_2019_compared_with_the_same_periods_of_2018_%28%25%29.png

27. Langemeyer, J., Benra, F., Nahuelhual, L., Zoderer, B.M.: Ecosystem services justice: the emergence of a critical research field. Ecosyst. Serv. **69**, 101655 (2024). https://doi.org/10.1016/j.ecoser.2024.101655

A Methodological Approach for Identifying Hotspots of Regulating Ecosystem Services: Insights from Campania and Sardinia, Italy

Federica Isola[1] , Bilge Kobak[1,2] , Sabrina Lai[1(✉)] , Francesca Leccis[1] , and Federica Leone[1]

[1] Dipartimento di Ingegneria Civile, Ambientale e Architettura (DICAAR), University of Cagliari, Cagliari, Italy
{federica.isola,bilge.kobak,sabrinalai,francesca.leccis, federicaleone}@unica.it
[2] IUSS, Pavia, Italy

Abstract. The assessment of ecosystem services (ESs) plays a vital role in spatial planning and land-use decision-making. While ecosystems provide both tangible and intangible benefits essential for sustaining life, land-use changes driven by spatial planning influence the distribution and health of ecosystems, thereby affecting ES provision. To effectively identify priority areas for ES supply, it is essential to analyze ES hotspots, i.e., clusters of areas where individual ESs or bundles of ESs are delivered at high levels. Within this context, this study introduces a methodological approach for delineating ES hotspots. The first step involves a biophysical assessment of ESs, which here focuses on three regulating ESs: habitat quality, reflecting ecosystems' capacity to provide niches and nurseries for wildlife; carbon storage and sequestration, indicating their role in climate mitigation; and land surface temperature, serving as a measure of local temperature regulation by vegetation and unsealed soils. In the second step, various spatial statistical techniques for hotspots identification are integrated to reduce the sensitivity associated with relying on a single method. The proposed approach is applied in the Italian regions of Campania and Sardinia, revealing significant differences in the extent and the spatial distribution of areas that serve as hotspots for all three ecosystem services. The proposed approach to ES delineation can be readily applied in any context where ES biophysical assessments are available. Besides aiding the identification of key areas for ES supply, it provides planners and decision-makers with robust, easily communicable information that can be effectively understood by a broader audience.

Keywords: Carbon storage and sequestration · Habitat quality · Land surface temperature · Regulating ecosystem services · Hotspots

1 Introduction

Ecosystem services (ESs) are defined as the benefits that humans receive from natural and semi-natural ecosystems [1, 2]. Specifically, regulating ESs are those provided by the regulation capacity of ecosystem processes [3], including the moderation of natural

O. Gervasi et al. (Eds.): ICCSA 2025 Workshops, LNCS 15890, pp. 156–173, 2026.
https://doi.org/10.1007/978-3-031-97606-3_11

phenomena, such as carbon sequestration and regulation of local climate [4]. The prerequisite for these functions is the very existence of suitable habitats for wild plants and animals, which enables the maintenance of biological and genetic diversity [2].

Research shows that, along with climate change, changes in land use land cover (LULC) are one of the primary causes which affect ESs [5, 6]. These in turn alter location and persistence of ES hotspots [7, 8], thus potentially impacting the effectiveness of sustainable conservation programs [9]. Mapping and assessing ESs is therefore essential for achieving biodiversity objectives and informing sustainable policies [10]; however, it is the identification of ES hotspots that is particularly crucial for spatial planning, as it enables the prioritization of conservation areas [11].

Initially, the term "hotspot" was exclusively referred to areas exhibiting rich variety of species [12, 13]; nowadays, an ES hotspot can be either interpreted as the areas with high levels of supply of one particular ES [14, 15], or as the areas where multiple ESs simultaneously present high levels of supply [16, 17]. When defining the second type of ES hotspots, it is crucial to ascertain the presence of synergistic interactions among the analyzed ESs, as this influences the purpose of the identified areas. Indeed, where synergies are absent or positive these areas can be valuably designated for conservation, whereas, the presence of negative interactions may lead to conflicts, thus necessitating integrated management to address trade-offs effectively [18].

This study refers to both current definitions and focuses on regulating ESs. It firstly maps the regulating ES hotspots of carbon storage and sequestration (CSS), habitat quality (HQ), and land surface temperature (LST) in the Italian regions of Campania and Sardinia; next, regional hotspots that simultaneously provide the three ESs examined are identified, leading to the identification of areas that could be targeted as priority sites for conservation.

The study unfolds through the following three stages. First, the regulating ESs of CSS, HQ, and LST are biophysically assessed and mapped. Second, hotspots for each single ES are identified. Third, multi-service hotspot cores, representing the spatial overlap of core hotspot areas for CSS, HQ, and LST, are delineated. Following this introduction, the materials and methods section provides information on the two case studies and illustrates the methodological approach developed to assess the three regulating ESs and identify ES hotspots. Finally, the results are presented and discussed, and conclusions are drawn.

2 Materials and Methods

This section is organized into three subsections. The first provides some information on the two case studies, i.e. the Italian regions of Campania and Sardinia; the second, further subdivided into three paragraphs, briefly describes how the three selected regulating ESs were assessed; finally, the third explains the methodological approach allowing for the identification of ES hotspots.

2.1 Study Areas: Sardinia and Campania

The region of Campania, located in southern Italy (Fig. 1, panel A), covers a total area of 13,700 square kilometers [19]. As of January 1, 2025, the total population of Campania was 5,575,025, making it the third most populous region, with Napoli, the regional capital, accounting for 908,082 inhabitants [20]. The region is bordered by Lazio to the northwest, Molise to the north, Apulia to the northeast, and Basilicata to the east, with the Tyrrhenian Sea to the south and west. The region's landscape is mostly made up of hills (51%) and mountains (35%), while the plains, covering 14% of the area, are alluvial and were formed in ancient times by the two main rivers, Volturno and Sele. The Campanian landscape is characterized by a diverse range of relief features, including limestone mountains such as the Matese, Sannio, Irpinia, and Alburni ranges, clay-based hills prone to landslides, and the dormant Vesuvius volcano, all of which are subject to seismic activity. Average altitude is 322 m [21]. A GIS analysis considering the first-level 2018 Corine Land Cover (CLC) classes reveals that slightly less than 40% of the regional territory is covered by woodland and semi-natural environments.

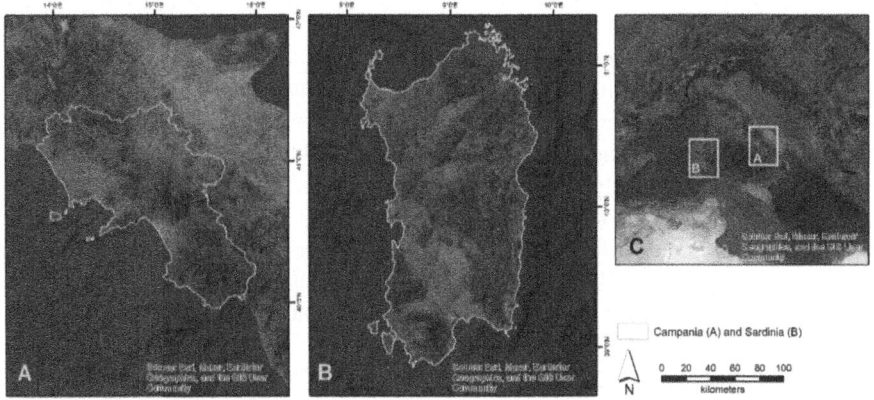

Fig. 1. Study areas: Campania (panel A) and Sardinia (panel B) in the Italian context (panel C).

The region of Sardinia, also situated in southern Italy (Fig. 1, panel B), is an island spanning a total area of 24,100 square kilometers [19]. The total number of inhabitants was 1,581,339 as of January 1, 2025 [20], and the capital city of the region is Cagliari with 146,627 inhabitants [20]. The island is bordered by the Tyrrhenian Sea to the east and south, and the Mediterranean to the west. The region is largely mountainous, characterized by several isolated mountain ranges, including Gennargentu, Sette Fratelli, and Limbara, along with hilly terrains, plateaus, and a few plains [22]. The average altitude is 300 m [23]. Major rivers like Coghinas, Tirso, and Flumendosa, which follow tectonic fractures and have carved deep valleys due to past uplifts, exhibit a predominantly torrential flow reflecting the island's dry summers and limited rainfall [22]. Considering the first-level CLC classes, around 49% of the total regional land area is occupied by woodland and semi-natural environments.

2.2 Ecosystem Service Mapping

Carbon Storage and Sequestration. The assessment of CSS was conducted using the Carbon storage and sequestration model of the InVEST (the Integrated Valuation of

Ecosystem Services) suite, a free and open-source modeling tool created by the Natural Capital Project [24] to map and assess ESs. InVEST helps compare alternative land use scenarios by evaluating their environmental impact [25] and integrates data on the often-overlooked, intangible benefits of ecosystems into decision-making processes, especially for local and regional planning [26]. In particular, the CSS model estimates total carbon storage across four carbon pools: aboveground and belowground biomass (within the top 30 cm of soil), dead organic matter, and soil organic matter. According to the InVEST User Guide, above-ground biomass (AGB) includes all living plant material above ground, while below-ground biomass (BGB) refers to the living roots of AGB. Dead organic matter (DOM) consists of leaf litter and dead wood. Soil organic matter (SOM), the largest carbon pool, includes organic material within the soil.

The CSS model has been applied in a variety of studies around the world. For instance, García-Ontiyuelo et al. [27] use it to estimate carbon sequestration in the coastal forests of southern Galicia to support sustainable forest management. Rachid et al. [28] evaluate the CSS benefits provided by urban greening in Nador for climate action. The CSS model is instrumental in studying how land use changes impact on carbon storage in the Sariska Tiger Reserve in India [29]. Moreover, the CSS model is useful to evaluate biodiversity and ES changes [30], to analyze the economic value of carbon sequestration [31], and to assess hurricane-related carbon and timber losses [32]. Other applications include examining urban development impacts, as in the Changzhutan area [33], and evaluating how land-use policies affect carbon storage in mixed-use landscapes [34].

The CSS model requires two key input datasets: i., a csv table with carbon density values assigned to each land cover class for at least one carbon pool, expressed in megagrams per hectare (Mg ha⁻1), and, ii., a land cover map. In this study, three carbon pools were analyzed within InVEST, with belowground biomass incorporated in the final phase by overlaying the NASA Oak Ridge National Laboratory Distributed Active Archive Center (ORNL DAAC) map onto the InVEST results and aggregating the values. The carbon density values for the csv table were derived from multiple sources, including NASA's Oak Ridge National Laboratory Distributed Active Archive Center (ORNL DAAC) [35], which provides the Global Carbon Map for AGB and BGB pools. Additional sources include the 2015 National Inventory of Forests and Carbon Pools [36], datasets from ISPRA, the Italian Institute for Environmental Research and Protection [37], data from the Regional Agricultural Research Agency of Sardinia [38], and classifications from the CLC map [39]. Data inputs are summarized in Table 1.

Habitat Quality. The InVEST Habitat quality model was used to assess HQ, informed by the work of Sallustio et al. [40], who provide expert-based data on threats, sensitivity, and habitat suitability. The model requires four key inputs: i., a land cover map (TIFF); ii., a folder of threat maps (TIFF); iii., a sensitivity table (CSV); and, iv., a threats table (CSV). Data inputs are summarized in Table 1. Habitat types in the study area were classified based on the 2018 CLC map: the existing categories were grouped into 12 broad categories based on [40], with an additional "mixed forest" category included to account for this specific type in Sardinia, hence totaling 13 categories.

The parameters needed for the threats table include maximum influence distance (MAX_DIST), indicating the extent of a threat's impact (km); relative weight (WEIGHT), ranking threats from 0 (low) to 1 (high); and decay parameter (DECAY),

Table 1. Data inputs and sources (last access date for all sources: 2025/04/07).

Ecosystem service	Data input	Data source
Carbon storage and sequestration	CSV table with carbon density values assigned to each land cover class	Aboveground biomass • ORNL DAAC (https://daac.ornl.gov/cgi-bin/dsviewer.pl?ds_id=1763) • INFC2015 (https://www.inventarioforestale.org/it/il-contenuto-di-carbonio-della-vegetazione-carbon-stock-in-the-aboveground-living-biomass)
		Belowground biomass • ORNL DAAC (https://daac.ornl.gov/cgi-bin/dsviewer.pl?ds_id=1763)
		Dead organic matter • INFC2015 (https://www.inventarioforestale.org/it/il-contenuto-di-carbonio-della-vegetazione-carbon-stock-in-the-aboveground-living-biomass)
		Soil organic carbon • INFC2005 (https://www.sian.it/inventarioforestale/jsp/dati_carquant_tab.jsp?menu=3) • ISPRA (https://www.mase.gov.it/sites/default/files/archivio/normativa/linee_guida_ISPRA_implementazione_RED_II.pdf) • AGRIS Sardegna (http://www.sardegnaportalesuolo.it/opendata/carta-della-distribuzione-del-carbonio-organico-del-progetto-cut-alla-scala-150000.html)
	Land cover map	Copernicus - Corine Land Cover 2018 (https://land.copernicus.eu/en/products/corine-land-cover/clc2018)
Habitat quality	Threats table	Sallustio et al. (2017) [40]
	Sensitivity table	Sallustio et al. (2017) [40]

(*continued*)

Table 1. (*continued*)

Ecosystem service	Data input	Data source
	Threat maps	Geofabrik. OpenStreetMap Data Extracts – Italy (https://download. geofabrik.de/europe/italy/Geo fabrik)
	Land Cover map	Copernicus - Corine Land Cover 2018 (https://land.copernicus.eu/ en/products/corine-land-cover/clc 2018)
Land surface temperature	Landsat 8–9 OLI/ TIRS Collection 2, Level 2	USGS Earth Explorer (https://ear thexplorer.usgs.gov/)

describing whether a threat's effect diminishes linearly or exponentially over space. While other values follow Sallustio et al. [40], the decay parameter was here assumed to be linear due to data limitations, therefore providing a conservative worst-case estimate of the threat's impact.

The sensitivity table lists habitat types and their sensitivity scores to each threat, with values derived from [40]. For the newly added "mixed forest" category, the score was calculated as the average of the "broadleaved" and "conifers" categories.

Land Surface Temperature. As per the Global Climate Observing System (GCOS) [41], LST is a key parameter for assessing land surface conditions and land-atmosphere exchange thermal emissions processes. The analysis of LST provides a solid base for spatial prioritization within sustainable spatial planning strategies aimed at climate regulation through LST mitigation [42]. In this subsection, the identification of areas where LST take on significantly high or low values in Campania and Sardinia is presented. Despite their differing geographical characteristics, both regions have experienced a marked increase in the frequency and intensity of heat waves in recent years [43].

The analysis was performed on satellite imagery; LST was mapped by using Landsat 2-Level 2 collection (Landsat 8–9 OLI/TIRS C2 L2 with a spatial resolution of 30 m, see Table 1) satellite images [44] retrieved from the United States Geological Survey (USGS) Earth Explorer platform. The image search was limited to the Summer of 2023 (time frame from June 25, 2023 to September 2, 2023) with a 6 percent maximum threshold on cloud cover. LST values were calculated using the Landsat B10 thermal band. Due to limitations in the spatial coverage of satellite imagery, multiple raster images from different acquisition scenes were collected. Among the retrieved images, those with the highest mean LST values were selected to generate the final composite LST maps.

As regards the Campania region, a total of 21 satellite images were retrieved; because no single-date images covering the whole region were available due to the configuration of satellite images, three sets of three/four images were used to fully cover the region. Once the raster images belonging to the same scene and date were merged, those with the highest mean values were subsequently selected. The final LST map for Campania was constructed using four Landsat images, as detailed in Table 2.

Regarding Sardinia, the same selection criteria (time frame and cloud cover) yielded 51 satellite images. Five of these images were required to ensure complete coverage of the region, as illustrated in Table 2.

Table 2. Selected Landsat images to create LST map for Campania and Sardinia Regions.

Region	Image code	Scene	Date
Campania	LC09_L2SP_189031_20230717_20230719_02_T1_ST_B10	189	July 17, 2023
	LC09_L2SP_189032_20230717_20230719_02_T1_ST_B10	189	July 17, 2023
	LC09_L2SP_190031_20230825_20230827_02_T1_ST_B10	190	August 25, 2023
	LC09_L2SP_190032_20230825_20230827_02_T1_ST_B10	190	August 25, 2023
Sardinia	LC08_L2SP_192033_20230730_20230805_02_T1_ST_B10	192	July 30, 2023
	LC08_L2SP_192032_20230730_20230805_02_T1_ST_B10	192	July 30, 2023
	LC09_L2SP_193033_20230814_20230817_02_T1_ST_B10	193	August 14, 2023
	LC09_L2SP_193032_20230814_20230817_02_T1_ST_B10	193	August 14, 2023
	LC09_L2SP_193031_20230814_20230817_02_T1_ST_B10	193	August 14, 2023

2.3 Hotspot Mapping

Various methods have been used in the literature for hotspot detection; according to Bagstad et al. [45], they can be grouped in three categories as follows: i., based on local spatial autocorrelation-based indices; ii., ES quantile-based; iii., area-based. Moreover, different approaches for identifying multi-service areas, which serve as hotspots for a plurality of ESs, have been proposed; for a classification of such approaches, the reader can refer to Schröter and Remme [18]. Both [45] and [18] show how different methods yield different hotspots. In this regard, Anselin [46, ch. 17.5], who focuses on approaches based on spatial statistic indexes, argues that "interesting locations" are those that remain detected as clusters regardless of the method or of the criteria used. Therefore, four methods were applied and integrated in this study to identify hotspots for each single ES: Local Index of Spatial Autocorrelation (LISA), median LISA, Getis-Ord (G*), and, finally, top-richest cells (i.e., quantile-based segmentation).

LISA, as per Anselin's definition, is an umbrella term for any statistics that "for each observation gives an indication of the extent of significant spatial clustering of similar values aggregation around that observation" [47, p.94], and for which a proportionality link between the sum of LISAs for all observations and a global indicator of autocorrelation exists. As implemented in GeoDa [48], LISA consists of a local application of Moran's index of spatial autocorrelation (I), by using a moving window that centers in a spatial unit and whose size and shape depend on the contiguity criterion in use. The result is a cluster map that, at assigned significance levels, categorizes clusters into four groups (HH, or hotspots; LL, or coldspots; HL and LH, spatial outliers) depending on whether the values in the observed spatial unit and in its surrounding area, as defined by the contiguity criterion, are higher (H) or lower (L) than the average. An extension of the traditional LISA, also implemented in GeoDa [48], is the median LISA statistics, which operates in a similar manner, but uses the median value instead of the mean, therefore reducing the impact of outliers.

The third statistic here used is the local G* proposed by Getis and Ord [49, 50] and widely used in cluster analysis. Similarly to LISA, local G* uses a moving window centered in the spatial unit being observed; it is defined as the ratio of the sum of the values within the window to the sum of values in the entire dataset. In contrast to LISA, local G* only yields hotspots and coldspots, but not spatial outliers [46, ch. 17.4].

For all the three above-mentioned local statistics, in this study, the queen criterion at the first level of contiguity was used.

The fourth method applied in this study is the quantile-based method, with a cut-off value set at the 90th percentile, hence focusing on the top 10% of grid cells with the highest values.

A four-step approach was applied in this study. The first step involved creating a vector grid composed of square cells with 200-m sides and covering the two study areas; for each cell, the mean values of the three selected ESs were calculated through zonal statistics and assigned to the cells as attributes. In the second step, the four selected methods for hotspot delineation were applied to the three ES maps in the two study areas; as a result, four hotspot maps were obtained for each ES. In the third step, for each ES the four corresponding hotspot maps were intersected, with a view to identifying those cells that remain identified as hotspot cores regardless of the method. Finally, in the fourth step a further intersection was applied so as to identify the cells that perform simultaneously as hotspot cores for CCS, HQ, and LST.

3   Results

This section is organized into four subsections. The first three sections describe the spatial distribution of the three selected ESs in Campania and in Sardinia, whereas the fourth accounts for ES hotspots in the two study areas.

3.1   Carbon Storage and Sequestration

Figure 2, panel A illustrates the distribution of carbon storage across the Campania Region, with values ranging from 0 to 21.55 megagrams per 900 square meters. The highest carbon storage values are grouped in distinct clusters, particularly in the central and southern parts of the region. These high values are mostly located within protected natural areas, like Regional Park of Roccamonfina - Garigliano Outfall, Matese Regional Park, area of Trebulani Mountains, Taburno-Camposauro Regional Park, and Partenio Regional Park in the north-west; Vesuvius National Park, Natural Reserve of Tirone Alto Vesuvius, Lattari Mountain Regional Park, Picentini Mountain Regional Park and Natural Reserve of Eremita-Marzano Mountains in the central area; and, finally, National Park of Cilento and Vallo di Diano in the south. In contrast, medium to low carbon storage values are found in more urbanized or cultivated zones, such as the Metropolitan City of Naples and the surrounding plains and hills. The data also shows that broad-leaved (CLC 311), coniferous (CLC 312), and mixed forests (CLC 313) have the highest average carbon storage, whereas artificial areas and watercourses show the lowest levels.

Carbon storage values in Sardinia vary from 0 to 16 megagrams per 900 square meters. All four carbon pools exhibit the same spatial pattern, with the largest concentrations occurring in the mountainous and forested areas of eastern and southwestern Sardinia, as seen in Fig. 2, panel B, including Sette Fratelli and the Gennargentu mountain chain as well as the two National parks of Asinara and of La Maddalena, and the three Regional Natural Parks of Porto Conte, Tepilora, and Gutturu Mannu. The land cover classes with the highest mean carbon storage values are coniferous and mixed forests (CLC 312 and 313), with averages of 11.4 and 11.1 megagrams per 900 square meters, respectively. Conversely, in every pool, the average values of broadleaved forests (CLC 311) are consistently lower than those of the other forest types in this region, the total average value being 9.9 megagrams per 900 square meters. Inland water bodies, artificial surfaces (CLC 111, 112, 121, 122, 123, 124, 131, 132, 133, 422, 511, 512, 521, 522, 523) have the lowest carbon storage values with values lower than 2 megagrams per 900 square meters, followed by agricultural areas (CLC 211, 212, 213, 241) with mean values below 4 megagrams per 900 square meters and vineyards, fruit trees and complex cultivation patterns (CLC 221, 222, 223, 242) below 5 megagrams per 900 square meters.

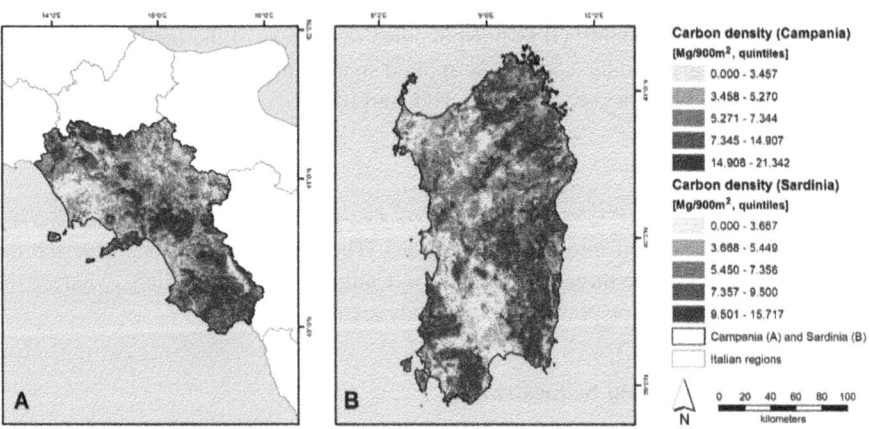

Fig. 2. Carbon storage and sequestration in Campania (panel A) and Sardinia (panel B).

3.2 Habitat Quality

The spatial distribution of habitat quality values is depicted for the Campania Region in Fig. 3, panel A, and for the Sardinia Region in Fig. 3, panel B.

In the Campania region, the average habitat quality value is 0.49. Specifically, 40.61% of the region consists of low-quality habitats ($0 < HQ \leq 0.33$), 27.96% exhibits medium-quality habitats ($0.33 < HQ \leq 0.66$), and the remaining 31.43% is comprised of high-quality habitats ($0.66 < HQ \leq 1$). These highest values are predominantly concentrated in green spaces, especially forested areas, frequently protected by parks and reserves. Conversely, the lowest values are observed in extensive urban areas and those dominated by intensive agriculture. Although 13 habitat types were intended for analysis, mixed forests were not found within the boundaries of the Campania region. Among the analyzed habitats, broadleaved forests showed the highest average quality (mean = 0.85), closely followed by grasslands (mean = 0.80). In contrast, the lowest mean score, approaching zero, is recorded in buildings and other artificial areas or impervious soils (aggregated from CLC 111, 112, 121, 122, 123, 124, 131, 132, 133) with a score of 0.09. The second-lowest values are observed in open urban areas (aggregated from CLC 141, 142) and intensive agricultural lands (aggregated from CLC 211, 212, 213, 221, 222, 223), with mean values of 0.22 and 0.24, respectively.

Figure 3, panel B, depicts the spatial distribution of HQ values across the Sardinia region. The average habitat quality value is 0.54. When examining the distribution of habitat quality across the region—categorized as low (values ranging from 0 to 0.33), medium (0.33 to 0.66), and high (0.66 to 1)—it emerges that 31.05% of the area is characterized by low-quality habitats. Medium-quality habitats account for 28.06% of the region, whereas high-quality habitats represent the largest share, covering 40.86% of the total area. The highest values are concentrated on forest areas scattered around the eastern part of the island. The highest mean habitat quality values are observed in broadleaved forests (CLC 311), with an average value of 0.85. This is followed by mixed forests (CLC 313) at 0.78, grasslands (CLC 321) at 0.77, and coniferous forests (CLC 312) at 0.75. Conversely, the lowest mean value, 0.09, is associated with artificial surfaces (CLC 111, 112, 121, 122, 123, 124, 131, 132, 133), followed by open urban areas (CLC 141 and 142). These results suggest that urban green spaces make a limited contribution to the provision of this type of ecosystem service.

3.3 Land Surface Temperature

In Campania, the LST values are within the range of 27.8–64.5 °C, as shown in Fig. 4, panel A. The highest LST values are observed in urban and artificial areas in the north-western part of the region, with reference to the Metropolitan City of Naples and in the north-eastern sectors of the provinces of Avellino and Benevento. The lowest LSTs are found in the green belt along the "Dorsale Appenninica" from the northeastern border, in mountainous and hilly areas. Regarding CLC classes, the highest mean values (47.6–53.3 °C) are associated with artificial surfaces, specifically continuous and discontinuous urban fabrics (CLC 111, 112). An exception is represented by urban green areas (CLC 141), which exhibit lower mean temperatures. The lowest mean values (34.3–39.4 °C)

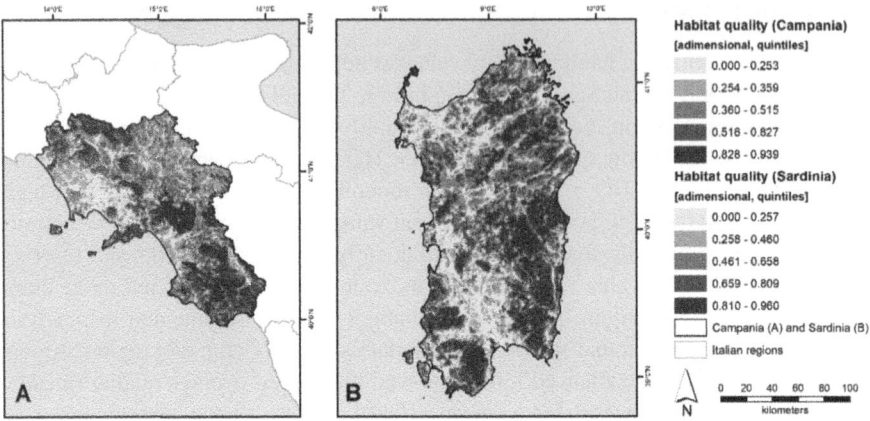

Fig. 3. Habitat quality in Campania (panel A) and Sardinia (panel B).

are observed in coastal wetlands and water bodies (CLC 521 and 512), forests (CLC 311, 312, 313), and areas covered by scrubs and herbaceous vegetation (CLC 323, 324).

In Sardinia, LST values range from 29.8 to 61.9 °C, as illustrated in Fig. 4, panel B. The highest values are observed in agricultural areas on the eastern part of the island as seen in three big clusters. Low values are observed in areas characterized by mountains, forests, and regional parks such as Mounts Limbara and Sulcis-Iglesiente, Gennargentu massif and Sette Fratelli. Regarding the corresponding CLC classes, agricultural areas (CLC 211, 212, 221, 222–231, 241–244) generally exhibit high mean LST values (46.9-51.5 °C). However, the category with the highest mean value is recorded in artificial areas (CLC 111, 112, 121–124, 131–133, 141, 142), reflecting the urban heat island effect. Urbanized areas show high values (44.4–54.0 °C) except for the "sports and leisure facilities" class (CLC 142), showing a mean value of 42.1 °C. The lowest mean values are observed in water-related classes (CLC 512, 521–523) with mean values ranging from 32 °C to 36 °C, and in forest areas (CLC 311–313) with the average LST ranging between 39.1 and 40.2 °C, possibly due to shading and evapotranspiration.

3.4 Ecosystem Services Hotspot

Core areas of the hotspots, defined here as cells that simultaneously exhibit high values across all three ESs (i.e., above the 90th percentile in each distribution) and that are consistently identified as cluster cores with a confidence level of 95% regardless of the spatial statistics applied, are presented in Fig. 5 for Campania (panel A) and Sardinia (panel B). The smaller panels (A1-A3 and B1-B3) provide the spatial layout of hotspots identified for each ES.

Cells that perform as hotspots simultaneously for the three regulating ESs assessed in this study make up a total of 643.68 km^2 in Campania and 208.6 km^2 in Sardinia, thus 4.7% and 0.08% of their land masses, respectively. Furthermore, the exclusion of small hotspots, i.e., those measuring less than 20 hectares, results in a reduction of the total

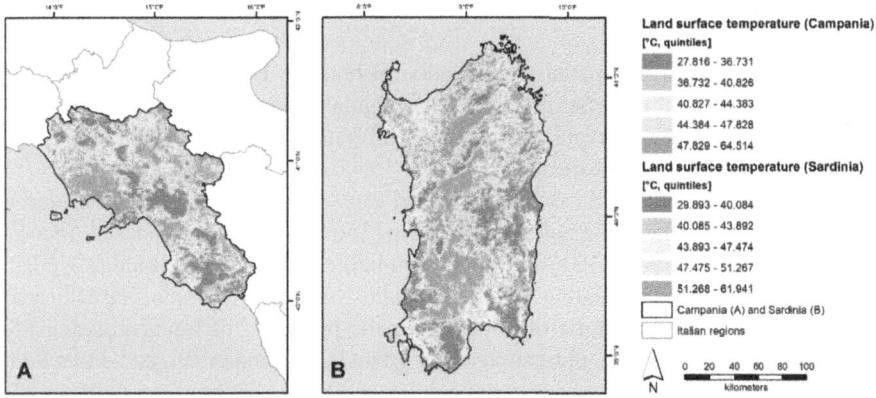

Fig. 4. Land surface temperature in Campania (panel A) and Sardinia (panel B).

area interested by hotspot cores to 606.20 km^2 in Campania and 149.4 km^2 in Sardinia, therefore equaling 4.4% and 0.06% of the two regions.

As clearly visible in Fig. 5, hotspots in panels A and B tend to be much larger in size in Campania than in Sardinia, with average sizes of 0.78 km^2 and 0.18 km^2, respectively; this feature reflects i., the spatial aggregation of individual ES hotspots, and, ii., higher levels of synergy between the three ESs; both aspects are more significant in Campania than in Sardinia (panels A1-A3 and B1-B3). Moreover, notable differences concern their spatial layout: while in Campania large hotspots form a sort of north-west to south-east inner belt, in Sardinia smaller and scattered hotspots are mostly found in the eastern and southern parts of the region.

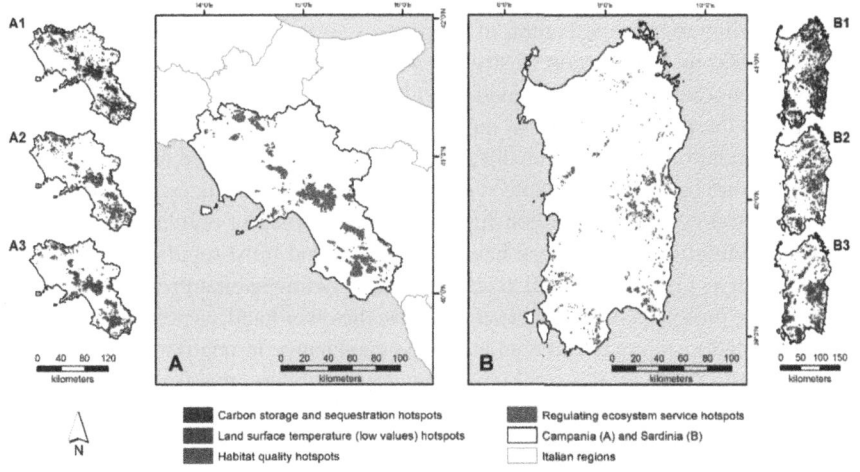

Fig. 5. Regulating ecosystem services hotspots in Campania (panel A) and Sardinia (panel B).

4 Discussion

This study focuses on the spatial identification of hotspots capable of simultaneously providing three regulating ESs: global climate regulation through carbon storage and sequestration, local climate regulation through LST measurement, and habitat provision through habitat quality assessment.

Several studies have addressed the issue of hotspot identification by considering different ESs. Although some authors, including [3] and [51, 52], consider all four ES groups as classified by MA [3] (provisioning, regulating, supporting and cultural), others [53–57] concentrate on regulating services, as in this study. For example, Nardella et al. [57] focus on the identification of hotspots for the provision of four regulating ESs (PM_{10} removal, O_3 removal, mitigation of the urban heat island effect, and urban flood risk mitigation) in order to assess the synergies and trade-offs between the four ESs in seven coastal Italian metropolitan cities. Moreover, according to Zheng et al. [58], the interactions between various regulating ecosystem services can vary significantly, depending on which services are considered, the scale at which they are analyzed, and the methods used for their assessment.

Our analysis shows that hotspots capable of simultaneously providing the three regulating ESs represent 4.4% of the regional territory in Campania and 0.06% in Sardinia. This different percentage is due to the fact that in Sardinia patches showing the highest values are scattered and not clustered as in the case of Campania. In Campania major hotspots create an internal corridor stretching from north-west to south-east. These areas correspond to the forested areas inside some protected areas, starting from the Matese Regional Park in the north to the Cilento and Vallo di Diano National Park in the south. This result is consistent with the results provided by Lin et al. [53], who identified hotspots related to the provision of six ESs, including carbon storage and habitat quality, and show that hotspots related to carbon storage and habitat quality are located in forested areas. This is also valid in the case of Sardinia, where the hotspots, although not corresponding to protected areas, in many cases concern forested areas, whose altitude exceeds 900 m. Furthermore, a strong synergy between habitat quality and carbon storage and sequestration values is evident in both Sardinia and Campania. This result is in line with the results reported in the study by Lee and Lautenbach [59], who analyze pairwise relationships between different typologies of ESs based on a review of the existing literature in order to promote synergies between the ESs themselves; they show that the strongest synergistic relationships concern the group of regulating ESs, and in particular, the relationship between habitat provision and most regulating ES. This is consistent with de Groot et al.'s [2] assertion, as they define habitat provision as a basic element for the provision of the other services. On the other hand, as pointed out in other studies, the relationship between regulating ESs can change in relation to other factors, such as vegetation and soil type, or human-environment interactions expressed in terms of land uses and socio-economic factors [59, 60].

5   Conclusions

The methodological approach proposed in this study enables the identification of hotspots of three key regulating ESs, i.e., areas having high ecological values. This information is of relevance to planners and decision-makers for two reasons. First, the outcomes highlight the need for the protection and conservation of regulating ES hotspots, as these areas are rich in natural resources that might be subject to increasing pressure. Targeted conservation measures are therefore needed to ensure the long-term sustainability of their ecosystem functions, in the context of rapid land use and land cover changes driven, for instance, by increasingly intense urbanization processes. Second, the identification of areas characterized by high levels of ES supply provides a significant foundation for policies aimed at enhancing these regulating ESs by improving the ecosystem's functional capacity to deliver ESs. In this context, enhancement refers to the implementation of strategies to improve the management and performance of natural ecosystems that possess high biophysical value and deliver considerable benefits to humans.

A potential future direction for this research involves the broader application of the proposed framework to identify ES hotspots, by introducing further key regulating ESs. This would be of particular importance, for example, in areas that have undergone substantial soil sealing, where remaining patches of unsealed soil and vegetated areas play a crucial role in addressing hydrogeological hazards or climate-related phenomena such as land degradation, desertification, or drought. In such areas, identifying ES hotspots and implementing spatial strategies aiming at their conservation, enhancement, and expansion can contribute to mitigating pressures from growing urbanization and can effectively foster climate adaptation. Finally, the proposed methodology is adaptable and could be applied to other contexts with different biophysical characteristics, as well as to other regions, provided that similar input datasets are available.

Acknowledgments. F. Isola, B. Kobak, S. Lai, F. Leccis, and F. Leone collaboratively designed this study. Individual contributions are as follows: F. Isola: Sect. 5; B. Kobak: Sect. 2.2; S. Lai: Sects. 2.3 and 3.4; F. Leccis: Sect. 1; F. Leone: Sect. 4. Joint contributions are as follows: Sect. 2.2 (CCS) and 3.1: F. Leone & B. Kobak; Sect. 2.2 (HQ) and 3.2: F. Leccis & B. Kobak; Sect. 2.2 (LST) and 3.4: F. Isola & B. Kobak This study was carried out: i., within the RETURN Extended Partnership and received funding from the European Union NextGenerationEU (National Recovery and Resilience Plan — NRRP, M4C2, Investment 1.3—D.D. 1243/2022, PE0000005); ii, with the financial support under the NRRP, M4C2, Investment 1.1, Call for tender 1409/2022 by the Italian Ministry of University and Research (MUR), funded by the European Union—NextGenerationEU—Project Title "Definition of a guidelines handbook to implement climate neutrality by improving ecosystem service effectiveness in rural and urban areas"—CUP F53D23010760001—Grant Assignment Decree 1378/2023, by MUR; iii, within the research grant CUP F73C23001680007 for the project "Geodesign for climate change mitigation and adaptation in the Mediterranean region" funded in 2022 by Fondazione di Sardegna. B. Kobak's scholarship at the PhD program "Sustainable Development and Climate Change" (IUSS Pavia) is financed by MUR through Ministerial Decree no. 118/2023, based on the NRRP - funded by the NRRP, M4C1, Investment 4.1 "Extension of the number of research doctorates and innovative doctorates for public administration and cultural heritage".

Disclosure of Interests.   The authors have no competing interests to declare.

References

1. Helliwell, D.R.: Valuation of wildlife resources. Reg. Stud. **3**(1), 41–47 (1969). https://doi.org/10.1080/09595236900185051
2. de Groot, R.S., Wilson, M.A., Boumans, R.M.J.: A typology for the classification, description and valuation of ecosystem functions, goods and services. Ecol. Econ. **4**(3), 393–408 (2002). https://doi.org/10.1016/S0921-8009(02)00089-7
3. MA (Millennium Ecosystem Assessment): Ecosystems and human well-being: A framework for assessment. Island Press: Washington, DC, US (2003)
4. Balasubramanian, M.: Economic value of regulating ecosystem services: a comprehensive at the global level review. Environ. Monit. Assess. **191**, 616 (2019). https://doi.org/10.1007/s10661-019-7758-8
5. Sun, L., Yu, H., Sun, M., Wang, Y.: Coupled impacts of climate and land use changes on regional ecosystem services. J. Environ. Manag. **326**, 116753 (2023). https://doi.org/10.1016/j.jenvman.2022.116753
6. Kohestani, N., Rastgar, S., Heydari, G., Jouibary, S.S., Amirnejad, H.: Spatiotemporal modeling of the value of carbon sequestration under changing land use/land cover using InVEST model: a case study of Nour-rud Watershed. Northern Iran. Environ. Dev. Sustain. **26**, 14477–14505 (2024). https://doi.org/10.1007/s10668-023-03203-2
7. Runting, R.K., et al.: Incorporating climate change into ecosystem service assessments and decisions: a review. Glob. Change Biol. **23**(1), 28–41 (2017). https://doi.org/10.1111/gcb.13457
8. Spake, R., et al.: Unpacking ecosystem service bundles: towards predictive mapping of synergies and trade-offs between ecosystem services. Glob. Environ. Change **47**, 37–50 (2017). https://doi.org/10.1016/j.gloenvcha.2017.08.004
9. Dong, X., et al.: Entwining ecosystem services, land use change and human well-being by nitrogen flows. J. Clean. Prod. **308**, 127442 (2021). https://doi.org/10.1016/j.jclepro.2021.127442
10. Maes, J., et al.: An indicator framework for assessing ecosystem services in support of the EU Biodiversity Strategy to 2020. Ecosyst. Serv. **17**, 14–23 (2016). https://doi.org/10.1016/j.ecoser.2015.10.023
11. Mitchell, M.G.E., et al.: Identifying key ecosystem service providing areas to inform national-scale conservation planning. Environ. Res. Lett. **16**, 014038 (2021). https://doi.org/10.1088/1748-9326/abc121
12. Myers, N.: Threatened biotas: "Hot spots" in tropical forests. Environmentalist **8**, 187–208 (1988). https://doi.org/10.1007/BF02240252
13. van Jaarsveld, A.S., et al.: Biodiversity assessment and conservation strategies. Science **279**(5359), 2106–2108 (1998). https://www.science.org/doi/https://doi.org/10.1126/science.279.5359.2106
14. Cimon-Morin, J.Ô., Darveau, M., Poulin, M.: Fostering synergies between ecosystem services and biodiversity in conservation planning: a review. Biol. Conserv. **166**, 144–154 (2013). https://doi.org/10.1016/j.biocon.2013.06.023
15. Egoh, B., Reyers, B., Rouget, M., Richardson, D.M., Le Maitre, D.C., van Jaarsveld, A.S.: Mapping ecosystem services for planning and management. Agric. Ecosyst. Environ. **127**(1–2), 135–140 (2008). https://doi.org/10.1016/j.agee.2008.03.013
16. Gos, P., Lavorel, S.: Stakeholders' expectations on ecosystem services affect the assessment of ecosystem services hotspots and their congruence with biodiversity. Int. J. Biodiversity Sci. Ecosystem Serv. Manage. **8**(1–2), 93–106 (2012). https://doi.org/10.1080/21513732.2011.646303

17. Geneletti, D., Scolozzi, R., Adem Esmail, B.: Assessing ecosystem services and biodiversity tradeoffs across agricultural landscapes in a mountain region. Int. J. Biodiversity Sci. Ecosyst. Serv. Manage. **14**(1), 188–208 (2018). https://doi.org/10.1080/21513732.2018.1526214
18. Schröter, M., Remme, R.P.: Spatial prioritisation for conserving ecosystem services: comparing hotspots with heuristic optimization. Landsc. Ecol. **31**(2), 431–450 (2016). https://doi.org/10.1007/s10980-015-0258-5
19. ISTAT [National Institute of Statistics] Superficie di comuni, province e regioni italiane al 9 ottobre 2011 [Area of Italian local municipalities, provinces and regions as of 9 October 2011]. https://www.istat.it/classificazione/principali-statistiche-geografiche-sui-comuni/. Accessed 2025/04/07
20. ISTAT [National Institute of Statistics]. Popolazione residente al 1° gennaio [Resident population as of January 1st]. http://dati.istat.it/Index.aspx. Accessed 2025/04/07
21. Capozzi, V., Rocco, A., Annella, C., Cretella, V., Fusco, G., Budillon, G.: Signals of change in the Campania region rainfall regime: an analysis of extreme precipitation indices (2002–2021). Meteorol. Appl. **30**(6), 1–27 (2023). https://doi.org/10.1002/met.2168
22. Pungetti, G., Marini, A., Vogiatzakis, I.: Sardinia. In: Vogiatzakis, I., Pungetti, G., Mannion, A.M. (eds.) Mediterranean Island Landscapes. Landscape Series, vol. 9. Springer, Dordrecht, Germany (2008). https://doi.org/10.1007/978-1-4020-5064-0_8
23. Berio, A.: Aspetti generali delle montagne sarde [General features of Sardinian mountains]. In: Camarda, I. (ed.). Montagne di Sardegna, pp. 9–25. Carlo Delfino Editore, Cagliari, Italy (1993)
24. Natural Capital Project: InVEST User Guide. http://releases.naturalcapitalproject.org/invest-userguide/latest/en/carbonstorage.html. Accessed 2025/04/07
25. Jiang, W., Deng, Y., Tang, Z., Lei, X., Chen, Z.: Modelling the potential impacts of urban ecosystem changes on carbon storage under different scenarios by linking the CLUE-S and the InVEST models. Ecol. Model. **345**, 30–40 (2017). https://doi.org/10.1016/j.ecolmodel.2016.12.002
26. Isely, E.S., Isely, P., Seedang, S., Mulder, K., Thompson, K., Steinman, A.D.: Addressing the information gaps associated with valuing green infrastructure in West Michigan: integrated valuation of ecosystem services Tool (INVEST). J. Great Lakes Res. **36**(3), 448–457 (2010). https://doi.org/10.1016/j.jglr.2010.04.003
27. García-Ontiyuelo, M., Acuña-Alonso, C., Valero, E., Álvarez, X.: Geospatial mapping of carbon estimates for forested areas using the InVEST model and Sentinel-2: A case study in Galicia (NW Spain). Sci. Total. Environ. **992**, 171297 (2024). https://doi.org/10.1016/j.scitotenv.2024.171297
28. Rachid, L., Elmostafa, A., Mehdi, M., Hassan, R.: Assessing carbon storage and sequestration benefits of urban greening in Nador City, Morocco, utilizing GIS and the InVEST model. Sustainable Futures **7**, 100171 (2024). https://doi.org/10.1016/j.sftr.2024.100171
29. Babbar, D., Areendran, G., Sahana, M., Sarma, K., Raj, K., Sivadas, A.: Assessment and prediction of carbon sequestration using Markov chain and InVEST model in Sariska Tiger Reserve. India. J. Clean. Prod. **278**, 123333 (2020). https://doi.org/10.1016/j.jclepro.2020.123333
30. Nelson, E., et al.: Modeling multiple ecosystem services, biodiversity conservation, commodity production, and tradeoffs at landscape scales. Front. Ecol. Environ. **7**(4), 4–11 (2009). https://doi.org/10.1890/080023
31. Chu, X., Zhan, J., Li, Z., Zhang, F., Qi, W.: Assessment on forest carbon sequestration in the Three-North Shelterbelt Program region. China. J. Clean. Prod. **215**, 382–389 (2019). https://doi.org/10.1016/j.jclepro.2018.12.296
32. Delphin, S., Escobedo, F., Abd-Elrahman, A., Cropper, W.: Mapping potential carbon and timber losses from hurricanes using a decision tree and ecosystem services driver model. J. Environ. Manage. **129**, 599–607 (2013). https://doi.org/10.1016/j.jenvman.2013.08.029

33. Wu, F., Wang, Z.: Assessing the impact of urban land expansion on ecosystem carbon storage: a case study of the Changzhutan metropolitan area. China. Ecol. Indic. **154**, 110688 (2023). https://doi.org/10.1016/j.ecolind.2023.110688

34. Lahiji, R.N., Dinan, N.M., Liaghati, H., Ghaffarzadeh, H., Vafaeinejad, A.: Scenario-based estimation of catchment carbon storage: linking multi-objective land allocation with InVEST model in a mixed agriculture-forest landscape. Front. Earth Sci. **14**, 637–646 (2020). https://doi.org/10.1007/s11707-020-0825-1

35. Spawn, S.A., Sullivan, C.C., Lark, T.J., Gibbs, H.K.: Harmonized global maps of above and belowground biomass carbon density in the year 2010. Sci. Data **7**, 112 (2020). https://doi.org/10.1038/s41597-020-0444-4

36. INFC. Inventario Nazionale delle Foreste e dei serbatoi forestali di Carbonio – INFC. Inventario forestale nazionale italiano [National Inventory of Forests and Forest Carbon Reservoirs]. https://www.inventarioforestale.org/it/statistiche_infc/. Accessed 2024/04/07

37. ISPRA (Istituto Superiore per la Protezione e la Ricerca Ambientale) [Institute for Environmental Protection and Research]. Linee guida per la redazione dei piani di monitoraggio o di gestione dell'impatto sulla qualità del suolo e sul carbonio nel suolo [Guidelines for preparing monitoring or management plans concerning impacts on soil quality and soil carbon] (2022). https://www.mase.gov.it/sites/default/files/archivio/normativa/linee_guida_ISPRA_implementazione_RED_II.pdf. Accessed 2024/04/07

38. AGRIS. Carta della distribuzione del carbonio organico del progetto CUT alla scala 1:50.000 [Organic Carbon Distribution Map, scale 1:50,000] (2016). http://www.sardegnaportalesuolo.it/opendata. Accessed 2024/04/07

39. Copernicus Land Monitoring Service. CORINE Land Cover – CLC 2018. https://land.copernicus.eu/en/products/corine-land-cover/clc2018. Accessed 2024/04/07

40. Sallustio, L., Pettenella, D., Romano, R., Marchetti, M.: Assessing habitat quality in relation to the spatial distribution of protected areas in Italy. J. Environ. Manage. **201**, 129–137 (2017). https://doi.org/10.1016/j.jenvman.2017.06.031

41. Global Climate Observing System (GCOS). Land Surface Temperature. https://gcos.wmo.int/site/global-climate-observing-system-gcos/essential-climate-variables/land-surface-temperature. Accessed 2024/04/07

42. Hernández, R.C., Camerin, F.: The application of ecosystem assessments in land use planning: a case study for supporting decisions toward ecosystem protection. Futures **161**, 103399 (2024). https://doi.org/10.1016/j.futures.2024.103399

43. ISPRA (Istituto Superiore per la Protezione e la Ricerca Ambientale) [Institute for Environmental Protection and Research]. Rapporto di sostenibilità 2020 [Sustainability report 2020]. ISPRA, Roma, Italy (2020). https://www.isprambiente.gov.it/files2020/pubblicazioni/documenti-tecnici/rapporto-2020-ispra-settembre.pdf. Accessed 2024/04/07

44. USGS EROS Archive - Landsat Archives - Landsat 8–9 OLI/TIRS Collection 2 Level-2 Science Products (2020). https://doi.org/10.5066/P9OGBGM6. Accessed 2024/04/07

45. Bagstad, K.J., Semmens, D.J., Ancona, Z.H., Sherrouse, B.C.: Evaluating alternative methods for biophysical and cultural ecosystem services hotspot mapping in natural resource planning. Landsc. Ecol. **32**(1), 77–97 (2017). https://doi.org/10.1007/s10980-016-0430-6

46. Anselin, L.: An Introduction to Spatial Data Science with GeoDa. Volume 1: Exploring Spatial Data. CRC/Chapman&Hall, Boca Raton, FL, US (2024). https://lanselin.github.io/introbook_vol1/. Accessed 2024/04/07

47. Anselin, L.: Local indicators of spatial association—LISA. Geogr. Anal. **27**(2), 93–115 (1995). https://doi.org/10.1111/j.1538-4632.1995.tb00338.x

48. GeoDa. An introduction to spatial data science. https://geodacenter.github.io/documentation.html. Accessed 2024/04/07

49. Getis, A., Ord, J.K.: The analysis of spatial association by use of distance statistics. Geogr. Anal. **24**(3), 189–206 (1992). https://doi.org/10.1111/j.1538-4632.1992.tb00261.x

50. Ord, J.K., Getis, A.: Local spatial autocorrelation statistics: distributional issues and an application. Geogr. Anal. **27**(4), 286–306 (1995). https://doi.org/10.1111/j.1538-4632.1995.tb0 0912.x
51. Wang, Y., Chang, Q., Fan, P.: A framework to integrate multifunctionality analyses into green infrastructure planning. Landscape Ecol. **36**, 1951–1969 (2021). https://doi.org/10.1007/s10 980-020-01058-w
52. Orsi, F., Ciolli, M., Primmer, E., Varumo, L., Geneletti, D.: Mapping hotspots and bundles of forest ecosystem services across the European Union. Land Use Policy **99**, 104840 (2020). https://doi.org/10.1016/j.landusepol.2020.104840
53. Lin, Y.-P., et al.: Systematically designating conservation areas for protecting habitat quality and multiple ecosystem services. Environ. Model Softw. **90**, 126–146 (2017). https://doi.org/10.1016/j.envsoft.2017.01.003
54. Lin, Y.-P., Chen, C.-J., Lien, W.-Y., Chang, W.-H., Petway, J.R., Chiang, L.-C.: Landscape conservation planning to sustain ecosystem services under climate change. Sustainability **11**, 1393 (2019). https://doi.org/10.3390/su11051393
55. Huang, H., et al.: Comprehensive evaluation of island habitat quality based on the invest model and terrain diversity: a case study of Haitan Island. China. Sustainability **15**, 11293 (2023). https://doi.org/10.3390/su151411293
56. Zhi, L., Li, X., Bai, J., Shao, D.: Prioritizing multifunctional conservation zones with dominant function based on comprehensive hotspots and bundles of ecosystem service. Ecol. Indic. **171**, 113122 (2025). https://doi.org/10.1016/j.ecolind.2025.113122
57. Nardella, L., Sebastiani, A., Stafoggia, M., Buonocore, E., Franzese, P.P., Manes, F.: Modeling regulating ecosystem services along the urban–rural gradient: a comprehensive analysis in seven Italian coastal cities. Ecol. Indic. **165**, 112161 (2024). https://doi.org/10.1016/j.ecolind.2024.112161
58. Zheng, D., Wang, Y., Hao, S., Xu, W., Lv, L., Yu, S.: Spatial-temporal variation and trade-offs/synergies analysis on multiple ecosystem services: a case study in the Three-River Headwaters region of China. Ecol. Indic. **116**, 106494 (2020). https://doi.org/10.1016/j.ecolind.2020.106494
59. Lee, H., Lautenbach, S.: A quantitative review of relationships between ecosystem services. Ecol. Indic. **66**, 340–351 (2016). https://doi.org/10.1016/j.ecolind.2016.02.004
60. Oliver, I., et al.: Land systems as surrogates for biodiversity in conservation planning. Ecol. Appl. **14**, 485–503 (2004). https://doi.org/10.1890/02-5181

Climate Change and Urban Open Spaces: A Spatial-Statistical Analysis of Adaptive Capacity in Naples

Gerardo Carpentieri, Carmela Gargiulo, Tonia Stiuso, and Floriana Zucaro[✉]

Department of Civil, Building and Environmental Engineering, University of Naples Federico II,
P.le Tecchio 80, 80125 Naples, Italy
{gerardo.carpentieri,gargiulo,tonia.stiuso,
floriana.zucaro}@unina.it

Abstract. Extreme weather events are natural phenomena, occurring at considerable distances in time, and have always been part of human experience and people's historical memory. These events are characterized as rare at a particular place and time of year, with unusual characteristics in terms of magnitude, location, timing, or extent. Over the past 10 years, we have been witnessing these phenomena more conspicuously in terms of frequency and intensity, annually reporting at least one phenomenon that emerges on a global scale and connotes itself as "the phenomenon of the year," sometimes earning a familiar household name, such as Charon or Katrina. These epochal events, nevertheless, although surprising in terms of magnitude, do not come unexpectedly. Not surprisingly 2024 was the hottest year on record since the pre-industrial age, with the global average temperature reaching +1.54 °C, even exceeding the limit identified as an extreme not to be surpassed in the Paris Agreements. Urban open spaces, both green and built-up, play a key role in improving thermal comfort and soil permeability, contributing to reducing energy consumption. Differing from most of the studies focused on just one of the two main issues affecting urban areas (energy and climate change), this work considers the open space system as the driver to strengthen the adaptive capacity of cities. The work aims to classify the urban area according to the relationships among the climatic, physical, environmental, and social characteristics of the fabrics where open spaces are located and the inner features of these built environment elements. Spatial-statistical analysis based on a cell grid is developed and applied to the study area of Naples. This paper represents a first step in a larger PRIN-funded research project 'Definition of a handbook of guidelines for implementing climate neutrality by improving the effectiveness of ecosystem services in rural and urban areas', aimed at defining an energy-efficient decision support tool based on urban and open space characteristics.

Keywords: Climate Change Adaptation · Urban Open Spaces · Green Areas · GIS · UHI · Flooding · Energy saving

1 Introduction

In recent years, the increasing complexity of contemporary urban phenomena, particularly with regard to climate change and growing energy demand, has stimulated the development of increasingly sophisticated analytical tools aimed at classifying and understanding the morphological, climatic and energy characteristics of cities [28]. Such tools are particularly effective in the field of urban planning, where the need to identify homogeneous urban typologies in terms of micro-climate and energy behaviour allows for more precise targeting of climate mitigation and adaptation strategies. In the scientific literature, the most widespread urban classification methodologies are based on data mining techniques, most notably cluster analysis, used to group spatial entities (neighbourhoods, blocks, urban areas) based on the similarity of a set of physical, functional, morphological, climatic, energy and socioeconomic variables. The objective is not only descriptive but operational: to identify urban fabric models on which to apply targeted intervention strategies and evaluate urban transformation scenarios. Among the most widely used techniques is the K-means method, appreciated for its computational efficiency and simplicity of implementation [1–3]. However, the need to define the number of clusters a priori, the sensitivity to outliers and the requirement to znormalize variables constitute non-negligible limitations. To overcome these critical issues, alternative approaches such as hierarchical clustering or hybrid techniques have been developed, including the two-step method, which is zcharacterized by its ability to automatically determine the optimal number of clusters. This approach allows the analysis of complex datasets comprising both continuous and categorical variables and is particularly suitable for use in urban settings [4, 5]. Applications of classification techniques are developed on different spatial scales, i.e. at the macro level, cities or regions are zanalyzed in terms of emissions, climate vulnerability and urban morphology [5, 6], while at the local level, the focus is on urban fabric characteristics, through physical (building density, building height), geomorphological (tree cover, permeable vegetation), microclimatic (surface temperature, thermal comfort) indicators, often supported by GIS technologies, remote sensing and microclimate simulations [3, 7, 8]. A crucial aspect in the methodological differentiation of this study from the previous ones is the set of the indicators as it is in line with the systemic approach of the governance of urban transformations. Indeed, some studies zemphasize the ecological component, assessing the capacity of green areas to mitigate the urban heat island effect [1, 9]. In contrast, others focus on the adaptive potential of urban open spaces, estimating the physical and functional capacity to accommodate adaptive solutions [3]. In still other cases, classifications focus on building forms, integrating bottom-up energy models to estimate thermal requirements in relation to urban form and local climatic conditions [10, 11, 29]. A recent methodological development concerns the integration of three-dimensional components, thanks to the use of high-resolution 3D maps obtained from LiDAR data, which allow volumetric variables to be included in classification models [4]. The flexibility offered by the variety of available approaches makes these techniques indispensable tools for integrating spatial analysis, climate adaptation and energy demand management. In particular, two-step clustering proves to be particularly suitable for complex urban contexts, thanks to the possibility of dealing with mixed variables, supporting the generation of urban typologies useful for subsequent microclimate simulation phases.

The present work consists of four main phases: (i) the variable selection and calculation, which consists in the identification of the most relevant physical, functional, microclimatic, geomorphologic and socioeconomic indicators for classification purposes, and the measurement of data through open source sources, integrating official databases, satellite data in GIS; (ii) the definition of minimum unit of reference for calculating the indicators; (iii) the cluster analysis with the application of the two-step method for the spatial classification of urban fabrics according to the detected characteristics. Finally, (iv) the interpretation of results, reading of the identified clusters and definition of urban typologies, focusing on the implications of climate adaptation, andenergy-saving potential.

Compared to the cluster analysis developed in the previous studies, this work includes a wide set of indicators that are all open data and easy available to collect, to guarantee the replicability of the analysis to different urban contexts. This feature allows to interpret the obtained outputs in a very detailed way, allowing to define the characteristics of the different parts of the city at a micro-level.

2   GIS-Based Methodology

2.1   The Minimum Reference Unit

In the preliminary phase of urban spatial analysis, the definition of the minimum reference unit plays a strategic role in constructing a robust and coherent methodological framework. This unit needs to have a level of detail that allows the detection of morphological and functional variations of the urban fabric while maintaining operational compatibility with the scale of the urban planning tools and databases available [7]. Among the main approaches are methods that divide the territory into sectors based on directions and quadrants [12, 13], and geometrical based ones, where the urban area is segmented into regular rings around the urban center to study spatial gradients linked to landscape fragmentation or urban growth [14, 15]. Another approach, instead, is based on the classification of urban areas based on the functional zoning defined by local authorities [16], or another prevalent methodology is the one that considers morphological, compositional and surface coverage parameters to define climatically homogeneous units [17–20]. Finally, subdivisions based on administrative units are particularly useful for interoperability with urban development plans and for analyses on an institutional scale [21, 22].

Despite the variety of approaches, the use of a regular grid has proven to be particularly effective, as it allows for an objective and replicable subdivision of the territory, useful for both spatial analysis and environmental modelling [23, 24].

2.2   The Indicators Selection and Measurement

The definition of the set of indicators to be used for urban fabric classification needs to be based on an in-depth systematic review of the scientific literature, with the aim of identifying the most relevant variables to analyze the relationships between morphological and functional characteristics of the urban environment and microclimatic phenomena, territorial vulnerability and energy consumption. Numerous studies highlight the importance of adopting an integrated and multidimensional approach in defining indicators, which considers local dynamics and evolving climatic conditions [1, 2]. Therefore, the selected indicators aim to coveringa plurality of dimensions, including demographic, socioeconomic, infrastructural, environmental, climatic, morphological and functional, to provide a representation of the urban context as complete and articulated as possible. In selecting variables, it is appropriate to favor those theoretically solid indicators that have revealed relevance in urban evaluation models, but also accessible in open format or easily derived from geospatial proxies [4, 6].

The spatial granularity of the information is a further critical element: the indicators need to be consistent with the minimum reference unit and guarantee interoperability between heterogeneous datasets, avoiding misalignments in the units of measurement and reference systems. The calculation of the indicators occurs through spatial analysis techniques implemented in a GIS environment, which include intersection operations, element counting, aggregation, zonal analysis and raster statistics, depending on the nature of the data [7]. Once calculated, the indicators must be normalized on homogeneous scales, using formulas that allow their integration into subsequent multivariate models or spatial classifiers.

2.3 The Cluster Analysis Two Step

The most widely applied methodology for urban analysis and classification consists of the use of clustering algorithms, with the aim of identifying homogeneous groups of spatial units, based on the urban characteristics that emerge from the set of selected indicators. The cluster-based approach allows to overcome rigid classifications based on single parameters or arbitrary thresholds, returning instead a segmentation of the territory that reflects characteristics emerging from the data themselves. Scientific literature underlines the effectiveness of this approach for complex spatial analysis, as it allows for the coherent synthesizing of the interaction between morphological, climatic, functional, and socioeconomic dimensions [3, 5, 10]. Among the most widespread techniques for clustering urban spatial units are k-means, particularly suitable for large numerical datasets; hierarchical analysis, useful for preliminary explorations and dendrogrammatic representations; fuzzy clustering, which allows the probabilistic attribution of units to multiple clusters simultaneously; DBSCAN (Density-Based Spatial Clustering of Applications with Noise), suitable for data with irregular distributions and presence of noise; and finally, two-step clustering, a more recent but very effective technique for the simultaneous management of continuous and categorical variables [10]. In the two-step multivariate cluster analysis, the process is divided into two main phases. In the first, the units are preliminarily grouped into small subgroups through a pre-clustering procedure, which reduces computational complexity even in the presence of large datasets. In the second phase, these subgroups are aggregated into final clusters through a hierarchical procedure, with the optimal number determined automatically based on the internal coherence of the groups and the penalization of the complexity of the model. This approach allows to obtain a robust, reproducible and statistically based classification. Once the classification has been performed, the results must be represented cartographically, returning the spatial distribution of the obtained clusters. Each cluster must be interpreted based on the average values of the indicators that characterize it to attribute a synthetic name and build a typological profile that is easily understandable and operationally useful.

3 Application to the City of Naples

The proposed methodology is applicated to the City of Naples, Italy (Fig. 1). The city is selected as a case study for its morphological complexity, the variety of microclimatic and socioeconomic conditions, as well as for the availability of detailed geospatial data, deriving from both institutional sources and open databases. Furthermore, the application of the urban classification methodology to the city of Naples allows to compare the obtained results with the main classification of the current spatial planning tools and interpret them according to the available information sources and the technical tools accessible for the analysis.

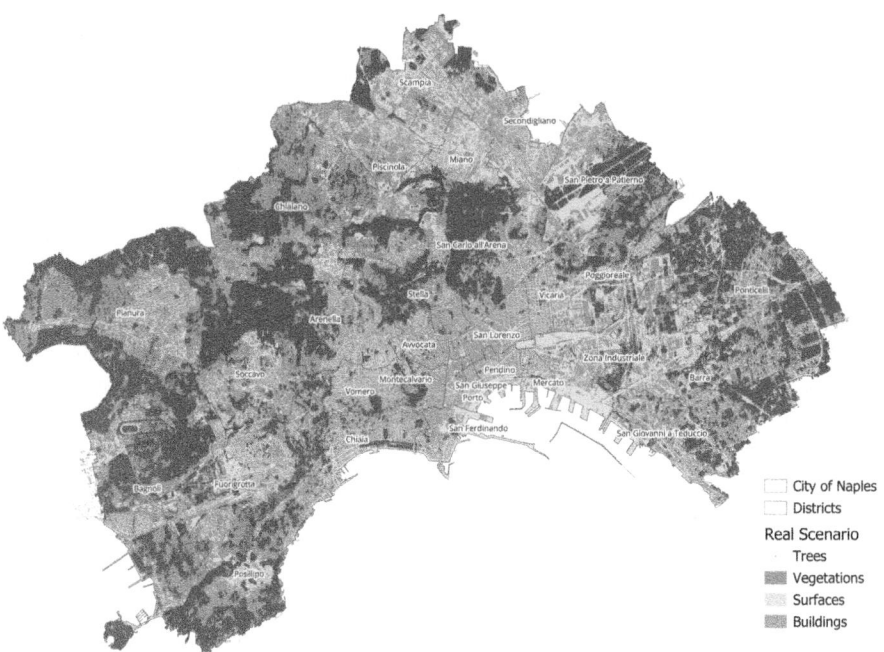

Fig. 1. The built and unbuilt surfaces distributed in the different districts of Naples.

For the case study of Naples, the minimum reference unit adopted is a regular grid with square cells of 250 × 250 meters. This choice is based on several reasons, including the need to have a unit consistent with the grids already adopted in official documents such as the PAESC (Sustainable Energy Action Plan) and the PRG (General Regulatory Plan) [25], allowing for direct integration between environmental analysis and urban planning tools. The grid is georeferenced based on the union frameworks prepared by the Campania Region, covering the entire municipal territory. Each grid cell represents a homogeneous portion of urban fabric on which a set of physical, functional, socioeconomic, geomorphological, and microclimatic indicators have been calculated. This methodological approach allows the integration of data from different sources and scales, ensuring the detailed analysis of urban phenomena and supporting the definition of climate mitigation and adaptation strategies on a local basis.

In the case study of the city of Naples, the indicator selection process follows a literature review aimed at identifying the most recurrent variables in urban classification models oriented towards climate adaptation and energy efficiency, in addition to these indicators, additional data were added that were necessary to further deepen the spatial analysis, that are: acclivity from the calculations on contour lines and slope, typology of inner courtyards continuity of urban fabric from Copernicus Data, for example Urban Atlas and Corine Land Cover [27], Runoff coefficient from PRG, cooling effect area [26, 31] and Real Estate Market Observatory zones from Agenzia delle Entrate. Subsequently, the indicators are adapted to the local context, considering the data's availability and quality.

Finally, 35 indicators are selected (Table 1), discarding those not available at the municipal level, the specific ones of a microclimatic nature, and the redundant socio-demographic ones, such as the average age, replaced by an indicator that is more explanatory of the incidence of vulnerable groups (<15 and >65 years).

Table 1. The system of indicators.

Characteristics		Variables	Indicators	ID
Open SpaceSystem	Vegetation and Greenery	Trees	Tree-lined areas	OS1.1
		Urban Forest	Forest areas	OS1.2
		Urban Greenery	General Vegetation	OS1.3
	Surface Area	Squares	Public Green areas	OS2.1
			Impermeable open spaces	OS2.2
		Parking	Parking areas	OS2.3
		Street orientation and geometry	Road surfaces	OS2.4
			Acclivity	OS2.5
		Courtyards in urban areas	Inner courtyards	OS2.6
			Green inner courtyards	OS2.7
Urban Context	Land Use	Functional urban areas	Industrial area	UC1.1
			Historical areas	UC1.2

(continued)

Table 1. (*continued*)

Characteristics		Variables	Indicators	ID
			Residential area	UC1.3
		Natural and Agricultural areas	Forest areas	UC1.4
			Agricultural land	UC2.1
	Building Density	Building coverage ratio	Built-up area Naples	UC2.2
		Mobility infrastructure	Local Public Transport stops	UC2.3
		Building material	Density of building in reinforced concrete	UC2.4
			Density of building in brickwork	UC2.5
			Density of building in steel, wood, etc.	UC2.6
		Neighborhood compactness and layout	Continuous urban fabric SL more 80%	UC2.7
			Discontinuous medium density urban fabric SL 30%–50%	UC2.8
			Low urban density and SL less 30%	UC1.1
Microclimatic and Geomorphology	Solar Radiation	Radiant temperature	Mean Radiant Temperature (MRT)	MG1.1
	Energy	Energy use consumption	Density of residential energy consumption	MG1.2
	Flooding	Flooding and Precipitation Tendency	Runoff coefficient	MG2,1
			Flooding Tendence	MG2.2

(*continued*)

Table 1. (*continued*)

Characteristics		Variables	Indicators	ID
	Temperature	Thermal indexes	Universal Thermal Climate Index (UTCI)	MG3,1
			Cooling Effect Area	MG3.6
			Land Surface Temperature (LST)	MG3.2
	Geomorphological features	Distance to coasts	Cartographic marine coastline	MG4.1
Socioeconomic and Demographic Indicators	Socioeconomic data	Total population	Density of total population	SED1.1
		Education	Density of the population with a specific education	SED2.1
		Income	Income per capita	SED2.2
		Real estate value	Real Estate Market Observatory zones	SED2.3
		Vulnerable Population	Density of vulnerable population	SED2.5
		Worker population	Density of general workers	SED2.6

The main data sources include the PAESC and the PRG of the Municipality of Naples, the Territorial Information System (SIT) of the Metropolitan City, national open data databases, the Copernicus Land Monitoring Service (Urban Atlas, HRL), OpenStreetMap (for buildings, roads and public green areas) and the Corine Land Cover. The indicators were calculated on the regular 250 × 250 m grid already defined, using zonal statistics functions for raster data (such as those from Copernicus) and vector operations for discrete spatial data.

In this work, the classification of spatial units of the city of Naples is carried out through multivariate cluster analysis using the two-step algorithm implemented in the SPSS software. This methodological choice is driven by the dataset's mixed nature, which included numerical variables (e.g. building density, percentage of impervious soil, runoff index) and categorical variables (e.g. land use class, type of land cover). The two-step algorithm stands out for its ability to simultaneously process data of different types, automatically estimating the optimal number of clusters. This feature makes it particularly suitable for complex urban contexts, where the variety of information sources and the multidimensionality of phenomena require a flexible and scalable approach [5].

The application of the algorithm produces eight distinct clusters, each characterized by a specific combination of mean values of the indicators, which defines its functional and morphological profile (Table 2). The analysis allows the outline a functional map of the Neapolitan urban territory, highlighting critical issues, opportunities and local specificities in an integrated and quantitative way. The interpretation of the clusters occurred through the analysis of the centroids and the distribution of the values of the variables for each group. Each cluster has then named on the basis of the prevalent characteristics, with the aim of facilitating the operational understanding of the results. The classification obtained represents a solid basis for defining climate adaptation strategies, orientation of urban solutions and interventions, and support for integrated territorial planning [30]. Figure 2, below displays the map resulting from the classification, highlighting the spatial distribution of the clusters throughout the territory of Naples.

3.1 Results

Cluster 1 – Green Lungs

The areas included in this cluster are mainly located in the north-western part of the city and represent the main green lungs of Naples. Their distinctive feature is the strong presence of vegetation, which translates into particularly high values compared to the other clusters for the "vegetation and greenery" category. Here the building density is extremely low, and the impermeable surfaces are reduced to a minimum (Table 2). The PRG confirms that many of these areas are classified as "Zone F - Areas intended for parks and public greenery". Temperatures are on average lower than in the rest of the city, thanks to the mitigating effect of the vegetation. The population living in these areas has an average income higher than the city average. From an urban planning point of view, it is crucial to preserve and enhance these areas to guarantee their contribution to the reduction of the heat island effect, such as the ecological function.

Cluster 2 – Residential Areas in Green Areas

This cluster is located mainly in the immediate vicinity of Cluster 1, in adjacent areas in the north-western strip, with some scattered portions in the city's eastern part. These are areas where vegetation is present, although to a lesser extent than in the previous cluster, and where land use is strongly oriented towards agricultural activities. The PRG classifies these areas as "Zone E - Agricultural areas", "Zone F - Sub-zone Fb - residential areas in the park" and, in some cases, as "Zone D - New production settlement areas". The building density is low, and the presence of natural surfaces is significant, even if a certain fragmentation of the urban fabric is observed. Temperatures are slightly higher than in Cluster 1, partly due to the lower tree cover (Table 2).

From a socioeconomic point of view, these areas have a low population density and an average income slightly higher than the city average. These parts need to be preserved according to their agricultural and naturalistic vocation and prevent the uncontrolled expansion of built-up areas.

Table 2. Cluster analysis output matrix showing the average values of indicators for each cluster.

N	159	396	201	386	133	220	445	166	2106
%	7.5%	18.8%	9.5%	18.3%	6.3%	10.4%	21.1%	7.9%	100.0%
Cluster	1	2	3	4	5	6	7	8	TOT
OS1.1	0.224	0.037	0.016	0.009	0.025	0.006	0.011	0.003	0.032
OS1.2	0.563	0.056	0.018	0.006	0.009	0.008	0.003	0.001	0.058
OS1.3	0.711	0.456	0.135	0.155	0.186	0.043	0.167	0.067	0.238
OS2.1	0.005	0.002	0.014	0.026	0.112	0.001	0.005	0.009	0.016
OS2.2	0.000	0.0002	0.006	0.003	0.075	0.001	0.001	0.022	0.008
OS2.3	0.003	0.002	0.005	0.010	0.110	0.015	0.017	0.013	0,016
OS2.4	0.034	0.081	0.154	0.183	0.179	0.022	0.126	0.218	0.123
OS2.5	0.340	0.209	0.251	0.081	0.072	0.088	0.039	0.086	0.133
OS2.6	0.002	0.002	0.018	0.025	0.034	0.002	0.011	0.249	0.031
OS2.7	0.000	0.001	0.003	0.008	0.009	0.002	0.004	0.105	0.012
UC1.1	0.000	0.006	0.000	0.009	0.074	0.001	0.144	0.030	0.040
UC1.2	0.014	0.014	0.357	0.099	0.174	0.074	0.019	0.825	0.144
UC1.3	0.012	0.062	0.385	0.619	0.245	0.031	0.141	0.097	0.219
UC1.4	0.089	0.367	0.041	0.063	0.018	0.023	0.057	0.014	0.108
UC2.1	0.003	0.010	0.056	0.049	0.039	0.005	0.017	0.218	0.040
UC2.2	0.009	0.014	0.099	0.031	0.167	0.012	0.023	0.096	0.043
UC2.3	0.103	0.145	0.107	0.102	0.036	0.010	0.041	0.096	0.083
UC2.4	0.092	0.118	0.080	0.090	0.094	0.023	0.138	0.072	0.096
UC2.5	0.072	0.176	0.186	0.143	0.051	0.019	0.085	0.037	0.109
UC2.6	0.001	0.002	0.043	0.046	0.067	0.004	0.012	0.063	0.025
UC2.7	0.017	0.087	0.155	0.084	0.009	0.008	0.010	0.008	0.052
UC2.8	0.055	0.061	0.003	0.001	0.002	0.000	0.000	0.000	0.016
MG1.2	0.051	0.049	0.201	0.154	0.070	0.012	0.029	0.200	0.088
MG2.1	0.197	0.312	0.626	0.664	0.661	0.427	0.602	0.850	0.535
MG2.2	0.330	0.471	0.606	0.718	0.744	0.192	0.713	0.877	0.590
MG1.1	0.202	0.582	0.480	0.571	0.619	0.562	0.796	0.632	0.591
MG3.1	0.806	0.833	0.730	0.736	0.776	0.194	0.815	0.527	0.705
MG3.2	0.689	0.802	0.785	0.782	0.826	0.701	0.846	0.769	0.786
MG4.1	0.002	0.001	0.019	0.000	0.036	0.217	0.002	0.005	0.028
SED1.1	0.042	0.068	0.293	0.179	0.065	0.010	0.050	0.154	0.105

(*continued*)

Table 2. (*continued*)

N	159	396	201	386	133	220	445	166	2106
%	7.5%	18.8%	9.5%	18.3%	6.3%	10.4%	21.1%	7.9%	100.0%
Cluster	1	2	3	4	5	6	7	8	TOT
SED2.1	0.021	0.028	0.311	0.067	0.037	0.005	0.020	0.072	0.062
SED2.2	0.451	0.407	0.745	0.370	0.438	0.109	0.331	0.397	0.390
SED2.3	0.381	0.386	0.813	0.398	0.459	0.082	0.286	0.529	0.392
SED2.5	0.041	0.063	0.305	0.175	0.067	0.009	0.047	0.145	0.103
SED2.6	0.004	0.004	0.008	0.004	0.064	0.003	0.010	0.009	0.010

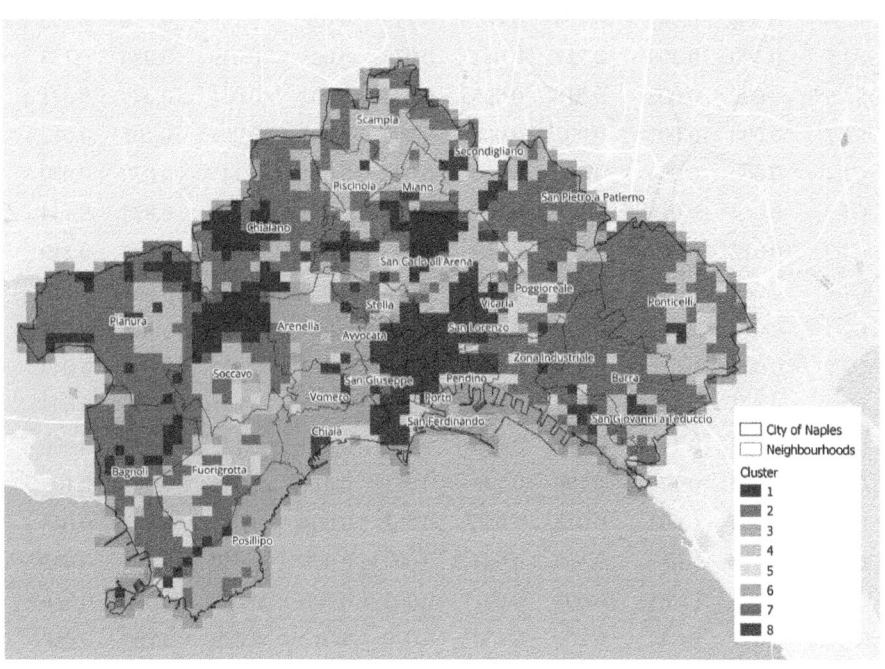

Fig. 2. Cluster Analysis map for the case study of the city of Naples.

Cluster 3 – Hillside Residential Areas

These areas include the coastal strip of Posillipo and Chiaia, extending to Vomero. They are characterized by a low presence of vegetation, compensated by a high environmental quality and a strong residential attractiveness. The PRG classifies these areas mainly as "Zone A - Settlements of historical interest" and "Zone B - Areas of urban completion". Land use is predominantly residential and characterized by a less dense built fabric than other city central areas. The population living in these areas has the highest income among all the clusters, with property values well above average (Table 2). From a climatic point of view, temperatures remain in line with the city average, while the risk of flooding is high. In these areas urban planning should focus on mitigating the effects of climate change by increasing soil permeability to reduce hydrogeological risk.

Cluster 4 – Vulnerable Areas

This cluster includes the northern areas of the city, such as Scampia and Secondigliano, and extends eastwards towards neighborhoods such as Barra and Ponticelli, as well as including some portions of Soccavo, Pianura and Fuorigrotta. These are areas characterized by a lack of greenery and a high building density (Table 2). Most of the buildings are social housing, and the urban fabric is the result of expansions that are often carried out in a disorganized way. The PRG classifies these areas as "Zone B - Recent Expansion" and "Zone C - Areas of low-cost and social housing". The socioeconomic indicators highlight a population with low incomes and high social vulnerability. The microclimatic conditions are, on average, worse than other areas of the city, with temperatures and levels of solar radiation above average. To improve the quality of life in these neighborhoods, it would be necessary to implement urban regeneration strategies, increasing the provision of green spaces and improving existing infrastructure.

Cluster 5 – Open Space Areas

These areas are distributed in a fragmented manner throughout the city and are characterized by the presence of large open surfaces, including parking lots and public spaces. The building density is low and the soil permeabilization is particularly high. The PRG classifies many of these areas as "Zone F - Areas for parking and public infrastructure". From a climatic point of view, temperatures above average and high solar radiation are recorded, due to the lack of vegetation cover (Table 2). These areas need to be redeveloped through urban forestation interventions and the creation of multifunctional areas capable of reducing urban overheating.

Cluster 6 – Border Areas

The areas that comprise this cluster are located on the edges of the consolidated urban fabric and represent a transition area between the built-up area and the more open areas and between the municipal border and the neighboring municipalities. The PRG classifies them mainly as " Zones B - Urban completion areas". The building density is medium-low, and the urban fabric is rather fragmented (Table 2). Socioeconomic indicators show that a population with incomes is generally lower than the city average. From an urban planning point of view, these areas could benefit from targeted interventions to improve urban cohesion and encourage the presence of services and public spaces connecting the different municipalities.

Cluster 7 – Productive and Abandoned Areas

These areas are mainly concentrated in the eastern part of the city, including neighborhoods such as Poggioreale, Barra and Ponticelli, as well as portions of Fuorigrotta and Bagnoli. These are areas with a productive vocation, often characterized by the presence of abandoned industrial infrastructures. The PRG classifies them as "Zone D - Productive Areas". The building density is relatively low, but the soil permeability is very high. The hydrogeological risk is significant, and temperatures are on average higher than the city average (Table 2). An adequate urban redevelopment strategy could transform these areas into new centers of sustainable economic development.

Cluster 8 – Consolidated Historic Areas
This cluster includes the historic center and surrounding areas, characterized by a high building density and a very low presence of vegetation. The PRG classifies these areas as "Zone A - Settlements of historical interest". The heat island effect is particularly pronounced, with high temperatures and strong soil sealing (Table 2). Urban planning strategies should focus on increasing urban green spaces and on solutions to mitigate summer overheating.

4   Conclusions

In conclusion, the application of the urban classification methodology to the case study of the city of Naples highlights the effectiveness and flexibility of the adopted approach, both from a methodological and operational point of view.

The choice of using a regular grid of 250×250 m as the minimum unit of analysis allows a homogeneous and detailed reading of the urban fabric, facilitating the integration of heterogeneous indicators from institutional sources and open data. This approach guarantees the possibility of developing solutions at a local scale, making the analysis directly readable in a holistic perspective. Furthermore, this methodological coherence facilitates direct comparison with indicators already adopted in official documents such as the PRG, strengthening the validity and operational utility of the results.

The definition and measurement of 35 indicators, considering the availability, quality and significance of the data for the City of Naples urban context, has allowed us to provide a complex and multidimensional picture of the territory. The use of Two-Step Cluster Analysis represents a methodological choice consistent with the mixed nature of the dataset, allowing the identification of eight functionally and morphologically distinct clusters, capable of exhaustively describing the urban complexity of the city. The results of the analysis highlight a marked territorial heterogeneity, returning a multifaceted image of the city of Naples, divided into eight functionally and morphologically distinct clusters. We move from areas with a prevalent environmental vocation, such as Cluster 1, which represents the large green lungs of the city, fundamental for climate regulation and environmental quality, to heavily built-up areas with high social vulnerability, such as Cluster 4, which require urgent interventions for urban redevelopment and strengthening of social resilience. Cluster 2 includes agricultural and peri-urban areas, with low building density and a rural vocation, which pose interesting prospects in terms of urban agriculture and landscape protection. Cluster 3, composed of prestigious hillside neighborhoods, highlights high real estate values and an average high environmental quality, although it presents critical issues related to hydrogeological risk. Cluster 5 is made up of fragmented areas, dominated by impermeable surfaces and underused public spaces, which represent a strategic potential for interventions on open spaces. Cluster 6 occupies the transition zones along municipal edges, often characterized by discontinuous fabrics and low real estate value, where planning can play a crucial role in strengthening urban cohesion. Cluster 7 identifies disused industrial areas, with high impermeability and poor environmental quality. Finally, Cluster 8 includes the densely built historic center, with high climatic criticalities due to the heat island effect and the lack of urban greenery. This segmentation not only highlights areas characterized by a high presence of green spaces or, on the contrary, by high building density and impermeable surface but also highlights socioeconomic and microclimatic criticalities, which are fundamental information for the identification of targeted interventions for climate adaptation.

Furthermore, this methodology proves solid and replicable and capable of providing an operational representation of the urban territory [33], useful for supporting strategic decisions aimed at adapting to climate change, UHI and flooading in particular [32], and energy saving. The analysis developed in the city of Naples provides a model that can be exported to other metropolitan contexts characterized by urban complexity, representing a useful tool for the governance of urban and territorial transformations.

Acknowledgments. The research leading to these results has received funding from the project "Definition of a guidelines handbook to implement climate neutrality by improving ecosystem service effectiveness in rural and urban areas" CUP E53D23018970001 funded by EU in the NextGenerationEU Plan through the Italian "Bando Prin 2022-D.D. 1409 del 14-09-2022".

References

1. Liu, W., Zhao, H., Sun, S., Xu, X., Huang, T., Zhu, J.: Green space cooling effect and contribution to mitigate heat island effect of surrounding communities in Beijing Metropolitan Area. Front. Publ. Health **10**, 870403 (2022). https://doi.org/10.3389/fpubh.2022.870403
2. Sützl, B.S., Strebel, D.A., Rubin, A., Wen, J., Carmeliet, J.: Urban morphology clustering analysis to identify heat-prone neighbourhoods in cities. Sustain. Cities Soc. **107**, 105360 (2024). https://doi.org/10.1016/j.scs.2024.105360
3. Villaverde, A., Álvarez, I., Rojí, E., Garmendia, L.: Categorization of urban open spaces for heat adaptation: a cluster based approach. Build. Environ. **263**, 111861 (2024). https://doi.org/10.1016/j.buildenv.2024.111861
4. Song, H., Cervini, G., Shreevastava, A., Jung, J.: Reshaping landscape factorization through 3D landscape clustering for urban temperature studies. Sustain. Cities Soc. **115**, 105809 (2024). https://doi.org/10.1016/j.scs.2024.105809
5. Peng, C., Li, Z., Xu, Q., Li, X., Li, X., Chen, H.: Spatial distribution of energy consumption: Integrating climate and macro-statistics for insights from clustering and sensitivity analysis. Energy Build. **318**, 114446 (2024). https://doi.org/10.1016/j.enbuild.2024.114446
6. Solecki, W., et al.: A conceptual framework for an urban areas typology to integrate climate change mitigation and adaptation. Urban Clim. **14**, 116–126 (2015). https://doi.org/10.1016/j.uclim.2015.07.001
7. Patle, S., Ghuge, V.V.: Urban fragmentation approach for assessing thermal environment dynamics: a case study of semi-arid city from a comfort perspective. Urban Clim. **53**, 101784 (2024). https://doi.org/10.1016/j.uclim.2023.101784
8. Diz-Mellado, E., López-Cabeza, V.P., Roa-Fernández, J., Rivera-Gómez, C., Galán-Marín, C.: Energy-saving and thermal comfort potential of vernacular urban block porosity shading. Sustain. Cities Soc. **89**, 104325 (2023). https://doi.org/10.1016/j.scs.2022.104325
9. Anderson, C.C., Uhr, J.S., Schmidt, S.: Visitor motivations and design feature use for thermal comfort on hot days in Bochum City Park. Germany. Urban Forestry Urban Greening **102**, 128564 (2024). https://doi.org/10.1016/j.ufug.2024.128564

10. Zou, Y., et al.: Comprehensive analysis on the energy resilience performance of urban residential sector in hot-humid area of China under climate change. Sustain. Cities Soc. **88**, 104233 (2023). https://doi.org/10.1016/j.scs.2022.104233

11. Cui, P., Lu, J., Wu, Y., Tang, J., Jiang, J.: Effect of urban morphology on microclimate and building cluster energy consumption in cold regions of China. Sustain. Cities Soc. **115**, 105838 (2024). https://doi.org/10.1016/j.scs.2024.105838

12. Kumar, S., Ghosh, S., Singh, S.: Polycentric urban growth and identification of urban hot spots in Faridabad, the million-plus metropolitan city of Haryana (2022)

13. Ullah, W., et al.: Analysis of the relationship among land surface (2023)

14. Chandra, S., Sharma, D., Dubey, S.K.: Linkage of urban expansion and land surface temperature using geospatial techniques for Jaipur City. India. Arab. J. Geosci. **11**(2), 31 (2018). https://doi.org/10.1007/s12517-017-3357-6

15. Zhao, Z.-Q., He, B.-J., Li, L.-G., Wang, H.-B., Darko, A.: Profile and concentric zonal analysis of relationships between land use/land cover and land surface temperature: case study of Shenyang. China. Energ. Build. **155**, 282–295 (2017). https://doi.org/10.1016/j.enbuild.2017.09.046

16. Kafy, A.-Al., Faisal, A.-A., Al Rakib, A., Fattah, Md.A., Rahaman, Z.A., Sattar, G.S.: Impact of vegetation cover loss on surface temperature and carbon emission in a fastest-growing city, Cumilla, Bangladesh. Build. Environ. **208**, 108573 (2022). https://doi.org/10.1016/j.buildenv.2021.108573

17. Bechtel, B., et al.: SUHI analysis using local climate zones—a comparison of 50 cities. Urban Clim. **28**, 100451 (2019). https://doi.org/10.1016/j.uclim.2019.01.005

18. Khamchiangta, D., Dhakal, S.: Future urban expansion and local climate zone changes in relation to land surface temperature: case of Bangkok metropolitan administration, Thailand. Urban Clim. **37**, 100835 (2021). https://doi.org/10.1016/j.uclim.2021.100835

19. Li, L., Zhao, Z., Wang, H., Shen, L., Liu, N., He, B.-J.: Variabilities of land surface temperature and frontal area index based on local climate zone. IEEE J. Select. Top. Appl. Earth Observ. Remote Sens. **15**, 2166–2174 (2022). https://doi.org/10.1109/JSTARS.2022.3153958

20. Zhao, C., Jensen, J.L.R., Weng, Q., Currit, N., Weaver, R.: Use of local climate zones to investigate surface urban heat islands in Texas. GISci. Remote Sens. **57**(8), 1083–1101 (2020). https://doi.org/10.1080/15481603.2020.1843869

21. Bera, D., et al.: Integrated influencing mechanism of potential drivers on seasonal variability of LST in Kolkata municipal corporation, India. Land **11**(9), 1461 (2022). https://doi.org/10.3390/land11091461

22. Yu, P., Yung, E.H.K., Chan, E.H.W., Wang, S., Chen, Y., Chen, Y.: Capturing open space fragmentation in high–density cities: towards sustainable open space planning. Appl. Geogr. **154**, 102927 (2023). https://doi.org/10.1016/j.apgeog.2023.102927

23. Sharma, R., Pradhan, L., Kumari, M., Bhattacharya, P.: Assessing urban heat islands and thermal comfort in Noida City using geospatial technology. Urban Clim. **35**, 100751 (2021). https://doi.org/10.1016/j.uclim.2020.100751

24. Vasanthawada, S.R.S., Puppala, H., Prasad, P.R.C.: Assessing impact of land-use changes on land surface temperature and modelling future scenarios of Surat. India. Int. J. Environ. Sci. Technol. **20**(7), 7657–7670 (2023). https://doi.org/10.1007/s13762-022-04385-4

25. Comune di Napoli - Piano Regolatore Generale (PRG). www.comune.napoli.it, https://www.comune.napoli.it/flex/cm/pages/ServeBLOB.php/L/IT/IDPagina/1023

26. Gargiulo, C., Sgambati, S., Zucaro, F.: The analysis of the urban open spaces system for resilient and pleasant historical districts. In: Lecture Notes in Computer Science, pp 564–577 (2023)

27. Dinç, G., Gül, A.: Estimation of the future land cover using Corine Land Cover data. TeMA **14**(2), 177–188 (2021)

28. Isola, F., Leone, F., Pittau, R.: Evaluating the urban heat island phenomenon from a spatial planning viewpoint. A systematic review. TeMA **2**, 75–93 (2023)
29. Guida, C.: Energy saving and efficiency in urban environments: integration strategies and best practices. TeMA **15**(3), 517–531 (2022)
30. Mazzeo, G., Polverino, S.: Nature-based solution for climate change adaptation and mitigation in urban areas with high natural risk. TeMA **16**(1), 47–65 (2023)
31. Carpentieri, G., Gargiulo, C., Stiuso, T., Zucaro, F.: Greening and cooling urban areas: the Open Space System contribution for energy saving and climate change adaptation. In: Lecture Notes in Computer Science, pp. 412–429 (2024). https://doi.org/10.1007/978-3-031-65273-8_27
32. Lai, S., Isola, F., Leone, F., Zoppi, C.: Assessing the potential of green infrastructure to mitigate hydrogeological hazard. TeMA, pp. 109–133 (2021)
33. Mobaraki, O.: Spatial analysis of green space use in Tabriz metropolis, Iran. TeMA **2**, 55–73 (2023)

The 15th International Workshop on Future Information System Technologies and Applications (FiSTA 2025)

Proposal for Japan's Community Bus Location System Using Blockchain

Toshihiro Uchibayashi[1(✉)], Chinasa Sueyoshi[2], Yoshihiro Yasutake[3],
Hideyuki Satomura[4], Yuto Tsumagari[4], Yuya Fukuyama[4],
and Kentaro Inenaga[3]

[1] Research Institute for Information Technology, Kyushu University, Fukuoka, Japan
uchibayashi.toshihiro.143@m.kyushu-u.ac.jp
[2] Industry-Academic Co-innovation and Research Promotion Headquarters, Kyushu
Sangyo University, Fukuoka, Japan
sueyoshi@is.kyusan-u.ac.jp
[3] Faculty of Science and Engineering, Kyushu Sangyo University, Fukuoka, Japan
{yasutake,inenaga}@is.kyusan-u.ac.jp
[4] Graduate School of Information Science, Kyushu Sangyo University, Fukuoka,
Japan
{k24gjk03,k25gjk08,k25gjk10}@st.kyusan-u.ac.jp

Abstract. In recent years, Japan's regional public transportation systems, particularly in rural areas, have been affected by population decline and aging. The expansion of areas with no public transportation due to the abolition or reduction of bus routes has become a serious problem. To address this issue, many local governments have introduced community buses. However, operating these services efficiently within limited budgets and human resources remains a challenge. Meanwhile, advancements in information and communication technology (ICT) have led to the development of new methods for improving the convenience of public transportation. Digital technologies that use standard formats, such as general transit feed specifications, are currently in progress. However, their use in regional public transportation remains limited. In this study, we developed and supported the implementation of ICT-based bus location system (BLS) and passenger counting system (PCS) to address regional public transportation issues. The BLS tracks real-time vehicle locations using mobile applications, providing passengers and operations with up-to-date information to improve convenience. The PCS enables drivers to record the number of passengers on and off through an application and analyze the data to optimize operation routes and timetables. These systems improve the convenience of regional public transportation and streamline local governments' operational management. However, to ensure data management and prevent tampering, certain issues must be addressed when implementing such systems. In particular, because public-transport data, such as general transit feed specifications (GTFS), are directly linked to passenger-movement information, there are concerns about the risk of unauthorized access and tampering. In this study, we improve the data reliability and strengthen tamper resistance by storing some GTFS data in a blockchain. Blockchain is

O. Gervasi et al. (Eds.): ICCSA 2025 Workshops, LNCS 15890, pp. 193–204, 2026.
https://doi.org/10.1007/978-3-031-97606-3_13

distributed ledger technology that enables highly transparent data management while preventing data tampering. The proposed system was tested in a real-world operational environment to verify its effectiveness. The results demonstrated that introducing a blockchain improved the reliability of GTFS data and reduced the risk of unauthorized data modification. However, adding or updating data takes time due to the blockchain feature. In this study, we analyze the current challenges of regional public transportation in Japan and explain the proposed BLS and PCS in detail. In addition, we discuss data management methods that utilize blockchain technology and verify their effectiveness through system evaluation. Finally, we propose a sustainable development model for regional public transportation based on the results of this research.

Keywords: Blockchain · Community Bus · Regional Public Transportation · Bus Location

1   Introduction

In recent years, the quality of public transportation in Japan has become a significant issue. In urban areas, public transportation, such as trains and buses, is well developed, and many people can enjoy convenient means of transport. However, in rural areas, a decline in population and the aging of society have reduced revenue, making public transportation difficult to maintain. In particular, in depopulated areas, main bus routes are being closed or reduced because of unprofitability, increasing the number of areas with no public transportation. In this situation, local governments are increasingly implementing community buses to ensure that residents have a means of transportation. However, these services face significant challenges, such as limited budgets and human resources. There is a need for a system to facilitate efficient operation management and use.

However, with the advancement of information and communication technology (ICT), new methods to improve the convenience of public transportation are gaining traction. In particular, the widespread use of smartphones has made it easier to search for and use transportation information. The use of real-time operational information is becoming increasingly common. Many public transportation organizations are responding to these trends by using standard formats, such as general transit feed specifications (GTFS), to provide operational details [1]. However, the use of such digital technology in regional public transport is lagging, and issues such as the inability to grasp the operational status of buses, failure to find bus stops, and reliance on manual record-keeping by bus crew members remain.

To address these challenges, we examined two areas of support for regional public transport using ICT: the bus location system (BLS), which uses location information from mobile device applications, and the passenger counting system (PCS), which uses mobile device applications. The BLS collects real-time location information on buses in operation and provides it to passengers and operation managers, thereby improving convenience and streamlining operations. The PCS is used by drivers to record the number of passengers on and off the bus. The collected data are then analyzed to optimize bus routes and timetables. These systems can improve the convenience of regional public transportation and make the operation management of local governments more efficient.

However, data management and security are significant challenges when implementing these systems. In particular, public-transport data, such as GTFS, contain essential information directly linked to passengers' movement, and the risk of unauthorized access and tampering must be considered. Conventional centralized database management remains vulnerable to server administrator errors or cyberattacks, which requires measures to ensure safety. In this study, we propose a method to strengthen data reliability and tamper resistance using blockchain technology. Blockchain is distributed ledger technology (DLT) that enables highly transparent management while preventing data tampering. Based on these, we construct a system that improves safety by storing part of the GTFS on a blockchain to ensure the accuracy of the operation information.

We summarize the current situation and issues of regional public transportation in Japan and introduce initiatives to support regional public transit. We detail the proposed BLS and PCS, highlighting how blockchain technology can improve safety and reliability. Finally, we evaluate the proposed system by verifying its effectiveness and demonstrating a new approach to contributing to the sustainable development of regional public transportation.

2 State of Regional Public Transportation

Regional public transportation is a public transportation service operated by local governments, such as railways, fixed-route buses, passenger ships, community buses, demand-response transportation, and passenger taxis [2,3]. In Japan, many regions, including major cities such as Tokyo and Osaka, have large-scale bus services operated by municipalities with ample funds or by companies that operate railways that form significant transportation arteries. However, outside city centers, population declines and aging have significantly impacted public transportation. Major railway and bus routes sometimes withdraw because of unprofitability. As a result, an increasing number of areas with no public transportation are becoming a problem [4]. Those without private vehicles cannot use public transport, thereby reducing their quality of life. Therefore, ensuring transport for residents is a significant issue. To solve this problem, municipal governments have taken the lead in operating regional public transport, such as small-scale community buses [5–7]. This allows residents to travel to their destinations without using cars. Regional public transportation is particularly important for people with difficulty moving around, such as the elderly and disabled because it enables them to participate in society. Local governments that operate them are also considered an essential part that contributes to the sustainable development of local communities and the improvement of mobility by incorporating them into urban planning and transport policy through regional public-transport planning [8–11].

In recent years, checking the means of transport and routes to your destination and then using websites or smartphone map apps to get there has become common. To include route information and other data in map apps, it is necessary to support GTFS, and more regional public-transport services are doing so, creating an environment that is easy to use for residents and visitors from outside the area. In addition, technologically advanced services, such as electronic payments and the ability to pay fares using IC cards, are also being developed. Many public transportation services are linked to other transport services at railway stations and bus terminals, providing more effective mobility. However, in many cases, regional public-transport services continue to operate with limited budgets, human resources, and equipment. In addition, GTFS and other systems are not yet fully developed. This means that the operation status is unknown to anyone other than residents, the location of bus stops is unknown, and operation records are written manually.

3   A System to Provide Support

Therefore, our research group has been supporting regional public transport to local governments in Fukuoka Prefecture, Japan, where we are based [12–16]. We focus on two main areas: support for developing regional public-transport data and regional public transport using ICT.

3.1   Support for Developing Regional Public-Transport Data

GTFS is a standard format for providing public-transport operation information, including timetables, routes, and bus stops. It is an essential format for standardizing public-transport data and enabling developers and service providers to handle data efficiently. It is also used to improve transit information and traffic system optimization. It is designed to be easily used by developers and systems and is particularly useful for transportation applications and related services. To date, we have provided support to 15 local governments. This support includes the development of GTFS and a standard bus information format (GTFS-JP) [17]. In particular, we create and validate the necessary files for GTFS or GTFS-JP and send them to companies that provide map applications, such as Google Maps, which are used to publish route information.

3.2   Support for Regional Public Transport Using ICT

We have supported 11 local governments, including questionnaire surveys using tablets, BLSs using mobile positioning data, passenger count surveys using mobile device applications, guidance display systems using in-vehicle monitors, and digital signage using monitors installed at major bus stops. These supports are made possible by the ACE system, comprising applications that run on the mobile devices and various servers we have built in our laboratory.

This study examines the BLS, which uses location information from mobile device applications, and the survey to track the number of passengers on and off using mobile device applications to support regional public transportation using ICT.

4   A System to Provide Support

This study introduces a system for implementing a BLS using location information from mobile device applications and a survey to track the number of passengers on and off. The system configuration is shown in Fig. 1.

The server provides two services for managers: booking and vehicle operation status for demand transportation. For community bus drivers, a service called passenger count records was also provided. For passengers using local buses, two services are provided: a simplified questionnaire survey and an on-board information display. For passengers waiting for local buses, two services are provided: display timetable/operation status and provision of vehicle location (bus location). Regional governments can access services that display operation history and geographic information system data. The infrastructure system was hosted on two physical servers running Apache and Cron, and the services were mainly developed in PHP.

We developed the SHINGU application (Fig. 2) to send bus location information and track the number of passengers on and off the bus. The application has a bus location function that sends location information to the cloud and records the number of passengers on and off the bus for each bus route. Smartphones with the SHINGU application installed are placed on the community bus to collect location information. The devices are powered by USB from inside the community bus. However, to conserve the battery during off-hours, such as during nighttime, the power is automatically turned off outside business hours. To collect the location information, the operator ID and bus number are configured in the application settings (Fig. 3). Once the application is activated, it transmits the current time, operator ID, bus number, battery level, and GPS coordinates to the cloud every three seconds. To count the number of passengers on and off the bus, the driver selects the operating route within the application and records the number of passengers on and off the bus on a dedicated screen. The application requests a list of routes that will begin operating approximately 30 min before the current time from the server, displaying the option to assist in route selection. This route information is based on GTFS data stored in the server database. The GTFS is often published as open data and is not confidential. However, when used in a way directly linked to operations, as in our system, threats of data tampering due to unauthorized access or server administrator errors remain. Therefore, we propose using the blockchain as a secure database that can track changes to store GTFS.

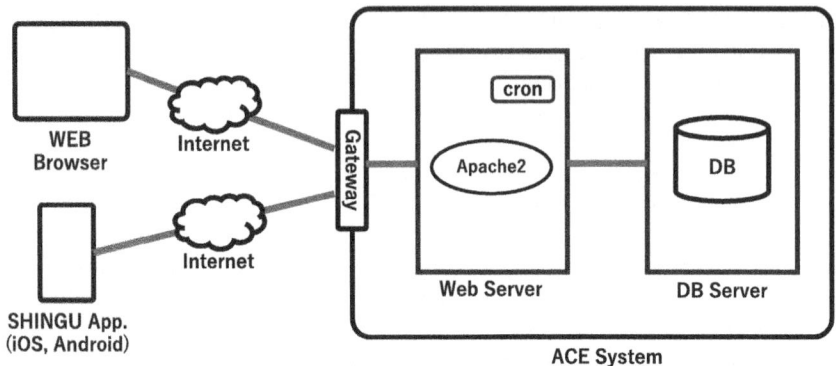

Fig. 1. ACE System Components.

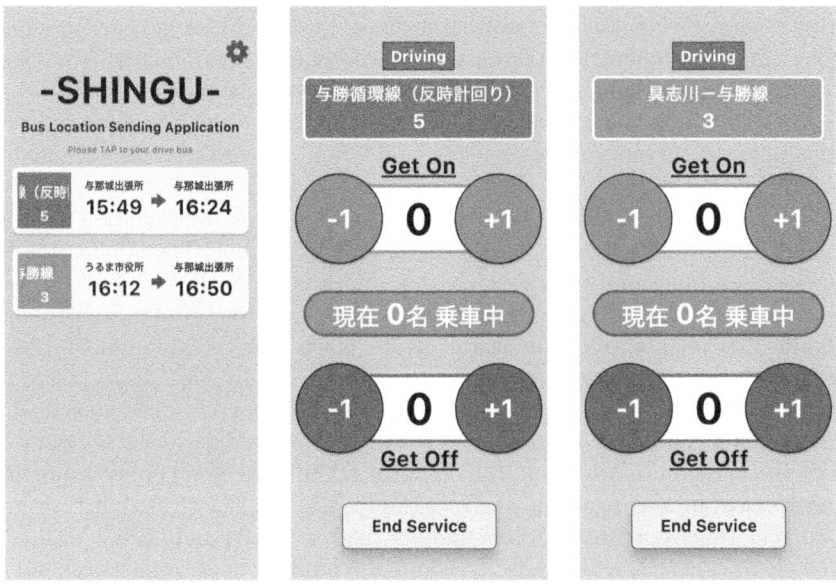

Fig. 2. SHINGU Application

5   Strengthening Through Blockchain

Blockchain is a DLT for securely managing data and recording transactions transparently and tamperproof [18]. As shown in Fig. 4, a blockchain is made up of blocks, which are the basic unit, a chain connecting these blocks in sequence, a distributed network comprising multiple nodes that store blockchain data, verify transactions, add new blocks on computers within the network, and smart contracts that are executed automatically when certain conditions are met. The system configuration enhanced by blockchain technology is shown in Fig. 5. In

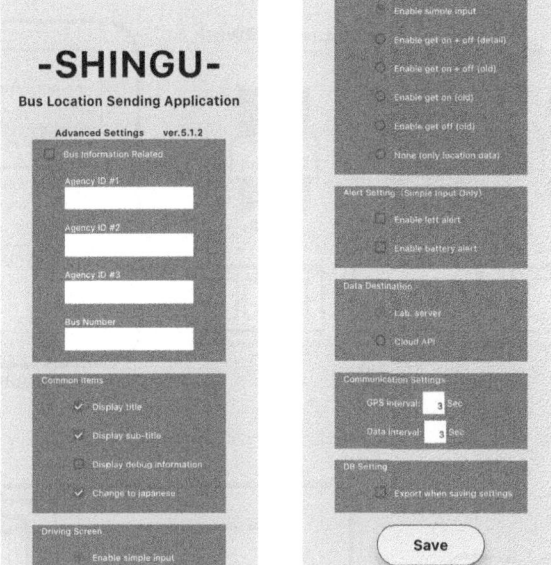

Fig. 3. SHINGU Application Settings

addition to a conventional database, the proposed system includes a blockchain with three nodes. Only a portion of the database data can be moved to the blockchain. The GTFS comprises nine different files (Table 1). The data that significantly impact operations due to tampering, such as agency, routes, shapes, stops, and trips, are stored in the blockchain. Only the server administrator can add, change, or delete this data.

Changes that were previously made directly in the database are now processed using the smart contract of the blockchain, which generates and connects a block to complete the storage process. Therefore, this method takes time to add, change, or delete data.

6   Verification and Discussion

We verify the proposed method for managing GTFS data using blockchain technology by constructing and evaluating an actual system. Blockchain provides resistance to data tampering and enhance transparency. This study improved the accuracy of operational information and ensured data safety. In addition, we tested BLS and PCS, which were developed in collaboration with local governments in Fukuoka Prefecture, in a real-world operating environment. Specifically, we stored some of the GTFS data (routes, stops, trips, etc.) on the blockchain and evaluated the impact of adding, updating, and deleting data compared to conventional database management.

The implementation environment was entirely built using Amazon web services. The web server and blockchain nodes were built using EC2 virtual

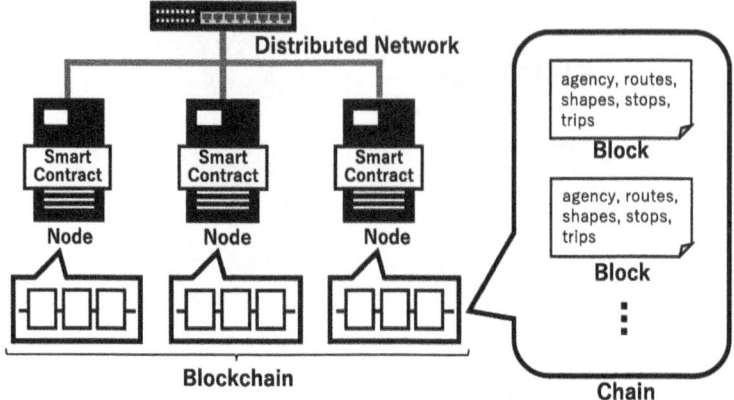

Fig. 4. Blockchain Construction

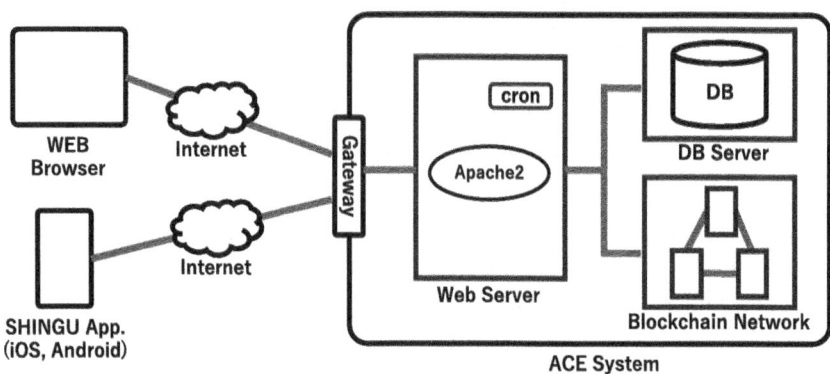

Fig. 5. System Strengthened by the Blockchain

machines. The web server configuration is t2 micro, memory, and 30 GB storage. The blockchain node configuration is t 3 medium, Memory, and 20 GB Storage. Figure 6 illustrates the data flow from the moment the web server requests the GTFS data to the time it is returned. We measured the time from data request to data return for the old system (without blockchain) and the new system (with blockchain). We ran each simulation 20 times, and the average results are shown in Fig. 7. The old system took an average of 15.5 ms, whereas the new system took an average of 283.4 ms. Moving to blockchain improves reliability and processing time.

The old system is vulnerable to data tampering due to administrator errors or unauthorized access. In contrast, the proposed system records all past data histories in the blockchain, which makes it easier to detect unauthorized changes. However, we observed that the time required to add and update data increased because data processing via smart contracts is required. We also examined the system's operational speed, data integrity, and tamper resistance. One of the

Table 1. GTFS Components

agency.txt	Contains information about the transit agencies, such as The agency's name, URL, and timezone
stops.txt	Contains information about the stops, including the stop's name, location (latitude and longitude), and time-zone
routes.txt	Contains information about the routes, including route names, route IDs, and types (e.g., bus, subway, etc.)
trips.txt	Contains information about trips, such as trip IDs, associated routes and service IDs
stop_times.txt	Contains detailed stop times for each trip, including arrival and departure times at each stop
calendar.txt	Defines the operating days for each service, including start and end dates and the days of the week on which the service operates
calendar_dates.txt	Provides exceptions to the service calendar, such as holidays or special operating days
fare_attributes.txt	Contains information about fare attributes, including fare types, price, and currency
fare_rules.txt	Defines the fare rules, mapping fares to specific routes or fare attributes

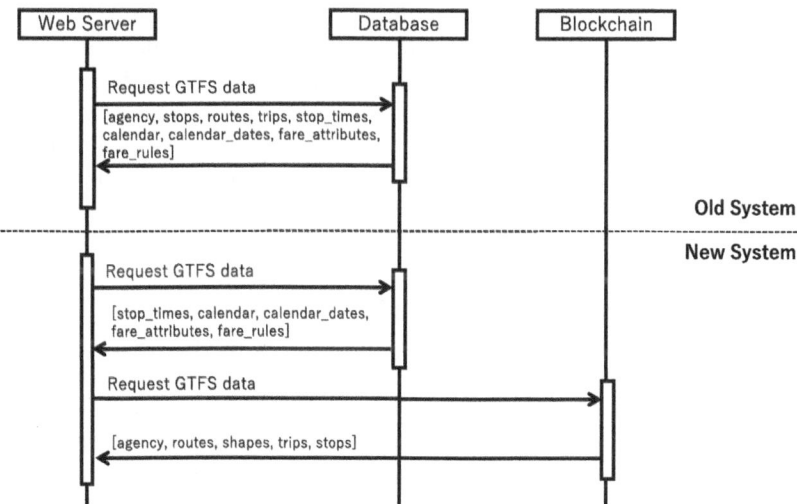

Fig. 6. Flow of a GTFS Data Request

advantages of implementing blockchain technology is its ability to prevent unauthorized data modifications because the history of changes is recorded on it. The recording of changes in operational information allows local governments and residents to check the validity of the data. In addition, the decentralized management approach reduces the risk of data loss due to server failures or admin-

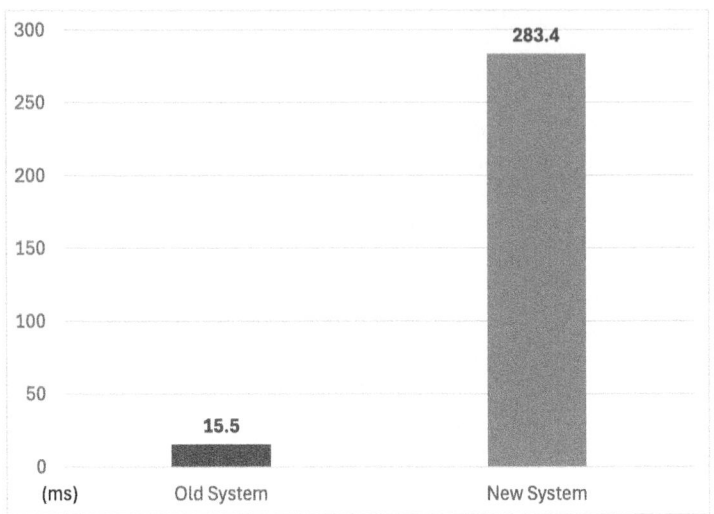

Fig. 7. Comparison results

istrator errors. However, reduced data processing speed was observed because data writing to the blockchain takes longer than immediate updates in traditional databases. This latency must be considered when implementing a real-time processing system. Although we achieved specific results in improving data reliability, we also identified issues such as delays in real-time processing and operating costs. In future work, we plan to consider hybrid operations that combine blockchain storage for critical operational data with traditional databases and methods to improve processing speed.

7   Conclusion

In this study, we developed BLS and PCS that use ICT to address the issues faced by regional public transportation in Japan. To improve data reliability and prevent tampering, we implemented blockchain technology to manage GTFS data. To ensure the safety of public transportation data, we stored key components of GTFS data on a blockchain. Blockchain technology allows us to manage data history and improve reliability transparently; conventional databases are vulnerable to tampering due to unauthorized access or management errors. However, blockchain takes a longer time to add and update data.

Our comparative analysis between the proposed system and conventional approaches demonstrates significant improvement in the convenience of regional public transportation and streamlining operations. However, the inherent latency in blockchain processing should be addressed in future work. In particular, to solve the problem of delays in data management using blockchain, a hybrid operation method that manages large real-time data and data essential for historical management separately is necessary.

In the future, we will collaborate with more local governments to expand the implementation of this system. We will also improve the technology to contribute to the sustainable development of regional public transportation. These efforts will advance the digital transformation of regional public transit while promoting the safety and comfortable movement of residents.

Acknowledgment. Our gratitude extends to Kyushu Sangyo University for their financial support through the Practical Application Support Research Funds. Additionally, we appreciate the backing provided by JSPS KAKENHI under Grant Number JP 24K14915.

References

1. Google: GTFS Static Overview. https://developers.google.com/transit/gtfs/
2. Bass, P., Donoso, P., Munizaga, M.: A model to assess public transport demand stability. Transp. Res. Part A Policy Pract. **45**(8), 755–764 (2011)
3. Hansson, J., Pettersson, F., Svensson, H., Wretstrand, A.: Preferences in regional public transport: a literature review. Eur. Transp. Res. Rev. **11**(1), 1–16 (2019). https://doi.org/10.1186/s12544-019-0374-4
4. Watari, K., Gao, W.: Present assessment of public traffic system based on GIS in Kitakyushu. Open J. Civil Eng. **4**(4), 397 (2014)
5. Ministry of Land, Infrastructure, Transport, and Tourism: Concept and type of community bus. http://www.mlit.go.jp/singikai/koutusin/rikujou/jidosha/bus/01/images/06.pdf
6. Ministry of Land, Infrastructure, Transport, and Tourism, Current status of regional public transportation in Japan. http://wwwtb.mlit.go.jp/kinki/content/000010186.pdf
7. Cabinet Office: Public opinion survey on public transportation. https://survey.gov-online.go.jp/h28/h28-kotsu/2-2.html
8. Li, Y., Xiang, C., Liu, N.: Planning and layout method for community bus stops based on carbon reduction benefits. Promet-Traffic Transp. **37**(1), 170–184 (2025)
9. Kim, S.: Decomposition analysis of greenhouse gas emissions in Korea's transportation sector. Sustainability **11**(7), 1986 (2019)
10. Lv, Y., Lv, W., Ren, Y., Ouyang, Q.: Optimizing the bus operation plan based on deep learning. Microprocess. Microsyst. **10404** (2021)
11. Wu, X., Feng, Q., Bai, C., Lai, C.S., Jia, Y., Lai, L.L.: Novel fast-charging stops locational planning model for electric bus public transport system. Energy **224** (2021)
12. Uchibayashi, T., Sueyoshi, C., Yasutake, Y., Satomura, H., Inenaga, K.: Construction of a regional public transportation management support system using the cloud. In: The 11th Asia-Pacific Conference on Computer Science and Data Engineering (CSDE 2024) (2024)
13. Uchibayashi, T., Sueyoshi, C., Yasutake, Y., Satomura, H., Inenaga, K.: Crew management support application for operation managers and boosting system security. In: 2024 IEEE Conference on Dependable, Autonomic and Secure Computing (DASC), pp. 73–77 (2024)

14. Satomura, H., Yasutake, Y., Uchibayashi, T., Sueyoshi, C., Inenaga, K.: A support tool for converting community bus operation data to GTFS format. In: The 39th International Technical Conference on Circuits/Systems, Computers, and Communications (ITC-CSCC 2024), pp. 1–6 (2024)

15. Uchibayashi, T., Sueyoshi, C., Takagi, H., Yasutake, Y., Inenaga, K.: A usage and analysis of measured CO_2 levels in Japanese community buses with IoT sensors. In: Proceedings of the 23rd International Conference on Computational Science and Its Applications (ICCSA 2023). Lecture Notes in Computer Science (LNCS), vol. 13957, pp. 242–255. Springer (2023)

16. Uchibayashi, T., Sueyoshi, C., Takagi, H., Yasutake, Y., Inenaga, K.: Proposal for an employee management support system for regional public transportation based on health data. In: Proceedings of Asia Pacific Computer Systems Conference 2021(APCS 2021). Lecture Notes in Electrical Engineering (LNEE), vol. 978, pp. 85–98. Springer (2023)

17. Ministry of Land, Infrastructure, Transport, and Tourism: GTFS-JP. http://www.mlit.go.jp/common/001283244.pdf

18. Nakamoto, S.: Bitcoin: a peer-to-peer electronic cash system. https://bitcoin.org/bitcoin.pdf

ShieldNetMapper: Internet of Things Powered Predictive Model for Real-Time Network Threat Detection and Response

R. Krishnamoorthy[1]([envelope]) [ID], Kazuaki Tanaka[2] [ID], and M. Amina Begum[3] [ID]

[1] Centre for Advanced Wireless Integrated Technology, Chennai Institute of Technology, Chennai 600069, Tamilnadu, India
`krishnamoorthyr@citchennai.net`
[2] Computer Science and System Engineering, Kyushu Institute of Technology, Kitakyushu, Japan
[3] Department of Electronics and Communication Engineering, Sri Venkataswaraa College of Technology, Chennai, Tamilnadu, India

Abstract. Numerous of IoT devices are in fact vulnerable to cyber threats. These vulnerabilities may be exploited over the internet and by remote access by the malefactors. Motivated by this, we suggest a reliable, knowledgeable IoT networks threat detection system. In this research, it aims at evaluating the integration of dual key design concepts in the development of a deep learning based intelligent threat detection system located at the edge of the IoT network. Given these notions, we introduce the ShieldNetMapper (SNM-Rand-N-MMOA) model. Finally, real time IoT traffic data is pre-processed using Spark, Enhanced Random Neural Network (Rand-NN) and Multifaceted Mayfly Optimization Algorithm (MMOA). A deep model is extracted by MMOA from the range of significant weights and bias values for the purpose of reconstructing the optimal network traffic data. On the other hand, we are utilizing Rand-NN for classification as well as to avoid the deep learning model from overfitting. This hereby proposes the model that evaluates IoT real time dataset using the recall rate of 99.78 % and average accuracy is 99.81%. With these impressive results, this is proof that the model can actually separate between different types of IoT traffic and this can help enhance the security and efficiency of operations in the network. Therefore, by integrating MMOA and Rand-NN, not only are data processed in an optimal manner but also the robust classification in dynamic environments is also guaranteed.

Keywords: Detecting IoT Threats · IoT Network Data Traffic · Improved Rand-NN · Multifaceted Mayfly Optimization

K. TanSaka and M. Amina Begum—These authors contributed equally to this work.

O. Gervasi et al. (Eds.): ICCSA 2025 Workshops, LNCS 15890, pp. 205–216, 2026.
https://doi.org/10.1007/978-3-031-97606-3_14

1   Introduction

As the numbers of IoT devices keep increasing, this also resulted in a large increase of the attack surface, making these networks an easy target for sophisticated cyberattacks. The main objective is to make the Internet of Things (IoT) networks and devices unusable by those people whom it is supposed to serve by flooding these networks or devices with too many requests. Basic network resource flooding and other more elaborate types of attacks, exploiting vulnerabilities in certain protocols or services are possible in these attacks [1]. A rather big threat to the IoT networks is represented by botnets networks of devices that were compromised by a single attacker (bot herder). It is done to execute DDoS attack, spread malware, etc. on compromised devices, which are usually small low powered IoT devices lacking adequate security mechanisms [2]. Due to the nature of botnets as being decentralized and spread, they are difficult to locate and deactivate. The use of deep learning models enables botnet traffic patterns to be effectively detected as they feature the specific communication patterns and the main command and control framework of botnets [3]. However, the design and communication method of botnets will continue to improve the problem is that botnet designs and communication methods are always improving so deep learning models need to adapt to new botnet behaviours [4]. Furthermore, there is a need for developing deep learning models to detect botnet for the same reason that most IoT devices have very limited resources, and deep learning models should be light and effective to run on the devices that have limited memory and processing power [5]. Lastly, the immense difficulty remains in detecting zero day exploits, which are not present in training datasets. Advanced Persistent Threats (APTs) are established and long lasting attacks, caused to hide from detection for a very long duration. Many of these assaults have many phases and methods, which makes them hard to perceive with traditional security tools. The deep learning models, and especially those that are able to identify very small changes in a long term behavior pattern can be used to detect APTs. Proficient APT identification requires the capacity to recognize and associate apparently irregular cases over the long haul. Even today, the creation of deep learning models that can detect APTs with high precision in real-time with very low false positives remains to be a problem. When threat intelligence is merged with contextual data, APT detection systems are much better and more accurate. It is the sequential nature of network traffic data that makes RNN's, LSTMs and GRUs perfect at evaluating it [6]. These models can capture time dependencies in the data which is important to detect the threats which develop with time [7]. There are advanced types of RNNs, LSTMs and GRUs, which have solved the problem of vanishing gradients. It enables them to learn long dependencies in data faster than RNNs. To identify slow moving attacks such as APTs, it's even more critical. Botnet assaults and other kinds of intrusions have already been successfully identified using LSTMs [8]. The combination of CNNs with RNNs, LSTMs or GRUs makes threat detection systems perform better in hybrid models. This method improves accuracy and flexibility because it combinations of the finest protocol of both CNNs and RNNs. Extracting spatial patterns are done with CNNs, and temporal dependencies are modelled by RNNs. However, even though RNN models based on RNNs might come with high computational costs as well, if the data sequences are long, they will not be as effective in IoT settings with limited resources.

2   Related Study

This research [9] examines the difficulties associated with managing and safeguarding the expansive Internet of Things (IoT) network, noted for its substantial scale and data flow. It is shown to provide intrinsic challenges in terms of the reliability and security in this context and innovative approaches that need to be taken to the network infrastructure management. These functions cannot be supported by the present dependence on individual IoT devices. The model's input layer examines characteristics of network traffic, and forwards their results to many hidden layers that can spot complicated patterns in the data. To avoid overfitting, a dropout strategy is used. A softmax activation function is used by them on output layer for classification of network traffic as normal or abnormal and hence as a multi class discrimination. The results indicate that it is important to process data carefully and to run a structured evaluation process that uses several performance criteria. The proposed model is compared with existing anomaly detection algorithms to validate its effectiveness in terms of accuracy and efficiency of handling IoT network data flow. In this study [10], the author identify and improve from Distributed Denial of Service (DDoS) attacks involving botnet drive attacks against Internet of Things (IoT) networks. As IoT devices become bigger and more sophisticated; it creates a growing landscape weak to cyber-attack and data breaches. Directly, research addresses the steady growing threat from botnets within the augmented IoT environment. The research makes use of a multidimensional method that leverages multiple ML models to accomplish its task. More details of the examination involves many techniques such as K-Nearest Neighbor (KNN), KMeans clustering, Fuzzy clustering, and deep learning models like Convolutional Neural Networks (CNN), Recurrent Neural Networks (RNN) and Long Short Term Memory (LSTM) networks. These models are assessed on the Bot-IoT dataset and we show their effectiveness. To aid in algorithm selection, the method employs preprocessing of data as well as a performance guided selection that is aided by accuracy percentages. Additionally, the study makes the machine learning algorithms work better and uses feature selection and the Synthetic Minority Over-sampling Technique (SMOTE). This suggests the suggested architecture is effective in determining botnet related attacks of the IoT network. In [11], the author examine the issue of growing security being faced in the stoopid growing Internet of Things (IoT) ecosystem more specifically, and how botnet assault is a big risk to IoT network operations. New approach, GA HDLAD (Genetic approach with Hybrid Deep Learning based Anomaly Detection) is proposed in the study for increasing security with Anomaly Detection for Botnet activities. In this approach, genetic algorithm is used to select feature for the high dimensionality existed in the IoT network data. Before effective and precise defects identification is possible, that requires this dimensionality reduction. HDL element is the essence (core) of the GA-HDLAD system. The advantage of multiple strategies is used by this component to achieve the result of effective botnet detection. At the same time, feature extraction techniques (FETs) are used to efficiently and effectively extract relevant features from the spatial data that is available in IoT network traffic. Attention mechanisms are integrated into the model so that the model can pay greater attention to the most significant part of the data and this leads to higher accuracy. Simulated annealing (SA) of the HDL method guarantees the optimal performance of the deep learning model, and hyperparameter optimization is performed for the HDL method with simulated annealing. Empirical assessment of the effectiveness of the proposed GA-HDLAD system based on a standardized benchmark botnet dataset is performed. Results from the experimental study show that the GA-HDLAD algorithm surpasses existing botnet detection techniques and thus has the promise of being a valuable addition to IoT security. In [12], the researcher proposed to advance the field of study by investigating how to utilize AI to address crucial cybersecurity problems, particularly from the point of view of enhancing security in the Internet of Things (IoT) environment. This objective is accomplished by an innovative architecture based on Cognitive Digital Twin Systems (CDTS) introduced by the research. Using AI methods to a high degree of sophistication, CDTS enables the digitalization of actual IoT devices, real time monitoring, real time prediction, real time pre-emptive security. It is a result of integrating cognitive learning ability, anomaly detection and machine learning capabilities to predict and counter security issues. In the adopted methodology, the patterns of security incidents are analyzed to reduce response time to 87.5% based on cognitive computing and predictive security techniques, and on detecting zero day attacks with accuracy rate of 92.4%. As expected, these results strongly indicate that the proposed CDTS architecture can provide a comprehensive solution to the issue of adaptive and intelligent threat control in complex IoT networks.

3   Proposed Methodology

The datasets are referred to as $'ToN_IoT'$ since they consist of such data sources drawn from Telemetry datasets of IoT and IIoT sensors. Furthermore, the dataset contains created new Industry 4.0 test-bed network consisting of both IoT and IIoT networks. In order to make easier talking between three levels of IoT, Cloud and the Edge/cloud system, the test-bed was created with bunch of virtual machines and hosts running numerous of Windows platform, Linux and Kali. Different types of threats, like DoS, DDoS, as well as ransomware, were to be used against web apps, Traffic ofIoT networks. The dataset creation was used parallel processing to collect network traffic, Windows audit logs, Linux audit logs and IoT service telemetry data for both normal and threat events. In this proposed method, termed ShieldNetMapper (SNP-Rand-NN-MMOP), should employ Random Neural Networks and Mayfly in conjunction, and it has many parts. An Artificial Neural Network (ANN) known as the Random Neural Network (Rand-NN) places its neurons in such a way that connection weights are randomly allocated in the middle of its neurons. Unlike traditional neural networks, the epitome of the Rand-NN differs in that its architecture is realized randomly. It is unique in the sense that it makes it easier to experiment with a whole accumulation of network architectures. The Rand-NN consists of an input layer, number of hidden layers, and an output layer. The neurons of the Rand-NN are interconnected in a random manner and thus, allow for efficient data flow through the network. The goal of Rand-NN is to discover the essence of neuronal interconnections and activation functions in a network. Rand-NN has the advantage that is easier to use to make random patterns, study properties of neural networks, etc. because their weights are randomized at the beginning. The particle swarm optimization algorithm enhances the multifaceted Mayfly optimization algorithm (MMOA). This bridges between the advantages of evolutionary as well as swarm intelligence algorithms and produces a high power hybrid algorithmic framework, which is applicable to solve both continuous and discrete problems. This method was derived from mayflies' flying and reproductive behaviours. We applied MMOA to a set of 20 test functions with 20 different test functions including fixed dimensional, unimodal, multimodal and multi object optimization functions for which we compare it to seven of the best performing meta heuristic algorithms. The proposed method synergizes the benefits of swarm intelligence and on one hand evolutionary computation.

Figure 1 shows that there are many phases in Rand-NN-MMOA. Scrambling, initialization, scheming the fitness function, selection of the best location, global best evaluation, and updating are the procedures. To obtain better solutions, the most important step in swarm intelligence processes is the exhibition of potential solutions. This work provides a solution to this problem by encoding the Rand-NN weights and biases as swarm mayflies. The three types of weights that can be modified in a Rand-NN network with respect to input activation state weights are: input weights (In W), neuron weights (NW), and bias. A particle has an initial velocity of $V_{ini} = 0$. The mayfly needs to be set up with a number of parameters. They consist of the total number of population for the swarm (S_{pop}), the maximum number of iterations or generations (Max$_{iter}$), the individual coefficient (k_{in}), the social ratio (k_{so}), and the inertia coefficient ($\mho$). The proposed Multifaceted MAO will be differentiated from the traditional MOA by using the inertia component x, the direction that linearly changes from $\mho_{max}$ to $\mho_{min}$ over time.

$$\mho = \mho_{max} - \frac{(\mho'_{max} - \mho'_{min})t}{T} \tag{1}$$

The variable t in Eq. (1) represents the current iteration number and the Variable T represents the total number of iteration counts. Calculation of the cost function in the middle of the actual and perceived values is the measure by which any population solution is effective. Position Best of each mayfly is used to find out its fitness, while Global Best value is the optimal location which is occupied by any mayfly in the swarm. The positions and velocities of the mayflies

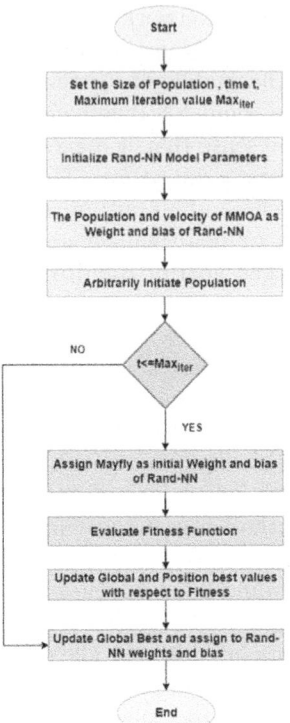

Fig. 1. Proposed Rand-NN-MMOP Flow Diagram.

are modified so that Pos_{best} and Glo_{best} are optimised in each iteration. This is an iterative process which continues till a stop criterion Max_{iter} is met. In the end, it produces the optimum solution that serves as the swarm's collective intelligence in its quest for solve problem in the shortest time possible.

The velocity and position of the ith mayfly at time t are denoted by $(Vel)_t^i$ and $(Pos)_t^i$. Subsequently, the equations cause modifications in the velocity $(Vel)_{t+1}^i$ and the position $(Pos)_{t+1}^i$ of the ith mayfly at the time $(t+1)$. Equations (2) and (3) represent their designated locations.

$$(Vel)_{t+1}^i = v \times (Vel)_t^i + k_{in}r_1 \times (Pbest)^i - (Pos)_t^i + k_{so}r_2 \times (Gbest)^i \times (pos)_t^i \quad (2)$$

$$(Pos)_{t+1}^i = (Pos)_t^i + (Vel)_{t+1}^i \quad (3)$$

To continue the exploitative and exploratory characteristics of the multi-faceted mayfly, we use the velocity of the complex mayfly, which is known to be the local and global optimum. The Pbest, Gbest, location, and speed of a mayfly are updated during the subsequent process until the iteration number exceeds the maximum (max_{iter}) or the tolerance reaches the specified threshold. The

Rand-NN, with all weights and biases calibrated and the feedforward layer fully regulated, yields the final Gbest, which is the optimal solution. The weights and biases of the MMOA-Rand-NN are taken as the starting point of the Rand-NN as well as Feed-forward RNN. They are then improved with Adam optimiz-er.

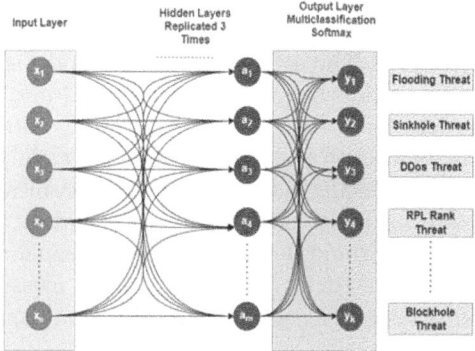

Fig. 2. IoT Network Threat Detection using Proposed SNM: Rand-NN-MMOP Model.

The suggestion is to have the input and output neurons and all of the posi-tive and negative weights relating to each of the neurons. It also has clusters that denote highly interconnected cells. The neurons of each cluster are assem-bled differ-ently and may be inhibited by external cellular units. The Rand-NN-MMOA architec-ture is depicted in Fig. 2 MMOA decodes how likely a single cell in a cluster is to become active and therefore model suggests the likeliness by exploiting strengths and weaknesses of inputs that stimulate and inhibit with MMOA. With back-propagation over the specified interval, different character-istics and initialization weights were establishedbeginning of input neurons, link matrices, information knowledge rate and total count of epochs, and the algo-rithms were run. It stores and retrieves weights, calculates firing rates of neurons and computes loss, correctness. The proposed Architecture which has a dual lay-ered framework and three layers of concealing layers considered for binary and multiclass classification. The model employs learning rates of 0.10, and 0.010 over 120 epochs. For binary classification the input X is a dimension of 72 and for multiclass classification 78. It is in the connectivity and weight matrices that the iterative updates of the MMOA optimal value weights of neurons, hence the prediction output, are dictated. A novel approach to simulating network risks is developed by Rand-NN-MMOA through the use of multiple attacks. The pro-posed architecture is based on a different way of sending data where path where the suspicious attack happened is blocked to flow data and is aware of quality of service (QoS). To protect the network from intrusion, this data is housed in two databases: one for defensive purposes and another for mitigation purposes. It is an active approach, increases the real time responsiveness of network defenses and also allows real time changes based on evolving threat set. The system can learn from these suggested algorithms, so that it con-tinues to learn how it finds threats and how it responds to it in order to have the strongest defenses against future attacks.

4   Result and Discussions

At the beginning of experiment analysis, the IoT routing network dataset is gener-ated from normal and Threat classes. Table 1 and Fig. 3 of 3D heat map show that there possible more than 6,375 instances, 12 meaningful characteris-tics, and 48 sub-class characteristics of the final routing dataset.

The three groups of the processed data are the training, validation, and testing, on the feature processing stage. For binary classification data, the data has 64 dimen-sions and for multi class classification data it has 69 dimensions. These sets have the labels within them, which refer to regular and attack threats. This representation is depicted in Fig. 4. Evaluation measures are used from mainstream literature, name-ly accuracy, precision, recall and F1 score in order to evaluate the proposed model.

Accuracy: This term is used to indicate the level of correctness of a model's pre-dictions. In other words, the accuracy rate is calculated as the number of

Table 1. Proposed Simulation Dataset Collection

S. No	Type of Data	No. of Samples
1	Normal Data	6375 (25*25)
2	Threat Data – DDoS	375
3	Threat Data – Flood	165
4	Threat Data – Sinkhole	186
5	Threat Data – RPL Rank	148
6	Threat Data – Blockhole	119

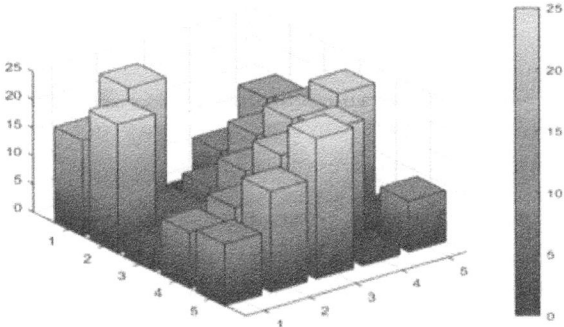

Fig. 3. 3D Heatmap Visualization of Proposed Model"s Input Dataset

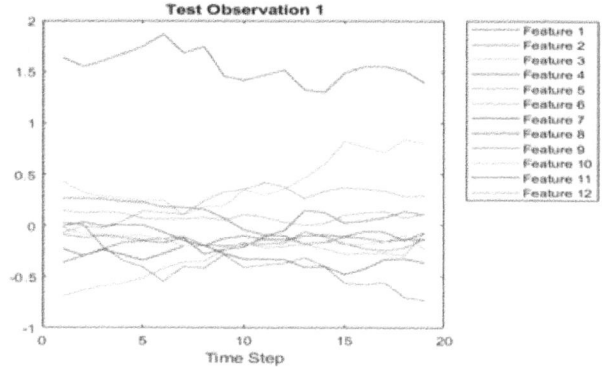

Fig. 4. Proposed Model Test observation Feature counts

correctly classified instances (true positives, true negatives) divided by total instances. We compute it using Eq. (4).

$$\text{Accuracy} = \frac{TP + TN}{TP + TN + FP + FN} \tag{4}$$

- **TP** It is a count of *'correct'* identified cases as positive.
- **TN** The number of correctly identified instances as negative.
- **FP** Number of positive incorrectly classified instances.
- **FN** The number of incidents misclassified as negative.

Precision is the number of the extent of accuracy in optimistic forecasts. The pro-portion of expected positive occurrences (both real and false) to actual positive oc-currences is known as the false positive rate. A measure of accuracy, precision may be expressed as the proportion of correct results to the total number of results, includ-ing both true and false positives. The ratio of the number of positively identified events to the total number of positive events (including both true positives and false negatives) is called recall, which is sometimes called sensitivity or the true positive rate. It is also a statistic that can be used to define precision and recall as the same. Hence, there is a need to find a F1 score in the middle of two metrics. Using accuracy and memory average is beneficial in case of imbalanced precision and recall score. As a categorization model, this method is commonly used by machine learning, deep learning, and statistical analysis; to determine an effective categorization model. Our proposed optimization involves the mathematical expression that the neces-sary losses is for to minimize with respect to the iteration and an iteration is a single step in an algorithm assessing the objective function towards the optimal solution step by step. In the Fig. 5, exemplify the objective function which shows that pro-posed M-MOA optimization has such characteristics and the iterations stands for the repeated steps followed to find the best possible value of the objective function.

Setting up experiments on the suggested models and using three benchmark datasets, we perform experiments on both multiclass and binary classification.

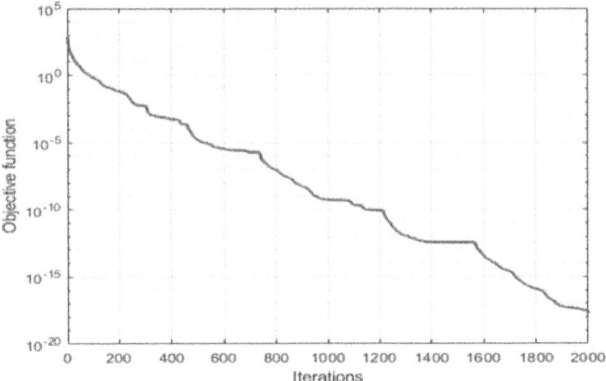

Fig. 5. Proposed Model Objective Function with respect to Iterations

To exhibit efficiency, we used the MATLAB 2022b Tool on a PC with a 2.4 GHz Xeon processor, 16 GB RAM, and NVIDIA Basic GPU for training and deployment of our suggested models. Its evaluation was performed on Windows 11. The stages of an assessment of a neural network include training, validation, and testing. The classification takes preference for the majority class if the dataset is unevenly distributed. In order to fix the problem of imbalanced class distribution in the datasets, we used class weights and AdaSyn for that purpose. The instance quantity of a class has an effect on the class weights, and a class with a small fraction of instance count will be under substantial weight. For the Multifaceted Mayfly Optimizer (MMOA), we trained each Rand-NN classifier for iterations with batch size one.

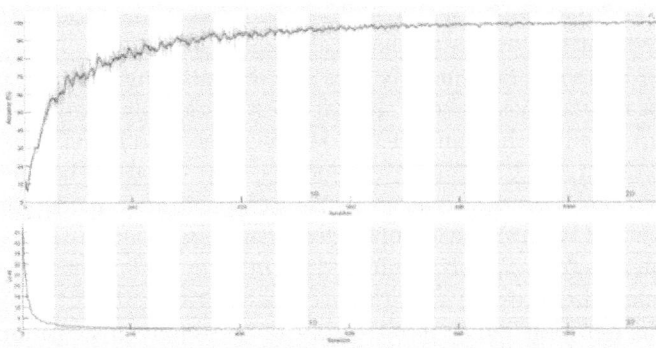

Fig. 6. Proposed Model Training Accuracy and Loss Function of Real Time Dataset

In this work, we employ a dual-type method for training and evaluating our proposed Rand-NN-MMOA model. In this experiment, we allocated 70% of the

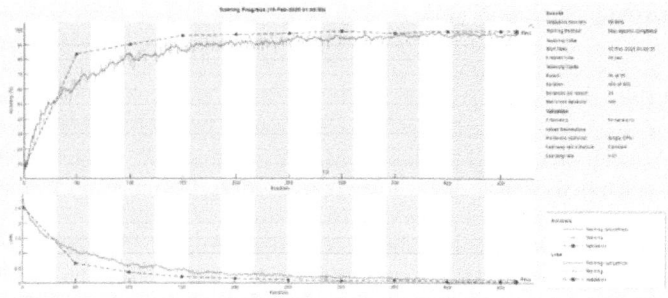

Fig. 7. Proposed Model Testing and Validation Accuracy and Loss Function of Real Time Dataset

data for training and the remaining 30% for testing. In the first case, results are obtained with the best of the standard MOA-based Rand-NN weight and bias assignment. During the evaluation, the Multifaceted Mayfly Technique (MMOA) uses sample points as an activation function to fine-tune hyperparameter values. During the tuning procedure, we also identified the epoch with the ideal learning rate and performance batch size as the best optimizers. Specifically, Figs. 6 and 7 illustrate accuracy and error rate of detection in training and validation as a function of testing data, in which the accuracy and loss components come from a separate set of testing data. Tests indicate that the model performance has considerably improved, especially under complex data distribution conditions. The comparative analysis also shows the robustness of the proposed method in improving the overall predictive capacity of the model on most of the datasets.

5   Conclusion

This is especially true when evaluating the effectiveness of the proposed SNM-Rand-NN-MMOA strategies, as shown by the fact that they can achieve near-optimal results under various data distribution complexities. A comparison investigation showing the efficacy of several strategies usually attaining performance metrics between 0.97 and 0.98 is performed. Notably, we also assessed the IoTReal time dataset for which the recall rate obtained is 99.78% and the average accuracy is 99.81%. Therefore, these results give confirmation that these methods are also practical in real-life applications and can be further improved in data analysis and machine learning to obtain more advanced decision-making processes in threat detection systems. These findings indicate that operational efficiency would be greatly increased by the use of modern data processing methods. With the continued development of these data-driven strategies becoming more and more necessary as the cycle of challenges and opportunities continues to rise in these firms, they will be essential in the ongoing enhancement.

Conflicts of Interest. The authors declare that they have no conflict of interest.

Ethics Approval. Not applicable.

References

1. Nuhu, A.A., Raffei, A.F.M., Razak, M.F.A., Ahmad, A.: Distributed denial of service attack detection in IoT networks using deep learning and feature fusion: a review. None (2024). https://doi.org/10.58496/mjcs/2024/004
2. Haque, S., El-Moussa, F., Komninos, N., Rajarajan, M.: A systematic review of data-driven attack detection trends in IoT. In: Italian National Conference on Sensors (2023). https://doi.org/10.3390/s23167191
3. Alsoufi, M.A., et al.: Anomaly-based intrusion detection systems in IoT using deep learning: a systematic literature review. In: Multidisciplinary Digital Publishing Institute (2021). https://doi.org/10.3390/app11188383
4. Abdullahi, M., et al.: Detecting cybersecurity attacks in internet of things using artificial intelligence methods: a systematic literature review. Multidisciplinary Digital Publishing Institute (2022). https://doi.org/10.3390/electronics11020198
5. Yaras, S., Dener, M.: IoT-based intrusion detection system using new hybrid deep learning algorithm. Electronics (2024). https://doi.org/10.3390/electronics13061053
6. Manimaran, A., Kartheesan, L., Kumutha, D., Surendran, R.: An optimized hybrid deep learning framework for monitoring botnet attacks in IoT networks (2024). https://doi.org/10.1109/ICICNIS64247.2024.10823344
7. Tekleselassie, H.: DDoS detection on internet of things using unsupervised algorithms. EDP Sciences (2021). https://doi.org/10.1051/e3sconf/202129701005
8. Avci, S., Koca, M.: Predicting DDoS attacks using machine learning algorithms in building management systems. Multidisciplinary Digital Publishing Institute (2023). https://doi.org/10.3390/electronics12194142
9. Singh, N.J., Hoque, N., Singh, K.R., Bhattacharyya, D.K.: Botnet-based IoT network traffic analysis using deep learning. Secur. Priv. (2023). https://doi.org/10.1002/spy2.355
10. Clinton, U.B., Hoque, N., Singh, K.R.: Botnet-based IoT network attacks identification using LSTM. In: Proceedings of International Conference on Computing Communication and Networking Technologies (ICCCNT) (2023). https://doi.org/10.1109/ICCCNT56998.2023.10307716
11. Kumar, A.K., et al.: Enhanced hybrid deep learning approach for botnet attacks detection in IoT environment (2024). https://doi.org/10.1109/ICSPIS63676.2024.10812621
12. Alkhudaydi, O.A., Krichen, M., Alghamdi, A.D.: A deep learning methodology for predicting cybersecurity attacks on the internet of things. Multidisciplinary Digital Publishing Institute (2023). https://doi.org/10.3390/info14100550

Whisper, Translate, Speak, Sync: Video Translation for Multilingual Video Conferencing Using Generative AI

Amirkia Rafiei Oskooei[1]([✉])(iD), Eren Caglar[2], Ibrahim Şahin[1], Ayse Kayabay[1],
and Mehmet S. Aktas[1](iD)

[1] Department of Computer Engineering, Yildiz Technical University,
Istanbul, Turkey
{amirkia.oskooei,ibrahim.sahin1,ayse.kayabay}@std.yildiz.edu.tr,
aktas@yildiz.edu.tr
[2] Aktif Bank, R&D Center, Istanbul, Turkey
eren.caglar@aktifbank.com.tr
https://www.aktifbank.com.tr/

Abstract. This paper addresses the growing need for seamless communication in multilingual video conferencing by presenting a novel, computationally efficient methodology for real-time video translation. While advancements in neural networks have enabled accurate speech translation and voice cloning, integrating these with lip synchronization for realistic talking head generation remains a challenge, particularly for real-time applications. This paper introduces a comprehensive video translation pipeline leveraging open-source deep learning models. We further propose a scalable system architecture incorporating a "Token Ring" mechanism to manage speaker turns and minimize computational load, addressing key challenges related to latency, scalability, and personalization in multilingual settings. A segmented batched processing protocol with inverse throughput thresholding and overlapping buffering is implemented to achieve near real-time performance. A simplified, universal prototype is developed to demonstrate the feasibility and efficacy of our approach, providing a foundation for building next-generation multilingual video conferencing systems. This work offers a practical framework for developers and businesses aiming to create inclusive and effective communication platforms.

Keywords: Video Translation · Computer Vision · Deep Learning · Generative AI · Human-AI Interaction · Video Conferencing

1 Introduction

In today's digital world, communication is increasingly taking place in online environments. With global collaborations on the rise, the need for technology that can overcome language barriers has become a pressing challenge. Video

O. Gervasi et al. (Eds.): ICCSA 2025 Workshops, LNCS 15890, pp. 217–234, 2026.
https://doi.org/10.1007/978-3-031-97606-3_15

conferencing has emerged as a cornerstone of modern communication, widely used in education, business, and work settings. The recent COVID-19 pandemic further accelerated the adoption of these platforms, enabling people to work and study remotely from home. When people with different native languages interact, challenges arise. Expressing oneself in a foreign language can be difficult, and understanding someone speaking in a non-native language can slow down and complicate the conversation. In an interconnected world, seamless communication across linguistic and cultural boundaries is essential, which drives the demand for real-time, multilingual video conferencing systems.

Recent advances in neural networks and deep learning have enabled rapid and accurate translation of both written and spoken language in virtual environments. Modern neural models are now capable of translating text and speech between multiple languages while preserving the tone and style of the speaker through voice cloning techniques. However, while these models can translate speech and adjust voice characteristics, the video component still presents a challenge. In video conferences, even if the translated speech sounds natural, the speaker's lip movements and facial expressions remain in the source language. Recent progress in lip synchronization, or audio-driven talking head generation, now allows for the generation of video where the speaker's lip movements match the translated speech. In simple terms, this means that a speaker's lips can be effectively "translated" along with their words. The complete process of translating all aspects of communication—including language, voice tone, facial expressions, and lip movements—is often called "Video Translation" or "Face-to-Face Translation" or simply "Face Translation".

Video Translation concept is gaining significant momentum as a potentially revolutionary communication paradigm. Its broad applicability spans diverse sectors including entertainment through video dubbing, film translation, immersive Augmented and Virtual Reality (AR/VR) experiences, telemedicine [6], and, crucially, multilingual video conferencing. Despite the acknowledged potential and numerous applications highlighted in current research, concrete methodologies for effectively deploying video-translation pipelines within real-world video conferencing systems remain underdeveloped. Furthermore, the practical challenges inherent in real-world implementation, and strategies to effectively address these challenges, require in-depth exploration. A primary obstacle lies in the computational demands of video-translation pipelines. The integration of multiple deep learning models, particularly computationally intensive generative models for computer vision tasks like lip synchronization, necessitates substantial processing resources, often requiring high-performance GPUs. Moreover, the imperative for real-time and uninterrupted communication in video conferencing environments exacerbates these computational pressures. Simply scaling computational resources by adding more or more powerful GPUs presents scalability concerns, especially in large multilingual meetings where numerous participants require real-time translation into their respective native languages, potentially demanding parallel execution of the entire pipeline multiple times.

Currently, a detailed exploration of these practical challenges is lacking in the existing literature, leaving a significant gap in actionable guidelines for developers and businesses. In response to these challenges, this paper presents a novel methodology that is computationally cost-effective, universal, and easy to implement. Our approach is designed to integrate with any video conferencing client while delivering near real-time performance. We propose a framework that includes a comprehensive video translation pipeline, a new system architecture, and strategies to address the computational and scalability challenges that have so far limited real-world applications. This work contributes to the literature by guiding developers and businesses toward building next-generation communication systems that enable seamless, multilingual interaction.

The subsequent sections of this paper are organized as follows: Sect. 2 provides a review of the current, albeit limited, literature on neural models and lip synchronization techniques applied to Video-translation. Section 3 details our proposed methodology, delineating the identified challenges and presenting our pipeline and system architecture as solutions. Section 4 describes the development of a universal and simplified prototype designed to validate the feasibility and efficacy of our approach. Finally, Sect. 5 presents a comprehensive evaluation of our system, encompassing both objective performance metrics and subjective user assessments, followed by an in-depth analysis of the results obtained.

2   Related Works

Speech-to-Speech Translation (S2S) has emerged as a pivotal technology for breaking down communication barriers in a globalized world. At its core, S2S systems typically involve a sequential pipeline comprising Automatic Speech Recognition (ASR), Machine Translation (MT), and Speech Synthesis (SS) modules. ASR transcribes spoken language into text, which is then translated into a target language by the MT module, and finally, the translated text is converted back to speech using SS. The advent of neural networks has revolutionized each of these components, leading to significant improvements in accuracy and naturalness compared to traditional statistical methods. Neural ASR models, often employing architectures like recurrent neural networks and transformers, have achieved remarkable performance in transcribing diverse accents and noisy environments [9,15,20]. Similarly, Neural Machine Translation (NMT) has surpassed phrase-based statistical MT in fluency and translation quality, leveraging encoder-decoder architectures and attention mechanisms [31,34]. More recently, the rise of large language models (LLMs) and their cpabilities in various tasks such as language and code understanding, has further pushed the boundaries of MT and even end-to-end S2S, demonstrating the potential for more contextually aware and human-like translations [19,40]. Neural Text-to-Speech (TTS) systems have also significantly improved the naturalness and expressiveness of synthesized speech, often incorporating voice cloning or voice conversion techniques to maintain speaker identity or style [4,13]. These advancements in neural models and LLMs have collectively propelled S2S towards more seamless and practical applications. The concept of Video Translation, sometimes referred to as Face Translation or Face-to-Face Translation, extends the capabilities of

S2S by addressing the visual aspects of communication, particularly in video settings. This area, while nascent compared to traditional S2S, is gaining increasing attention due to its potential to enhance video conferencing, film dubbing, and immersive experiences.

Extending S2S to the visual domain requires language-independent Lip Sync or Talking Head Generation models. This language independence is essential for integrating these models into video translation pipelines. Recent advances in neural language-independent Lip Sync models have been key to progress in face-to-face translation, shifting focus primarily to the lip sync module itself. A foundational work in language-independent lip sync using neural models was presented in [11]. This work spurred research into GAN-based lip sync models [3,7,8,10,21,33,39]. Subsequent research has explored Diffusion-based [12,14, 26,29,35] and NeRF-based [27,30,36–38] approaches. Some studies have also examined the generalizability and language independence of these models [23], a crucial requirement for video translation pipelines.

Having covered the necessary modules and models for Video Translation, we now focus on works specifically utilizing lip sync and S2S pipelines for this task. This area remains underexplored, but we highlight some prominent examples. One of the earliest attempts at Video Translation was [24], which developed a full face-translation pipeline before the advent of neural models. The [11] discussed the concept of automatic face-to-face translation and its applications, but did not provide specific guidance for real-world scenarios. The [28] integrates Multilingual TTS with Lip Sync, but lacks focus on real-world application and comprehensive experimental evaluation. [5] presents a notable effort in end-to-end face translation, developing a model that avoids cascading modules. However, this end-to-end approach, while advantageous in some ways, lacks modularity, which can limit control over individual steps and raise scalability concerns. The [22] implements a blazing-fast real-time pipeline and addresses concerns regarding latency, but does not address the system-level challenges.

While speech and video translation components have advanced significantly, deploying and evaluating complete video translation pipelines for real-world video conferencing remains a challenge. Existing work often focuses on individual modules like lip synchronization, neglecting system-level integration issues for real-time, scalable, and user-friendly applications. Computational demands and architectural considerations, especially for multilingual settings, are also under-explored. This paper addresses these gaps by presenting a novel, cost-effective, and universally applicable methodology for video translation tailored for multilingual video conferencing. We propose a complete pipeline, a scalable architecture, and practical strategies to overcome computational and scalability bottlenecks that have limited the adoption of video translation in real-world communication.

The authors of [1] proposed a fault-tolerant information service architecture for managing dynamic Web and Grid resources. The authors of [25] conducted a systematic mapping study demonstrating structured methodologies for evaluating application reliability. Research efforts in [17,18] modeled user behavior through embedding-based representations of clickstream sequences, while the authors of [32] introduced a provenance-enabled data infrastructure to improve transparency in scientific workflows. In parallel, the authors of [2,16] addressed collaborative grid portals for high-performance computing applications. While these studies emphasize distributed system architectures, user modeling, and provenance integration, none of them address the real-time orchestration of generative AI models for speech, translation, and video synchronization in multilingual communication.

3   Methodology

In this section, we detail our methodology for designing a video translation pipeline utilizing deep learning models specifically for video conferencing systems. Our methodology prioritizes minimal computational resource and budgetary demands, aiming to facilitate the development of multilingual video conferencing systems that are cost-effective, universally accessible, and scalable. In the Subsect. 3.1, we describe the proposed pipeline workflow, which integrates readily available open-source deep learning models. Considering the application of this pipeline within video conferencing environments, the Subsect. 3.2 presents a scalable system architecture that leverages the proposed pipeline.

3.1   Pipeline

Our video translation pipeline leverages state-of-the-art open-source deep learning models, selected for their efficacy and broad accessibility. From a high-level perspective, the objective of this modular pipeline is to process an input video and generate a talking head of a specified identity—either the original individual or a novel identity—where the original speech is translated into a target language while preserving the original voice tone, and the lip movements are synchronized with the translated speech. This pipeline constitutes a deep learning-based video translation system, also referred to in the literature as Face Translation or Face-to-Face translation, designed for portable and versatile deployment.

We now detail the components and modules of our proposed pipeline, as depicted in Fig. 1. The input is a video featuring a talking head, or more generally, any speaking individual. The initial module in the pipeline is an **Automatic Speech Recognition (ASR)** model. This module is responsible for detecting and transcribing speech from the video's audio track. Depending on the specific requirements of the ASR model, an audio extraction sub-module may extract and pre-process the audio to ensure compatibility with the ASR module specifications. This step functions as an audio-to-text conversion. Subsequently, a **Machine Translation (MT)** module is invoked. Given the transcribed text, this component translates it from the source to the target language, completing the second stage, performing a text-to-text translation.

With the translated text obtained, the next stage involves **Speech Synthesis (SS)**. This stage utilizes a **Text-to-Speech (TTS)** sub-module, and optionally incorporates a **Voice Cloning (VC)** sub-module, depending on the TTS sub-module's capabilities in voice conversion to maintain the original tone and style. The ASR, MT, and TTS modules collectively achieve Speech-to-Speech translation from the source to the target language.

To address the visual communication aspects, we employ a **Lip Synchronization (lip-sync)** model. Given an input audio track and a reference identity (e.g., a human face), this component generates a talking head where lip movements are synchronized with the translated speech. This finalizes our video translation pipeline, resulting in a translated video encompassing all facets of communication.

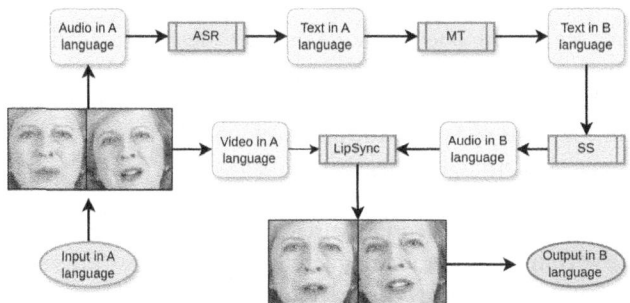

Fig. 1. Workflow of the Pipeline for Video Translation.

3.2   System Architecture

The proposed pipeline exhibits universal applicability across diverse domains, including video conferencing systems. However, its efficient utilization necessitates a rigorous system design due to inherent challenges.

Challenges. First, latency presents a significant concern in real-time environments such as video conferencing. This is particularly pertinent given that the pipeline incorporates multiple generative models processing various modalities: video, audio, and text. Each modality demands substantial computational resources, potentially disrupting the streaming process and compromising the real-time nature of the video conferencing experience, thereby impeding conversational fluidity. Second, the processing of these modalities requires considerable computational power, often necessitating high-performance GPUs to parallelize computations across models. This requirement is amplified by the pipeline's sequential nature, wherein each component's input depends on the preceding component's output. Consequently, standard parallel execution strategies such as round-robin are ineffective for enhancing performance and mitigating latency. Therefore, a meticulously designed execution strategy is crucial. Third, scalability in multi-user scenarios constitutes a critical challenge. Video conferencing typically involves multiple participants, each requiring real-time processing.

Scaling the system to accommodate numerous users exponentially increases computational demands, underscoring the need for optimized GPU utilization and scheduling strategies. While augmenting the number or power of GPUs can offer some mitigation, this approach is neither scalable nor cost-effective in the long term. Fourth, turn-taking and speaker management complexity pose a further challenge. Dynamic conversations are characterized by frequent speaker interruptions and transitions. The system must efficiently manage speaker changes while minimizing processing lag and ensuring seamless language switching. Fifth, personalization based on each participant's language preference is essential. A system hard-coded for specific source and target languages caters only to a limited subset of stakeholders, primarily those speaking the predetermined target language. In multilingual video conferencing, language agnosticism is a fundamental requirement.

To address these challenges, we designed a system architecture intended for integration with the proposed or similar pipelines to facilitate the development of a multilingual video conferencing system. This system aims to be cost-effective, modular, scalable, language-agnostic, and personalized, while maintaining uninterrupted real-time conversation. Figure 2 illustrates our proposed architecture.

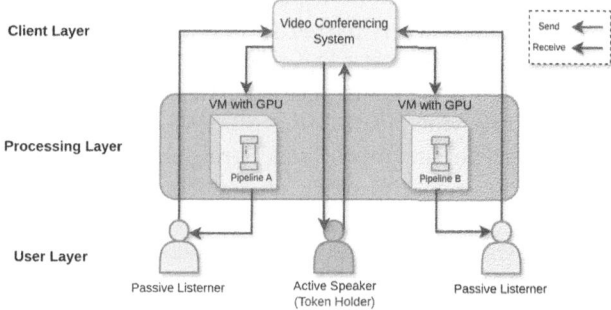

Fig. 2. Both the sending and receiving streams of the Active Speaker (in yellow) bypasses the processing layer, while the receiving stream of the Passive Listeners (in blue) passes through a GPU instance, which hosts the Video-translation pipeline that translates the video of the Active Speaker to target language (A or B) of the passive listeners. (Color figure online)

Layers. From a high-level perspective, the proposed architecture comprises three primary layers. The uppermost layer is the Video Conferencing System (Client Layer). This layer encompasses any video conferencing platform or interface, such as Jitsi, Teams, Google Meet, or Zoom, and manages user connections, video/audio transmission, and user interactions. The lowermost layer is the User Layer, where participants choose their preferred language for receiving translated video and interact directly with the conferencing client, mirroring the user interaction model of conventional video conferencing systems. An intermediate Video-translation System (Processing Layer) is introduced to translate the video stream (encompassing both video frames and audio). This layer intercepts and processes media streams between users and the client before delivery to the end user.

Token Ring Mechanism. To clarify the operational principles, consider the following illustrative scenario. Initially, participants connect to the video meeting platform and interact with its user interface. Prior to initiating speech, based on meeting protocols or administrative decisions, one participant is assigned a 'Token' to speak, while others remain passive listeners. The token holder transmits and receives data via the media stream without intermediary processing. Conversely, passive participants select their desired target language for translation of the token holder's video. Each passive participant (listener) is allocated a dedicated GPU or a cloud-based GPU-equipped virtual machine from a pool of available GPUs. More specifically, each passive user is allocated a GPU instance upon selecting their target language. While listeners receive the video stream of the token holder, their incoming stream is routed through their allocated GPU instance, which hosts the pipeline. This pipeline translates the video into the listener's chosen target language before displaying it to the user. Upon completion of the speaker's turn, the token is passed to another participant, either by the current token holder or by request. The previous token holder, now a passive listener, is then allocated a GPU instance, and their incoming stream is subsequently processed by the video-translation pipeline, translating the video into their chosen language. The new token holder transmits and receives data without stream interception or intermediary processing. We term this turn-taking mechanism the 'Token Ring' strategy, as shown in Fig. 2.

The Token Ring strategy offers several advantages and effectively mitigates many of the aforementioned challenges. Crucially, by designating a single active speaker (token holder), each GPU assigned to a user is responsible for translation into only one target language. This approach addresses potential bottlenecks associated with concurrently operating multiple models within the pipeline in real-time environments. This single-target language focus is critical due to the pipeline's sequential and cascaded architecture, which precludes GPU parallelization of intra-pipeline model execution. Furthermore, without the Token Ring mechanism, if multiple speakers were active concurrently, system scalability would be compromised. A single GPU would necessitate running multiple pipeline instances, each with a different input language, introducing synchronization issues. The variable length of translated speech across languages would result in unordered delivery of translated videos from multiple speakers, disrupting conversational coherence. Our Token Ring turn-taking strategy not only resolves these challenges but also enhances scalability. To further quantify this, consider a video conferencing system without the Token Ring strategy with N participants. In a worst-case scenario where each participant speaks a different language, a single passive listener would require N-1 GPU instances. Scaling this to an entire meeting with N participants, a total of $N \times (N-1)$ GPU instances would be required, resulting in a computational complexity of $O(N^2)$. However, with our Token Ring strategy, each allocated GPU is responsible for translation into only one target language, reducing the complexity to $O(N-1)$, which simplifies to $O(N)$. This approach is particularly advantageous when multiple passive listeners select the same target language. In this case, the number of allocated GPUs can be even smaller than the number of passive listeners, as multiple users will benefit from a single GPU instance that translates to the common target language, making the complexity $O(1) = \Omega(1)$. By decoupling the number of GPU instances from the number of participants, the Token Ring strategy ensures computational efficiency without sacrificing personalization. It guarantees that translated streams are delivered in sync with the speaker's turn, preserving conversational fluidity even in large meetings. This approach not only resolves the inherent challenges of latency, scalability, and dynamic speaker management but also provides a practical framework for deploying multilingual video conferencing systems in real-world settings. The combination of rigorous architectural design and strategic resource allocation makes our solution both robust and adaptable, addressing the demands of real-time communication.

Segmentation, Thresholding and Overlapping Buffering. Achieving low-latency, real-time communication in multimodal systems incorporating computationally intensive deep learning modules, such as generative lip-sync, presents a significant challenge. While optimization strategies targeting individual pipeline components and token-ring arbitration mechanisms offer partial mitigation, the inherent computational demands of these models remain a bottleneck to seamless user experience. Psycholinguistic studies establish a latency threshold of 100–300 ms as perceptually real-time, a benchmark commonly observed in video conferencing applications. However, the integration of supplementary pipelines with complex functionalities, particularly those involving generative image processing, necessitates innovative approaches to maintain comparable latency.

Our inference time analysis of the proposed pipeline, processing video chunks of varying duration (t), reveals a distinct relationship between chunk length and processing time (p). We observe a threshold (T) beyond which the processing time transitions to a logarithmic trend. This relationship is formally described by Eq. 1:

$$p(t) = \begin{cases} p > t : & t < T \\ \log t : & t \geq T \end{cases} \tag{1}$$

Prior to the threshold $T(t < T)$, the pipeline inference time p exceeds the video chunk duration t, indicating a system throughput less than unity. Conversely, for video chunk lengths surpassing $T(t \geq T)$, the inference time p becomes less than t, signifying improved throughput.

Based on this observation, we developed a segmented batched processing protocol to ensure continuous, near real-time conversational flow. This methodology introduces an initial latency equivalent to T. Subsequently, the active speaker's video stream is segmented into fixed-duration chunks of length T. The initial pipeline iteration for the first segment incurs an inference time of $p = log(T)$. Upon completion of processing, the translated video segment is transmitted to the passive listener. While the listener consumes this T-second segment, subsequent video segments from the active speaker undergo concurrent processing within the pipeline.

As established by Eq. 1, for $t \geq T$, we have $p < t$, and specifically in our implementation with chunk size T, we have $p = log(T) < T$. This ensures that subsequent segments are processed in less time than the playback duration of the preceding segment. Consequently, despite the initial latency of T seconds introduced at the onset of the speaker's turn, continuous playback is achieved thereafter, providing a perceptually near real-time conversational experience characterized by uninterrupted translated video for the listener.

To sustain smooth playback, our segmented batched processing protocol leverages inverse throughput thresholding and overlapping buffering. We define reciprocal (inverse) throughput, $\tau(t)$, as the ratio of processing time to video chunk duration, as shown in Eq. 2:

$$\tau(t) = \frac{p(t)}{t} \tag{2}$$

The threshold T is determined as the minimum video chunk duration for which the inverse system throughput, $\tau(t)$, falls below 1.0 s. This condition, formalized in Eq. 3, ensures that the pipeline generates 1.0 s of translated video in less than 1.0 s processing time for $t \geq T$, thereby facilitating continuous playback after the initial latency. The condition for smooth playback and perceptually real-time communication is shown in Eq. 3:

$$\textbf{Condition: } \tau(t) < 1.0 \textbf{ for } t \geq T \tag{3}$$

By integrating token-ring turn-taking, input segmentation into fixed-duration chunks (T), inverse throughput thresholding to determine T, and overlapping buffering, the proposed system effectively addresses the challenges of latency in computationally intensive real-time multimodal communication. This integrated approach provides a robust and perceptually near real-time user experience.

4   Proof-of-Concept

In order to demonstrate the feasibility of implementing our proposed pipeline, we developed a simple yet comprehensive prototype that includes all the components outlined in the Pipeline subsection. This prototype was designed to run on modest and widely available computational units, such as GPUs, to ensure accessibility and scalability. By analyzing its performance and quality, we aim to provide a foundational framework for developers and businesses to build upon, enabling the development of next-generation video conferencing systems equipped with real-time multilingual video translation capabilities.

To simulate a real-world video conferencing environment, we implemented a simple user interface (UI) that mimics the experience of a multilingual video conferencing system. The prototype was intentionally kept as simple as possible, as our primary goal is to provide a general guide for developers and businesses. By maintaining simplicity, we ensure that the prototype is modular, scalable, cost-effective, and, most importantly, universal. By "universal," we mean that the system is both language-agnostic and platform-agnostic. Regardless of the selected models or video conferencing platform, developers can build upon this prototype to deploy a conferencing system equipped with video translation. This universality ensures that the system can be adapted to various use cases and environments, making it a versatile solution for real-world applications. As a result, simplicity is a key design principle throughout the development of this prototype.

4.1 Prototype

The prototype consists of four main modules: Automatic Speech Recognition (ASR), Machine Translation (MT), Text-to-Speech Synthesis (SS), and Lip Synchronization (LipSync). Each module was implemented using state-of-the-art open-source models to ensure high performance and adaptability. The ASR module utilizes the Whisper-Small model for speech recognition and language detection, chosen for its balance between speed and accuracy. The MT module employs the SeamlessM4T-Large model, which excels in producing accurate translations across multiple languages. For speech synthesis, the XTTS-v2 model was selected due to its ability to generate natural-sounding speech that closely mimics the original speaker's voice. Finally, the LipSync module uses the Wav2Lip-GAN model to synchronize the synthesized speech with the speaker's lip movements, ensuring a realistic viewing experience. The pipeline was implemented in a modular fashion, allowing each component to be tested and optimized independently before integration. This modular design not only facilitates performance tuning but also ensures scalability and flexibility, enabling future updates and enhancements. The entire system was deployed on Google Colab, leveraging its free-tier Nvidia T4 GPU capabilities for computational efficiency during the development and testing phases.

To simulate a real-world video conferencing environment, we developed a simple user interface (UI) using React.js, CSS, and HTML. The UI allows users to initiate video calls, select target languages for translation, and view the translated video with synchronized lip movements. Real-time communication between users was facilitated using Socket.io, while peer-to-peer video and audio streaming was implemented with the Simple-Peer library. The prototype was designed to be platform-agnostic, meaning it can be integrated into any existing video conferencing platform with minimal modifications. This universality ensures that the system can be adapted to various use cases and environments, regardless of the underlying technology stack.

4.2 Evaluation

The evaluation of the prototype was conducted using a combination of objective and subjective methods to assess both its technical performance and user experience. The objective evaluation focused on measuring the inference times of each module and the overall system throughput, which are critical for determining the system's suitability for real-time applications. The subjective evaluation, on the other hand, involved user surveys to gather qualitative feedback on the system's usability, translation quality, lip sync accuracy, and overall user experience.

For the objective evaluation, we designed an experimental setup using a dataset of 8-second-long videos in various languages. The videos were segmented into clips of 1, 2, 3, 5, and 8s to test the system's performance under different input lengths. Each module's inference time was measured three times for each segment, and the average inference time along with the standard deviation was calculated. This approach allowed us to identify potential bottlenecks and assess the system's scalability.

The subjective evaluation involved ten participants who were asked to rate the translated videos based on several criteria, including Lip Sync Accuracy (LSA), Motion Naturalness (MN), Visual Quality (VIQ), and Vocal Quality (VOQ). Participants provided their feedback using a 5-point Likert scale, and the results were analyzed using the Mean Opinion Score (MOS) protocol.

5 Experiments and Results

Our experimental evaluation was designed to rigorously assess the proposed system across two critical dimensions: computational efficiency and user perception. These axes are paramount to validating the practicality and user-centricity of our multilingual video conferencing solution.

5.1 Objective Evaluation Results

The objective evaluation focused on quantifying the computational performance of our pipeline through precise measurements of module execution times and overall system throughput. To specifically examine the efficacy of our segmented batched processing protocol, described in Subsect. 3.2, we constructed a test dataset comprising 8-second video samples featuring speakers in various languages. These samples were meticulously segmented into clips of varying durations: 1, 2, 3, 5, and 8s. This segmentation strategy was not arbitrary; it was deliberately chosen to empirically validate the predicted logarithmic-like trend in processing time relative to segment length, a core hypothesis underpinning our optimization strategy. By testing across these segment lengths, we aimed to identify the operational characteristics of our pipeline and confirm the benefits of segmented processing.

Each segment was then processed by the pipeline, instrumented with timers to capture module-specific inference times – for Automatic Speech Recognition

(ASR), Machine Translation (MT), Speech Synthesis (SS), and Lip Synchronization (LipSync) – alongside the total system processing duration. To ensure the robustness of our findings and account for potential variations in model inference times, each experiment was iterated three times, and standard deviations were calculated to assess the consistency of the recorded values. The primary metric for this objective assessment was inference time, directly reflecting the computational cost and real-time feasibility of each module and the integrated pipeline. For a representative analysis of Inference Time, we selected a German language video as input and targeted English as the translation output. This served as a benchmark scenario to illustrate the pipeline's typical performance profile. The detailed results of this analysis are presented in Table 1.

Table 1. Results of Inference Time Analysis (in seconds)

Length	ASR	MT	SS	LipSync	Total Inference	Reciprocal Throughput
1	0.2474	0.4280	0.6190	7.6944	8.9888	8.9888
2	0.2917	0.5524	1.3250	8.1047	10.2738	5.1369
3	0.3011	0.6691	1.4820	8.4715	10.9237	3.6412
5	0.3607	0.7651	1.9452	8.9386	12.0096	2.4019
8	0.4817	0.7648	2.1174	9.3346	12.6985	1.5873

The data presented in Table 1 robustly supports our hypothesis, detailed in Subsect. 3.2 and Eq. 1, that the total inference time p of the pipeline exhibits a non-linear, logarithmic-like relationship with the video chunk length t. This trend is clearly evidenced by the diminishing rate of increase in total inference time as video segment length increases. For example, while tripling the video length from 1 to 3 s, the total inference time only increases by approximately 22%, far below the 200% increase expected under linear scaling. Further extending the video length nearly threefold from 3 to 8 s results in a more modest increase of approximately 16% in inference time, far below the 166% increase expected under linear scaling. This sublinear scaling characteristic is precisely what our segmented batched processing protocol is designed to exploit to enhance efficiency within latency-constrained applications like video conferencing. The observed trend confirms the approximation $p \approx log(t)$, validating the core principle of our segmentation strategy for mitigating the computational burden of deep learning pipelines in real-time settings and fostering perceptually real-time communication with smooth playback.

It is important to note that, due to computational resource constraints inherent in utilizing a consumer-grade GPU (NVIDIA T4) – intentionally chosen to demonstrate accessibility and scalability on readily available hardware – our experiments did not achieve a Reciprocal Throughput (Inverse Throughput) value below the critical threshold of 1.0 s across the tested video lengths. Achieving $\tau(t) < 1.0$ for $t \geq T$, as stipulated in Eq. 3, represents the ideal smooth playback condition. Extrapolation suggests that smooth playback ($\tau < 1$) would occur at $t \approx 14$ on this hardware, demonstrating the protocol's scalability.

However, the observed trend of decreasing Reciprocal Throughput with increasing video length convincingly demonstrates the effectiveness of our fixed-length video segmentation and initial latency approach in substantially improving system efficiency and moving towards real-time performance, even within resource-constrained environments. This aligns with our prototyping philosophy of prioritizing open-source software and computationally economical processing units, underscoring the scalability and broad applicability of our proposed methodology, even when deployed on modest hardware configurations. Further optimization and deployment on higher-performance GPU infrastructure are anticipated to readily achieve the desired real-time throughput target.

To further assess the robustness of our pipeline performance, we conducted an analysis of the variability in inference times across repeated runs. Specifically, we examined the standard deviations of the inference times for each module across the three iterations performed for each video segment length. These standard deviation values, presented in Table 2, provide insights into the consistency and stability of the individual modules within the pipeline.

Table 2. Standard Deviations of Inference Times

Video Length	ASR	MT	SS	LipSync
1	0.0070	0.0013	0.1295	0.0972
2	0.0409	0.0130	0.2135	0.0873
3	0.0058	0.0145	0.1437	0.0586
5	0.0035	0.0065	0.1260	0.1195
8	0.0054	0.0044	0.2056	0.0827

The magnitude of standard deviation in inference times directly indicates module performance consistency. Notably, the Speech Synthesis (SS) module exhibited significantly higher standard deviations compared to ASR, MT, and LipSync, suggesting greater inference time variability and a potential need for system design considerations like buffering. Conversely, the consistently low standard deviations of ASR, MT, and LipSync indicate their stable and predictable performance across varying video lengths.

Furthermore, linguistic similarity between translated languages significantly influences pipeline performance, particularly in MT and SS modules. Linguistically closer languages may lead to faster processing, while distant languages can increase processing times and introduce variations in translated text length, potentially impacting output video duration and real-time synchronization. Future research should explore a wider range of language pairs to fully understand and address these language-dependent performance variations.

5.2 Subjective Evaluation Results

Subjective evaluation, crucial for gauging user perception and overall system usability, complemented our objective measurements. Recognizing the limitations of quantitative metrics in capturing nuanced aspects of user experience, we employed a survey-based approach to gather qualitative feedback on key perceptual attributes of the translated videos. This evaluation aimed to assess the system's performance in real-world communication scenarios and to quantify user satisfaction across several critical dimensions. We defined the following criteria for subjective assessment:

The subjective evaluation employed four key criteria to assess user perception: Lip Sync Accuracy (LSA), gauging the temporal alignment of lip movements with the synthesized audio; Motion Naturalness (MN), evaluating the realistic and natural quality of lip movements beyond mere synchronicity; Visual Quality (VIQ), appraising the overall aesthetic fidelity of the generated video; and Vocal Quality (VOQ), assessing the synthesized voice's naturalness and similarity to the original speaker, especially considering voice cloning.

Survey participants were instructed to rate 8-second translated video segments within our video conferencing prototype environment across diverse language pairs using a 5-point Likert scale for each criterion. Collected responses were analyzed using the Mean Opinion Score (MOS) protocol to aggregate and interpret user feedback. The summarized subjective evaluation results, presented for each criterion and language pair, are detailed in Table 3. A more granular analysis, segmented by individual language pair, is presented below.

Table 3. Source - Target Translation Scores Based on Evaluation Criteria

Source - Target	LSA	MN	VIQ	VOQ	Overall
English – Turkish	3.2	3	3.2	3.4	3.2
Turkish – English	3.4	3.6	2.8	3.2	3.25
French – Spanish	4.6	4.8	4.8	4.8	4.75
Spanish – French	3.8	4.2	4.2	4.8	4.25
Arabic – German	4	4.4	2.8	4.6	3.95
German – Arabic	4.2	4.6	3.2	4.8	4.2

In summary, subjective evaluation revealed varying performance across language pairs. English-Turkish translations showed moderate user satisfaction with strong vocal quality but needing improvement in lip sync accuracy, motion naturalness, and visual quality. French-Spanish translations, particularly French-to-Spanish, demonstrated high user satisfaction across all metrics, likely due to linguistic similarity, with both directions achieving excellent vocal quality and lip sync accuracy. Arabic-German translations exhibited intermediate performance, with good motion naturalness and vocal quality, but consistently lower visual quality scores, indicating a clear area for future enhancement across these language pairs.

Overall, the subjective evaluation effectively highlighted performance variations across different language pairs, underscoring the influence of linguistic factors on user perception. Specifically, visual quality and, to a lesser extent, lip synchronization accuracy emerged as key areas for targeted improvements in future iterations of the video translation pipeline, particularly for language pairs with greater linguistic divergence.

6   Conclusion

This paper introduced a novel, computationally efficient video translation method for multilingual video conferencing. Our pipeline, using open-source deep learning models, achieves perceptually real-time face-to-face translation. A "Token Ring" architecture and segmented batched processing protocol address latency and scalability. A simplified prototype demonstrated feasibility, with objective tests validating efficiency and subjective evaluations showing user satisfaction. Future work will optimize modules and improve visual quality and lip-sync, particularly for diverse language pairs. While a simplified prototype demonstrates the feasibility of our approach, future work will focus on rigorous evaluation with diverse datasets, exploring advanced lip sync models, and optimizing the system for large-scale deployments. We believe this work contributes a valuable framework for developing next-generation multilingual communication platforms.

Acknowledgments. This research paper has utilized Generative AI tools solely for the purpose of enhancing the readability and clarity of the manuscript. The AI was employed to refine sentence structure and improve grammatical flow, without altering the original content, introducing new ideas, or impacting the research findings. The authors retain full responsibility for the accuracy and integrity of the presented work. This research was made possible by the collaborative environment provided by **Aktif Bank**. The authors extend their appreciation for their support.

References

1. Aktas, M.S., Fox, G.C., Pierce, M.: Fault tolerant high performance information services for dynamic collections of grid and web services. Futur. Gener. Comput. Syst. **23**(3), 317–337 (2007)
2. Aydin, G., Aktas, M.S., Sayar, A.: Servogrid complexity computational environments CCE integrated performance analysis. In: 2005 6th International Workshop on Grid Computing (GRID), pp. 256–261 (2005)
3. Bao, H., et al.: MILG: realistic lip-sync video generation with audio-modulated image inpainting. Vis. Inform. **8**(3), 71–81 (2024)
4. Casanova, E., et al.: XTTS: a massively multilingual zero-shot text-to-speech model. arXiv preprint arXiv:2406.04904 (2024)
5. Cheng, X., et al.: Transface: unit-based audio-visual speech synthesizer for talking head translation. arXiv preprint arXiv:2312.15197 (2023)
6. Chu, S.N., Goodell, A.J.: Synthetic patients: simulating difficult conversations with multimodal generative AI for medical education. arXiv preprint arXiv:2405.19941 (2024)

7. Das, D., Biswas, S., Sinha, S., Bhowmick, B.: Speech-driven facial animation using cascaded GANs for learning of motion and texture. In: Computer Vision–ECCV 2020: 16th European Conference, Glasgow, UK, 23–28 August 2020, Proceedings, Part XXX 16, pp. 408–424. Springer (2020)

8. Hong, F.T., Zhang, L., Shen, L., Xu, D.: Depth-aware generative adversarial network for talking head video generation. In: Proceedings of the IEEE/CVF Conference on Computer Vision and Pattern Recognition, pp. 3397–3406 (2022)

9. Kheddar, H., Hemis, M., Himeur, Y.: Automatic speech recognition using advanced deep learning approaches: a survey. Inf. Fusion 102422 (2024)

10. Kim, M., Hong, J., Ro, Y.M.: Lip to speech synthesis with visual context attentional GAN. Adv. Neural. Inf. Process. Syst. **34**, 2758–2770 (2021)

11. KR, P., Mukhopadhyay, R., Philip, J., Jha, A., Namboodiri, V., Jawahar, C.: Towards automatic face-to-face translation. In: Proceedings of the 27th ACM International Conference on Multimedia, pp. 1428–1436 (2019)

12. Li, C., et al.: Latentsync: audio conditioned latent diffusion models for lip sync. arXiv preprint arXiv:2412.09262 (2024)

13. Li, R., Pu, D., Huang, M., Huang, B.: Unet-TTS: improving unseen speaker and style transfer in one-shot voice cloning. In: ICASSP 2022-2022 IEEE International Conference on Acoustics, Speech and Signal Processing (ICASSP), pp. 8327–8331. IEEE (2022)

14. Lin, G., Jiang, J., Yang, J., Zheng, Z., Liang, C.: Omnihuman-1: rethinking the scaling-up of one-stage conditioned human animation models. arXiv preprint arXiv:2502.01061 (2025)

15. Malik, M., Malik, M.K., Mehmood, K., Makhdoom, I.: Automatic speech recognition: a survey. Multimedia Tools Appl. **80**, 9411–9457 (2021)

16. Nacar, M.A., Aktas, M.S., Yuen, D.A.: Vlab: collaborative grid services and portals to support computational material science. Concurr. Comput. Pract. Exp. **19**(12), 1717–1728 (2007)

17. Olmezogullari, E., Aktas, M.S.: Representation of click-stream data sequences for learning user navigational behavior by using embeddings. In: 2020 IEEE International Conference on Big Data (Big Data), pp. 3173–3179 (2020)

18. Olmezogullari, E., Aktas, M.S.: Pattern2vec: representation of clickstream data sequences for learning user navigational behavior. Concurr. Comput. Pract. Exp. **34**(9) (2022)

19. Oskooei, A.R., Babacan, M.S., Yağcı, E., Alptekin, Ç., Buğday, A.: Beyond synthetic benchmarks: assessing recent LLMs for code generation. In: 14th International Workshop on Computer Science and Engineering, WCSE (2024)

20. Prabhavalkar, R., Hori, T., Sainath, T.N., Schlüter, R., Watanabe, S.: End-to-end speech recognition: a survey. IEEE/ACM Trans. Audio Speech Lang. Process. (2023)

21. Prajwal, K., Mukhopadhyay, R., Namboodiri, V.P., Jawahar, C.: A lip sync expert is all you need for speech to lip generation in the wild. In: Proceedings of the 28th ACM International Conference on Multimedia, pp. 484–492 (2020)

22. Rafiei Oskooei, A., Aktaş, M.S., Keleş, M.: Seeing the sound: multilingual lip sync for real-time face-to-face translation. Computers **14**(1), 7 (2024)

23. Rafiei Oskooei, A., Yahsi, E., Sungur, M., S. Aktas, M.: Can one model fit all? An exploration of wav2lip's lip-syncing generalizability across culturally distinct languages. In: International Conference on Computational Science and Its Applications, pp. 149–164. Springer (2024)

24. Ritter, M., Meier, U., Yang, J., Waibel, A.: Face translation: a multimodal translation agent. In: AVSP'99-International Conference on Auditory-Visual Speech Processing. Citeseer (1999)
25. Sahinoglu, M., Incki, K., Aktas, M.S.: Mobile application verification: a systematic mapping study. In: Computational Science and Its Applications–ICCSA 2015. Lecture Notes in Computer Science, vol. 9159, pp. 147–163 (2015)
26. Shen, S., et al.: Difftalk: crafting diffusion models for generalized audio-driven portraits animation. In: Proceedings of the IEEE/CVF Conference on Computer Vision and Pattern Recognition, pp. 1982–1991 (2023)
27. Shin, A.H., Lee, J.H., Hwang, J., Kim, Y., Park, G.M.: Wav2nerf: audio-driven realistic talking head generation via wavelet-based nerf. Image Vis. Comput. 105104 (2024)
28. Song, H.K., et al.: Talking face generation with multilingual TTS. In: Proceedings of the IEEE/CVF Conference on Computer Vision and Pattern Recognition, pp. 21425–21430 (2022)
29. Stypułkowski, M., Vougioukas, K., He, S., Zięba, M., Petridis, S., Pantic, M.: Diffused heads: diffusion models beat GANs on talking-face generation. In: Proceedings of the IEEE/CVF Winter Conference on Applications of Computer Vision, pp. 5091–5100 (2024)
30. Sun, X., et al.: Vividtalk: one-shot audio-driven talking head generation based on 3D hybrid prior. arXiv preprint arXiv:2312.01841 (2023)
31. Team, N., et al.: Scaling neural machine translation to 200 languages. Nature **630**(8018), 841 (2024)
32. Tufek, A., Gurbuz, A., Aktas, M.S.: Provenance collection platform for the weather research and forecasting model. In: 2018 14th International Conference on Semantics, Knowledge and Grids (SKG), pp. 17–24 (2018)
33. Vougioukas, K., Petridis, S., Pantic, M.: End-to-end speech-driven realistic facial animation with temporal GANs. In: CVPR Workshops, vol. 887, pp. 37–40 (2019)
34. Wang, H., Wu, H., He, Z., Huang, L., Church, K.W.: Progress in machine translation. Engineering **18**, 143–153 (2022)
35. Xu, S., et al.: Vasa-1: lifelike audio-driven talking faces generated in real time. arXiv preprint arXiv:2404.10667 (2024)
36. Ye, Z., et al.: Geneface++: generalized and stable real-time audio-driven 3D talking face generation. arXiv preprint arXiv:2305.00787 (2023)
37. Ye, Z., et al.: Mimictalk: mimicking a personalized and expressive 3D talking face in minutes. arXiv preprint arXiv:2410.06734 (2024)
38. Ye, Z., et al.: Real3d-portrait: one-shot realistic 3D talking portrait synthesis. arXiv preprint arXiv:2401.08503 (2024)
39. Yin, F., et al.: Styleheat: one-shot high-resolution editable talking face generation via pre-trained stylegan. In: European Conference on Computer Vision, pp. 85–101. Springer (2022)
40. Zhu, W., et al.: Multilingual machine translation with large language models: empirical results and analysis. arXiv preprint arXiv:2304.04675 (2023)

Autonomous Network Reconstruction Using LPWA for Disaster Prevention

Kou Nakakubo[1]([✉]), Kazuaki Tanaka[1][iD], and R. Krishnamoorthy[2][iD]

[1] Kyushu Institute of Technology, Fukuoka, Japan
nakakubo.ko922@mail.kyutech.jp, kazuaki@ics.kyutech.ac.jp
[2] Chennai Institute of Technology, Chennai, India
krishnamoorthyr@citchennai.net

Abstract. In recent years, the use of IoT networks for environmental data collection by local governments has been increasing. However, these networks face a critical issue: when relay points are lost due to disasters, most communications are disrupted. In this study, we propose a system that utilizes Low Power Wide Area (LPWA) communication technology to autonomously reconstruct communication networks. The proposed system employs a tree-structured LPWA network that dynamically reconfigures itself in the event of a failure. Specifically, each node assesses the health of its upstream node based on relayed uplink packet information and dynamically selects an optimal alternative route. We evaluate the effectiveness of our method through field experiments, confirming that network prevention can be appropriately performed even in the presence of node failures.

Keywords: LPWA · Disaster Prevention · Autonomous Network Reconstruction

1 Introduction

1.1 Background

In recent years, local governments and public institutions have increasingly adopted IoT devices for environmental data collection [1]. In particular, Low Power Wide Area (LPWA) technology has played a crucial role in environmental monitoring and smart city projects due to its ability to cover wide areas while maintaining low power consumption. In practice, LPWA has been actively utilized in atmospheric and water quality monitoring by the Ministry of the Environment and in smart city initiatives promoted by the Ministry of Economy, Trade, and Industry. However, conventional LPWA networks face a significant challenge: if a relay node fails, the entire network communication is disrupted. This issue becomes particularly severe in disaster scenarios, where multiple nodes may fail simultaneously, making network prevention difficult.

O. Gervasi et al. (Eds.): ICCSA 2025 Workshops, LNCS 15890, pp. 235–246, 2026.
https://doi.org/10.1007/978-3-031-97606-3_16

1.2   Existing Technologies and Challenges

In conventional LPWA networks, when a failure occurs, relay points must be manually reconfigured, which requires time and hinders immediate communication prevention [2]. Various solutions, such as mesh networks and communication reconstruction using drones, have been proposed. However, these solutions pose challenges in terms of cost and power consumption, making them difficult to implement in practical scenarios. Additionally, traditional LPWA networks risk losing data from leaf nodes when intermediate relay nodes fail, leading to disruptions in information transmission during disasters. Thus, there is a need for a communication method that enables autonomous network reconstruction while ensuring reliable data transmission from leaf nodes.

1.3   Objective of This Study

To address this issue, this study proposes an autonomous network reconfiguration method for communication continuity in the event of a failure [5]. In this method, nodes monitor uplink communication and assess the health status of their upstream nodes. If a failure is detected, nodes autonomously select the optimal relay node and retransmit the lost packets. By doing so, this method ensures that data from leaf nodes reaches the root node, thereby enhancing communication continuity in disaster scenarios. The effectiveness of this method is evaluated through real-world experiments.

2   LPWA Technology and Characteristics

2.1   Overview of LPWA Technology

Low Power Wide Area (LPWA) is a wireless communication technology designed for the Internet of Things (IoT) that enables long-range communication with low power consumption. Unlike conventional Wi-Fi or cellular networks (LTE, 5G), LPWA provides a balance between extended coverage and energy efficiency (Fig. 1).

However, LPWA has certain limitations, such as low data transmission speed and long communication intervals. Therefore, an appropriate routing control protocol is required depending on the use case. Table 1 compares the characteristics of LPWA (LoRa) with cellular communication (4G/5G).

Table 1. Limitations of LPWA

	LPWA (LoRa)	4G/5G (Cellular Network)
Data Rate	0.016 Mbps	290 Mbps
Communication Interval	≤4400 ms	≤1 ms

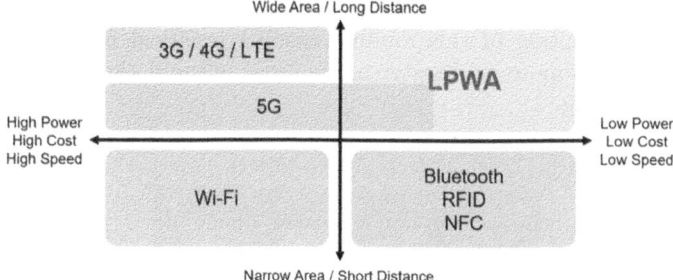

Fig. 1. Comparison of Communication Characteristics: Wi-Fi, LTE, and LPWA.

2.2 Major LPWA Standards Overview

LPWA includes multiple communication standards, and an appropriate standard must be selected depending on the application. Table 2 summarizes the characteristics of major LPWA standards.

Table 2. Major LPWA Standards and their Characteristics

LoRa	Promoted by the LoRa Alliance and freely available for private use. Only the modulation method is specified.
LoRaWAN	Communication network based on the LoRa system, which requires the use of LoRa Alliance-certified equipment.
NB-IoT	Using the mobile carrier band. Available only in the carrier's service area.
Sigfox	Ultra-narrowband network managed globally by UnaBiz. Available in multiple countries via international roaming.
LTE-M	LTE for machine-type communication. Same area as LTE service. Relatively high speed communication.

2.3 LPWA Module Used in This Study

This study adopts LoRa due to its license-free nature and low power consumption [4], making it suitable for remote sensing applications with energy constraints.

For implementation, we used the ES920LR3 module, which supports LoRa modulation and is optimized for ultra-low power operation. This module integrates a Cortex-M4 MCU and RF transceiver, enabling compact, power-efficient, and autonomous deployments in the field.

Although power consumption was not the primary focus of evaluation in this study, the adoption of this module ensures practical feasibility for long-term operation in remote or disaster-prone areas without the need for frequent maintenance [3] (Fig. 2).

Fig. 2. ES920LR3 module and its development board.

3   System Design

3.1   Structure of the Tree-Based LPWA Network

The proposed communication network adopts a tree topology consisting of a root node (HQ; Head Quarter named in this study) and multiple relay nodes and leaf nodes. Each node selects a single optimal parent node based on RSSI (Received Signal Strength Indicator) and node depth information to construct the tree structure, ensuring that data flows along a unique path to the HQ. As shown in Fig. 3, the structure comprises HQ, relay nodes, and leaf nodes.

In this configuration, data originating from leaf nodes is sequentially forwarded through one or more relay nodes until it reaches the HQ node. Because each node communicates only with its selected parent, this hierarchical transmission model simplifies routing and eliminates redundant transmissions, making it highly suitable for power-constrained LPWA environments.

3.2   Dynamic Path Selection Method

Each node constantly monitors packets transmitted by upper-layer nodes (closer to the HQ) and extracts RSSI, depth, and node ID information. Using this information, the node determines the optimal communication path and maintains multiple alternative routes to enable rapid switching in case of a failure. By maintaining a table of multiple uplink routes, the system ensures rapid path switching when a failure occurs.

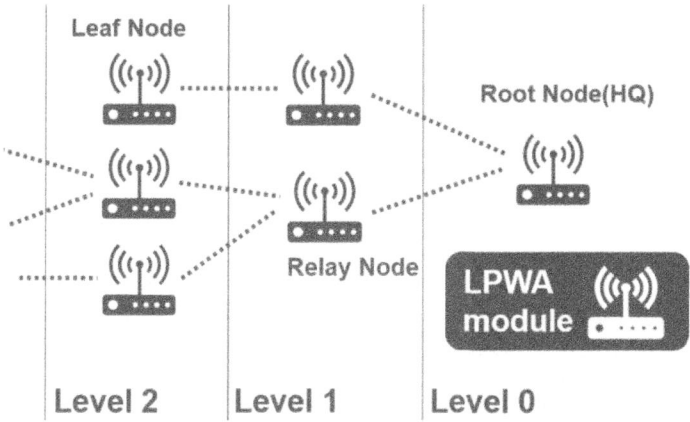

Fig. 3. Structure of the Tree-Based LPWA Network.

To enhance the responsiveness of the system to environmental changes such as signal obstruction or interference, the routing table is not based on historically maximum RSSI values but is instead dynamically updated with the latest observed RSSI readings for each uplink candidate. This design avoids overfitting to outdated or temporary signal conditions and ensures that the selected route reflects the most current network status.

Algorithm 1. Candidate Table Maintenance Algorithm

1: **Input:** Received packet from node i with RSSI $rssi_i$ and level $level_i$
2: **Data:** Candidate table $T = \{(ID_j, RSSI_j, Level_j)\}$
3: **for all** entry $(ID_j, RSSI_j, Level_j)$ in T **do**
4:     **if** $ID_j = i$ **then**
5:         $RSSI_j \leftarrow rssi_i$
6:         $Level_j \leftarrow level_i$
7:         **return**
8:     **end if**
9: **end for**
10: Insert new entry $(i, rssi_i, level_i)$ into T

To avoid unnecessary structural disruptions in the overall tree topology, each node prioritizes candidate uplink nodes from the layer directly above its own (i.e., level $n - 1$). This hierarchical constraint minimizes the likelihood of triggering cascading reconfigurations across subordinate nodes, which would otherwise be required to update their own uplink paths in response to their parent node's level change.

Algorithm 2. Parent Node Selection Algorithm (Hierarchical Fallback)

1: **Input:** Candidate table $T = \{(ID_j, RSSI_j, Level_j)\}$, current node level L
2: **Output:** Selected parent node ID (or `null` if not found)
3: **for** $d = 1$ to $L - 1$ **do**
4:     $C \leftarrow \{(ID_j, RSSI_j) \in T \mid Level_j = L - d\}$
5:     **if** C is not empty **then**
6:         Sort C by descending $RSSI_j$
7:         **return** ID of the first element in C
8:     **end if**
9: **end for**
10: **return null**   ▷ No valid parent found

3.3   Node Health Check and Retransmission Mechanism

The proposed system enables nodes to assess the health of their parent nodes based on the relayed uplink packet information, ensuring network stability. Additionally, after switching the uplink destination, failed transmission data is retransmitted. The selection of the new uplink destination in this process follows the routing policy described in Sect. 3.2, which is based on the most recent RSSI values and hierarchical level constraints. The operational algorithm is as follows:

1. The leaf node (n+2 layer) sends an uplink packet to the relay node (n+1 layer).
2. The sent packet is recorded, and **a timer is started**.
3. The relay node (n+1 layer) receives the packet and forwards it to the root node (HQ, n layer).
4. Determine the status of the relay node
   – **If the relay node is operational (Relay Success):**
     Within the set time, the leaf node receives the forwarded packet sent by the relay node to the root node. If the received packet matches the recorded packet, the record is deleted, and the relay node is deemed functional. This normal relaying process is illustrated in Fig. 4.
   – **If the relay node is down (Relay Failure):**
     If the leaf node does not receive the forwarded packet within the set time, it detects a failure in the relay node and selects a new uplink destination. Using the stored information in the table, it attempts to reconnect to a new uplink node. Once a new uplink destination is established, the recorded packet is retransmitted. The reconfiguration and retransmission flow is illustrated in Fig. 5.

4   Experiments and Evaluation

4.1   Experimental Setup

The experimental network consists of one root node (ID:00), three relay nodes (ID:01, ID:02, ID:03) at Level 1, two intermediate nodes (ID:04, ID:05) at Level 2, and one leaf node (ID:06) at Level 3, as illustrated in Fig. 6.

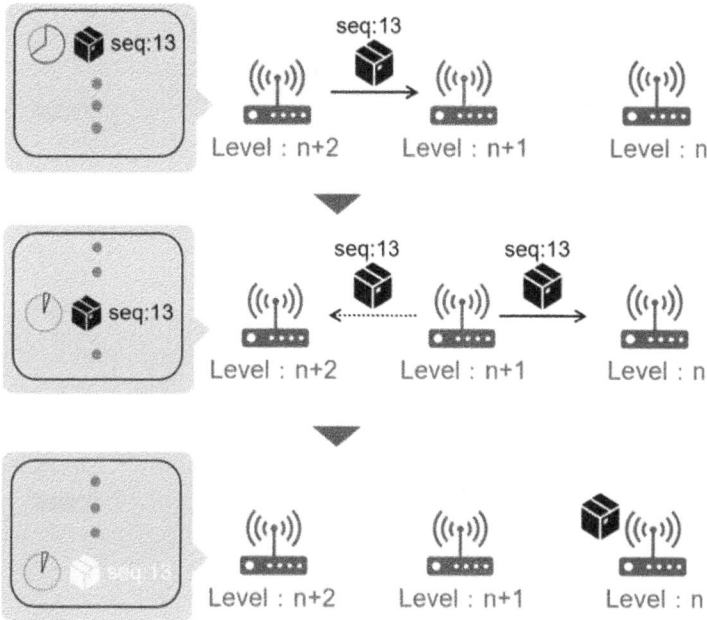

Fig. 4. Normal Relaying Process.

Initially, each node was manually configured to connect with a designated parent node based on deployment location and predefined ID mapping. This initial setup allowed control over the network's logical topology, ensuring that nodes began with the intended hierarchical structure. The experiment later evaluates the system's capability to autonomously reconfigure paths upon node failure, according to the routing policy discussed in Sect. 3.2.

4.2   Failure Scenario and Reconfiguration Test

To evaluate the fault tolerance of the system, we simulated a failure of relay node ID:03.

Node ID:05 was pre-configured with multiple uplink candidates and, upon detecting the failure, was expected to autonomously select a new uplink using its stored RSSI and level information.

Table 3 lists the actual uplink candidate entries stored by node ID:05 before the failure of ID:03. As shown, node ID:02 had the strongest RSSI among nodes at Level 1.

The network configuration during the failure scenario is depicted in Fig. 7.

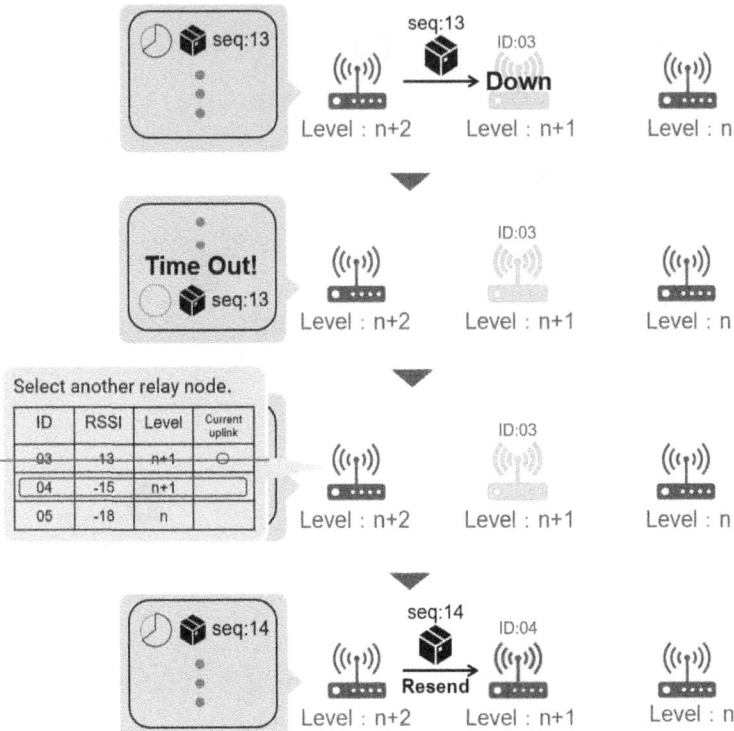

Fig. 5. Retransmission Process.

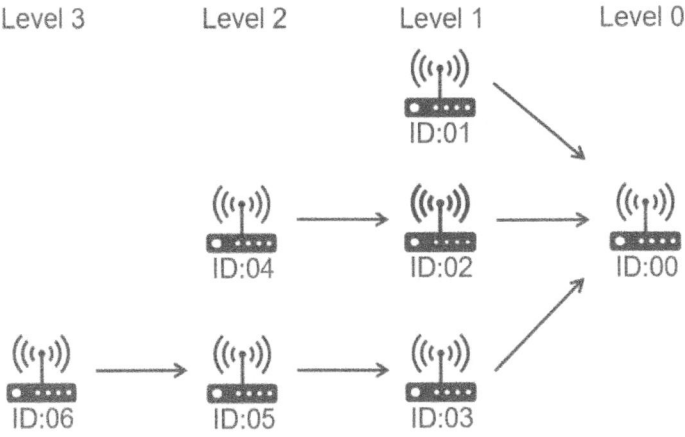

Fig. 6. Initial uplink paths of each node.

Table 3. Stored Uplink Candidates in Node ID:05 (Before Failure)

ID	RSSI	Level
01	−23	1
02	−20	1
03	−18	1
04	−19	2
06	−18	3

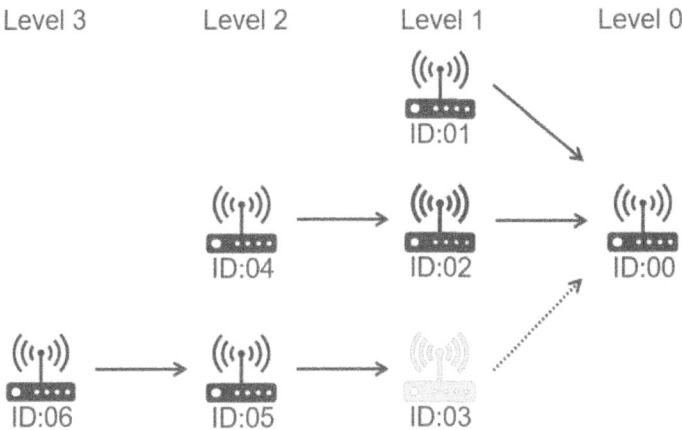

Fig. 7. Network Configuration During Failure.

4.3   Results and Recovery Performance

After ID:03 failed, node ID:05 autonomously selected ID:02 as the new uplink node. This selection was based on the highest RSSI and level consistency with the hierarchical constraint defined in the routing policy. Subsequently, the packet from ID:06 was successfully routed through ID:05 and ID:02 to the HQ (ID:00).

These results demonstrate that the proposed system can autonomously reconfigure the network in response to node failure and maintain uninterrupted data delivery. Figure 8 illustrates the reconfigured network topology.

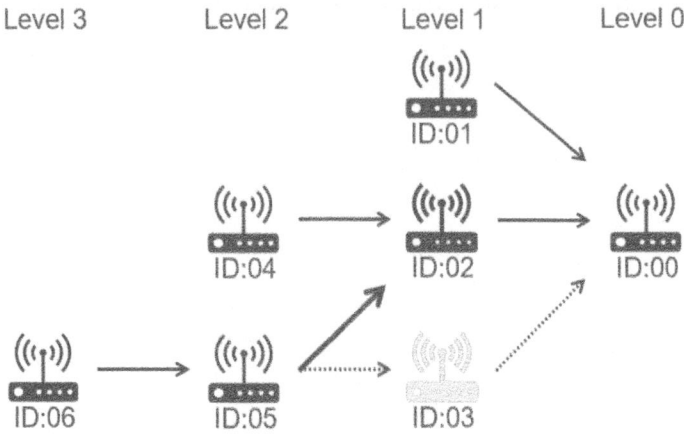

Fig. 8. Network Topology After Reconfiguration.

5   Discussion

This section outlines how the proposed system operates under real-world disaster scenarios, focusing on the failure conditions and the autonomous recovery process executed at each node.

5.1   Expected Failure Conditions

The system is designed to address the following common failure cases:

– A relay node becomes unreachable due to physical damage (e.g., landslides, flooding, or power outages).
– Temporary signal loss or obstruction causes upstream acknowledgment packets (ACKs) to be undelivered within the timeout period.

In such situations, each node autonomously executes a predefined recovery sequence to restore communication and continue data delivery.

5.2   Autonomous Recovery Steps

1. **Failure Detection:** The node monitors the return of acknowledgment packets. If no ACK is received within the specified timeout period, the uplink is considered failed.
2. **Candidate Lookup:** The node refers to its locally maintained table of candidate uplink nodes, which includes each candidate's RSSI and hierarchical level.
3. **Prioritized Selection:** Among candidates at the upper layer (i.e., level $n - 1$), the node selects the one with the strongest RSSI as the new parent.

4. **Uplink Reconfiguration:** The node reconfigures its uplink path to the newly selected parent node.
5. **Data Retransmission and Confirmation:** Buffered data is retransmitted through the new uplink. Upon receiving an acknowledgment, the node deletes the corresponding buffered packet.

This fully distributed and lightweight recovery mechanism allows the network to self-heal without any centralized coordination or manual intervention, thereby preserving communication continuity even under partial infrastructure failures (Fig. 9).

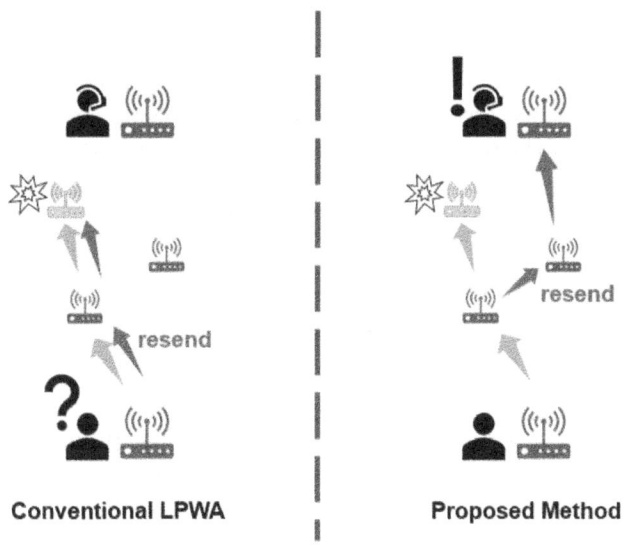

Fig. 9. Comparison between Conventional LPWA and Proposed Method in failure scenarios.

5.3   Practical Scenario: Disaster-Affected Regions

A typical real-world application is in disaster-stricken evacuation shelters equipped with LPWA-enabled sensors. These sensors transmit emergency alerts or environmental data to the municipal headquarters (HQ), which acts as the root node. Even if intermediate relay nodes become inoperable, the shelter (leaf node) can autonomously reconfigure its path and continue transmitting critical information—such as survivor counts or hazard warnings—without confirming delivery status or relying on external support.

6   Conclusion

In this study, we proposed an autonomous communication network reconstruction method using LPWA to restore communication infrastructure in disaster scenarios. The proposed method enables each node to dynamically assess the health status of its upper-layer node and select an alternative relay node when a failure occurs, ensuring network continuity.

The experimental results demonstrated that even in the event of a node failure, end nodes could autonomously select an appropriate relay node and successfully transmit data to the root node. Specifically, when a relay node became inoperable, an alternative uplink path was dynamically selected, ensuring successful data delivery from the end node to the root node. These findings confirm the effectiveness of the proposed method in maintaining network integrity under failure conditions.

For future work, evaluations in larger-scale network environments and verification of interoperability with different LPWA technologies are necessary. Additionally, optimizing the dynamic path selection algorithm could further enhance the speed and stability of network reconstruction, contributing to the realization of a more resilient LPWA-based communication network.

References

1. Ministry of Internal Affairs and Communications: Latest Trends in Wireless Communication Technologies for the IoT Era (2023). https://www.soumu.go.jp/menu_news/s-news/01kiban05_02000114.html
2. Tanaka, K., Maeda, H., Yamashita, K., Liu, Y., Hazarika, H.: Implementation and proof experiment of communication network for disaster prevention using LPWA. In: Gervasi, O. et al. (eds.) ICCSA 2022 Workshops, LNCS, vol. 13379, pp. 42–55. Springer, Cham (2022). https://doi.org/10.1007/978-3-031-10545-6_4
3. EASEL Co., Ltd.: ES920LR3 Product Overview. https://www.easel5.com/products/es920lr3/
4. Noreen, U., Bounceur, A., Clavier, L.: A study of LoRa low power and wide area network technology. In: 2017 International Conference on Advanced Technologies for Signal and Image Processing (ATSIP), pp. 1–6. IEEE (2017). https://doi.org/10.1109/ATSIP.2017.8075570
5. Kinoshita, S., Tanaka, K.: Tree topology communication network construction of LPWA. In: Proceedings of the 11th International Symposium on Applied Engineering and Sciences (SAES2023), pp. 305–306 (2023)

Geogames for Sustainable Development (GeoGames 2025)

Emotions Geogame: Developing a Game for Mapping Emotions and Evaluating Places

Alenka Poplin[1]([✉]) [iD], Niall Sharma[1], Kumar Siddharth[3], and Chiara Garau[2] [iD]

[1] Iowa State University, Ames, USA
apoplin@iastate.edu
[2] University of Cagliari, Cagliari, Italy
[3] Bangalore, India

Abstract. This paper demonstrates the state-of-the-art development of the Emotions Geogame. The main goal of the Emotions Geogame is to motivate users/players to go on an adventure, explore their built environment, socialize with other residents and report about the emotions they feel related to the visited places. This research is based on the three pillars of the previous research, which include research on emotions and their meaning, mapping emotions related to places, and location-based games that inspired this test implementation. The core component of the Emotions Geogame is its invitation to the users/players to record their emotions. It is accomplished in a two-step process. In the first step the user selects the emotion felt at the selected place. In the second step the user can provide a more comprehensive response to the reasons for the recorded feeling that stems from the environment. In the next steps of the implementation, the formal and dramatic elements of the Emotions Geogame will be further developed. The testing and data collection will be organized in the USA, Italy and India. The paper concludes with a discussion and directions for further research and implementation.

Keywords: Geogame · Emotions · Places · Unity · Data Collection

1 Introduction

Humans are emotional beings but often have difficulties expressing the emotions they feel or even finding words that would describe emotions. Studying emotions as this intangible sensation and feeling is complex and rather difficult. It is close to impossible to know if "sad" or "joyful" means the same to different people and how they perceive it. Studies on emotions take on different perspectives. An evolutionary theory on emotions stresses the impact of the survival mechanism. The somatic theory of emotions concentrates on senses and feelings, while the cognitive theory on emotions concentrates on mind and cognition while processing emotions.

This research attempts to link three different aspects and unite them in the form of the Emotions Geogame. These three aspects are places, emotions, and games. It investigates if a game can be created that may encourage residents to play and experiment.

O. Gervasi et al. (Eds.): ICCSA 2025 Workshops, LNCS 15890, pp. 249–259, 2026.
https://doi.org/10.1007/978-3-031-97606-3_17

It is envisioned as a location-based game that takes the player into the environment to explore. It is an adventure game that incorporates the elements of the environment and invites the player to explore this environment; outside the player and inside. The outside environment consists of places that, by definition, have fuzzy boundaries. These places may evoke emotions, and the residents may also visit them when they feel in a particular way. Can these emotions be captured? How should a game be designed to motivate users to visit and explore places and record emotions they feel related to these places? The focus of this research is on exploring how to design a geogame that may help to capture how people actually feel in response to given stimuli and what eliciting factors may be responsible for evoking certain emotions. Understanding inhabitants' perceptions of locations can assist urban planners and designers in interpreting the impact of urban morphologies on residents' well-being. This work builds on the previous research on mapping emotions [1], GIS analysis of places and emotions [2], engaging residents [3], and games related to empathy and emotional conditions such as loneliness and depression [4, 5], and location-based games such as Pokémon Go [6]. The main research challenges include questions related to geogame design and implementation, as well as the integration of a geogame's playfulness with serious aspects of emotions felt at certain places.

The Emotions Game is currently in the pilot phase of completion of the first prototype. It is implemented in the game engine environment Unity which utilizes Open Street Map geospatial data used for navigation in the environment. The game is an adventure and exploration geogame that enables the users to socialize and map emotions related to places they visit. This paper summarizes the main results of the current implementation and concludes with discussion and further research directions.

2   Emotions, Games and Places

2.1 Emotions and Applications

Emotions are difficult to study, and several theories attempt to explain them from their perspective. These theories of emotions include evolutionary, somatic, and cognitive theories. The evolutionary theory suggests that emotions serve as a survival mechanism and may be essential in their protection [7–10]. Ekman particularly studies face and facial expressions associated with emotions. The somatic theory of emotion concentrates on the experience and the senses in the body [11, 12]. The cognitive theory of emotion studies cognitive processes that may generate emotions [13]. Emotions have also been studied in the design research community to address how the understanding of emotions can be used to create designs and conditions for evoking, modulating or prohibiting certain emotions in user experience.

Some applied research, for example by the Apple team, studies how to empower people to live a healthier day by using innovative technologies that may support personal health and self-care to achieve overall well-being [14]. Figure 1 shows the user interface and how users can record how they feel and use the slider to indicate how pleasant this emotion is. The Mood Meter developed by the HopeLab [15, 16] in collaboration with Yale Center for Emotional Intelligence uses an emotions grid, which is then implemented on a mobile application as shown in Fig. 1 on the right. Emotions are organized along the x-axis indicating pleasantness, and, on the y-axis, indicating the level of energy as shown in Fig. 2. An interesting fact is that HopeLab was co-founded by Pam Omidyar who had an idea to create a video game to help young cancer patients with treatment compliance. At the time she was working as a researcher in an immunology lab and a video game enthusiast.

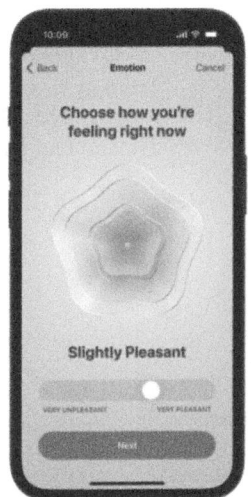 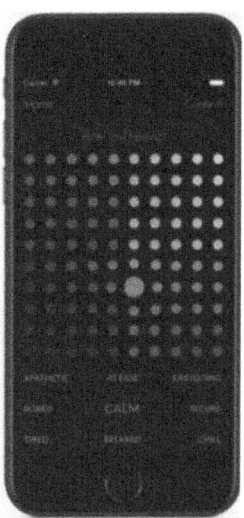

Fig. 1. Apple application (left); HopeLab implementation (right)

Enraged	Panicked	Stressed	Jittery	Shocked	Surprised	Upbeat	Festive	Exhilarated	Ecstatic
Livid	Furious	Frustrated	Tense	Stunned	Hyper	Cheerful	Motivated	Inspired	Elated
Fuming	Frightened	Angry	Nervous	Restless	Energized	Lively	Excited	Optimistic	Enthusiastic
Anxious	Apprehensive	Worried	Irritated	Annoyed	Pleased	Focused	Happy	Proud	Thrilled
Repulsed	Troubled	Concerned	Uneasy	Peeved	Pleasant	Joyful	Hopeful	Playful	Blissful
Disgusted	Glum	Disappointed	Down	Apathetic	At Ease	Easygoing	Content	Loving	Fulfilled
Pessimistic	Morose	Discouraged	Sad	Bored	Calm	Secure	Satisfied	Grateful	Touched
Alienated	Miserable	Lonely	Disheartened	Tired	Relaxed	Chill	Restful	Blessed	Balanced
Despondent	Depressed	Sullen	Exhausted	Fatigued	Mellow	Thoughtful	Peaceful	Comfortable	Carefree
Despairing	Hopeless	Desolate	Spent	Drained	Sleepy	Complacent	Tranquil	Cozy	Serene

← LOW PLEASANTNESS → ← HIGH PLEASANTNESS →

Fig. 2. Mood Meter (Mood Meter, 2025) [17, 18]

Research on games and emotions mostly concentrates on understanding players' experience of games and how they can be utilized to elicit, evaluate and express emotions [19]. Knutz and Markussen [20] describe the Child Patient Game (CPgame) developed for pediatric patients at a Danish hospital [20]. The players/users are 4 - 6-year-old hospitalized children who can learn about their emotions and their emotional reactions to medical treatment by using the game which can also inform health personnel about their emotional state.

2.2 Emotions and Places

Places may evoke emotions and residents may also attach emotions to certain places. Out of the whole literature on place and attachment we are selecting publications that are directly related to mapping emotions to places, specifically our previous research on mapping emotions and places. Poplin and her collaborators (Poplin et al. [1]) mapped emotions related to places in Germany, Austria, Iowa (USA) and Brazil. They only concentrated on positive evocative places, places that help residents to feel relaxed and recharged.

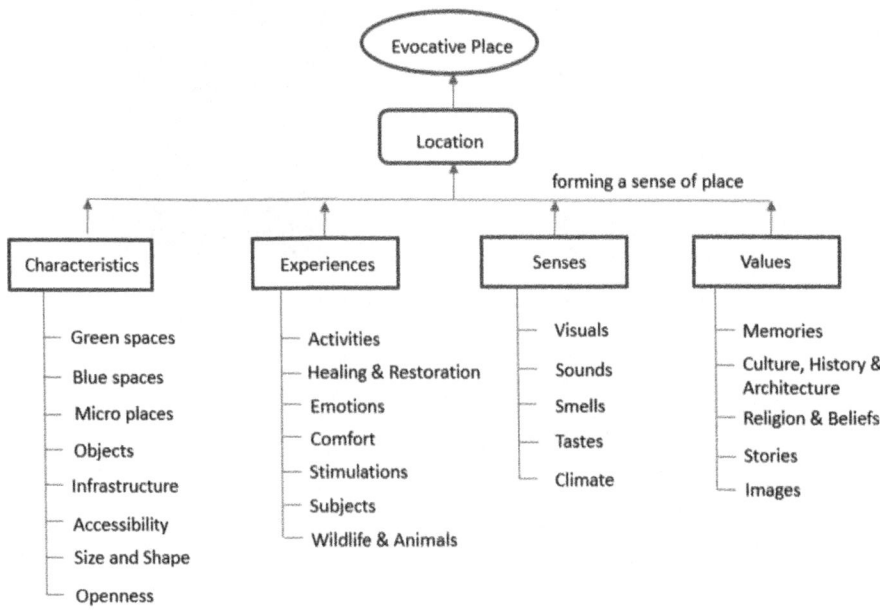

Fig. 3. Conceptual Model of an Evocative Place (Poplin et al. [1])

Figure 3 shows the conceptual model of an evocative place. It summarizes descriptions of evocative places as expressed by the residents in their interviews using paper or online maps and a questionnaire in which the residents described evocative places with three words. A categorization of these descriptions was proposed as a model, verified with a new dataset from Vienna (Austria) which resulted in the version presented in Fig. 3. Evocative places are described with their affordances in terms of physical characteristics of this place, experiences residents may have at this place, what they can sense and remember associated with values.

2.3 Commercial Location-Based Games

Location-based games that use geospatial information and maps and are not serious games include Pokémon Go, Minecraft Earth, Pikmin Bloom, Monster Hunter Now, and Dragon Quest Go, among others.

Pokémon Go   First released in 2016, is an augmented reality (AR) game. Players create their own avatar, which is then displayed on a map visualized on their mobile device. As players move in the real world, they also see their moves visualized on the map. They meet characters called Pokémons which can be viewed in AR mode or with a live-rendered background. Technology such as AR using a camera and gyroscope on the player's mobile device helps display characters as if they would appear in the real world. The map on the mobile device also stimulates players to go to certain selected places as indicated on the map.

Minecraft Earth   Was released in 2019 as an augmented reality game that utilized OpenStreetMap data and was built on Microsoft Azure. It operated as a sandbox game where players can build and explore the real world with augmented reality objects. Players were encouraged to complete adventures in the form of specific tasks and puzzles to solve or to defeat entities at virtual locations.

Pikmin Bloom   Is a 2021 augmented reality game that invites players to play outside. They can wander outside, grow or feed Pikmin creatures, and create a trail of blossoming flowers on the map. Local landmarks can be represented as big flowers or mushrooms. Collaborative events bring players together facing challenges in the game. The player can also take real photographs with virtual Pikmin.

Monster Hunter Now   Is a 2023 augmented reality mobile game. It uses the player's real location, who can place an avatar on the gameplay map. The game environment in the form of a map is represented with different options including forest, swamp, and desert. The terrain map is refreshed every 24 h, and available monsters vary depending on the terrain. This game addresses more the "killer" playstyle in which players interact with monsters placed on the map and can initiate fights with them.

3   Research Focus

Based on this brief summary of previous research, the research team decided to explore if it would be possible to create a game that would enable the users to register emotions related to places. The research team summarized the key research questions as follows:

- How to develop a geogame that will invite players to explore places and map emotions?
- How can the geogame be designed to motivate players to keep returning to the game?

The focus of this contribution is in the geogame design and implementation that allows players to log their emotions at specific self-selected locations. The exploration is in the concept of a game, possibility to implement it a game involving real-world geospatial data and the design and inclusion of a module that will enable the user to register emotions.

4 Research Methodology

The research methodology consists of the following steps: literature review, conceptualizations, prototyping and implementations, user testing, data collection, and geospatial analysis. This section summarizes the accomplished in each of these steps. It, in principle, follows Boehm's [21] spiral model of software development, which suggests repeating the cycles from ideation and definition of goals to prototyping and testing in the form of a spiral. Every phase – or loop – results in an improved version of the developed software, resulting in constant improvements and production of new prototypes till the last one satisfies the requirements and specifications. The main research phases composing a research methodology are described as follows.

Literature Review. The initial exploration is in the form of a literature review, which concentrates on understanding emotions and mapping them on smart devices. This phase also includes studying location-based games and their concepts, implementations, and formal elements.

Conceptualization. This phase involved brainstorming online and in person. I included the selection of the platform for implementation. Unity was selected due to the possibility of using OpenStreetMaps for cartographic and spatial visualization. This phase also included initial designs of the game, which included the idea of the game loop. Guardiola defines the game loop as "the set of actions the player will iterate the most, and in which the winning/losing condition are real outcomes" [22]. This idea is then envisioned in ways in which the user/player interacts with the mobile application as she/he visits the places of choice, logs emotion(s), and is then rewarded for this activity. The next design decision was related to the implementation of emotions. The very early prototype was based on six selected emotions, which included joy, tranquility, trust, worry, anger, and regret. Three of them were on the negative spectrum, and three of them were on the positive spectrum. This design choice was then changed as the team discovered the Mood Meter and decided to experiment with its use and implementation in the Emotions Game.

Figure 4 shows the emotions as they appear in the research by Garau and Annunziata [2], and Poplin and her colleagues (Poplin et al. [1]) are mapped on the Mood Meter. The emotions on the gird (Fig. 4) that are marked with circles also appeared in the research on emotions and places as previously explored by Garau, Poplin and their colleagues. This mapping then informed the choice of emotions selected for the implementation of the initial user interface for the Emotions game.

Prototyping and Implementations. The prototyping includes the back-end and front-end prototyping. The map system was implemented in Unity. Figure 5 shows the visualization of maps in the selected game engine. The server-side of the Emotions Geogame (back-end) was written in JavaScript, uses NodeJS, and features the use of CRUD operations to manipulate the data that was then stored in a MySql database. The important information stored in this database includes the geospatial location of the player, date and time, and the answers to the two questions the player answers. Unity then talks to the NodeJS server and uses CRUD operations to add new points players log to the database. Several prototypes were implemented to test a variety of options.

					Surprised	Upbeat	Festive	Exhilarated	Ecstatic
Enraged	Panicked	Stressed	Jittery	Shocked	Surprised	Upbeat	Festive	Exhilarated	Ecstatic
Livid	Furious	Frustrated	Tense	Stunned	Hyper	Cheerful	Motivated	Inspired	Elated
Fuming	Frightened	Angry	Nervous	Restless	Energized	Lively	Excited	Optimistic	Enthusiastic
Anxious	Apprehensive	Worried	Irritated	Annoyed	Pleased	Focused	Happy	Proud	Thrilled
Repulsed	Troubled	Concerned	Uneasy	Peeved	Pleasant	Joyful	Hopeful	Playful	Blissful
Disgusted	Glum	Disappointed	Down	Apathetic	At Ease	Easygoing	Content	Loving	Fulfilled
Pessimistic	Morose	Discouraged	Sad	Bored	Calm	Secure	Satisfied	Grateful	Touched
Alienated	Miserable	Lonely	Disheartened	Tired	Relaxed	Chill	Restful	Blessed	Balanced
Despondent	Depressed	Sullen	Exhausted	Fatigued	Mellow	Thoughtful	Peaceful	Comfortable	Carefree
Despairing	Hopeless	Desolate	Spent	Drained	Sleepy	Complacent	Tranquil	Cozy	Serene

←————————LOW PLEASANTNESS ————————→ ←————————HIGH PLEASANTNESS ————————→

Fig. 4. Mapping emotions captured related to places (Poplin et al. [1]) on the Mood Meter

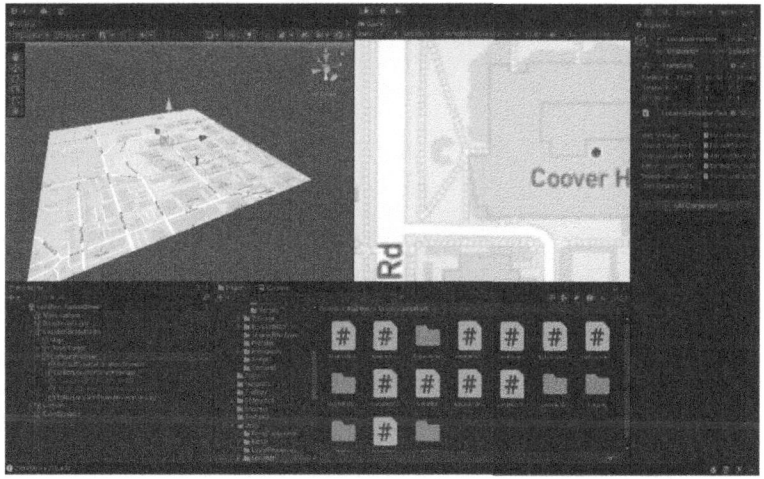

Fig. 5. Use of maps in the game engine Unity

User Testing and Data Collection and Geospatial Analysis. The initial tests of the system were performed after the test implementation. The data collected were first exported from Unity and then fed into the backend server created for data management. A Python script was used to convert the JSON data file taken from the server into a GeoJSON format, which can then be imported into a geographic information systems (GIS) software. Once the team implements the final version of the game, more comprehensive user testing is planned. The data collected will then be imported into a geographic information system and used for geospatial analysis of places in the selected cities.

5   The Concept of the Emotions Geogame

The Emotions Geogame is designed as an adventure and exploration game. Users/players go on a quest to explore their environment. A socializing component will add excitement for players who want to meet at certain places, socialize and visit those places, or meet other people. They will go on quests and missions.

Mapping emotions within the Emotions Geogame is currently concentrated on two main questions. The first question inquires how this place makes the user/player feel. The second question explores what in the environment makes the user/player feel this way. The implementation and the initial mock-ups for the mapping emotions part of the game are illustrated in Fig. 6.

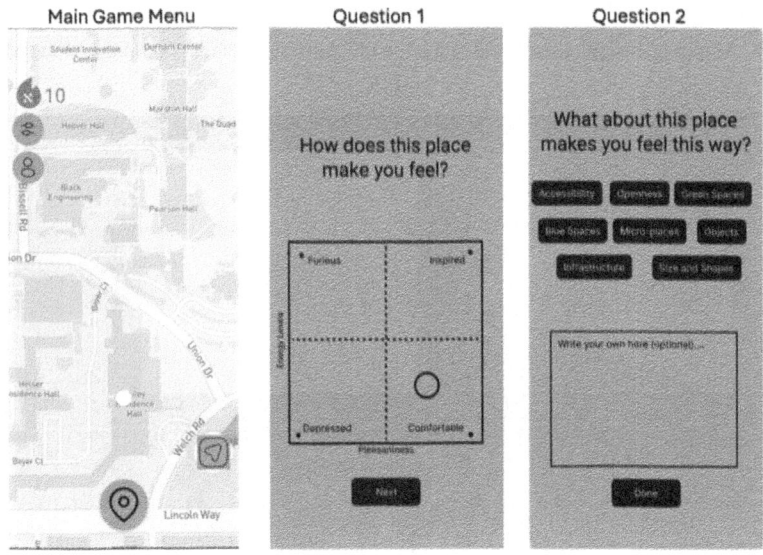

Fig. 6. Initial mock-up user interface for the Emotions Game

Question 1: How does this place make you feel?

The first question will present a grid with an x and y axis to the player. The x-axis will be "pleasantness," and the y-axis will be "energy levels". Four "landmark emotions" will be given to the player at four of the extremes on the graph as a way to orient themselves. The x-axis is scaled from $(-25, 0)$ to $(25, 0)$, while the y-axis is scaled from $(0, -25)$ to $(0, 25)$.

Question 2: What about this place makes you feel this way?

The second question will give the player the ability to understand why they feel the way they do, as well as give us the data to understand why they feel in a specific way. The user will also have the ability to input their own answer in a textbox if the provided answers are not enough.

In the further brainstorming about the implementation two additional ideas to Question 1 emerged. They are visualized on Fig. 7. On the left-hand side: Adding a grid for easier navigation in indicating emotions on the unpleasant – pleasant and low energy – high energy axes. On the right-hand side: Writing words for emotions that were most often expressed based on the previous research.

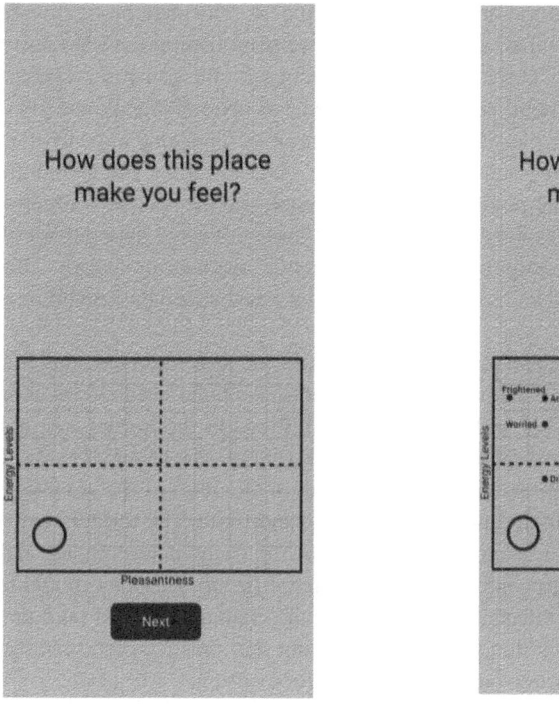
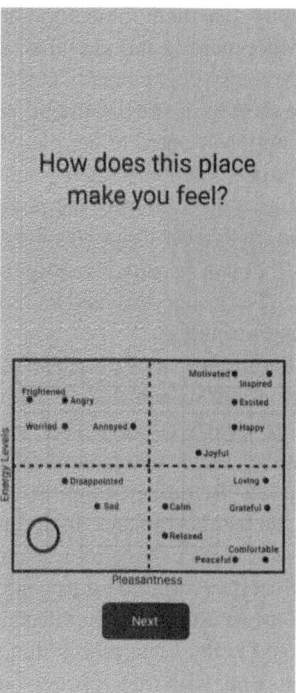

Fig. 7. Adding a grid and extracted words expanding the user interface of the Emotions Game

6   Conclusions and Further Research

This paper overviews the current state of the development and implementation of the Emotions Game, game designed to engage users/players in exploring their city, meet other residents, and take on an adventure. The Emotions Geogame also aims to motivate them to record their emotions related to places they visit. It is being developed in a collaboration of researchers from the USA, Italy and India in fruitful and regular project meetings.

The main concept was first developed for the section on emotions and mapping emotions. A set of location-based games served as inspiration for a mobile game. Previous research on emotions and mapping emotions and places inspired this implementation. The Emotions Geogame is still in its experimental phase and further development and implementation will be needed. More work needs to be invested in defining the main goals and missions/quests of the game. They are particularly important as they may significantly impact users/players' retention and the willingness and motivation to return to the game and play it repeatedly.

The game engine Unity was selected for its implementation due to its ability to integrate real-world data in the form of interactive maps. The map layer is provided by the Open Street Map organization, which unites mappers from around the world to create a geospatial database of places. The users of the Emotions Game can view these maps, use them for navigation, and search for places. The main motivation behind the development is the idea that a game can be a very motivating and attractive tool for community engagement. Through this engagement with the game the residents can explore their living environment, visit their preferred and favorite places, and also share their emotions related to the places visited. The Emotions Geogame aims to enable its users/players to capture their longitude and latitude, date and time, and an emotion ID representing the x and y of the point chosen on the graph and the reasons for feeling this emotion. A Python script was developed to convert these collected data into GeoJSON format that can be directly imported into a geographic information system. This data will then be further analyzed and combined with other geospatial data depending on the goals of the analysis.

In the further steps of research, the final version of the user interface and its implementation will be selected. The concept of the Emotions Game needs to be expanded and more clearly defined. This will include the definitions of the formal and dramatic geogame elements and a more specific premise of the game. The research team intends to complete the implementation and organize testing in the cities of the countries from which the team originates, including the USA, Italy, and India. The further goal of this research is to contribute to a better understanding of the living environments and how they affect the emotional states and well-being of their citizens. This data should further inform urban designers, architects, and planners of the characteristics of built environments and help create places that result in well-being and positive emotions for their residents and, with that, a better-built environment for everyone.

Acknowledgments. Chiara Garau thanks the support of the project "RAMÉ RegCITIES: spatial analyses foR co-creAting the future of sMartest and happiEst REGions/CITIES. Comparisons between Cagliari in Italy and Des Moines in the US", founded by the program "Bando 2023 Mobilità Giovani Ricercatori (MGR)," financed by the Autonomous Region of Sardinia (under the Regional Law of 7 August 2007, n. 7 "Promotion of Scientific Research and Technological Innovation in Sardinia").

Disclosure of Interests. The authors have no competing interests to declare that are relevant to the content of this article.

References

1. Poplin, A., Duffer, E., Gartner, G.: Well-being evocative places: validating the conceptual model of an evocative place (CMEP) based on the inter-rater reliability test. Int. Cartograph. J. **9**(1) (2022). Taylor and Francis. https://doi.org/10.1080/23729333.2022.2091740
2. Garau, C., Annunziata, A.: Supporting children's independent activities in smart and playable public places. Sustainability **12**(20), 8352 (2020)

3. Stembert, N., Mulder, I.J.: Love your city! An interactive platform empowering citizens to turn the public domain into a participatory domain. In: International Conference Using ICT, Social Media and Mobile Technologies to Foster Self-Organisation in Urban and Neighbourhood Governance, Delft, The Netherlands (2013)

4. Cheng, Z., Greenwood, B.N., Pavlou, P.A.: Location-based mobile gaming and local depression trends: a study of Pokémon Go. J. Manag. Inf. Syst. **39**(1), 68–101 (2022). https://doi.org/10.1080/07421222.2021.2023407. Accessed 12 Jan 2025

5. Karpouzikis, K., Yannakakis, G.N. (eds.): Emotion in Games: Theory and Praxis. Springer, Cham (2016)

6. Wang, A.I., Skjervold, A.: Health and social impacts of playing Pokémon Go on various player groups. Entertain. Comput. **39**, 100443 (2021). https://ntnuopen.ntnu.no/ntnu-xmlui/handle/11250/2984964. Accessed 27 Jan 2025

7. Plutchik, R.: A general psychoevolutionary theory of emotion. In: Plutchik, R., Kellerman, H. (eds.) Emotion: Theory, Research and Experience, Theories of Emotion, vol. 1, pp. 3–33. Academic Press, New York (1980)

8. Plutchik, R.: A psychoevolutionary theory of emotions. Soc. Sci. Inf. **21**(4–5), 529–533 (1982). https://doi.org/10.1177/053901882021004003.S2CID144109550

9. Tomkins, S.: Affect Imagery Consciousness: Cognition, vol. 4. Springer, New York (1992). 9780826104458

10. Ekman, P.: Facial expression and emotion. Am. Psychol. **48**(4), 384–392 (1993). https://doi.org/10.1037/0003-066X.48.4.384

11. Lang, P.J.: The varieties of emotional experience: a meditation on james-lange theory. Psychol. Rev. **101**(2), 211–221 (1994). https://doi.org/10.1037/0033-295x.101.2.211

12. Damasio, A.: Descartes' Error: Emotion, Reason, and the Human Brain, Putnam (1994). ISBN 0-399-13894-3

13. Arnold, M.B.: Memory and the Brain. L. Erlbaum Associates, Hillsdale, N.J. (1984). ISBN 0-89859-290-9. OCLC 10275461

14. Apple: Empowering people to live a healthier day Innovation using Apple technology to support personal health, research, and care (2022). https://www.apple.com/newsroom/pdfs/Health-Report-October-2023.pdf. Accessed 12 Feb 2025

15. HopeLab: Mood Meter development In partnership with Yale Center for Emotional Intelligence (2025). https://hopelab.org/case-study/mood-meter/. Accessed 20 Mar 2025

16. YCEI: Yale Center for Emotional Intelligence (2025). https://medicine.yale.edu/childstudy/services/community-and-schools-programs/center-for-emotional-intelligence/. Accessed 18 Mar 2025

17. Mood Meter: Mood Meter (2025). https://unhconnect.unh.edu/s/1518/images/gid4/editor_documents/moodmeter-2020.pdf?gid=4&pgid=61&sessionid=1bb73457-5514-4c64-9482-329849e69901&cc=1. Accessed 25 Mar 2025

18. Hernandez, J., Hoque, M., Drevo, W., Picard, R.W.: Mood meter. In: Proceedings of the 2012 ACM Conference on Ubiquitous Computing – UbiComp '12, 5–8 September 2012. ACM, Pittsburgh, USA (2012)

19. Yannakakis, G.N., Paiva, A.: The Oxford Handbook of Affective Computing. Oxford University Press (2015)

20. Knutz, E., Markussen, T.: Measuring and communicating emotions through game design. In: Proceedings of Design and Emotion: Proceedings of the 7th International Conference on Design and Emotion (2010). http://www.id.iit.edu/de2010/index.html. Accessed 12 Feb 2025

21. Boehm, B.: A spiral model of software development and enhancement. IEEE Comput. **21**(5), 62–72 (1988)

22. Guardiola, E.: The gameplay loop: a player activity model for game design and analysis. In: Proceedings of the 13th International Conference on Advances in Computer Entertainment Technology, pp. 1–7. ACM, New York, NY, USA (2016)

Geographical Analysis, Urban Modeling, Spatial Statistics 2025 (Geog-And-Mod 2025)

Real-Time Monitoring and Active Control of Autonomous Agricultural Robot Trajectories Using an Edge-Fog Architecture

Mohammad Kassir[1,3], Sandro Bimonte[1,3]($\boxtimes$), Robert Wrembel[1,3], Mohamed El-Ouati[1,3], and Mahmoud Sakr[2,3]

[1] INRAE, Clermont-Ferrand, France
{sandro.bimonte,mohamed.el-ouati}@inrae.fr,
robert.wrembel@cs.put.poznan.pl
[2] Poznan University of Technology, Poznan, Poland
mahmoud.sakr@ulb.be
[3] Université libre de Bruxelles, Brussels, Belgium

Abstract. Smart farming concerns the usage of autonomous robots and sensors in the field to implement agro-ecology practices. Agriculture stake-holders are supported by supervision and control systems that allow for monitoring real-time data by means of Data Stream Management Systems (DSMSs), and remotely control robots in the field. However, processing in real-time streaming trajectory data that come from autonomous robots presents significant challenges due to the large volume of data generated by robots, and their bad quality since communication networks deployed in rural area can present several problems (e.g., instability and congestion). Furthermore, existing lightweight DSMSs do not support spatial data, and the proposed supervision systems are based on cloud-fog architectures, which do not provide effective solutions for trajectory data stream analysis within bad quality communication network. Therefore, in this paper, we extend [14], by proposing a hybrid edge-fog architecture and computation framework for robotic trajectory data analysis, which combines distributed and non-distributed DSMSs to manage trajectory data more efficiently. In particular, we extend the lightweight DSMS *Esper* with spatial operators, and dynamic frequency mechanism, at the edge level to process complex queries over trajectory data stream of the robots. Our architecture uses *Geoflink* at the fog, i.e., in the farm. A distributed computation approach for complex queries has therefore been implemented to split queries over the edge and the fog. We validate our proposals using experiment in real-life conditions.

Keywords: Data stream management systems · agricultural robots · anomaly detection · continuous queries · real-time data processing · edge processing

© The Author(s), under exclusive license to Springer Nature Switzerland AG 2026
O. Gervasi et al. (Eds.): ICCSA 2025 Workshops, LNCS 15890, pp. 263–280, 2026.
https://doi.org/10.1007/978-3-031-97606-3_18

1   Introduction

Agricultural robots are autonomous machines designed for farm works. They are equipped with sensors to perceive their environment and actuators to carry out tasks, in order to operate independently of other robots and requiring no direct human intervention. These robots typically consist of a mobile base with a navigation system and a set of agricultural tools that can be mounted directly, semi-mounted, or towed. These robots are more and more frequently used in agro-ecology. Agro-ecology emphasizes environmentally sustainable farming practices. To support this, farmers and stakeholders need a robust system for supervising and remotely control agricultural robots [14]. Such a system should allow remote monitoring of robot progress in the field, as well as ingesting and analyzing data from various field devices, that can be classified as:

- *sensor data*, which are delivered in real-time from environmental sensors, e.g., temperature, wind speed, soil humidity;
- *odometry data*, which represent robot's position, movement, and other mechanical parameters; such data are continuously updated, reflecting current positions of robots in fields;
- *contextual data*, including spatial information (e.g., agro-field boundaries), and other farmer-specific details (e.g., the type of crops being harvested).

Sensors and odometry data are continuously generated as data streams and they are accessed in real-time, requiring a system that can efficiently handle these dynamic streams. For instance, it is crucial to track a robot's movement (speed, GPS location) and monitor weather conditions (temperature, humidity), since farmers should be able to control the right execution of agricultural tasks, monitor the robots performance and avoid any security human and animal risks. Moreover, such supervision systems must also provide remotely control capabilities to allow farmers to action robots from their working position to change the robots behavior when it deviates from the planed trajectory (e.g., robot has a delay), to guide it when robot is not able to autonomously continue its work (e.g., robot stops in presence of a obstacle), etc.

Data Stream Management Systems (DSMSs) are used in various application domains, such as traffic control, health, etc. to process scalable streaming data in real-time. DSMSs process data streams by means of continuous queries. A continuous query runs repeatedly at a predefined frequency. It incrementally processes results on data collected within a specified time window. For instance, a query might be configured to calculate the minimum speed of each robot every 5 s (i.e., frequency), based on data collected within the preceding 20 s (i.e., time window). Common aggregation operators, such as min, max, avg are used to summarize numerical values within a given time window.

However, handling agricultural robotic data with DSMSs raises some significant challenges, resulting from: (1) the high frequency of ingested data, (2) the need for real-time computation, and (3) poor quality (network instability and congestion) of a communication network deployed in agricultural fields, which can cause data loss. This loss deteriorates the integrity of the data, resulting in inaccurate monitoring indicators, which is critical to maintaining operational safety and efficiency. Moreover, DSMSs come with a set of predefined queries, and they do not allow end-users to modify them, for example, changing the frequency of the query or the aggregation functions used.

To overcome these challenges, in this paper we extend the architecture proposed in [14] with a new **edge-fog** approach for monitoring of agricultural robotic data. Edge computing refers to processing data closest to the data source, e.g., on a device itself. It minimizes latency, improves real-time performance, and reduces bandwidth needs. Fog computing is a layer between an edge and cloud. It provides a balance of processing power and centralized management. In particular, we extend [14] with the computation of queries on streams of robot trajectory data in a distributed way between the edge and the fog. To this end, we extend the analysis capabilities of the *Esper* DSMS with trajectory types and operations. This is achieved viaintegrating it with the in-memory spatial DBMS *H2GIS*. We deploy it at each robot (i.e., edge level) to execute local queries. At the fog level, we use the Spatial DSMS *GeoFlink* to compute and aggregate data and Esper query results coming from the robots.

Moreover, we propose a dynamic time frequency mechanism that allows to change the frequency that robots send data to *GeoFlink*, in order adapt the monitoring system to the on-going situation of the robots. This dynamic time frequency mechanism can be controlled using a rich palette of predefined rules at the robot level that are automatically triggered. We also have implemented a mechanism allowing the end-users to remotely change the frequency of the continuous queries when need to support advanced control capabilities. To evaluate our proposal, a set of representative trajectory queries is proposed for robots monitoring in the experiments.

The paper is structured in the following way: Sect. 2 presents the motivation scenario and the definition of trajectory data and queries. Section 3 presents the architecture we extended, and the implementation of the continuous queries is shown in Sect. 4. Experiments are presented in Sect. 5.

2   Robots Trajectory Stream Queries for Monitoring Agricultural Autonomous Robots

In this section, we present the definition of a robot trajectory data and different kinds of continuous queries over such data for the supervision and control of agricultural autonomous robots.

2.1   Monitoring and Control of Agricultural Autonomous Robots

An agricultural robot is an unmanned ground vehicle equipped with sensors and actuators, capable of autonomously and safely performing one or multiple tasks in a farm field. It typically consists of a locomotion system integrated with a navigation module and an agricultural component, which may include mounted, semi-mounted, or towed implements. These robots can be designed for a specific

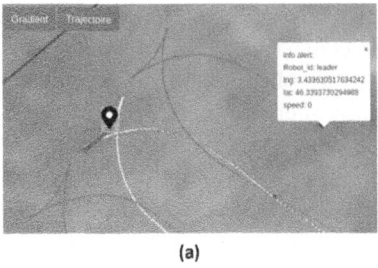 

(a)   (b)

Fig. 1. Visualization of robots data. (a) The display show the robot pre-defined trajectory, and the robot real-time location. The depicted U-turn maneuver is one of the complex movements the robot can do, which might incur problems in implementing it. In (b) the end-user has a control device and a camera view to be able to control the robot trajectory when needed.

task, such as weeding or harvesting, or they can function as tool carriers for various equipment configurations for tasks like tillage and seeding. Monitoring and control systems must provide end-user support with a visual interface that is able to show in real-time different indicators, and to remotely control the robots in the field as shown in Fig. 1. In particular, it is necessary to monitor:

- *Robot malfunction and risks*: Agricultural robots operate in rural environments, often under harsh weather conditions and on challenging terrains (e.g., uneven or rocky ground), which may lead to technical failures. Moreover, robots can work in risks situations, such as the collision of robots, or with humans, etc.
- *Task alerts*: Robots are programmed to a particular predefined task in the field. Although robots are programmed to follow the predefined trajectories, they can autonomously adjust their paths to avoid obstacles like animals, tree branches, and rocks. These adjustments, however, may cause delays, or deviating from the predefined trajectory.

Fig. 2. Field configuration.

Typically, robots are deployed in the field, which is equipped with some communication networks as shown in Fig. 2. These communication networks can be

Internet, Wi-Fi ad-hoc network, etc. These networks are particularly challenging in farms since cellular network coverage may be not sufficient, or the bandwidth is low, which can generate data loss and by consequence a bad computation of monitoring indicators and impossibility to remotely control the robots. In the context of robots supervision, we have identified some relevant data-based indicators defined as a set of continuous queries:

- *Robot malfunction and risks*:
  - **Q1**: *Every 5 s, find robot Alpo's top speed in the last 5 s*;
  - **Q1a**: *Every 5 s, find top speed of all robots in the last 5 s*;
  - **Q2**: *Every 5 min, compute the total number of robots in a particular geometrical zone of the field in the last minute.*
  - **Q4** *Every 10 s, find possible collisions among all robots.*
- *Agricultural tasks' alerts*:
  - **Q3**: *Every 5 min, compute the delay of every robot according to their predefined trajectories in the last minute.*
  - **Q6**: *every minute, compute the traveled distance for every robot in 'Plot1' in the last 120 s.*

A visual interface for a supervision system must implement the *perception* level of the *situation awareness* (SA). Perception has been defined as *the level responsible for perceiving the status, attributes, and dynamics of relevant elements in the observed environment. The most elementary level of SA, involves the processes of sensing, monitoring and simple recognition, which lead to an awareness of multiple situational elements objects, people, systems, environmental factors and their current states and characteristics* [18]. The goal at this level is to maintain a constant and accurate understanding of the environment, which is foundational for higher levels of SA that involve comprehension and projection of future states.

In practical terms, for a supervision system overseeing robots in a field, the implementation of this SA can be achieved via continuous queries that report on the robots' status. For instance, a query (**Q1**) might check whether a robot has ceased movement for the past five seconds, potentially indicating a mechanical issue. Here, Continuous monitoring is key for real-time situational awareness.

However, the stream update frequency (*frequency parameter*) impacts user cognitive load. To address this, a **dynamic frequency** approach adjusts frequency based on result normality. For instance, if a robot's speed drops to zero (**Q1**), the system increases updates to every second, boosting situational awareness and enabling timely interventions.

To further optimize data flow and situational response, the concept of a backward channel from Fog to Edge in the typical edge-fog-cloud architecture is introduced. Unlike the traditional one-directional flow (from edge to fog, then fog to cloud), this two-way communication allows for adaptive data transmission based on the context, which could be governed by rules such as:

- *Spatial rules:* Certain zones, like near a field's boundary or a water body within it, may require more frequent updates to prevent the robots from straying off course or entering hazardous areas.

- *Event-based rules:* An increase in a robot's speed beyond a predefined threshold could trigger more frequent data transmissions.
- *Pattern-based rules:* Complex maneuvers, like a U-turn, which might increase the risk of incidents, could necessitate a higher data update rate to closely monitor and control the robot's actions.
- *Fog-control:* Fog, as farm controller, should be able to override default settings to adjust data flow as needed.

2.2   Robot Trajectory Point Data Type

In batch processing of trajectories—e.g., at the fog or cloud—a trajectory type maps time to space (e.g., in [15, 21]). A robot trajectory is a time-ordered list of trajectory points. Figure 3 shows two example trajectories. In a streaming setting, trajectory points arrive incrementally, and the DSMS groups them into windows for processing. A trajectory point includes the following main attributes:

- *longitude* and *latitude* represented in the WSG84 coordinate system;
- *the set of numerical attributes*, which represent odometry data collected by the robot, as for example the *speed*;
- *timestamp* when data was collected by the robot, i.e., valid time.

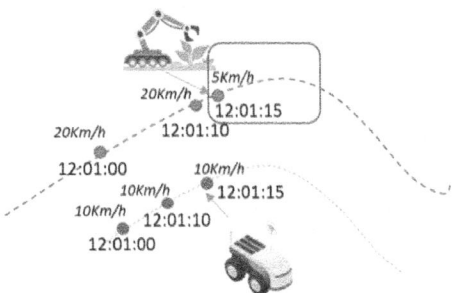

Fig. 3. Example of two robots trajectories, where one is represented in blue and the other one in green. The GPS position is represented by a colored point with the associated timestamp and their associated speed values (e.g., for robot blue: *12:01:00*-20 km/h at the first position; *12:01:10*-20 km/h at the second position; and *12:01:15*-5 km/h at the third position). (Color figure online)

2.3   Continuous Queries on Robots Trajectories Streams

A *continuous query* over a stream of robot trajectories involves the following:

- **data sources** - the specification of a table(s) (e.g., relational data describing an agro-field) and a stream(s) (e.g., a robot trajectory) to be queried, including means for joining them (if applicable);

– **data selection** - the definition of attributes to be extracted from the data sources (e.g., speed). In particular, *data selection* can imply different kinds of selection predicates, like: *alphanumeric* (e.g., robot name is "Alpo"), *spatial*, i.e., the usage of topological operators (e.g., the blue robot position is inside the red polygon, as depicted in Fig. 3), and *spatio-temporal* i.e., the usage of spatial and temporal operators (e.g., are robots blue and green at the same position at time *12:01:00?*).

– **data aggregation** - aggregation functions can be numerical or spatio-temporal. *Numerical aggregation* computes values like max, min, or avg using standard SQL functions or complex algorithms. *Spatio-temporal aggregation* focuses on the trajectory's points and timestamps.

– **windowing** - the definition of a time window (e.g., sliding, tumbling) and its parameters for evaluating a query (e.g., withing the last 10 sec);

– **dynamic frequency** - the definition of a frequency used to trigger the query (e.g., every 2 sec). The frequency can be defined using a set of rules evaluated on the trajectory data or can be remotely set up by the end-user.

An example of a continuous query using a numerical aggregation is: *every 5 s (frequency), compute the max speed of robot blue within 15 sec (window)*". Referring to the scenario shown in Fig. 3, at time *12:01:15*, the result is 20 km/h, since from *12:01:00* to *12:01:15* the max speed is 20 km/h at time *12:01:00* and at time *12:01:10*.

3   System Architecture

In this section, we present the main components of the *LambdAgrIoT* proposed in [14] (Sect. 3.1), and then we detail our extension for the effective edge-fog processing of robots' trajectories stream queries (Sect. 3.2).

3.1   LambdAgrIoT Overview

LambdAgrIoT has been proposed by [14] for collecting, integrating, and analyzing agricultural robotic data. It is a multi-layered architecture based on the *Lambda* architecture, and it is composed of the following main layers:

– **Data Producers Layer** includes a meteorological station and autonomous robots, feeding the system for real-time and historical analysis.

– **Speed Layer** processes real-time data streams produced by the *Data Producers* layer for decision-making. It is based on the DSMS *Apache Spark Streaming* coupled with *Apache Sedona*. *Apache Sedona* allows spatial data processing. The results of continuous queries are then visualized by means of **Real-Time Monitoring Dashboard**, which is a visual web interface.

– **Message Queuing Layer** serves as the backbone for data flow management within the architecture, ensuring efficient and reliable data transmission across different layers. It is based on *Apache Kafka*.

- **Batch Layer** supports long-term storage and analysis of historical data using *PostGIS* for spatial data management, and it implements a data warehouse for supporting OLAP queries.
- **Serving Layer** merges data from the *Batch* and *Speed* layers that feed an online scheduling algorithm implemented with CPLEX.

3.2   Extended Edge-Fog Layers

In this section, we detail the extension of *LambdAgrIoT* for computing continuous queries over trajectory data stream by means of an edge-fog approach. In particular, we have redefined the *Data producers* and *Speed* layers as shown in Fig. 4. The main idea is to compute the continuous query using the partial computation approach as described in [13], which consists in splitting the computation of the query in different parts at the edge level, and then aggregate them at the fog level. In our proposal, a continuous query can be computed: (i) totally at the robot level (i.e., edge), (ii) totally at the fog level (i.e., at the farm), or (iii) split accross the edge and fog levels.

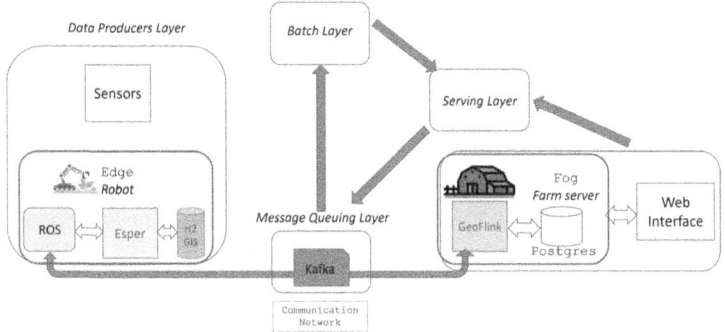

Fig. 4. Extended *LambdAgrIoT* architecture: in red rectangles the modified components of the architecture.

Data Producers Layer. A main contribution in this paper is that it extends [14] with the capabilities of Edge processing. In the extended architecture, edge devices are considered as processing units, in addition to their function as data producers. We therefore design a software stack for the edge devices, i.e., robots, in order to equipe them with query answering capabilities. Processing streaming query at the edge level needs for DSMS that are lightweight. Indeed, robots come with common laptop machine that have no-high performance physical devices such as RAM, CPU and disks. Moreover, the maintenance of the software of robots fleets is a tedious and time consuming task when the number of robots is high or this task is left to the farmers. Then, the usage of complex DSMS such as distributed one is not adapted for deploying the DSMS at the robot level. This criteria plus the active maintenance of the DSMS software, and the need for the usage only of open-source software in our architecture lead to use *Esper*. A comparison of existing DSMS is provided in Sect. 6. From this analysis, *Esper* appears to be the most suitable choice because it is lightweight and can be deployed on robots. Furthermore, it has advanced pattern recognition capabilities, which are necessary for processing complex data (such as robots data), and it is actively maintained and updated.

However, Esper does not support spatial data processing. Therefore, we extend Esper by creating a new trajectory point data type and an associated set of methods. These methods implement spatial operators by means of the native functionalities offered by *H2GIS*. *H2GIS* is an in-memory database supporting the storage and querying of spatial data. It provides better performance for data access than classical disk databases [17], then it is compliant with real-time performance required by robots monitoring queries. Moreover, it is a lightweight system and by consequence its maintenance is also easier. Then, these spatial operators are used in the continuous queries methods offered by Esper to set frequency and window. Implementation details are provided in Sect. 4.

Further, our robots are equipped with ROS (Robotic Operating System). ROS provide a software framework for robots control and management. ROS uses a message subscribe protocol, which we use as a message queue that to handle messages from the fog. Other light message brokers systems could be also deployed. However, ROS allows to develop ad-hoc functionalities, it does not come with DSMSs functionalities. Thus, the usage of Esper plus HGIS allows to easy deploy continuous queries on robots without any additional ROS implementation. Moreover, this loosely coupled solution with Esper plus HGIS on the top of the robot software allow for exploiting also other robots that do not use ROS, which makes our proposal more generic and flexible.

Speed Layer. The original *LambdAgrIoT* architecture uses Apache Sedona, which is a DSMS supporting spatial data within a distributed architecture. However, a more detailed analysis is needed to establish the best system being used. For that reason, we have compared GeoFlink, GeoMesa, and Apache Sedona according to different criteria as detailed in Sect. 6.1. This analysis reveals that *GeoFlink* seems to be the most suitable solution as it excels in real-time processing, which is a priority for detecting anomalies in robot trajectories. Additionally, it offers good scalability and spatial support capabilities, while requiring only moderate resources. Then, we adopt GeoFlink in our new *Speed* layer implementation.

4   Implementation

In this section, we detail the implementation of the continuous queries and the dynamic window approach.

4.1   Esper Extension for Spatial Data

Esper does not support spatial data. Therefore, to implement the *data sources* layer, we have extended the functionalities of Esper. We have implemented a trajectory point data type (i.e., *trajectoryPoint*) in Esper using a Java class.

This class comes with a set of methods that implement spatial operators using HGIS. An example of the spatial operator 'inside a polygon' for the trajectory data point type is shown in Fig. 5. The Esper Java function *IsStreamPointInsid-ePolygon* takes as a trajectory point data type and the identifier of a polygon. A set of predefined polygons is stored in a table named *Polygons*. The method creates the H2GIS inside spatial query, using the longitude and latitude of the input trajectory point data. Finally, it executes the query. The other spatial operators have been implemented in the same way.

```
public static IsStreamPointInsidePolygon (trajectoryPoint
trajectoryp, integer idpolygon) {

    String query = "SELECT ST_Contains((SELECT geom FROM
                    Polygons
                    WHERE id = idpolygon, " +
                    "ST_GeomFromText('POINT('|| ? || ' '
                    ||   ? |T ')', 4326))";

    try (PreparedStatement stmt =
        conn.prepareStatement(query)) {
            stmt.setDouble(1, trajectory.getLatitude());
            stmt.setDouble(2, trajectoryp.getLongitude());
    }
    ResultSet rs = stmt.executeQuery();

}
```

Fig. 5. Spatial inside operator.

4.2   Continuous Queries Implementation

In the following we describe the implementation of the continuous queries at the edge, fog, and edge-fog levels.

Continuous queries over robots data can be classified into mono-trajectory queries, involving individual trajectories, and multiple trajectory queries involving a group of trajectories. An example of mono-trajectory query is query **Q1** (Every 5 s, find robot Alpo's top speed in the last 5 s), while query **Q1a** (Every 5 s, find top speed of all robots in the last 5 s) is a multiple-trajectory query.

Another classification, orthogonal to the classification described above, is based on the aggregation functions used:

- A *distributive* aggregation query can be decomposed in sub-(aggregation) queries. For example the query **Q1a** (Every 5 s, find top speed of all robots in the last 5 s) can be computed as follows: (1) compute the max speed for each robot and then (2) select the max of these precomputed values.

– A *non-distributive* aggregation cannot be computed based on partially aggregated values. An example of non-distributive aggregation is query Q2 (every 5 min, compute the total number of robots in a particular geometrical zone of the field within the last minute) since a distinct count aggregation, which is not distributive, must be applied.

Using the above described classifications of the continuous queries, we describe their implementation in the edge, fog and edge-fog levels.

Edge. Queries totally implemented at the edge level are mono-trajectory queries, since they need only data of one robot to being computed. Therefore, they are implemented exclusively using Esper and HGIS.

```
1.   String epl = "select window(*) as points
                   from TrajectoryPointDataType.win:time_batch(5 sec)";
2.   EPStatement statement =
         runtime.getDeploymentService().deploy(epl).getStatements()[0];
3.   statement.addListener((newData, oldData, stat, rt) ->
         isTrajectoryPointInsidePolygon(newData));
```

Fig. 6. Esper implementation of query Q1.

Figure 6 illustrates the implementation of query **Q1** as an example for this class. Every 5 s (i.e., frequency), this query processes all events within the last 5 s (window) using the spatial *IsStreamPointInsidePolygon* method. Esper query language is inspired from SQL with *select* and *from* clauses. The *select: window(*)* clause in Line-1 selects all stream data generated by one robot and gives it the alias *points*. In the *from* clause, *TrajectoryPointDataType* Specifies the event type being processed, which is the robot point trajectory. Recall that this class includes the attributes longitude, latitude, speed, and timestamp. The operation *win:time_batch(30 sec)* sets the window size and the frequency to 30 s. Other kinds of windows exist in Esper. Once the Esper query defined, a listener is attached to this query (Line-2). The *isTrajectoryPointInsidePolygon* is executed each time new data arrive (Line-3).

More complex queries have been implemented at the edge level with Esper and HGIS. For example, the delay query **Q3** (every 5 min, compute the delay of each robot according to their predefined trajectories within the last minute) as shown in Fig. 7a. In order to compute the delay of a robot, it is needed to compare the real time data with the predefined trajectory in this way: compute the distance between the real time GPS position and the planned one, then using the speed compute the time needed to reach planned position from the real one.

In the example of Fig. 7a the robot at time 12:01:20 has a speed of 5 km/h and it is 100 m far from the planned trajectory. Then, its delay is of 72 s.

Fog. Queries implemented exclusively at the fog level are multi-trajectory and non-distributive aggregation queries. This is because their computation need for

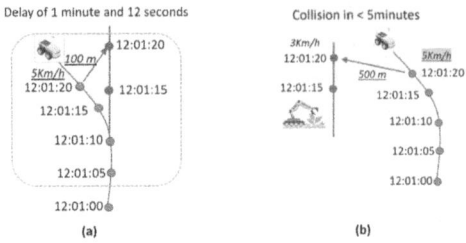

Fig. 7. a) Trajectory delay query example; b) Trajectories collision query example.

all data of different robots, preventing partial computation at the edge. Thus they are implemented at the fog level using only GeoFlink. An example is the collision query **Q4** (Each 10 s, compute if there is a possible collision among all robots) (Fig. 7b). To compute the collision indicator, the distance between pairs of robot trajectories is computed. Then using the maximum speed value, the time for the collision is extrapolated. A threshold is defined in order to trigger a warning or an alert. In the example of Fig. 7b the blue robot has the max speed (5 km/h) and it is 500 m far from the green robot. Thus there is no collision, at least in the next 5 min.

Edge-Fog. Queries that are multi-trajectory queries, thus fog is involved. To being partially computed on the edge level, these queries must involve distributive aggregations. The main idea is to let the robot locally compute a sub-aggregation, and then use the fog level to aggregate these sub-aggregations. An example is the query **Q1a** (every 5 s, compute the max speed of all robots in 5 s). This query can be computed as the max of the result of the local max speed computation of all robots, since the max is a distributive aggregation.

The edge-fog approach can also be used for optimize non-distributive multi-trajectory queries. The main idea is to split the query computation by letting the edge level perform a partial computation that reduce the data sent to the fog for the total aggregation. An example is the optimization of the collision query. To reduce the volume of data that GeoFlink must compute, we have implemented a query optimization technique based on the usage of a buffer zone around the predefined trajectory of each robot. This buffer zone represents a safety area for the robot, where there is no possibility of collisions with the other robots as shown in Fig. 8. Thus, the robot checks that it is within this buffer zone, before sending data to GeoFlink. If this spatial inside computation is positive, then a low frequency is used to transmit data to the fog, as there is no nearby risk of collision. Conversely, when a robot is outside the buffer zone and the error is increasing, a higher frequency is used, resulting in more frequent data transmission from the edge to the fog.

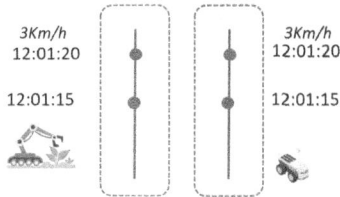

Fig. 8. Collision query optimization at the edge using a safety buffer.

5   Experiments

The edge-fog and the dynamic frequency mechanisms allow for reducing the volume of data sent through the network from the edge to the fog. As counterpart, the fog level receives only a subset of the robotic data, which means that a low frequency simplifies the robots' trajectories. For some simple tests with frequencies 3 s, 15 s, 30 s, we obviously observe that a high frequency does not distort the robot's trajectory, contrary to a low frequency that approximate too much the geometries of the trajectory. More smart frequency sampling approaches can be defined using our dynamic frequency approach, for example when robot maneuver to turn in the field.

In this experiment, we quantify the error according to the frequency used. The error is computed be comparing the distance between the result of the edge-fog query implementation with different frequencies. The experiment is conducted using two machines, one on the robot and the other one at the farm. The farm machine has 32 GB RAM and a quad-core 64-bit i5 processor. The robot machine has 4 GB of RAM and an AMD FX 4100 @3.6 Ghz 64-bit Quad core processor. Trajectory data are sensed by ROS with a frequency of 10 Hz (i.e., 1 data each 0.1 s). We run the query for 30 min, and every 15 s the collision query using 2 robots is triggered. The error is calculated based on MAPE (Mean Absolute Percentage Error).

Figure 9 shows the results of the experiment. It confirms the impact of the frequency on the error. For 15 s the error is under 20%, which is safe for a supervision task. The error decreases to 4% when frequency is high. Thus, we can consider that the collision query can effectively support SA perception in such supervision system.

Next, we compare the query time performance of the proposed edge-fog distribution of the collision query v.s., traditional centralized evaluation at the fog (Fig. 10). Our edge-fog approach is clearly faster than the fog one, thanks to distributed computing and to the reduced data size. The above results show that the edge-fog architecture, including dynamic window resizing mechanisms, query optimization, and in-memory database, has reduced computation time while controlling error, thereby preserving the architecture's reliability.

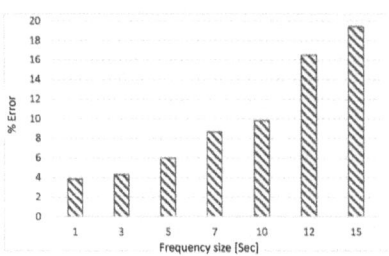

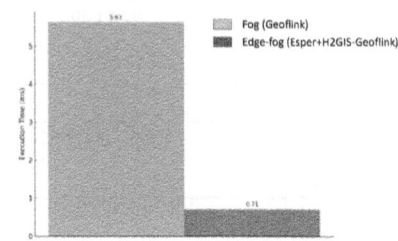

Fig. 9. Edge-fog collision query: Error percentage according to the frequency.

Fig. 10. Collision query: Execution time of edge-fog vs fog approaches.

In the following experiment, we measure how well the edge layer performs, since it plays a key role in helping robots respond in real time. We focus on the processing speed (throughput) of two spatiotemporal functions, using different sliding window sizes, or equivalently different data update rates. The TrajectoryInsidePolygon function checks if a robot stays inside a predefined area by making sure that all its location points within a given time window are inside the given polygon. The Speed function tracks the robot's average speed in real time. It does this by calculating the speed between each pair of points and then averaging these values over the window. We experiment with the two functions using different observation frequencies ranging from 1 to 15 s. As illustrated in Fig. 11, the cost is clearly affected by the observation frequency (notice the exponential scale on Y-axis). Still, with the highest rate of 15 s, the robot is able to combine the two functions in a query, and respond in less than one second. We believe this throughput is good for the real-time operations of agriculture robots, and that it would even give room for more complex operations and queries.

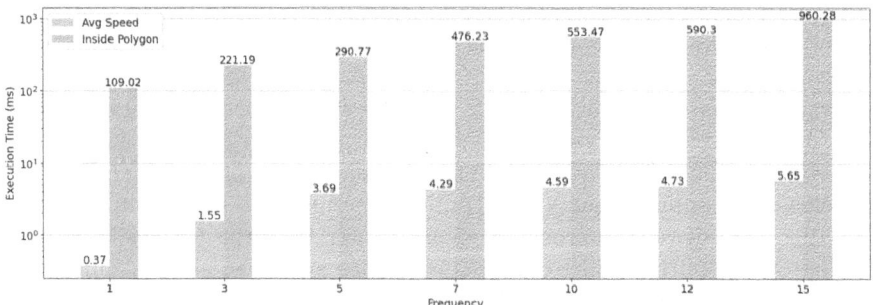

Fig. 11. Execution time of spatial functions in Esper, i.e., in the edge.

6   Related Work

Architectures for Processing Trajectory Data. Agricultural robots, equipped with a variety of sensors, collect vast amounts of spatiotemporal data, including GPS coordinates, speed, and odometry information. This data is streamed in real-time from the robots to be analyzed by a system capable of handling dynamic, high-volume data flows. To manage and analyze this continuous stream of information, a Data Streaming Management System (DSMS) is essential.

A DSMS is designed to efficiently process real-time data streams, making it ideal for agricultural robotics applications. These systems are specifically built to manage large-scale data, support real-time analysis, and execute complex queries on streaming data. In the case of agricultural robots, the trajectory data generated during operations can be sent to the DSMS, which will facilitate advanced analytics, such as detecting anomalies and optimizing performance.

Data Stream Management Systems. DSMS engines are crucial for detecting anomalies in robot trajectories due to their ability to process continuous queries that require scalability and real-time capabilities that traditional databases cannot provide. For this reason, we focus our study on two types of DSMS, namely: (1) *distributed engines* that operate on multiple nodes and (2) *non-distributed engines* that operate on a single node. To assess the compatibility of each solution with the requirements of this project, we highlight the capabilities of these engines in terms of scalability and real-time performance for distributed systems, and lightweight operation for non-distributed systems.

Distributed Engines. For trajectory distributed streaming engines, we have identified eight main solutions that can be used for our project, namely: *GeoFlink, Apache Sedona, GeoMesa, GeoTrellis, LocationSpark, Magellan, NebulaStream,* and *Gelly Streaming,* which are outlined below.

GeoFlink - its main strength is its ability to process real-time spatial data by leveraging *Apache Flink's streaming architecture* and *grid indexing*, enabling efficient continuous queries like range and kNN [20]. Its critical disadvantage is the lack of support for batch processing and persistent storage, which limits its ability to analyze historical spatial data effectively.

Apache Sedona excels at processing large-scale spatial data efficiently in a distributed environment by leveraging *Apache Spark,* with support for batch operations like spatial joins, range queries, and distance calculations. However, it lacks real-time processing capabilities and support for window temporal queries, as it is specifically designed for batch processing workflows [23].

GeoMesa provides storage and query massive spatio-temporal data [6], by leveraging distributed NoSQL databases like *Apache HBase, Accumulo,* or *Google Bigtable.* Its main disadvantages include high resource requirements and complex deployment, due to its reliance on these distributed NoSQL databases.

GeoTrellis excels in processing raster data efficiently, but it has limited real-time processing capabilities because it is primarily designed for batch processing

[7]. Additionally, it has limited support for vector data, which restricts its applicability for tasks like robot trajectory analysis.

LocationSpark offers good real-time spatial query capabilities using efficient spatial indexing techniques like R-trees and Quadtrees [22]. However, it has high resource requirements, relies on *Apache Spark's* micro-batch processing architecture, and has been outdated for over 8 years, limiting its applicability for modern real-time applications.

Magellan integrats with *Spark*, enabling batch processing of large-scale vector data [8]. However, it lacks real-time processing capabilities and has limited support for advanced spatial operations such as proximity analysis and buffering.

NebulaStream has high capabilities in processing real-time spatial data for IoT applications [9]. However, its immaturity and complexity in deployment make it an unfavorable choice for large-scale distributed projects.

Gelly Streaming has high real-time capabilities for graph data, but it has limited support for spatial operations and spatio-temporal queries, as it was primarily designed for graph-based data processing [5].

Non-Distributed Engines. Regarding non-distributed streaming engines we identified two main solutions, i.e., *Esper* and *Apache Edgent.*

Esper provides complex event processing (CEP) with advanced support for real-time temporal queries and pattern recognition, as well as its lightweight design and simplicity of deployment, operating with minimal dependencies [3]. Unfortunately, it does not inherently support spatial data, requiring additional tools or custom implementations for geo-spatial processing.

Even though *Apache Edgent* is optimized for streaming data processing on IoT edge devices [4], it has been retired since 2019, and it lacks advanced features like complex event processing (CEP) and pattern recognition. As a consequence, its functionality is limited to less sophisticated real-time data processing tasks (Table 1).

Table 1. Comparison of the fundamental features of *GeoFlink, Sedona,* and *GeoMesa*

Feature	GeoFlink	Apache Sedona	GeoMesa
Scalability	High	High	Very High
Real-time capabilities	Very High	Low	Moderate
Spatial support	Moderate	High	Very High
Computational resources	Moderate	Moderate	High

Light-weight Geospatial Databases: in this paper, we needed geospatial processing capabilities at the edge. Due to the resource constraints, traditional database engines would be out of the scope being too heavy, and way beyond the data management at the edge. A vaiable option is thus to use a light-weight in-memory database. Emerging technologies significantly enhance geospatial data management capabilities, particularly for edge computing environments.

DuckDB and *H2GIS* are notable for their lightweight, in-memory architectures that facilitate rapid spatial data processing. DuckDB, known for its embedded OLAP capabilities and spatial extensions, integrates with open-source libraries like GEOS to support complex spatial queries and operations. H2GIS extends the H2 database, providing robust spatial data handling, especially in Java environments [12,19].

Additionally, *Apache GeoParquet*, *Apache Iceberg*, and *Apache IoTDB* offer advanced solutions for managing large-scale spatial datasets across distributed systems. GeoParquet standardizes spatial data storage in an optimized columnar format, while Iceberg facilitates schema evolution and complex data ecosystem management. IoTDB is tailored for time series data in IoT applications, demonstrating significant utility in real-time geospatial processing [1,2,21].

Further alternatives in the landscape, in-process databases such as *Apache Derby*, *Progress OpenEdge*, and *RaimaDB* provide efficient embedded systems with geospatial extensions, suitable for mobile and IoT applications [10,11,16].

7   Conclusion and Future Work

Modern smart farming utilizes autonomous robots and sensors to enable agro-ecological practices. Effective management requires real-time monitoring and control through Data Stream Management Systems (DSMSs). However, the vast volume and potential inaccuracies of robot trajectory data, due to unreliable rural communication networks, pose significant challenges. Existing lightweight DSMSs lack spatial data capabilities, and cloud-fog architectures struggle with poor network conditions. To address this, we propose a hybrid edge-fog architecture and computation framework, building upon our previous work. This framework combines distributed (Geoflink) and extended non-distributed (Esper with spatial operators and dynamic frequency adjustment) DSMSs to efficiently analyze robot trajectory data. A partial computation approach distributes query processing between the edge and fog. Real-world experiments validate the effectiveness of our solution. Our ongoing work concerns the full benchmarking of the proposed solutions. Moreover, we plan to test the usage of different in-memory databases such as DuckDB at the edge level, and benchmark them. Future work is the extension of spatial operators we have implemented in Esper with trajectory operators in order to improve analysis capabilities of our supervision and control system.

Acknowledgements. This work is supported by the French National Research Agency project ANR Ninsar and ANR-24-CHR4-0004-03, French government IDEX-ISITE initiative 16-IDEX-0001 (CAP 20–25) Superob2. Co-author SAKR is partially supported by the EU's Horizon Europe research and innovation programs under Grants No. 101070279 MobiSpaces and No. 101093051 EMERALDS.

References

1. Apache GeoParquet. https://geoparquet.org/. Accessed 21 Mar 2025
2. Apache iceberg. https://iceberg.apache.org. Accessed 21 Mar 2025
3. Complex event processing streaming analytics. https://www.espertech.com/. Accessed Jan 2025
4. Edgent. https://incubator.apache.org/projects/edgent.html. Accessed Jan 2025
5. Gelly streaming. https://github.com/vasia/gelly-streaming. Accessed Jan 2025
6. Geomesa. https://www.geomesa.org/. Accessed Jan 2025
7. Geotrellis. https://geotrellis.io/. Accessed Jan 2025
8. Magellan. https://github.com/harsha2010/magellan. Accessed Jan 2025
9. Nebulastream documentation. https://docs.nebula.stream/. Accessed Jan 2025
10. Progress openedge. https://www.progress.com/openedge. Accessed Mar 2025
11. Raimadb for high-performance embedded databases. https://www.raima.com. Accessed Mar 2025
12. A spatial extension of the h2. http://www.h2gis.org/. Accessed Mar 2025
13. Abdullah, F., Peng, L., Tak, B.: A survey of IoT stream query execution latency optimization within edge and cloud. Wirel. Commun. Mob. Comput. **2021**(1), 4811018 (2021)
14. André, G., et al.: Lambdagriot: a new architecture for agricultural autonomous robots' scheduling: from design to experiments. Cluster Comput. **26**(5), (2023)
15. Bakli, M., Sakr, M., Zimányi, E.: Distributed spatiotemporal trajectory query processing in sql. In: Proceedings of the 28th International Conference on Advances in Geographic Information Systems, pp. 87–98 (2020)
16. Deligiannis, I.: Apache derby: an introduction to security features in an open source database. In: Open Source Systems: Integrating Communities, pp. 158–167. Springer (2016)
17. Dincă, A.-M., Axinte, S.-D., Bacivarov, I.C.: In-memory versus on-disk databases: best practices, use cases and architectural designs. In: 2023 15th International Conference on Electronics, Computers and Artificial Intelligence (ECAI), pp. 1–6. IEEE (2023)
18. Endsley, M.R.: Situation models: an avenue to the modeling of mental models. Proc. Hum. Fact. Ergon. Soc. Ann. Meeting **44**(1), 61–64 (2000)
19. Raasveldt, M., Mühleisen, H.: Duckdb: an embeddable analytical database. In: Proceedings of the 2019 International Conference on Management of Data (2019)
20. Shaikh, S.A., Kitagawa, H., Matono, A., Mariam, K., Kim, K.: Geoflink: an efficient and scalable spatial data stream management system. IEEE Access **10**, (2022)
21. Shuai, X., Wang, J., Zou, J., Tsotras, V.: Apache iotdb: time series database for industrial IoT. In: Proceedings of the 2020 ACM SIGMOD International Conference on Management of Data, ACM (2020)
22. Tang, M., Yu, Y., Mahmood, A.R., Malluhi, Q.M., Ouzzani, M., Aref, W.G.: Locationspark: in-memory distributed spatial query processing and optimization. Front. Big Data **3**, (2020)
23. Yu, J., Wu, J., Sarwat, M.: Geospark: a cluster computing framework for processing large-scale spatial data. In: SIGSPATIAL International Conference on Advances in Geographic Information Systems, ACM (2015)

A Hydrodynamic Model of the Mississippi Sound, USA

Vladimir J. Alarcon[1]([⊠]) [iD], Paul F. Mickle[1], and Ruben A. Alvarado[2]

[1] Northern Gulf Institute, 1021 Balch Blvd.,, Stennis Space Center, Mississippi 39529, USA
{valarcon,pmickle}@ngi.msstate.edu
[2] Universidad Católica de Salta, 4400 Salta, República Argentina
Ruben.a.alvarado@gmail.com

Abstract. In this paper, an initial hydrodynamic model for the Mississippi Sound is presented. The paper presents the conceptualization of the problem, the computational mesh and boundary conditions, results of on-going model calibration, and a computational experiment for estimating Lake Pontchartrain flushing time. In addition, existing observed data on nutrients, salinity, suspended solids, and chlorophyll-a are presented to support the framework on which a future water quality model will be developed.

Keywords: Mississippi Sound · Groundwater · Salinity · Southeast Florida · Karst · Aquifer · MODFLOW

1 Introduction

The largest anthropogenically induced hypoxic area in North American coastal waters forms every summer in the northern Gulf of Mexico requiring load reductions of up to 63% in total nitrogen, and 48% in total phosphorus to reach a hypoxic area of 5000 km^2 [1]. In the Mississippi Sound (Fig. 1), Sankar et al. [2] identified seasonal changes in phosphate and ammonia concentrations. Observed concentrations were higher by 800% during both summers of 2018 and 2019 than in winter of 2018.

Nutrient loadings are clearly linked to anthropogenic nutrient inputs [1] and have strong implications for the health of oyster reefs' habitats in the Mississippi Sound (MS Sound) that support the economy of the State of Mississippi coastal area [2]. A better understanding of nitrogen and phosphorus loading to MS coastal waters, and their circulation through hydrodynamic processes is necessary to support sound management strategies that take into account the hydrological, hydraulic, and biochemical connectivity between estuaries and their watersheds [3].

Moreover, bacterial pollution risks in the Northern Gulf of Mexico are evident. Powers et al. [4] found that one third out of 66 beaches in the area were 'hotspots' of bacterial pollution. Enterococci were correlated with time, urban population size, and sea level, although additional factors influencing enterococci levels stressed the need for targeted studies to pinpoint drivers of fecal pollution. Zhang et al. [5] identified six independent environmental variables, including rainfall, tide, wind, salinity, temperature,

O. Gervasi et al. (Eds.): ICCSA 2025 Workshops, LNCS 15890, pp. 281–294, 2026.
https://doi.org/10.1007/978-3-031-97606-3_19

and weather type, as important to characterize fecal coliform levels at Louisiana beaches. Brewton et al. [6] found that septic system- groundwater- surface water couplings are a crucial factor for coastal waters bacterial contamination along Florida's Gulf Coast.

In addition to the anthropogenic sources of pollution, the Mississippi Sound also receives pollutant loads from the Bonnet Carré Spillway (Louisiana). The Bonnet Carré Spillway (BCS) is a flood control structure operated by the United States Army Corp of Engineers in the Lower Mississippi Valley that allows floodwaters from the Mississippi River to flow into Lake Pontchartrain (Louisiana). The Lake is an estuary connected to the Gulf of Mexico through the Rigolets strait. Over the past few decades, the impacts of BCS openings to adjacent estuaries have been scientifically investigated [7]. Biological response and habitat alteration from spillway outflows have the potential to degrade essential fish habitat as defined by federal law [8].

The Magnuson-Stevens Fishery Conservation and Management Act is the principal law governing marine fisheries in the United States. The Act defines Essential Fish Habitat (EFH) and identifies modeling studies as potential research to support fishery conservation and management [9].

Identifying the sources of pollution and characterizing the circulation of pollutants throughout the Mississippi Sound requires a thorough understanding of hydrodynamic processes throughout the study area (Fig. 1). This research present initial steps in this direction.

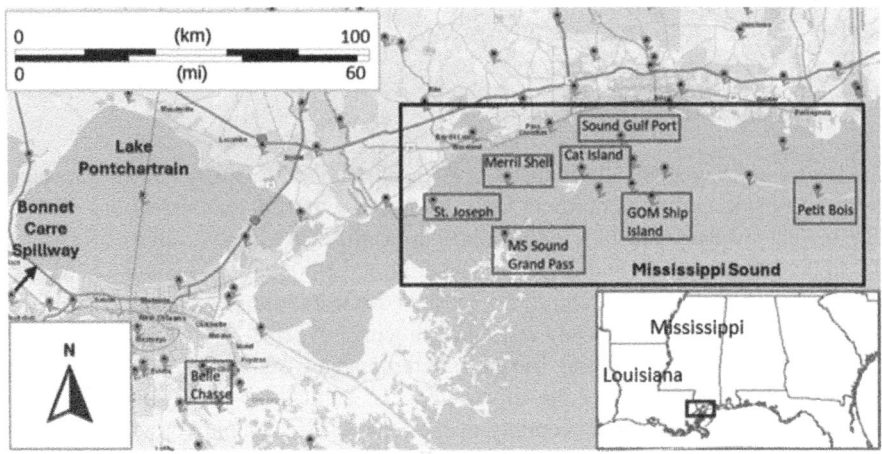

Fig. 1. Study area. The Mississippi Sound, Lake Pontchartrain and the Bonnet Carré Spillway are shown. United States Geological Survey (USGS) water quality stations in the area are shown as red rectangles.

In this paper, a partially calibrated hydrodynamic model for the MS Sound is presented. A comprehensive analysis of observed data including salinity, nutrients, coliform, suspended solids, and chlorophyll-a is performed to determine the spatial reach and boundary conditions of the model. A computational grid is presented, including preliminary hydrodynamic calibration results. The model is used for estimating Lake Pontchartrain flushing times under hypothetical BCS openings.

2 Methods

2.1 Study Area

Figure 1 shows the study area for this research. Lake Pontchartrain (located in Louisiana) at the western border of the figure, and Petit Boise USGS station (located at eastern Mississippi Sound) constitute the geographical limits for the study. Figure 2 shows the predominant land use and land cover in the inland watersheds that drain to the Mississippi Sound. The location of economically important oyster reefs is also shown. As depicted, urban areas along the Mississippi coast are significantly close to the oyster reefs. While densely populated areas are clearly potential sources of pollution, the dense network of rivers and minor streams in the land area may also collect non-point source pollutants from agricultural areas (cultivated crops, pasture/hay) located outside of the urban sprawl.

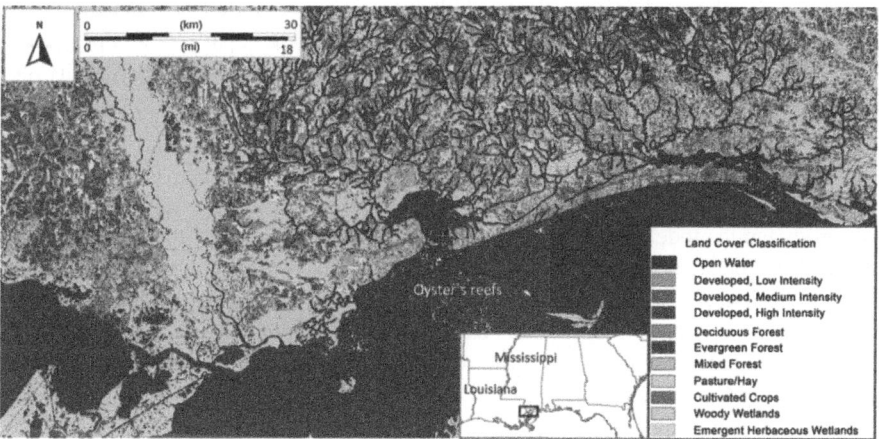

Fig. 2. Land use and land cover in the Mississippi Sound. Land use/land cover in urban areas draining to the MS Sound are shown.

2.2 Observed Water Quality Data

The Mississippi Department of Environmental Quality (MDEQ) and the United States Geological Survey (USGS) perform routine water quality analyses in the Mississippi Sound and Pontchartrain Lake. Nutrients and bacteria are considered indicators of potential water contamination from human and animal waste. Under the MDEQ Mississippi Beach Monitoring Program, water is monthly tested for the presence of fecal bacteria and nutrients. USGS stations collect monthly data although some stations are not operational and provide incomplete records with data gaps of several years or even a decade. The datasets obtained from these organizations are described in the following sections.

MDEQ Data

Monthly observed Total Kjeldahl Nitrogen (TKN), Total Phosphorus (TP), Total Suspended Solids (TSS), and salinity are used in the analysis. Basic statistical indicators were calculated for each of the water quality variables. In particular, we were interested on detecting the effects of the Bonnet Carré Spillway openings on the water quality of the MS Sound. Those openings occurred in years 2016, 2018 and 2019.

USGS Data

Total Kjeldahl Nitrogen (TKN), Total Phosphorus (TP), Total Suspended Solids (TSS), chlorophyll-a (chl-a), salinity (SAL), are analyzed. In this research, due to the very low NO_3 and NO_2 concentrations observed at all water quality stations, TKN observations are treated as surrogates of Total Nitrogen since it includes ammonia as well as organic N. Since the USGS stations collect water quality data sparingly (some stations collect data only a couple of months in the year), descriptive statistics (median, quartiles, minimum and maximum) were calculated using all observed data collected at selected stations. Nevertheless, salinity data for selected USGS stations were used at higher temporal resolution to detect effects of BCS opening on salinity. A comparison was performed for years 2014 (no BCS opening) and 2016 (BCS was opened for 23 days). Salinity data for years 2017 through 2019 were incomplete and a comparison was not possible.

2.3 Hydrodynamic Modeling

A hydrodynamic model that simulates the hydrodynamic and salinity regime for the area encompassed between Bonnet Carré Spillway (BCS) at Lake Pontchartrain and the Petit Bois USGS station (see Fig. 1) has been developed. In this model, freshwater inputs from the BCS, Pass Manchac, Tchefuncte, Pearl, Jourdan, and Wolf Rivers, will be set up as freshwater boundary conditions. Three open ocean boundaries are setup between the Grand Pass USGS St. and Petit Bois USGS Station are implemented to capture salinity and tidal effects throughout the MS Sound and Lake Pontchartrain.

3   Results

3.1   Water Quality at USGS Stations

Figure 3 shows a map that provide a geographical reference to the results shown in this section. Figure 4 shows boxplots for water quality data collected at the USGS stations. Salinity is shown to increase eastwards, while stations that are located close to Lake Pontchartrain (St. Joseph, Merrill Shell, Grand Pas and Cat Island) report salinity values below 25 parts per thousand (PPT), with episodical lows close to 0.0 PPT. These may be related to freshwater being hydrodynamically transported from the lake to those locations during rain events or BCS openings. The decrease in salinity is relevant because concentrations below 5 PPT may have strong implications for the health of key habitats that require higher salinity levels.

This spatial trend is also shown by TSS and turbidity observations. While turbidity at two locations on the Mississippi River (Baton Rouge and Belle Chase) ranges between 20 and 100 NTU, most turbidity values at the MS Sound stations are reported to be below 20 NTU. This seems to suggest that during BCS openings (BCSO), turbid waters from the Mississippi River may be diluted through mixture with less turbid waters from Lake Pontchartrain and/or the ocean, thereby decreasing turbidity at the MS Sound. The dilution effect is also observed in TSS concentrations, which slightly decrease eastwards.

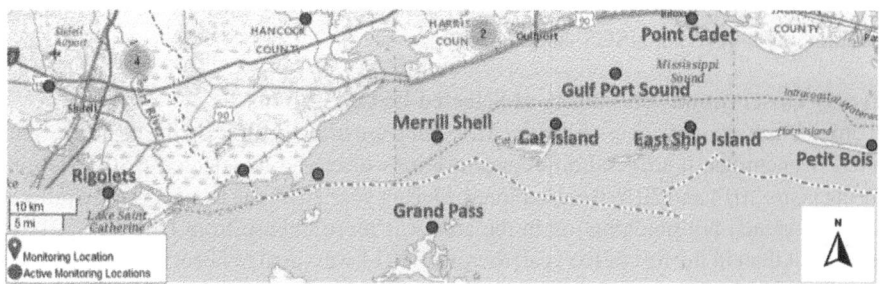

Fig. 3. Reference map for USGS stations results.

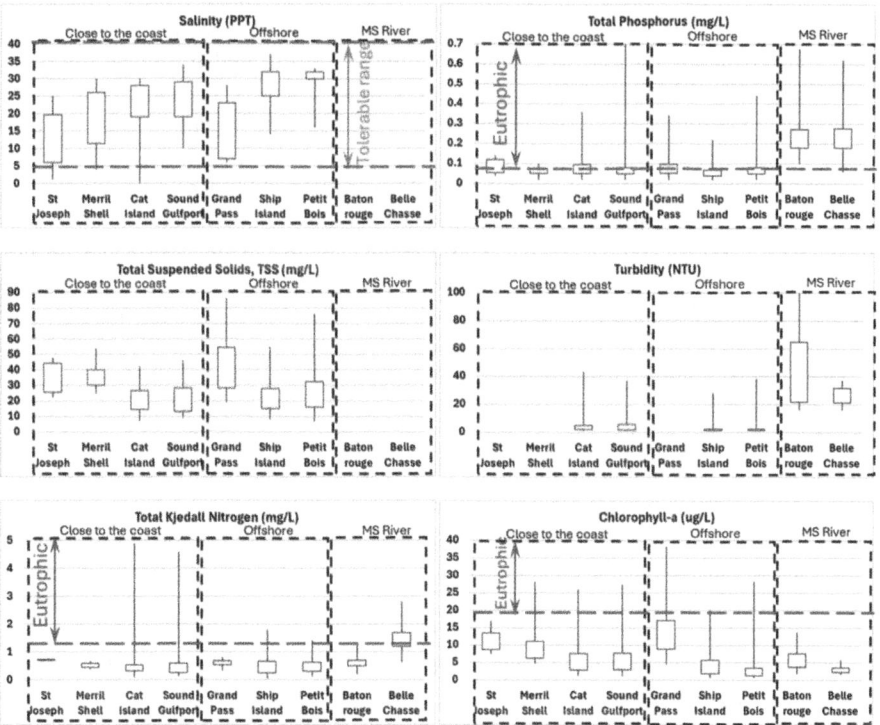

Fig. 4. Salinity and water quality at USG stations.

TKN and TP show a slight eastward decrease in concentrations. Most TKN concentrations are smaller than 2 mg/L which indicates mild eutrophication. The majority of TP concentrations are above 0.04 mg/L in the MS Sound ND above 0.15 mg/L in the Mississippi River, which indicates that eutrophication is a potential risk.

Chlorophyll-a concentrations are also shown to decrease eastwards. The majority of the concentration values are below 20 ug/L indicating that algal biomass is not substantial. Nevertheless, there are chlorophyll-a episodical peaks that are above 20 mg/L indicating that eutrophic conditions were observed in the past.

In general, there seems to be an eastward dilution effect for most of the water quality parameters observed at USGS stations.

Hourly Observations of Salinity at Selected USGS Stations

In order to ascertain if waters from the MS Sound are directly affected during rain events or BCS openings, hourly salinity concentrations observed at selected USGS stations during years 2014 and 2016 were explored. During year 2014, the Bonnet Carré Spillway was not opened but precipitation in the area was more intense from February 2014 to June 2014 than in the rest of the year, therefore 2014 was ideal to observe rainfall effects on salinity in the MS Sound. During 2016, there was a short opening of BCS (22 days during January 2016).

During year 2014 (when no BCSO occur), the sustained rain events that took place from February to June decreased salinity below 5 PPT at the exit of Lake Pontchartrain (Rigolets) during the same period (Fig. 5). At the most eastward station (Point Cadet), salinity also decreases below 5 PPT but from mid-March to mid-June. These stations are located at the MS Sound coast and are primarily affected by runoff from inland watersheds; therefore, it was expected to observe the decrease in salinity due to rainfall alone.

During 2016, the BCS was opened from January 10 to February 1 (22 days). The effect of BCSO on salinity is evident in Rigolets station even though lower than mean precipitation was observed concurrently. A gradual decrease to less than 5 PPT salinity values was observed (Fig. 5). A slight decrease is also observed at Point Cadet station (the most eastward monitoring location) although the salinity variation may also be attributed to the January precipitation events.

Since water quality constituents such as Nitrogen or Phosphorus in the water column react, transform, or are up taken by other biological organisms, it is unlikely that the effects of the short 2014 BCSO on nutrients will reach the Point Cadet station. Nitrogen and Phosphorus related concentrations at coastal locations will most likely depend on contaminants carried by inland runoff or leaked from urban areas.

Stations that are located in mid MS Sound (Merrill Shell and Gulf Port) show a similar trend as the coastal stations (Rigolets and Point Cadet) in year 2014 (Fig. 6). Nevertheless, salinity at Gulf Port station is greater than 7 PPT during the rainy months (February-June) and the rest of the year. Salinity at Merrill Shell station decreases episodically to less than 5 PPT during April and May, probably because this station is located close to Bay Saint Louis (an estuary that receives freshwater from two rivers).

During 2016 (year in which BCSO occur), salinity decreases gradually (at Merrill Shell station) to less than 5PPT during the BCSO (Fig. 6), evidencing the effect of the Bonnet Carré spillway openings. For Gulf Port station, however, salinity is greater than

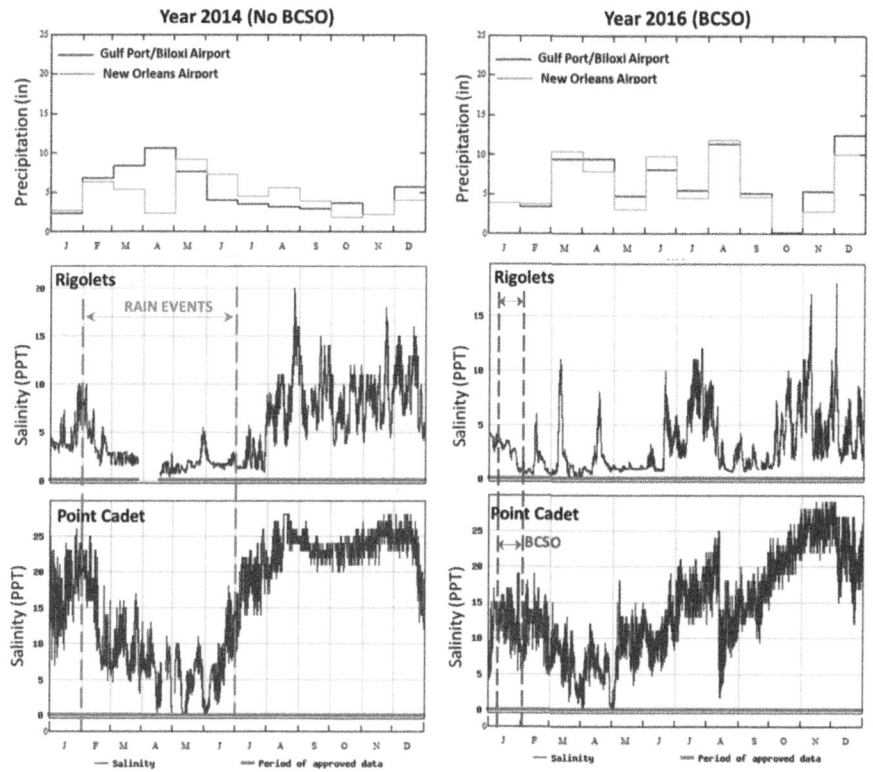

Fig. 5. Hourly salinity at coastal stations: Rigolets and Point Cadet.

10 PPT during all the BCS opening event, showing that the BCSO effects at this location are mild to none. Therefore, from a water quality modeling perspective, at Gulf Port station nitrogenous and phosphorus compounds concentrations in the water column will not likely be affected by short BCSO events such as the 2014's.

At offshore stations (Fig. 7), the effects of either rain events or BCSO are milder than in mid MS Sound or the coast. During 2014, salinity at Grand Pass station is mostly greater than 5 PPT during the rainy months and greater than 18 PPT during the rest of the year. At East Ship Island station, salinity seems to be not affected by rain events since it is shown to be greater than 10 PPT year-round. In January 2016 (month in which BCSO occurred) salinity at Grand Pass station decreases gradually to less than 5 PPT but also increases episodically to 10 PPT after January 20 (mid BCSO). This indicates a moderate effect of the BCSO at this location. At East Ship Island station (Fig. 7), salinities increase during the 2016 BCSO evidencing that the spillway opening does not affect salinities at this location. Therefore, water quality constituents will most likely be not affected by BCSO at locations as far as East Ship Island.

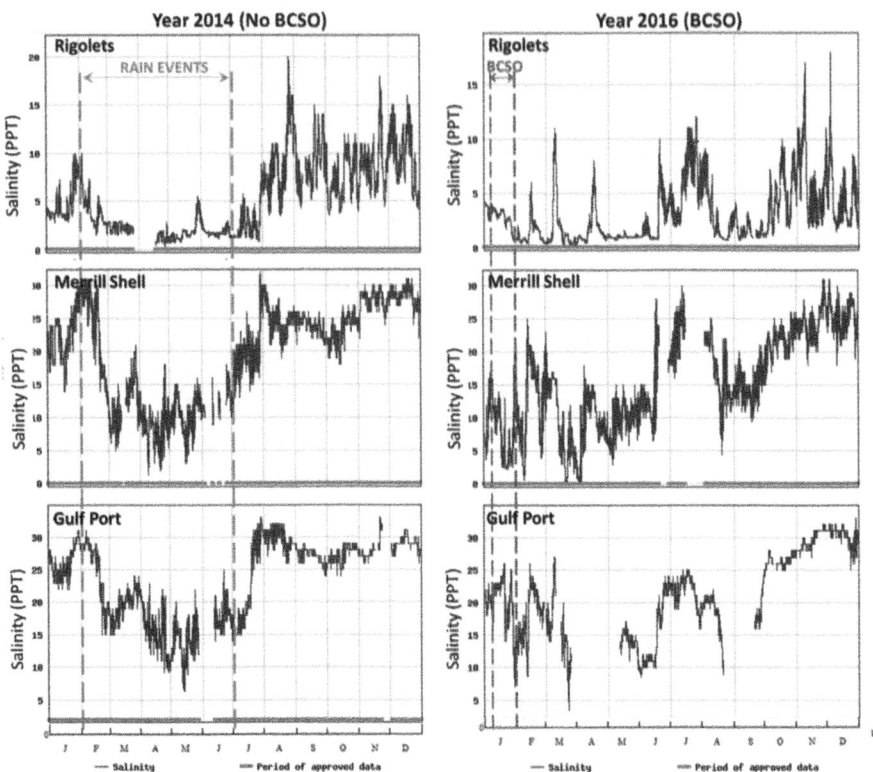

Fig. 6. Hourly salinity at stations close to the coast: Merrill Shell, Gulf Port Sound.

3.2   Water Quality at MDEQ Stations

As explained in previous sections, the MDEQ stations collect salinity and water quality data at a monthly frequency. Those stations are located at the MS Sound coast and are probably strongly affected by coastal surface runoff. Nevertheless, since it was detected that at the Point Cadet USGS coastal (the easternmost USGS station) salinity is decreased during rain events and/or BCSO, analyzing salinity data at MDEQ stations may help to providing bounds to BCSO effects at coastal waters of the MS Sound. Figure 8 shows the locations of selected MDEQ water quality stations which data was analyzed in this research.

Stations 1, 4, 7 and 8 are denominated "eastern stations" in this paper, while stations 11A, 12A, 14 and 20 are denominated "western stations". Western stations are geographically located close to Pontchartrain Lake, the Bonnet Carré Spillway, and the Saint Louis Bay estuary. Eastern stations are located close to Biloxi and Pascagoula rivers.

Figure 9 shows monthly salinity data at eastern and western MDEQ stations. As shown, salinity decreases during BCSO and/or sustained precipitation. The most extended BCSO (that took place in 2019) decreased salinity at western MDEQ stations

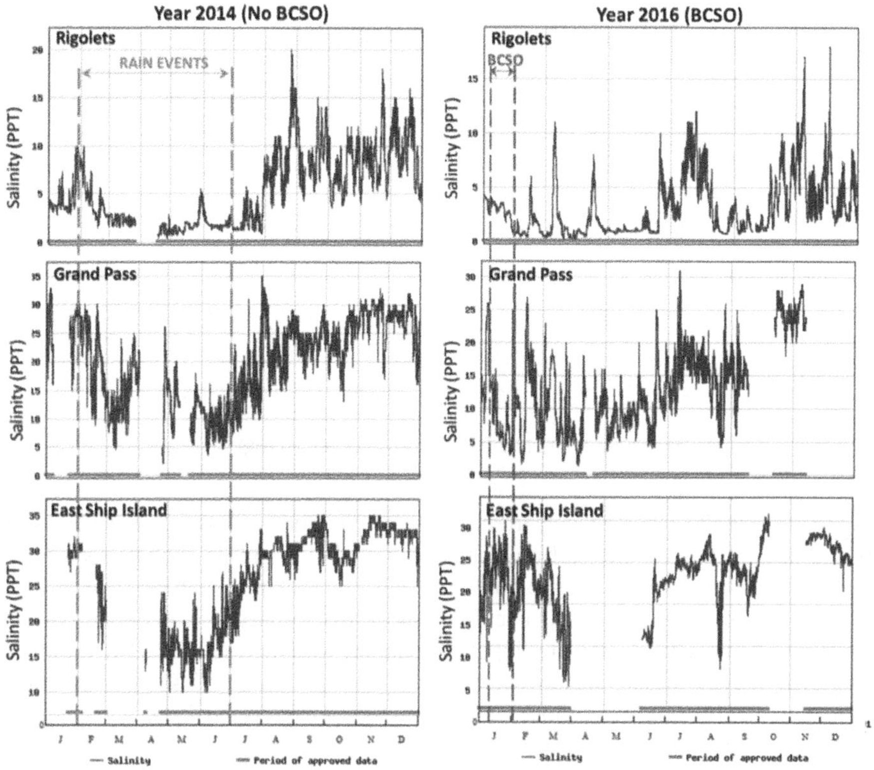

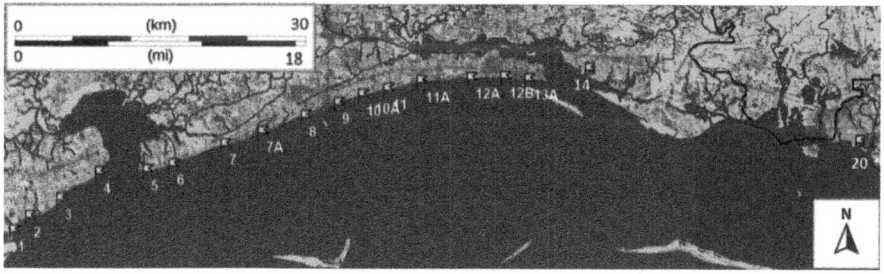

Fig. 7. Hourly salinity at offshore stations: Grand Pass, East Ship Island.

Fig. 8. Reference map for MDEQ stations results.

(MSDB01to MSDB 08) to less than 5 PPT. The 2016 and 2018 also decreased salinity below the 5 PPT threshold but only at western MDEQ stations MSDB01 and MSDB04. These results indicate that the spatial impact of short BCSO in salinity reaches MSDB04, while extended BCSO effects reach MSDB08. Salinity at all western stations is not less than 4.8 PPT.

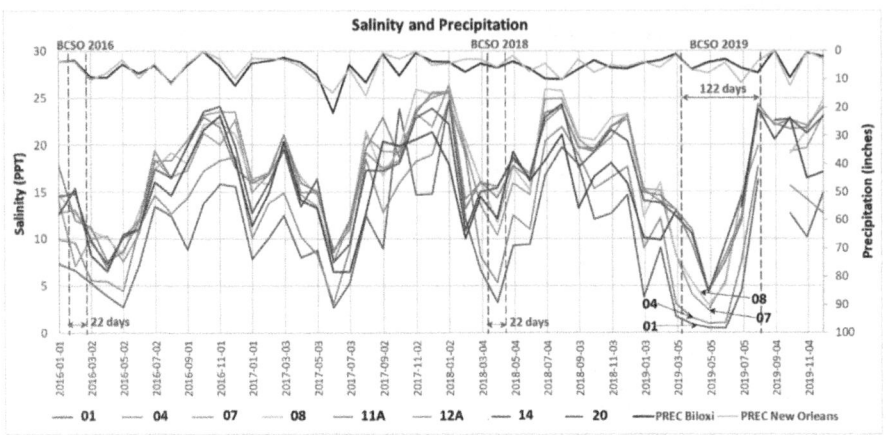

Fig. 9. Salinity and precipitation at selected MDEQ stations.

Since all BCSO occurred concurrently with precipitation events (see Fig. 9), assessing the actual effect of the spillway opening on salinity and its spatial reach is not straightforward. However, the precipitation events that took place during June and July 2017 (a year in which no BCSO occurred) show that salinity may decrease below 5 PPT because of coastal freshwater inputs, at stations MSDB01 and MSDB04. Salinity at western MDEQ stations that are not close to a river is above 7.5 PPT. Since during the longest BCSO salinity at those stations reached 4.8 PPT, therefore maximum the effect of precipitation alone is approximately 2.7 PPT during an extended opening of the Bonnet Carré spillway.

3.3 Computational Grid

Based on the previous discussion the proposed computational grid to simulate hydrodynamics and water quality in the study area is shown in Fig. 10.

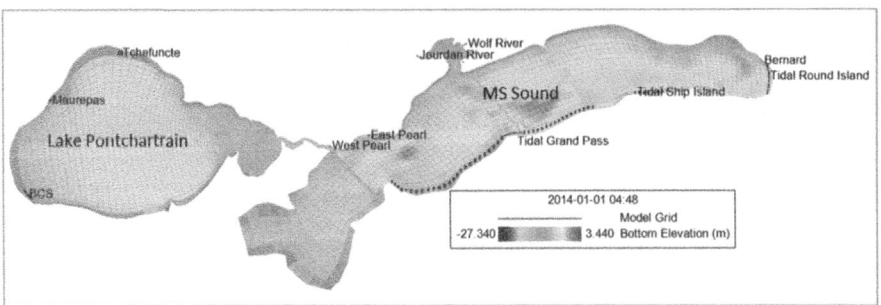

Fig. 10. Computational grid, bathymetry, and boundary conditions.

The model will simulate hydrodynamics covering the area encompassed between Bonnet Carré Spillway (BCS) at Lake Pontchartrain (Fig. 10 left) and the Round Island

USGS station (Fig. 10 right). In this model, freshwater inputs from the BCS, Lake Maurepas' Pass Manchac River, and Tchefuncte River will be set up as freshwater boundary conditions for the grid area representing Lake Pontchartrain.

West Pearl River freshwater boundary drains to the Rigolets (a strait that connects Lake Maurepas to the MS Sound. Fresh water boundaries for the MS Sound, are East Pearl, Jourdan and Wolf rivers. Those freshwater boundaries are setup using observed flow at USGS stations located on the rivers or area-averaged estimates in ungauged watersheds.

Three open ocean boundaries are setup between the Grand Pass USGS St. and Round Island USGS Station. Through these boundaries, salinity and tidal effects throughout the MS Sound and Lake Pontchartrain will be estimated. This modeling approach has been used for similar purposes in the MS Sound area [10–12], and other coastal water bodies in the Southeastern USA [13, 14].

The computational grid and corresponding hydrodynamic model were developed using the EEMS Modeling System (https://eemodelingsystem.com/). The curvilinear grid shown in Fig. 10 consists of 7255 grid cells and covers an area 3943.39 km^2.

3.4 Hydrodynamic Calibration

Hydrodynamic calibration is on-going. Nevertheless, Fig. 11 shows the current status of the calibration process showing simulated versus observed tidal elevations charts. Representative results for three USGS stations are shown: Rigolets (western station), Gulfport Light (central station), and Biloxi Point (eastern station).

The model successfully captures the tidal trend and magnitudes at central locations (Gulfport), captures trends and average magnitudes at western locations, and noticeably overestimates tidal elevations at eastern locations (Biloxi Point).

3.5 Lake Pontchartrain Flushing Time

A computational experiment for estimating Lake Pontchartrain flushing time was performed using the partially calibrated hydrodynamic model. Initial salinity in all the computational domain was setup to 2 PPT. Four Bonnet Carré Spillway openings (BCSO) inflow simulations were implemented in the model. Each simulation mimicked a real 43-day long BCS opening that occurred in year 2019. This spillway was the first of two openings during that year. During the first 2019 opening, gradually increasing flows from the Mississippi River were diverted towards Lake Pontchartrain. The maximum flow was 6031.5 m^3/s. After reaching the maximum, flows were decreased gradually until reaching 0.0 m^3/s. In this research, the historical flow timeseries was multiplied by 1.0, 0.75, 0.5, and 0.25, to explore the effect of flow magnitude in Lake Pontchartrain flushing time and salinity in the MS Sound. Figure 12 shows the scenario simulations.

Figure 13 shows that Lake Pontchartrain flushing time ranges between 24 days (for 100% of maximum flow, 6031.5 m^3/s) and 33 days for 75% of maximum flow. Figure 13 shows that after 43 days of BCSO, the Lake Pontchartrain would not be completely flushed for 50% and 25% of maximum inflow. Salinity at the Bay Saint Louis entrance (MDEQ stations 4 and 5 in Fig. 8) and coastal locations to the east of Bay Saint Louis

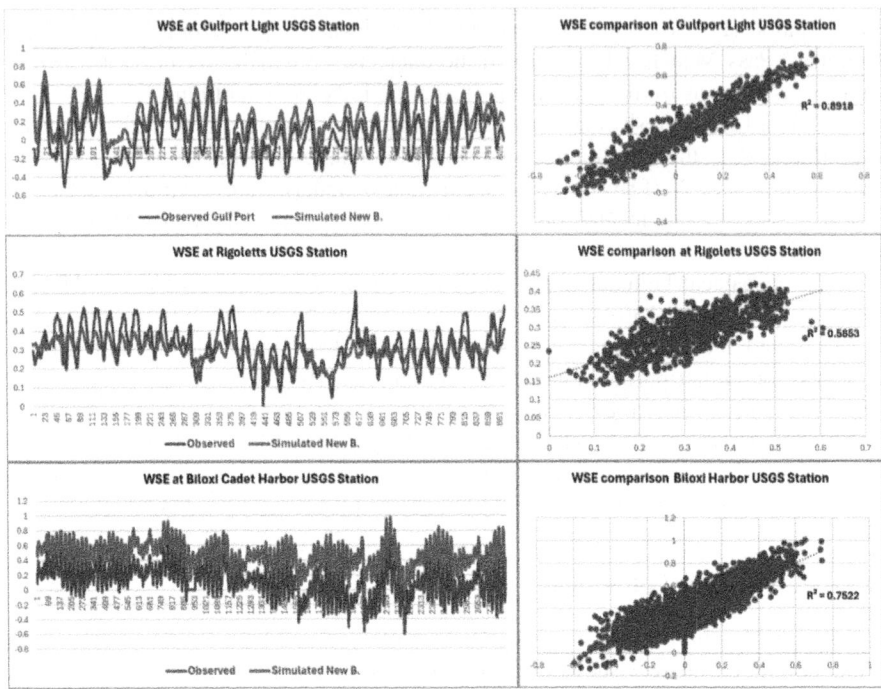

Fig. 11. Hydrodynamic calibration.

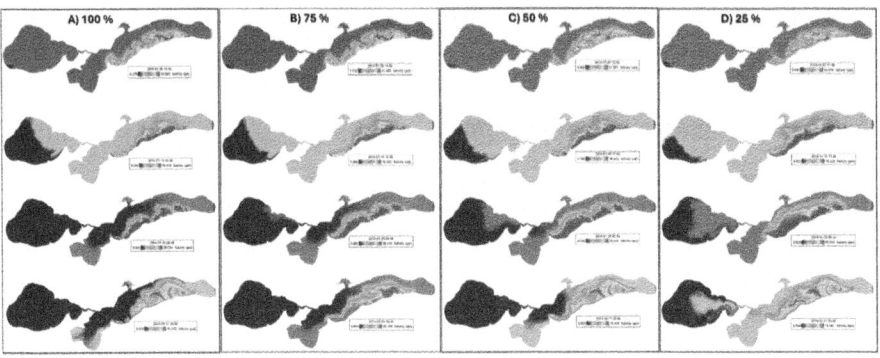

Fig. 12. Lake Pontchartrain flushing time and salinity in the MS Sound. A 2019 Bonnet Carré opening in which gradually increasing flows from the Mississippi River were diverted towards Lake Pontchartrain (maximum flow 6031.5 m^3/s). The historical flow timeseries was multiplied by A) 1.0, B) 0.75, C) 0.5, and D) 0.25, to simulate the effect of flow magnitude in Lake Pontchartrain flushing time and Mississippi Sound salinity.

(MDEQ stations 6 to 14 in Fig. 8) are above 6 PPT for scenarios where Lake Pontchartrain is not completely flushed. On the other hand, for scenarios where the Lake is flushed, salinities are between 1 PPT and 4 PPT. In particular, when BCS flows are not decreased

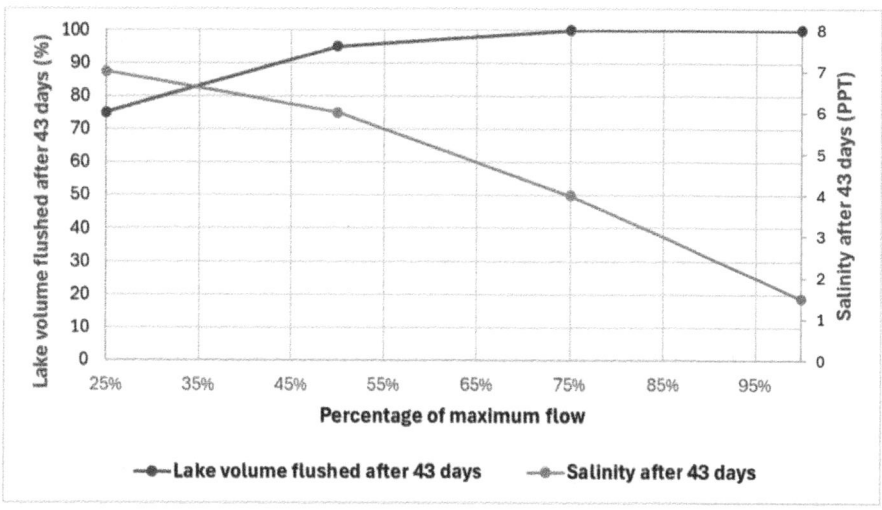

Fig. 13. Flushing time and salinity at MDEQ stations 4 and 5 (Saint Louis Bay entrance).

(Fig. 12 A), simulated salinities at MDEQ station locations 1 to 20 are similar to those observed in 2019 (Fig. 9).

The results shown in Figs. 12 and 13 are significant because they show that MS Sound's extreme decreases in salinity (< 5 PPT) occur after full flush of Lake Pontchartrain. Several biological species depend on salinity ranges above 5 PPT and their survival would be impaired.

4 Conclusions

Observed precipitation, salinity, TKN, TP, suspended solids, chlorophyll-a, and turbidity data collected at USGS and MDEQ monitoring stations in the Mississippi Sound indicate that Bonnet Carré Spillway openings may affect water quality as eastward as Gulf Port (Mississippi), and with lower intensity up to Biloxi. The effects seem to reach as southward as Grand Pass USGS stations and Cat Island (Mississippi). The hydrodynamic model presented in this paper simulates the effects of Bonnet Carré Spillway openings successfully. Also, a preliminary estimation of Lake Pontchartrain flushing times shows that it ranges between 24 days (for maximum flow $= 6031.5$ m^3/s) to 45 days (for maximum flow $= 1507.9$ m^3/s), and consequently, decreases in salinity in the MS Sound after BCSO will occur more slowly for BCSOs that divert smaller flows into Lake Pontchartrain.

Acknowledgements. This research was funded by grant MS GOMESA 2022 MS-363507.

References

1. Fennel, K., Laurent, A.: N and P as ultimate and proximate limiting nutrients in the northern Gulf of Mexico: implications for hypoxia reduction strategies. Biogeosciences **15**(10), 3121–3131 (2018). https://doi.org/10.5194/bg-15-3121-2018
2. Sankar, M.S., Dash, P., Lu, Y.H., Hu, X., Mercer, A.E., Wickramarathna, S., Moorhead, R.J.: Seasonal changes of trace elements, nutrients, dissolved organic matter, and coastal acidification over the largest oyster reef in the western Mississippi sound, USA. Environ. Monit. Assess. **195** (1) (2023). https://doi.org/10.1007/s10661-022-10719-z
3. Camacho, R.A., Martin, J.L., Watson, B., Paul, M.J., Zheng, L., Stribling, J.B.: Modeling the factors controlling phytoplankton in the St. Louis Bay estuary, Mississippi and evaluating estuarine responses to nutrient load modifications. J. Environ. Eng. **141**(3) (2015). https://doi.org/10.1061/(ASCE)EE.1943-7870.0000892
4. Powers, N.C., Pinchback, J., Flores, L., Huang, Y., Wetz, M.S., Turner, J.W.: Long-term water quality analysis reveals correlation between bacterial pollution and sea level rise in the Northwestern Gulf of Mexico. Mar. Pollut. Bull. **166** (2021). https://doi.org/10.1016/j.marpolbul.2021.112231
5. Zhang, Z., Deng, Z., Rusch, K.A.: Modeling Fecal Coliform Bacteria Levels at Gulf Coast Beaches. Water Qual. Expo Health **7**, 255–263 (2015). https://doi.org/10.1007/s12403-014-0145-3
6. Brewton, R.A., Kreiger, et al.: Septic system–groundwater–surface water couplings in waterfront communities contribute to harmful algal blooms in Southwest Florida. Sci. Total Environ. **837**, 155319 (2022). https://doi.org/10.1016/j.scitotenv.2022.155319
7. Beck, R., Xu, M., Zhan, S., et al.: Comparison of satellite reflectance algorithms for estimating turbidity and cyanobacterial concentrations in productive freshwaters using hyperspectral aircraft imagery and dense coincident surface observations. J. Great Lakes Res. **45**(3), 413–433 (2019). https://doi.org/10.1016/j.jglr.2018.09.001
8. Gledhill, et al.: Mass mortality of the Eastern Oyster Crassostrea Virginica in the Western Mississippi sound following unprecedented Mississippi River Flooding in 2019. J. Shellfish Res. (2020). https://doi.org/10.2983/035.039.0205
9. NOAA: Magnuson-Stevens fishery conservation and management act. https://media.fisheries.noaa.gov/dam-migration/msa-amended-2007.pdf
10. Alarcon, V.J., Johnson, D., McAnally, W.H., et al.: Nested hydrodynamic modeling of a coastal river applying dynamic-coupling. Water Resour. Manag. **28**, 3227–3240 (2014). https://doi.org/10.1007/s11269-014-0671-6
11. Alarcon, V.J.: The role of boundary conditions in water quality modeling. Lecture Notes in Computer Science, vol. 8581, pp. 721–733 (2014). https://doi.org/10.1007/978-3-319-09150-1_53
12. Alarcon, V.J., Johnson, D., McAnally, W., van der Zwaag, J., Irby, D., Cartwright, J.: Design and deployment of a dynamic-coupling tool for EFDC. Lect. Notes Comput. Sci. **8581**, 615–624 (2014). https://doi.org/10.1007/978-3-319-09150-1_45
13. Alarcon, V.J., et al.: Coastal inundation under concurrent mean and extreme sea-level rise in Coral Gables. Nat. Hazards **2022**, 1 (2022). https://doi.org/10.1007/s11069-021-05163-0
14. Alarcon, V.J., Linhoss, A., Kelble, C., Mickle, P.: Potential challenges for the restoration of Biscayne Bay (Florida, USA) in the face of climate change effects revealed with predictive models. In: Elsevier (ed.) Ocean Coast. Manag. **247**, 25–33 (2024). https://doi.org/10.1016/j.ocecoaman.2023.106929

Analyzing Zipf's Law: Reflections on Power Law or Sigmoid Distribution

Giampiero Lombardini[1]([✉]) [iD] and Simone Lombardini[2] [iD]

[1] Genoa University, Stradone di Sant'Agostino 37, 16123 Genoa, Italy
giampiero.lombardini@unige.it
[2] Genoa University, Via Vivaldi 5, 16126 Genoa, Italy
simone.lombardini@edu.unige.it

Abstract. The Urban hierarchy has often been explained with Zipf's law, a particular form of the power law where the shape parameter tends to equal 1. There is a large literature on the applicability of Zipf's law to different spatial and historical contexts, which is generally valid but not optimal. In fact, there is a wide debate about whether the mathematical form expressed by Zipf's Law is the best distribution to represent urban hierarchies since this function seems to decline in its ability to represent the "fat tail" of the distribution curve. The objective of this study is to show there is a distribution function potentially better than Zipf that is based on a sigmoid function. This particular function represents the hierarchy between urban centers, even the smallest ones, in a much more accurate way. The use of this function overcomes the problems arising when adopting a Pareto function - which is valid only for the group of major cities - either a log-normal one or a combination of both. The sigmoid function has been applied to a sample of European countries, showing constant application validity.

Keywords: Rank-size Rule · Zipf's Law · Sigmoid · City-Size · Distribution

1 Exploring Rank-Size Distribution of Cities

1.1 Limits of Zipf's Rank-Size Law

The history of Zipf's law dates back to Felix Auerbach [1] who first observed that the Pareto distribution could fit well for cities sizes. This preliminary evidence of Auerbach, received success only later, thanks to George Kingsley [2], to whom the law also owes its name. Zipf postulated the size of cities is inversely proportional to their rank. From that moment, this type of regularity, which is found in many phenomena of different nature, took the name of "rank-size rule" or "power law". This relationship implies that, in a system of cities, the largest one is about twice the size of the second, about three times the size of the third, and so on (when the exponent of the power law is 1). Deviations from Zipf's law are considered as evidence of distortions in urban systems, such as aggregations, segregations and efficiency losses [3].

According to most scholars, one of the limits of Zipf's law is its static nature. The double logarithmic scale graphs illustrating the rank-size relationship represent instant photographs of an urban system at a precise time. However, from a historical perspective, it could be helpful to represent the temporal dynamics of distribution. Most scholars agree that the exponent of the power law tends to remain constant. An urban system, indeed, needs a long time to change its hierarchical structure significantly: in this sense, considering "instant" photos can have a more general value [4, 5].

A second limit is that the Zipf distribution correctly estimates the rank of a city through its population only for the top cities [6]; depending on the country's demographic extension - and thus on the number of cities there, this cut-off can range from 90% to 99.5% of all the other cities. In addition, it is widely demonstrated that the chosen cut-off heavily influences the value of the estimated parameter. Another crucial point is the level of "coherence" that city data must possess to observe Zipf's law. A surprising feature that characterizes "Zipfian" sets is that in general (as observed by [7], subsets or union of Zipfanian sets are no longer Zipfanian. Examples from cities in the US and EU provide strong evidence to support this view. While Zipf's law holds approximately for the size of the cities of each European country (France, Italy, Germany, Spain, etc.), it totally fails in the European Union as a whole. On the other hand, considering all the cities of each state of the Confederation, the distribution of US cities as a whole closely follows Zipf's law (as noted by Krugman, 1996), although the data set of the cities of each state (e.g., California, New York, Illinois, Massachusetts) does not generate a Zipf distribution. These two examples suggest a general property that could be defined as "coherence" or "integration," thus recalling a characteristic of "homogeneity", an expression of a shared history. This means that Zipf's Law must be strongly connected to the evolutionary history of the entire urban system. For Europe, the geographic level consistent with the data is the nation-state when an integrated evolution is observed, whilst in the United States, the entire Confederation represents the consistency, but not each independent state. The American urban system, in fact, has evolved collectively and organically, generating an ordered distribution of cities complying with Zipf's Law.

The scholars who more recently have addressed the question of the validity (and therefore usability) of Zipf's law [1, 3, 8, 9] have highlighted empirical evidence that Zipf's law is not always a good estimation function, even by limiting the study to the most populated cities of a country/region. The contribution of this paper consists in the proposal of a new distribution function which best approximates the urban hierarchy, overcoming the limits of the Zipf's law. Furthermore, in this study we only adopt the functional definition of cities, postponing the discussion for the case of "natural" cities, to further works.

1.2 Zipf's law applied to European Countries

To test Zipf's Law, the study conducts a comparative analysis across territorially coherent European countries, focusing on continental Europe. Data is sourced from Eurostat, covering census years from 1961 to 2021. The dataset includes all data available in the Eurostat database (30 countries), excluding only Cyprus due to missing data. Therefore, we did not select a specific group of countries, but we preferred to include all for the completeness of the analysis. Most countries provide census data at ten-year intervals, starting in 1961 and ending with the most recent census in 2010–2011. Although very small nations like Malta and Luxembourg cannot reliably support Zipf's Law testing due to their limited number of cities, their data is still included for completeness. The limited urban structure in such countries poses statistical challenges for accurate estimations. The study acknowledges that the historical political landscape of Europe-particularly the existence of former unified entities like Austria-Hungary, which included modern states such as Austria, Hungary, Slovakia, and the Czech Republic could have influenced urban development and population distribution. However, these historical factors are noted but not analyzed within the scope of this paper.

The Zip's Law parameters are estimated at different truncations; in Table 1 we also show the standard deviation of residuals, and the arithmetic mean of residuals in absolute value[1]. Each column of Table 1 refers to the estimations with different truncation levels[2].

The countries in the table have been sorted into three groups: the first block concerns the top 5 nations comparable for the high number of cities (>8000); the second group of nations concerns states that are small either territorially or demographically but with a dense network of cities (between 2000 and 6000); the third group concerns small nations with few cities (from around 50 to 1000).

The analysis of Zipf's Law in urban systems reveals several recurring issues, particularly when applied to heterogeneous groups of cities. Previous studies [10] have shown that non-homogeneous distributions are common and can distort results, regardless of how strong the correlation is between observed and expected data. One key problem is the atypical behavior of the largest cities, which often do not conform to Zipf's Law. Another frequent issue arises with medium and small cities, where, beyond a certain population threshold, the distribution abruptly diverges from Zipf's expected trend. In such cases, only the largest urban agglomerations tend to align with Zipf's Law, forming a relatively homogeneous system where the distribution exponent is close to 1.

To address this, many studies apply a cutoff, including only the largest cities and excluding smaller ones, thus focusing on the homogeneous upper tail of the distribution. However, this practice raises questions about the general applicability of Zipf's Law across an entire national urban system. Another limitation lies in the assumption - common in City Size Distribution (CSD) studies - that cities within a given country represent a single coherent system. This disregards historical changes in national borders and administrative structures, which may have shaped city development in fundamentally different ways [11].

A further complication involves the concept of "primacy cities" - extremely dominant capital cities that cannot be statistically grouped with the rest of the urban system. Even in cases where Zipf's Law seems to apply, such outliers violate its core assumptions.

Despite these challenges, the analysis of data from 30 European countries reveals consistent patterns. One key finding is that the fit of Zipf's Law tends to worsen as smaller cities are included in the sample. This supports previous research [12, 13] indicating that Zipf's Law becomes less valid without data truncation. Without a cut-off, regression residuals show strong leftward asymmetry (asymmetry < 0) and high leptokurtosis (kurtosis > 0), meaning that the model systematically overestimates lower-ranked cities

---

[1] The lower the error standard deviation is the better the estimation is. The same holds for the residuals arithmetic mean in absolute value.

[2] All estimation has run through Gretl, an Italian software of econometric estimation.

Table 1. Zip's Law at different thresholds

Country No. Cities	tr-135	tr-500	tr-2000	No-threshold	Av. | Residuals|	Dev.St. Residuals
France (FR) - 36565	−1.4863	−1.4896	−1.2650	0.7125	0.2123	0.3051
R^2	(0.9837)	(0.9937)	(0.9909)	(0.9068)		
Italy (IT) - 8092	−1.3422	−1.4450	−1.3183	−0.6850	0.2758	0.3870
R^2	(0.9857)	(0.9930)	(0.9945)	(0.8494)		
Germany (DE) - 11255	−1.2324	−1.2831	−1.2765	−0.6113	0.2633	0.3755
R^2	(0.9918)	(0.9961)	(0.9978)	(0.8583)		
Spain (ES) - 8116	−1.3100	−1.17363	−0.9490	−0.5104	0.2232	0.3249
R^2	(0.9884)	(0.9936)	(0.9810)	(0.8938)		
U. Kingdom (GB) - 8923	−0.1609	−0.2059	−0.2347	−0.6217	0.2556	0.3244
R^2	(0.9343)	(0.9745)	(0.9755)	(0.7851)		
Austria (AT) - 2357	−1.1406	−1.3811	−1.3020	−1.0219	0.2522	0.3175
R^2	(0.9388)	(0.9684)	(0.9756)	(0.8783)		
Bulgaria (BG) - 4598	−0.9235	−0.9366	−1.0145	−0.5765	0.3168	0.4278
R^2	(0.9910)	(0.9951)	(0.9954)	(0.8153)		
Czech R. (CZ) - 6258	−1.4711	−1.4466	−0.9727	−0.7611	0.1571	0.2487
R^2	(0.9721)	(0.9904)	(0.9465)	(0.9377)		
Denmark (DK) - 2114	−4.6102	−2.2370	−0.7798	−0.7102	0.2769	0.4334
R^2	(0.9732)	(0.8714)	(0.8339)	(0.8090)		
Ireland (IE) - 3402	−2.4623	−1.9895	−1.2232	−0.938374	0.2029	0.3160
R^2	(0.9792)	(0.9775)	(0.9414)	(0.9026)		
Slovakia (SK) - 2926	−1.2101	−1.0598	−1.0599	−0.7832	0.2445	0.3316
R^2	(0.9101)	(0.9706)	(0.9877)	(0.8886)		
Swiss (CH) - 2495	−1.47113	−1.4466	−0.9467	−0.6863	0.2919	0.4088

(*continued*)

Table 1. (*continued*)

Country No. Cities	tr-135	tr-500	tr-2000	No-threshold	Av. | Residuals|	Dev.St. Residuals
R^2	(0.9721)	(0.9904)	(0.9362)	(0.8304)		
Hungary (HU) - 3176	−1.2242	−1.0172	−0.9492	−0.6730	0.2407	0.3365
R^2	(0.9345)	(0.9748)	(0.9872)	(0.8854)		
Poland (PL) - 2479	−1.2704	−1.3322	−1.3053	−1.1954	0.1152	0.1586
R^2	(0.9953)	(0.9971)	(0.9968)	(0.9744)		
Romania (RO) - 3181	−1.0200	−1.1087	−1.3658	−1.1957	0.1845	0.2520
R^2	(0.9719)	(0.9817)	(0.9741)	(0.9357)		

Note: The Average of Residuals in modulus and Standard Deviation are referred to the Residuals of OLS Zip's Law estimation run on the complete dataset of cities

and exhibits extreme variations at the distribution's tails. This challenges the power law's adequacy in modeling city rank versus population size.

Moreover, scatter plots comparing actual city ranks to those predicted by the Zipf model reveal its limitations. Only the top-ranked cities are estimated with reasonable accuracy, while lower-ranked cities are increasingly overestimated. Specifically, beyond the top 20% of cities, the model's accuracy declines sharply. Interestingly, when comparing the logarithm of estimated ranks with observed ranks, it becomes clear that the expected logarithmic trend of city ranks does not align with the mathematical behavior of the Zipf estimate. The log of the estimated rank follows a different pattern - closer to the inverse of a sigmoid function - further emphasizing the model's limitations in representing full urban systems.

2   The Sigmoid Distribution Function

2.1   Zipf and Sigmoid (Sig) Distributions

The sigmoid function is initially characterized by an increasing trend, approximating a Pareto function; after that, however, the para-exponential growth slows down until it stops at an asymptotic value. Zipf's Law is:

$$y_i = A \bullet x_i^{\beta} \tag{1}$$

A sigmoid function is of the type:

$$y_i = \frac{A}{1 + e^{\beta x}} \tag{2}$$

Table 2. Zip's Law at different thresholds

Country No. Cities	tr-135	tr-500	No-threshold	AV. IResidualsI	Dev.St. Residuals
Belgium (BE) - 589	−1.6348	−1.3727	−1.0421	0.2651	0.3780
R^2	(0.9938)	(0.9667)	(0.8508)		
Croatia (HR) - 556	−1.1649	−1.0954	−0.9736	0.1610	0.2338
R^2	(0.9883)	(0.9882)	(0.9428)		
Estonia (EE) - 226	−1.0088	−0.8398	-	0.1648	0.2784
R^2	(0.9981)	(0.9156)	-		
Finland (FI) - 336	−1.0995	−0.7566	-	0.2130	0.3162
R^2	(0.9926)	(0.8933)	-		
Greece (EL) - 1034	−1.4321	−1.1119	−0.6917	0.2808	0.4127
R^2	(0.9601)	(0.9749)	(0.8248)		
Latvia (LV) - 119	−0.9197	-	-	0.1681	0.2304
R^2	(0.9394)	-	-		
Lithuania (LT) - 60	−0.9847	-	-	0.2815	0.3621
R^2	(0.8385)	-	-		
Luxemburg (LU) - 106	−1.0378	-	-	0.1409	0.1736
R^2	(0.9652)	-	-		
Malta (MT) - 68	−0.8366	-	-	0.3327	0.4707
R^2	(0.7313)	-	-		
Netherlands (NL) - 415	−1.5578	−1.0903	-	0.2173	0.3379
R^2	(0.9911)	(0.8793)	-		
Norway (NO) - 429	−1.2497	−0.7976	-	0.2219	0.2972
R^2	(0.9899)	(0.9067)	-		
Portugal (PT) - 309	−1.2176	−0.8029	-	0.2005	0.3120
R^2	(0.9526)	(0.8957)	-		
Slovenia (SI) - 58	0.3783	-	-	0.1109	0.1692

(*continued*)

Table 2. (*continued*)

Country No. Cities	tr-135	tr-500	No-threshold	AV. |Residuals|	Dev.St. Residuals
R^2	(0.9646)	-	-		
Sweden (SE) -290	−1.3342	−0.9853	-	0.1854	0.2603
R^2	(0.9779)	(0.9272)	-		
Turkey (TR) - 957	−0.4616	−0.8532	−1.1885	0.3496	0.4208
R^2	(0.8870)	(0.9083)	(0.8677)		

Note. The Average of Residuals in modulus and Standard Deviation are referred to the Residuals of OLS Zip's Law estimation run on the complete dataset of cities

In a sigmoid function $\beta < 0$; in Zipf's function $\beta > 0$. As x increases in (6), the mathematical function tends to the asymptotic value A, vice versa, in Zipf's law, when x increases, the function grows to infinity. The asymptotic point A in the sigmoid function represents the total number of cities (the city with the highest rank is the last in the ranking in order of population), x is the population while the dependent variable is the rank (for a comparison see: [14]). Rewriting (2) with the aforementioned variables:

$$R_i = \frac{R_{max}}{1 + e^{a+bln(POP_1)}} \qquad (3)$$

From the empirical analysis, it seems that the population depends on the rank according to a function that is actually the inverse of the sigmoid; therefore, to correctly estimate (7), we must solve (7) for POP. Through the application of logarithms in a natural base, we obtain the following linearized function:

$$\ln(POP_i) = \alpha + \beta \ln\left(\frac{R_{max}}{R_i} - 1\right) \qquad (4)$$

where $\alpha = -\frac{a}{b}$ and $\beta = \frac{1}{b}$. Now, we note that by construction[3], the arithmetic mean of $ln\left(\frac{R_{max}}{R} - 1\right) = 0$. If, in general, we use an OLS estimator to estimate the dependent variable y_i with a single regressor ($y_i = \alpha + \beta x_i$), the estimation parameter for "the constant model" is ($\alpha = \bar{y} - \beta\bar{x}$) [15]. Therefore, in this case where $y_i = \ln(POP_i)$ and $x_i = \ln\left(\frac{R_{max}}{R} - 1\right)$, the deduce that $\alpha = \overline{\ln(POP)} - \beta \overline{\ln\left(\frac{R_{max}}{R_i} - 1\right)}$, but, as just recalled, the average of $ln\left(\frac{R_{max}}{R} - 1\right) = 0$, so that:

$$\alpha = \overline{\ln(POP)} \qquad (5)$$

The parameter α is, therefore, depending on the magnitude of the population. More interesting, on the opposite, is the interpretation of β which does not depend on the

---

[3] Firstly, by definition of logarithm we simplify the Eq. (4) as follow: $POP_i = e^{\overline{\ln(POP)}} \cdot \left(\frac{R_{max}-R_i}{R_i}\right)^{\beta}$, $e^{\overline{\ln(POP)}} = e^{\frac{1}{n}(POP_1)+\cdots+\frac{1}{n}\ln(POP_n)} = \sqrt[n]{\prod_{i=1}^{n} POP_i}$. This last finding is the geometric mean of population.

population's size. β is totally independent of the country-size, therefore it can be used to compare different nations. The parameter β expresses the degree of population concentration among the cities of a nation. β varies in a range between $(0; +\infty)$. By construction, in fact, an increasing number (rank) is linked by a decreasing number (the population of the corresponding city); therefore, this inverse relationship forces the parameter b of Eq. (3) to be positive. By this way, a sigmoid curve decreases as the logarithm of the population increases, $b \in (0; +\infty)$. Since $\beta = \frac{1}{b}$ also $\beta \in [0; +\infty)$, varying in the opposite direction to b. If $\beta \to 0$, $\ln(POP_i) = \overline{\ln(POP)}$ $\forall i$. This is the case of a perfect distribution of the population in each city; each urban agglomeration has the same number of inhabitants. Algebraically, this means that the sigmoid of Eq. (3) degenerates into a vertical line with abscissa $\overline{\ln(POP)}$. By difference, the opposite limiting case, i.e. when $\beta \to +\infty$ implies $b \to 0$ and $a \to 0$, i.e., observing Eq. (3), the sigmoid degenerates into a straight line horizontal of height $R_i = R_{max}$, i.e. the rank does not change when the cities population varies. This is the extreme case in which the entire population of a nation is concentrated in a single city, so the rank i cannot change because there is a single city. But there is also another way to interpret parameter β.

Rearranging the Eq. (4) we get:

$$POP_i = \overline{POP_g} \bullet (R_{max} - R_i)^\beta \bullet \left(\frac{1}{R_i}\right)^\beta \qquad (6)$$

We can also rearrange the Zipf in this way:

$$POP_i = A \bullet \left(\frac{1}{R_i}\right)^\beta \qquad (7)$$

Equations (6) and (7) are similar; they have a pre-multiplied constant (POPg and A); and exponent β, the rank of city i in the denominator. However, in the Sigmoid's Law there is the factor $(Rmax - R)^\beta$ that varies according to R; this factor is quite constant for small values of R^4. This means that, for the greatest cities of a country, whose rank is close to 1, the Zip's Law well approximates the Sig's Law. However, when the rank raises (i.e., medium-sized cities), the factor $(Rmax - R)^\beta$ is no more close to its initial value so it reduces significantly the final outcome (POP). This factor corrects the Zip's Law that as already observed overestimates the medium-size and small cities. With this rearrangement, the meaning of β in the Sig's Law is similar to the meaning of β in the Zipf's law. If $\beta = 1$, also for the Sig's Law, the second city is approximately the half of the first one and so on. However when R increases, this rule, that remain valid for Zipf's Law, is no more true for the Sig's Law: the factor $(Rmax - R)^\beta$, indeed, gains importance reducing the city-size faster than in the Zip's law. In this case the factor becomes simply $(Rmax - R)$ since $\beta = 1$. If $\beta < 1$, it means that the city-size of the second city is less than the half of the first one, i.e. there is a less hierarchical distribution of population among cities. Moreover, the city population decreases slower by increasing the rank R since the factor $(Rmax - R)^\beta$ is smaller when β pass from 1 to < 1. Finally, if $\beta > 1$, the opposite is true: there is a distribution more hierarchic than in a power law, for the

---

[4] Image a country like Italy with more than 8000 cities; with small R, 8000-R is however very close to 8000.

biggest cities. Meanwhile, the city population decreases faster by increasing the rank R since the factor $(Rmax - R)^{\beta}$ is higher when β pass from 1 to > 1. To sum up, β provides information not only about the distribution of a country population among its cities, but also the rate at which cities decline as their rank increases.

2.2 The Rank-Size City Distribution: A Logistic Theoretical Interpretation

The variation in the natural landscape may usefully be regarded as random, and that this random variation could produce a sigmoid law. The logistic regression model of estimation for the relationship rank-urban population, has been initially thought looking to the data available (data- driven approach). However, there are significant theoretical reasons to support the hypothesis of a sigmoid distribution for the cities population. We assume two relevant hypotheses widely confirmed by the empirical literature:

Hp 1) the population growth of a city follows a logistic curve[5];

Hp 2) irregularity in resources distribution and in territory (plains, mountains, rivers, lakes, row materials, fertile lands, etc.) follows a Gaussian spatial-distribution.

As for Hp 1), Northam [16] demonstrated the increase in the urbanization level over time exhibits an S-shaped curve that can be formulated as a sigmoid function (also called known as model). For several years, the UN assumed that the urban-rural growth difference of countries follows a logistic path and estimated it based on the experience of numerous countries [17, 18]. According to this hypothesis the population growth for a generic city i would be:

$$POP_{it} = \frac{K_i}{1 + A \bullet e^{-rt}} \tag{8}$$

where POP_{it}, is the population of city i at time t; r is the population growth rate, assumed fixed for simplicity, A is a constant parameter, t is the number of year passed from the starting point and K_i is the carrying capacity of the environment to sustain humankind in a specific area. In any given country, there are a limited number of areas, denoted as K_i, that are potentially suitable for urbanization. Each area, based on its geographic features and natural resources, can support a city or a system of cities with up to K_i inhabitants. Initially, not all of these areas are populated; early settlers tend to choose the most favorable locations, leading to the concentration of populations in select areas. As rural populations grow - driven by technological advancement, social stratification, and wealth accumulation - some of the other potentially urbanized areas may eventually become inhabited. The population growth of cities is generally assumed to follow a logistic pattern under normal conditions. However, external disruptions such as wars, climate shifts, or plagues can halt or reverse growth, sometimes destroying cities entirely. Despite these short-term shocks, the analysis focuses on long-term urban development and distribution, as these exogenous events are ultimately neutralized over time.

As for Hp 2) Geostatistics literature widely employ Gaussian function to model the spatial distribution of natural resources. Geostatistics was born in the 1960s from the

---

[5] Near the upper asymptote threshold of the logistic curve, the population of a city reaches a state of equilibrium which remains stable until technological shocks occur. Also war or environmental (famines and plagues) shocks may shift the population city out of its logistic equilibrium.

need to estimate reserves in mineral deposits [19]. If the continuous spatial phenomenon $\{z(u), u \in A\}$ is generated by the sum of a (not too large) number of independent sources $\{yk(u), u \in A\}$, $k = 1,..., K$, with similar spatial distributions, then its spatial distribution can be modeled by a multivariate Gaussian RF model. Multivariate Gaussian models are highly effective and well-established in spatial analysis, with a strong record of successful applications [20]. In the classical Kriging model, which is widely used for spatial estimation, a normal distribution is assumed. Kriging is a regression technique that interpolates quantities in space by minimizing the mean square error, based on the assumption that similar values are geographically close to each other, as per Tobler's law. Several studies have applied Gaussian and plurigaussian models in resource estimation, including Betzhold and Roth [21], who used plurigaussian simulations for copper deposits in Chile, and Veliz [22], who studied geological uncertainty in copper deposits. Other applications include simulating uranium mineralization [23] and lithological resource evaluation [24]. Sadeghi [25] combined fractal theory and Gaussian simulation for mineral resource classification. Gaussian copulas, used in water resource estimation [26], also account for spatial variability in unsampled locations.

According to Hp 1) and 2), our thesis is that the final population distribution among cities is close to a Sigmoid distribution. The brief demonstration (logic) is the following.

1) At the starting point, in a generic country, there are K area that can be potentially urbanized.
2) Each area has its specific demographic carrying capacity K_i.
3) the carrying capacity Ki depends on natural resources distribution and on territories distribution.
4) Therefore, for Hp 2, the distribution of Ki follows a Gaussian distribution.
5) We start simulation with only 2 inhabitants per each area K.
6) We let cities population grow according to a logistic function, following the Hp 1).
7) The more time passes, the more the population grows unevenly between cities; those with small K tend to stabilize at low values while those with large K grow faster; however, cities stabilize at the same speed.
8) For t tends to infinity the distribution of population among cities reach the carrying capacity, therefore its distribution coincide to the distribution of K_i, i.e. it is Gaussian.
9) By ordering the observations of a Normal random variable from smallest to largest, we obtain the cumulative distribution function.
10) The cumulative distribution function of a Gaussian density function is very close to a logistic function.

In conclusion, the theoretical interpretation of the sigmoid distribution for population among cities is the following: Single cities grow according to a logistic curve that reflects natural demographic dynamics, but each city has its own carrying capacity of inhabitants which depends on external conditions (natural resources and type of territory on which city lies). The logistical distribution of cities therefore reflects the random (Normal) distribution of resources and the random type of environments and territories that exist within the same country.

Human activity can influence the "natural" pathways of territorial development in two key ways.

Technological progress can increase a territory's carrying capacity (K_i) by enhancing productivity, allowing populations to exceed previous limits. However, this doesn't alter the distribution of Ki, as innovations spread evenly across a country or region, benefiting all cities proportionally.

Human activity also affects population concentration within cities. While the fundamental distribution remains unchanged, the degree of urban concentration can shift. Institutions play a role in this by influencing how resources are distributed. For example, unilateral transfers, such as those from natural resource rents, can concentrate wealth in specific regions. Additionally, governmental transfers, like taxes, are often directed to capital cities from border areas, where public services are more concentrated. These persistent transfers lead to ongoing population concentration in a few cities. The spatial allocation of natural resource rents depends on property rights, not just resource distribution [27].

2.3 Comparison Between Zipf's Law and the Sigmoid Function

This section shows the application of the Sigmoid function to the same data previously used to study Zipf's Law. The Eq. (4) is used to estimate the city population, getting the parameters α and β. Together with the parameters in Tables 3 and 4, we report some fundamental statistics that measure the goodness of the estimates: the R^2 index, the arithmetic mean of the absolute value of the residuals and the standard deviation of residuals. By comparing these three variability indices with those found in Tables 1 and 2, it is possible to appreciate the improvement to which the estimation model proposed in this paper leads.

3 A Statistical Comparison Between Zipf's Law and Sig's Law

The equations estimated without truncation, have much lower residuals standard deviations, for all countries, compared to the Zip's law. The comparison between the Zipf's model and the Sigmoid model (from now, for convenience, we call it Sig's Law) can be better appreciated through a quick graphical inspection of the Fig. 1 proposed below. The graphs are a scatter plot between the statistical index R2 referred to as both Zip's Law and Sig's Law estimates. The bisector of the 1st and 3th quadrant is drawn to help the visual inspection of the outcomes; on the abscissas, there is the R2 referred to the Zip's Law; on the ordinate there are the R2 values for the estimates run with Sig's Law. In this way, when a point of the scatter plot (representing a country) lies above the bisector line, it means that the R2 is greater when we use the sigmoid estimate; vice versa, if a point of the scatter plot lies below the bisector Zipf's Law estimates fit better.

Figure 1.A compares the goodness of fit index (R2) for the Zips' Law and the Sig's Law regression without setting any threshold. What graphical inspection suggests is a noticeable overall improvement in estimates when applying Sig's Law. This new estimation method obtains precise estimates ($0.95 < R^2 < 1$) even when no threshold is set. On the opposite the R^2 indices of the Zip's Law are between 0.8–0.9. Almost every country lies above the bisector, and almost all the dots are aligned to the horizontal line

Table 3. Sig's Law at different thresholds

Country & No. Cities	tr-135 β	tr-500 β	tr-2000 β	No-treshold β	Av. |Residuals|	St.Dev. Res
France - 36565	0.6612	0.6646	0.7728	0.7318	0.1255	0.1769
R^2	(0.9837)	(0.9938)	(0.9922)	(0.9825)		
Italy - 8092	0.7309	0.6759	0.7052	0.7389	0.0670	0.1057
R^2	(0.9853)	(0.9927)	(0.9979)	(0.9938)		
Germany - 11255	0.8022	0.7672	0.7452	0.8476	0.1028	0.1257
R^2	(0.9920)	(0.9957)	(0.9984)	(0.9931)		
Spain - 8116	0.7512	0.8332	0.9694	1.0045	0.2395	0.3243
R^2	(0.9886)	(0.9944)	(0.9901)	(0.9692)		
UK - 8923	0.1603	0.2030	0.2216	0.3865	0.0812	0.1202
R^2	(0.9352)	(0.9745)	(0.9837)	(0.9704)		
Austria - 2357	0.8085	0.6582	0.5256	0.5000	0.0500	0.1102
R^2	(0.9356)	(0.9616)	(0.9798)	(0.9853)		
Bulgaria - 4598	1.0647	1.0312	0.8559	0.8836	0.0784	0.1110
R^2	(0.9914)	(0.9938)	(0.9871)	(0.9946)		
Czech R. - 6258	0.6566	0.6704	0.8970	0.6916	0.2177	0.2710
R^2	(0.9714)	(0.9912)	(0.9675)	(0.9543)		
Denmark - 2114	0.2076	0.3692	0.7236	0.6886	0.1862	0.2438
R^2	(0.9756)	(0.8954)	(0.9627)	(0.9623)		
Ireland - 3402	0.4419	0.5048	0.6636	0.5562	0.1502	0.1953
R^2	(0.9871)	(0.9907)	(0.9846)	(0.9636)		
Slovakia - 2926	0.7439	0.8744	0.8395	0.7278	0.0777	0.1414
R^2	(0.9137)	(0.9728)	(0.9843)	(0.9894)		
Swiss - 2495	0.6503	0.6478	0.7414	0.7379	0.0527	0.0744
R^2	(0.9703)	(0.9918)	(0.9954)	(0.9968)		
Hungary - 3176	0.7554	0.9198	0.8395	0.7655	0.0866	0.1138
R^2	(0.9371)	(0.9795)	(0.9928)	(0.9894)		
Poland - 2479	0.7716	0.7061	0.5465	0.4372	0.1489	0,2230
R^2	(0.9952)	(0.9939)	(0.9746)	(0.9259)		
Romania - 3181	0.9423	0.8459	0.5622	0.4286	0.1253	0.2183
R^2	(0.9732)	(0.9772)	(0.9334)	(0.9263)		

(*continued*)

Table 3. (*continued*)

Country & No. Cities	tr-135 β	tr-500 β	tr-2000 β	No-treshold β	Av. IResidualsl	St.Dev. Res
Belgium - 589	0.5666	0.4967	0.4817	0.0404	0.1064	
R^2	(0.9902)	(0.9947)	(0.9849)			
Croatia - 556	0.7872	0.5916	0.5357	0.1342	0.1953	
R^2	(0.9847)	(0.9692)	(0.9599)			
Estonia - 226	0.7821	0.6054	-	0.1631	0.2493	
R^2	(0.9760)	(0.9479)	-			
Finland - 336	0.7946	0.6797	-	0.0985	0.1240	
R^2	(0.9968)	(0.9894)	-			
Greece - 1034	0.6473	0.7558	0.7193	0.0745	0.0936	
R^2	(0.9649)	(0.9885)	(0.9945)			
Latvia - 119	0.5555	-	-	0.1530	0.2378	
R^2	(0.9418)	-	-			
Lithuania - 60	0.4844	-	-	0.1572	0.2162	
R^2	(0.9334)	-	-			
Luxemburg - 106	0.4976	-	-	0.1367	0.2181	
R^2	(0.9386)	-	-			
Malta - 68	0.5417	-	-	0.1277	0.1789	
R^2	(0.9629)	-	-			
Netherlands - 415	0.5747	0.4663	-	0.0753	0.1170	
R^2	(0.9903)	(0.9805)	-			
Norway - 429	0.7191	0.6477	-	0.1137	0.1587	
R^2	(0.9918)	(0.9814)	-			
Portugal - 309	0.6858	0.6353	-	0.1521	0.1910	
R^2	(0.9769)	(0.9719)	-			
Slovenia - 58	0.3783	-	-	0.1525	0.2175	
R^2	(0.8938)	-	-			
Sweden - 290	0.6306	0.5261	-	0.1170	0.1632	
R^2	(0.9878)	(0.9700)	-			
Turkey - 957	0.4463	0.7356	0.6902	0.1602	0.2168	
R^2	(0.8999)	(0.9515)	(0.9705)			

Note. The Average of Residuals in modulus and Standard Deviation are referred to the Residuals of OLS Sig's Law estimation run on the complete dataset of cities close to 1, i.e. Sig's Law improves the estimates, reaching a high level of accuracy. The concrete advantage is that these outcomes without the necessity to insert any threshold.

In Fig. 1.B the R^2 estimates using Zipf's and Sig's Law were compared, applying the threshold to the first 135 cities, as a large part of the literature suggested. In this case, two facts stand out. The first is that both models estimate rank with high accuracy: 0.94 $< R^2 < 1$. The second empirical evidence is that the points of the scatter plot lie with great precision on the bisector line, that is, for very narrow thresholds, the Zipf's Law and the Sig's Law are equivalent. This is also consistent with the model algebra used in this work. In fact, mathematically, the sigmoid function assumes a para-exponential trend before slowing down its growth stabilizing close to its asymptote.

In Fig. 1.C the goodness of fit of both models was compared with a broader threshold, grouping the top 500 cities. Almost all the points of the scatter plot lie above the bisector. Therefore, the situation is similar to Fig. 1.A. Sig's Law replicates the observed trend better than Zip's Law, already slightly expanding the range of cities considered (from 135 to 500). In addition, it was observed that Sig's Law increases the goodness of fit of estimations for all countries up to a value of 0.95 $< R2 < 0.99$ except for one country. The improvement is even more evident from Fig. 1.D, when the threshold bar is raised to the top 2000 cities6. Also in this case the Sigs' Law is associated with goodness of fit indices that are significantly better than the Zip's Law, passing from $R^2 = 0.85$ to $R^2 = 0.98$.

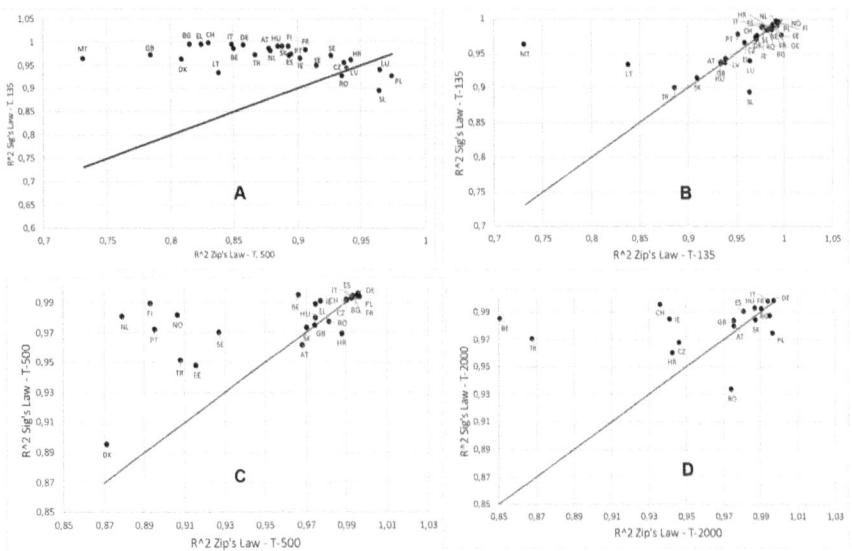

Fig. 1. Scatter Plot Dev.St. Residuals, Zip's Law vs Sig's Law (No Threshold).

Lastly, the researchers show that Sig's Law can also be employed to study how the population concentration among cities has changed over time, in the same country. To this aim, the 4 countries with the most cities according to available Eurostat data, namely Italy, France, Germany and Spain, were considered. The data available refer to the decennial censuses conducted since 1961. The table shows only the value of the parameter β, always estimated through an OLS estimator, using always the Eq. (4).

Table 4. The population distribution among cities over Time 1961–2011 (β)[6]

	Italy	France	Germany	Spain
1961	0.5974 (0.0024)***	0.6225 (0.0013)***	0.8111 (0.0012)***	0.6859 (0.0034)***
1971	0.6411 (0.0025)***	0.6697 (0.0014)***	0.8353 (0.0011)***	0.7810 (0.0033)***
1981	0.6733 (0.0023)***	0.7057 (0.0014)***	0.8545 (0.0013)***	0.8831 (0.0033)***
1991	0.6933 (0.0022)***	0.7243 (0.0013)***	0.8588 (0.0016)***	0.9348 (0.0036)***
2001	0.7196 (0.0020)***	0.7295 (0.0013)***	0.8560 (0.0013)***	0.9536 (0.0042)***
2011	0.7389 (0.0019)***	0.7318 (0.0018)***	0.8672 (0.0014)***	1.0045 (0.0046)***
Observations	8092	36565	11755	8116

Table 4 highlights a steady rise in population inequality among cities, reflecting broader socio-economic changes since the 1960s. Industrialization and increased capital and labor productivity have led to population concentrating in fewer urban centers, where economies of scale are more effectively utilized. France and Italy show similar trends in both the value of the inequality parameter (β) and its evolution over time. In contrast, Germany and Spain demonstrate divergent patterns. Germany had a high level of urban population concentration as early as the 1960s, surpassing the levels that France and Italy would only reach decades later, though its inequality grew slowly over time. Spain, by comparison, began with a more balanced population distribution but experienced a sharp rise in inequality. By 1981, Spain had already surpassed Germany, and by 2011, it had reached one of the highest β values, indicating a significant shift toward urban population concentration.

---

[6] Notes (Table 4):

1. Significance Level: * 10%, ** 5% and ***1%

2. Standard errors in parentheses. Full tables are available from the authors upon request.

3. As for α coefficients, they are not reported for ease of exposition.

4   Conclusion

While Zipf's Law is commonly used to describe the hierarchical structure of urban systems, it fails to accurately represent the full distribution of cities, from the largest to the smallest. Instead, the sigmoid function provides a more precise model. Tested across 30 European countries with diverse urban histories and varying city sizes, the sigmoid function consistently outperformed Zipf's Law in statistical accuracy. This suggests the existence of a deeper, underlying regularity in the development of urban systems. Early city formation likely followed a hierarchical structure based on environmental factors such as climate, terrain, and resource availability. As urban areas expanded over time, they maintained this inherent hierarchy. Beyond this structural consistency, the organization of cities within each country has also been shaped by its unique economic and civil development. Thus, both historical foundations and modern socio-economic trajectories influence how urban systems evolve and distribute populations.

Acknowledgments. This study was funded by University of Genoa.

Disclosure of Interests.   The author has no competing interests to declare that are relevant to the content of this article.

References

1. Rybski, D., Ciccone, A.: Auerbach, Lotka, and Zipf: pioneers of power-law city-size distributions. Archive for History of Exact Sciences (2023)
2. Florence, P.S., Zipf, G.K.: Human behaviour and the principle of least effort. Econ. J. **60**(240) (1950)
3. Arshad, S., Hu, S., Ashraf, B.N.: Zipf's law and city size distribution: a survey of the literature and future research agenda. Physica A **492**, 75–92 (2018)
4. Batty, M.: Inventing Future Cities. The MIT Press, Cambridge (MA) (2018)
5. Mori, T.: Spatial pattern and city size distribution. In: Oxford Research Encyclopedia of Economics and Finance (2020)
6. Eeckhout, J.: Gibrat's law for (all) cities. Am. Econ. Rev. **94**(5) (2004)
7. Cristelli, M., Batty, M., Pietronero, L.: There is more than a power law in Zipf. Sci. Rep. **2**(1), 812 (2012)
8. Modica, M., Reggiani, A., Nijkamp, P.: Methodological advances in Gibrat's and Zipf's laws: a comparative empirical study on the evolution of urban systems. In: Socioeconomic Environmental Policies and Evaluations in Regional Science: Essays in Honor of Yoshiro Higano, pp. 37–59 (2017)
9. Verbavatz, V., Barthelemy, M.: The growth equation of cities. Nature **587**(7834) (2020)
10. Benguigui, L., Blumenfeld-Lieberthal, E.: The end of a paradigm: is Zipf's law universal? J. Geograph. Syst. **13** (1) (2011)
11. Giesen, K., Südekumy, J.: Zipf's law for cities in the regions and the country. J. Econ. Geogr. **11** 4) (2011)
12. Fazio, G., Modica, M.: Pareto or log-normal? Best fit and truncation in the distribution of all cities. J. Region. Sci. **55**(5) (2015)
13. González-Val, R., Lanaspa, L., Sanz-Gracia, F.: New evidence on Gibrat's law for cities. Urban Stud. **51**(1) (2014)

14. González-Val, R., Ramos, A., Sanz-Gracia, F., Vera-Cabello, M.: Size distributions for all cities: which one is best? Papers Region. Sci. **94**(1) (2015)
15. Stock, J.H., Watson, M.W.: Introduction to Econometrics. Pearson (2020)
16. Northam, R.M.: Urban Geography. Wiley, New York (2013)
17. United Nations: World Urbanization Prospects: the 2001 Revision. United Nations, New York (2002)
18. United Nations: World Urbanization Prospects: the 2011 Revision. United Nations, New York (2012)
19. Goovaerts, P.: Geostatistics for Natural Resources Evaluation. Oxford University Press, Oxford (1997)
20. Journel, A.G., Deutsch, C.V.: Rank order geostatistics: a proposal for a unique coding and common processing of diverse data. Geostatistics Wollongong **96**(1) (1997)
21. Betzhold, J., Roth, C.: Characterizing the mineralogical variability of a Chilean copper deposit using plurigaussian simulations. J. South Afr. Inst. Min. Metall. **100**(2), 111–119 (2000)
22. Veliz, V., Maleki, M., Madani, N., Soltani-Mohammadi, S., Mery, N., Emery, X.: Plurigaussian modeling of non-stationary geological domains to assess geological uncertainty in a porphyry copper deposit. Ore Geol. Rev. 105707 (2023)
23. Skvortsova, T., et al.: Simulating the geometry of a granite-hosted uranium orebody. In: Geostatistics Rio 2000: Proceedings of the Geostatistics Sessions of the 31st International Geological Congress, Rio de Janeiro, Brazil, 6–17 August 2000, pp. 85–99. Springer, Netherlands (2002)
24. Ekolle Essoh, F., Emery, X., Meying, A.: Assessing the uncertainty in lithology, grades and recoverable resources in an iron deposit in Southern Cameroon. Nat. Resour. Res. **32**(6), 2515–2540 (2023)
25. Sadeghi, B., Madani, N., Carranza, E.J.M.: Combination of geostatistical simulation and fractal modeling for mineral resource classification. J. Geochem. Explor. **149**(Supplement C), 59–73 (2015)
26. Bárdossy, A.: Copula-based geostatistical models for groundwater quality parameters. Water Resourc. Res. **42**(11) (2006)
27. Dentinho, T.P.: Urban concentration and spatial allocation of rents from natural resources: a Zipf's curve approach. Region **4**(3), 77–86 (2012)

Multicriteria Analysis Based on GIS for the Potential Zoning of Artisanal Tilapia Aquaculture (Oreochromis sp)

Marcelo Fonseca[1] ⓘ, Marcelo Leon[2](✉) ⓘ, David Almeida[3] ⓘ,
Franklin Rodriguez[1,2] ⓘ, and Fabricio Echeverria[4] ⓘ

[1] Universidad Estatal Peninsula de Santa Elena, La Libertad, Ecuador
[2] Universidad ECOTEC, Samborondón, Ecuador
marceloleon11@hotmail.com
[3] Ministerio de la Producción, Quito, Ecuador
[4] Corporación Universitaria de Asturias, Bogotá, Colombia

Abstract. The present research is entitled "MULTICRITERION ANALYSIS BASED ON GIS FOR THE POTENTIAL ZONING OF ARTISANAL TILAPIA AQUACULTURE (Oreochromis eng) IN GUAYAS, ECUADOR" and bases its application on the establishment of a significant potential to improve the productivity and sustainability of tilapia aquaculture by identifying suitable areas within the geographic and environmental factors through the use of the geographic information system (GIS) to represent and overlay the cartographic information. 1) The identification of geographic and environmental factors allowed to identify the best areas for aquaculture. Data were collected and categorized on natural and artificial water sources, temperatures (from 23 °C to 30 °C), altitudes (from 0 to 1,200 m above sea level), slope levels from 0 to 7%, and exclusion zones that included protected areas, anthropogenic zones, and flood zones. 2) Representation of Cartographic Information, this was carried out through the GIS, which provided the elements required to implement a detailed spatial analysis, where the areas were classified as "Suitable", "Moderately Suitable" and "Not Suitable". On the other hand, the zoning criteria were integrated, which allowed the design of individual maps of each of the variables identified in advance, which facilitated the spatial visualization for the development of aquaculture in the province of Guayas. 3) Application of the Cartographic Information Overlay System, in this process multiple layers of geospatial data were combined, considering the suitability criteria for the determination of fish farming areas and performing a presence-absence check to corroborate the identified spatial data, which allowed the categorization and integration of the polygons, facilitating the identification of the most suitable areas (with a range of 0 to 6, where 6 is the most suitable area) for tilapia aquaculture in the province of Guayas. According to the overlay of geographic data, of the 15,338.06 km^2 that make up the province of Guayas, 7,606.64 km^2, or 49.28%, are suitable for tilapia aquaculture. Zones of geographic-environmental suitability and exclusion zones (protected areas, protective forests and vegetation, anthropic zones and flood zones) were established. Finally, the reality that the area presents particular conditions in terms of flood zones where both agricultural and aquaculture activities are carried out is highlighted, and that these must be considered and analyzed, especially within the 4,501.80 km^2 that make up the "Prone" area (river overflow or heavy rainfall).

Keywords: Multicriteria analysis · GIS (Geographic Information System) · Potential zoning · Artisanal aquaculture · Tilapia (Oreochromis sp)

1 Introduction

The Organic Law for the Development of Aquaculture and Fisheries (LODAP, 2020) defines aquaculture as the activity of reproduction, breeding and cultivation of hydro-biological resources in continental areas, inland waters and marine zones. This implies, on the one hand, intervention in the breeding process to improve production, and on the other, individual or business ownership of the cultivated stock. On the other hand, it characterizes aquaculture carried out by individuals, family groups or communities, peoples, nationalities and actors of the popular economy and solidarity, oriented to the consumption familiar for he improvement nutritional and Small-scale trade is considered as: "Artisanal aquaculture", if its production scale generates a volume maximum of six (6) tons of total biomass per year and that don't be greater than three (3) hectares; and "Artisanal subsistence aquaculture" when it is of a family nature for self-consumption and whose maximum production is five hundred (500) kilograms of fish per year and area productive equal either minor to three hundred (300) meters squares (RLODAP, 2022).

The production fish farming of the country is a of the activities with a good profitability that can be exercised throughout the national territory, with easy access especially for the population of the popular and solidarity economy. According to data from the fishing census (2010) at the national level there were about 4.514 producers fish farming, of the which he 97% were cataloged as artisanal producers with the breeding of cachama, trout and tilapia. In base to the data of producers fish farms identified in 2017 show a 15% growth in fish farming activity nationwide (MPCEIP, 2020). By 2022, an estimated 5,022 productive units with 937.45 hectares used are estimated (MPCEIP, 2020).

The aim is for suitable zoning to allow for a more optimal planning of land spaces based on the compatibility and incompatibility with the multiple uses that are carried out on them and the specific cultivation to be carried out for an effective promotion of any productive activity whose purpose is the cultivation or breeding of living organisms. This zoning must be approved by the national authority (LODAP, 2020). Determining a potential distribution through study and analysis is another effective way of determining the areas of interest for specific cultivation of hydrobiological species, which determines a distribution potential, by through the study and analysis of the optimal physical requirements for their growth, which conditions them to various factors, mainly associated with the climate, topographic variations, availability of resources such as water and temperature It constitutes one of the determining factors in the distribution of species (Márquez & Chacón-Moreno, 2021).

Success in aquaculture production depends largely on the correct choice of the site for the project. In order to select the area or land, it is important to have as much information as possible about the area where the facilities will be located. Consider the availability of water, topography of the land, access, hand of local work, basic services (water, electricity, communication) and type of agricultural practices (MAG-Paraguay & FAO, 2011).

Tilapia (*Oreochromis sp*) is a teleost fish, of the Perciforme order belonging to the Cichlidae family, endemic to the African continent. They are poikilothermic organisms of warm waters, with a natural temperature range of between 20 to 30 °C that stop growing if the temperature drops below 15 °C and die if it drops below 10 °C (Martin and Guerrero, 2004; Saavedra, 2006; Cantor, 2007). Rural artisanal fish farming with tilapia is an important activity for food security and the diversification of the economy of the sector, due to the characteristics of the species that make it attractive for this type of farming, such as: rapid growth, closed cycle, good reproduction, easy handling, adaptation to a diversity of foods, resistant to diseases and supports high crop densities (Saavedra, 2006).

1.1 Problem of Investigation

Tilapia production not only contributes significantly to the local economy, but also has a positive impact on rural communities within projects and programs of support to the aquaculture sustainable, this includes the promotion of practices responsible aquaculture, which strengthens the technical capacity of producers and improves the infrastructure and access to markets, which fixed a potential of development of the economy of those involved in this activity.

Considering it indicated, inside of the problem of investigation HE established the need to determine the geographic zoning factors suitable for the establishment of tilapia production pools as a tool for the development of aquaculture (Wicki and Gromenida, 2016).

The objetive: apply a multicriteria analysis based on GIS to determine the suitable areas for rural artisanal aquaculture with tilapia (*Oreochromis sp*) in the province of Guayas, Ecuador

Identify the geographic and environmental factors of potential areas for tilapia aquaculture

Representing cartographic information to establish spatial distribution for tilapia aquaculture

Apply a cartographic information overlay system to determine areas suitable for tilapia aquaculture

2 Methodology

The methodology for the determination of suitable areas for the aquaculture rural artisan with tilapia In the province of Guayas, it allowed to establish the geographic-environmental characteristics linked to the administrative division of the province. In addition, with the aim of spatially representing the official cartographic information, and subsequently achieving the determination of zoning, through a multivariate superposition system of the characteristics main for the development of the aquaculture (suitable, moderately suitable, unsuitable), compared with a presence-absence study (if they intercept, do not intercept) within a geographic region (concepto, 2024).

2.1   Research Design in Function of the Goals

The line of the investigation HE I structure in base to the categorization, he guy and he level investigative, that is, each factor (element - variable) was operationalized according to each level of aptitude, or presence - absence relationship(Fonseca et al., 2015).

Inside of the categorization the multicriteria research based on GIS, was structured in base to the items of area and aspect field, like this:

Field: Rural Geography **Area:** Planning territorial **Aspect:** Aquaculture

The type of research was structured using quantitative methods, in this way the measurements and coordinates were ensured, resulting in precision and objectivity in the results. Within the georeferenced modeling, HE employment he software of geoprocessing ArcGIS for to identify coordinates, patterns and correlations between geographical elements and environmental factors for tilapia production. The level of research proposed was exploratory, descriptive, relational (multivariate) because HE focused in characterize the factors geographic and environmental that influence the production of tilapia as the coordinates, the sources water and restrictions that each element had to meet to understand the relationships between these factors and determine the polygons (X, Y) of the suitable areas (Cantor, 2007).

Finally, the investigation fulfills a level of application, by how much he deliverable end is a tool of planning territorial, is say, a system which was programmed on the territorial layers (overlay of cartographic information) of each incorporated variable (Espinoza, 2001).

2.2   In Function of the Requirements and Factors

According to the requirements cartographic, HE analyzed the characteristics fit physical and their ranges for each established element (Water source, Temperature, Altitude, Slope, Exclusion zones) for the development of aquaculture with tilapia (*Oreochromis sp*) described by the Food and Agriculture Organization of the United Nations, as well as tilapia breeding manuals (MAG-Paraguay & FAO, 2011). With these ranges, the cartographic areas suitable for the location of ponds for aquaculture were defined. The elements analyzed were:

2.2.1   Factors

To determine the areas suitable for artisanal rural tilapia aquaculture, multiple geographic zoning variables were considered. (Garza-Martínez et al., 2021). According to management manuals for tilapia farming, the main geographic and environmental conditions to be analyzed were determined: water sources, temperature, altitude and slope. for their cartographic representation, suitability ranges were determined, categorizing them into: suitable, Moderately Suitable and not Suitable, assigning them a color in traffic light format

Geographically and administratively, there are areas where it is not possible to carry out productive activities such as fish farming, either because they are natural conservation areas, they are risk areas or they already have other anthropogenic activities incompatible with rural artisanal aquaculture with tilapia. These areas were determined as Exclusion Zones and are made up of: natural System of Protected Areas SNAP, Forests and Protective Vegetation BVP, Anthropic Zones and Flood Zones.

In this way, the zoning for rural artisanal fish farming with tilapia was established in the province of Guayas, geographically detailing the areas of suitability and the exclusion zones, according to the following table (**Error! Reference Source not Found.**).

Factors Geographic - Environmental

Water Sources: Regarding water sources, both the origin and type of source were assessed. Suitable natural rivers and estuaries were located, providing a favorable environment due to their constant flow and natural conditions (Ramírez et al., 2019). Artificial canals were also considered, offering control over water supply, although additional caution is needed to maintain water quality and minimize environmental risks.

Temperature: This parameter is considered essential for aquaculture, its variations are linked to the types of fish that develop according to their temperature and altitude, such as cold water fish, temperate water fish and warm water fish. Its ranges will determine the optimal conditions for the effective breeding of tilapia (Cantor, 2007). The country does not have maps with territorial temperature ranges, so it was taken as a reference for the temperature environmental, related to the temperature of the water (AUNAP & FAO, 2013).

Altitude: Altitude is a geographical factor that limits the distribution of aquaculture in general, not because of the pressure changes that may occur but because of its relationship with the ambient temperature, therefore, the water temperature. Altitudes between 0 and 1,200 m above sea level were identified as suitable, providing stable and favorable climatic conditions for aquaculture production (Cantor, 2007).

This relationship between ambient temperature and altitude is represented in Table 1, where the water temperature is referenced for the analysis in zoning.

Table 1. Altitude relationship with ambient temperature.

FISH	HEIGHT	TEMPERATURE
Cold waters	2000 to 3000	8 to 18 °C
Temperate waters	1200 to 2000	18 to 22 °C
Warm waters	0 to 1200	22 to 30 °C

Fountain: (Cantor, 2007).

Earring: The inclination of the floor is important already that facilitates either makes difficult the functionality of the ponds and has a direct relationship with the construction costs. If possible, completely flat land should also be avoided, (Martin and Guerrero, 2004) since a slight slope facilitates the management of the water flow with the action of gravity. It was classified between the following ranges: 26–99%, 8–25%, 0–7% (AUNAP & FAO, 2013).

Table 2. Cartographic information

Factors	Classification / Rank	Categories	
Water source	Origin (FH)	Rivers	
		Estuary	
		Channel	
		Ravine	
	Type (FH)	Artificial	
		Natural	
Temperature	23 - 30 ^{0}C	Suitable	
	18 - 22 ^{0}C	Moderately suitable	
	8 - 17 ^{0}C	Unfit	
Altitude	0 to 1,200 meters above sea level	Suitable	
	1,201 to 2,000 meters above sea level	Moderately suitable	
	2,001 to 3,000 meters above sea level	Unfit	
Earring	0 – 7 %	Suitable	
	8 – 25 %	Moderately suitable	
	26 - 99 %	Unfit	
Exclusion zones	Protected areas	SNAP Areas	
		BVP Areas	
	Anthropic zone	Populated areas	
		Areas with infrastructure	
	Flood zones	Permanent (Mangroves and swamps)	
		Storms (rainy seasons)	
		Prone (river overflows or heavy rainfall)	

Exclusion Areas: Finally, exclusion areas were delimited, such as protected areas of the National System of Protected Areas (SNAP) and protective forests and vegetation (BVP), as well as anthropogenic zones with populations and structures, which are not suitable for aquaculture due to human interference and the need for environmental conservation (suia.ambiente, 2024). Flood zones, both permanent (such as mangroves and swamps) and temporary and prone to overflow, were also identified as unsuitable due to the risks associated with abrupt changes in water level.

Area of Those Involved. For carry to cape the activities of investigation HE considered to the project emblematic: Improving the Competitiveness of the Aquaculture and Fisheries Sector, from the Ministry of Production, Foreign Trade, Investments and Fishing, approved by Agreement No. MPCEIP-DMPCEIP-2020–0029 and developed between 2019 and 2022. Where, its main objective was to increase the competitiveness

Table 3. Official sources of the Shapes

Factors			Fountain
Water source	Origin (FH)		IGM
	Type (FH)		IGM
Temperature			SEMPLADES
Altitude			RASTER-INV
Earring			RASTER-INV
Exclusion zones	Protected areas	SNAP Areas	MAATE-SUIA
		BVP Areas	MAATE-SUIA
	Anthropic zone	Populated areas	MAATE-SUIA
		Areas with infrastructure	MAATE-SUIA
	Flood zones	Permanent (Mangroves and swamps)	IGM
		Storms (Rainy seasons)	IGM
		Prone (River overflows or heavy rainfall)	IGM

Table 4. Water Sources

Variable	Perennial/permanent	Non-perennial/intermittent/fluctuating	Dry
Water Sources	11,474.51 km (78.76%)	2,867.74 km (19.68%)	226.47 km (1.55%)

Table 5. Temperature

Variable	Suitable 23–30 °C	Moderately suitable 18–22 °C	Unfit <17–>31 °C
Temperature	15,207.52km^2 (99.15%)	122.50 km^2 (0.85%)	8.03 km^2 (0.05%)

Table 6. Altitude

Variable	Suitable 0–1,200 masl	Moderately suitable 1,201–2,000	Unfit >2.001
Altitude	15,184.73 km^2 (99.00%)	134.93 km^2 (0.88%)	18.40 km^2 (0.12%)

Table 7. Slopes

Variable	Suitable 0–7%	Moderately suitable 8–25%	Unfit 26/99%
Earring	15,001.75 km^2 (97.81%)	325.02 km^2 (2.12%)	11.29 km^2 (0.07%)

Table 8. Protected Areas

Variable	Exclusion area	Suitable area
SNAP - BVP	1,048.06 Km^2 (6.83%)	14,290.00 Km^2 (93.17%)

Table 9. Anthropic Zones

Variable	Exclusion area	Suitable area
Anthropic zones	1,864.66 km^2 (12.16%)	13,473.00 Km^2 (87.84%)

Table 10. Flood Zones

Variable	Exclusion area	Suitable area
Flood zones	6,413.50 km^2 (45.59%)	8,345.27 km^2 (54.41%)

Table 11. Zoning (Temperature, altitude and slope)

Assessment	Area Km^2
6	14,327.72
5	259.28
4	251.96
3	58.76
2	424.98
1	14.30
0	1.06
Total	15,338.06

of the national and export aquaculture and fishing sector of Ecuador through promotion, regulation, control and monitoring, where, as component 2, it established: promote

Table 12. Overlap Area Presence Absence (Exclusion Zones)

Variable	Exclusion area	Suitable area
Exclusion zones	7,829.66 km^2 (51.05%)	7,508.06 km^2 (48.95%)

Table 13. Overlap Zone - Area Presence Absence

Assessment	Area Km^2
6	7,134.92
5	150.25
4	220.92
3	41.45
2	52.42
1	6.29
0	0.39
Total	7,606.64

the productivity and competitiveness of the aquaculture and fishing sector (production. 2023).

The Undersecretariat of Aquaculture is the in charge of the promotion aquaculture in the country, benefiting to fish farmers framed in the economy popular and solidarity, of the which annually are About 2,000 fish farmers nationwide receive training and assistance services technique in topics of aquaculture. Through the project HE look for increase in 40% the production average annual for attend it required by the sector fish farmer that HE supplies fry (trout, tilapia, cachama) through the supply and sale processes.

Finally, the project of investment Strengthening Comprehensive and Sustainable of the Sector Aquaculture and Fishing, is a project of the Ministry of Production, Trade Abroad, Investments and Fishing, approved through Agreement No. MPCEIP-MPCEIP-2022-0037-A projected for his execution in the period 2023 to 2025. Its main objective is to promote the development of aquaculture and fishing activities in all their production phases, for achieve the sustainability of the sector and guarantee access to new markets.

From the geographical location, the fish farmers related to the project were considered of the Ministry of Production, Trade Abroad, Investments and Fishing framed, with a record of 56 representatives of families and an association that are recorded within the cantons of the province and that have received, according to the capacity of their pools, a quantity of fry as part of the project of production (MPCEIP, 2020). Saying record allowed identify the coordinates of georeferencing and others information, the same that allowed provide of a Updated data matrix on the 57 locations between swimming pools in the province of Guayas.

P = 57 locations (X, AND).

Geographical Area. From a spatial perspective, the province of Guayas was considered with its geographical and environmental characteristics and its already established aquaculture activity, for this reason the province presents a favorable scenario for the development of artisanal rural production of tilapia (*Oreochromis sp*). Availability of water sweet, is presented as the "sine qua non" condition that enhances the success of this activity in the region (Maestu, 2015).

He climate of the province of the Guayas is tropical monsoonal (bioweb, 2024), with a temperature average annual average of 25 °C. The average annual rainfall is 1,000 mm, concentrated mainly in the months of winter (January to April). The relief of the province of the Guayas is varied, with mountainous areas in the east, hills in the centre and plains in the west. The mountainous area corresponds to the Western Cordillera of the Andes, while the plains form part of the lower basin of the Guayas River.

The province of the Guayas account with a extensive hydrographic network, composed by rivers, estuaries and channels. The main rivers are he Guayas, Daule, Babahoyo and Vinces. Account with several important estuaries, in addition to a fundamental hydrographic network for the development of aquaculture activities, including tilapia production.

The soils of the province of Guayas are mostly sandy loam or clay loam, with good permeability and drainage. The clay loam soils are suitable for tilapia farming, provided they are properly managed to prevent erosion and salinization.

2.3 Data Collection Instruments

Geographic Information Systems (GIS): Using GIS software (such as ArcGIS or QGIS) to map and analyze geospatial data (aeroterra, 2024).

Geospatial Database: For the creation and management of a database containing all relevant variables to complement and verify the information collected.

Site Suitability Analysis: To carry out the evaluation of potential areas by weighing the geographic and environmental factors of the polygons related to the suitable areas. Finally, the data analysis process was carried out to effectively identify and evaluate the zoning for tilapia aquaculture in the province of Guayas, providing a cartographic basis for the identification of the coordinates of the suitable areas by means of:

1. Data collection
2. Data preparation
3. Exploratory data analysis
4. Spatial distribution analysis
5. Overlay system
6. Verification of polygons

3 Results

3.1 Identification of Geographical and Environmental Factors

The identification of geographic and environmental factors represented a crucial stage in determining the zoning for rural artisanal tilapia aquaculture in the province of Guayas. The geographic distribution of these factors (water source, temperature, altitude, slope, exclusion areas), related to the geography of the province of Guayas, is essential to establish, after its multivariate analysis, the suitable, moderately suitable and unsuitable areas for the promotion of rural artisanal aquaculture in Guayas (FAO, 2013).

3.2 Representation of Cartographic Information

The cartographic representation facilitated the prior visualization of the spatial distribution for the sustainable development of aquaculture in the province of Guayas (Dias & Oliveira, 2022).

3.2.1 Areas

Water Sources The water source conditions in the province of Guayas are favorable for rural artisanal aquaculture of tilapia (*Oreochromis sp*) due to the availability of various natural and artificial water sources. The province has artificial canals that provide a controlled and constant water supply, which is ideal for the efficient management of aquaculture. In addition, there are natural estuaries and rivers that enrich the aquatic environment, offering quality water. These natural water sources are essential for sustainability and food productivity (CELAC, 2023), as they provide a water supply for tilapia farming in pools.

Water sources were grouped into three categories: perennial/permanent, non-perennial/intermittent/fluctuating, and dry. The majority of water sources, totaling 11,474.51 km (78.76%), are perennial or permanent, indicating a constant availability of water in these areas. A total of 2,867.74 km (19.68%) are non-perennial, intermittent, or fluctuating, indicating that these water sources are not available throughout the year and may vary depending on the season or weather conditions. Finally, a total of 226.47 km (1.55%) correspond to dry sources, where, for a large part of the year, water is not available.

Temperature The province of Guayas has temperature conditions mostly suitable for rural artisanal aquaculture of tilapia (*Oreochromis sp*), with 99.15% of its surface (15,207.52 km^2) within the optimal range of 23–30 °C. This wide extension ensures a favorable environment for tilapia productivity, since these temperatures promote efficient growth and development of the fish. However, a small percentage of the province, specifically 0.85% (122.50 km^2), is within the moderately suitable temperature range (18–22 °C), which could imply certain limitations in productivity without being completely unfavorable. Only a tiny fraction, 0.05% (8.03 km^2), has unsuitable temperatures (<17 °C–>31 °C), suggesting a minimal risk of unsuitable areas for tilapia farming in this region. It is highlighted that the province of Guayas offers highly favorable thermal conditions for tilapia aquaculture, which positions it as a strategic area to promote its productivity.

Altitude The province of Guayas has altitude conditions predominantly suitable for rural artisanal aquaculture of tilapia (*Oreochromis sp*), with 99.00% of its surface (15,184.73 km²) located between 0 and 1,200 m above sea level, a range considered suitable for the development of this activity. These altitudes favor tilapia farming due to the stable and adequate environmental conditions for its growth. A small percentage of the province, 0.88% (134.93 km²), is located at moderately suitable altitudes (1,201–2,000 m above sea level), which may present certain restrictions, but is still viable for aquaculture with adequate management. Finally, only 0.12% (18.40 km²) of the province is at altitudes above 2,001 m above sea level, considered unsuitable for tilapia farming due to extreme conditions that can negatively affect its development. It is noteworthy that the province of Guayas has highly favorable altitudinal conditions for tilapia aquaculture, which contributes significantly to its productive potential in the region.

Pending The province of Guayas shows slope conditions mostly suitable for rural artisanal aquaculture of tilapia (*Oreochromis sp*), with 97.81% of its surface (15,001.75 km²) having slopes between 0 and 7%, an optimal range for this activity due to the ease of management and construction of ponds, as well as the minimization of erosion and sedimentation risks. 2.12% of the province (325.02 km²) has moderately suitable slopes (8–25%), where, although aquaculture is possible, more careful management is required to prevent stability and erosion problems. Finally, only 0.07% (11.29 km²) has unsuitable slopes (26–99%), which make aquaculture impossible due to the difficulty of building and maintaining adequate infrastructure. It is noteworthy that the province of Guayas has highly favorable slope conditions for tilapia aquaculture, consolidating its productive potential in the region.

3.2.2 Exclusion Zones

Protected Areas Only 6.83% of the area (1,048.06 km²) is designated as exclusion zones, which include the National System of Protected Areas (SNAP) and protective forests and vegetation (BVP). The province of Guayas has a vast majority of its territory suitable for rural artisanal aquaculture of tilapia (*Oreochromis sp*), with 93.17% of its surface (14,290.00 km²) available for this activity. These areas are protected due to their ecological value and biodiversity, and are not suitable for aquaculture in order to preserve the environmental balance. The availability of a large suitable surface ensures the potential to expand tilapia aquaculture in the province, as long as the protected areas are respected to maintain sustainability and the conservation of the natural environment.

Anthropic Zones In the province of Guayas, the conditions of anthropic zones reflect that 12.16% of the area (1,864.66 km²) is occupied by exclusion zones, which include populated areas and infrastructure, and 87.84% of the territory (13,473.00 km²) is suitable for rural artisanal aquaculture of tilapia (*Oreochromis sp*), indicating a wide availability of areas that can be used for this activity. These anthropogenic areas are unsuitable for aquaculture due to population density and the presence of structures that do not allow the development of ponds and other aquaculture facilities. Despite these restrictions, the extensive suitable area offers significant potential for increasing rural artisanal tilapia aquaculture in the region, always considering appropriate planning to avoid conflicts with urbanized areas and existing infrastructure.

Flood Zones In the province of Guayas, the conditions of the flood zones show that 45.59% of the area (6,413.50 km^2) is subject to flooding, including permanent areas (mangroves and swamps), temporary areas (during rainy seasons) and areas prone to river overflows or heavy rainfall; and 54.41% of the territory (8,345.27 km^2) is suitable for rural artisanal aquaculture of tilapia (*Oreochromis sp*), offering a considerable extension of suitable areas for this activity. These exclusion zones present significant challenges for aquaculture due to the instability of the terrain and the risk of loss of infrastructure and fish. Despite these limitations, the considerable proportion of suitable areas provides opportunities for the development and expansion of tilapia aquaculture in the province, provided that appropriate management and mitigation strategies are implemented to minimize the risks associated with flooding.

3.3 Application of the Cartographic Information Overlay System

This overlay system allowed the integration of polygons in a precise manner, facilitating the identification of the most suitable areas for artisanal rural tilapia aquaculture in the province of Guayas. In turn, it allowed combining and analyzing multiple layers of geospatial data with their respective criteria (suitability, presence - absence) to combine and identify the general suitable areas for tilapia aquaculture in the province of Guayas.

3.3.1 Consolidation Suitability Zone (Temperature, Altitude and Slope)

Consolidation of the data overlay of suitable areas for rural artisanal tilapia aquaculture reveals a varied layered distribution through the establishment of range/colors (See Table 14) of suitability in different areas. Out of the 15,338.06 km^2 assessed, a small portion of 1.06 km^2 was classified as unsuitable for aquaculture. An area of 14.30 km^2 is considered moderately suitable, while 424.98 km^2 and 58.76 km^2 are suitable and moderately suitable, respectively. Areas with clear and definite suitability for aquaculture cover 251.96 km^2 and 259.28 km^2. The largest portion of land, 14,327.72 km^2, was identified as suitable, establishing that the majority of the provincial territory has favorable geographical conditions for tilapia farming. Under these conditions and up to this point, the analysis indicates that the province of Guayas would have a large area suitable for promoting aquaculture production in the region.

3.3.2 Overlapping Exclusion Zones (Protected Zones, Anthropic Zones, Flood Zones)

To optimize the productivity of tilapia aquaculture in the province of Guayas, it is crucial to analyze the suitable and excluded areas according to the identified geographic factors. According to the established data, the exclusion zones, which include protected areas, anthropic zones and flood zones, occupy approximately 51.05% of the studied territory, totaling 7,830 km^2. On the other hand, the areas considered suitable for aquaculture occupy the remaining 48.95%, equivalent to 7,508.06 km^2. This overlap reveals a delicate balance between environmental preservation and productive use of space, highlighting the need for integrated management strategies that maximize productive potential without compromising the environmental sustainability of the region.

3.3.3 Overlapping Suitability Zones Without Exclusion Zones

The overlay of data to determine suitable areas and the presence or absence of favourable geographical factors shows a diverse distribution of suitability (by layers). Out of a total of 7,606.64 km^2 assessed, only 0.39 km^2 was classified as unsuitable, while 6.29 km^2 are considered moderately suitable and unsuitable. The areas that combine suitability and medium suitability cover 52.42 km^2 and 41.45 km^2, respectively. The clearly suitable and moderately suitable areas for aquaculture total 220.92 km^2 and 150.25 km^2, respectively. The majority of the territory, with 7,134.92 km^2, was identified as fully suitable, confirming that the province has a large area for tilapia farming, providing a solid basis for the development and expansion of this activity in the region.

3.3.4 Checking the Suitability Zones and Exclusion Zones on Site

Of the 57 tilapia pools registered in the province of Guayas, 31 pools are located in the Zone of Greater Suitability (Rating 6) and 26 in the Exclusion Zone. Of the 26 in the exclusion zone, all are in the Yahuachi canton and almost all (25) are located in the exclusion zone because it is an area prone to flooding due to river overflow. One pool is located in a temporary flood zone due to the rainy season.

4 Conclusions

The identification of geographic and environmental factors allowed to outline the most suitable areas for rural artisanal tilapia aquaculture in the province of Guayas. Variables such as types of water sources, temperature, altitude, and slope of the terrain were considered, in addition to exclusion zones (protected areas, anthropogenic zones and flood zones), which were linked with the sequence to define zones that presented optimal conditions for aquaculture productivity.

The use of geographic information system (GIS) provided detailed spatial data of the areas into suitability categories ("Suitable", "Moderately Suitable", and "Unsuitable") based on established indices. The cartographic representation allowed a clear visualization of the spatial distribution of these areas, providing a fundamental tool for planning and management of aquaculture in the province.

The cartographic information overlay technique allowed the integration and analysis of multiple layers of information, consolidating the polygons of the areas suitable for tilapia aquaculture. Using this technique, it was established that, of a total of 15,338.06 km^2 that make up the province of Guayas, of which 7,606.64 km^2 (49.28%) are suitable for aquaculture. The overlay methodology highlighted a balance between geographical suitability and the exclusion of protected or anthropogenic areas, confirming that the province of Guayas has a solid base for the development of tilapia aquaculture. It is highlighted that this area presents particular conditions in terms of flood zones where aquaculture activities are currently carried out, and that they must be considered and analyzed, particularly within the 4,501.80 km^2 that make up the "Prone" area (river overflows or heavy rainfall).

A total of 57 pools, the zoning of geographical and environmental factors has allowed to identify suitable and unsuitable areas for the implementation of cultivation pools. The results reveal that 54.39% of the pools are located in suitable areas, which represents a favorable environment for the development of aquaculture. However, 45.61% of the pools (most of them with a barrage system) are located in areas prone to flooding due to river overflow, where environmental conditions would present significant risks. Of these, 1.75% are located in areas that are temporarily flooded during the rainy season.

References

aeroterra (2024). https://www.aeroterra.com/es-ar/que-es-gis/introduccion#:~:text=A%20geog raphic%20information%20system%20(GIS)%20is%20a%20framework,using%20maps% 20and%203D%20scenes, https://www.aeroterra.com/es-ar/que-es-gis/introduccion#:~:text= A%20geographic%20information%20system%20(GIS)%20is%20a%20framework,using% 20maps%20and%203D%20scenes

AUNAP & FAO: Zoning of National Aquaculture. Bogotá. FAO. (2011). Basic Manual of Fish Farming for Paraguay. Bogotá (2013). https://www.aunap.gov.co/documentos/OGCI/Zonifi caci%C3%B3n-de-la-Acuicultura-en-Colombia.pdf

Bioweb: fungiweb/GeografiaClima/ (2024). https://bioweb.bio/fungiweb/GeografiaClima/

Cantor, F.: TILAPIA PRODUCTION MANUAL. Puebla: Secretariat of Rural Development of the State of Puebla (2007). https://docplayer.es/35165080-Manual-de-produccion-de-tilapia. html

CELAC: CELAC Plan for food security, nutrition and hunger eradication 2030. FAO (2023). https://openknowledge.fao.org/server/api/core/bitstreams/31c8be1b-1dcc-44aa-a956-f5555624763f/content

Concept: region-geografica/ (2024). https://concepto.de/region-geografica/

Dias, M., Oliveira, E.: Spatial circuits of tilapia production in the regional contexts of northern and western Paraná, Brazil. Tierra Plural **19** (2022). https://doi.org/10.5212/TerraPlural.v.16. 2217547.016

Espinoza, G.: Fundamentals of environmental impact assessment. Santiago de Chile: Inter-American Development Bank (IDB) (2001). file:///C:/Users/WINDOWS/Downloads/Analisis_multitemporal_de_las_coberturas_vegetales.pdf

FAO, A. d. (ed.): Climate change, fisheries and aquaculture in Latin America: potential impacts and challenges for adaptation, p. 335. Concepción: University of Concepción, Concepción, Chile (2013). https://d1wqtxts1xzle7.cloudfront.net/37676161/proceedings_climate_change_ in_latin_american_fisheries_and_aquaculture-libre.pdf?1432024259=&response-content-disposition=inline%3B+filename%3DCambio_climatico_pesca_y_acuicultura_en.pdf&Exp ires=1721262324&Si

Fonseca, M., García, H., Rueda, C., Merino, M.: METHODOLOGY: Before, During and After RESEARCH. Latacunga, Cotopaxi, Ecuador: Technical University of Cotopaxi (2015). https:// isbn.cloud/9789978395134/metodologia-antes-durante-y-despues-de-la-investigacion/

Garza-Martínez, M., et al.: Territorial suitability for tilapia (Oreochromis niloticus) farming with biofloc technology in the state of Durango, Mexico. (U. d. Juarez, Ed.) Agricultural Ecosystems and Resources (2021). 13. https://era.ujat.mx/index.php/rera/article/view/3049/1485

LODAP: Organic Law for the Development of Aquaculture and Fisheries. Decree No. 187. Quito, Pichincha, Ecuador: Official Registry (2020). https://www.gob.ec/sites/default/files/regula tions/2022-05/Documento_Ley-Org%C3%A1nica-para-Desarrollo-Acuicultura-y-Pesca.pdf

Maestu, J.: Water and Sustainable Development. United Nations Office (2015). https://www.un.org/spanish/waterforlifedecade/pdf/WM_IIIESP.pdf

MAG-Paraguay & FAO: Basic Manual of Fish Farming for Paraguay. Montevieo (2011). https://openknowledge.fao.org/server/api/core/bitstreams/277125fe-ec16-4d2f-8b3a-3836ef28329d/content

Márquez, Y., Chacón-Moreno, E.: Potential distribution of agricultural crops in the state of Mérida (Venezuela), under climate change scenarios. Venezuelan Geogr. J. (2021)

Martin, P., Guerrero, B.: Tilapia Culture Manual. Lima, Peru (2004)

MPCEIP: Flagship Project to Improve the Competitiveness of the Aquaculture and Fisheries Sector. Guayaquil, Guayas, Ecuador: Agreement No. MPCEIP-DMPCEIP-2020-0029 (2020). https://www.produccion.gob.ec/wp-content/uploads/downloads/2020/07/Proyecto-Mejora-Competitiva-del-Sector-Acu%C3%ADcola-y-Pesquero.pdf

Production: MPCEIP-Improvement-in-the-Competitiveness-of-the-Aquaculture-and-Fishing-Sector.pdf. MPCEIP (2023). https://www.produccion.gob.ec/wp-content/uploads/downloads/2023/01/K001-MPCEIP-Improvement-in-the-Competitiveness-of-the-Aquaculture-and-Fishing-Sector.pdf

Ramírez, B., González, A., Valdivia, R., Salas, J., García, A.: Efficient rates for water for agricultural use in the Comarca Lagunera. (RM Agrícolas, Ed.) (2019). https://typeset.io/pdf/tarifas-eficientes-para-el-agua-de-uso-agricola-en-la-t852u0jgny.pdf

RLODAP: General regulations of the organic law for the development of aquaculture and fisheries. Decree No. 362. Quito, Pichincha, Ecuador: Official Registry (2022). https://www.produccion.gob.ec/wp-content/uploads/downloads/2022/03/Decreto-Ejecutivo-No.-362-Reglamento-General-a-la-Ley-Organica-para-el-Desarrollo-de-la-Acuicultura-y-Pesca.pdf

Saavedra, M.: Tilapia Farming Management. Managua, Nicaragua (2006)

suia.ambiente. https://suia.ambiente.gob.ec/

Wicki, G., Gromenida, N.: STUDY OF TILAPIA (Oreochromis niloticus) DEVELOPMENT AND PRODUCTION (2016). https://www.semanticscholar.org/paper/ESTUDIO-DE-DESARROLLO-Y-PRODUCCION-DE-TILAPIA-Wicki-Gromenida/42eb24d81afaf264c7075243f32231b4964103ad

Harnessing AI for Future Scenarios: Exploration Approaches for Sustainable Planning in Taranto, Italy

Domenico Camarda(⊠)

Polytechnic University of Bari, 70125 Bari, Italy
domenico.camarda@poliba.it

Abstract. This paper explores the perspectives of traditional, human-centered Scenario Building (SB) and AI-driven Scenario Building (AISB) techniques. The context of study is to devise a sustainable regeneration strategy for Taranto by navigating its challenges through a hybrid methodological approach. While AISB methodologies swiftly process data and model future scenarios, traditional SB methods excel in capturing local knowledge. The study thus suggests the potential of a hybrid approach, emphasizing a methodological balance that harmonizes data-centric insights with human expertise, showcasing the potential for resilient and inclusive urban planning in Taranto.

Keywords: Sustainable planning · Decision support · Scenario building · Artificial intelligence

1 Introduction

The city of Taranto, in the Italian Mezzogiorno (Fig. 1), has undergone significant industrial and urban changes over years.

Fig. 1. Taranto in the national context.

© The Author(s), under exclusive license to Springer Nature Switzerland AG 2026
O. Gervasi et al. (Eds.): ICCSA 2025 Workshops, LNCS 15890, pp. 328–340, 2026.
https://doi.org/10.1007/978-3-031-97606-3_22

This case exemplifies how urban and industrial planning can profoundly impact a region's social, spatial and natural environment organization. Taranto was planned as a development pole in the 1960s. Since then, it has experienced rapid and often controlled expansion, which brought complex and intertwined issues. Admittedly, anticipating future outcomes, a core aspect of planning, frequently introduces shifts that complicate the diverse and detailed nature of available information. This can lead to subjective interpretations of varied and fragmented data. Researchers and practitioners have made numerous efforts to organize this intricate information for better decision-making [1]. In recent times, increasing popularity has been gained by methodologies that blend qualitative and quantitative approaches to organize distributed knowledge. This has long been an area of activity for the field of the so-called futures studies. Notably, the future workshop methodological approach stands out because it allows for the integration of individual and group perspectives, both critical and forward-thinking, to develop potential strategies and alternative future possibilities [2].

In this background, the present study is an attempt to explore whether innovative technologies and approaches can better mirror this complexity to derive alternative research and operational perspectives. In particular, hybrid methods have been explored for building up future scenarios oriented to Taranto's sustainable regeneration. The purpose was to combine traditional (SB) and technological (AISB) scenario-building approaches to address the city's multiform challenges.

After this introduction, the paper is structured as follows. Section 2 examines Taranto's evolution from a development pole to an environmentally and socioeconomically problematic city. Section 3 delves into both traditional and AI-driven scenario-building methodologies experimental sessions for Taranto. Section 4 analyzes some strengths and weaknesses of SB and AISB approaches, with key findings and insights for future research in Sect. 5.

2   Taranto Case Study: From Development Pole to Troubled City

In the mid-20th century, Taranto became a key industrial center for Italy, inspired by François Perroux's growth pole theory [3]. According to this theory, focusing resources and investments in selected areas and particular sectors could spur economic progress. But following a first apparent confirmation of this concept, Taranto's evolution diverged from expectations for various reasons [4]. While physical and industrial growth continued, quality of life and environmental sustainability have started to decline severely.

Taranto has received explicit association in recent years to one of the European Union's socioeconomically shrinking industrial cities, a paradox for a region meant to be a growth model. From the perspective of physical growth, which experienced substantial urban and industrial expansion, the shrinkage issue was not apparent (Fig. 2) [5].

This development led to increased environmental issues and a decline in quality of life, showing evidence of a development that ignored environmental sustainability and social needs (Fig. 3). Taranto's rapid expansion severely impacted the environment. The 2000s saw dangerously high levels of pollution, with Taranto recording Europe's highest dioxin emissions, which are notoriounsly very toxic. This pollution directly affected public health, increasing respiratory diseases and pollution-related health problems. Taranto became one of Europe's most affected areas in terms of pollution-related morbidity and mortality [5].

Fig. 2. The state of industrial and urbanized areas in Taranto in 2024

Citizens' quality of life has been increasingly worsened by environmental pollution, contributing to urban malaise and reduced livability. The environmental crisis was exacerbated by inadequate mitigation measures and industrial expansion without considering environmental impacts.

Taranto's economic and employment deterioration significantly affected its social frame. After initial growth and industrial employment, Taranto saw flimsy stabilization and then a reduction in jobs since the 1970s. Central city residents, once integral to the industrial sector, now represent just about a third of total employees, leading to economic and social cohesion decline.

This employment decline spurred suburbanization. In pursuit of improved living circumstances and economic prospects, residents have migrated from core regions to suburban and provincial communities. The population distribution has changed as a result of this transition, with the urban core becoming less populated and the outlying settlements becoming overcrowded. This has caused an imbalance and significantly deteriorated the urban condition [5].

Fig. 3. A daytime snapshot of Taranto pollution days (2012).

Suburbanization posed further challenges, particularly in infrastructure and transport. Despite demands for better public transport and urban infrastructure, developments were poorly implemented, increasing reliance on private transport, traffic congestion, and pollution. Inadequate public transport worsened livability issues, causing pollution and traffic to spiral out of control.

This puzzling paradigm emphasizes the necessity of integrated approaches to urban planning that take into account the demands of infrastructure and transportation as well as sustainable physical growth.

3 Envisioning Scenarios of Futures

3.1 A Traditional Perspective of Scenario-Building

In order to address these complex and interrelated issues, the Municipality asked the Polytechnic University of Bari to set up a process for building up scenarios for the future of Taranto.

The process aimed at involving the local community in identifying new visions and strategies for the city's future. Scenario building uses participatory approaches integrating expert knowledge and community contributions to identify and valorize the city's socio-environmental resources (Table 1) [6].

Community involvement ensures proposed solutions align with citizens' needs and expectations. This participatory approach builds shared visions for the city's future, fostering community and responsibility among local knowledge agents and stakeholders. The process of building up future scenarios originally involved exchanging messages on paper (Fig. 4).

Our process, using digital platforms (as is normally the case today: PC-based SB), involved various Taranto neighbourhoods and a wide range of participating people, including citizens, institutional agents, and industry representatives (Table 2).

The experiment highlighted the ideas put forward by the participants, summarized as follows:

Table 1. A traditional future workshop layout [1].

Future Workshops		
PHASE	CONTENTS	EXPECTED RESULTS
1. Preparation	The issue to be analysed is decided and the structure and environment of sessions are prepared	Summary of contributions
2. Critique	Clarification of the issue selected, of dissatisfactions and negative experiences in the present situation	Problematic areas for the following discussion
3. Fantasy	Free idea generation (as an answer to the problems) and of desires, dreams, fantasies, opinions concerning the future. The participants are asked to forget the practical limitations and the obstacles of their present reality	Indication of a collection of ideas and choice of some solutions and planning guidelines
4. Implementation	Going back to the present reality, to its power structures and to its real limits, to analyse the actual feasibility of the previous phase solutions and ideas. Identification of obstacles and limits to the plan implementation and definition of possible ways to overcome them	Creation of strategic lines to be followed in order to fulfil the traced goals. Action plan and implementation proposal drawing

Fig. 4. Experimental sessions of traditional SB.

Table 2. Participants of Taranto SB sessions

Place			Participants	
Sched	District	Location	#	Profiles
1	Inner city	public hall	150	residents; local associations; fish sector
2	Lama San Vito	church yard	50	residents; students
3	Lido Torretta	public playground	50	residents; tourists
4	Talsano	church hall	15	residents
5	Paolo VI	church hall	30	residents; industrial workers
6	Salinella	church hall	30	residents; students
7	Tamburi	public hall	5	public officers; local associations
8	City Centre	public library	30	residents; scholars; students

- Redevelopment of Coastal Areas. Participants emphasized transforming the San Vito coastal district into a tourist area, improving the beach, and building tourist villages. Remediating polluted waters near the military port was a priority.
- Revision of the Master Plan. Participants discussed the need to update Taranto's Master Plan, suggesting reducing landscape constraints from 300 m to 150 m to support tourism and housing development.
- Promotion of Tourism and Cultural Activities. There was strong interest in promoting cultural and historical tourism, with proposals for creating city brands and organizing cultural events to attract tourists and enhance Taranto's historical heritage.
- Improvement of Infrastructures and Services. Participants highlighted the importance of improving urban infrastructure, including sewerage networks, roads, and integrating cycle paths for sustainable mobility.
- Environmental Sustainability and Innovation. Participants recognized the need for sustainable technologies, such as renewable energy for new housing and converting the local economy towards agriculture, technology, and tourism. They also discussed retrofitting existing buildings and introducing energy efficiency measures.
- Community Involvement and Participatory Planning. Continuous community involvement in urban planning was a central aspect, allowing for a wide range of opinions and scenarios reflecting local needs and aspirations.

In summary, the traditional SB process resulted in specific visions and practical suggestions for urban regeneration. A synthesized report is shown below, with alternative final visions grouped by participants.

1) *Taranto city of green and cultural renaissance*

   – Redevelopment and use of abandoned state-owned areas for cultural, tourist, and environmental projects, with particular attention to the Cheradi Islands. The restoration of monuments and historic buildings will be accompanied by initiatives to improve urban mobility and encourage sustainable mobility.

2) *A city tailored for future youth*

- Allocate abandoned areas to create youth centers and meeting spaces, encouraging young people to actively participate in urban redevelopment. Projects include converting abandoned buildings into social centers and opening new sports and cultural activities.

3) *Taranto city of sea tourism and culture*

- Return the seafront to the city to promote tourism and maritime trade, enhancing natural and historical resources through the creation of museums, thematic routes, and tourist attractions. The promenade will be made pedestrian-friendly and bicycle-friendly, with services for visitors.

4) *A city of innovation and sustainable technology*

- Invest in renewable energies, sustainable mobility, and waste management to make Taranto an environmentally cutting-edge city. Converting old phone booths into charging stations for electric cars and improving air quality monitoring systems are part of this plan.

5) *Taranto historical heritage and identity*

- Recover and enhance Taranto's historic center, transforming it into an open-air ecomuseum and encouraging repopulation. The old town will be restored with targeted interventions to preserve popular architecture and noble palaces, while promoting economic and social activities related to local traditions.

This SB process collected structured ideas and suggestions for addressing Taranto's main challenges. These results could be seen as a useful basis for future planning processes, showing the importance of a distributed and integrated knowledge-based approach in addressing the city's socioeconomic and environmental challenges.

Scenario-building itself shows up as a useful approach for exploring future options and evaluating the possible impacts of political and urban decisions. Using PC-based software and models allows for detailed simulations of complex scenarios, supporting more informed decisions based on comprehensive data.

3.2   Experiments Using Generative AI (AISB)

An ex-post experimentation was conducted on this context, using generative AI tools (Google's Gemini and OpenAI's ChatGPT) [7]. The same traditional SB scheme was followed (Fig. 4) and the same questions were asked to the AI module. In the end, the AISB process showed up as a kind of structured interview with available GPT models. An excerpt of one of the sequential steps from the AISB process is shown in Fig. 5.

The AI-driven scenario-building process for Taranto delivered meaningful insights, providing somehow comprehensive projections of the city's potential futures. By massively analyzing historical, demographic, economic, and environmental documents from online sources [8], the AI identified key trends shaping Taranto's trajectory:

- Demographic decline: Ongoing population reduction, particularly in central districts, driven by internal migration to suburban areas and emigration to other regions.

```
PROMPT>>> Imagine that the Municipal Administration of Taranto is
creating the new Master Plan, needing your participation and
knowledge support to build together scenarios and strategies for
the future of the city. We ask you to look at Taranto's history,
at what has happened over years. What do you think are the
critical issues of Taranto, the small as well as the big problems
according to your knowledge? (PHASE 1 - CRITICALITIES)

AI>>>> Certainly! Addressing the critical issues of Taranto
involves looking at both historical and current contexts. Here are
several key issues that have been prominent in the city's history
and remain relevant today:

Environmental Degradation
     1. Industrial Pollution: Taranto has been heavily impacted by
```

Fig. 5. The *criticalities* phase of the AISB process (excerpted from the output image)

- Environmental challenges: Continuing high pollution levels, especially affecting air quality and water systems.
- Suburban Expansion: Growth of residential areas on the periphery, coupled with increased dependence on private vehicles for transportation.

The AI employed integrated predictive modeling to generate multiple urban regeneration scenarios, evaluating various political, economic, and infrastructure interventions. Among the diverse scenarios examined, three emerged as particularly significant.

1) *Taranto as a green city*

   – Taranto is envisioned as a hub for substantial investments in renewable energy, environmental restoration, and green infrastructure. This vision promises a marked enhancement in air quality and a decrease in emigration rates. Additionally, it forecasts an uptick in tourism and a surge in employment opportunities within the green sector.

2) *Industrial reboot*

   – This involves the industry's rebirth through technological advancements, including the adoption of clean production technologies. It is linked to moderate economic growth, yet it continues to face ongoing challenges related to pollution and waste management.

3) *A city of cultural renaissance*

   – Taranto prioritizes enhancing its cultural and historical heritage, fostering tourism, and nurturing creative industries. This leads to a surge in cultural events and improved community well-being, significantly boosting the city's appeal.

An initial socio-economic assessment by AISB analyzed potential impacts across various scenarios. Key findings include:

- Employment: Scenarios prioritizing environmental sustainability and technological innovation are projected to generate new employment opportunities, notably in renewable energy, technology, and tourism.

- Living quality: Scenarios emphasizing green and cultural regeneration are anticipated to enhance quality of life, evidenced by improved social well-being indicators, a decline in pollution-related illnesses, and stronger community bonds.
- Spatial Equity: The assessment warns of potential increases in regional disparities without strategic interventions, with suburban areas likely to expand at the expense of central urban areas.

Within this framework, AISB methodology produced targeted policy suggestions, derived from the modeled simulations. These encompass:

- Promotion of eco-friendly enterprises: Suggestions for tax and monetary encouragement to stimulate investment in environmentally sound and renewable technologies.
- Restoration of former industrial lands: Proposals for transforming abandoned industrial zones into environmentally friendly communal areas or technological centers.
- Enhancement of communal transit: Formulation of a cohesive public transportation strategy to lessen reliance on personal vehicles, strengthen connections between urban core and outlying districts, and diminish contamination.

The AI-driven process examined a broad spectrum of potential future scenarios for Taranto, offering valuable insights to aid strategic planning and informed decision-making. It proposed visions for sustainable urban development, emphasizing urban regeneration and enhancements to the quality of life for residents. However, this innovative approach, and the broader application of simulation-based (SB) methods, carries both benefits and challenges, including limitations and critical issues. The following section will delve into the implications of these aspects.

4 SB vs. AISB: An Open Comparison

In general terms, scenario building is a strategic approach that helps decision-makers envision various potential futures, allowing them to better navigate opportunities and uncertainties. Both traditional and AI-driven methods have their own strengths and weaknesses when it comes to scenario planning. Below is a general overview of each approach.

Traditional SB relies on direct engagement among stakeholders and local experts, leveraging historical data, past experiences, and collective insights to explore possible futures. The participatory sessions highlighted a set of crucial issues: the necessity to regenerate the coastal areas, with a particular focus on the San Vito neighborhood; the revision of urban planning instruments to support a more balanced development; the promotion of cultural tourism; the advancement toward a more sustainable and innovative economy. This approach offers several insights, as reported in research literature [1, 9, 10]. One key point of strength is that face-to-face interaction facilitates the capture of nuanced, context-specific knowledge, which might be overlooked in purely data-driven analyses. Additionally, discussions among diverse participants can lead to new perspectives and innovative strategies that are more aligned with local needs. Another benefit is flexibility—traditional scenarios can be adapted throughout the process, integrating real-time feedback and new information as it becomes available. Moreover, the active involvement of local actors fosters a stronger sense of ownership, leading to greater acceptance and implementation of proposed decisions.

However, traditional SB also has limitations. The process often demands significant time and resources, especially when involving large groups or repeating sessions to incorporate evolving variables. Furthermore, human intuition—while valuable—can introduce biases, potentially distorting the perception of possible futures and leading to inaccurate predictions. This issue becomes particularly relevant in highly complex and dynamic contexts like Taranto, where oversimplification or overlooked factors could compromise scenario accuracy.

AISB has also generated alternative visions for the city, encompassing: Taranto as a green city, a city with Industrial reboot, and a City of Cultural Renaissance. These scenarios are complemented by socioeconomic impact evaluations, highlighting the potential creation of new employment opportunities in green and cultural sectors, enhancements in quality-of-life indicators, and risks of emerging spatial disparities. Generative AI utilizes advanced algorithms and predictive modeling to produce such automated future scenarios. One major advantage of our AISB experimentation was the ability to process vast amounts of documents at high speed. AI could rapidly analyze publicly available information on a given topic, detect hidden patterns, and consider a broader range of influencing factors. Since these projections are rooted in mathematical models and algorithms, they reduce subjective biases and can be consistently replicated across different scenarios. As a result, AISB proves to be particularly useful in managing complex, interconnected systems, such as urban environments where economic, social, technological, and environmental factors interact. This approach also allows for long-term simulations, assessing the possible outcomes of political or economic decisions.

Despite these advantages, AISB comes with challenges. First, AI models heavily depend on the quality and availability of documents to be 'statistically' processed. If the data used are incomplete, outdated, or unreliable, the resulting predictions may be misleading or incorrect. Another critical issue is transparency: AI systems typically function as "black boxes," making it difficult to trace how conclusions are reached. In our case, this lack of clarity can create skepticism and hinder trust in AI-generated scenarios. Lastly, AISB may undervalue human expertise, particularly the ability to contextualize data, incorporate ethical considerations, and assess moral and social implications within scenario planning – elements that, conversely, are a hallmark of traditional SB. All these aspects, both positive and negative, were observed in the ex-post AISB experimentation on the Taranto case and compared with the traditional SB approach.

It is important to emphasize that the *raison d'être* of this experimental comparison stems from a purely exploratory intent. Ultimately, the SB process represents the account of a real and institutionally situated framework, while the AISB process remains solely a proof of concept. Nevertheless, this comparison brings to light reflections, perspectives (and limitations) of practical implementability, potentially valuable for spatial planning, synthetically outlined in the following discussion.

5   Discussion and Conclusion

The future of Taranto hinges on its capacity to sustainably manage resources while actively engaging the community in strategic planning and decision-making. The Polytechnic University of Bari has taken a significant step toward urban regeneration by employing hybrid scenario-building approaches, aiming for a more resilient and sustainable transformation of the city.

The case study revealed both benefits and drawbacks of the two methods. First it must be said that the use of generative AI has not a conceptual but a lexical foundation. This in itself determines problems of interpretation of the meanings upstream and downstream of the interactions and the questions asked. The upstream problems concern the writing/structure of each question, which must be asked in a suitable way to obtain a useful answer. This determines a possible iterative cycle of calibration of the question towards the answer - possibly paradoxical for common sense, yet studied through specific lines of research (Prompt Engineering) [11, 12]. Downstream of the interactions, the problems concern the very consistency of the meanings of the answers obtained. These are in fact the result of computational models and algorithms of machine learning that analyze statistical frequencies and redundancies of individual words and letters through stochastic approaches. It is therefore evident that the aim of the elaborations is not the conceptual accuracy of the answers but their statistical coherence with the (very numerous) data analysed [8, 13, 14]. However, one key advantage of AISB is its speed—our experiment generated scenarios within hours, whereas traditional SB workshops can take days or even weeks. This rapid turnaround is particularly beneficial when time is a limiting factor in urban planning. However, AISB struggles with capturing the complexities of human insight and the nuances of specific local contexts. In our study, the AI model often generalized issues, overlooking important contextual factors that human participants would naturally consider. This makes scenarios generated by people potentially more realistic and relevant, as they incorporate diverse perspectives and lived experiences. Essentially, the fundamental distinction between these methods lies in how they handle knowledge: traditional SB workshops foster new knowledge through interaction and the exchange of ideas, whereas AISB relies on existing data sources, such as information available online (as in the case of GPT-based models). This limitation can reduce the potential for creativity and innovation in scenario development.

Despite these constraints, AISB presents intriguing opportunities for the future of decision-making, particularly in spatial planning. Currently, its main strength lies in trend analysis and supporting data-driven insights. Policymakers often need preliminary assessments of different courses of action, and AISB can provide valuable foresight that can later be refined through human expertise and collaborative knowledge-sharing.

The future of AISB likely depends on its integration with dynamic sensor data and multi-agent knowledge systems. For instance, incorporating real-time environmental data from sensor networks could enable AISB to develop microclimate-related scenarios. Additionally, linking AISB to external knowledge frameworks—such as multi-agent architectures—could expand the range of options available to decision-makers.

Ongoing research is focused on improving AISB's knowledge management, shifting from purely statistical methods to more conceptual approaches. One promising direction involves the use of ontologies—formal knowledge representations that help structure and share information (e.g., OntoGPT) [15]. By integrating ontological frameworks, AISB could enhance its understanding of relationships between different data points, resulting in more comprehensive and refined scenario development.

Given the strengths and weaknesses of both methods, a hybrid scenario-building approach appears to be the most effective. This would leverage AI's capability to process vast amounts of data while incorporating the expertise, creativity, and contextual awareness of stakeholders.

In the context of Taranto's urban planning, such a hybrid approach could involve AI-driven analysis of environmental and demographic trends, complemented by input from local experts and residents based on their lived experiences and aspirations. This combination would ensure that the resulting scenarios are not only data-driven but also culturally and socially relevant.

In the end, Taranto's future will be shaped by its ability to balance sustainable resource management with inclusive, community-driven planning. The exploration of hybrid scenario-building methods represents a crucial step toward achieving long-term resilience and sustainability for this evolving urban region.

Acknowledgement. The work has been partially supported by the ICSC National Research Centre for High Performance Computing, Big Data and Quantum Computing (CN00000013), under the NRRP MUR program funded by NextGenerationEU.

References

1. Khakee, A., Barbanente, A., Camarda, D., Puglisi, M.: With or without? Comparative study of preparing participatory scenarios using computer-aided and traditional brainstorming. J. Future Res. **6**, 45–64 (2002)
2. Jungk, R., Mullert, N.: Future Workshop: How to Create Desirable Futures. Institute for Social Inventions, London (1996)
3. Perroux, F.: A note on the notion of growth pole. Econ. Appl. **1**(2), 307–320 (1955)
4. Maretti, M.: Urban crisis within environmental and industrial policies in Italy: the case of the steel industry in Taranto. In: Holt, W.G. (ed.) From Sustainable to Resilient Cities: Global Concerns and Urban Efforts, pp. 103–124. Bingley, Emerald (2014)
5. Camarda, D., Rotondo, F., Selicato, F.: Strategies for dealing with urban shrinkage: issues and scenarios in Taranto. Eur. Plan. Stud. **23**, 126–146 (2014)
6. Camarda, D.: Building sustainable futures for post-industrial regeneration: the case of Taranto, Italy. Urban Res. Pract. 1–9 (2018)
7. Bhardwaz, S., Kumar, J.: An extensive comparative analysis of Chatbot technologies-ChatGPT, Google BARD and Microsoft Bing. In: IEEE (ed.) 2nd International Conference on Applied Artificial Intelligence and Computing (ICAAIC2023), pp. 673–679. IEEE, Salem, India (2023)
8. Wolfram, S.: What is ChatGPT doing... and why does it Work? Wolfram Writings. February (2023)
9. Borri, D., Camarda, D.: Dealing with multi-agents in environmental planning: a scenario-building approach. Stud. Reg. Urban Plann. **10**, 89–98 (2004)
10. Grassini, L., Monno, V., Khakee, A.: Evaluating strategic metropolitan planning in Bari and Taranto. Eur. Plan. Stud. **26**, 1682–1700 (2018)

11. White, J., et al.: A prompt pattern catalog to enhance prompt engineering with chatgpt. arXiv preprint arXiv:2302.11382. (2023)
12. Giray, L.: Prompt engineering with ChatGPT: a guide for academic writers. Ann. Biomed. Eng. **51**, 2629–2633 (2023)
13. Schlagwein, D., Willcocks, L.: 'ChatGPT et al.: The ethics of using (generative) artificial intelligence in research and science. J. Inf. Technol. **38**, 232–238 (2023)
14. Floridi, L., Chiriatti, M.: GPT-3: its nature, scope, limits, and consequences. Mind. Mach. **30**, 681–694 (2020)
15. Caufield, J.H., et al.: Structured prompt interrogation and recursive extraction of semantics (SPIRES): a method for populating knowledge bases using zero-shot learning. Bioinformatics. **40**, btae104 (2024)

Classifying Human Activities in Urban Spaces with a Multimodal AI: Towards a Massive Assessment of Urban Affordances

Ivan Blečić[1]([⊠]), Alessandro Floris[1], Giulia Giliberto[1], and Giuseppe A. Trunfio[2]

[1] Department of Civil and Environmental Engineering and Architecture, University of Cagliari, Cagliari, Italy
{ivanblecic,a.floris62,giulia.giliberto}@unica.it
[2] Department of Biomedical Sciences, University of Sassari, Sassari, Italy
trunfio@uniss.it

Abstract. We present a tool that leverages a Multimodal Large Language Model (MLLM) for the automatic classification of human activities from images of urban scenes. Starting from an image of spaces populated with people, the tool is capable to classify them according to five features: age group, sex, bodily posture, activity level and social configuration. The tool implements a sequential pipeline consisting of Faster R-CNN for person detection, followed by postprocessing and two consecutive applications of GPT-4o models for refined image description and information extraction.

In the paper we also present an experimental test used to preliminary validation of the tool, comparing the ground truth on 24 images of urban scenes with the estimates provided by the tool, yielding a good degree of alignment.

The tool is part of the wider research programme of massive assessment of urban affordances, within the framework of the capability approach.

Keywords: urban affordances · capability approach · urban space analysis · Multimodal Large Language Model · urban evaluation modelling

1 Introduction

Public spaces play an important role in shaping human experiences, social interactions, and people's capabilities [1]. Understanding how people use and interact with urban spaces is fundamental for designing inclusive and enabling environments [2–4].

Since the 1960s, pioneers such as Jane Jacobs [5], William H. Whyte [6], and Jan Gehl [7, 8] highlighted the importance of creating urban spaces adopting a human-centred perspective, rather than overly relying on formal "aesthetic" forms or technical solutions for the built environment.

Building on these foundational ideas, there has been a growing demand for methods identifying relationship between people and their urban environments, aiming to better understand how urban spaces are used in everyday life, and to provide insights to inform policies and guide the physical transformation of cities.

© The Author(s), under exclusive license to Springer Nature Switzerland AG 2026
O. Gervasi et al. (Eds.): ICCSA 2025 Workshops, LNCS 15890, pp. 341–357, 2026.
https://doi.org/10.1007/978-3-031-97606-3_23

Empirical methods within this domain often employ direct observation as a tool for surveying, mapping, and categorising how urban spaces are used by people [9].

Traditionally, such observational studies on the use of public spaces have been conducted through direct human observation. While this approach offers valuable qualitative insights, it is inherently time-consuming, difficult to scale up, and possibly subject to observer bias. In response to such challenges, recent advancements in machine learning and artificial intelligence provide new opportunities for automating and enhancing behavioural analysis in urban contexts [10]. Indeed, the past decade has seen a growing adoption of computer vision and machine learning techniques for automating behavioural analysis in urban contexts.

In this paper we present one such tool, leveraging a Multimodal Large Language Model (MLLM), for the automatic classification of human activities from images of scenes of urban spaces. Specifically, starting from an image of urban space populated with people, the tool is capable to classify them according to five features: age group, sex, bodily posture, activity level and social configuration.

As we will more extensively present in the Background section, besides automatising and hence allowing for massive assessment of activities in urban spaces, the tool is instrumental for the development of a wider research programme of the systematic assessment of urban capabilities [11–14], within which a relevant role is played by the physical affordances [15] of urban space, conceptualised as a subset of urban opportunities which are directly perceivable and actionable in the urban physical environment.

The paper is organised as follows: the following Sect. 2 presents some relevant background both on the theoretical and methodological framework, as well as on the techniques and technologies employed for the development on the tool; Sect. 3 provides more details on the observation protocol and technical details on the functioning of the tool; in Sect. 4 we present the experimental test and discuss its results; finally, Sect. 5 offers some concluding remarks and perspectives for future development.

The present study was carried out within the TERSICORE (Technologies for Evaluation and Research for Sustainability Innovation: a Community-Oriented Regenerative Evolutions) research project, the aim of which is to develop a set of protocols for the assessment of the psycho-social dimension of urban space in order to support projects of urban regeneration and to evaluate their impacts.

2 Background

This background section is subdivided into two subsections. The first is dedicated to theoretical and methodological framework liveable which to situate the tool for automatic assessment of human activities in urban spaces. The second subsection presents background on techniques and technologies that were employed for the development of the tool.

2.1 Urban Capabilities, Opportunities and Affordances

In cities people engage in activities, they perform different behaviours in different urban spaces. These activities are characterised by the interaction of people with objects, other people, and the environment, with the intention of achieving goals and the attainment of certain functionings.

The term "functioning" is here used specifically in the context of the capability approach [16, 17], in which a human functioning is attained among those within individual's set of capabilities.

A capability may be defined as a person's substantive freedom to choose among various options of doing and being that they have reason to value. A capability presupposes two constitutive elements: (1) individual ability, understood as the internal capacity—possessed though not necessarily exercised—to act or to be in particular ways; and (2) opportunity, referring to the external conditions that render the exercise of such capacity feasible. A person may be said to possess a given capability only when both components—internal and external, ability and opportunity—are concurrently present. The physical configuration of urban space—the material infrastructure of the city—affects capabilities primarily through its impact on the opportunity component.

The opportunities relevant to attain urban capabilities may in principle be a broad set of circumstances, including institutional, economic, social, and spatial conditions. Within these, the *affordances* in Gibson's sense [15] may be conceptualised as a subset of opportunities, in particular those that are directly perceivable and actionable in the urban physical environment.

Hence, the functionings attained within their capability set comprise activities people perform within urban space, so these activities are the "mediating factor" between the people and the physical urban environment. Concrete actions are goal-oriented, driven, and adjusted to the circumstances. Even while a goal and a reason might not change, the approach used to get there might, depending on the situation and on the environment [18]. And this possibility of action hinges critically on the available affordances of urban space.

While the objective of a massive assessment of affordances of urban spaces provides the general drive to our research programme, the assessment tool presented here is just a stepping stone to that more general aim. Instead of actually assessing affordances of physical spaces, it performs a more limited task of assessing people's activities, which are directly observable. In other words, it observes actual spatial functionings taking place in urban spaces.

To this end, behavioural mapping represents a methodological approach based on structured observation, combining various detection, mapping, and quantification techniques of activities performed at different times by people occupying a defined space. This method enables the identification of patterns in space utilisation, social interactions, and activity distributions [19].

From a human-centred perspective, the approach helps explore both the quantity and quality of the various activities performed by people who move, stay, play, and spend their time in different ways. The data collection process through observation, analysis, and visualisation can highlight the presence of different social groups in the study area and their behaviour and thus of the affordances relating to that public space. The information gathered about practices in a particular urban context potentially describes the general framework in terms of socialisation, time budgets, and physical activity. The results, therefore, provide an understanding of user dynamics in specific places [20].

So, the objective of urban analysis is twofold: it is both an observational and a documental process, and it should also lead to positive change in the built environment [21]. The outcomes can serve as inputs for formulating urban regeneration programs and for evaluating the effectiveness of transformative interventions.

2.2 AI-Based Tools: Techniques and Technologies

In recent times, conventional observational methods such as direct observation and enumeration are being complemented by technological advancements including GPS, GIS, skin sensors, remote sensing, and closed-circuit television (CCTV), amongst others. The rapid advancements in computer processing speed and power have rendered it feasible to integrate diverse sensing and observation modalities in ways that were hitherto inconceivable.

Many recent studies have focused on person detection, employing *object detection* models to localise individuals in images or video streams. For example, in [22], the authors used an advanced variant of the YOLO (You Only Look Once) series of real-time object detectors to identify individuals in a public square and classify them according to demographic and behavioural attributes, achieving approximately 83% accuracy across categories such as walking, sitting, and exercising. A complementary approach is presented in [23], where the authors employed YOLOv4 [24] for person detection and CNN-based classifiers (*ResNet-18* [25] and *EfficientNet* [26]) for gender classification, trained on a custom-annotated dataset. Rather than directly recognising physical activities or postures, their method inferred usage patterns in an urban park based on the spatial distribution, gender, and temporal presence of detected individuals. This enabled the identification of behavioural trends—such as which demographics utilised specific areas of the park—without the need for explicit action or posture recognition.

Another line of research gaining traction in public space analysis involves *pose estimation*, which enables the automatic classification of bodily postures (e.g., upright, seated, recumbent) by extracting and analysing skeletal keypoints. However, deploying such techniques in uncontrolled outdoor environments remains challenging due to factors such as occlusion, variable lighting, and background complexity. As highlighted by Cormier et al. in [27], the lack of large-scale datasets tailored for public surveillance settings has hindered the development of generalisable pose estimation models, and there is a continued need for lightweight systems capable of operating in real-time with limited computational resources.

A key innovation in the field has come with the emergence of Multimodal Large Language Models (MLLMs)—extensions of Large Language Models (LLMs), which are deep neural networks trained on vast corpora of text to generate and understand human language. While LLMs, operate solely on textual input, MLLMs are designed to process and reason over multiple modalities, particularly combining visual and textual inputs, allowing them to interpret images and extract structured semantic information in a zero-shot fashion, that is without requiring task-specific training. This enables scene understanding, extracting semantic and structured information from visual content without the need for task-specific training. An early application in the context of urban analysis is found in [28], who used a MLLM to assess walkability from Google Street View imagery, demonstrating the ability of these models in multimodal reasoning. Also,

[29] explored the use of GPT-4 Vision in the automated analysis of urban morphology and public space usage using both Google Street View and CCTV imagery. Their approach consisted of prompting the model to generate structured JSON outputs describing elements such as the presence and activities of people, built environment quality, and public safety indicators. To address inconsistencies and hallucinations—such as incorrect detection of "danger" from suggestive elements like traffic cones, or fluctuating labelling of features like "mixed-use areas"—they submitted each image five times and aggregated the outputs to improve reliability. Despite these efforts, the authors emphasise that the system's outputs should be treated as "suspected" rather than definitive detections, requiring human verification and not suitable for critical decision-making.

These limitations point to a key challenge in applying general-purpose MLLMs directly for fine-grained urban behavioural analysis: while they are flexible and powerful, their outputs can be inconsistent, ambiguous, or overly sensitive to context. Our approach follows this recent line of research leveraging MLLMs and LLMs for urban scene understanding, explicitly addressing these issues by introducing a structured pipeline designed to enhance robustness and interpretability. Specifically, it extracts consistent and reliable information on individuals' bodily posture, activity level, social configuration, age range, and sex from images captured in public spaces.

After extensive experimentation with several multimodal strategies—including LLaVA [30], Gemini [31], and GPT-4o [32]—we identified the most effective approach as a sequential pipeline consisting of Faster R-CNN [33] for person detection, followed by postprocessing and two consecutive applications of GPT-4o models for refined image description and information extraction. The details of our approach are presented below in Sect. 3.1.

3 Observation Protocol

The presented AI tool is based on and aims at reproducing an observation protocol designed to be performed by human auditors/observers. The protocol, more extensively presented in [34], has the purpose to gather information about what people do in public spaces, and has been tested in real-world contexts.

The observation protocol was designed to control for different variables, such as time of day, day or week, season, location and so on. A controlled observation follows a clear set of steps. These steps include what, where, when, who, how and how long to observe.

In relation to the object of study, i.e. people's actions in open spaces, the observation is quantitative as it generates numerical outputs of frequency counts.

The research method is founded upon a series of systematic questions, enabling the articulation of diverse activities undertaken by various groups of people across multiple levels. Specifically, context-specific questions are derived from the integration of five fundamental questions [19]:

- *How many people?* – The first question concerns the number of people in relation to the space, i.e. how many people are present in the observed scene.
- *Who?* – The second question aims to categorise the actors in the space, dividing them into different groups according to two variables:

- *age*, classified on a generational basis (child, adult, senior);
- *gender* (male, female).

– *Where do people carry out their activities?* – The third question focuses on the activities people perform in space, with a particular emphasis on the mapping of locations that offer opportunities for action. The data collected enables the description of the positioning of individuals according to the activities they perform and the elements present.
– *What activities take place?* – The fourth question explores the nature of the activity, with respect to a specific taxonomy of activities, subdivided in three features:

- *body posture*, describing physical position or bodily configuration of the person, classified into "upright" (standing, leaning, squatting), "seated" (sitting on a bench, ground, ledge, stairs, wall, etc.), and "recumbent" (lying down, lounging);
- *physical activity*, movement, or exertion; the classes are "sedentary" (stationary, minimal movement while standing/sitting/lying, for example resting, reading, eating, playing cards or a board game), "moderate" (walking, slow ambulatory movement), and "vigorous" (running, jumping, playing, exercising);
- *social configuration*, indicating the social context in which the individual is situated; the classes are "solitary" (alone, no direct social interaction, solitary presence), "dyadic" (in a pair, interacting with one other person), and "group" (in a group of three or more, engaged socially).

– *How long does the activity last?* – The fifth question considers the temporal component associated with activities performed in public space. Specifically, it assesses the duration of the activities. Duration can provide insights into the quality of the spaces.

3.1 The Tool: A Multimodal AI Pipeline for Automatic Observation of Activities in Urban Spaces

The purpose on the tool presented here is to implement an AI pipeline for automatic observation of activities in urban spaces, based on the observation protocol briefly presented in the previous subsection. The tool accepts images of urban scenes populated with people, and automatically classifies people in the scene according to five features: age group (child, adult, senior), sex (female/male), bodily posture (upright, seated, recumbent), activity level (sedentary, moderate, vigorous) and social configuration (solitary, dyadic, group).

After extensive experimentation with several multimodal strategies—including LLaVA [30], Gemini [31], and GPT-4o [32]—we identified the most effective approach as a sequential pipeline consisting of Faster R-CNN [33] for person detection, followed by some postprocessing detailed below and two consecutive applications of GPT-4o models for refined image description and information extraction.

A schematic overview of this workflow is shown in Fig. 2, which visually represents each step from person detection to the final structured output.

The pipeline initiates with the detection of individuals within the image, for which we used Faster R-CNN, from Detectron2. Faster R-CNN is an advanced object detection model utilising a Region Proposal Network (RPN) to identify potential bounding boxes that might contain objects. The adopted version of the model employs a ResNeXt-101 backbone architecture, known for its superior performance in extracting rich visual features, and Feature Pyramid Networks (FPN), which enhance detection accuracy across multiple scales by leveraging features at various resolution levels. The model is trained for extended epochs ($3\times$), improving its robustness and accuracy in detecting complex objects, especially humans, across diverse environments.

Detectron2 is a state-of-the-art, open-source platform developed by Facebook AI Research (FAIR) for building, training, and deploying object detection, segmentation, and other visual perception models. It provides modular, highly customisable components and pre-trained models that facilitate rapid experimentation and deployment of advanced computer vision applications. Note that, in views of the subsequent steps, identified bounding boxes undergo padding to ensure complete encapsulation of the detected individuals. In the present application, padding values are calculated proportionally, extending each bounding box by 40% horizontally and 20% vertically, thus providing sufficient contextual visual information for following analysis.

As shown in Fig. 1, to reduce the complexity of the visual input passed later to the language model, bounding boxes intersecting or closely positioned are clustered into singular bounding boxes.

This clustering employs an iterative approach, merging overlapping bounding boxes until no further merges are possible, significantly enhancing the coherence and clarity of subsequent image cropping and analysis. Importantly, this step does not necessarily isolate single individuals or single groups of interacting people but rather aims to ensure that cropped regions passed to the language model do not contain an excessive number of distinct people. In fact, overcrowded crops tend to reduce the precision of the multimodal language model's descriptive capacity. Clustering therefore plays a crucial role in optimising the quality of the generated image descriptions, preserving a balance between sufficient context and visual clarity.

Subsequently, the clustered bounding boxes are used to crop sub-images from the original frame. Each cropped image is then independently analysed by a MLLM, which was GPT-4o in the present application, to produce detailed descriptions, capturing essential visual attributes and contextual cues. GPT-4o's proved quite robust in vision understanding and could ensure precise interpretations of visual content, addressing even partially visible individuals.

Generated textual descriptions from the MLLM are further processed through a secondary LLM pass to extract structured information systematically. For this step also we used GPT-4o after some experimentation with alternative models. This step assigns definitive values for bodily posture (upright, seated, recumbent), activity level (sedentary, moderate, vigorous), social configuration (solitary, dyadic, group), age range (child, adult, senior), and sex (male, female) for each individual, even under conditions of visual uncertainty.

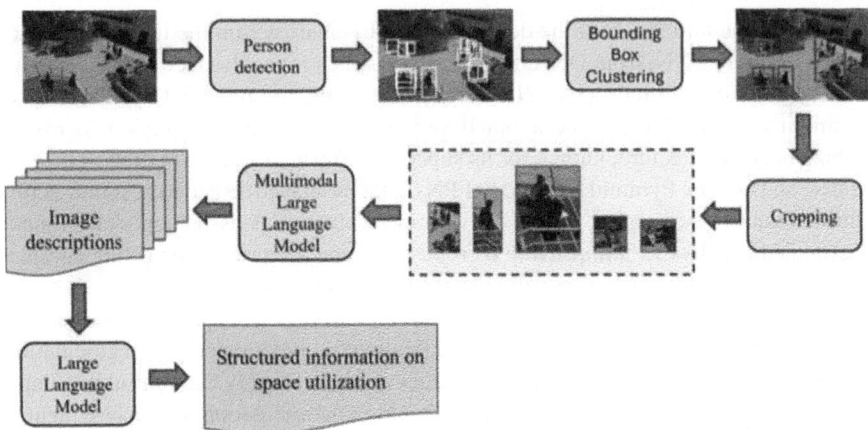

Fig. 1. Multimodal AI pipeline for structured observation of public spaces. Individuals are detected with Faster R-CNN and grouped by bounding box overlap. Cropped regions are expanded and analysed by GPT-4o, which generates descriptions later parsed to extract posture, activity level, social configuration, age group, and gender.

Extracted data are compiled into structured JSON files, facilitating downstream statistical analysis and comparative evaluations. These files comprehensively document each individual's characteristics and the total count of visible persons per analysed image.

The approach described above effectively mitigates several issues reported in [29], including the inconsistency of outputs and hallucination of scene elements. In contrast to their single-step prompting method, our two-stage pipeline decouples image interpretation from structured data extraction. This reduces ambiguity, ensures more accurate attribute labelling, and facilitates validation against observational data. Furthermore, the use of bounding box clustering and context padding contributes to increased robustness when analysing crowded scenes or partially occluded individuals.

The following sections present a comparative evaluation of this pipeline against manually annotated data, to assess its accuracy and reliability in real-world scenes.

4 Experimental Test

To test the tool, we have collected images from 24 different scenes across 5 open urban public spaces in the city of Cagliari (Italy). The images were captured under favourable weather conditions and during daylight hours over the course of three days in March 2025.

Each image was classified by a human auditor according to five features:

- age group ("child", "adult", "senior");
- sex ("female" or "male");
- body posture ("upright or "seated"); the "recumbent" category from the original protocol was not present in the sample;

- activity level ("sedentary" or "moving"); "moving" category comprised of only "moderate" activity levels, since "vigorous" level was not present in the sample;
- social configuration ("solitary" or "group"); the "group" category aggregates "dyadic" and "group" categories from the original protocol.

Figure 2 presents an example of the procedure applied for the manual evaluation of a sample images. The images were then submitted to the classification algorithm, providing the estimate classifications for the same four features.

Fig. 2. Example of manual evaluation of the captured scenes. The image presents seven social configurations (a–g), within which individual components are observed. *Configuration a* (solitary): 1 male, upright, sedentary; *configuration b* (group): 2 males, seated, sedentary; *configuration c* (group): 2 females, seated, sedentary; *configuration d* (solitary): 1 male, upright, moving; *configuration e* (group): 4 males, upright, moving; *configuration f* (solitary): 1 female, upright, moving; *configuration g* (group): [1 male, seated, sedentary], [1 male, upright, sedentary], [1 female, seated, sedentary].

The overall count of people in the two samples, ground truth and estimates, together with essential descriptive statistics, are summarised in Fig. 3.

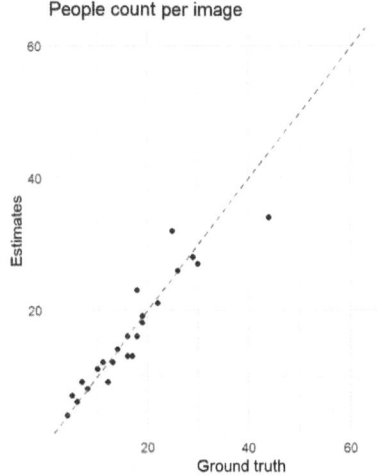

People count per image

Statistics	Ground truth	Estimates
Total count of people	462	438
Min	4	4
Median	16.50	15.00
Mean	19.25	18.25
Max	73	60

Fig. 3. People count: scatterplot (left); descriptive statistics (right)

The figures in the following pages – from Figs. 4, 5, 6 and 7 – show scatterplots and Bland-Altman plots, reporting the counts per each feature's category with respect to the two samples (ground truth and estimates).

To assess the alignment and distributional similarity between the ground truth and the estimates, several per-category error metrics and global divergence measures are calculated on relative data (i.e. percentages), comparing estimated and ground-truth category distributions.

MAE (Mean Absolute Error) and RMSE (Root Mean Squared Error) quantify the average absolute and squared deviations, respectively, between estimated and true proportions for each category. Bias indicates the mean signed error, capturing over- or under-estimation.

As global metrics, Chi-square distance, Kullback–Leibler (KL) divergence and Jensen–Shannon (JS) divergence are calculated for each of the four features. Chi-square distance measures the average relative squared difference between estimated and observed proportions, normalised by the observed values. Kullback–Leibler (KL) divergence quantifies the information loss when using the estimated distribution to approximate the ground truth. Jensen–Shannon (JS) divergence is a symmetric and smoothed version of KL, bounded between 0 and 1.

For the three global metrics, we estimated the confidence intervals using a nonparametric bootstrap resampling procedure. Specifically, we performed 1,000 bootstrap iterations, in each of which the set of samples (i.e., per-image predictions) was resampled with replacement, and the target metrics (i.e., Chi-square distance, KL divergence, Jensen-Shannon divergence) were recomputed. The 95% confidence interval was then computed as the 2.5th and 97.5th percentiles of the resulting bootstrap distribution.

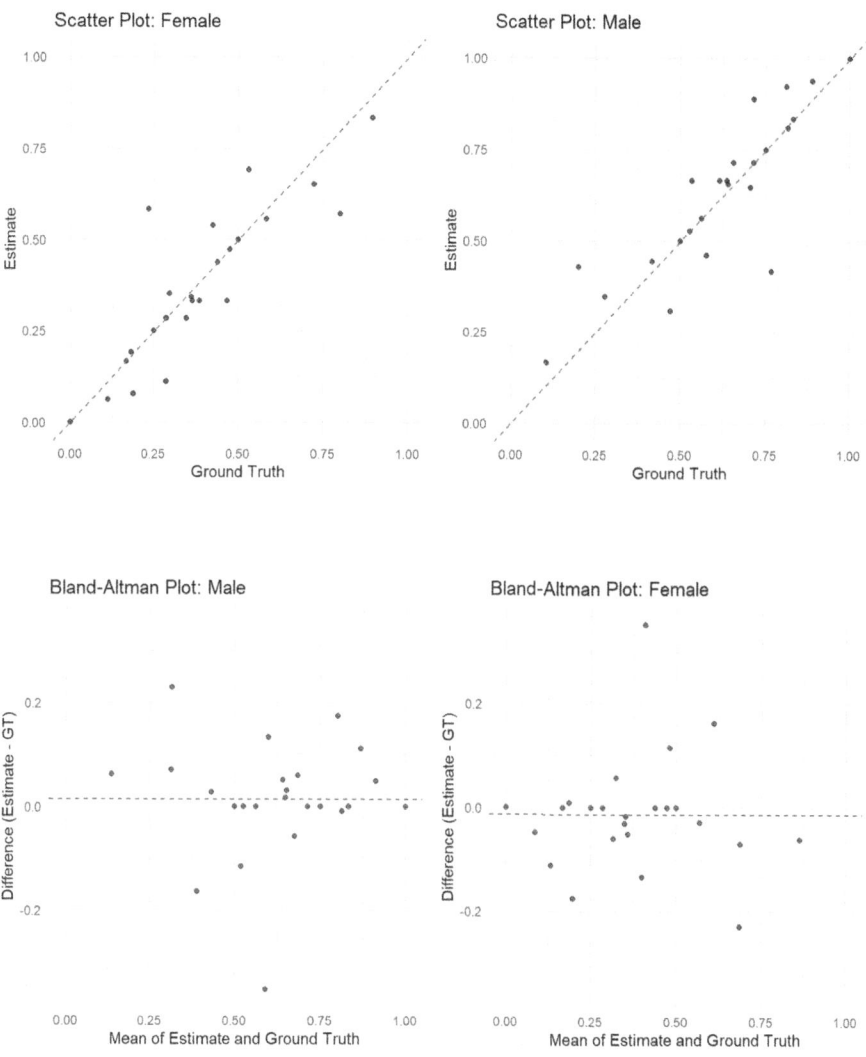

Fig. 4. Feature: Sex (female or male); values expressed in percentages (%).

All the metrics and confidence intervals are reported in Table 1. In the table, we report values just for one category within each feature, given that all the features hold only binary categories (e.g. female/male, upright/seated, etc.), so the values reported for MAE and RMSE are identical for both categories of each feature, while the Bias is sign-inverted (e.g. for the "Sex" feature, the estimate bias for "female" $-.0132$, hence the estimate bias for "male" is $.0132$).

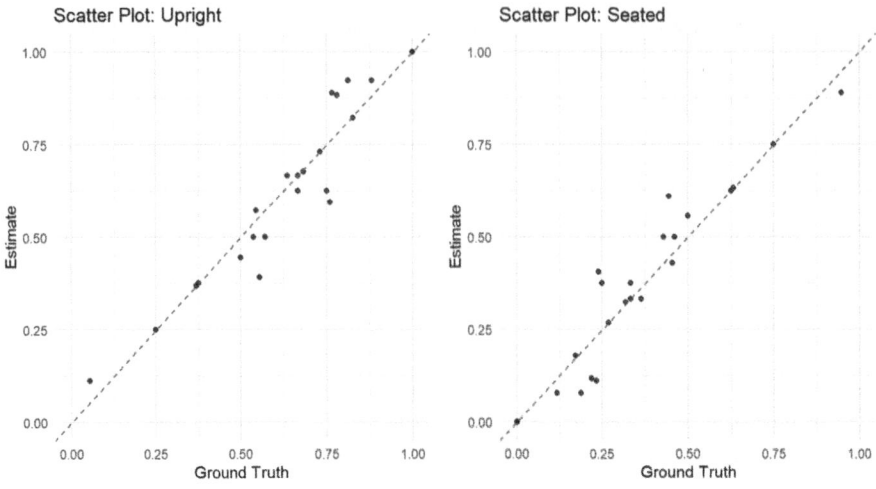

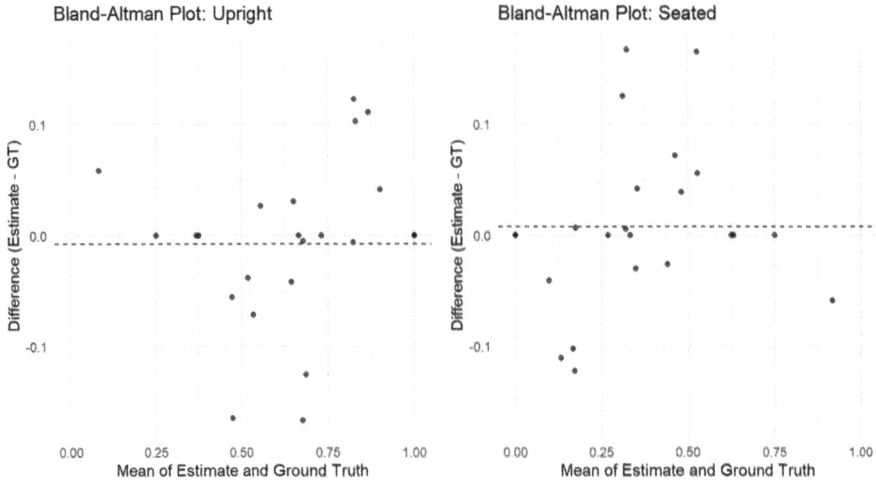

Fig. 5. Feature: Body posture (upright or seated); values expressed in percentages (%).

4.1 Discussion

The per-category error metrics (MAE, RMSE, Bias), as well as the global divergence metrics reveal satisfactory, although not uniform degrees of alignment between estimated and ground-truth distributions. The lowest divergence values were observed for Sex (Chi-Square = .07, KL = .03, JS = .01) and Body Posture (Chi-Square = .03, KL = .02, JS = .00), indicating high consistency between algorithmic estimates and actual category proportions for these features.

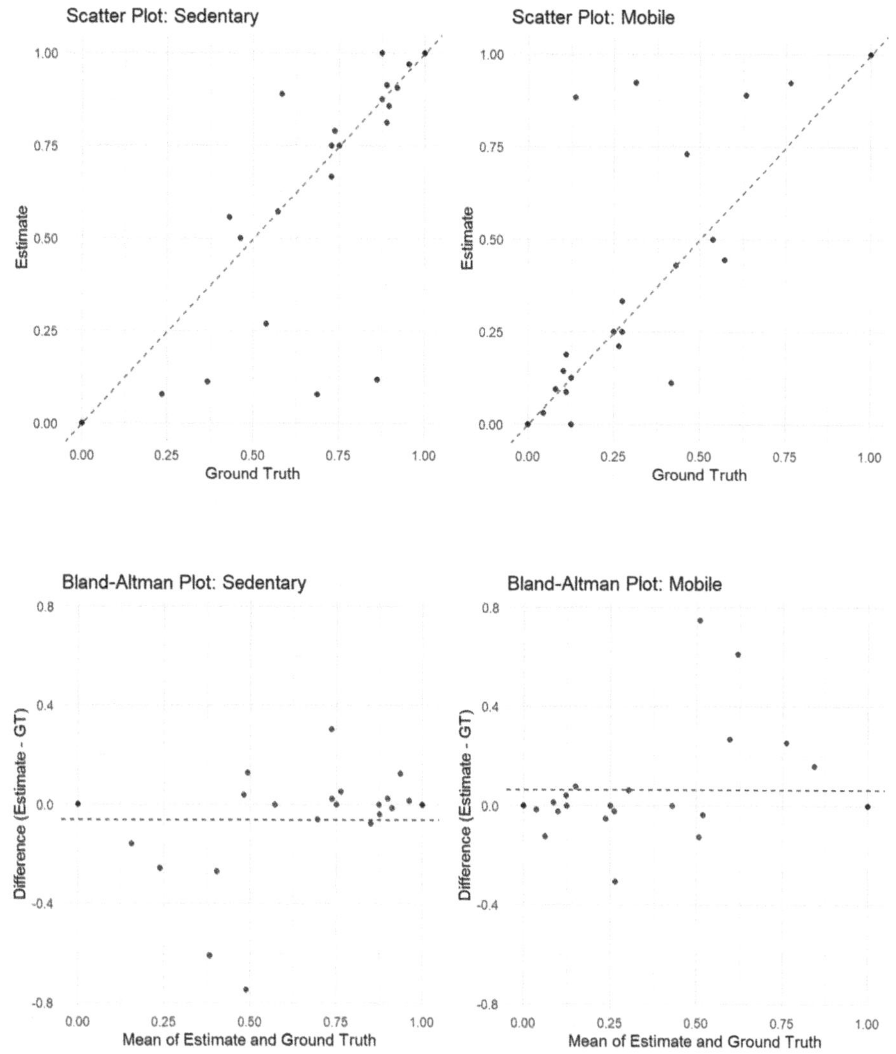

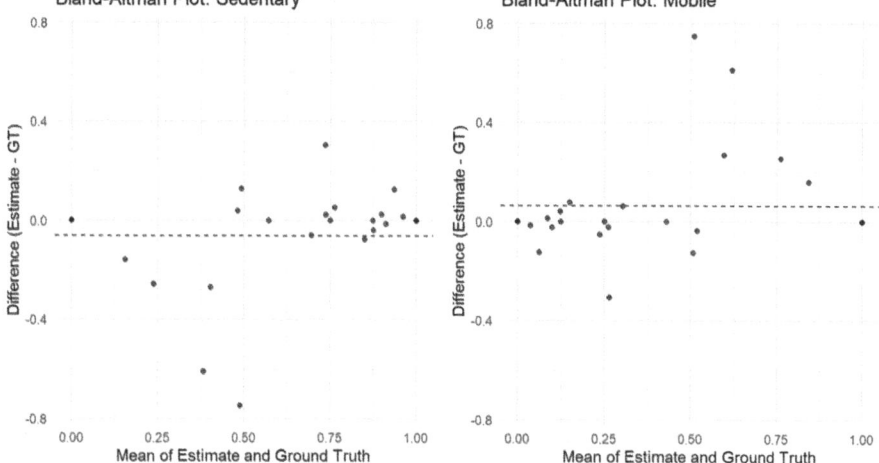

Fig. 6. Feature: Activity level (sedentary or mobile); values expressed in percentages (%).

In contrast, Activity Level exhibited higher divergence across all three measures (Chi-Square = .33, KL = .20, JS = .03), suggesting that the classification algorithm performed somewhat worse with estimating the distribution of sedentary vs. mobile individuals. Social Configuration showed somewhat intermediate divergence (Chi-Square = .10, KL = .19, JS = .02), indicating some discrepancies, though less pronounced than for Activity Level.

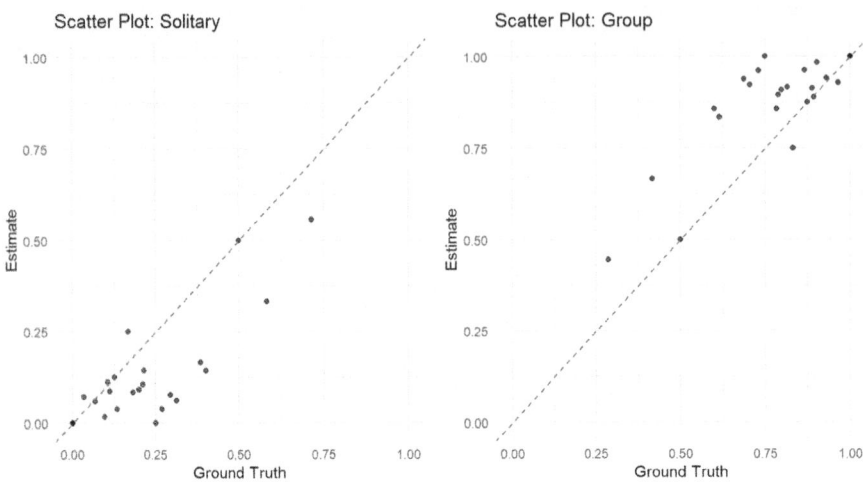

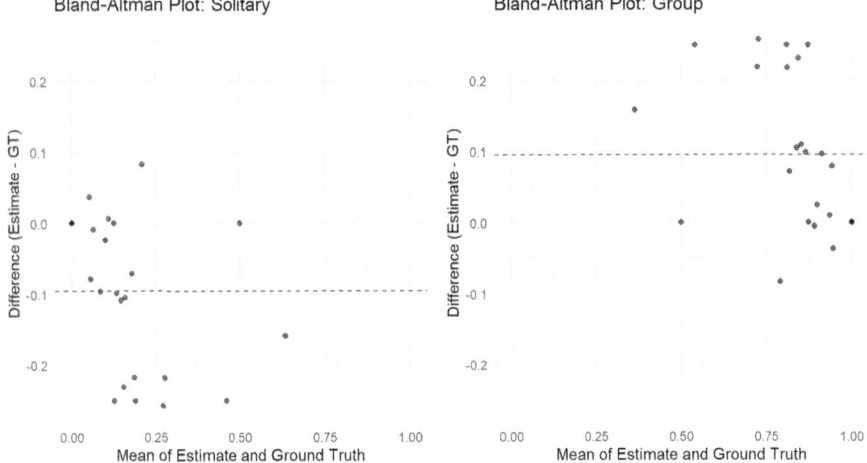

Fig. 7. Feature: Social configuration (solitary or group); values expressed in percentages (%).

Table 1. Per-category error metrics and global divergence measures comparing ground-truth and estimated category distributions. MAE: Mean Absolute Error; RMSE: Root Mean Squared Error; CSq: Chi-square distance; KL: Kullback–Leibler divergence; JS: Jensen–Shannon divergence; CSq I KL I JS CI: respective 95% confidence intervals.

Feature	MAE	RMSE	Bias	CSq	CSq CI	KL	KL CI	JS	JS CI
Sex (female/male)	.0711	.1114	− .0132	.07	.02-.14	.03	.01-.06	.01	.00-.01
Body posture (upright/seated)	.0485	− .0725	− .0076	.03	.01-.05	.02	.00-.03	.00	.00-.01
Activity level (sedentary/mobile)	.1226	.2268	− .0633	.33	.04-.84	.20	.05-.38	.03	.01-.06
Social configuration (solo/group)	.1063	.1428	− .0958	.10	.06-.15	.19	.05-.45	.02	.01-.03

5   Conclusions

The results presented suggest that the algorithm performs very well in estimating distributions for sex and posture, while further refinement may be needed for activity level and social configuration, although also in those cases the performance of the classification algorithm is fairly acceptable.

The relative greater difficulty to estimate the activity level (sedentary vs. mobile) is likely inherent to the nature of the input data, i.e. still images of urban scenes. In these, the mobile or sedentary status of people can often be intrinsically ambiguous, add hence hard to interpret or altogether impossible to discern. Should a child goalkeeper playing football but standing still in the image be classified as sedentary or as performing a vigorous physical activity? Likely, to improve the classification performance here it would be necessary to submit a video clip, or a sequence of frames shot in close time succession to better assess the dynamics of the activity.

Both these paths lie before us, rich with potential for further development of the tool.

Acknowledgments. This study was funded by:

References

1. Qi, J., Mazumdar, S., Vasconcelos, A.C.: Understanding the relationship between urban public space and social cohesion: a systematic review. Int. J. Com. WB. **7**, 155–212 (2024). https://doi.org/10.1007/s42413-024-00204-5
2. Mitchell Tada, G.: Socially just public spaces are crucial to flourishing societies (2023)
3. Low, S.: Why Public Space Matters. Oxford University Press, Oxford (2022)
4. Tigran, H., Littke, H., Elahe, K.: Urban form and human behavior in context of livable cities and their public realms. SJPBS **3**(4), 325–339 (2020). https://doi.org/10.32474/SJPBS.2020.03.000167
5. Jacobs, J.: Death and Life of Great American Cities. Random House, New York (1961)

6. Whyte, W.H.: The social life of small urban spaces. In: Project for Public Space, New York (1980)
7. Gehl, J.: Life Between Buildings: Using Public Space. Island Press, Washington, DC (1971)
8. Gehl, J.: Cities for People. Island Press, Washington, DC (2010)
9. Szczepańska, A., Pietrzyk, K.: An evaluation of public spaces with the use of direct and remote methods. Land **9**, 419 (2020). https://doi.org/10.3390/land9110419
10. Weng, Q., et al.: How will ai transform urban observing, sensing, imaging, and mapping? NPJ Urban Sustain. **4**, 1–9 (2024). https://doi.org/10.1038/s42949-024-00188-3
11. Blečić, I., Cecchini, A., Talu, V.: The capability approach in urban quality of life and urban policies: towards a conceptual framework. In: Serreli, S. (ed.) City Project and Public Space. Springer, Dordrecht (2013). https://doi.org/10.1007/978-94-007-6037-0_17
12. Blečić, I., Cecchini, A., Congiu, T., Fancello, G., Talu, V., Trunfio, G.A.: Operationalising urban capabilities: the case of walkability. In: Proceedings of the 2015 HDCA Conference-Capabilities on the Move: Mobility and Aspirations, Washington, September 10, p. 2015 (2015)
13. Blečić, I., Cecchini, A., Talu, V.: Capability approach and urban planning. Fertile urban capabilities and quality of urban life of the most disadvantaged inhabitants. Archivio di Studi Urbani e Regionali **48**, 34–52 (2018). https://doi.org/10.3280/ASUR2018-122003
14. Blečić, I., Cecchini, A., Congiu, T., Fancello, G., Talu, V., Trunfio, G.A.: Capability-wise walkability evaluation as an indicator of urban peripherality. Environ. Plann. B Urban Anal. City Sci. **48**, 895–911 (2021). https://doi.org/10.1177/2399808320908294
15. Gibson, J.: The Ecological Approach to Visual Perception. Psychology Press, New York (1979)
16. Sen, A.: Development as Freedom. Oxford University Press, Oxford (1999)
17. Sen, A.: The Idea of Justice. Harvard University Press, Harvard, MA (2009)
18. Bærentsen, K.B., Trettvik, J.: An activity theory approach to affordance. In: Nordichi 2002. Proceedings of the Second Nordic Conference on Human-Computer Interaction, pp. 51–60 (2002)
19. Gehl, J., Svarre, B.: How to Study Public Life. Island Press, Washington, DC (2013)
20. Byrne, J.A.: Observation for data collection in urban studies and urban analysis. In: Baum, S. (ed.) Methods in Urban Analysis, pp. 127–149. Springer, Singapore (2021). https://doi.org/10.1007/978-981-16-1677-8_8
21. Ye, Y., Li, D., Liu, X.: How block density and typology affect urban vitality: an exploratory analysis in Shenzhen. China. Urban Geogr. **39**, 1–22 (2017). https://doi.org/10.1080/02723638.2017.1381536
22. Wang, L., He, W.: Analysis of community outdoor public spaces based on computer vision behavior detection algorithm. Appl. Sci. **13**, 10922 (2023). https://doi.org/10.3390/app131910922
23. Gravitz-Sela, S., Levy, A., Zehavi, S., Bryt, O., Shach-Pinsly, D., Plaut, P.: Analyzing usage patterns from video data through deep learning: the case of an urban park. Comput. Environ. Urban Syst. **117** (2025). https://doi.org/10.1016/j.compenvurbsys.2024.102229
24. Bochkovskiy, A., Wang, C.-Y., Liao, H.-Y.M.: YOLOv4: optimal speed and accuracy of object detection. arXiv preprint arXiv:2004.10934 (2020)
25. He, K., Zhang, X., Ren, S., Sun, J.: Deep residual learning for image recognition. In: 2016 IEEE Conference on Computer Vision and Pattern Recognition (CVPR), pp. 770–778 (2016). https://doi.org/10.1109/CVPR.2016.90
26. Tan, M., Le, Q.V.: EfficientNet: rethinking model scaling for convolutional neural networks. arXiv preprint arXiv:1905.11946 (2020)
27. Cormier, M., Clepe, A., Specker, A., Beyerer, J.: Where are we with human pose estimation in real-world surveillance? In: 2022 IEEE/CVF Winter Conference on Applications of Computer Vision Workshops (WACVW). pp. 591–601. Waikoloa, HI, USA (2022)

28. Blečić, I., Saiu, V., A. Trunfio, G.: Enhancing urban walkability assessment with multi-modal large language models. In: Gervasi, O., Murgante, B., Garau, C., Taniar, D.,C. Rocha, A.M.A., Faginas Lago, M.N. (eds.) Computational Science and Its Applications – ICCSA 2024 Workshops, pp. 394–411. Springer, Cham (2024). https://doi.org/10.1007/978-3-031-65282-0_26
29. Komar, T., James, P.: LLM-vision in enhancing the understanding of public spaces. Abstr. ICA. **8**, 1–4 (2024). https://doi.org/10.5194/ica-abs-8-15-2024
30. Liu, H., Li, C., Wu, Q., Lee, Y.J.: Visual instruction tuning. arXiv preprint arXiv:2304.08485 (2023)
31. Gemini Team Google: Gemini: a family of highly capable multimodal models. arXiv preprint arXiv:2312.11805 (2024)
32. OpenAI: GPT-4°. https://platform.openai.com/docs/models/gpt-4o
33. Ren, S., He, K., Girshick, R., Sun, J.: Faster R-CNN: towards real-time object detection with region proposal networks. IEEE Trans. Pattern Anal. Mach. Intell. **39**, 1137–1149 (2017). https://doi.org/10.1109/TPAMI.2016.2577031
34. Manunza, A., et al.: Build it and they will stay: assessing the social impact of self-build practices in urban regeneration. Urban Sci. **9**(2) (2025). https://doi.org/10.3390/urbansci9020030

Trajectory Analysis Applied to Crime Incidence

Rodrigo Tapia-McClung[1]([✉])(iD), Rodrigo Lopez-Farias[2,3](iD),
and Camilo Caudillo-Cos[1](iD)

[1] Centro de Investigación en Ciencias de Información Geoespacial CDMX, Contoy
137, 14240 Lomas de Padierna, Tlalpan, Mexico
{rtapia,ccaudillo}@centrogeo.edu.mx

[2] Centro de Investigación en Ciencias de Información Geoespacial Querétaro, Pedro
Escobedo, 76709 Querétaro, Mexico
rlopez@centrogeo.edu.mx

[3] Secretaría de Ciencia, Humanidades, Tecnología e Innovación, Insurgentes Sur
1582, Crédito Constructor, 03940 Benito Juárez, Mexico

Abstract. In the study of criminal incidence, the lack of graphical specialized tools makes it difficult to properly communicate in a consistent
way, and with simple terms, its spatio-temporal evolution. In this work,
we propose the application of a count-based trajectory time series analysis to study the spatio-temporal evolution of larceny theft in Mexico
City. This framework helps describing the spatio-temporal evolution of
an event by identifying and grouping the individual location dynamics
that contribute in the description of the types and magnitude of different changes in space. These changes can be expressed in terms of gains,
losses, and possible alternations that generate exchange of criminal incidence without observing significant gross loss or gain in incidence. We
highlight the characteristics that are beneficial to the interpretation of
the spatio-temporal evolution of crime incidence and the drawbacks of
using this technique. We conclude that while there is a general decreasing trend of crime incidence, the graphical method is sensitive to show
internal patterns such as gains, losses and alternation, that are important
to analyze key spatio-temporal patterns throughout the years. This approach is intended to be useful for evaluating strategies for the reduction
of criminal incidence.

Keywords: Trajectory analysis · Crime incidence · Spatio-temporal
time series

1 Introduction

The main objectives of criminology are understanding, communicating, and
delineating strategies to minimize criminal incidence. Understanding criminal
phenomena requires the articulation of diverse areas of work like sociology, such
as psychology, anthropology, political science law [3], and any other discipline

© The Author(s), under exclusive license to Springer Nature Switzerland AG 2026
O. Gervasi et al. (Eds.): ICCSA 2025 Workshops, LNCS 15890, pp. 358–370, 2026.
https://doi.org/10.1007/978-3-031-97606-3_24

that contributes to study the phenomena such as statistics and geospatial sciences. In this work we propose applying a Trajectory Analysis, that is descriptive statistics method oriented to visualize the magnitude of criminal incidence in terms of its quantity and spatial change.

A trajectory, in the broad sense, is defined as "the path that a moving object follows through space as a function of time" [14]. In geospatial sciences, the trajectory analysis of criminal incidence is the study of its patterns and describing its characteristics of importance in the spatio-temporal domain.

A count-based Trajectory Analysis approach for binary cover maps series put forward in [2] is applied in this work for the study of the evolution of criminal events through space and time in terms of gain and loss components. This approach is based on the classification of every location of the map according to the type of temporal trajectory of a binary variable taken throughout time. Then, the size of the gain and loss component is obtained as the contribution of different trajectories.

We posit that this kind of description would allow the classification of the type of change in criminal incidence in an area of study. In this sense, it would be possible to identify whether crime incidence shows a general increase, decrease, if it alternates in space or if it is only being exchanged from one place to another without observing an apparent loss. Specifically, we carry out this analysis and find it useful in recognizing crime patterns in Mexico City.

This paper is organized as follows. We first present the background and previous work that justifies the connection between the study of larceny theft and the count-based trajectory analysis. We then introduce the basic concepts of the trajectory analysis of spatio-temporal data used in this contribution along with the study area and data used. Then, we present the processed data used to make conclusions regarding the dynamics of the crime incidence in Mexico City. Lastly, we present some constructive criticism highlighting the areas for improvements for this kind of application and future work.

2   Background and Related Work

Time series analysis, longitudinal analysis, and trajectory analysis are all methods for analyzing data over time, but they each have different purposes. In a time series analysis, data points are collected and analyzed at regular intervals over time to identify patterns and trends. Usually, one can expect to predict future values. In a longitudinal analysis, the interest is on studying how variables change over time for a group of subjects. The goal is commonly identify cause-and-effect relationships. In a trajectory analysis, the objective is usually to describe how a variable changes over time or age. It can be used to study how covariates affect the shape of a variable [8].

In the social sciences, sequence analysis has been translated into a set of longitudinal data methods [1]. Surveys like this one, focus on highlighting the application of qualitative methods that study the population and their changes throughout time, also referred to as life course trajectories or event history trajectories [9]. Over time, computational approaches have been emphasized to characterize complex successions of different states [12], finding that social organization derives from spatial, hierarchical, and other ordered phenomena.

Trajectory analysis is a sub-discipline commonly used for exploratory analysis and to develop hypotheses to explain differences between certain groups. In criminology, it has been used to examine how large samples of individuals could be grouped according to crimes throughout life [10]. More recently, longitudinal analyses have also been applied at the place scale to identify trends and clusters of street segments in terms of crime incidences [16] and microgeographic hotspots [15]. Cluster analysis methods have also been adapted to extend to spatio-temporal patterns, resulting in the characterization of trajectories in other longitudinal studies of crime [5]. This last example implements the classification of trajectories with a longitudinal k-means algorithm, which identifies groups of spatial units with similar behaviors. This work also strongly suggests to retain the resource allocation information regarding the time and place of occurrence and use count-based methods to measure the frequency of events in specific locations.

Examples of the application of the count-based Trajectory Analysis include measuring and tracking the trajectories of losses and gains of soybean cultivation [11] and to cross comparing the marsh evolution in three sites within the United States Long-Term Ecological Research Network [2]. Both use the proposed count-based methodology for a time series trajectory analysis to describe spatio-temporal changes in land cover to elucidate details and differences of the evolution of certain types of cover.

The methodology proposed in [2] is a relatively new approach and, thus, the diversity of applications is yet scarce. In this sense we propose using this methodology for a spatio-temporal graphical analysis of the dynamics of larceny theft. But first, we briefly explain this methodology in the next section.

3   Count-Based Trajectory Analysis of Spatio-Temporal Discrete Data

The count-based time series trajectory analysis consists of analyzing and classifying the sequences of all the individual locations in the area of interest of cover maps.

The characteristic of this approach is the preservation of both qualitative and quantitative information. The qualitative information is associated with the classification of the dynamic described by the sequence of presence and absences of a variable for each location. The quantitative information is associated with the total of gains and looses of a variable in the space for each time interval through the time. Other approaches, such as trajectory identification through unsupervised learning, have the disadvantage that the quality of the clusters will depend on an arbitrary number of classes defined a priori. The approach summarizes the possible trajectories (changes over time) in six classes, providing a synthetic view of the crime incidence behavior.

Initially, every local trajectory is a sequence of binary labels representing the presence or absence of a variable of interest at different moments in time. The method classifies trajectories into one of eight different types, depending on the number of time intervals considered. The possible trajectories defined with this approach appear when considering a minimum set of four maps [M_1, M_2, M_3, M_4] and are shown in Table 1.

Table 1. Schematic representation of the different types of space time trajectories. White and black cells represent the absence and presence of the variable of interest, respectively.

ID	M_1	→	M_2	→	M_3	→	M_4	Trajectory Classification
One time interval								
1	□	→	□					Stable Absence
2	□	→	■					Gain without Alternation
3	■	→	□					Loss without Alternation
4	■	→	■					Stable Presence
Two time intervals								
5	□	→	■	→	□			All Alternation Gain First
6	■	→	□	→	■			All Alternation Loss first
Three time intervals								
7	■	→	□	→	■	→	□	Loss with Alternation
8	□	→	■	→	□	→	■	Gain with Alternation

The first column shows the ID of the location, the second one indicates the map sequence, and the last one contains the corresponding trajectory classification.

Location with IDs {1, 2, 3, 4} only have one time interval available and their representation is limited to four possible trajectories: stable absence, stable presence, gain and loss without alternation. For locations with IDs {5, 6}, having two time intervals, the representation is extended in addition to the previous trajectories, with presence or absence at the initial and final time intervals. However, these additional trajectories exhibit alternation. They are aptly named: all alternation gain first and all alternation loss first. Lastly, for location IDs {7, 8}, with three time intervals, apart from the previous trajectories also being represented, it is possible to include one for gains or losses with alternation in the entire time interval. For practical and descriptive purposes, in the case of four or more time intervals, the method considers the same classes with the disadvantage of loosing details regarding the temporality and number of the changes of the events.

While it is possible to map every trajectory class, it only gives a simplified idea regarding the description of the dynamics of the phenomena because it hides temporal information details. It is here that the need of a Trajectory Plot arises.

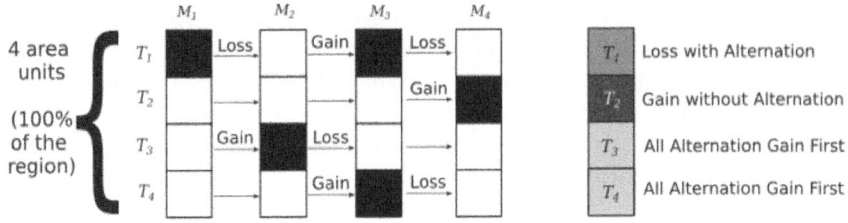

Fig. 1. Example of binary maps with trajectories and their classification.

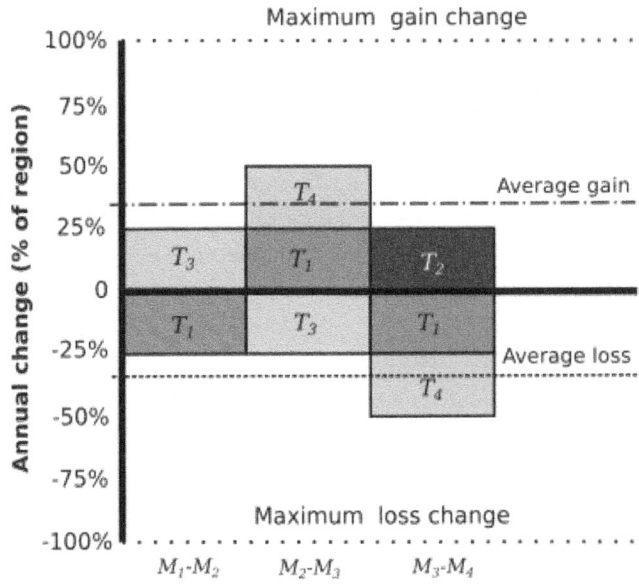

Fig. 2. Example of a trajectory plot.

This plot essentially records the contribution of the changes to the magnitude of gains or losses of change for every time interval.

These trajectories contribute to the overall gains and looses for every time interval. A trajectory plot is a way to graphically and visually represent these contributions and easily and quickly convey how these overall changes behave through time. The only trajectories that do no contribute to changes in the trajectory plot are "Stable Presence" and "Stable Absence".

Figure 1 shows an example of the evolution of four maps M_1, M_2, M_3, and M_4 with an extent of four areal units located implicitly in space. Each unit i has a corresponding trajectory T_i. In this example we see that trajectory T_1 is of the kind "Loss with Alternation", trajectory T_2 is "Gain without Alternation", and trajectories T_3 and T_4 are of type "All Alternation Gain First".

The gross gains and losses for each time interval in this example are depicted in the trajectory plot in Fig. 2.

The trajectory plot shows change in terms of gross gains and losses for each time interval. It presents the contribution source associated with each trajectory observed in Fig. 1. The horizontal axis represents the time intervals, while the vertical one indicates the gross gains and losses for each corresponding time interval as an annual percentage of the area of study. The dash-dotted line shows the average gain, while the dotted one shows the average loss over the full time interval. This graphical representation summarizes all the trajectories and their respective changes with an idea of the size and the year of occurrence.

4   Study Area and Data

We apply the time series trajectory analysis methodology in Mexico City. Located in the south-central portion of the country, it is the capital, and covers an area of about 1495 km^2 (roughly 0.1% of the country), making it the smallest state. It is also divided into 16 municipalities and has a population of about 9.2 million, representing 7.3% of the total population of the country.

According to results from the most recent National Survey on Victimization and Public Safety Perception carried out by the National Institute of Statistics and Geography (Instituto Nacional de Estadística y Geografía - INEGI), roughly one third of households in the city reported being victims of crime incidence [7]. Additionally, crime incidence has been consistently reported with decreasing trends in the last five years.

It, then, becomes interesting to explore the spatio-temporal pattern of this reported decrease. Because not all crime types behave the same way and some have higher "dark" or "hidden figures" (the gap between reported and unreported crimes), we focus on those that have the lowest dark figures.

We use yearly larceny incidence in Mexico City from 2019 to 2023 that contain little over 55,000 data points distributed in the city reported by the Office of the Attorney General of Mexico City [4].

Mexico City's Secretariat of Citizen Security divides the city in 71 territorial units (equivalently to coordinations or jurisdictions in other countries) to monitor and serve policing. They have varying sizes and areas that range from 1.08 to 73.43 km^2, with a mean area of 12.70 km^2 and a standard deviation of 9.68 km^2. This variation can hinder an easy and straightforward comparison of larceny incidence with respect to population at risk and police areas of attention.

For that reason, a regular tessellation was preferred over the original jurisdiction geometries. The H3 hierarchical tessellation of level 7 was deemed a reasonable choice, with an average area of 5.16 km^2 and average edge length of 1.41 km (https://h3geo.org/). Mexico City is covered by 301 hexagons and we count the number of observed incidences in each hexagon for each year. It is important to note that using cells of the same size gives the advantage of avoiding the modifiable areal unit problem, and that they allow for efficient data aggregation and classification of similar groups [13].

Figure 3 shows the locations of Mexico City, its public safety territorial units together with the extend of the city's administrative boundary, and the data points considered for 2019–2023 on top of the H3 units. The number of data points considered for each year is shown in Table 2.

5   Results

This section describes the count-based Trajectory Analysis applied to larceny data in Mexico City from 2019 to 2023. First, the H3 level 7 tessellation that covers the study area was created and the number of observation inside each cell was summarized by year. Next, a raster stack with a 50 m spatial resolution was created. The result is a series of images depicting the distribution of larceny in

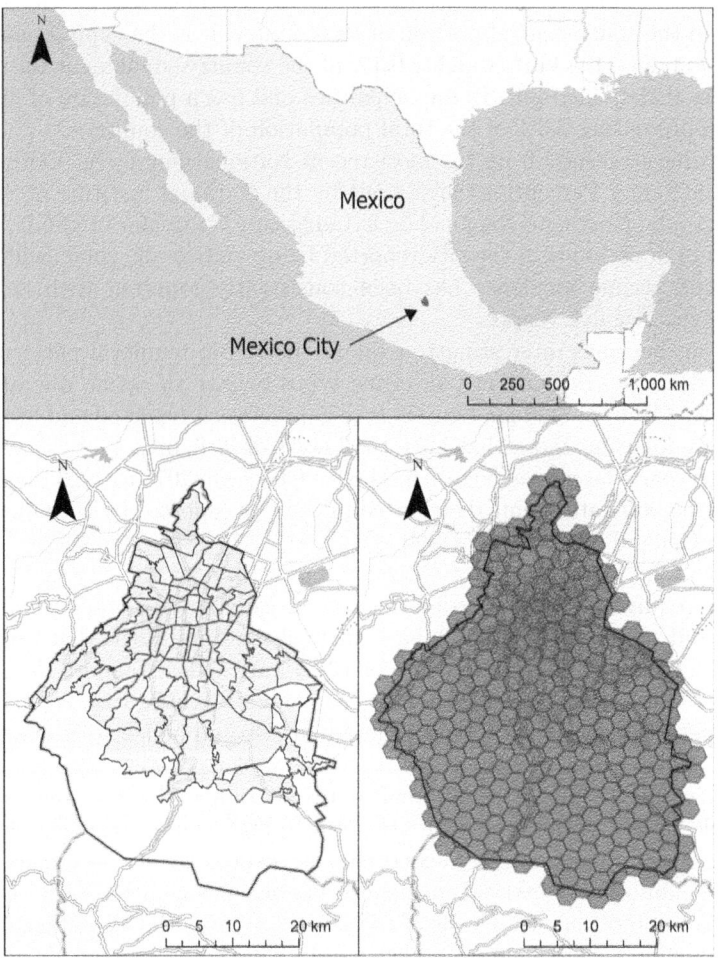

Fig. 3. Area of study and data: The location of Mexico City, its public safety territorial units, H3 level 7 hexagons and data points.

Table 2. Number of data points considered for each year.

Year	Data points
2019	15,440
2020	10,122
2021	10,762
2022	10,273
2023	8,600
Total	55,197

space and time. It is important to note that, while the original methodology is carried out in terms of presence or absence of a given class (binary data), here we apply the methodology to integer (counts) data.

Yearly hex binned incidence count is rasterized and stacked together as input for the `timeseriesTrajectories` R package [6]. By analyzing the values in each cell for consecutive years, it is possible to quantify the magnitude and direction

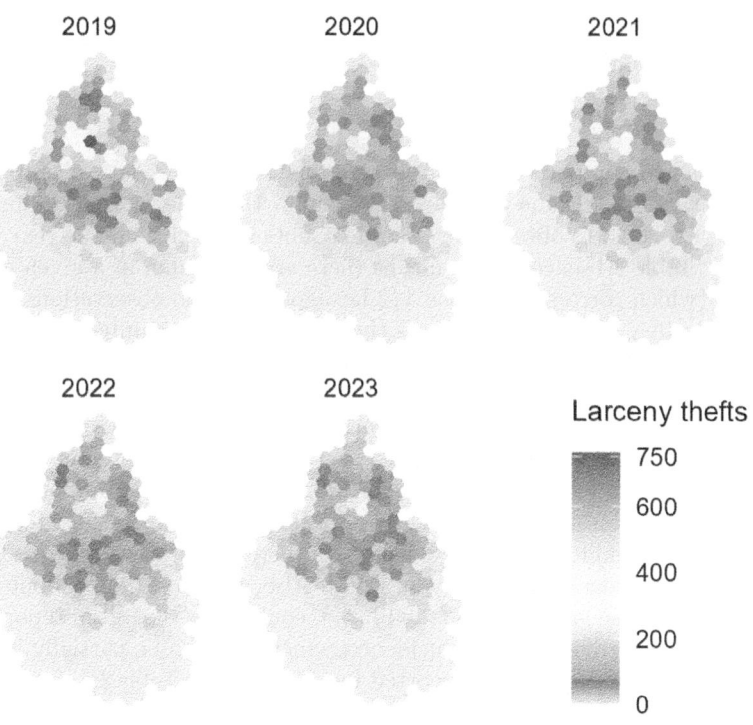

Fig. 4. Spatial and temporal distribution of larceny counts in H3 hexagons covering Mexico City.

of changes in larceny. Figure 4 shows the yearly distribution of counts inside the tessellation.

It can be seen that 2019 has a significant drop in counts. Two cells show high values compared to the rest of that year and all of the subsequent years. Of the 301 hexagons that cover the study area, only 189 have reported incidences and the remaining 112 have no observations. Because it can be overwhelming to try and follow the changes for any given hexagon, trajectories are calculated and classified into one of the categories introduced in Sect. 3. The number of hexagons classified in each type of trajectory are shown in Table 3.

Table 3. Number of hexagons classified in each trajectory.

Trajectory	Number of hexagons
Loss without Alternation	21
Loss with Alternation	117
Gain without Alternation	3
Gain with Alternation	31
All Alternation Loss First	6
All Alternation Gain First	11
Stable Absence	112

In contrast to [2], here we do not observe the "Stable Presence" class because observing exactly the same counts every year in the time interval is unlikely, therefore is expected to observe variation in counts in a cell from one year to the next. The "Stable Absence" value means there are no counts in a given cell for every year (which correspond to the 112 hexagons with no observations).

The trajectory plot in Fig. 5 shows that while there certainly are gains and losses at the end of the interval, there are also variations in between. For instance, the significant change that had already been identified for the 2019–2020 time interval in Fig. 4 can be quantified in terms of the annual change expressed as a percentage of the region of study. In this case, the overall loss is greater than 30%, and the overall gain is less than 1%. Then, 2020–2021 shows an important gain of larceny theft accompanied of a slightly decrement. Then, from 2020 to 2023, a consistent drop trend for gains and a consistent increase for loss is observed. This change is much harder to appreciate in Fig. 4. Also, the gross gain (about 3.5%) is much less than the gross loss (about 14.3%), confirming the initial reports of a general decreasing trend of crime incidence, which can also be partially inferred from the number of data points reported for each year in Table 2.

The trajectory plot also describes that the major source of alternation comes from loss with alternation trajectories. This means that, in general, larceny thefts decrease but there are fluctuations. Another important component is "Loss without Alternation", which shows a solid decrement in this regard in approximately 5% of the region for the time interval 2019–2020. Then, the contribution of this trajectory class for subsequent time intervals is remarkably less. Then the "All Alternation Gain First", "All Alternation Loss First", and "Gain with Alternation" trajectories have smaller contributions in general to gains and losses in the plot.

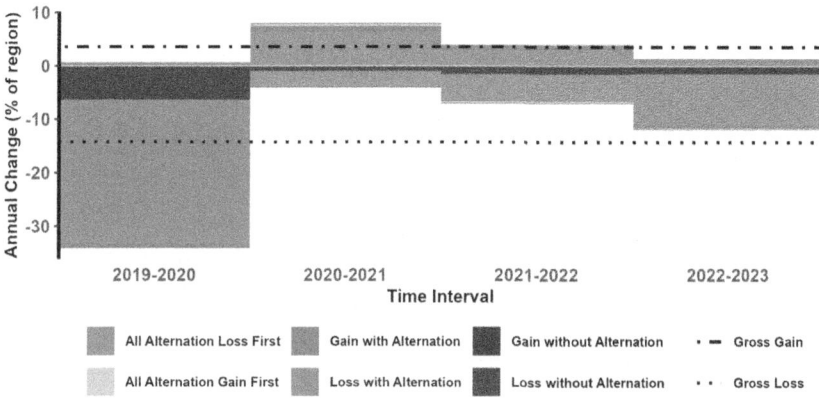

Fig. 5. Results of time series trajectory analysis with different types of gains and losses for each year.

Figure 6 shows the trajectories in space and it is possible to discern which cells had an overall gain, loss, or an alternating behavior. As mentioned before, cells that had no observations are classified as "Stable Absence". It is interesting to note that the region of the city where reports are consistently higher shows a decreasing trend over time, mostly classified as losses with and without alternation. Equally interesting is to find that towards the south there are more gains with alternation rather than losses. This could be an indication that due to more operatives in the central region of the city, some activity may be shifting towards other locations.

Figure 7 shows the trajectories for each cell. The lines depict the yearly behavior, clearly showing if a particular cell had gains, losses or an alternating behavior. It can be seen that there are few cells with pure gains, and the most populated one correspond to "Loss with Alternation" followed by "Gain with Alternation" and "Loss without Alternation".

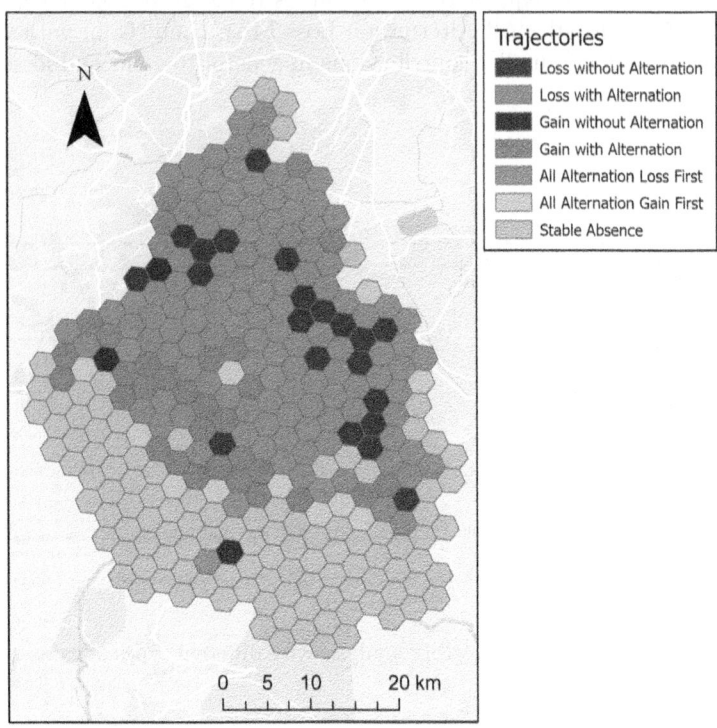

Fig. 6. Trajectories for larceny in Mexico City from 2019 to 2023.

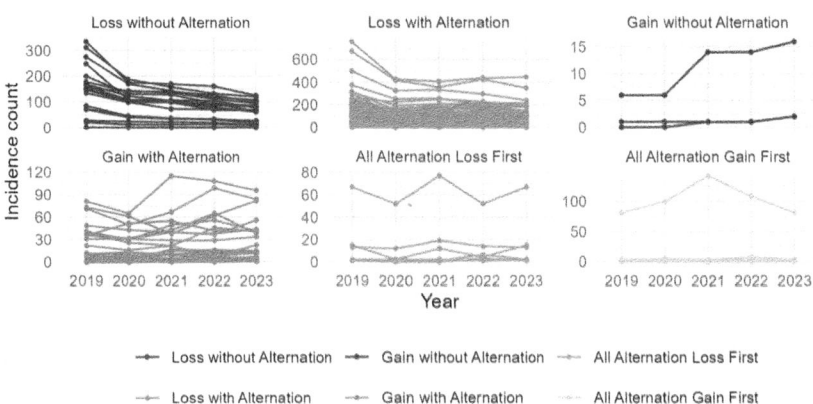

Fig. 7. Incidence count for each type of trajectory and year. Each line corresponds to one cell from the H3 tessellation used.

6   Conclusions and Future Work

We applied a time series trajectory analysis to larceny data in Mexico City and conclude that, indeed, there is a descending trend in general the last five years, but with slight area with increments of this crime. While it is complicated to visually assess these changes both through space and time with regular maps (like in Fig. 4), a trajectory plot provides additional details on the yearly dynamics of the incidence under study.

By identifying which areas are classified under each type of trajectory, it is possible to start asking questions about how is larceny incidence behaving at a more local scale. Some regions are fluctuating, but the trajectories alone are not enough to show the magnitude. By considering the incidence count for each type of trajectory it is then possible to put these changes into perspective, both in terms of other regions with the same trajectory and the rest of the cells; that is, it gives a first glimpse about the local and global behavior of the trajectories.

We have only scratched the surface of this methodology applied to studying crime incidence. It will be worth carrying out a temporal sensitivity study to assess how significant are these results in terms of their permanence or fluctuation through coarser or finer periods. In this sense it will be interesting to aggregate larceny data on a monthly or weekly basis instead of a yearly one and compare the resulting trajectory plots.

On the same sensitivity note, it could be possible to explore how changing the cell and time interval sizes affects these results. That is, study the dependence on their spatial and temporal scale. It is expected that there will be a critical cell size that will reveal interesting shifts in the distribution of reported crimes. Unfortunately, H3 tessellations' sizes are fixed in terms of their hierarchical structure and thus may not be the best option for this sensitivity analysis. It may be beneficial to use square grids for this purpose.

On the other hand, how valid could our conclusions be if data are noisy and there is a lot of alternation? It would then be difficult to guarantee that gains or losses are authentic. For that purpose, an initial exploration can be carried out by studying the behavior of counts shown in Fig. 7. This data sets does not seem to be too noisy as behavior within trajectories does not differ much. It would be, however, interesting to develop more refined tests of noise in data.

Lastly, it could also be interesting to confront these results and associated conclusions with alternate ways of accounting for the observed larceny. For instance, it could be relevant to study the spatial distribution of clusters of high or low values of observed counts and their associated trajectories to compare them with the ones presented here.

Disclosure of Interests. The authors have no competing interests to declare that are relevant to the content of this article.

References

1. Abbott, A.: Sequences of social events: concepts and methods for the analysis of order in social processes. Hist. Methods **16**(4), 129–147 (1983). https://doi.org/10.1080/01615440.1983.10594107
2. Bilintoh, T.M., Jr, R.G.P., A.Z.: Methods to compare sites concerning a category's change during various time intervals. GISci. Remote Sens. **61**(1), 2409484 (2024). https://doi.org/10.1080/15481603.2024.2409484
3. Brazil, K.J., Whittingham, L.M.: Criminology. In: Shackelford, T.K., Weekes-Shackelford, V.A. (eds.) Encyclopedia of Evolutionary Psychological Science, pp. 1–15. Springer, Cham (2019). https://doi.org/10.1007/978-3-319-16999-6_3193-1
4. Fiscalía General de Justicia: Carpetas de investigación FGJ. https://datos.cdmx.gob.mx/dataset/carpetas-de-investigacion-fgj-de-la-ciudad-de-mexico   (2024), Accessed 20 Sep 2024
5. Harinam, V., Bavcevic, Z., Ariel, B.: Spatial distribution and developmental trajectories of crime versus crime severity: do not abandon the count-based model just yet. Crime Sci. **11**(1), 1–15 (2022). https://doi.org/10.1186/s40163-022-00176-x
6. timeseries Trajectories. https://github.com/bilintoh/timeseriesTrajectories (2024), Accessed 15 Jan 2025
7. Instituto Nacional de Estadística y Geografía: Encuesta Nacional de Victimización y Percepción sobre Seguridad Pública (ENVIPE). https://www.inegi.org.mx/programas/envipe/2024/ (2024), Accessed 20 Feb 2025
8. Longford, N.T.: Longitudinal and Time-Series Analysis, pp. 335–370. Springer, New York, NY (2008). https://doi.org/10.1007/978-0-387-73251-0_11
9. Mills, M.: Sequence Analysis. In: Introducing Survival and Event History Analysis, chap. 11, pp. 213–226. SAGE Publications Ltd, London (2012). https://doi.org/10.4135/9781446268360
10. Nagin, D.S., Tremblay, R.E.: Analyzing developmental trajectories of distinct but related behaviors: a group-based method. Psychol. Methods **6**(1), 18–34 (2001). https://doi.org/10.1037/1082-989X.6.1.18
11. Pontius Jr, R., Bilintoh, T., Oliveira, G., Shimbo, J.Z.: Trajectories of losses and gains of soybean cultivation during multiple time intervals in Western Bahia, Brazil. In: Anais da Space Week Nordeste 2023. Campinas. Galoá (2023)
12. Ritschard, G., Studer, M. (eds.): Sequence Analysis and Related Approaches. LCRSP, vol. 10. Springer, Cham (2018). https://doi.org/10.1007/978-3-319-95420-2
13. Sadahiro, Y.: Analysis of the relations among spatial tessellations. J. Geog. Syst. **13**(4), 373–391 (2011). https://doi.org/10.1007/s10109-010-0127-3
14. Shoval, N.: Trajectories: analysis. In: International Encyclopedia of Geography, pp. 1–5. John Wiley & Sons, Ltd (2017). https://doi.org/10.1002/9781118786352.wbieg0611
15. Weisburd, D.: The law of crime concentration and the criminology of place. Criminology **53**(2), 133–157 (2015). https://doi.org/10.1111/1745-9125.12070
16. Weisburd, D., Bushway, S., Lum, C., Yang, S.M.: Trajectories of crime at places: a longitudinal study of street segments in the city of seattle. In: Quantitative Methods in Criminology, pp. 443–481. Routledge (2017). https://doi.org/10.4324/9781315089256-19

Impact of Climate Change on Agricultural Productivity in the East African Community

Dahir Mohamed Ali[1]([✉]) [iD] and Giuseppe Borruso[2] [iD]

[1] Faculty of Economics, Accounting, Statistics and Management Science, Somali National University, Gaheyr Afgoye Street, Mogadishu, Somalia
`dahireco@snu.edu.so`
[2] DEAMS - Department of Economics, Business, Mathematics and Statistics "Bruno de Finetti", University of Trieste, Via A. Valerio 4/1, 34127 Trieste, Italy
`giuseppe.borruso@deams.units.it`

Abstract. This study explores the influence of climate change on agricultural productivity in the East African Community (EAC), a region heavily dependent on agriculture for food security and economic stability. The study employs a mixed-methods strategy to analyse the impact of crucial climate factors such as carbon dioxide (CO_2) levels, rainfall, higher temperature, and sun radiation on cereal yields across EAC member states over the last three decades. Applying dynamic panel data techniques, this study Implemented first-order differencing to remove unobserved effects and employ the Generalized Method of Moments (GMM) estimation for robust analysis. Based on 192 observations from six countries, the fixed-effects model reveals that CO_2 concentration positively affects cereal yields, with a rise of nearly 2000.87 units per unit increase in CO_2 ($p = 0.002$). Conversely, maximum temperature and solar radiation negatively affect production, declining it by 37.42 and 467.72 units, respectively ($p = 0.062$ and $p = 0.007$). This research discovers compelling evidence of homoskedasticity ($Chi2(6) = 1755.38$, $p < 0.001$) and no serial correlation ($F(1, 5) = 6.570$, $p = 0.0504$). To address potential endogeneity, the study implemented GMM estimation using lagged response Variables as instruments. The Arellano-Bond test shows no significant second-order autocorrelation ($z = -0.87$, $p = 0.384$), validating my approach. The two-step GMM results expose that all variables are essential, highlighting the complex interactions between climate variables and agricultural productivity.

Keywords: Climate change · agricultural productivity · cereal yields · dynamic Panel Data · Generalized Method of Moments · East African Community

1 Introduction

Climate change is one of the world's leading challenges, and its impact on global agricultural productivity cannot be ignored, particularly in vulnerable states such as East Africa. The East African Community (EAC) consists of six countries: Kenya, Uganda,

O. Gervasi et al. (Eds.): ICCSA 2025 Workshops, LNCS 15890, pp. 371–386, 2026.
https://doi.org/10.1007/978-3-031-97606-3_25

Tanzania, Rwanda, Burundi, and Somalia. The EAC mainly relies on agriculture for economic stability and food security. The region's economy is strongly linked to agriculture, which constitutes a substantial part of the Gross domestic product and offers careers for numerous populations, operating as the social core of economic growth. The EAC climate change master plan offers a framework for partner nations to enforce climate change and migration industries through the East African Community Protocol on Environment and Global Accords [1]. A significant relationship links agricultural productivity in the East African Community (EAC) and the region's agro-environmental landscapes, with temperature crucial in influencing crop growth or failure. In lowland regions with high temperatures and inconsistent rainfall, heat-tolerant crops like maize, sorghum, and cassava dominate [2]. As climate conditions shift, characterised by higher temperatures, changing precipitation, and the escalation in frequency and severity of extreme weather events, the implications for agricultural output in the EAC worsen progressively. [3] approved a 2.3 billion program to improve food security in Eastern and Southern Africa. The agricultural sector is the backbone of the EAC economy, significantly enhancing job opportunities and overall economic development [4].

However, it is increasingly becoming more fragile due to the effects of climate change, which is altering essential environmental elements like temperature, rainfall patterns, and the regulars of extreme weather events [5]; these shifts present influential obstacles to agriculture output, particularly for staple produce such as maize, wheat, and beans, which are positively exposed on climatic interpretations. Although some research has explored the global implications of climate change agriculture [6], little emphasis has been placed on the region-specific threats to the agriculture of the East African Community.

2   Literature review

The East African community's agriculture industry is grappling with many difficulties. Climate change remains a global issue in the current century. This literature review explores the established framework and observed data considering the impact of climate change on agriculture output. The Arllano-Bond method, developed by [7], has effectively examined mixed variable data agronomic investigation. This model has been considerably applied to explore the impacts of climate adaption on farming productivity as it considers both temporal dynamics and unnoticed heterogeneity [8]. Similarly, [9] and [10] employed this method to examine the impact of climate finance and climate change on food security and economic results, respectively. [11] explore Somalia's farming landscape, observing that while precipitation can boost long-term crop yields, it adversely impacts short-term production due to increasing temperatures.. [12] examine how variations in temperature and rainfall affect crop yield, revealing the underlying mechanisms.

They advocate for funding irrigation systems and developing heat-tolerant crops as essential adaptation measures. Additionally, [13] emphasizes the critical role of the EAC in enhancing food security by sharing agricultural knowledge and Technology, particularly in rice farming. The agricultural and agri-food sector is the primary employer in East Africa and is a significant revenue source. [14] fills this void by investigating how fluctuations in temperature and rainfall affect agricultural production in East Africa by considering both intermediate and extended effects as well as regional disparities.

2.1 Empirical Evidence

Recent innovations in panel dynamic modelling, including advancement in GMM estimation techniques and integration of higher-precision climate change, improved its utilization in agricultural studies. For instance, [16] indicates that combining remote sensing data with the Arllano-Bond model provides a comprehensive study of how to achieve healthy crops and vegetation adapt to climate Variation. He emphasized the importance of innovative methods to enhance agricultural productivity and sustained capacity in East Africa. Likewise, [17] examined the impact of technological innovation and improved crop Varieties that contribute to overcoming obstacles like low productivity and regional climate shift. In addition, according to [18], the role of climate-smart agricultural extension services in Uganda is to assist farmers with adapting climate variability and improving sustainability.

Recent study by [19], has observed substantial changes in temperature and precipitation patterns in the East African Community. Data from the [20] revealed a marked Rise in temperature irregularity and seasonal precipitation changes, impacting crop production seasons and water availability. For example, [21] found inconsistent temperatures and variable precipitation during the maize growing season led to substantial yield decreases. Similarly, a study by [22] discovered that factors influencing rainfall patterns lead to decreased productivity and a higher rate of harvest loss in small-scale farming systems. [23] Personal Communication with the agricultural development officer, Uganda. The DAO contributed to food shortages due to insufficient early rains, delayed heavy rains, Locust swarms, and Escalating prices due to Sudanese refugees. [24] Uganda's diverse agroecological zones have contributed to the development of various farming technologies. [25] Their study focused on two nations in Eastern Kenya. [26] Tanzania has seven agroecological areas, with arid and semi-arid zones more at risk from climate change. In spite of these challenges,

[27] defines climate change as long-term temperature and rainfall changes. It is particularly alarming for East Africa, where [28] predicted that at the global warning level of 4.6 °C, many East African cities are expected to show an increase to 2000-fold increase in exposure to extreme heat (days > 40.6 °C) in contrast to covering the time from 1985 to 2005, including Blantyre-Limbe, Lusaka, and Kampala. [29] implemented advanced forecasting methods for wheat yields in the context of climate change, which projected a 27 per cent decrease in yield in North-West Victoria and a 14 per cent drop across Victoria by 2036–2065 in line with the IPCC's "Hotter & Drier" scenario. In contrast, findings from [30] highlight the importance of climate-resilient farming practices, such as incorporating drought-resistant crop varieties and enhancing irrigation methods. Complementing this, [31] investigated food security issues in East Africa, forecasting decreased crop yields in Sudan and potential increases in the Oromia region of Ethiopia due to climate change.

3   Descriptive Analysis

3.1   Country- Level Trends in Agricultural land use (% of Land Area) of EAC

Agricultural land use and productivity in the East African Community (EAC) have experienced significant changes over the years due to the interplay between socio-economic factors and climate change. According to [32] the Average temperature was 0.61 °C higher than the 1991–2020 mean and 1.28 °C higher than the 1961–1990 average. The African continent cautioned at the rate of + 0.3 °C/decade between 1991 and 2023, a slightly faster rate than the worldwide average.

The bar chart below compares longitude, latitude, and the maximum temperature together with latitude and longitude for the EAC nations; Somalia exhibits the highest maximum temperature due to its closeness to the equator, while other countries, like Rwanda and Burundi, have comparatively maximum temperatures, and both Kenya and Tanzania show moderate highest temperatures. South Sudan faced high temperatures, like Somalia, primarily due to its low elevations and conditions (Fig. 1).

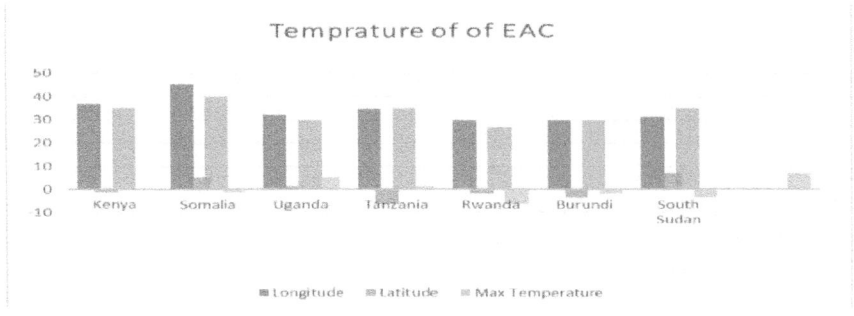

Fig. 1. Higher Temperature effect on Agricultural productivity

Figure 2 illustrates that the East African Community (EAC) comprises six member states: Burundi, Kenya, Rwanda, South Sudan, Tanzania, and Uganda. Situated across the tropical and subtropical zones, this varied terrain renders the region especially susceptible to the consequences of climate change, such as increasing temperature, irregular precipitation patterns and extreme weather occurrences.

Figure 2 demonstrates the agricultural land patterns in the East African Community nations from the past three decades (1990 to 2020), emphasizing the different socio-economic, political, and environmental pathways. In Kenya, agricultural land varied between 1990 and 2000, with phases of decline and recovery, likely because of changing policies or external pressures. From 2000 onwards, there was consistent growth, peaking between 2005 and 2010 and reaching stability with gradual expansion until 2020, stimulated by economic progress, population growth and land planning policies. Somalia displayed a gradual increase in agricultural land until 205, followed by a steep rise and decline between 2005 and 2010 due to political upheaval and conflict; after 2010, the trend stabilized, with slight upward growth by 2020, indicating recovery actions and progress in governance. Burundi saw a substantial decrease from around 80 in 1990

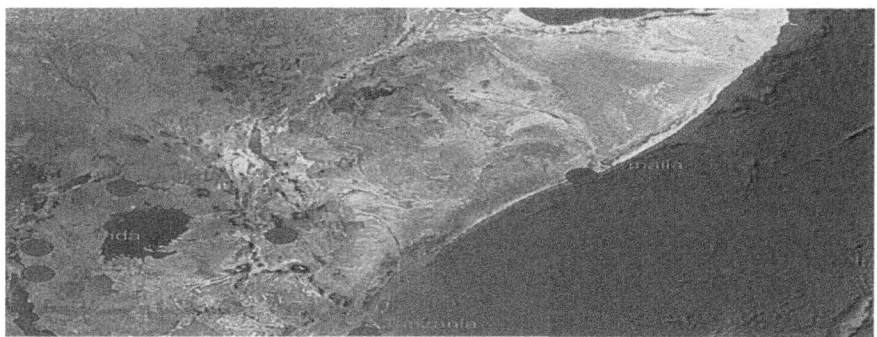

Fig. 2. Map location in EAC

to under 70 by 2005, probably because of land degradation, reforestation projects, and socio-economic issues (Fig. 3).

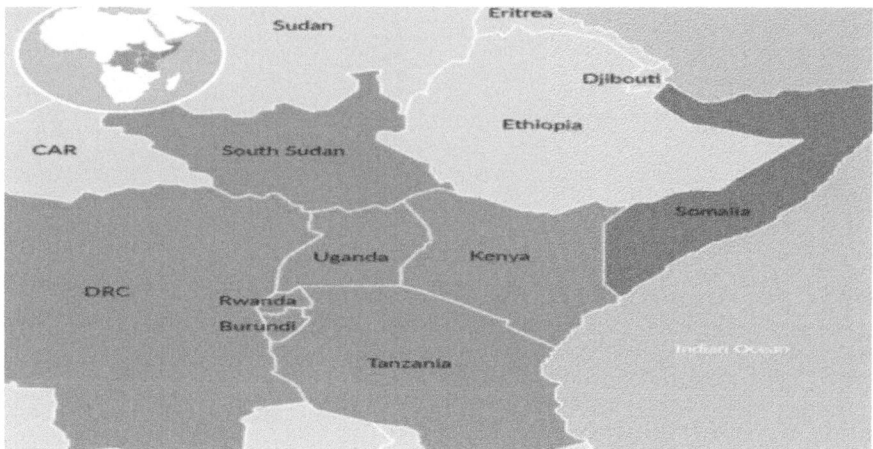

Fig. 3. Map of eight Countries currently part of the EAC regional Bloc

The East African Community countries consist of eight states: Burundi, DRC, Kenya, Rwanda, South Sudan, Tanzania, and Somalia. They have considerable areas of farmland, though their utilization varies greatly. States like Burundi and Rwanda have a higher percentage of agricultural land (more than 80%) and regular utilization of most of it due to dense populations and high-input farming. On the other hand, Somalia, South Sudan, and DRC have extensive regions classified as agricultural, but much remains underused because of political instability, inadequate infrastructure, and limited investment. Kenya, Uganda, and Tanzania fall in between, with significant agricultural areas ranging between 45% and 72% but only limited use. Uganda, for instance, Cultivates only roughly 21% of its arable land (Fig. 4).

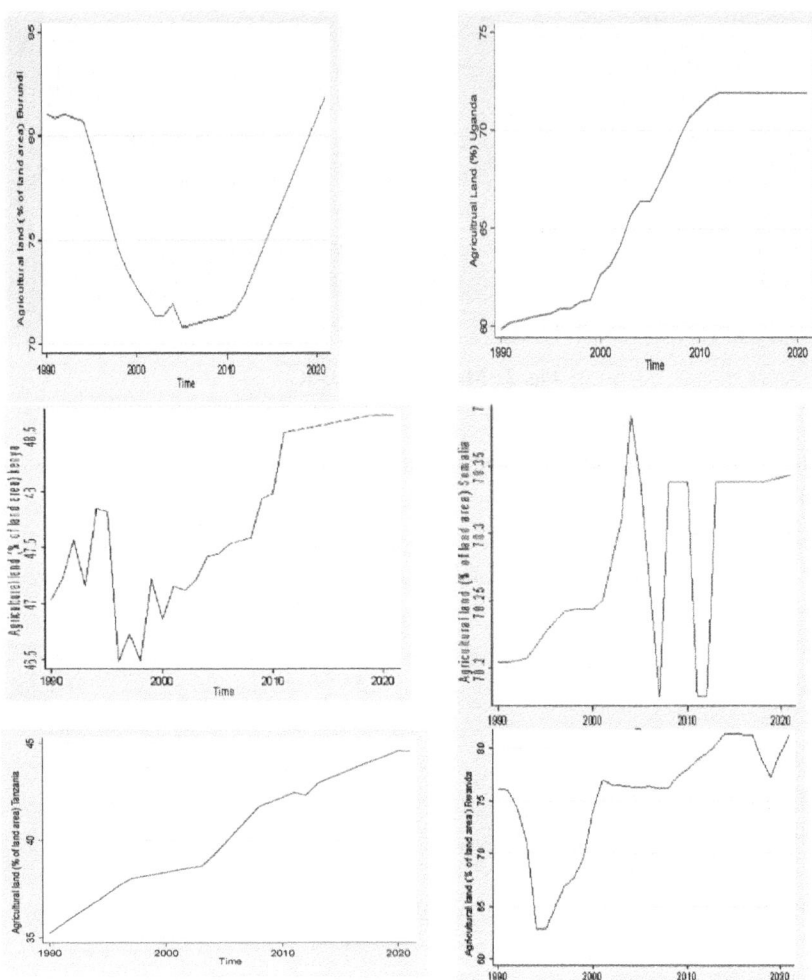

Fig. 4. Line chart showing Agricultural land trends for six EAC from 1990 to 2021

4 Materials and method

4.1 Data collection and Analysis

This study collected data from NASA and the World Bank from 1990 to 2020. Data gathered from NASA Power offered essential climate variables such as Maximum temperature, Precipitation, and Solar radiation, which are crucial for assessing the effect of weather conditions on agriculture. Agricultural output data, including Cereal yields and CO_2, are sourced from the World Bank. In the description part of the study, the GIS tool drew a map and investigated spatial trends, while statistical analysis was carried out using STATA. [33] challenged traditional econometric frameworks for their inadequacies in policy assessments, stemming from insufficient addressing of fluid linkages and causal interconnections. For the statistical analysis, this research is 1st differencing Generalized method of moments (GMM) estimator developed by [7]. On this, [34] criticized traditional econometric models for their insufficiencies in policy assessments arising from poor handling of dynamic relations and causal interactions.

Model Specification

Dynamic panel data Where: CY_{t-1} = cereal productivity of the state i at time t-1

The equation represents the linkage between cereal output (the dependent variable) and several independent variables, including rainfall, CO2 levels, solar radiation, and maximum temperature.

First Order Differencing to Eliminate Unobserved μ Effect

$$\begin{aligned}\Delta CY_{it} = CY_{it} - CY_{i(ti1)} &= \beta_1 \Delta CY_{i(t-1)} \\ &+ \beta_2 \Delta Tmax_{it} + \beta_3 \Delta PSA_{it} \\ &+ \beta_4 \Delta Solar\ Ra_{it} + \beta_5 \Delta CO2_{it} + \epsilon_{it}\end{aligned} \tag{2}$$

Specify Instruments. Employing $CY_{i(t-2)}$ and other lagged variables t-2 or previous as instruments for $\Delta CY_{i(t-1)}$. Utilizing $Tmax_{t(t-1)}$, $PSA_{i(t-1)}$, $SolarRadation_{i(t-1)}$, $CO2_{i(t-1)}$ as instrument for the consistent first differencing.

Moment Conditions

The condition can be expressed as:

$$E\left[\Delta_{it} \backslash CY_{i(t-2)}, Tmax_{t(t-1)}, PSA_{i(t-1)}, SolarRa_{i(t-1)}, CO2_{i(t-1)}\right] = 0 \tag{3}$$

GMM Estimation

$$\begin{aligned}Q(\beta) = &\left(\frac{1}{T}\sum_{T=2}^{T} \Delta CY_{it} - \beta_1 \Delta CY_{i(t-1)} - \beta_2 \Delta Tmax_{it} - \beta_3 \Delta PSA_{it} - \beta_4 \Delta Solar\ Ra_{it} - \beta_5 \Delta CO2_{it}\right)' \\ &W\left(\frac{1}{T}\sum_{T=2}^{T} \Delta CY_{it} - \beta_1 \Delta CY_{i(t-1)} - \beta_2 \Delta Tmax_{it} - \beta_3 \Delta PSA_{it} - \beta_4 \Delta Solar\ Ra_{it} - \beta_5 \Delta CO2_{it}\right)\end{aligned} \tag{4}$$

5 Results

Result contained in Table 1 shows that based on 192 observations across six countries in east African community, the fixed-effects regression analysis reveals that CO2 concentration positively impacts cereal output, with a significant increase of approximately 2000.87 units per unit rise in CO2 (p = 0.002). Conversely, two-meter maximum temperature and solar radiation negatively affect output, decreasing it by about 37.42 and 467.72 units, respectively, with both effects being statistically significant (p = 0.062 and p = 0.007). Precipitation showed no significant impact (p = 0.217).

The results in Table 2 show that the random effect of the (GLS) regression analysis of 192 observations from six countries shows that climate factors and cereal productivity are linked meaningfully. Carbon dioxide concentration positivity affects cereal output, with a coefficient of 2473.7 (P < 0.001) pointing to higher CO2 levels increasing output. Precipitation also has a positive effect, with a coefficient of 0.37990 (P < 0.001),

Table 1. Fixed-effects(within) regression

	Number of obs =					192
Group country	Number of groups =					6
R-sq:	Obs per group:					
within =0.139	min =					32
between =0.10	avg =					32
overall = 0.115	max =					32
	F (4,182) =					7.35
Corr (u_i, Xb) = -0.0548	Prob > F =					0.0000
Cereal Y	Coef.	Std. Err.	t	P>t	[95%	interval
T Max	-37.4234	19.923	1.8 76.7	0.06	-	1.8868
PSA	-0.1004	0.081	1.2 .260	0.21	-	0.059
C02	2000.8	629.9	3.1 757.8		0.002	3243.9
Solar Radi	-467.72	171.0	2.7 805	0.007	-	-130.3
_cons	4989	1223.4	4.08	0.00	257	7403
Sigma_u	412.8424					
Sigma_e	313.36255					
Rho	0.6344628	(Fraction of variance due to u_i)				

Source: our elaborations from NASA Data and World bank Data

while a two-meter maximum temperature is linked to a rise of approximately 93.89 units (P < 0.001), indicating potential regional adaptations. Conversely, solar radiation negatively affects productivity (coefficient: −259.0, P = 0.005). The model shows that country-specific factors account for around 48.29% of the total variability, with a substantial between-group R-squared of 94.66%. The result underscores the intricate relationships between climatic variables and the productivity of agriculture in the East African Community (EAC).

The result contained in Table 3 shows that the fixed effect estimate for higher temperature (T Max) is −37.423, while the random effect estimate is 93.88, a difference of −131.31. The fixed effect coefficient for participation (PSA) is −0.10041, while the random effect coefficient is −0.48035. The fixed effect estimate for carbon dioxide is 2000.8, which is −472.88 different from the random effect estimate of 2473.7, and the fixed effect estimate for solar radiation is −467.72, which is different from the random effect estimate of −259.04 by 208.67. The Hausman test statistic is χ^2 (4) = 97.08 with a corresponding P-value of 0.0000. Shows that the subject-specific effects are correlated with the predictors, violating the random effects assumption. Thus, the fixed effects model offers more consistent and robust estimates for investigating the effect of the climate factors on cereal output in the East African Community members.

Table 2. Random-effects GLS regression

Number of Obs =		192
Group country Number of groups =		6
R-sq: Obs per group:		
within = min =		32
0.0325		
between = avg =		32
0.946		
overall = max =		32
0.4829		
Wald chi2(4)		174.62
=		
Corr Prob > chi2 =		0.0000
(u_i, X)		
= 0		
(assumed)		

Cereal Y	Coef.	Std. Err.	z	P>t	[95% Conf.	Interval
TMax	93.888		5.65		0.000	126.482
	16.630		61.29			
PSA	0.37993		5.80		0.000	0.50833
	0.0655		0.2515	7.4	0.000	
C02	2473.7		1819			3127.79
	333.70		2.79	0.005	-	
Solar Rad	-259.0		441.3			-76.766
	92.999		1.17	0.241	-	
_cons	-863.59	7	230.7			580.311
	36.7					
Sigma_u		0				
Sigma_e		313.36255				
Rho		0 (fraction of variance due to u_i)				

Source: our elaborations from NASA Data and World bank Data

Table 4 illustrates that the adjusted Wald test for groupwise heteroskedasticity in the fixed-effects regression model strongly rejects the null hypothesis (H0) that the error variances are the same across groups. A test statistic of $X2 (6) = 559.98$ and a p-value of 0.0000 indicates significant evidence of heteroskedasticity. Using robust standard errors may be necessary to address this issue in the model estimation.

The results in Table 5 indicate that the Wooldridge test for autocorrelation in panel data assesses the null hypothesis (H0), which posits the lack of first-order autocorrelation. The results indicate an F-statistic of $F (1,5) = 10.142$ with a p-value of 0.0244. Given that the p-value is below the statistically significant threshold of 0.05, we reject H0, signifying the existence of first-order autocorrelation in the panel dataset.

Table 3. Hausman Fix Random

Coefficients -	(b)	(B)	b-B)	Sqrt (diag(V b-V_B))
	Fix	random	Difference	S.E.
T Max	37.423	93.88	- 131.31	10.971
PSA	- .10041	0.3799	- .48035	.0.04785
C02	2000.8	2473.7	- 472.88	534.34
SolarRa	-467.72	-259.04	-208.6	143.50

b = consistent under Ho and Ha; obtained from xtreg
Test: Ho: difference in coefficients not systematic
Test: Ho: difference in coefficients not systematic
            97.08

Prob>chi2 =   0.0000

(V_b-V_B is not positive definite)

Source; Authors Used STATA For this Analysis

Table 4. Hausman Fix Random

H0: sigma(i)^2 = sigma^2 for all	I
chi2 (6) = 559.98	
Prob>chi2 = 0.0000	

Source; Authors Used STATA For this Analysis

Table 5. Wooldridge' test for autocorrelation In Panel data

H0: no first-order autocorrelation
F (1, 5) = 10.142
Prob > F = 0.0244

Source: Authors Used STATA For this Analysis

The result in Table 6 shows that the higher temperature of the coefficient is 93.88 ($p < 0.001$), suggesting that for every 1 unit increase in high temperature, cereal output increases by approximately 93.88 units. The precipitation value of the coefficient is 0.3799 ($p < 0.001$), indicating that a 1-unit increase in rainfall is associated with an increase of about 0.38 units in cereal output. The coefficient for carbon dioxide is 2473.7 (p-value is less than 0.001), showing that for every additional unit of CO2, grain yield rises by around 2473.7 units. This shows a robust, helpful connection. The solar radiation coefficient is -259.0 ($p = 0.006$), reflecting that an increase in solar radiation relates to a decline of around 259 units in the production of cereals.

Table 6. Linear Regression Results

. reg CY TMax PSA C02 SolarRa,						
		Robust				
Linear regression			Number of obs =			192
			F(4, 187)	=		58.98
			Prob > F	=		0
			R-squared	=		0.4829
			Root MSE	=		375.42
Robust						
Cereal Y	Coef. Err.	Std.	t	P>t	[95% Conf.	Interval]
T Max	93.88 14.71		6.38	0	64.85275	122.92
PSA	0.3799 .0757		5.01	0	0.230441	0.5294
C02	2473	266.2	9.29	0	1948.47	2999.0
SolarRa	-259.0	93.67	2.77	0.006	443.83	-74.25
_cons	-863.	672.0	-1.2	0.2	2189.2	462.09

Table 7 demonstrates that high temperature strongly correlates positively with Cereal productivity (0.7191, the P value is less than 0.0001), showing that cereal yield also tends to rise with increasing the maximum temperature. High temperature is positively associated with Cereal productivity and has a moderate correlation with PT (0.3940, P-Value less than 0.0001) and Carbon dioxide (0.3564, P-value is less than 0.0001), indicating that higher temperatures are related to increases in precipitation and Carbon dioxide levels. Rainfall positively correlated with Cereal yield (0.3623, $p < 0.0001$), implying increased precipitation is associated with higher cereal production. However, there is a slight inverse relationship with radiation (-0.1208, P- value equals 0.0952), demonstrating that solar Radiation may decrease as precipitation rises, although this association is not statistically significant. CO2 has a positive correlation with cereal output Y (0.3366, $p < 0.0001$) and T2mMax (0.3564, $p < 0.0001$), showing that higher CO2 levels are associated with increased cereal productivity.

Table 7. Correlation Matrix Summary

	e	Cereal Y	T2mMax	PPT	CO2	Solar Rada
Cereal Y	0.7191* 0.0000	1.0000				
T Max	−0.0000 1.0000	0.3940* 0.0000	1.0000			
PSA	−0.0000 1.0000	0.3623* 0.0000	−0.1208* 0.0952	1.0000		
CO2	0.0000 1.0000	0.3366* 0.0000	0.3564* 0.0000	−0.3517* 0.0000	1.0000	
Solar Rada	0.0000 1.0000	−0.2616* 0.0002	0.1660* 0.0214	−0.6804* 0.0214	0.3909* 0.0000	1.0000

Source: Authors Used STATA For this Analysis

Table 8 show that Coefficient of the error(e) and Lagged Cereal output (L. Cerealy) is 0.522 with a p-value of 0.0000, indicating a strong positive correlation between the error term and lagged cereal output.

Table 8. Coefficient of error and lagged

	e L.Cere ~ y
e	1.0000
L.Cereal Y	0.5221* 1.0000
	0.0000

Source: Authors Used STATA For this Analysis

Table 9 presents the results of dynamic panel-data analyses using a single-step difference Generalized Method of Moments (GMM) approach, focusing on the variable "Cerealy" across six countries with a total of 174 observations. The Wald chi-squared statistic is 31.34, with a p-value of 0.003, indicating that the model is statistically significant. This suggests that the regressors collectively have a significant impact. The coefficient for lagged "Cerealy (L1) is significant at 0.7628 (P value is less than 0.001), emphasizing strong persistence in the Variable. "T2mMax" has a significant negative effect on "Cereal" (−36.41, P value is less than 0.001), suggesting that rises in temperature correlate with decreases in "Cerealy." The other Variable integrates lagged terms for "T2mMax", PPT," CO2", and "Solar radiation," which illustrates mixed significance and shows complex associations. Notably, the lagged impact of "Solar radiation" is essential and positive (L1: 297.69, P value = 0.042), while the second-order lag(L2) is significantly negative (−377.7, P value less than 0.001), indicating intricate dynamics over time. The Arellano-Bond tests demonstrate first-order autocorrelation (AR) (1) where Z

$= -2.25$, P value $= 0.024$) but no second-order autocorrelation AR (2), where $z = -0.97$, P value $= 0,188$), confirms the validity of the model's instruments.

Table 9. Dynamic panel-data estimation, one-step difference GMM

Group Variable: country		Number of obs =			174	
Time variable : year		Number of Groups =			6	
Number of instruments =		Obs per group: min =			29	
163						
Wald ch12 (13) = 31.34				avg =	29.00	
Pro > chi2 = 0.003				max=	29	
Cerealy	**Coef.** interval	**Robust Std. Err.**	**Z**	**P>|z|**		**[95% Conf.**
L1-	.762766	.16021	4.76	0.000	.4487594	1.07677
T max						
-- _	-36.409	8.6779	-4.20	0.000	-53-417	-1940
L1-	-29.16	16.731	-1.74	0.081	-61.961	3.623
L2-	13.823	9.57743	1.44	0.149	-4.9480	32.59
PSA						
-- _	-06292	-07011	-0.90	0.369	-2003591	0745
L1.	-04979	0527	-0.94	0.345	-15309	0534
L2.	04189	071995	0.58	0.561	-.0992168	.1830
CO2						
-- _	69.705	2371.26	0.03	0.977	-4577-89	4717.
L1.	-1689	4092.45	-0.41	0.680	-9710.714	6331.
L2.	2671.4	2324.22	1.15	0.250	-1883.965	7226.
SolarRa_						
	-250-2	156.280	-1.60	0.10	-556.527	56.08
L1.	297.6886	146.246	2.04	0.04	11.0500	584.32
L2.	-3.77.793	86.55858	-4.36	0.00	-547.4454	-208.1

Instruments for first differencing equations standard
D. (TMax PSA CO2 SolarRa)
GMM-type (missing = 0, separation instruments for each period unless collapsed)
L (2/31) _ L. Cereal y
Arellano-Bond test for AR (1) in first differencing: z = -2.25 pr > z = 0.024
Arellano-Bond test for AR (2) in first differencing: z = -0.97 pr > z = 0.332
Sargan test of overid_ restrictions: chi2(150) = 165.13 Prob > chi2 = 0.188
(Not roubust, but not weakened by many instruments)
Hansen test of overid. restrictions: chi2(150) = 0.00 Prob > chi2 = 1.000
(Robust, but weakened by many instruments.)

6 Recommendations and Conclusions

The outcomes of this research emphasize the need for strategic policy recommendations to reduce the adverse consequences of climate change on agriculture in the East African community. Development of Climate-adaptive crop types: The East African Community nations should invest in developing and transferring climate-resilient crop types. These crops should be heat-resistant, drought-tolerant, and adaptive to fluctuating temperatures and sunlight conditions. Research and development in this part should be prioritized, and seed pots and distribution channels should be set to ensure farmers can access these enhanced sorts. Establishment of integrated water management systems: Promotion of Climate-Smart Agriculture: Policymakers should encourage adopting climate-smart agricultural practices, like agroforestry, protection tillage, and mulching. This research offers significant data regarding the effects of climate changes on the agricultural productivity of the EAC. The results underscore the importance of understanding the intricate interactions between climatic conditions and agricultural practices. While CO_2 enhances yields in the short term, increasing temperatures and solar radiation pose significant threats to the region's food security.

Author Contributions. Dahir Mohamed Ali and Giuseppe Borruso contributed equally to the following aspects of the manuscript: Formulation, Verification, Supervision, and Writing—Original Draft preparation. Dahir Mohamed Ali was responsible for data collection, formal analysis, and research analysis using Stata software and visualization. Giuseppe Borruso handled mapping, Resources, and Review & editing which significantly enhanced the study's methodology framework. Further investigation is ongoing.

Conflict of Interest. Their authors declare no conflict of interest.

References

1. E. EAC, 'Climate Change Policy Framework'. Accessed 4 Feb 2025. https://www.eac.int/environment/climate-change/eac-climate-change-policy-framework
2. FAO, 'The State of Food and Agriculture 2020'. Accessed 6 Apr. 2025. https://www.fao.org/interactive/state-of-food-agriculture/2020/en/
3. W. World Bank, 'World Bank Approves $2.3 Billion Program to Address Escalating Food Insecurity in Eastern and Southern Africa', World Bank. Accessed 4 Fe. 2025. https://www.worldbank.org/en/news/press-release/2022/06/21/world-bank-approves-2-3-billion-program-to-address-escalating-food-insecurity-in-eastern-and-southern-africa
4. World Bank, 'Africa: Development news, research, data I World Bank'. Accessed 4 Feb 2025. https://www.worldbank.org/en/region/afr
5. NASA, 'Climate Change - NASA Science'. Accessed 04 Feb 2025. https://science.nasa.gov/climate-change/
6. Schmidhuber, J., Tubiello, F.N.: Global food security under climate change. Proc. Natl. Acad. Sci. U.S.A. **104**(50), 19703–19708 (2007). https://doi.org/10.1073/pnas.0701976104
7. Arellano, M., Bond, S.: Some tests of specification for panel data: monte carlo evidence and an application to employment equations. Rev. Econ. Stud. **58**(2), 277 (1991). https://doi.org/10.2307/2297968

8. Blundell, R., Bond, S.: Initial conditions and moment restrictions in dynamic panel data models (1997)
9. Doku, I., Phiri, A.: Climate finance and hunger among non-annex-1 parties: a lens on Sub-Saharan Africa. Int. J. Sustain. Econ. **14**(4), 380–398 (2022). https://doi.org/10.1504/IJSE.2022.125972
10. Geda, A., et al.: Unraveling the climate-macro conundrum: the macroeconomic impact of climate change in Eastern Africa, August 2023, Accessed 04 Feb 2025. https://hdl.handle.net/10568/135660
11. Warsame, A.A., Sheik-Ali, I.A., Ali, A.O., Sarkodie, S.A.: Climate change and crop production nexus in Somalia: an empirical evidence from ARDL technique. Environ. Sci. Pollut. Res. Int. **28**(16), 19838–19850 (2021). https://doi.org/10.1007/s11356-020-11739-3
12. 'Climate Change Impacts in Agriculture', SciSpace - Paper. Accessed 04 Feb 2025. https://typeset.io/papers/climate-change-impacts-in-agriculture-5e82q77q4t
13. 'Towards planet and people-positive agriculture in East Africa | FAO'. Accessed 04 Feb 2025. https://www.fao.org/family-farming/detail/en/c/1639928/
14. Mubenga, T.: Full article: climate variability impacts on agricultural output in East Africa. Accessed 04 Feb 2025. https://www.tandfonline.com/doi/full/10.1080/23322039.2023.2181281
15. Smith, K.: The anti-competitive effects of common institutional ownership in health insurance markets, 09 Mar 2022, Social Science Research Network, Rochester, p. 4053176, NY. https://doi.org/10.2139/ssrn.4053176
16. Warinda, E., Nyariki, D.M., Wambua, S., Muasya, R.M., Hanjra, M.A.: Sustainable development in East Africa: impact evaluation of regional agricultural development projects in Burundi, Kenya, Rwanda, Tanzania, and Uganda. Nat. Res. Forum **44**(1), 3–39 (2020). https://doi.org/10.1111/1477-8947.12191
17. Turyasingura, B., Chavula, P.: Climate-smart agricultural extension service innovation approaches in Uganda: review paper. IJFSA **6**(1), 35–43 (2022). https://doi.org/10.26855/ijfsa.2022.03.006
18. Kogan, F.: Remote Sensing Land Surface Changes: The 1981–2020 Intensive Global Warming. Springer Nature (2023)
19. A. D. Bank, 'Annual Report 2021', African Development Bank Group. Accessed: 24 Aug 2024. https://www.afdb.org/en/documents/annual-report-2021
20. Yasin, M., et al.: Climate change impact uncertainty assessment and adaptations for sustainable maize production using multi-crop and climate models. Environ. Sci. Pollut. Res. **29**(13), 18967–18988 (2022). https://doi.org/10.1007/s11356-021-17050-z
21. Adesina, O.S., Loboguerrero, A.M.: Enhancing food security through climate-smart agriculture and sustainable policy in Nigeria. In: Leal Filho, W., Luetz, J., Ayal, D. (eds.), Handbook of Climate Change Management: Research, Leadership, Transformation, Springer, Cham, pp. 1–17 (2020). https://doi.org/10.1007/978-3-030-22759-3_338-1
22. TIM ALLEN, 'Social upheaval and the struggle for community: a study of the Ugandan Madi - ProQuest'. Accessed 06 Apr 2025. https://www.proquest.com/openview/00e76f2403c1d4353a3bd2aaf516a5d7/1?cbl=2026366&diss=y&pq-origsite=gscholar
23. Peter, E., et al.: Drivers of land use change and household determinants of sustainability in smallholder farming systems of Eastern Uganda | Population and Environment. Accessed 06 Apr 2025. https://doi.org/10.1007/s11111-010-0104-2
24. Mburu, S.W., Koskey, G., Kimiti, J.M., Ombori, O., Maingi, J.M., Njeru, E.M.: Agrobiodiversity conservation enhances food security in subsistence-based farming systems of Eastern Kenya. Agric. Food Secur. **5**(1), 19 (2016). https://doi.org/10.1186/s40066-016-0068-2
25. Mkonda, M.Y.: Agricultural sustainability and food security in Agroecological Zones of Tanzania. In: Lichtfouse, E. (ed.) Sustainable Agriculture Reviews, vol. 52, Springer, Cham, pp. 309–334 (2021). https://doi.org/10.1007/978-3-030-73245-5_9

26. Masson-Delmotte, V.P., et al.: IPCC, 2021: summary for policymakers. In: Climate Change 2021: The Physical Science Basis. Contribution of Working Group I to the Sixth Assessment Report of the Intergovernmental Panel on Climate Change, Jan 2021, Accessed 04 Feb 04 2025. https://doi.org/10.1017/9781009157896.001
27. 'Projections of Human Exposure to Dangerous Heat in African Cities Under Multiple Socioe-conomic and Climate Scenarios - Rohat - 2019 - Earth's Future - Wiley Online Library'. Accessed 04 Feb 2025. https://doi.org/10.1029/2018EF001020
28. Bailey, N., Hochman, Z., Mao, Y., Silvapulle, M., Silvapulle, P.: Impact of climate change on agriculture in Australia: an interactive fixed effects model approach. Appl. Econ. 1–14 (2024). https://doi.org/10.1080/00036846.2024.2387361
29. 'Can we avert the looming food crisis of climate change?', ScienceDaily. Accessed 04 Feb 2025. https://www.sciencedaily.com/releases/2024/11/241126134816.htm
30. Choi, Y.-W., Eltahir, E.A.B.: Near-term climate change impacts on food crops productivity in East Africa. Theoret. Appl. Climatol. **152**(1), 843–860 (2023). https://doi.org/10.1007/s00 704-023-04408-1
31. World Meteorological Organization, State of the Climate in Africa 2023. Erscheinungsort nicht ermittelbar: United Nations (2024)
32. Sims, C.: Are forecasting models usable for policy analysis? Quart. Rev. **10**(Win), 2–16 (1986)
33. Sims, C.A.: Are forecasting models usable for policy analysis? Quart. Rev. **10**(Win), 2–16 (1986)

Assessing Local Human Development in Poland: Insights from 2010 and 2023

Veranika Kaleyeva$^{(\boxtimes)}$, Piotr A. Werner , and Mariusz Porczek

Faculty of Geography and Regional Studies, University of Warsaw, Warsaw, Poland
v.kaleyeva@gmail.com, {peter,mt.porczek}@uw.edu.pl

Abstract. The Local Human Development Index (LHDI) serves as a region-specific human development assessment tool measuring fundamental aspects like health, education and standard of living at the subnational level. This study explores the LHDI in Poland for the years 2010 and 2023, focusing on its spatial distribution and component variables. By analysing regional disparities, we identify trends and changes in LHDI across different areas. The findings provide insights into the evolving socio-economic landscape of Poland and highlight regions requiring targeted policy interventions.

Keywords: Local Human Development · LHDI · polarization · Poland

1 Introduction

The approach to human development measurement has changed substantially throughout history, moving away from exclusive reliance on economic metrics like GDP to more inclusive methods that evaluate social and human well-being factors. The Human Development Index (HDI) which originated from the United Nations Development Programme (UNDP) in 1990 stands as one of the most influential development measurement tools. Developed by economist Mahbub ul Haq, with conceptual contributions from Amartya Sen, the HDI was designed to provide a broader assessment of development by incorporating three key dimensions: health as measured by life expectancy at birth and education represented by average years of schooling and expected years of schooling along with standard of living evaluated through Gross National Income per capita adjusted for purchasing power parity [1, 2].

The HDI has successfully expanded development discussions past economic growth but hides substantial socio-spatial inequalities within countries according to national and regional HDI statistics [3]. Researchers and policymakers turned their attention to Local Human Development Index (LHDI) frameworks which modify HDI methodology for smaller regions like cities and districts because of this understanding [4]. By revealing subnational disparities, LHDI equips governments and organizations with insights into regional development, helping them craft targeted policies for specific local challenge [5, 6].

© The Author(s), under exclusive license to Springer Nature Switzerland AG 2026
O. Gervasi et al. (Eds.): ICCSA 2025 Workshops, LNCS 15890, pp. 387–401, 2026.
https://doi.org/10.1007/978-3-031-97606-3_26

The research investigates the importance of LHDI as well as its methodological approach and its role in evaluating socioeconomic differences to inform local policy strategies. Through spatial and comparative analysis of the Local Human Development Index (LHDI) in Poland for the years 2010 and 2023, we illustrate the robust analytical capacity of LHDI in assessing developmental progress and detecting disparities. These insights aim to provide a foundation for supporting sustainable development measures at local level.

2   Foundations and Analytical Perspectives of Local Human Development Index

2.1 Determinants of LHDI

The Local Human Development Index (LHDI) is a composite metric derived from a series of closely related economic, social, and governance factors important for economic growth, resource distribution, and overall quality of life. It incorporates both the traditional components of HDI and area-specific measures, considering the unique characteristics and development context of a given location.

The regional economic performance stands as the most reliable factor influencing LHDI through its measurement via Gross Regional Domestic Product (GRDP). The increase of income levels leads to better access to vital services and higher living standards which support human development processes [7–9]. Research has shown that public spending on health care, education, and infrastructure directly leads to better development results in local areas [10–12]. The distribution and operational effectiveness of these resources are often determined by the broader framework of fiscal decentralization, which, depending on the context, may either empower local authorities or generate coordination challenges and inefficiencies [13, 14].

Social factors including poverty incidence and unemployment rates play an essential role in determining the quality of life and future development prospects [15, 16]. The ability of people to obtain education and health care becomes restricted when poverty rates are high which reduces social mobility for both people and their communities. Moreover, the research highlights the role of social capital – such as trust, civic engagement, and institutional cooperation – emphasizing the importance of community participation and governance transparency in driving developmental outcomes [17, 18].

Infrastructure development and a reliable energy supply are also fundamental elements that drive economic growth, improve service delivery, and raise quality of life standards. Inequalities in these domains create deeper development gaps between regions [19].

Additional dimensions, such as migration patterns, demographic change, and environmental health risks may influence human development trajectories by reshaping access to services and shifting local priorities. Studies indicate that limited social networks among migrants can hinder access to essential resources [5]. Furthermore, local health conditions, such as cancer incidence and mortality rates, provide critical insights into regional disparities in healthcare access [20, 21].

Together, these determinants form a dynamic framework emphasizing that LHDI is not simply a statistical construct but a reflection of interconnected processes that shape the opportunities and well-being of local populations.

2.2 Expanding LHDI Dimensions

The traditional focus on health, education and income in LHDI has faced recent academic pressure to expand its scope for better understanding modern human development complexities. The proposed extensions into environmental sustainability, equity and cultural inclusion aim to enhance local indices for responding to new societal challenges.

A notable effort to reconceptualize the human development framework is the Human Sustainable Development Index (HSDI), which incorporates ecological sustainability into the assessment of development [22]. While still on the margins of mainstream research, such proposals recognize that sustainable access to natural resources and environmental resilience are increasingly essential to long-term human well-being.

Other studies have suggested incorporating less conventional elements – such as ethical values or religious practices – into localized indices. The Islamic Human Development Index (I-HDI), for example, includes cultural elements relevant to specific populations [23]. While such initiatives highlight the diversity of human development understandings, their applicability tends to remain context-specific and should be approached with caution when designing comparative metrics.

In the present study, we deliberately refrained from expanding the LHDI framework. Our primary objective was to ensure comparability with the original Polish LHDI report from 2012, which was based on 2010 data [24]. The arguments supporting the selection of particular sub-indicators were presented in detail in that foundational publication. The evaluation of temporal changes in this article used the same framework to maintain methodological consistency.

2.3 Methods to Study LHDI

The study of LHDI involves the application of diverse analytical methods, each chosen to reflect both the complexity of human development and the specificity of local contexts. Central to this approach is the construction of composite indices, which combine multiple normalized indicators into a single, interpretable metric. These composite indicators typically use geometric or arithmetic means and reflect normalized measures of health, education, and income dimensions. The flexibility of this method has allowed for its adaptation across various local and regional studies, including modifications for sector-specific assessments or population-targeted metrics [15, 17, 25, 26].

Beyond index construction, statistical techniques are widely employed to analyze patterns and disparities in LHDI scores. Regression analysis, correlation matrices, and multidimensional scaling help researchers identify the relationships among determinants and highlight areas of concern [27, 28]. More advanced econometric models, including panel data analysis and structural equation modelling, are increasingly used to investigate causal pathways and long-term trends in human development indicators.

Geospatial methods also play a vital role in LHDI research. Techniques such as Geographically Weighted Regression (GWR), spatial autocorrelation (e.g., Moran's I) and cluster analysis allow scholars to visualize and interpret the geographic distribution of development inequalities. These tools are particularly useful in identifying regional clusters of high or low development and exploring the spatial dependencies between variables [14, 18, 29].

Comparative approaches – both cross-regional and longitudinal – enable the assessment of development trajectories over time or across spatial units. By applying consistent metrics across different regions or timeframes, researchers can draw robust conclusions about structural shifts, policy impacts, and regional convergence or divergence in development [11, 30–33].

Overall, the methodological landscape of LHDI research continues to evolve, reflecting both the theoretical complexity of human development and the practical demands of policy evaluation. Future research may benefit from integrating emerging data sources and further refining tools for spatial-temporal analysis, while maintaining a commitment to transparency, comparability, and context sensitivity.

3   Methodology of Evaluation of Local Human Development Index (LHDI) in Poland

The key aspect of contemporary scientific studies is the ability to repeat the methodological steps. The approach aims to either verify previously obtained results or obtain new, comparable results for different time points or spatial locations, all using the same research schema. The first evaluation of LHDI in Poland (2012) has been precisely and in detail described in the published report [24]. Recently, these steps were repeated with the goal of comparing the final LHDI coefficients in 2023 across Polish counties, along with their three main components. The main reasons for repeating these research procedures were the 'wild cards' at the global and continental (European) scale, i.e., outbreaks of the COVID-19 pandemic (2020–2022, still marking its presence in 2023), and the ongoing war in Ukraine (from February 2022). These factors rearranged the main values and priorities as perceived by Polish society and have undoubtedly left their mark on the global and domestic economies.

The situation of Poland in the first years of the XXI century was shaped by two main global phenomena: the financial crisis (2007–2009) and the earthquake, tsunami, and nuclear crisis at Fukushima, Japan, which, in turn, changed the global perception of electric energy acquisition from nuclear plants (similarly to the nuclear catastrophe of the nuclear plant in Chernobyl, Ukraine, 1986). Two main phenomena emerged at the local scale. The first was Poland's accession to the European Union in 2004 and its continued negative foreign migration balance until 2015. Minor mass event, but important (at the continental scale, and from a recent historic perspective) was the 2012 UEFA European Football Championship (Euro 2012) co-hosted by Poland and Ukraine, which also marked itself in public opinion, different sectors of the local economy, and tourism. The publication of the 2012 LHDI report preceded this event, and it's likely that this initiative had a connection to it.

The 2012 Poland LHDI report presented local HDI coefficients by counties as the set of composite indices for the year 2010 that combined normalized indicators (geometric means, at the scale 1–100): life expectancy, education level, and per capita income, which in turn contained composite, detailed, absolute (also normalized) values of particular sub-indices. The 2023 approach is a replication of this procedure aimed at revealing time and spatial changes of these features.

3.1   Poland HDI 2010–2022

The methodology for evaluating a country's HDI differs from that of LHDI, though the overall approach to estimating the country's total coefficient is similar. Poland's HDI rose almost without breaks but slightly shrank during the COVID-19 pandemic (Fig. 1) [34], returning to its level in 2022.

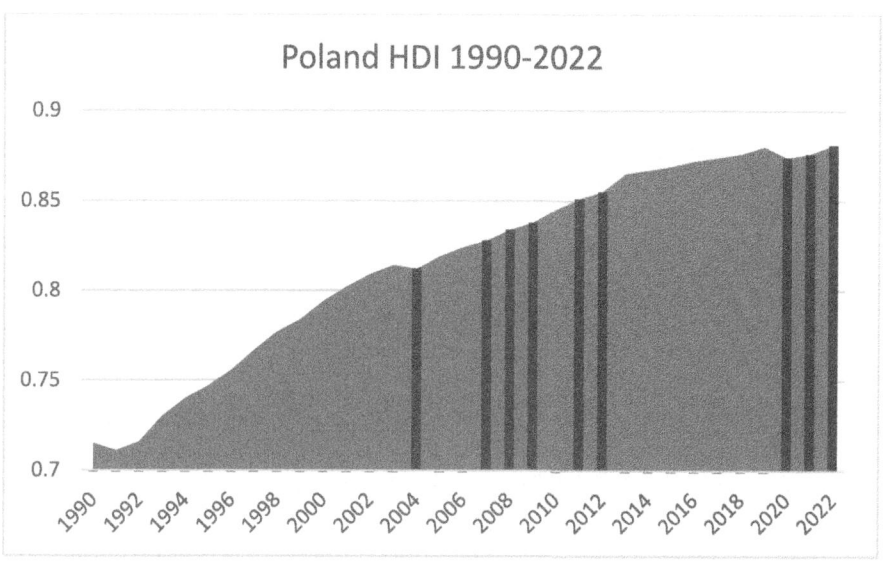

Fig. 1. HDI Poland 1990–2022, data source: [33]; 2004 Poland's accession to the EU; 2007–2009 global financial crisis; 2011 Fukushima; 2012 Euro 2012; 2020–2021 COVID-19; 2022 war in Ukraine.

4   LHDI in Poland: Changes from 2010 to 2023

The analysis begins with a brief overview of Poland's Human Development Index (HDI) at the national level to provide contextual background and highlight temporal trends. With its advantages, HDI has limits – such as masking internal disparities and omitting environmental or political dimensions, but it is still a robust tool for understanding and comparing human progress at an international level. It also serves as an appropriate introductory step to analyze the further Local Human Development Index at the subnational level.

There is a scatter matrix graph (Fig. 2) that shows the comparison of the final LHDI indices and their sub-indices for each county in Poland in 2010 and 2023. The diagonal charts display the self-dispersion of the indices themselves. The rest of the graphs show the comparison of particular indices (as variables) by counties (at the regional level, i.e., county – 'powiat'). The scatter matrix graph starts the analysis of LHDI in Poland at a local level, showing how each pair of LHDI subcomponents and LHDI itself changes over space and time. The footprints of each pair show the general tendency of spatial and time dispersion of the subcomponents. Each footprint shows where all 380 regions (counties) are located in relation to the compared subcomponents and the overall LHDI at specific times. The diagonal presents histogram of the LHDI subcomponents and overall LHDI strictly to the related point in time.

The Local Human Development Indices show the tendency to multidirectional polarization between the counties (LHDI 2023 vs. LHDI 2010) over the past thirteen years.

In spite of Educational sub-indices (LHDI_EI_2023 vs. LHDI_EI_2010), which display a certain linear trend with easily noticeable margins (which reveals stability between the counties). Conversely, the Health sub-indices (LHDI_HI_2023 vs. LHDI_HI_2010) reflect deeper and more varied polarization, indicating increasing divergence in health-related development. The Wealth sub-indices (LHDI_WI_2023 vs. LHDI_WI_2010) show an almost linear trend with a few top counties (with max values) as hot-spot outliers.

Local Human Development Index values (LHDI_year) by counties in Poland 2023 shows slight more dispersion than in 2010 looking at the particular indices using the box-plots (Fig. 3). There are more top (hot-spots) outliers as well a slight lower (bottom) outlier (that confirms again greater polarization between counties). But the first quartile

**Local Human Development Index (LHDI, 2023 vs 2010) in Poland.
Sub-indices: Educational (EI), Health (HI), Welfare (WI) 2023 vs 2010**

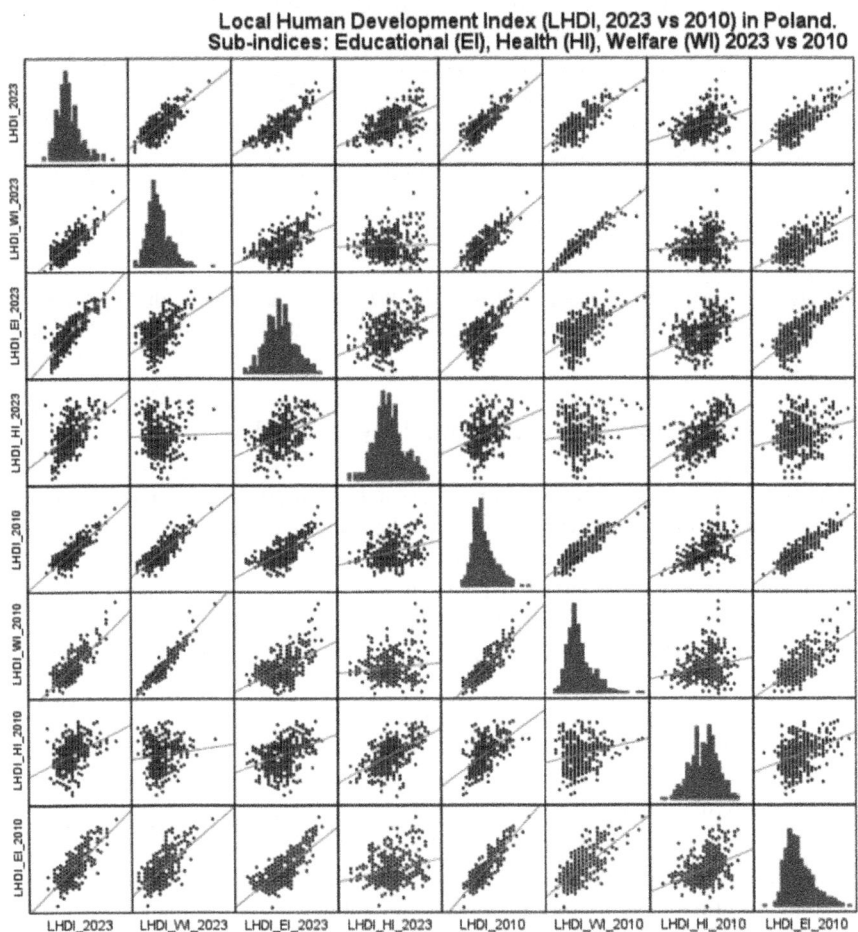

Fig. 2. Scatter matrix graph. Comparison of Local Human Development Indices (LHDI_year), and Educational (LHDI_EI_year), Health (LHDI_HI_year) and Wealth (LHDI_WI_year) Sub-Indices of 380 counties in Poland in 2023 and 2010. The data was processed using the PS IMAGO PRO software, with the analytical engine being IBM SPSS Statistics.

and median are a little bit greater in 2023 than in 2010. The reduction of polarization is visible for education by counties (LHDI_EI) in 2023 but dispersion shrunk and simultaneously, for set of education sub-indices of counties: first and third quartiles rose, as well as median. Conversely, the set of health sub-indices (LHDI_HI) in 2023 reveal greater dispersion, with top and low outliers, as well the lower values of all quartiles (greater polarization). This schema of greater polarization (greater dispersion) in 2023 is repeated also for set of wealth sub-indices by counties with rose of the quartiles and shrunk of former (in 2010) top outliers.

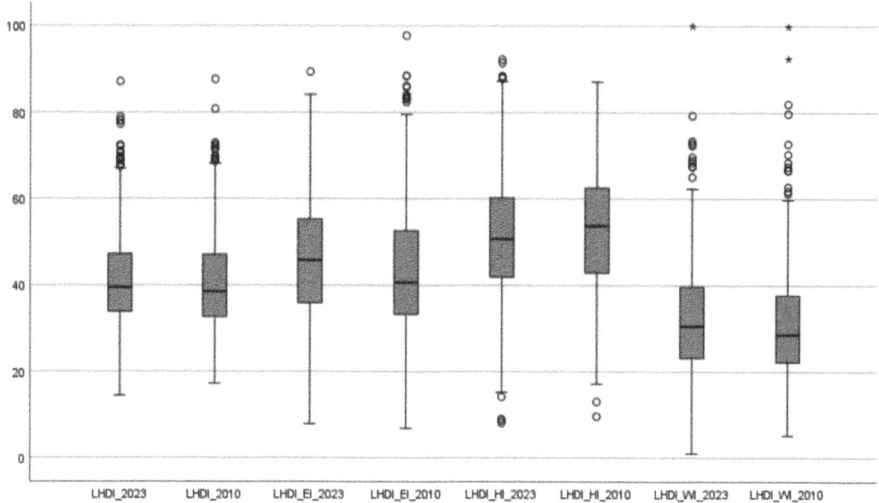

Fig. 3. Box-plots: comparison of Local Human Development Indices (LHDI_year), and Educational (LHDI_EI_year), Health (LHDI_HI_year) and Wealth (LHDI_WI_year) Sub-Indices of 380 counties in Poland in 2023 and 2010. The data was processed using the PS IMAGO PRO software, with the analytical engine being IBM SPSS Statistics.

Simple calculations of the difference, representing the decrease or increase in LHDI (Fig. 4), illustrate changes in the index over a 13-year period. An attempt to maintain uniform class sizes resulted in only five counties being classified in the highest category (counties: Wrocławski, Płocki, Pińczowski, Kazimierski, and Miechowski), marked in dark red, and one in the lowest category (Ciechanowski county), marked in deep blue. The increase observed among peri-urban counties indicates an improvement in the quality of life in metropolitan or agglomeration areas. In general, central urban areas do not exhibit significant growth, as their LHDI values were already high in 2010. Instead, the cities typically experience a decline in the index. It is also worth noting the decline in LHDI along anthropogeographical boundaries (e.g., the borders of the West Pomeranian and Greater Poland Voivodeships, as well as the Masovian and Warmian-Masurian Voivodeships), in Greater Poland, and in the Sudetes Mountains.

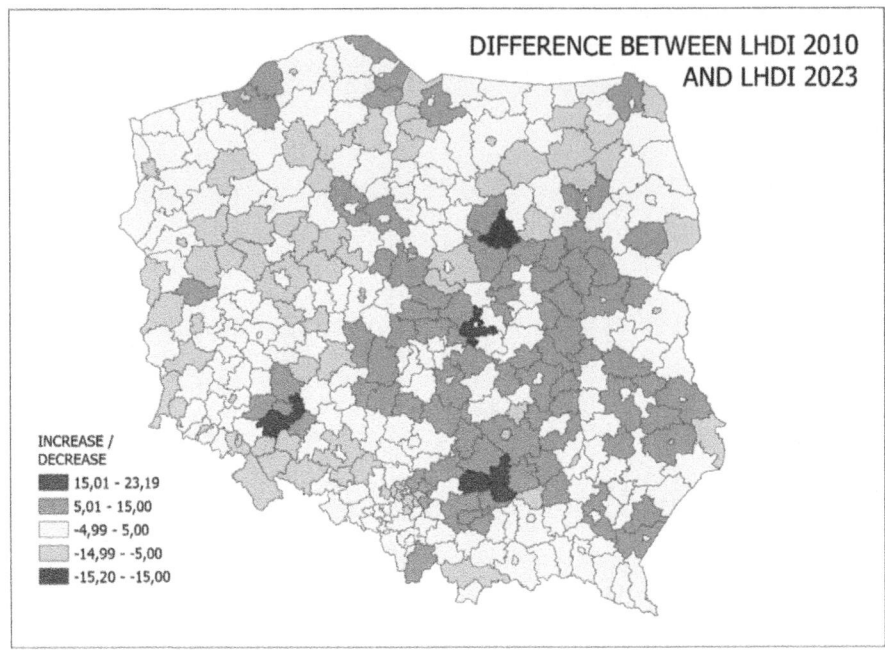

Fig. 4. Difference between LHDI in 2010 and 2023.

4.1 Cluster Analysis – Grouping Based on LHDI Coefficients

The analysis was conducted using SAGA GIS with a combined method for nine clusters, which were grouped by software based on similarities in LHDI parameters for 2010 and 2023. Due to the varying index values, clusters were assigned descriptive names to better illustrate their essence, relative rank, and trend direction. In every cluster's range, extreme values ('min' and 'max') and the average value ('avg') are presented in Table 1.

Table 1. Value ranges and colour representation in county clusters.

No. of Cluster	Cluster Name	Short Name	Trend Direction	LHDI Level	No. of Elements	Std. Dev.	2023 avg	2023 min	2023 max	Spread 2023	2010 avg	2010 min	2010 max	Spread 2010
0	Down Worst	DW	↓ Decline	Very Low	36	4,81	24,07	14,46	29,27	14,81	31,26	20,47	39,44	18,97
1	Up Worst	UW	↑ Increase	Low	41	5,04	31,75	24,39	41,30	16,91	25,99	17,24	31,08	13,84
2	Down Low	DL	↓ Decline	Medium-Low	50	3,48	32,89	28,04	36,88	8,84	36,79	31,68	42,55	10,87
3	Up Low	UL	↑ Increase	Low-Medium	50	3,88	38,90	34,44	48,99	14,55	32,38	23,24	36,26	13,02
4	Down Medium	DM	↓ Decline	Medium	37	3,73	39,18	34,38	43,57	9,19	44,65	40,71	51,30	10,59
5	Up Medium	UM	↑ Increase	Medium	59	3,65	42,53	38,33	51,28	12,95	38,61	33,70	42,70	9,00
6	Little High	LH	— Stable	Medium-High	48	4,81	48,76	41,78	56,48	14,70	48,65	41,70	57,12	15,42
7	Medium High	MH	— Stable	High	43	6,10	56,40	47,87	69,33	21,46	58,07	50,70	68,62	17,92
8	Very High	VH	— Stable	Very High	16	8,39	72,50	64,65	87,12	22,47	70,64	61,54	87,63	26,09

While this alone may not provide significant insights, the distribution is more clearly depicted in the following chart (Fig. 5).

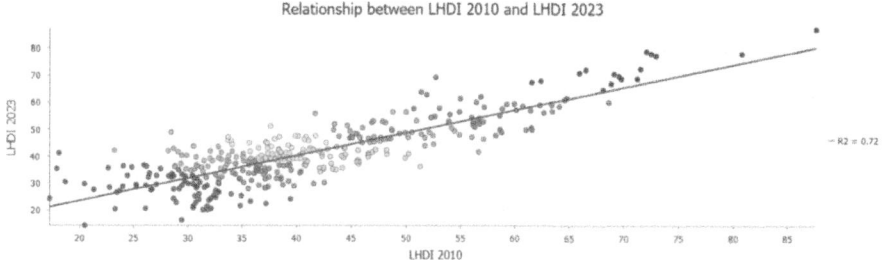

Fig. 5. Relationship between LHDI in 2010 and 2023.

The three most intensely red-shaded clusters are labelled as High (specifically Very High, Medium High, and Little High), representing counties with the highest LHDI values in both 2010 and 2023. The grouping of the remaining counties was based on the direction of LHDI change – either growth or decline. Each of the three object groups (Medium, Low, and Worst) was further divided according to LHDI trends: Up (increase) and Down (decrease). This classification clearly illustrates where the LHDI index has risen and where it has declined.

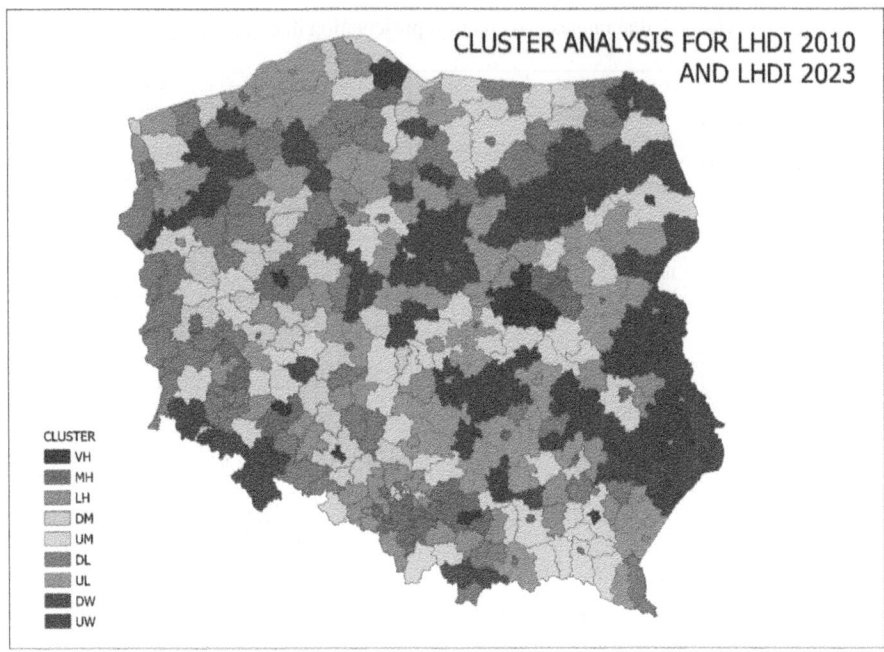

Fig. 6. Spatial distribution of county clusters for LHDI 2010 and 2023.

The map visualization (Fig. 6) indicates that the three High classes primarily represent cities and large metropolitan areas (e.g., the Silesian-Zagłębie Metropolis, Warsaw, the Tri-City, Poznań, Wrocław, etc.). While smaller cities exhibit high LHDI values, their surrounding areas do not necessarily follow this trend. However, most of these regions have noted LHDI growth. An exception is Opole and several smaller county towns. A decline in LHDI is mainly observed in peripheral areas, where the index was already low in 2010 and has since decreased further (Fig. 7).

4.2 Local Sub-Indices in Poland (2010 vs 2023)

Health Sub-index (HI). This parameter exhibited the most significant change among all three parameters. Growth is observed across all clusters. Notably, there is no decline in LHDI within the VH group, whereas a pronounced decrease is evident among DW counties, primarily located in northern Mazovia and the Sudetes. Among lower-performing counties, a substantial increase can be observed in the Lublin and Kielce regions.

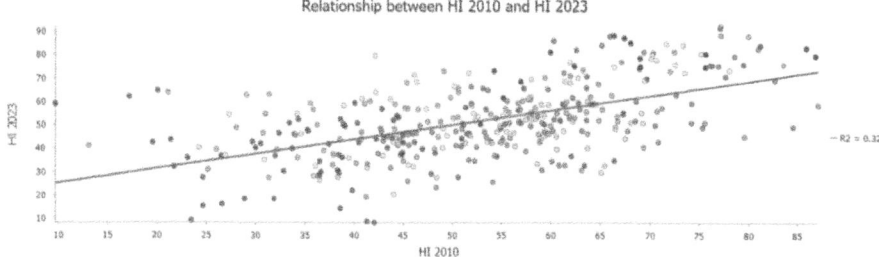

Fig. 7. Relationship between the health sub-index (HI) in 2010 and 2023.

Education Sub-index (EI). The education parameter exhibits significantly lower dispersion. Warsaw initially demonstrated the highest EI value in 2010; however, its subsequent decline allowed other units to reach comparable levels. At present, Kraków records the highest EI index. This parameter may also contribute to the observed decline in total LHDI value across a range of counties within the DW and DL groups, particularly in northern Poland. Conversely, a significant increase has been recorded in counties located in the eastern part of the country (UW cluster) (Fig. 8).

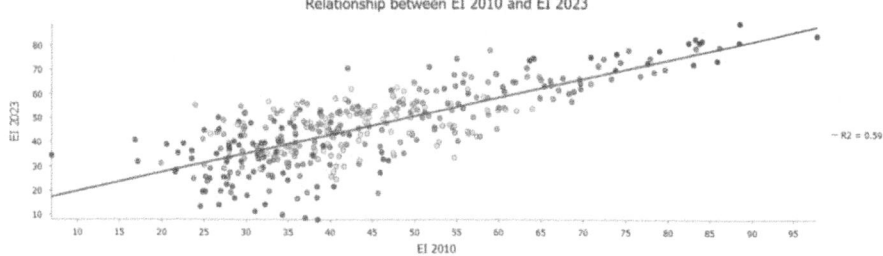

Fig. 8. Relationship between the education sub-index (EI) in 2010 and 2023.

Welfare Sub-index (WI). Among all three parameters, the WI parameter exhibits the lowest dispersion. There are no substantial fluctuations in values, which may indicate a certain stagnation among the poorest counties. A noticeable decline is observed among the wealthiest counties, particularly those surrounding Warsaw, as well as among the poorest ones. This pattern may offer an interesting insight into emerging regional dynamics and warrants further exploration (Fig. 9).

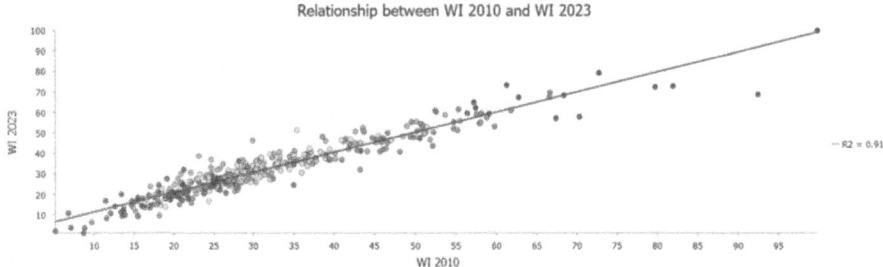

Fig. 9. Relationship between the welfare sub-index (WI) in 2010 and 2023.

5 Discussion

The LHDI in Poland exhibits a trend of multidirectional polarization among counties (LHDI 2023 vs. LHDI 2010). This pattern is concerning because it reflects increasing regional differences that may result in varied availability of resources, services, and opportunities. Such polarization may further exacerbate social and economic inequalities, compromise the overall development, and erode regional coherence [35, 36]. Persistent disparities can also contribute to political instability and weaken economic resilience [37].

The decline in LHDI values is primarily driven by decreases in specific parameters, particularly the health sub-index (HI) in northern Mazovia and the Sudetes, and the education sub-index (EI) in northern Poland. However, the overall trend of the education sub-indices remains relatively linear with well-defined margins, indicating stability across counties. The decline in LHDI is predominantly observed in peripheral areas, where index values were already low in 2010 and have further decreased. This trend may be linked to depopulation and the increasing closure of infrastructure in these regions.

Counties with the highest LHDI values in both 2010 and 2023 are primarily urban centres and large metropolitan areas. The observed increase in peri-urban counties suggests an improvement in quality of life within metropolitan and agglomeration zones, reflecting dynamic suburban expansion and the growth of urbanized regions. This strong suburbanization trend aligns with previous studies on urban development in Poland [38]. Central urban areas show limited LHDI growth, as their values were already high in 2010. In some cases, declines are evident, likely due to the natural urban life cycle and challenges related to overpopulation. Despite the fact that several small cities have high LHDI values and are still growing, their respective regions do not necessarily have similar patterns of suburbanization to those of large metropolitan areas.

Although the national Human Development Index (HDI) has increased positively in the last 10 years, the average Local Human Development Index (LHDI) for 2010 and 2023 has no significant upward or downward shift to justify further in-depth analysis. This lack of significant change in the overall LHDI highlights the limitations of relying solely on national averages and underscores the importance of examining the contextual factors that influence human development at the local scale.

There are numerous potential reasons for regional variation in LHDI, which deserve further exploration to better understand the uneven nature of human development across localities. To calculate and interpret the LHDI, it is crucial to consider local socio-economic, cultural, and environmental factors, as these are key determinants of human development outcomes. Our study outlines the dependencies between LHDI and urban development dynamics, which could benefit from further investigation. This underscores that, in line with well-established research, these dependencies may not always be immediately evident but provide valuable insights into LHDI research. For instance, cultural practices and traditional customs are essential in shaping social and economic behavior. Rajappa et al. (2023) explain that cultural practices, such as tobacco chewing, contribute to health inequalities in certain communities [39].

In conclusion, while the present study highlights key regional variations in LHDI, understanding the complex interplay of socio-economic, cultural, and institutional factors is crucial for developing more targeted policies aimed at fostering balanced human development.

6 Conclusion

The study demonstrates that the Local Human Development Index (LHDI) in Poland displays a pattern of multidirectional polarization among counties between 2010 and 2023.

The main challenge in the estimation of the LHDI is the lack of detailed information at the local scale. The constant evolution of the LHDI methodologies shows that it is crucial to align the measurement instruments with the local socio-economic and environmental realities. Future work should also keep on integrating innovation such as sustainability, equity, and cultural factors to the assessment to offer a better view of local human development.

Disclosure of Interests.   The authors have no competing interests to declare that are relevant to the content of this article.

References

1. Nations, U.: Human Development Report 1990. United Nations (1990)
2. Haq, M.: Ul: Reflections on Human Development. Oxford University Press, Oxford, New York (1995)
3. Conceição, P.: Human development report: beyond income, beyond averages, beyond today: inequalities in human development in the 21st century. UNDP (2019)
4. Rodríguez-Pose, A., Hardy, D.: Addressing poverty and inequality in the rural economy from a global perspective. Appl. Geograph. **61** (2015). https://doi.org/10.1016/j.apgeog.2015.02.005
5. Harttgen, K., Klasen, S.: A human development index by internal migrational status. J. Hum. Develop. Capab. **12**, 393–424 (2011). https://doi.org/10.1080/19452829.2011.576819
6. Harttgen, K., Klasen, S.: A household-based human development index. World Dev. **40**, 878–899 (2012)

7. Türk, U., Toger, M., Östh, J.: How can small-scale measures of human development index (HDI) be used to study the local potential for sustainable economic growth? In: Suzuki, S. and Patuelli, R. (eds.) A Broad View of Regional Science: Essays in Honor of Peter Nijkamp, pp. 161–173. Springer, Singapore (2021). https://doi.org/10.1007/978-981-33-4098-5_9

8. Sukri, A., et al: The effect of regional original income (PAD), balancing funds on economic growth through the human development index (IPM) in Central Mamuju regency. In: Presented at the 1st Australian International Conference on Industrial Engineering and Operations Management December 21 (2022). https://doi.org/10.46254/AU01.20220364

9. Susanto, J.: Infrastructure, gross regional domestic product, and convergence of human development index. J. Ekonomi Studi. Pembangunan. **22**, 244–255 (2021). https://doi.org/10.18196/jesp.v22i2.7619

10. Biao, I., et al.: The contribution of the human development index literacy theory to the debate on literacy and development. World J. Educ. **4**, 1–12 (2014)

11. Irani, D.D., Siers, M., Rice, M., Bast, E.: Human Development Index Disparities in Baltimore City

12. Iksan, U.M., Fajri, A.C., Tri, W.S.: The effect of capital allocations on economic growth, human development Index and poverty in North Maluku of Indonesia during 2010–2016. Russian J. Agricul. Socio-Econ. Sci. **80**, 11–18 (2018)

13. Karpi, I.K., Widayat, Y.Y., Ratnasari, N.E., Munajat, M.D.E.: Can Regional Spending Management Policies Improve Human Development Index?. J. Indon. Sustain. Develop. Plan. **3**, 177–191 (2022). https://doi.org/10.46456/jisdep.v3i2.309

14. Handayani, L., Seniorita, Anantajaya, S.P., Hendrawan, H., Tannady, H.: Analysis of the influence of fiscal decentralization, dependency ratio, and ratio of independence on the human development index in East region of Indonesia. JEMSI (Jurnal Ekonomi, Manajemen, dan Akuntansi). **9**, 140–147 (2023). https://doi.org/10.35870/jemsi.v9i1.914

15. Salim, S.S., Sathianandan, T.V., Mohamed, K.S., Narayankumar, R., Athira, N.R.: A fisher development index (FDI) for assessing human development in marine fishers of Kerala. India. Environ. Dev. Sustain. (2024). https://doi.org/10.1007/s10668-024-04923-9

16. Dahliah, D., Nur, A.N.: The influence of unemployment, human development index and gross domestic product on poverty level. Golden Ratio Soc. Sci. Educ. **1**, 95–108 (2021). https://doi.org/10.52970/grsse.v1i2.84

17. Khalifa, M., Connelly, S.: Monitoring and guiding development in rural Egypt: local sustainable development indicators and local human development indices. Environ. Dev. Sustain. **11**, 1175–1196 (2009). https://doi.org/10.1007/s10668-008-9173-0

18. Varlitya, C.R., Masbar, R., Jamal, A., Nasir, M.: Do Fiscal Decentralization and Human Development Index Affect Poverty in Indonesia? Presented at the 1st Aceh Global Conference (AGC 2018) January (2019). https://doi.org/10.2991/agc-18.2019.84

19. Ray, S., Ghosh, B., Bardhan, S., Bhattacharyya, B.: Studies on the impact of energy quality on human development index. Renew. Energy **92**, 117–126 (2016)

20. Khazaei, Z., et al.: The incidence and mortality of endometrial cancer and its association with body mass index and human development index in Asian population. World Cancer Res. J. **5**(4), e1174 (2018). https://doi.org/10.32113/wcrj_201812_1174

21. Namayandeh, S.M., Khazaei, Z., Lari Najafi, M., Goodarzi, E., Moslem, A.: global leukemia in children 0–14 statistics 2018, incidence and mortality and human development index (HDI): globocan sources and methods. Asian Pac. J. Cancer Prev. **21**, 1487–1494 (2020). https://doi.org/10.31557/APJCP.2020.21.5.1487

22. Bravo, G.: The human sustainable development index: new calculations and a first critical analysis. Ecol. Ind. **37**, 145–150 (2014). https://doi.org/10.1016/j.ecolind.2013.10.020

23. Lestari, D., Arumi, N.A.: Factors that influence the Islamic perspective human development index as evidence of the development of the Muslim community. J. Islamic Econom. Buss. Ethics. **1**, 75–93 (2024). https://doi.org/10.24235/jiesbi.v1i2.133

24. Arak, P., et al.: Krajowy raport o rozwoju społecznym. Polska 2012. Rozwój regionalny i lokalny. (2012)
25. Sheth, S., Bettencourt, L.: The community human development index as a precision vulnerability metric and risk indicator. https://papers.ssrn.com/abstract=4328885, (2023). https://doi.org/10.2139/ssrn.4328885
26. Wong, S.: Conceptual and methodological issues of developing a community and neighborhood human development index CHIPP Res. Paper No. 2. (2011)
27. Sasmita, N.,et al.: statistical assessment of human development index variations and their correlates: a case study of Aceh province, Indonesia. Grimsa J. Bus. Econ. Studies. 1, 12–24 (2023). https://doi.org/10.61975/gjbes.v1i1.14
28. Nayak, P., Mishra, S.K.: Efficiency of Pena's P2 distance in construction of human development indices. SSRN J. (2012). https://doi.org/10.2139/ssrn.2066567
29. Zangiacomi Martinez, E., da Roza, D.L.: Ecological analysis of adolescent birth rates in Brazil: association with human development index. Women Birth. 33, e191–e198 (2020). https://doi.org/10.1016/j.wombi.2019.04.002
30. Anderson, J., Gerber, J.: A human development index for the United States-Mexico border. J. Borderlands Studies. 19, 1–26 (2004). https://doi.org/10.1080/08865655.2004.9695624
31. Anderson, J.B., Gerber, J.: The US-Mexico border human development index (2023). https://doi.org/10.1080/08865655.2020.1855229
32. Sandu, D.: Validation of the local human development index for Romanian villages by their regional location: introducing a data basis. (2017)
33. Sandu, D.: Challenge and Response of Regional Disparities: Romania in a Comparative Perspective. Presented at the February, vol. 14 (2022). https://doi.org/10.1007/978-3-658-36343-7_13
34. Nations, U.: Documentation and downloads. United Nations
35. Piketty, Thomas: Capital in the Twenty-First Century. Harvard University Press (2014)
36. Rodríguez-Pose, A.: The revenge of the places that don't matter (and what to do about it). Camb. J. Reg. Econ. Soc. 11, 189–209 (2018). https://doi.org/10.1093/cjres/rsx024
37. Iammarino, S., Rodriguez-Pose, A., Storper, M.: Regional inequality in Europe: evidence, theory and policy implications. J. Econ. Geograp. 19, 273–298 (2019). https://doi.org/10.1093/jeg/lby021
38. Werner, P.A., Kaleyeva, V., Porczek, M.: Urban sprawl in Poland (2016–2021): drivers, wildcards, and spatial externalities. Remote Sens. 14, 2804 (2022). https://doi.org/10.3390/rs1412 2804
39. Rajappa, S., Singh, M., Uehara, R., Schachterle, S.E., Setia, S.: Cancer incidence and mortality trends in Asia based on regions and human development index levels: an analyses from GLOBOCAN 2020. Curr. Med. Res. Opin. 39, 1127–1137 (2023). https://doi.org/10.1080/03007995.2023.2231761

HERitage and CLIMAte Neutrality. Resilient Approach for Nature Centered/Based Sustainable Cities. (HERCLIMA 2025)

Analysis of Factors Influencing the Development of Health and Wellness Tourism in the Context of Sustainable Urban and Regional Development in Uzbekistan

Bahodirhon Safarov[1] ⓘ, Nargiza Mansurova[2] ⓘ, Habibullo Hasanov[3][✉] ⓘ,
Abdulatif Xayrullayev[1] ⓘ, Raxima Sanayeva[4] ⓘ, and Jie Yu[5] ⓘ

[1] Zarmed University, Q. Murtazoyev Street, Bukhara, Uzbekistan
[2] "Silk Road" International University of Tourism and Cultural Heritage, Boulevard 17, Samarkand 140100, Uzbekistan
[3] Samarkand Institute of Economics and Service, A. Temur Street. 9, Samarkand 140105, Uzbekistan
khabibulloeco@gmail.com
[4] Samarkand Regional Pedagogical Skill Center, H. Obiddinov Street. 7, Samarkand 140104, Uzbekistan
[5] Northwest University, Xi'an 710027, China

Abstract. This study examined the role and significance of wellness tourism in the advancement of sustainable urban and regional development in Uzbekistan. The combination of healthcare, environmental sustainability and economic development that characterizes wellness tourism ensures sustainability not only at the local level but also at the regional level. The study aims to study the main factors influencing the demand for wellness tourism in Uzbekistan and its role in regional sustainable development. The relationship of wellness tourism with economic, demographic and tourism-related factors was assessed using the OLS regression model based on data from the Agency for Statistics of the Republic of Uzbekistan for 2010–2023. The results showed that the most important factors in the demand for wellness tourism are population income, the volume of healthcare services, domestic and inbound tourism. An increase in these factors significantly contributes to higher demand for wellness tourism. At the same time, increasing the number of new sanatoriums and resorts does not directly affect the demand for wellness tourism. On the contrary, it is more important to increase the capacity of existing sanatoriums and improve the quality of service. These results provide useful recommendations for organizations responsible for state policy, investors and tourism specialists.

Keywords: Wellness Tourism · Sustainable Development · Sanatorium-Resort Services · Domestic Tourism · Inbound Tourism

O. Gervasi et al. (Eds.): ICCSA 2025 Workshops, LNCS 15890, pp. 405–414, 2026.
https://doi.org/10.1007/978-3-031-97606-3_27

1   Introduction

In recent years, health and wellness tourism has become an important part of how cities and regions can develop in a way that is good for the environment and society. This type of tourism combines healthcare services with travel experiences. According to the Global Wellness Institute (GWI), the global wellness tourism market was valued at 650.7 billion USD in 2022 [1]. The GWI anticipates that the market will reach 1.4 trillion USD by 2027 [1]. It does not only help the economy but also protects the environment and improves the well-being of society [2–4]. In many countries, wellness tourism is seen as an important sector that helps the local economy, supports public health initiatives, and creates international cooperation in the medical and hospitality industries. Uzbekistan is a country with great potential for wellness tourism [5]. The country's rich natural resources, healing springs, balneological sanatoriums and traditional medicine methods serve as a solid foundation for the development of wellness tourism [6]. However, this sector is not yet fully developed in Uzbekistan. Identifying the key factors influencing the demand for wellness tourism services is crucial for formulating effective development strategies.

Wellness tourism has been widely studied in terms of the interaction between economic development, healthcare infrastructure, and tourism demand [7, 8]. Studies show that quality healthcare services have a significant impact on the demand for wellness tourism [9, 10]. Domestic tourism is an important factor in the sustainability of this sector, and the preference of domestic tourists for short-distance travel increases the demand for wellness tourism [11]. At the same time, it has been observed that international wellness tourists tend to choose high-quality sanatoriums and natural healing resorts [9, 12]. However, empirical research on the factors influencing the demand for wellness tourism in Uzbekistan is lacking. This study aims to fill this gap by empirically assessing the impact of economic, demographic and other factors on wellness tourism.

This study aims to analyze the factors influencing the growth of wellness tourism in Uzbekistan and assess its role in sustainable regional development. Using the OLS regression model, the impact of factors such as population, income, number and capacity of sanatoriums, volume of health services and the level of domestic and foreign tourism on the demand for wellness tourism is assessed. A deeper understanding of this relationship provides important recommendations for state policymakers, entrepreneurs, and investors in the development of wellness tourism.

The analysis of the most influential factors that shape wellness tourism demand is beneficial to scholars and practitioners alike. While wellness tourism is a subject in international tourism studies, there is not enough focus on its particulars in Uzbekistan. This research hopes to fill that by providing actionable and data-informed strategies on how the sector can achieve growth and sustainability.

2   Materials and Methods

We use annual data from the Statistics Agency of Uzbekistan for the period 2010 to 2023 to identify factors influencing the number of people accommodated in sanatorium-resort institutions and recreation organizations (SanAccom) in Uzbekistan. The dataset includes key economic, demographic, and infrastructural variables expected to influence SanAccom. Table 1 provides an overview of these variables, their definitions, and units of measurement.

Table 1. Determinants of sanatorium-resort accommodation demand.

Acronym	Variable name	Unit of measure
SanOrg	Number of sanatorium-resort facilities and recreational organizations	Units
SanPlace	Number of available places in sanatorium-resort facilities and recreational organizations	Thousand units
Income	Real total income per capita	Thousand UZS
Population	Permanent population	Thousand people
RecBases	Number of recreational centers and tourist bases	Units
HospBeds	Number of hospital beds per 10,000 people	Units
HealthServ	Volume of healthcare services	Billion UZS
DomTourism	Domestic tourism	Persons
InbTourism	Inbound tourism	Persons
SanAccom	Number of people accommodated in sanatorium-resort institutions and recreation organizations	Thousand units

Before conducting regression analysis, it is necessary to examine the distribution of the main variables used in the study. Table 2 presents descriptive statistics for each variable for the period 2010–2023.

Table 2. Descriptive statistics of the variables.

Variable	Obs	Mean	Std Dev	Min	Max
SanAccom	14	582.871	157.432	285.6	887.4
SanOrg	14	414.714	85.725	278	591
SanPlace	14	57.857	13.592	34.7	99.5
Income	14	7834.107	5079.274	2038.7	18201.2
Population	14	33.914	12.858	16.9	72.3
RecBases	14	217	56.907	132	298
HospBeds	14	45.014	2.514	41.1	47.9
HealthServ	14	2565.921	2568.41	258	8621.7
DomTourism	14	348884.43	179968.62	150233	728581
InbTourism	14	184489.36	85112.557	21693	348731

The Income has high standard deviations from the mean, indicating a significant change in per capita income over time. Similarly, SanAccom ranges from 285.6 to 887.4 thousand, indicating a shift in the demand for wellness tourism. However, there was a sharp decline in 2020, when the number decreased to 285,600, primarily due to the COVID-19 pandemic and the associated travel restrictions. The sector recovered in the following years, reaching 887,400 in 2023 (Fig. 1)

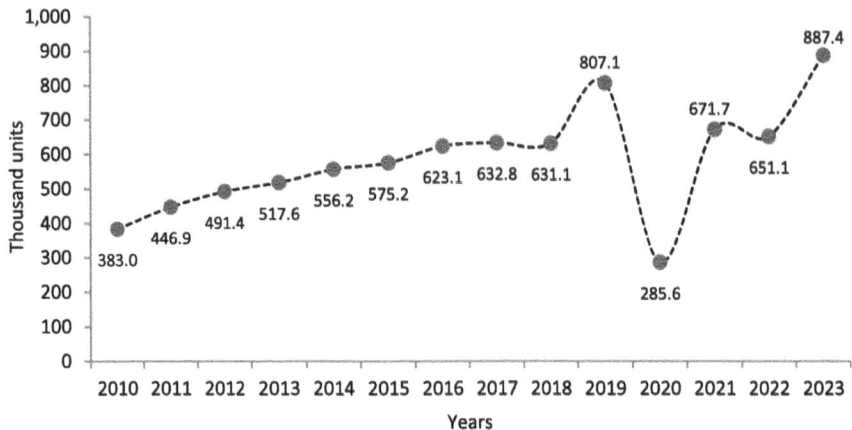

Fig. 1. Number of people accommodated in sanatorium-resort institutions and recreation organizations in Uzbekistan (2010–2023). Source: Statistics Agency of Uzbekistan

We can see that the variables DomTourism and InbTourism vary significantly, in particular, the number of DomTourism ranging from 150,233 to 728,581 and InbTourism ranging from 21,693 to 348,731 (Table 2). This variability reflects trends in tourism demand, potentially influenced by economic conditions, policy changes, and infrastructure development. In particular, DomTourism and InbTourism showed steady growth until 2019, before experiencing a sharp decline in 2020 due to COVID-19 restrictions. However, the variables have recovered significantly in the following years as the pandemic restrictions have eased (Fig. 2)

To analyze the relationship between SanAccom and the independent variables, we use the ordinary least squares (OLS) regression model. OLS is widely used to estimate linear relationships between a dependent variable and multiple independent variables due to its efficiency and interpretability [13]. The general form of the model is expressed as follows:

$$SanAccom_t = \beta_0 + \sum_{i=1}^{9} \beta_i X_{i,t} + \varepsilon_t \tag{1}$$

where: $SanAccom_t$— Number of SamAccom at time t; $X_{i,t}$— the explanatory variables from Table 1; β_i— the coefficients showing how much each explanatory variable influences SanAccom; ε_t— the error term, which accounts for other factors not included in the model.

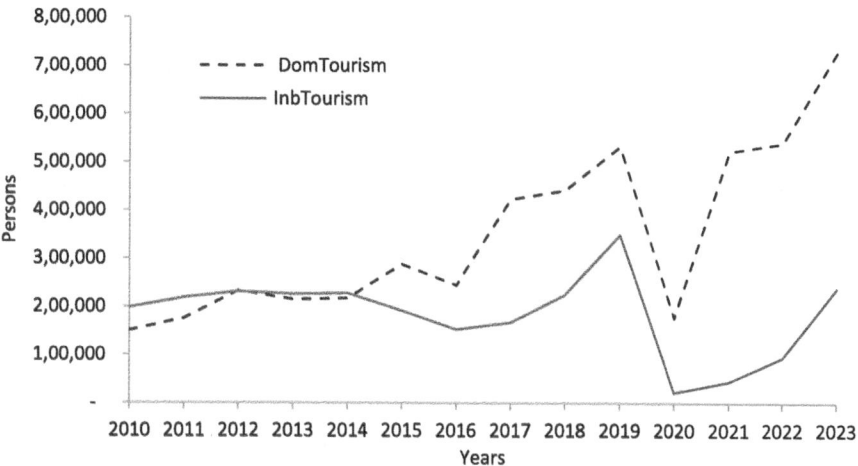

Fig. 2. Trends domestic tourism and inbound tourism in Uzbekistan (2010–2023). Source: Statistics Agency of Uzbekistan.

Regression analysis is performed using Stata 17 statistical software, which provides robust estimation and standard diagnostic tests for model validation. During the research, we test the following hypotheses:

H_0 – the factors in Table 1 do not have a statistically significant effect on SanAccom;
H_1 – the factors in Table 1 do have a statistically significant effect on SanAccom.

These hypotheses are tested using OLS regression. Robustness checks, including multicollinearity tests, heteroskedasticity tests, and residual analysis, will be performed to ensure the reliability of the results.

3 Results

Before conducting regression analysis, a correlation matrix (Table 3) was created to assess the relationships between variables.

To ensure the reliability of the regression analysis, it is necessary to resolve the multicollinearity problems between independent variables. To detect multicollinearity, we conducted a correlation analysis using the Chaddock scale [14], which classifies correlation coefficients above 0.7 as strong multicollinearity. From the correlation matrix (Table 3), we observed a high correlation (above 0.7) between several independent variables, particularly between Income and HealthServ (0.988), Income and DomTourism (0.847), Population and SanPlace (0.879) and DomTourism and SanAccom (0.888). To address this, we constructed three separate models, each incorporating different sets of independent variables to avoid severe collinearity while preserving the explanatory power of the regression. Furthermore, variables with low correlation (below the 10% critical value of 0.3613) with the dependent variable (SanAccom) such as Population (0.056), RecBases (0.058), and HospBeds (−0.099) were excluded from the regression models, as their inclusion would not meaningfully contribute to the explanation of wellness tourism demand.

Table 3. Matrix of correlations.

Variables	(1)	(2)	(3)	(4)	(5)	(6)	(7)	(8)	(9)	(10)
(1) SanAccom	1.000									
(2) SanOrg	0.563	1.000								
(3) SanPlace	0.373	0.068	1.000							
(4) Income	0.598	0.608	0.446	1.000						
(5) Population	0.056	-0.341	0.879	0.007	1.000					
(6) RecBases	0.058	0.573	-0.077	-0.136	-0.104	1.000				
(7) HospBeds	-0.099	-0.067	0.006	0.320	-0.128	-0.499	1.000			
(8) HealthServ	0.618	0.578	0.379	0.988	-0.064	-0.235	0.374	1.000		
(9) DomTourism	0.888	0.614	0.436	0.847	0.036	-0.041	0.205	0.856	1.000	
(10) InbTourism	0.386	0.161	-0.370	-0.333	-0.345	0.236	-0.094	-0.271	0.086	1.000

Note: 10% critical value (two-tailed) is 0.3613 n = 14

The first regression model (Table 4) examines the impact of SanOrg, SanPlace, Income and InbTourism on SanAccom. The model explains 82.7% ($R^2 = 0.827$) of the variation in wellness tourism demand.

Table 4. The results of (SanAccom | SanOrg, SanPlace, Income, InbTourism) OLS model.

SanAccom	Coef.	St.Err.	t-value	p-value	[95% Conf	Interval]	Sig
SanOrg	-0.008	0.373	-0.02	0.984	-0.851	0.836	
SanPlace	3.902	1.891	2.06	0.069	-0.376	8.179	*
Income	0.022	0.007	3.08	0.013	0.006	0.038	**
InbTourism	0.001	0.000	4.38	0.002	0.001	0.002	***
Constant	-62.994	170.227	-0.37	0.720	-448.075	322.086	
Mean dependent var		582.871	SD dependent var			157.432	
R-squared		0.827	Number of obs			14	
F-test		10.793	Prob > F			0.002	
Akaike crit. (AIC)		165.742	Bayesian crit. (BIC)			168.938	

Note: *** p<0.01, ** p<0.05, * p<0.1

According to the results of model 1, SanOrg (p = 0.984) is statistically insignificant, indicating that the number of sanatorium-resort facilities does not directly increase the number of visitors. SanPlace is marginally significant (p < 0.1), implying that facility capacity expansion positively affects accommodation numbers. Also, Income (p = 0.013) and InbTourism (p = 0.002) are statistically significant (p < 0.05), confirming that rising Income and InbTourism positively influence wellness tourism demand.

In the second model, HealthServ is added as a predictor (Table 5). The model slightly improves explanatory power ($R^2 = 0.829$), reinforcing that quality and availability of healthcare services are essential determinants of sanatorium-resort utilization.

The results indicate that an increase in healthcare services significantly enhances wellness tourism demand, with a statistically significant effect at the 5% level.

The final model replaces Income and HealthServ with DomTourism to evaluate its impact on SanAccom (Table 6).

Table 5. The results of (SanAccom | SanOrg, SanPlace, HealthServ, InbTourism) OLS model.

SanAccom	Coef.	St.Err.	t-value	p-value	[95% Conf	Interval]	Sig
SanOrg	0.128	0.340	0.38	0.716	-0.642	0.898	
SanPlace	4.498	1.815	2.48	0.035	0.393	8.604	**
HealthServ	0.038	0.012	3.11	0.012	0.010	0.065	**
InbTourism	0.001	0.000	4.25	0.002	0.001	0.002	***
Constant	-61.392	169.453	-0.36	0.725	-444.722	321.939	
Mean dependent var		582.871	SD dependent var			157.432	
R-squared		0.829	Number of obs			14	
F-test		10.924	Prob > F			0.002	
Akaike crit. (AIC)		165.602	Bayesian crit. (BIC)			168.797	

*Note: *** p<0.01, ** p<0.05, * p<0.1*

Table 6. The results of (SanAccom | SanOrg, SanPlace, DomTourism, InbTourism) OLS model.

SanAccom	Coef.	St.Err.	t-value	p-value	[95% Conf	Interval]	Sig
SanOrg	0.036	0.250	0.15	0.887	-0.528	0.601	
SanPlace	2.082	1.537	1.35	0.209	-1.395	5.56	
DomTourism	0.001	0.000	4.94	0.001	0.000	0.001	***
InbTourism	0.001	0.000	3.30	0.009	0.000	0.001	***
Constant	83.238	136.845	0.61	0.558	-226.328	392.804	
Mean dependent var		582.871	SD dependent var			157.432	
R-squared		0.905	Number of obs			14	
F-test		21.311	Prob > F			0.000	
Akaike crit. (AIC)		157.463	Bayesian crit. (BIC)			160.658	

*Note: *** p<0.01, ** p<0.05, * p<0.1*

DomTourism and InbTourism are highly significant ($p < 0.01$), emphasizing that both domestic and inbound tourism are crucial drivers of wellness tourism demand. The results indicate that the model achieves the highest explanatory power ($R2 = 0.905$), indicating that tourism variables explain over 90% of the variations in wellness tourism accommodation.

In this study, Variance Inflation Factor (VIF) values were calculated for the three models above to check whether there was a multicollinearity problem. The results showed that none of the variables exceeded the threshold value of VIF < 5 [15], which means that multicollinearity is not a serious problem. Although the highest VIF values were recorded for the variables Income (2.67), HealthServ (2.07) and DomTourism (2.25), they remained within the acceptable range. The average VIF values for the three models ranged from 1.64 to 1.93, confirming that there was no strong correlation between the independent variables. Thus, the results indicate that the regression estimates are reliable and do not suffer from significant bias due to multicollinearity.

4   Discussion

The results of this study helped to identify the main factors influencing the development of wellness tourism in Uzbekistan. The results of the research showed that domestic tourism has a greater impact on the demand for wellness tourism than inbound tourism. That is, the main customers of sanatoriums and resorts are local travelers because local tourists prefer short-distance trips [16, 17]. Therefore, to stimulate domestic tourism, it is necessary to implement programs to increase subsidies, discounts for local tourists, and transport amenities. At the same time, advertising campaigns and visa facilitation measures should be taken to attract international tourists.

The results of the study show that an increase in the income of the population leads to an increase in the demand for wellness tourism. People with higher incomes invest more in their health and are more likely to use sanatorium services [11]. Therefore, economic policies aimed at increasing the real income of the population, especially measures to support the middle-income group, will help develop wellness tourism.

The study found that the availability of quality medical services plays an important role in the development of wellness tourism. Scientific research confirms that the availability of quality medical services is an important factor for the development of wellness tourism [10, 18, 19]. Investments in healthcare infrastructure, ensuring that sanatoriums meet international standards, and expanding cooperation with medical centers play an important role in the development of wellness tourism. To attract international clients, it is necessary to develop medical tourism programs and introduce certified wellness programs.

The study showed that increasing the number of new sanatoriums and resorts does not directly affect the demand for wellness tourism. On the contrary, it is more important to increase the capacity of existing sanatoriums and improve the quality of service. Smith and Puczkó [12] also noted the importance of adapting sanatoriums and rehabilitation centers to world standards for the growth of wellness tourism. Therefore, state policy in the development of wellness tourism should be aimed at modernizing existing sanatoriums, improving the quality of service and introducing innovative medical and health programs. In addition, the integration of digital health services into wellness programs can increase guest convenience and further stimulate demand for wellness tourism.

5   Conclusion

This study aimed to study the main factors influencing the demand for wellness tourism in Uzbekistan. Based on the OLS regression model, the most important factors determining the demand for wellness tourism were identified, and the results were evaluated on a scientific basis.

The results of the study showed that domestic tourism, foreign tourism, population income and health services are the main driving factors of wellness tourism. In particular, it was found that domestic tourism has the greatest impact on the demand for wellness tourism, and it was emphasized that it is necessary to strengthen measures to attract domestic tourists. Also, an increase in population income and improvement of health services directly affect the increase in the demand for wellness tourism, which indicates the importance of economic development and investment in medical infrastructure.

One of the important conclusions is that it is more important to increase the capacity and improve the quality of service of sanatoriums than to increase the number of sanatoriums. Simply building new sanatoriums will not lead to an increase in the demand for wellness tourism. On the contrary, modernizing existing infrastructure, improving the quality of service, and expanding sanatorium capacity can yield more effective results.

Based on the results, the following policy recommendations are put forward:

- Develop special programs for the development of domestic tourism, including supporting tourist destinations, providing incentives and discounts, and improving transport infrastructure;
- Invest in health services and integrate wellness programs with high-quality medical services to develop medical and wellness tourism;
- Make sanatorium services more accessible and affordable for a wide range of the population, especially for middle-income groups;
- Prioritize quality over quantity, i.e. improve existing sanatoriums and recreation facilities in accordance with modern requirements and increase the level of services.

This study provides empirically based recommendations for the development of wellness tourism, enabling government agencies, entrepreneurs, and investors to make scientifically sound decisions. With the right strategies and targeted investments, Uzbekistan can become one of the leading countries in the region in the development of wellness tourism, attracting not only domestic but also international tourists.

Acknowledgments. The research undertaken was made possible by the equal scientific involvement of all the authors concerned.

Disclosure of Interests. The authors have no competing interests to declare that are relevant to the content of this article.

References

1. BridgetGWI: A Decade of Wellness Tourism: First-Ever Compilation of 10+ Years of Market Data. https://globalwellnessinstitute.org/global-wellness-institute-blog/2024/03/25/a-decade-of-wellness-tourism-first-ever-compilation-of-10-years-of-market-data/. Accessed 06 Feb 2025
2. Caciora, T., et al.: Digitization of the built cultural heritage: an integrated methodology for preservation and accessibilization of an art nouveau museum. Remote Sens. **15** (2023). https://doi.org/10.3390/rs15245763
3. Wendt, J.A., et al.: Natural sources in preventive conservation of naturally aged textiles. Fibres Text. Eastern Europe (2021). https://doi.org/10.5604/01.3001.0014.9309
4. Ilies, D.C., et al.: Indoor air quality perception in built cultural heritage in times of climate change. Sustainability **15** (2023). https://doi.org/10.3390/su15108284
5. Safarov, B., et al.: Prospects of agrotourism development in the region. Economies **12** (2024). https://doi.org/10.3390/economies12120321
6. Yelizarov, M.G.: Development of recreation in improving the health of the population. Acad. J. Digit. Econ. Stabil. **37**, 58–63 (2024). https://doi.org/10.51699/economics.v37i3.125

7. Zhong, L., Deng, B., Morrison, A.M., Coca-Stefaniak, J.A., Yang, L.: Medical, health and wellness tourism research—a review of the literature (1970–2020) and research agenda. Int. J. Environ. Res. Public Health **18**, 10875 (2021). https://doi.org/10.3390/ijerph182010875
8. Mukhammedov, M., Safarov, B., Hasanov, H., Isxakova, S., Buzrukova, M., Hassan, T.H.: Methods for optimizing property relations as a key aspect of stimulating the development of the tourism industry. Geojournal Tourism Geosites **58**, 484–491 (2025). https://doi.org/10.30892/gtg.58145-1430
9. Dimanche, F., Andrades, L.: Health and wellness tourism. In: Tourism in Russia: A Management Handbook. Emerald Group Publishing (2015)
10. Pan, H., Mi, H., Chen, Y., Chen, Z., Zhou, W.: Measurement and evaluation of the development level of health and wellness tourism from the perspective of high-quality development. Sustainability. **16**, 8082 (2024). https://doi.org/10.3390/su16188082
11. Lee, T.J., Han, J.-S., Ko, T.-G.: Health-oriented tourists and sustainable domestic tourism. Sustainability **12**, 4988 (2020). https://doi.org/10.3390/su12124988
12. Smith, M., Puczkó, L.: Health, Tourism and Hospitality: Spas, Wellness and Medical Travel. Routledge (2014)
13. Burton, A.L.: OLS (linear) regression. In: The Encyclopedia of Research Methods in Criminology and Criminal Justice. pp. 509–514. Wiley (2021). https://doi.org/10.1002/9781119111931.ch104
14. Chaddock, R.E.: Principles and Methods of Statistics (1925)
15. Studenmund, A.H.: Using Econometrics a Practical Guide. Pearson Education Limited (2014)
16. Nyaupane, G.P., Graefe, A.R.: Travel distance: a tool for nature-based tourism market segmentation. J. Travel Tour. Mark. **25**, 355–366 (2008). https://doi.org/10.1080/10548400802508457
17. Xue, L., Zhang, Y.: The effect of distance on tourist behavior: a study based on social media data. Ann. Tour. Res. **82**, 102916 (2020). https://doi.org/10.1016/j.annals.2020.102916
18. Aydin, G., Karamehmet, B.: Factors affecting health tourism and international health-care facility choice. Int. J. Pharm. Healthc. Mark. **11**, 16–36 (2017). https://doi.org/10.1108/IJPHM-05-2015-0018
19. Safarov, B., Janzakov, B.: Measuring competitiveness in tourism enterprises using integral index. GeoJournal Tourism Geosites **37**, 768–774 (2021). https://doi.org/10.30892/gtg.37305-707

From Tourism as an Opportunity for Growth to the Discomfort of Overtourism: The Erosion of Public Space and the Need to Rethink Coastal Cities

Clara Stella Vicari Aversa[1] , Giulia Fernanda Grazia Catania[2](✉) ,
Tatar Corina[3] , and Celestina Fazia[2]

[1] Department of Architecture and Design – dAeD, University "Mediterranea" of Reggio Calabria - UNIRC, 89124 Reggio Calabria, Italy
clarastella.vicariaversa@unirc.it

[2] Department of Engineering and Architecture, University of Enna "Kore", 94100 Enna, Italy
giuliafernandagrazia.catania@unikorestudent.it,
celestina.fazia@unikore.it

[3] Department of Geography, Tourism and Territorial Planning, Universitatii Street, 410087 Oradea, Romania

Abstract. The growth of tourism in coastal cities, once heralded as a catalyst for economic prosperity, has increasingly revealed its darker consequences in the form of overtourism. This study critically examines how unregulated tourism-driven urban development in Mediterranean Italian coastal cities of Taormina, Scilla and Tropea has led to the commodification and degradation of public spaces, social polarization, and environmental strain. Drawing from urban theory, historical context, and case analysis, the research explores the transformation of public space from a collective civic asset to a contested arena dominated by market interests. The paper argues that the pursuit of short-term economic gains has undermined urban habitability and inclusivity, necessitating a paradigm shift in urban planning and tourism policy. A rethinking of coastal city governance is urgently needed to prioritize public interest, spatial equity, and long-term sustainability.

Keywords: Sustainable Tourism · Overtourism · Territorial Vulnerability

1 Introduction

For some decades now, there has been an increasing awareness that tourism is indeed an opportunity for economic growth, but if it is not properly managed through suitable policies and measures, it generates the discomfort of the so-called Overtourism in the cities most affected by the phenomenon. The risks and critical issues are related to the urban load (consumption of resources, production of urban waste and emission of pollutants), the erosion of public space due to the progressive loss of land to be used for services and the optimization of flows. Hence the need to rethink cities.

O. Gervasi et al. (Eds.): ICCSA 2025 Workshops, LNCS 15890, pp. 415–431, 2026.
https://doi.org/10.1007/978-3-031-97606-3_28

It is necessary, in many Italian cities, with regard to the tourism phenomenon, a rethinking and in some cases almost a healthy reversal of course.

In order to illustrate the criticalities and effects of an (uncontrolled) explosion of the phenomenon, some cases of southern Italy, near the Strait of Messina, on both shores, the Calabrian and the Sicilian shores, are analyzed.

The choice of the three cities, Scilla, Tropea and Taormina, depends on the fact that they are coastal tourist cities united by some basic characteristics:

- Geographical aspect: they overlook the Tyrrhenian Sea and the Strait of Messina channel;
- Morphological-orographic conditions: the three selected cities have a "touristy" historic centre located on a rocky ridge overlooking the sea and a part connected to the coast, with sandy shores and beaches equipped for bathing; they have a small port and seabed of particular naturalistic interest;
- Multi-seasonal tourist offer. As summer holiday destinations, they are affected by diversified flows of visitors thanks to the presence of factors that exert a strong territorial attraction, such as: coastal landscape, nature, historical-cultural heritage, identity connotation of the sites linked to anthropological/identity aspects, food and wine and elements of material culture.

2 In-Depth Study, Materials

Overtourism refers to the excessive number of tourists visiting a destination, leading to negative impacts on the environment, local communities, and the overall tourist experience. This phenomenon has gained significant attention in recent years, particularly in popular destinations like Barcelona, Venice, and Dubrovnik [1]. The rapid growth of tourism, driven by factors such as low-cost airlines and the rise of short-term rental platforms, has exacerbated the issue. "Se "tutti" vogliono godere lo stesso panorama, la stessa spiaggia bianca e deserta, lo stesso rifugio di montagna, "nessuno" potrà più goderne" (If 'everybody' wants to enjoy the same panorama, the same deserted white beach, the same mountain hut, 'nobody' will be able to enjoy it any more), summarizes Elena Granata well when speaking of a phenomenon that, if it gets out of control, risks plundering territories, emptying them of their most intimate and profound meaning. "Tourists by chaos," as one column titles it, highlighting how this also changes the essence of travel.

Key impacts of overtourism include such issues as environmental degradation, increased pollution, waste, and damage to natural habitats; social tensions such as conflicts between residents and tourists, often due to overcrowding and the strain on local resources and economic effects such as the rising living costs and displacement of residents [2, 3].

Doxey's Irritation Index, also known as the Irridex, is a model developed by George Doxey in 1975 to describe the changing attitudes of local residents towards tourists as tourism development progresses [4]. The model outlines four stages such as euphoria which refers to an initial excitement and enthusiasm about tourism, with residents welcoming tourists and the economic benefits they bring; apathy referring to residents who become more indifferent, viewing tourists as a source of income rather than guests, as tourism grows; irritation which relates to how over time, the negative impacts of tourism become more apparent, leading to frustration and annoyance among residents; antagonism which is the final stage where residents may openly express hostility towards tourists, blaming them for various problems in the community [5].

Understanding these dynamics is crucial for developing sustainable tourism strategies that balance the needs of both visitors and local communities. Addressing overtourism requires a multifaceted approach, including better tourism management, regulation of visitor numbers, and efforts to distribute tourism more evenly across destinations. By models like Doxey's Irritation Index, policymakers and stakeholders can better understand and mitigate the negative impacts of tourism, ensuring a more sustainable and harmonious relationship between tourists and host communities.

3 Case Studies

3.1 Taormina

Taormina is the tourist destination by excellence in Sicily. It is an Italian municipality of over 10,000 inhabitants in the metropolitan city of Messina, on the eastern side of the island. It is known as the Pearl of the Ionian Sea and has always been one of the most well-known and loved places on the island by travelers from all over the world.

Characteristics of the territory, include culture, history and environment. Taormina boasts an enchanting position on the sea, a flourishing and luxuriant nature, a past capable of seducing and telling Greek myths, Arab influences, Spanish and Norman contaminations. It is a concentration of architectural, artistic, cultural and natural beauties in the heart of the Mediterranean, which has always inspired poets, writers, travelers, actors and internationally renowned celebrities.

The ancient history of Sicily has passed through here and Taormina has been able to jealously guard its signs, legacies, architecture. "The greatest masterpiece of art and nature", Johann Wolfgang Goethe defined Taormina in his "Journey to Italy" which contains the account of the Grand Tour that the famous German writer made in Italy between 3 September 1786 and 1788 [6]. Guy de Maupassant also spoke of Taormina in the following century. "Un homme n'aurait à passer qu'un jour en Sicile et demanderait: «Que faut-il y voir?» Je lui répondrais sans hésiter: «Taormine»". The historic French travel reporter emphasizes its beauty by highlighting its features, those of "un paysage où l'on trouve tout ce qui semble fait sur la terre pour séduire les yeux, l'esprit et l'imagination." [7].

The "Touristy" Urban Centre and the Neighbourhoods Most Affected

Tourism in Taormina has origins as old as the city, it is a phenomenon that has always grown over time until it has become the favorite destination of European nobles and artists of the nineteenth century and since 1900 becoming famous all over the world as the most elegant city in Sicily, the place where movie stars spent their holidays.

Corso Umberto I is the most important pedestrian street in the historic center and still the most affected by tourist flows. It is named after Umberto I of Savoy, King of Italy from 1878 to 1900, it was an integral part of the ancient Via Valeria that in ancient times connected Messina with Catania. Even today, two imposing gates, Porta Messina and Porta Catania, mark the entrances.

Along Corso Umberto I there are several squares, which have always represented the meeting place and the pulse of numerous recreational activities, especially Piazza IX Aprile with a breathtaking view of the sea with Mount Etna in the background, but also Piazza Santa Caterina, an ancient Greek agora then the Roman forum, or the center of political and social activities of the Greek-Roman civilization, overlooked by Palazzo Corvaja, owned by the municipality, used as a venue for exhibitions and cultural events, which in 1411 was the seat of the Sicilian Parliament and in the kingdom of Sicily elected the King. Although the tourist flow in the town generally decreases in winter, around February, the main street is confirmed all year round as a lively pedestrian promenade full of cafes, restaurants, and shops. However, it becomes almost unsustainable to travel in the summer months, especially close to August, when the tourist flow and concentration increase even for the arrival of groups coming in the same day such as those of cruise ships.

A few steps from Corso Re Umberto I, in an extraordinary panoramic area from which you can admire the bulk of Mount Etna and the Ionian Sea, is the Greek-Roman Theater "situated in such a wonderful position that there is probably no other comparable place in the whole world" [7] (Fig. 1).

Fig. 1. Taormina. Teatro Greco Romano with views of the sea and Mount Etna. Credit: Clara Stella Vicari Aversa

In the seaside part, Isola Bella is one of the symbolic places of Taormina, a very small island in a nature reserve in a protected area, full of exuberant vegetation between rock and transparent sea. A small islet, known as the Pearl of the Mediterranean for its unique characteristics, where it is easy, at certain times, to be able to walk from the beach, being connected to it by a narrow strip of land that is, depending on the timetable, more or less covered by the tides (Fig. 2).

Tourist flows, always growing steadily for the city, have increased after covid, also amplified by filming and TV series such as "The White Lotus 2", shot entirely in Taormina during covid and which brought and then multiplied US tourism. This has led many hotels to reposition themselves and some of the most historic have been purchased by international luxury groups, such as the Four Seasons Hotel group which bought the

Fig. 2. Taormina. Isola Bella, with umbrellas all the way on the strip of land that connects it to the mainland. Credit: Clara Stella Vicari Aversa.

San Domenico hotel and LVMH which bought the Grand Hotel Timeo and the Villa Sant'Andrea.

In line with this trend, even along Corso Re Umberto, especially around Piazza IX Aprile, an unstoppable race seems to have started between luxury companies to carve out a space. If on the one hand it is celebrated as an extremely positive fact, on the other, even just walking through the streets of Taormina, whose gait has always been a continuous immersion in beauty, lately, on some days or months of the year risks becoming difficult, devoid of the authenticity that distinguished it, becoming almost a hellish path.

Roads and Connections

The nearest airport is Catania Fontanarossa, the fifth busiest airport in Italy, from which it is easily connected by bus and train. Another airport that can guarantee the connection is in Reggio Calabria, beyond the Strait of Messina reachable by 40 km of motorway or railway. You can get to the city by car or bus (there are various lines from the main cities in the surrounding area) via the motorway exit of the same name on the A18 Messina-Catania motorway. The city has a railway station, the Taormina-Giardini station, one of the main stations of the Messina-Syracuse railway.

Among the other infrastructural endowments, there has been talk of a tourist port for years and there would be foreign groups that would look with interest at the initiative of the Municipality of Taormina. The attention, as is understandable given the enormous attractiveness of Taormina, goes beyond European borders.

Dynamics of Tourism

Much of the area of tourist interest is concentrated around Corso Re Umberto I, the main street of the city, which is a pedestrian area and therefore can be visited on foot.

If in some months Taormina seems to govern tourism well, in others it suddenly appears unprepared for overtourism, becoming more and more urgent to further strengthen public services, those of proximity, adapting the mobility system to the diversified demand for travel. The municipal administration, in recent months, in order to cope with ever-increasing tourism, has made several changes and innovations regarding the use and deseasonalization of the shows or the construction of new parking lots.

In some months, the number of visitors exceeds the city's carrying capacity, causing problems such as overcrowding of streets, squares and means of transport. There is an increase in the cost of living and pressure on rents. The risks of damage to the historical and natural heritage are increasing, but also a saturation of public services and a distortion of the local identity. It is no longer conceivable to overload the city only in certain months of the year but, on the contrary, also to avoid an urban load oversized compared to the capacity of the historic center, it seems inevitable to have to deseasonalize, reduce hit-and-run tourism, but also identify new strategies. In too many Calabrian and Sicilian cities, mass tourism is risking transforming and obscuring precious little pearls on the sea like Taormina. Several villages, once authentic, are now facing the challenges of out-of-control tourism, with an exponential increase in B&Bs, second homes for tourists and a progressive loss of the local population. This is the case of the phenomenon taking place in ancient villages such as Cefalù, between Messina and Palermo, investigated by Marcello Panzarella, so indignant as to call it "a city for sale", describing the dark side of mass tourism. "The so-called and trumpeted new plan of the historic center... Consists of the simple introduction of adjustments to changes in legal regulations... But it is totally devoid of a vision, of a purpose of service to the community of inhabitants, whose existence is forgotten. There is no project in it, just as there is none in the general urban plan". Panzarella, who already in the 80s, together with a group of young people, friends and intellectuals, including the sociologist Carlo Doglio and the architect Pasquale Culotta, found themselves reasoning together on the corrosive drift of tourism in Cefalù, argues that if Cefalù does not have an urban plan equipped with adequate infrastructural provisions (roads, rest areas, escape routes, intermodal connections) and is oppressed by overtourism the responsibility lies with the political and administrative choices of the government junta, and that a powerful commitment to description and knowledge of the sack of Cefalù is needed, preliminary to any act aimed at recovering what can now be feared irretrievable [8].

The intensification of tourism flows poses complex spatial challenges that touch on sustainability and the quality of life of residents. There is a need to explore sustainable management models that can mitigate the impact of mass tourism and preserve the cultural and environmental resources of destinations [9]. It is necessary not only to ensure that Taormina acts in time not to suffer the sack of cities like Cefalù but also that it tries to start becoming a model of response to the increasingly frequent phenomena of overtourism. A key issue, but also discussed, is the adoption of an entrance ticket as a regulation measure, already active in the parking lots in Taormina for cars and buses. Above all, strategies are needed to be able to transform Taormina into a smart city to be able to monitor tourist flows. This is also to maintain control of pollutant and CO_2 emissions, the production of urban waste and the water cycle, as well as their reuse. These also seem to be the strategies in which the city seems to want to move, whose goal, as underlined by the Councilor for Tourism Jonathan Sferra, is to become an example of a destination attentive to the environment and the quality of life, in which technology to monitor flows can become a fundamental ally to balance tourism and livability. Taormina could become a model of sustainable tourism, aiming to extend the offer even outside the summer season, also involving neighboring municipalities with the "Area Pact" and developing alternative tourist routes. It is necessary to work by analyzing and cross-referencing challenges and solutions to balance the influx of visitors with the livability of cities.

3.2 Scilla

In Calabria, Scilla is a few kilometers from Villa San Giovanni (bridgehead for the connection with Messina, then Sicily). Known for the myth of Scylla and Charybdis, it is closer to Bagnara Calabra (a maritime center with a port) and develops along the Costa Viola. It is morphologically similar to Tropea, but has a small fishing village called Chianalea, very characteristic, and a small port.

Characteristics of the Territory, Between Culture, History and Environment
Scilla represents the synthesis of history, myth and nature. It reserves for the visitor the story of a historic place through the particular morphology composed of urban fabrics that follow the orographic trend opening towards the coastal landscape, the panorama of the Strait of Messina and the archipelago of the Aeolian Islands, with the last slopes of the Aspromonte side behind it. The coast, closed between the vineyard terraces of the Costa Viola and the charming village of Chianalea, is among those most reached by the inhabitants of the neighboring cities and by tourists who flock to the beach of Marina Grande for 8 months a year. The crystal-clear water covers seabeds rich in biodiversity [10].

Classification of the Territory and Relations with the Context
Scilla is located on the rocky spur of the same name, the Scillèo Promontory, jutting out over the Strait of Messina, which rises north-east of the capital [11] at 113 m above sea level. The municipal territory occupies an area of 44.13 km^2, mainly for agricultural use and only minimally urbanized. As of 2023, there were 4,513 inhabitants [12].

Peculiarities: Scylla, Between History and Myth
The imposing cliff houses the Ruffo Castle, while the stretch of water that separates the Calabrian side from the Sicilian one [13] was the scene of the events of Ulysses and his crew on their way to Ithaca, grappling with the anthropophagous monster, Scylla, capable of grabbing and devouring six men, and the force of the whirlpool, Charybdis created by Zeus, capable of swallowing anything. Pirate assaults have marked these waters since the fifth century BC, such as the Tyrrhenians, skilled sailors, while there are widespread signs of the presence of the Greeks and Romans. The village of Chianalea houses the fishermen's boats in the basement, the port houses the swordfish used since ancient times for the hunting of swordfish, the "touristy" urban centre and the neighbourhoods most affected. The points of greatest tourist interest are the promenade named after Columbus, located in the Marina Grande -which in summer is reached by thousands of daily users and which is a meeting place until late at night-, the marina area and Chianalea with the internal axis that can be traveled on foot along Via Annunziata. The panoramic street of San Giorgio is the one that skirts the upper part of the city [14]. Four different parts of the territory define the urban layout of Scilla, characterized by their own social connotation. The San Giorgio district in which the church of San Rocco, patron saint

of Scilla, and the town hall are located, which encloses the historic center, from Piazza San Rocco to the ancient town of Bastìa, with the characteristic terraced houses that overlook steep alleys and which still retain some typical architectural elements of the place, including the lowered arch and the circular window. Jeracari, on the other hand, completes the upper part of Scilla and is exclusively residential. Marina Grande, which houses the sixteenth-century church of the Holy Spirit, acts as a backdrop to the coastline between the Belvedere Morselli and the gigantic fortress of the Ruffo Castle. Chianalea (in Chjanalèa) or Plain of the Galleys, from the name of an ancient swordfish fishing boat, is an ancient seaside district with typical alleys and houses lying on the sea and is included in the list of the most beautiful villages in Italy. Seasonal attractions, events and user base. For Scilla, the summer season represents the time when the beach of Marina Grande welcomes many tourists interested in the sea but also in the villages of Chianalea and San Giorgio. The food and wine tradition, linked to swordfish, takes shape in the numerous restaurants, typical bars, street food activities and in the refreshment places of the bathing establishments. The Ruffo Castle hosts the Scilla Jazz Festival, an event of great appeal for its artistic and cultural value, and is home to various public initiatives, and exhibitions. Naturalistic experiences can be enjoyed in Punta Pacì, a place with crystal clear and deep waters, ideal for diving enthusiasts and divers specialized in diving in the depths of the Strait; Cala delle Rondini is a difficult to access area, reachable by boat, it preserves an uncontaminated environment. A little further north, there are the beach of Favazzina and the Tremusa Caves, covered with marine fossils, of presumed karst origins.

Roads and Connections

The nearest airport is that of the Strait based in Reggio Calabria, but that of Lamezia Terme can also be reached; another airport that can guarantee the connection is that of Catania if the tourist chooses to continue from there by other means (train, bus or car) to Messina ferrying from Villa San Giovanni. Visitors can arrive in the city mainly via the A2 motorway exit of the same name and from the lower Tyrrhenian state road, which has been affected several times by landslides due to the widespread hydrogeological risk affecting the area. The city has a railway station; the trains that stop there are almost all regional, originating in Reggio Calabria, Paola or Cosenza, Rosarno, Lamezia Terme. Other infrastructural features include the Vico II Spirito Santo tourist-fishing port with 100 berths: it houses fishing boats and, during the summer, small and medium-sized pleasure boats.

Dynamics of Tourism

Much of the area of tourist interest is concentrated on the seafront, so it can be visited on foot. There is a pedestrian area in Chianalea. To go up from the seafront to the upper part there is a public lift. By car you can get around, there is a large area to park is the promenade with paid parking. Some local bus companies make scheduled stops departing and arriving in the city. There are a dozen restaurants by the sea between the marina and Chianalea, and as many kiosks in the seasonal beaches. A dozen hotels and 30 B&Bs [15], as many apartments offered with the AirBnB formula [16].The tourist-accommodation activities are unable to meet the demand for accommodation, so much so that the historic buildings in the center, even if they are not perfectly restored, are rented to tourists weekly with on-site reservations and are difficult to census through search engines dedicated to the supply/demand of tourist accommodation and short-term rentals. To improve the tourist offer (Hassan et alii, 2024) [17] and the ordinary management of the town, it is necessary to network the different locations and sort the flows to the external areas, in the surrounding area the cities that can be visited in Calabria are Reggio Calabria, Tropea and Bagnara and the system of foothill centers of Aspromonte, while in Sicily the cities of Messina and Milazzo are destinations of tourist interest; at a greater distance we find Capo d'Orlando, Taormina and Giardini Naxos, as well as Catania and the system of Etna centers. Implementation and urban transformation projects in progress. Chianalea has been the subject of widespread urban recovery interventions. The current General Regulatory Plan approved in 2005, is adapted with the amendments and limitations imposed by art. 65 of Regional Law no. 19/2002, has provided for three implementation plans that intervene only on the housing stock and historical recovery: Recovery Plan for the "A1" area in the Chianale Scilla district; Recovery Plan "A2" Spirito Santo Scilla district; Recovery Plan "A3" San Giorgio Scila district. Many private interventions have involved the recovery and maintenance of individual buildings which, if on the one hand, have contributed to improving urban quality, on the other hand have encouraged the process of gentrification [18] by replacing the old residents dedicated to fishing with seasonal users, almost always housed in short-term rental accommodation.

The supply of small accommodations rented even weekly has increased dramatically, the Structural Plan in Associated form, provided for by the Regional Urban Planning Law 19/02, is still being developed, consequently the city is unprepared to govern the process of overtourism by strengthening public services, those of proximity, adapting the mobility system to the diversified demand for travel [17] (Fig. 3).

Fig. 3. Borgo di Chianalea. Credit: Clara Stella Vicari Aversa, Celestina Fazia

The lack of an urban planning tool and an environmental monitoring plan (linked to the SEA, Strategic Environmental Assessment) does not allow us to assess the effects induced by a growing demand for housing, which does not correspond proportionally to the reorganization of network infrastructures, primary and secondary urbanization works. The result is an urban load that is oversized compared to the capacity of the coastal center of Scilla, a lack of control of pollutant and CO_2 emissions, the production of urban waste and the water cycle, as well as their reuse.

3.3 Tropea

Tropea, located on the renowned Costa degli Dei in Calabria, is a city that represents a perfect synthesis of natural beauty, historical heritage and cultural richness. Perched on a rocky promontory overlooking the Tyrrhenian Sea, Tropea offers breathtaking views that embrace the Aeolian Islands, the Gulf of Gioia Tauro and the immense blue expanse of the Mediterranean [14]. Its golden sandy beaches, lapped by clear waters, are framed by lush Mediterranean vegetation, which adds a touch of authenticity to the landscape. The historic center of the city is a veritable treasure trove of architectural treasures: narrow, winding alleys lead to hidden squares and noble palaces dating back to the 17th and 18th centuries, many of which are decorated with family coats of arms and loggias that tell a story of prestige and influence [19].

The city is deeply linked to myth and history. According to legend, Tropea was founded by Hercules on his return journey from the Pillars of Hercules. This tradition, although mythical, underlines the strategic and symbolic importance that the place has had over the centuries. The Church of Santa Maria dell'Isola, located on a rocky outcrop, is an iconic symbol of the city and represents a meeting point between spirituality and nature. Other notable monuments include the Norman Cathedral, which houses important works of sacred art, and numerous smaller churches, which testify to the religious fervour of the local community over the centuries.

Tropea is also one of the most visited destinations in southern Italy, recording over 500,000 tourists in 2023 [20]. This success, while confirming its international attractiveness, raises concerns related to overtourism. During the summer months, the resident population of around 6,000 multiplies exponentially, putting significant pressure on local infrastructure and services. The streets of the historic center, designed for limited foot traffic, are often congested with intense tourist flows. The lack of parking spaces and the lack of an integrated public transport system further aggravate the situation, creating inconvenience for both residents and visitors. This tourist pressure is also reflected in basic services, such as waste management, water consumption and accommodation capacity. During the high season, waste production grows exponentially, putting the urban collection and disposal system in crisis, which is often inadequate to cope with seasonal overload [21]. In addition, coastal erosion, aggravated by intensive beach use and climate change, poses a real threat to the territory. At the same time, the proliferation of unregulated short-term rentals has encouraged a process of gentrification: many historic buildings have been converted into accommodation facilities, often without adequate renovation interventions, altering the social and cultural fabric of the historic center [22]. Events such as the Tropea Blues Festival and the Red Onion Festival represent an opportunity to enhance local traditions and promote the food and wine of the area. The red onion of Tropea PGI is a symbol of Calabrian excellence and a strong identity element, which contributes to strengthening the image of the city as a quality tourist destination. However, the lack of strategies to seasonally adjust tourism limits the potential of these initiatives, concentrating flows in specific periods and leaving the city less active in the winter and spring months [23]. The need to distribute tourist flows throughout the year is one of the most urgent priorities for Tropea. The introduction of new attractions or events that enhance cultural and natural heritage during less frequented seasons could help reduce pressure on the environment and infrastructure. For example, hiking routes that explore the surrounding rural areas or cultural events related to local history and myths could attract visitors even in the cooler months. In addition, collaboration with tour operators to promote travel packages in the low season would represent an additional lever to mitigate the problem of overtourism. From the point of view of planning, the Municipality of Tropea has already started important interventions, such as the restoration of the Church of Santa Maria dell'Isola and the redevelopment of the seafront. However, the effectiveness of these interventions depends on the ability to integrate them into a broader and more coordinated strategy. The recent Municipal Structural Plan (PSC) includes measures to promote sustainable mobility, including the introduction of electric shuttles and the creation of cycle paths. However, it is crucial to ensure that these initiatives are accompanied by constant monitoring to assess their impact and optimize their results [24]. Another crucial aspect concerns raising awareness of the local community and visitors on the importance of environmental sustainability. Education and awareness campaigns, together with incentives for virtuous practices, such as waste recycling or the use of ecological means of transport, could help improve the management of tourist flows and preserve the authenticity of the territory.

Therefore, Tropea is an emblematic example of the challenges and opportunities related to contemporary tourism. Preserving its landscape and cultural uniqueness requires integrated strategic planning, which balances economic development with environmental and social sustainability. Only through a long-term vision, which actively involves institutions, tour operators and local communities, will the city be able to consolidate its role as a destination of excellence, ensuring a better quality of life for residents and an authentic experience for visitors (Fig. 4 and Table 1).

Fig. 4. Tropea in high season: between coastal charm and overtourism challenges. Source: Alamy Stock Photo – https://www.alamy.com/stock-photo/tropea-italy.html

Table 1. Case studies. Credit:Celestina Fazia, compiled: C.Fazia, C.Vicari Aversa e G.F.G. Catania

Criteria	Cities, case studies					
	Taormina		Scilla		Tropea	
Urban area "touristified"	Medium in relation to 13.13 km^2 of municipal surface		Minimal in relation to 44.13 km^2 of municipal surface		Minimal in relation to 3.66 km^2 of municipal surface	
Resident population	10.465 to 2024		4.513 to 2023		About 6.000 to 2023	
Tourists per season	0–70.000	70.000–1.300.000	0–5.000	5.001–20.000	0–20.000	20.001–250.000
1 - Autumn		x		x	x	
2-Winter	x		x		x	
3-Spring		x		x	x	
4-Summer		x		x		x
Greatest seasonal increase compared to resident population	☐1 ☐2 ☐3 X 4		☐1 ☐2 ☐3 X 4		☐1 ☐2 ☐3 X 4	
Most lacking type of public service	Parking Undersized connections		Parking Local public interest		Public transport and parking	
Actual offer of tourist infrastructure (qualitative-quantitative performance)	High		Low		Low, insufficient for peak tourist demand; predominance of unregulated short-term rentals	
Misure previste dall'amministrazione per la sostenibilità ambientale	Low		Very low		Recent interventions: electric shuttles, seafront redevelopment, cycling paths. However, measures remain limited compared to increasing tourist flows	
Emerging issues in managing tourist flows	Traffic pressure at some internal road junctions Shuttle bus services exist but are insufficient		Unresolved road network nodes Lack of shuttle bus services		Congested narrow streets in the historic centre Parking shortage Lack of integrated public transport	
Sectoral criticalities (priority order, from 1 to 5)	- Urban congestion (1) - (In)urban safety (4) - Environmental pollution (2) - Vehicular traffic (3) - Insufficient services (healthcare, culture, leisure, sports) (5)		- Urban congestion (2) - (In)urban safety (5) - Environmental pollution (1) - Vehicular traffic (3) - Insufficient services (4)		- Urban congestion - (In)urban safety (2) - Environmental pollution (1) - Vehicular traffic (3) - Insufficient services (4)	

3.4 Overview of the Three Case Studies

3.5 Methods. Irridex Concept (Doxey's Irritation Index) and Launch of Interviews

The current paper used the survey as a means of primary data collection which was applied online to Romanian and Italian markets and which got a response rate of 42 respondents of which 24 respondents are of Romanian and 18 respondents are of Italian origin. All respondents are aged over 18 years old and the period when the survey was applied was during the month of January 2025. The survey comprised 16 close and open-ended questions referring to overtourism introductory questions for defining overtourism terminology; visitation of Italian cities background and context; particular questions referring to the case studies of Tropea, Scilla and Taormina towns; overtourism analysis questions (overvisitation concerns, authenticity loss); strategy and measures to mitigate overtourism (mitigation practices, role played by decision-makers) and concluding questions referring to the willingness to collaborate with stakeholders to address overtourism challenges. The survey is both addressed to tourists as well as to residents from the three analyzed case studies of Tropea, Scilla and Taormina. For the resident respondents it is meant to highlight the visitation stage according to Doxey's Irridex concept. For the latter Irridex case studies few residents have provided their response so that there's barely 1–2 residents providing answers which comes as a study limitation.

4   Discussion of Results

The survey results reveal that, for the introductory questions related to the general awareness of overtourism's challenges and diverse patterns of visitation to Italian destinations, the majority of respondents associate overtourism with its negative impacts on local communities (88%). While most participants are at least somewhat familiar with the term, only a third (33%) are highly knowledgeable about it. In terms of travel habits, 50% of respondents visit Italian cities occasionally, with a smaller yet significant portion visiting either rarely (24%) or frequently (26%).

For the questions related to recent visitation of Italian cities, the respondents indicated Bergamo, Venice, Florence, Verona, Taormina, Sicily, Rome, Milano, Bologna showed that 85.7% of respondents noticed overcrowding or infrastructure strain, while 9.5% did not, and 4.8% were unsure. These findings highlight significant overtourism challenges in iconic destinations, emphasizing the urgent need for sustainable tourism solutions.

Awareness of the case study cities varied significantly, with low recognition for Tropea (68% not aware) and Scilla (61% not aware), while Taormina stood out with higher familiarity (28.5% very aware). These findings highlight Taormina's stronger visibility compared to the other two tourist destinations like Tropea and Scilla.

Respondents identified key challenges faced by Italian cities due to tourism, including impacts on public spaces (32%) and infrastructure limitations (29%), alongside rising accommodation demand. A significant 74% believe overtourism affects city authenticity, and 64% are somewhat concerned about overtourism in Italian cities, highlighting strong awareness of its potential negative effects.

Respondents identified key challenges faced by Italian cities due to tourism, including impacts on public spaces (32%) and infrastructure limitations (29%), alongside rising accommodation demand, no free parking, prices rise, waste and pollution as well as overcrowding (Fig. 5). A significant 74% of respondents believe overtourism affects city authenticity (Fig. 6a), and 64% are somewhat concerned about overtourism in Italian cities (Fig. 6b), highlighting strong awareness of its potential negative effects.

Respondents suggested key strategies for sustainable tourism management, with the most popular being promoting off-peak travel and limiting visitor numbers. Additionally,

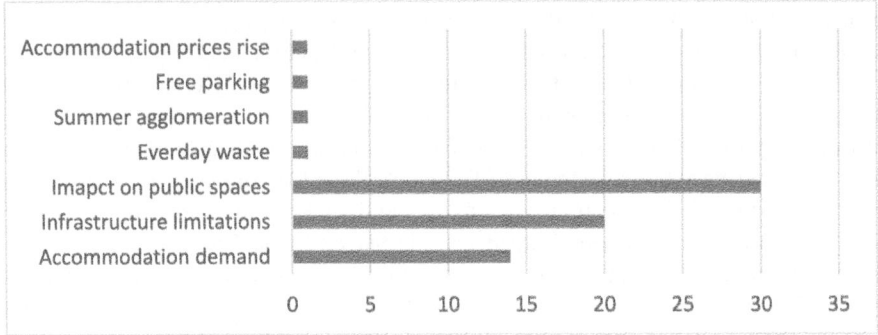

Fig. 5. Respondents' opinion survey with reference to the challanges faced by the Italian towns of Tropea, Scilla, Taormina due to overtourism. Source: Online survey applied by the authors in January 2025

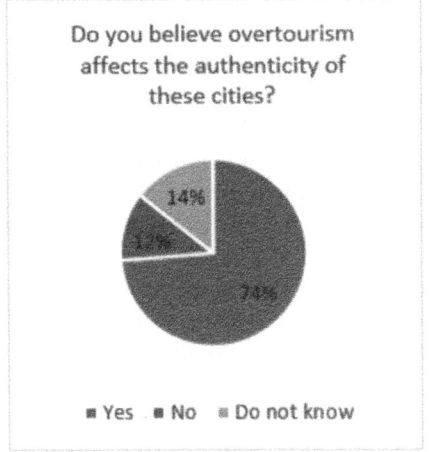 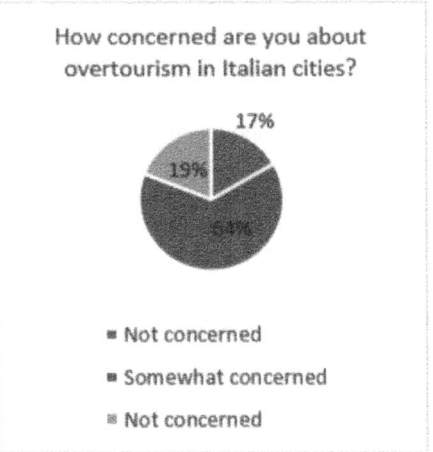

Fig. 6. a. Right: Respondents' opinion with reference to authenticity loss in Tropea, Scilla, Taormina.; b. Left: Respondents' opinion with reference to overtourism concern in Italian cities. Source: Online survey applied by the authors in January 2025

many supported enhancing public transport, cycling paths, and pedestrian-friendly areas (Fig. 7a). An overwhelming 83% agreed that informed decision-making should play a critical role in managing tourism effectively (Fig. 7b).

The majority of respondents were not residents of Taormina, Tropea, or Scilla, with minimal engagement from local perspectives, being one of the study limitations.

Among the few self-identified residents, reactions to tourism activity varied slightly but were predominantly negative, with sentiments like apathy, annoyance, or aggression reported by at least one respondent in each city. Enthusiasm for tourism was notably absent, reflecting potential concerns about its impact on local communities.

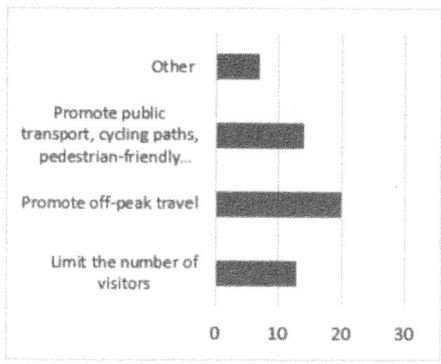 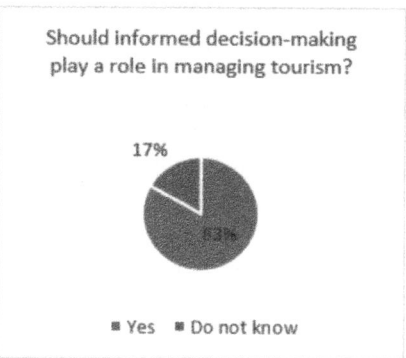

Fig. 7. a. Right: Respondents' opinion with reference to possible sustainable practices to mitigate overtourism in Tropea, Scilla and Taormina.; b. Left: Respondents' opinion with reference to informed decision-making role in tourism management. Source: Online survey applied by the authors in January 2025

5 Conclusion Outcomes

The current study has shown how the once-celebrated potential of tourism as a driver of urban and economic development has, in many Italian coastal cities, given way to a more problematic reality characterized by overtourism, privatization, and spatial injustice. The Italian case studies of Taormina, Scilla and Tropea illustrate how aggressive commodification of public space, driven by the interests of capital and governance models favoring growth, erodes the social fabric and threatens the character of the urban environment. This analysis underscores the need to move beyond growth-centric planning toward more inclusive, participatory, and ecologically responsible approaches to tourism development. Rethinking public space not as a secondary concern but as a central component of urban resilience and social equity is crucial. Only through this shift can coastal cities reclaim their role as spaces of shared life and collective identity, rather than mere assets in a global tourism economy. The survey results highlight significant challenges associated with overtourism in Italian cities, including impacts on public spaces, infrastructure strain, and concerns about authenticity loss. Awareness of overtourism varies, with iconic cities like Taormina receiving more recognition than the destinations of Tropea and Scilla. Respondents emphasized the need for sustainable practices, such as promoting off-peak travel and limiting visitor numbers, while strongly advocating for informed decision-making in tourism management. Local residents of Taormina, Tropea, and Scilla exhibit predominantly negative or indifferent attitudes toward tourism (i.e. apathy and annoyance according to Irridex concept), highlighting concerns about its impact on their communities. These results align with broader studies on overtourism, which consistently identify overcrowding, environmental degradation, and cultural authenticity as critical issues, emphasizing the urgency of implementing sustainable tourism policies in Italy's most visited cities [25–27]. These cases underscore the urgency for sustainable tourism policies to preserve Italy's cultural heritage and ensure the well-being of local communities.

Contribution Authors. Although the research is the result of the work carried out jointly by all the authors, which Clara Stella Vicari Aversa and Celestina Fazia and are the supervisor, the drafting of the essay is to be attributed differently to each of them: § Abstract by Clara Stella Vicari Aversa, Giulia F. G. Catania, Celestina Fazia; § 1. Introduction by Clara Stella Vicari Aversa and Celestina Fazia; § 2. In-depth study, Materials by Giulia F. G. Catania and Tatar Corina; § 3. Case studies: § 3.1. Taormina by Clara Stella Vicari Aversa; § 3.2. Scilla by Celestina Fazia, § 3.3. Tropea by Giulia F. G. Catania; § 3.4 Overview of the three case studies by Clara Stella Vicari Aversa, Giulia F. G. Catania, Corina Tatar, Celestina Fazia; § 3.5 Methods. Irridex concept (Doxey's Irritation Index) and launch of interviews by Clara Stella Vicari Aversa, Giulia F. G. Catania, Corina Tatar, Celestina Fazia; § 4. Discussion of results by Corina Tatar; § 4. Conclusions Outcomes, by Celestina Fazia, Corina Tatar and Clara Stella Vicari Aversa.

All the contributions are outcomes of some researches related to both the A.Ma.Te sponde convention, Agreement between the Department of Architecture and Territory of the Mediterranean University of Reggio Calabria and the Department of Engineering and Architecture of the Kore University of Enna, and the research group working on COastal Borders vs INland Areas_CO.IN., Projects in dialogue between coasts and inland across Mediterranean and Atlantic, in which are present, among others, both Italian Universities, Mediterranea of Reggio Calabria and Kore of Enna, and the University of Oradea in Romania.

References

1. Veríssimo, M., Moraes, M., Breda, Z., Guizi, A., Costa, C.: Overtourism and tourismphobia: a systematic literature review. Tourism **68** (2020). https://doi.org/10.37741/t.68.2.4
2. Falk, M.T., Hagsten, E., Lin, X.: Domestic tourism demand in the North and the South of Europe in the covid-19 summer of 2020. Ann. Reg. Sci. **69**, 537–553 (2022). https://doi.org/10.1007/s00168-022-01147-5
3. Hugo, N.C.: Overtourism at heritage and cultural sites. In: Séraphin, H., Gladkikh, T., Vo Thanh, T. (eds.) Overtourism, pp. 147–160. Palgrave Macmillan, Cham (2020). https://doi.org/10.1007/978-3-030-42458-9_10
4. Apollo, M., Cheer, J.M.: Irritation index in tourism. In: Jafari, J., Xiao, H. (eds.) Encyclopedia of Tourism, pp. 1–4. Springer, Cham (2024). https://doi.org/10.1007/978-3-319-01669-6_746-1
5. Pavlić, I., Portolan, A.: Irritation index, tourism. In: Jafari, J., Xiao, H. (eds.) Encyclopedia of Tourism, pp. 1–3. Springer, Cham (2015). https://doi.org/10.1007/978-3-319-01669-6_564-1
6. Goethe, J.W., Italienische, R.: (1817.) (ed.) Italiana Viaggio in Italia, Garzanti, (1997)
7. Maupassan, T., Guy de, L.S., 1886, In: La Vie, E. (1890). (ed.) italiana Viaggio in Sicilia, Sigma Edizioni (1998)
8. Panzarella, M.: Over Tourism. Cefalù una città in vendita, Edizioni Plumelia, Bagheria, Palermo (2025)
9. Pane, P.: Geografie dell'overtourism. Ambiente, paesaggio, e politiche territoriali, (2024), Aracne marchio editoriale di Adiuvare, Roma
10. Turismo, R.C.: Scilla, incontro eterno tra mito e bellezza. Alla scoperta della perla della Costa Viola e delle scogliere tra cui dimorava il mostro cantato da Omero. https://turismo.reggiocal.it/area-metropolitana/la-costa-tirrenica-di-reggio-calabria/scilla, Accessed 04 Mar 2025

11. Wiki Voyage: Scilla (Italia). https://it.wikivoyage.org/wiki/Scilla, (Italia), Accessed 04 Mar 2025
12. di Scilla, C.: Relazione PRG Comune di Scilla (2005)
13. Consolo, V.: Vedute dello Stretto di Messina. Sellerio, Palermo (1993)
14. Braudel, F.: Il Mediterraneo. Lo spazio, la storia, gli uomini, le tradizioni. Edizioni Bompiani, Milano (2017)
15. Booking.com: Hotel Scilla. Prenota ora il tuo hotel! https://www.booking.com, Accessed 04 Mar 2025
16. Airbnb: Trova case vacanze a Scilla. https://www.airbnb.it/host/homes?from_footer=1, Accessed 04 Mar 2025
17. Hassan, T.H., Fazia, C., Abdelmoaty, M.A., et al.: Sustainable pathways: understanding the interplay of environmental behavior, personal values, and tourist outcomes in farm tourism. Discov. Sustain. **5**, 153 (2024). https://doi.org/10.1007/s43621-024-00354-8
18. Coco, A.: Reggio Calabria: una ricostruzione della realtà urbana e sociale. In: Frudà, L. (ed.) Le città italiane tra spazio fisico e spazio socio-culturale, pp. 97–112. Franco Angeli, Milano (2007)
19. Consolo, V.: Il viaggio attraverso la Calabria: storia, mito e leggenda. Sicania Editrice, Messina (1993)
20. Ugeo Urbistat: Dati demografici e statistici del Comune di Tropea. https://ugeo.urbistat.com, Accessed 04 Mar 2025
21. Laporta, R.: Turismo e sviluppo sostenibile nelle città costiere calabresi. Editrice Calabrese, Vibo Valentia (2024)
22. Coco, G.: Gentrification e trasformazioni urbane: il caso della Calabria costiera. FrancoAngeli, Milano (2007)
23. Istat: Ottomila Census: dati sulla popolazione e sull'urbanizzazione in Italia. https://ottomi lacensus.istat.it, Accessed 04 Mar 2025
24. Comune di Tropea: Piano Strutturale Comunale e Regolamento Edilizio Urbanistico. Documento approvato. https://www.lapiazzatropea.it, Accessed 04 Mar 2025
25. Celata, F., Romano, A.: Overtourism and online short-term rental platforms in Italian cities. J. Sustain. Tour. **30**(5), 1020–1039 (2020). https://doi.org/10.1080/09669582.2020.1788568
26. Salerno, G.M., Russo, A.P.: Venice as a short-term city. Between global trends and local lock-ins. J. Sustain. Tour. **30**(5), 1040–1059 (2020). https://doi.org/10.1080/09669582.2020.1860068
27. Coconi, A., Bordacconi, M., Barbagli, C., Herold, G.: The effect of overtourism upon the ecology of florence's historic centre. In: Berr, K., Koegst, L., Kühne, O. (eds.) Landscape Conflicts, RaumFragen: Stadt – Region – Landschaft, pp. 273–288. Springer VS, Wiesbaden (2024). https://doi.org/10.1007/978-3-658-43352-9_13

Author Index

O. Gervasi et al. (Eds.): ICCSA 2025 Workshops, LNCS 15890, pp. 433–434, 2026.
https://doi.org/10.1007/978-3-031-97606-3

The manufacturer's authorised representative in the EU is Springer
Nature Customer Service Centre GmbH, Europaplatz 3, 69115 Heidelberg,
Germany. If you have any concerns regarding our products, please
contact ProductSafety@springernature.com

Printed and bound by CPI Group (UK) Ltd, Croydon, CR0 4YY
28/04/2026
02098515-0010